Lecture Notes in Computer Science 875

Edited by G. Goos, J. Hartmanis and J. van Leeuwen

Advisory Board: W. Brauer   D. Gries   J. Stoer

Dieter Gollmann (Ed.)

Computer Security – ESORICS 94

Third European Symposium on
Research in Computer Security
Brighton, United Kingdom, November 7-9, 1994
Proceedings

Springer-Verlag

Berlin Heidelberg New York
London Paris Tokyo
Hong Kong Barcelona
Budapest

Series Editors

Gerhard Goos
Universität Karlsruhe
Vincenz-Priessnitz-Straße 3, D-76128 Karlsruhe, Germany

Juris Hartmanis
Department of Computer Science, Cornell University
4130 Upson Hall, Ithaka, NY 14853, USA

Jan van Leeuwen
Department of Computer Science, Utrecht University
Padualaan 14, 3584 CH Utrecht, The Netherlands

Volume Editor

Dieter Gollmann
Department of Computer Science
Royal Holloway, University of London
Egham, Surrey TW20 0EX, United Kingdom

CR Subject Classification (1991): D.4.6, E.3, C.2.0, H.2.0, K.6.5

ISBN 3-540-58618-0 Springer-Verlag Berlin Heidelberg New York

CIP data applied for

© Springer-Verlag Berlin Heidelberg 1994
Printed in Germany

Typesetting: Camera-ready by author
SPIN: 10479219   45/3140-543210 - Printed on acid-free paper

Preface

This year for the first time ESORICS is being held outside France. This is an important step for a European Symposium, which should evidently not get fixed in any one country. Making the move revealed various unsuspected dependencies on the former organisational background, and we are all highly indebted to Dieter Gollmann and Pamela Bye who cheerfully and energetically made things happen when there was some local turbulence.

We are grateful to the Fondazione Ugo Bordoni for a grant to the IMA in support of their work for the Symposium, and to Codes & Ciphers Ltd for a timely loan. LAAS-CNRS, through the good will of Yves Deswarte, gave valuable assistance with a mailing, and distributed details electronically.

The Programme Committee coped uncomplainingly with the increased workload generated by the needed extension of submission date, and we are also greatly indebted to the referees who ensured at short notice that good professional opinions were always available.

I feel confident that we shall all have a valuable Symposium at Brighton.

Roger Needham
General Chairman

Programme Chair's Preface

Twenty-six papers were selected for the European Symposium on Research in Computer Security, ESORICS'94, held November 7-9, 1994 in Brighton, UK. This year's symposium is the third in the ESORICS series created in 1990 and renewed in 1992 by AFCET in France. The IMA organised ESORICS'94 in co-operation with AFCET, BCS Computer Security Specialist Group, CERT-ONERA, AICA and GI. Its proceedings are the object of this volume.

Progressively organised in a series of European countries, the symposium is confirmed as the European research event in Computer Security. The seventy-one submitted papers came from the five continents. Considering the high average quality of the submissions, the programme committee decided to select many of them, which led to a dense programme. The papers were grouped in sessions devoted to high security assurance software, key management, authentication, digital payment, distributed systems, access controls, databases and measures. As the evaluation of security was not sufficiently addressed in the submitted research papers, the programme committee organised a panel session devoted to it. In addition, to amplify the contribution to the symposium of the digital payment topic, it invited Professor Henry Beker to talk about "Security Research for the Financial Sector".

The authors of all submitted papers deserve the main acknowledgement. The successful continuation of a top-grade international symposium depends on them. The efficiency of the programme committee members made possible a timely review of quality. The signatories thank Professor Roger Needham for his help in the global review process they had to perform.

Gerard Eizenberg   Elisa Bertino
Programme Chair   Programme Vice-Chair

ESORICS'94

General Chair

Roger Needham   Cambridge University

Programme Committee

Bruno d'Ausbourg	CERT-ONERA
Elisa Bertino (Vice-Chair)	Universitá di Milano
Thomas Beth	Universität Karlsruhe
Joachim Biskup	Universität Hildesheim
Peter Bottomley	DRA
Yves Deswarte	LAAS-CNRS & INRIA
Klaus Dittrich	Universität Zürich
Gerard Eizenberg (Chair)	CERT-ONERA
Simon Foley	University College Cork
Dieter Gollmann	Royal Holloway, University of London
Franz-Peter Heider	GEI
Jeremy Jacob	University of York
Sushil Jajodia	George Mason University
Helmut Kurth	IABG
Teresa Lunt	DARPA
Giancarlo Martella	Universitá di Milano
Cathy Meadows	Naval Research Laboratories
Jonathan Millen	MITRE Corporation
Emilio Montolivo	Fondazione Ugo Bordoni
Roger Needham	Cambridge University
Andreas Pfitzmann	Technische Universität Dresden
Jean-Jacques Quisquater	Université de Louvain-la-Neuve
Einar Snekkenes	NDRE

Steering Committee Chair

Yves Deswarte   LAAS-CNRS & INRIA

Organising Committee

Pamela Bye	IMA
Dieter Gollmann	Royal Holloway, University of London

Referees

Ross Anderson *(Cambridge University)*, Bruno d'Ausbourg *(CERT ONERA)*, Elisa Bertino *(Universitá di Milano)*, Thomas Beth *(Universität Karlsruhe)*, Pierre Bieber *(CERT ONERA)*, Joachim Biskup *(Universität Hildesheim)*, Peter Bottomley *(DRA Malvern)*, Christel Calas *(CERT ONERA)*, Silvana Castano *(Universitá di Milano)*, Jacques Cazin *(CERT ONERA)*, John Clark *(University of York)*, Frédéric Cuppens *(CERT ONERA)*, Marc Dacier *(LAAS)*, Robert Demolombe *(CERT ONERA)*, Yves Deswarte *(LAAS-CNRS & INRIA)*, Gerard Eizenberg *(CERT ONERA)*, Simon Foley *(University College, Cork)*, Alban Gabillon *(CERT ONERA)*, Dieter Gollmann *(Royal Holloway, University of London)*, Franz-Peter Heider *(GEI)*, Jeremy Jacob *(University of York)*, Sushil Jajodia *(George Mason University)*, Dirk Jonscher *(Universität Zürich)*, Detlef Kraus *(GEI)*, Helmut Kurth *(IABG)*, Michel Lemoine *(CERT ONERA)*, Jean-Henri Llareus *(ENSAE)*, Mark Lomas *(Cambridge University)*, Teresa Lunt *(DARPA)*, Betty Mackman *(DRA Malvern)*, Giancarlo Martella *(Universitá di Milano)*, John McLean *(NRL)*, Catherine Meadows *(NRL)*, Jonathan Millen *(MITRE Corporation)*, Chris Mitchell *(Royal Holloway, University of London)*, Emilio Montolivo *(Fondazione Ugo Bordoni)*, Roger Needham *(Cambridge University)*, Colin O'Halloran *(DRA Malvern)*, Andreas Pfitzmann *(Technische Universität Dresden)*, Jean-Jacques Quisquater *(Universite Catholique de Louvain)*, Clare Robinson *(DRA Malvern)*, John Rushby *(SRI)*, Pierangela Samarati *(Universitá di Milano)*, Ravi Sandhu *(George Mason University)*, Chris Sennett *(DRA Malvern)*, Marek Sergot *(Imperial College)*, Einar Snekkenes *(NDRE)*, Jacques Stern *(Ecole Normale Superieure)*, Erich Van Wickeren *(GEI)*, Simon Wiseman *(DRA Malvern)*, John Wood *(DRA Malvern)*, Raphael Yahalom *(The Hebrew University of Jerusalem)*, Kioumars Yazdanian *(CERT ONERA)*

Contents

Measures

High Assurance Software

Key Management I

Authentication

Key Management II

Digital Payment

Distributed Systems

Access Controls

Database I

Database II

List of Authors

Measures

Valuation of Trust in Open Networks

Thomas Beth   Malte Borcherding*   Birgit Klein

European Institute for System Security
University of Karlsruhe, Germany

Abstract. Authentication in open networks usually requires participation of trusted entities. Many protocols allow trust to be obtained by recommendation of other entities whose recommendations are known to be reliable. To consider an entity as being trustworthy, especially if there have been several mediators or contradicting recommendations, it is necessary to have a means of estimating its trustworthiness. In this paper we present a method for the valuation of trustworthiness which can be used to accept or reject an entity as being suitable for sensitive tasks. It constitutes an extension of the work of Yahalom, Klein and Beth ([YKB93]).

Keywords: Trust values, Trust measures, Distributed systems

1 Introduction

Communication in open networks often requires information about the trustworthiness of the participating entities, especially when authentication protocols need to be performed. If, for example, user A receives a message signed allegedly by user B without having B's verification data at hand[1], she can ask a trusted *authentication server* (AS) of her choice to confirm the signature. In large distributed networks it will frequently happen that this AS does not have the required data in its database and will have to ask another trusted AS for assistance. This AS, in turn, can repeat this procedure until eventually a sufficiently informed AS is reached and the data can be handed to A. For A to believe in the received data being authentic she has to trust the terminal AS and hence the sequence of mediating ASs (the *recommendation path*). The longer the path becomes, the less trustworthy the final entity intuitively will be.

Depending on the task which A wants an entity of such a path to perform, she has to decide whether it is sufficiently trustworthy. Usually there is a maximum value one is willing to risk within a certain trust relationship. To determine such a maximum value, one has to estimate *degrees* of trust.

A valuation of trustworthiness also becomes relevant when different entities offer different allegedly authentic data of the same entity. In such cases the trustworthiness of these entities needs to be compared.

---

* Now working at the Institute of Computer Design and Fault Tolerance, University of Karlsruhe, Germany

[1] B's verification data corresponds to its public key when using a digital signature scheme.

In the past there have been several approaches to describe trust formally (e.g. [BAN89, GNY90, Ran92, YKB93]). The result were logics which can be used to draw conclusions from given initial trust relationships like who is trustworthy and which public data belongs to whom. These logics lack the notion of degrees of trust; an entity is considered either trustworthy or not.

In [TH92] Tarah and Huitema propose a valuation of *certification paths* (which are related to the recommendation paths mentioned above) and give some hints on how to perform such a valuation. As examples for measures they suggest the minimum of the involved trust values or the length of the certification path.

Some questions remain open, e.g. the meaning of an actual value of trustworthiness and how different recommendations about an entity with different degrees of trustworthiness can be combined to yield a unique value.

In this paper we introduce a measure of trustworthiness based on the work of Yahalom, Klein and Beth ([YKB93]) and consider the aforementioned questions. Further work on this topic can be found in [Bor93].

The paper is organized as follows. In section 2 we introduce a formal representation of valued trust relationships, in sections 3 and 4 we show how new relationships and their values can be derived from already existing ones. This method of derivation is demonstrated by an example in section 5. In section 6 we show how the actual decision whether to trust an entity or not can be made. We conclude with a summary in section 7.

2   Formal Representation of Trust Relationships

In this section we introduce a formal representation of valued trust relationships. It is an extension of the representation used in [YKB93]. We assume the following underlying model of a distributed system:

The system consists of entities which communicate via links. Each entity has a unique identifier and may have a secret which can be used for authentication purposes. The entities can generate, read and modify any message on any link. Entities may have some computational power e.g. for the encryption and decryption of messages. Some entities are distinguished as *authentication servers (AS)* as they support the authentication of other entities.

To model degrees of trust, we need the notion of *numbers of positive/negative experiences*. We assume that an entity can assign a certain number (value) to each task it entrusts to another entity. This number can be thought of as the number of ECU being lost when the task is not fulfilled. Each lost or not lost entrusted ECU increments the number of positive or negative experiences by one.

2.1   Trust Classification

In [YKB93] it is pointed out that there is no need to trust an entity completely if one expects it only to perform a limited task. After examining some authentication protocols, the following classes were identified:

- **key generation**: Providing good quality keys to be used with some agreed upon cryptographic function.
- **identification**: Correctly associating entities (respectively their unique identifiers) with their identifying data, e.g. public or shared keys.
- **keeping secrets**: Keeping classified information secret.
- **non interference**: Not interfering in other entities' sessions (e.g. by eavesdropping or impersonating).
- **clock synchronization**: Maintaining close clock synchronization.
- **performing algorithmic steps**: Following protocol specifications correctly.

Trust with respect to one of these classes is independent of trust with respect to other classes. It may be perfectly reasonable to trust an authentication server in a different domain with respect to identifying entities in that domain without trusting its key generation capabilities.

2.2   Direct Trust and Recommendation Trust

For each of the classes of trust there are two *types* of trust: direct trust and recommendation trust. To trust an entity directly means to believe in its capabilities with respect to the given trust class. Recommendation trust expresses the belief in the capability of an entity to decide whether another entity is reliable in the given trust class and in its honesty when recommending third entities.

Recommendation trust can be granted in a restricted manner. Constraints can be imposed on the properties of the recommending entities further along the path as well as on the entities which are eventually recommended as being directly trustworthy. These properties can include the very names of entities, their domains or the number of entities on the path so far. The constraints are used to express *distrust* towards entities.

Due to the different notions of direct trust and recommendation trust, we present their formal representations separately.

Direct Trust

$$P \; trusts_x^{seq} \; Q \; value \; V$$

A direct trust relationship exists if *all* experiences with Q with regard to trust class x which P knows about are positive experiences. *seq* is the sequence of entities who mediated the experiences[2] (the recommendation path) excluding P and Q. V is a value of the trust relationship which is an estimation of the probability that Q behaves well when being trusted. It is based on the number of positive experiences with Q which P knows about.

Let p be the number of positive experiences. The value v_z of these experiences is computed as follows:

$$v_z(p) = 1 - \alpha^p \; . \tag{1}$$

---

[2] We regard a recommendation as propagation of positive experiences.

This value is the probability that Q has a *reliability* of more than α, founded on the information P possesses about Q. The reliability is the probability that Q turns out to be reliable when being entrusted with a single task, i.e. a task of value 1. α should be chosen reasonably high to ensure sufficiently safe estimations.

Proposition 1: *Let ok be a variable for the number of positive experiences and* r *be the reliability of an entity. Assume further that* r *is distributed uniformly over the set of all entities. Then the probability that* r *is greater than* α *on the condition that ok equals* p *is* $1 - \alpha^{p+1}$.

Proof:

$$
\begin{aligned}
P(r > \alpha | ok = p) &= \frac{P(r > \alpha, ok = p)}{P(ok = p)} = \frac{\int_\alpha^1 x^p \, dx}{\int_0^1 x^p \, dx} \\
&= \frac{(p+1)^{-1}(1 - \alpha^{p+1})}{(p+1)^{-1}} \\
&= 1 - \alpha^{p+1}
\end{aligned}
\tag{2}
$$

$\square$

We use the formula $1 - \alpha^p$ in our model instead of $1 - \alpha^{p+1}$ to enforce a trust degree of zero for an unknown entity. This slight deviation from the stated semantics (which is meaningless for large p) buys us a much more convenient model for the trust values.

The value of direct trust has the following (realistic) property: A single additional positive experience has more influence on a low value than on a high value. Obviously, a positive experience with a stranger offers more information than the same experience with a reliable friend.

If there have been negative experiences, there is no trust relationship. We did not model *values of distrust* since a distrusted entity should not be trusted with anything at all, no matter how small the non-trustworthiness may be. Instead, a distrusted entity can be excluded from being recommended by other entities by using the target constraints described in the next paragraph.

Recommendation Trust

$P \; trusts.rec_x^{seq} \; Q \; when.path \; S_p \; when.target \; S_t \; value \; V$

A recommendation trust relationship exists if P is willing to accept reports from Q about experiences with third parties with respect to trust class x. This trust is restricted to experiences with entities in S_t (the *target constraint set*) mediated by entities in S_p (the *path constraint set*). Again, *seq* is the sequence of entities who mediated the recommendation trust. V is the value of the trust relationship. It represents the portion of offered experiences that P is willing to accept from Q and is based on the experiences P has had with the entities *recommended* by Q.

Given numbers of positive and negative experiences p and n, respectively, with the recommended entities, the recommendation trust value v_r is computed according to the following formula:

$$v_r(p, n) = \begin{cases} 1 - \alpha^{p-n} & \text{if } p > n \\ 0 & \text{else} \end{cases}.$$

This value can be regarded as a degree of similarity between P and Q, taking into account that different entities may have different experiences with a third party. An entity which usually sends unclassified messages will less often be confronted with treachery than an entity which transmits secret information. Given such a dissimilarity, the latter entity will not put much weight on what the former is telling about other entities' discretion.

The experiences with the recommending entity are formed by the experiences with the recommended entities. If a recommended entity behaves well, we have the experience of a valuable recommendation. Otherwise, the recommendation seems to be questionable, but we cannot deduce that the recommending entity has been lying from its point of view. Hence there is no immediate reason to reject further recommendations; it is sufficient to state a certain dissimilarity and to lower the trust value. This is modeled by the following properties of the given formula:

- $v_r(p, n) = 0$ for $p = 0$.
- $v_r(p, n)$ approaches 1 with growing p and fixed n.
- $v_r(p, n)$ approaches 0 with growing n and fixed p.

If the negative experiences outnumber the positive experiences, the value becomes zero and the entity is excluded from the recommendation constraint set.

Representation of the Constraint Sets
The constraint sets need not be stated explicitly. It suffices to specify predicates which decide the membership of an entity to the set in question. Such a predicate could be "is-child-of(x, A)" which would be true if x is a child of A in a given hierarchy and hence describes implicitly the set of all children of A. These predicates have to be decidable to be useful in this context.

The predicates may depend on the trust expressions they are evaluated in. If the predicate in the example above is changed into "is-child-of(x, *current-entity*)" it defines the set of children of the trusted entity. As will be described later, predicates can be taken over from initial trust expressions into derived ones with different trusted entities so that the same predicate applies to different instances of *current-entity*. When used as path constraint set, the given sample predicate would restrict the recommendation path to a descending path in the given hierarchy.

3 Deriving Trust Relationships

The representation of trust by trust expressions leads to rules which describe how new trust comes into being when recommendation is performed. With the help of these rules one can derive new trust relationships from a given set of initial relationships. Since the trust model itself offers no inherent strategy to derive a trust relationship between two entities, derivation algorithms need to be added. In this section we introduce the rules of inference and describe two derivation algorithms.

3.1 Description of the Rules of Inference

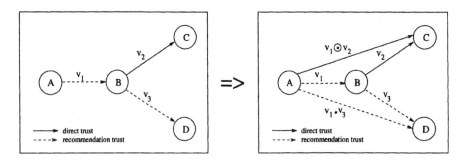

Fig. 1. Derivation of Trust Relationships

Before we introduce the rules of inference formally, we will describe them by the help of an example (see figure 1).

We start with the following initial trust relationships:

1. A $trusts.rec_x^{seq_1}$ B $when.path$ S_{p_1} $when.target$ S_{t_1} $value$ V_1
2. B $trusts_x^{seq_2}$ C $value$ V_2
3. B $trusts.rec_x^{seq_3}$ D $when.path$ S_{p_3} $when.target$ S_{t_3} $value$ V_3

Deriving Direct Trust

From 1. and 2. a new direct trust relationship from A to C can be derived provided that

- C is in S_{t_1} (C is a possible target)
- All entities in seq_2 are also in S_{p_1} (no mediator of the direct trust is excluded by the recommendation trust)
- seq_1 contains no entity from seq_2 (noncyclicity)

The new recommendation path is composed of seq_1, B and seq_2 to $seq_1 \circ B \circ seq_2$. The value of the new relationship is computed according to the following formula:

$$V_1 \odot V_2 = 1 - (1 - V_2)^{V_1} . \tag{3}$$

This formula is a result of the computation of the direct trust values following 2.2 and the semantics of the recommendation trust values. If V_2 is based on p positive experiences, the following equation holds:

$$V_1 \odot V_2 = 1 - (1 - (1 - \alpha^p))^{V_1} = 1 - \alpha^{V_1 \cdot p} .$$

Thus the new value is based on the equivalent of "$p \cdot V_1$" experiences.

Deriving Recommendation Trust

From 1. and 3. a new recommendation trust relationship from A to D can be derived, provided that

- D and all entities in seq_3 are also in S_{p_1} (D and the mediators of the trust in D are not excluded)
- D and all entities in seq_3 are not in seq_1 (noncyclicity)

The new trust relationship has a recommendation path of $seq_1 \circ B \circ seq_3$, a path constraint set of $S_{p_1} \cap S_{p_2}$, a target constraint set of $S_{t_1} \cap S_{t_2}$ and a value of $V_1 \cdot V_3$.

The multiplication of the values ensures that the trust value descends as the recommendation path grows. The proposition "If someone whose recommendations are rather useless to me recommends someone whose recommendations are rather useless to him, then the recommendations of the recommended one are even less useful to me" may not be true in all cases since the usefulness of the recommendation may well be higher, but it helps to stay on the safe side.

We have required noncyclicity for the following reason: Cycles would lead to an infinite number of possible recommendation paths between two entities with trust values approaching zero as the pathlength increases. In section 4 we introduce a method on how to combine values of trust relationships between two entities which would be undermined by an arbitrary number of arbitrarily small trust values. Since cycles add no new information on who is trustworthy, they can safely be left out.

The intersection of the constraint sets is intended to preserve the type of representation used in the original constraint sets. Thus, when using the implicit representation, the new set is the conjunction of the predicates in the two sets. This is necessary to retain the meaning of the variables which depend on the context (the trust expression) they are evaluated in. The intersection of explicit sets yields another explicit set, as one might expect.

If the sets to be intersected are of different type, the explicit set can easily be transformed to an implicit representation, e.g. the explicit set "$\{A, B\}$" can be transformed to "$x = A$ or $x = B$".

3.2 The Rules of Inference

Here we present the rules of inference formally:

RULE1: (NEW DIRECT TRUST)

P $trusts.rec_x^{seq_1}$ Q $when.path$ S_p $when.target$ S_t $value$ V_1
$\wedge$ Q $trusts_x^{seq_2}$ R $value$ V_2
$\wedge$ $R \in_s S_t$
$\wedge$ $\forall X : (X \in_l seq_2 \Rightarrow (X \in_s S_p \wedge X \notin_l P \circ seq_1))$
$\Rightarrow P$ $trusts_x^{seq_1 \circ Q \circ seq_2}$ R $value$ $(V_1 \odot V_2)$

RULE2: (NEW RECOMMENDATION TRUST)

P $trusts.rec_x^{seq_1}$ Q $when.path$ S_{p_1} $when.target$ S_{t_1} $value$ V_1
$\wedge$ Q $trusts.rec_x^{seq_2}$ R $when.path$ S_{p_2} $when.target$ S_{t_2} $value$ V_2
$\wedge$ $\forall X : (X \in_l seq_2 \circ R \Rightarrow (X \in_s S_{p_1} \wedge X \notin_l P \circ seq_1))$
$\Rightarrow P$ $trusts.rec_x^{seq_1 \circ Q \circ seq_2}$ R
$when.path$ $(S_{p_1} \cap S_{p_2})$ $when.target$ $(S_{t_1} \cap S_{t_2})$ $value$ $(V_1 \cdot V_2)$

The symbol $\circ$ denotes concatenation of sequences or appending of elements to a sequence, the predicates $\in_l$ and $\in_s$ denote the membership of elements to a sequence or to a set, respectively.

3.3 Associativity of the Derivation Rules

The choice of the derivation strategy has no influence on the derivable trust expressions. That means that from a given sequence of trust expressions one can either derive a unique trust expression from the first trusting entity to the last trusted entity or none at all, independent of the order of rule application.

Thus it does not matter whether one first derives the recommendations along a path and then the desired direct trust, or whether one derives direct trust expressions from the end of a path towards its beginning.

To show this, we start with

Definition 2: Let $\mathcal{R}$ and $\mathcal{D}$ denote the sets of recommendation trust expressions and direct trust expressions, respectively. We define two functions $R_1 : \mathcal{R} \times \mathcal{D} \to \mathcal{D}$ and $R_2 : \mathcal{R} \times \mathcal{R} \to \mathcal{R}$ as

$$R_1(rx_1, dx_2) := \begin{cases} \text{Result of Rule1 when applied to } rx_1 \text{ and } dx_2 \text{ if applicable} \\ \bot \qquad\qquad\qquad\qquad\qquad\qquad\qquad\qquad\qquad\qquad \text{else} \end{cases}$$

$$R_2(rx_1, rx_2) := \begin{cases} \text{Result of Rule2 when applied to } rx_1 \text{ and } rx_2 \text{ if applicable} \\ \bot \qquad\qquad\qquad\qquad\qquad\qquad\qquad\qquad\qquad\qquad \text{else} \end{cases}$$

Proposition 3: *For* $rx_1, rx_2, rx_3 \in \mathcal{R}$ *and* $dx_3 \in \mathcal{D}$ *the following equations hold:*

(1) $R_1(R_2(rx_1, rx_2), dx_3) = R_1(rx_1, R_1(rx_2, dx_3))$
(2) $R_2(R_2(rx_1, rx_2), rx_3) = R_2(rx_1, R_2(rx_1, rx_3))$

Proof:

For the proof of (1), we consider trust relationships $rx_1, rx_2 \in \mathcal{R}$ and $dx_3 \in \mathcal{D}$:

$rx_1 = P_1\ trusts.rec_x^{seq_1}\ Q_1\ when.path\ S_{p_1}\ when.target\ S_{t_1}\ value\ V_1$
$rx_2 = P_2\ trusts.rec_x^{seq_2}\ Q_2\ when.path\ S_{p_2}\ when.target\ S_{t_2}\ value\ V_2$
$dx_3 = P_3\ trusts_x^{seq_3}\ Q_3\ value\ V_3.$

First we show the equality in case the rules are applicable:

$R_1(R_2(rx_1, rx_2), dx_3) = P_1\ trusts_x^{(seq_1 \circ Q_1 \circ seq_2) \circ Q_2 \circ seq_3}\ Q_3\ value(V_1 \cdot V_2) \odot V_3$
$R_1(rx_1, R_1(rx_2, dx_3)) = P_1\ trusts_x^{seq_1 \circ Q_1 \circ (seq_2 \circ Q_2 \circ seq_3)}\ Q_3\ value V_1 \odot (V_2 \odot V_3)$

These two expressions are equal because the concatenation of sequences is associative and

$$V_1 \odot (V_2 \odot V_3) = V_1 \odot (1 - (1 - V_3)^{V_2})$$
$$= 1 - (1 - (1 - (1 - V_3)^{V_2}))^{V_1} = 1 - (1 - V_3)^{V_1 \cdot V_2}$$
$$= (V_1 \cdot V_2) \odot V_3.$$

We now show that the conditions for $R_1(R_2(rx_1, rx_2), dx_3) \neq \bot$ are equivalent to the conditions for $R_1(rx_1, R_1(rx_2, dx_3)) \neq \bot$:

Conditions for $R_2(rx_1, rx_2) \neq \bot$:
   (1) $Q = P_2$
   (2) $x \in seq_2 \circ Q_2 \Rightarrow x \in S_{p_1} \wedge x \notin P_1 \circ seq_1$
Additional conditions for $R_1(R_2(rx_1, rx_2), dx_3) \neq \bot$:
   (3) $Q_2 = P_3$
   (4) $Q_3 \in S_{t_1} \cap S_{t_2}$
   (5) $x \in seq_3 \Rightarrow x \in S_{p_1} \cap S_{p_2} \wedge x \notin P_1 \circ seq_1 \circ Q_1 \circ seq_2$

Conditions for $R_1(rx_2, dx_3) \neq \bot$:
   (6) $Q_2 = P_3$
   (7) $Q_3 \in S_{t_2}$
   (8) $x \in seq_3 \Rightarrow x \in S_{p_2} \wedge x \notin P_2 \circ seq_2$
Additional conditions for $R_1(rx_1, R_1(rx_2, dx_3)) \neq \bot$:
   (9) $Q_1 = P_2$
  (10) $Q_3 \in S_{t_1}$
  (11) $x \in seq_2 \circ Q_2 \circ seq_3 \Rightarrow x \in S_{p_1} \wedge x \notin P_1 \circ seq_1$

$\{(1), (2), \ldots, (5)\} \Rightarrow \{(6), (7), \ldots, (11)\}$ holds because (3) $\Rightarrow$ (6), (4) $\Rightarrow$ (7), (1) $\wedge$ (5) $\Rightarrow$ (8), (1) $\Rightarrow$ (9), (4) $\Rightarrow$ (10) and (2) $\wedge$ (5) $\Rightarrow$ (11).
$\{(6), (7), \ldots, (11)\} \Rightarrow \{(1), (2), \ldots, (5)\}$ holds because (9) $\Rightarrow$ (1), (11) $\Rightarrow$ (2), (6) $\Rightarrow$ (3), (7) $\wedge$ (10) $\Rightarrow$ (4) and (8) $\wedge$ (9) $\wedge$ (11) $\Rightarrow$ (5).

The proof of proposition (2) can be carried out in a similar manner and is thus omitted.   □

3.4 Trust Derivation Algorithms

To track down all entities which can be trusted by an entity P with respect to a trust class x, one has to go along all noncyclic paths in the network which consist of trust relationships of the desired class, start at P, follow the collected constraints and end with a direct trust relationship.

For this purpose a trust derivation algorithm is proposed in [YKB93] which derives all possible direct trust relationships with an entity P as trusting entity from a given set of initial trust relationships. The algorithm tries for each recommendation trust expression to derive as many new trust expressions as possible. Then the considered recommendation trust is removed from the set and the new recommendation trusts are inserted into it. This process is continued until the set is empty (which happens in finite time since the paths are not to contain cycles).

The trusted entities in the derived direct trust expressions are collected in an extra set which finally contains all entities P may trust in the given trust class.

A disadvantage of this algorithm is its exponential complexity (in the number of nodes) with no remedy to be expected since the problem has proven to be NP-complete ([Bor93]). So it was necessary to make use of some sensible heuristics.

In [YKB94] a distributed algorithm is proposed which can handle all types of networks but is especially designed for tree-like structures as they frequently appear in the real world. In the case of a pure tree, the complexity is logarithmic. To accelerate the search when the tree structure is disturbed, it makes use of routing tables which store information about shortcuts in the structure.

These algorithms can easily be adopted to support the extended model of valued trust relationships.

4 Combination of Trust Values

Since there are not necessarily unique recommendation paths, there will sometimes be several (derived) trust relationships of the same trust class between two entities. They will usually have different values, so one has to find a way to draw a consistent conclusion. The introduced semantics of the trust values lead to the result that different values do not imply a contradiction, but can be used as collective information to compute a combined value. In this section we show how this combination can be performed. Again, we consider recommendation trust and direct trust separately.

4.1 Recommendation Trust

Suppose A has several recommendation trust relationships to B. That means it has different estimations about its similarity with B which could have been derived via different recommendation paths. To combine these values to a unique value one has a choice of possible averages. This family is represented by

$$\bar{V} = \left(\frac{\sum\limits_{i=1}^{n} V_i^{\beta}}{n} \right)^{1/\beta}$$

with $\beta \in \mathbf{R} \setminus \{0\}$ as free parameter. Special cases are maximum and minimum with $\beta \to \infty$ and $\beta \to -\infty$, respectively, harmonic, geometric and arithmetic mean with $\beta = -1$, $\beta \to 0$ and $\beta = 1$, respectively.

In order to avoid relationships with extreme values to determine the combination completely, we decided to use neither minimum nor maximum. When using the maximum of the values, a single unjustified trust with a high value could override any amount of low valued recommendations. A similar argument holds for the minimum. So the best choice seemed to be the arithmetic mean which regards all values equal.

Given n values of recommendation trust relationships between the same entities and with respect to the same trust class V_i ($i = 1 \dots n$), $V_i \neq 0$, their combination V_{com} is computed according to the following formula:

$$V_{com} = \frac{1}{n} \sum_{i=1}^{n} V_i \; . \tag{4}$$

4.2 Direct trust

Here we have several direct trust relationships between two entities with respect to the same trust class. It is necessary to classify the trust expressions with respect to the last recommending entity on the recommendation path to get a result which conforms to the semantics of the trust values.

Let P_i ($i = 1 \dots m$) be the different last entities on the recommendation paths and, in case of empty paths, the trusting entity and $V_{i,j}$ ($i = 1 \dots m$, $j = 1 \dots n_i$), $V_{i,j} \neq 0$ the values of the trust relationships (with n_i denoting the number of relationships having P_i as last recommending entity). The $V_{i,*}$ represent classes of trust values with each class containing the values of trust relationships with the same last recommending entity P_i.

The values of the direct trust relationships are combined according to the following formula:

$$V_{com} = 1 - \prod_{i=1}^{m} \sqrt[n_i]{\prod_{j=1}^{n_i}(1 - V_{i,j})} \tag{5}$$

This formula follows from the meaning of a recommendation: There exists an entity which has had some experiences with the entity to be recommended. These experiences have been propagated along the recommendation paths, undergoing a reduction corresponding to the values of the recommendation trusts on their way. Since there are not necessarily unique paths from one entity to another, the same experiences may be propagated to an entity several times via different paths and with different reductions. In the previous paragraph we pointed out that these reductions can be averaged to yield a unique value.

In particular, we can split the $V_{i,j}$ into their inherent positive experiences p_i directly from entities P_i and diminishing factors $\tilde{V}_{i,j}$ which fulfill the equation

$$V_{i,j} = 1 - \alpha^{\tilde{V}_{i,j} \cdot p_i} .$$

The combined trust value is computed to

$$V_{com} = 1 - \prod_{i=1}^{m} \sqrt[n_i]{\prod_{j=1}^{n_i}(1 - V_{i,j})} = 1 - \prod_{i=1}^{m} \sqrt[n_i]{\prod_{j=1}^{n_i} \alpha^{\tilde{V}_{i,j} \cdot p_i}}$$

$$= 1 - \prod_{i=1}^{m} \alpha^{\frac{1}{n_i}(\sum_{j=1}^{n_i} \tilde{V}_{i,j}) \cdot p_i} = 1 - \alpha^{\sum_{i=1}^{m} \frac{1}{n_i}(\sum_{j=1}^{n_i} \tilde{V}_{i,j}) \cdot p_i}$$

and hence corresponds to experiences of $\sum_{i=1}^{m} \frac{1}{n_i}(\sum_{j=1}^{n_i} \tilde{V}_{i,j}) \cdot p_i$ which is exactly what we described above.

4.3 Nonmonotonicy of the Combination

The combination of values has the property of being *nonmonotonic*. If the set of trust relationships between two entities with respect to the same trust class grows, the behaviour of the combined values cannot be predicted. This property is a result of the averaging of the recommendation trust values. The average can increase or decrease as new relationships arise.

If it is unknown whether all possible trust relationships have been derived, an estimation of possible effects of new relationships on the combined value would be necessary. Hence the combination of values would imply the consideration of probability densities. Otherwise, when using the "incomplete" combined value, one can but hope that no significant changes will appear.

Considering these alternatives, the combined value should only be computed from a complete set of trust relationships. We suppose that in real world scenarios this is not a problem since the paths are few and rather determined by the existing hierarchies. Another, somewhat optimistic, solution would be not to use the arithmetic mean as average, but the maximum of the values.

5 An Example

In this example we demonstrate the derivation of trust relationships and the combination of their values. Since the example focuses on the values, we make no use of the path constraints. For simplicity, we replace the part "*when.path*[true] *when.target*[true]" in each recommendation trust expression by dots (...).

We start with the following trust relationships (see figure 2):

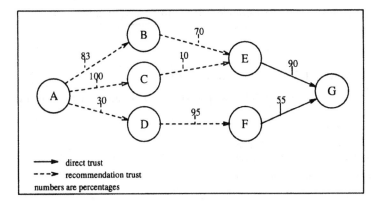

Fig. 2. Combination of Trust Values

(r1) $A\ trusts.rec_x^{\emptyset}\ B\ \dots\ value\ 0.83$
(r2) $A\ trusts.rec_x^{\emptyset}\ C\ \dots\ value\ 1$
(r3) $A\ trusts.rec_x^{\emptyset}\ D\ \dots\ value\ 0.30$
(r4) $B\ trusts.rec_x^{\emptyset}\ E\ \dots\ value\ 0.70$
(r5) $C\ trusts.rec_x^{\emptyset}\ E\ \dots\ value\ 0.10$
(r6) $D\ trusts.rec_x^{\emptyset}\ F\ \dots\ value\ 0.95$
(d1) $E\ trusts_x^{\emptyset}\ G\ value\ 0.90$
(d2) $F\ trusts_x^{\emptyset}\ G\ value\ 0.55$

Derivation of a Direct Trust Relationship

There are two basic strategies for the derivation of a direct trust relationship from A to G (e.g. via B and E): iterative and recursive. Both yield the same trust expressions (with the same values) as was pointed out in section 3.3. The values in this example are rounded to three digits.

Iterative Derivation: We first derive a recommendation trust from A to E, followed by the derivation of the direct trust from A to G:

(r1), (r4), Rule2 $\Rightarrow$ (r7) $A\ trusts.rec_x^B\ E\ \dots\ value\ \underbrace{0.83 \cdot 0.7}_{=0.581}$

(r7), (d1), Rule1 $\Rightarrow$ (d3) $A\ trusts_x^{B \circ E}\ G\ value\ \underbrace{0.581 \odot 0.9}_{=0.738}$

Recursive Derivation: Here we start with the derivation of the direct trust from B to G which is then used to derive the direct trust from A to G:

(r4), (d1), Rule1 $\Rightarrow$ (d4) $B\ trusts_x^E\ G\ value\ \underbrace{0.7 \odot 0.9}_{=0.800}$

(r1), (d4), Rule1 $\Rightarrow$ (d5) *A trusts$_x^{B \circ E}$ G value* $\underbrace{0.83 \odot 0.800}_{=0.738}$

Combination of Direct Trust Relationships:

The following direct trust relationships from A to G can be derived using either strategy:

(d3) *A trusts$_x^{B \circ E}$ G value 0.738*
(d4) *A trusts$_x^{C \circ E}$ G value 0.206*
(d5) *A trusts$_x^{D \circ F}$ G value 0.204*

There are two different entities at the end of the recommendation paths: E and F. So we identify two classes of trust expressions, the first consisting of (d3) and (d4), the second being solely (d5).

The computation of the combined value yields

$$V_{com} = 1 - \sqrt{(1 - 0.738) \cdot (1 - 0.206)} \cdot (1 - 0.204) = 0.637.$$

6 How to Use the Values

In this section we show how the introduced values can be used to decide whether or not an entity is sufficiently trustworthy with respect to a certain task.

As mentioned earlier, we assume that the value of each task can be measured in units, e.g. in ECU which are lost when the task is performed incorrectly. Our estimations about the reliability of entities were made relative to tasks consisting of a single unit. If we wish to entrust a task consisting of T units, the trusted entity has to fulfill T "atomic" tasks in order to complete the whole task. Bearing that in mind, we can estimate the risk when entrusting a task to an entity.

Let f denote the density of an entity's reliability r provided it passed p tests successfully ($ok = p$). Since $P(r \le \alpha | ok = p) = \alpha^{p+1}$ (see equation (2)), we have that $f = (p + 1)r^p$. From this equation and equation (1) follows that when T units are entrusted to an entity with trust value v, the average loss l is

$$l(\alpha, v, T) = \int_0^1 (log_\alpha(1 - v) + 1) \cdot r^{log_\alpha(1-v)} \cdot T \cdot (1 - r^T) \, dr$$

$$= \frac{T^2}{log_\alpha(1 - v) + T + 1}.$$

If, for example, $\alpha = 0.99$, $v = 0.637$ and we wish to entrust a task worth 100 units then we must be willing to risk $l(0.99, 0.637, 100) = 49.5$ units.

7 Summary

In this paper we introduced the notion of valuated trust as an extension of the trust model of Yahalom, Klein and Beth [YKB93]. We pointed out that the semantics of direct trust values differ from that of recommendation trust values: the former expresses the probability that an entity is working with a certain minimum reliability, the latter states how useful the recommendations of the trusted entity are expected to be.

The introduction of trust values gives rise to the problem that recommendations about one entity can differ in value, depending on the recommending entities. We have shown that these different values are not contradictory but can be combined to a single value which considers the information of all the respective recommending entities.

When trust values are to be used in real systems, it is necessary to evaluate the entrusted tasks. We have shown how the trust values can be used to estimate the risk when such a task is to be assigned to an entity.

Using the trust values, a flexible policy can be applied which allows to select appropriately trustworthy entities depending on the task's value. Combined with the notion of different trust classes the requirements for trusted entities can be kept to a minimum.

Acknowledgment

We would like to thank Raphael Yahalom and the anonymous referees for their valuable comments.

References

[BAN89] M. Burrows, M. Abadi, R. Needham, "A Logic of Authentication", *Proc. of the 12th ACM Symposium on Operating Systems Principles*, Litchfield Park, Arizona, 1989. Published as ACM Operating Systems Review, 23 no 5 (1989).

[Bor93] M. Borcherding, "Ermittlung verschieden vertrauenswürdiger Pfade in offenen Netzen", Diploma thesis at the European Institute for System Security, University of Karlsruhe, 1993 (in German).

[GNY90] L. Gong, R. Needham, R. Yahalom, "Reasoning about Belief in Cryptographic Protocols", *Proc. 1990 IEEE Symp. on Research in Security and Privacy*, 234-248.

[Ran92] P. V. Rangan, "An Axiomatic Theory of Trust in Secure Communication Protocols", *Computers and Security* 11 (1992) 163-172, Elsevier Science Publishers Ltd., Oxford 1992.

[TH92] A. Tarah, Ch. Huitema, "Associating Metrics to Certification Paths", *Proceedings of the Second European Symposium on Research in Computer Security (ESORICS) 1992*, 175-189, Springer LNCS 648, Berlin 1992.

[YKB93] R. Yahalom, B. Klein, Th. Beth, "Trust Relationships in Secure Systems – A Distributed Authentication Perspective", *Proc. 1993 IEEE Symp. on Research in Security and Privacy*, 150-164.

[YKB94]   R. Yahalom, B. Klein, Th. Beth, "Trust-based Navigation in Distributed Systems", to appear in: Special issue "Security and Integrity of Open Systems" of the journal "Computing Systems", 1994.

Security versus Performance Requirements in Data Communication Systems

Vasilios Zorkadis

FZI Forschungszentrum Informatik an der Universität Karlsruhe, Germany.

Abstract. The research activities in secure computer networks have paid little attention to the tradeoff between security and other quality requirements of the communication service. This paper aims to introduce performance aspects regarding secure computer networks. First, we attempt to quantify the tradeoff between security and performance in secure data communication systems by means of queueing theory. Our second target is to reduce the performance degradation caused by the security mechanisms and protocols. For this purpose, optimization concepts are proposed. The key points in the optimization concepts are: preprocessing, message segmenting and compression. They have to be integrated or considered in secure communication protocols to improve their performance characteristics. Preprocessing aims to exploit the idle periods of the system (e.g., computer or special crypto-chip), to take the stochastic nature of such communication processes into consideration, e.g., using the OFB-mode for generating (pseudo) random bit sequences after connection establishment. Segmenting is proposed for long messages in order to better exploit the pipeline nature of communication systems. Also, compression is discussed as a means to further improve the performance measures of secure communication.

1 Introduction

Computer network systems provide data transfer services for computer systems. Further requirements such as performance, security, and reliability characterize the quality of the transfer service. However, these requirements affect each other such that a decision has to be made for cases in which all or some of the requirements are desired but cannot be fulfilled. As an example, consider the case when confidentiality over a 155 Mb/s network is desired, but no encipherment devices of such speed are available. Another example could be firewalls (e.g. Interlock, 500 Kbit/s encipherment and 1,2 Mb/s authentication [13]) whose security functions (authentication and encipherment) are the system bottlenecks when communicating over a T1 link. Furthermore, the additional traffic generated through the firewalls must be considered since its performance impact could be prohibitive for their employment. In this section we will introduce briefly the most important security service classes. In the second section we will study the tradeoff between security and performance, and in the third section we will describe and analyze the optimization concepts.

There are five classes of security services in the field of secure data communication systems: authentication, access control, confidentiality, integrity and non-repudiation services. Table 1 shows the classification of the security services according to the OSI Security Architecture 7498-2 [11].

Authentication services refer to one-sided or mutual authentication of peer entities as well as to the authentication of the data origin. They mostly involve trusted third parties and are based on symmetrical or asymmetrical methods. They can be simple like the exchange of unprotected passwords or complex like the three-way-authentication in the Authentication Framework [12]. We refer to [3,9] and the references therein for information about authentication, authentication services and mechanisms, and authentication servers like Kerberos. Authentication of the peer entities takes place before the message exchange begins and data origin authentication during the data transfer phase. Authentication affects the performance of a data communication association this way at its beginning and during the data transfer phase.

Tab 1. Classification of the OSI Security Services

Security services	Subclasses
Authentication	Peer entities Data origin
Access Control	Communication services, Hosts, Networks, Subnets etc.
Confidentiality	Data (connection-oriented,-less, selective field) Traffic-related data
Integrity	Data (connection-oriented,-less, selective field)
Non-repudiation	Data (origin and/or delivery)

Access control services may be employed in the connection establishment phase with connection-oriented communication and for each message with connectionless communication. These services are local in the form of outgoing access control and remote with respect to different security domains and intermediate systems through which the communication is routed. Access Control is based on authentication and integrity, in addition to authorization table look-ups (e. g., checking the related information in the access control lists). From our performance point of view, it is apparent that access control services introduce computing costs either at the connection establishment phase or during the data transfer phase.

Confidentiality services may be employed for whole or parts of messages as well as for traffic-related information, as who communicates with whom and when and how many messages are exchanged and how long they are (traffic analysis). We refer to [1,7] for further information on efficient concepts for anonymous networks. Confidentiality services are based on cryptographic algorithms. From our performance point of view, the confidentiality services always impose processing costs at the end systems (and maybe at the intermediate nodes when link-by-link encipherment is employed). Further costs are related to the key exchange and other cryptographic parameters, like initialization variable, cryptographic algorithm names, mode of operation, etc. Also, costs result from expanding the messages being enciphered due to block-oriented modes of operation. The latter costs could be avoided [2].

Integrity services, like confidentiality services, may be employed for whole or parts of messages and message streams. They include the calculation of check sums and the appending of these and message sequence numbers to the messages. Timestamps and challenge/response mechanisms may be used against the replay attack.

The performance costs result from the check sum calculations and the expansion of the message length.

Non-repudiation services provide for one-sided (origin or delivery) or mutual (both origin and delivery) protection of the communicating parties with respect to each other. They always include authentication and integrity services and may include confidentiality as well. They have juridical character and therefore may be of rare usage in non-commercial networks. Their performance costs as the costs for authentication and integrity, and confidentiality services arise from the additional traffic, the processing and the message length expansion due to the several check sums.

2 Security versus Performance

In the introduction, we addressed the performance costs that arise due to the different security mechanisms. Table 2 contains security services and their corresponding performance costs. The performance costs can be local and/or remote according to the security model used, including the specific security mechanisms, such as access control and encipherment concepts, the use of trusted third parties (e.g., Kerberos), the use of firewalls, security-related routing control, etc.

Table 2. Security services and their associated performance costs

Security services	Performance costs
Authentication	Additional traffic arising at the connection establishment phase processing costs during the data transfer phase
Access control	Processing costs at connection establishment or data transfer phase
Confidentiality	Processing costs in the end systems (end-to-end encipherment) or the end and the intermediate systems (link-by-link encipherment)
Integrity	Message length expansion and calculation costs
Non-repudiation	Like authentication and integrity costs with respect to the kind (and confidentiality costs in case of confidential communication)

In connection-oriented communication, the connection establishment and the data transfer phase are of importance, as opposed to the connection release phase, unless a new communication association is immediately requested. The most important performance measures are throughput and delay. In the connection establishment phase, only the delay is reasonable as a performance measure. Both performance measures are of interest in the data transfer phase for the connection-oriented as well as for the connectionless communication.

The performance analysis of the connection establishment phase involves the analysis of the delay that elapses from the time the connection is requested until the time data transfer can begin, and depends on the concrete authentication mechanisms that are employed. Yet the delay for the communication with the authentication server (e.g., Kerberos) has to be considered when trusted third parties are involved in the authentication protocols. The delay depends on the number of authentication messages to be exchanged (one-way, two-way or three-way authentication, number of intermediate systems to be involved, etc.), their length and the computational costs of the security functions to be employed. (encipherment, generation of random bit sequences, like challenge, etc.)

In the following, we will consider only the data transfer phase for performance analyses. As an example of a secure communication protocol, we will briefly describe the S-SNMP (Secure Simple Network Management Protocol [8]). Network management comprises protocols related to fault, accounting, configuration and name, performance, and security management. The security services that are provided by S-SNMP are: data integrity (against duplication, insertion, modification, resequencing, or replays), data-origin authentication (for corroboration of a message's source), access control and data confidentiality. The message formats are as shown in Fig. 1 [8]. The MD5 message-digest algorithm is used to calculate the 128-bit digest and DES for encryption. A D(estination)-timestamp as well as a S(ource)-timestamp are used to simplify clock synchronization and the context parameter to enable access control. PDU is the acronym for Protocol Data Unit and privDest is the destination party identifier. When privacy is required the privDest field remains in plaintext form to enable the receiving entity to determine the privacy characteristics (e.g., which key to use for decryption) of the D-Party. The timestamps are 32 bits long (but the associated fields are 2 octets longer due to encoding-specific reasons) and the other fields may be of variable length (minimum 3 octets).

privDest	digest	D-time-stamp	S-time-stamp	D-Party	S-Party	Context	PDU

(a) Authenticated but not private

privDest	field of 0 length		D-Party	S-Party	Context	PDU

(b) Private but not authenticated

privDest	digest	D-time-stamp	S-time-stamp	D-Party	S-Party	Context	PDU

(c) Private and authenticated

Fig. 1. Message formats for S(ecure)-SNMP (version 2)

2.1   A Simple Performance Model of Communication Systems

In the following, we want to model a communication system, first without and then with security mechanisms employed. The model comprises three components: two communicating open systems (OS1 and OS2) and the communication subsystem (CS, see Fig. 2). Each of the ovals OS1, OS2 and CS in the Fig 2 describes a queueing system. As an example consider the communication of two firewalls over a T1 link (ca. 1,5Mbps in USA and 2 Mbps in Europe). The product Interlock [13] provides for 500 Kbps encryption and for 1,2 Mbps data integrity and data origin authentication. We assume that the external arrival process is Poisson distributed with parameter λ

(arrival rate) and the service times are constant with corresponding service rates μ_1 μ_2 and μ_3 respectively. When considering secure communication, the arrival parameter λ remains the same but the service rates, which are now μ'_1, μ'_2 and μ'_3 respectively, change due to the additional processing for encryption and integrity in the gateways, and due to longer messages or packets for the data integrity and data origin authentication in the communcation subsystem.

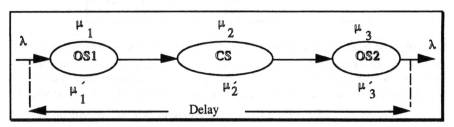

Fig. 2. A simple model of a communication system

2.2 Performance Analysis

The maximum throughput is determined by the bottleneck queue, with parameter $\mu_b = \min_{i \in \{1,2,3\}} (\mu_i)$. The maximum throughput is then equal to μ_b. In the case of our example above, when considering insecure communication, the bottleneck component is the T1 link, and when considering secure communication, the bottleneck component is the gateway (or firewall or open system) due to the encryption or the integrity and authentication functions required.

The component utilizations are $\rho_i = \lambda/\mu_i$. The definition $s_i = \mu_i/\mu'_i$ leads to

$$\rho'_i = \lambda/\mu'_i = s_i(\lambda/\mu_i) = s_i\rho_i .$$

The average delay spent in the system by a packet is equal to the sum of the times spent in each of the queueing systems. For our model (i.e., a tandem net with constant service times and external arrivals Poisson distributed) we can calculate the delay by only considering the bottleneck component as an M/D/1 [6] queueing system regardless of its position in the model chain (i.e., regardless of the actual arrival process of the bottleneck component) and adding to this result just the service times spent in the other components.

Thus, we have the average time T for insecure and T' for secure communication spent in the system as the sum of the time spent in the bottleneck components plus the service times in the other components:

$$T = \frac{1}{\mu_b} + \frac{1}{\mu_b} \frac{\rho_b}{2(1-\rho_b)} + \sum_{\substack{i=1 \\ i \neq b}}^{3} \frac{1}{\mu_i} = \frac{1}{\mu_b} \frac{\rho_b}{2(1-\rho_b)} + \sum_{i=1}^{3} \frac{1}{\mu_i}$$

$$T' = \frac{1}{\mu_b'} + \frac{1}{\mu_b'} \frac{\rho_b'}{2(1-\rho_b')} + \sum_{\substack{i=1 \\ i \neq b}}^{3} \frac{1}{\mu_i'} = \frac{1}{\mu_b'} \frac{\rho_b'}{2(1-\rho_b')} + \sum_{i=1}^{3} \frac{s_i}{\mu_i}$$

Example. The factors s_i depend not only on the security functions employed, but also on the message lengths. When communicating 60-bytes-long messages, the additional 24 bytes (16 bytes digest plus 8 bytes timestamps) for data authentication result in a 40% expansion of the message length. In this case we obtain: $s_2 = 1,4$. For longer messages we obtain smaller values for s_2. According to literature reports on traffic statistics (e.g., [5], these statistics follow the same general pattern of statistics collected on general-purpose networks) 52,8% of the total number of packets have a length of 60-98 bytes, approximately 69% of total packets have a length of 60-138 bytes and ca. 87% of them a length of 60-566 bytes. Although many of the packets that are less than 200 bytes are either acknowledgements or control packets [5], it is obvious that a significant percentage of the traffic consists of small packets. Note that acknowledgements are much fewer than packets sent since connectionless communication does not require acknowledgement and that, with connection-oriented communication, one acknowledgement packet acknowledges more than one user packet. Furthermore, we want to point out that s_2 also depends on the specific communication protocols regarding packet formats. For example, frames in CSMA/CD-based LANS must have a minimum length of 60 bytes along with the protocol-related data as opposed to ATM-based networks, where the communicating data unit is a cell with a constant length of 53 bytes (48 bytes payload). So messages which are less than 60 bytes along with their associated protocol overhead must be padded up to 60 bytes for communication over an ethernet-based network. These padding-bytes can be substituted by the integrity check sum without resulting in communication costs. Therefore, the factor s_2 depends on the communication protocols, the traffic characteristics and the security mechanisms employed.

The message expansion, due to the security mechanisms, leads to longer service times for communication protocol functions, like CRC (Cyclic Redundancy Check), but does not for others, like routing. In order to calculate the new service rates and their associated factors, s_1 and s_3, we must add the computing times for the specific security functions to the new service times for the communication protocol functions.

The following diagram (see Fig. 3) contains the response times for:

1) $\mu_1 = \mu_2 = \mu_3 = 1920$ packets/s, insecure communication for 100 byte long packets,

2) $\mu_1' = \mu_3' = 1920$ packets/s and $\mu_2' = 1548$ packets/s, only data integrity and origin authentication,

3) $\mu_1' = \mu_3' = 625$ packets/s and $\mu_2' = 1920$ packets/s, only encryption for 100 byte long packets,

4) $\mu_1' = \mu_3' = 504$ packets/s and $\mu_2' = 1548$ packets/s, authentication and encryption for 100 (+24) byte long packets,

where in the cases 2 and 3 only the encryption service times of the stations OS1 and OS2 (500 Kbps) are considered.

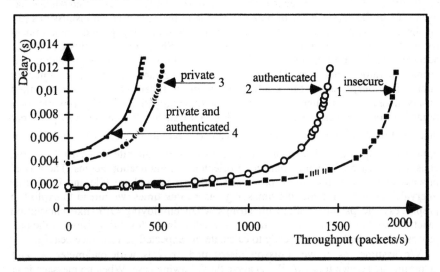

Fig. 3. The average system time as a function of the throughput for insecure (case 1), for authenticated (case 2), for confidential (case 3) and for confidential and authenticated communication (case 4).

For an intuitive explanation of the exponential growth of the response times for $\rho_b \to 1$ or $\rho_b' \to 1$, for each case consider that the random arrival process results in bursts of traffic and we must pay an extreme penalty when attempting to run the system near $\rho = 1$ [6].

3 Optimizations

In this chapter we deal with optimization concepts that do not involve substituting the hardware or software components by faster ones. The question in this chapter is: how can we improve the performance measures of secure communication? First, we observe that we cannot increase the maximum throughput, which requires the above-mentioned substitution of slow components with faster ones. However, we can improve the delay for equal values of achieveable throughput. Observing, in a differentiated way, the optimization possibilities for integrity, authentication, and encryption, we come to following: For integrity and authentication the goal can be to decline the length of the check sums and other parameters used rather than to reduce the associated processing costs and for encryption to reduce the processing needed. In the following, we deal with optimization concepts for security services requiring encryption.

3.1 Preprocessing

We remind first that the OFB (output feedback) operation mode was mainly intended for applications in which the error-extension properties of CBC (cipher block chaining) and CFB (cipher feedback) were troublesome [2]. A further advantage has been seen in the applicability of bulk encryption to multiple user´s transmissions [5]. As disadvantages were seen an increased sensitivity to bit slippage and a requirement for more complex synchronization procedures [5]. When employing this OFB operation mode, the cryptographic functions are actually used as a pseudo-random bit-string generator. When using OFB or any other strong random number generator for encryption purposes in the application-oriented layers, the above-mentioned disadvantages are no longer present since the transport-oriented layers provide for a reliable error-free message or packet end-to-end transfer. We should also point out that traditional transmission media possess an error bit rate between 10^{-4} and 10^{-6} as opposed to optical transmission media with an error bit rate of ca. 10^{-13}. Now, consider the case of when a connection-oriented communication begins. The arrival process of the messages to be processed and sent is random. Idle and busy time intervals alternate. It is the idle times, e.g., user think times, we intend to exploit to preprocess the pseudo-random bit strings when employing OFB-like encryption functions so that we can improve the average delay. In the following, we treat the pre-processing concept mathematically to calculate the expected performance benefit.

We assume, as above, Poisson distributed arrivals with parameter λ and deterministic service times d. We analyze the following case: When no message is in the queue and the last message in service leaves the server (i.e., the queueing system would enter in an idle period), the server begins to preprocess the random bit sequence for the next message to arrive. For simplifying the analysis, we will consider only the case where the server preprocesses the relevant pseudo-random bit sequence for the next message when the system would be otherwise idle. When the random bit sequence for a message is processed before its arrival, the system enters in an idle period. We neglect the time for the XOR-operation.

Analysis. We observe that when a new message arrives, the system is in one of the following states:
1)   With probability, say now p, the server is busy with messages that arrived prior to the new message, which has to wait until all of the messages which arrived earlier are processed. In that case the server needs the time d (the same as without preprocessing) to completely serve the new arrived message.
2)   With probability $(1-p)$, the server preprocessed either all or part of the processing required for the new arrived message. Thus, its new service time depends on the elapsed time since the last message left the system. It ranges from 0 to d, i.e., 0 when the elapsed time since the last message left the system was longer than d and a value less than d when the elapsed time was shorter than d.

The idle periods are exponentially distributed since we assumed a Poisson arrival process and implicitly an exponential distribution for the interarrival times as they are in an M/G/1 system [6]. Let $g(y)$ be the pdf (probability density function) describing the new service time and its Laplace transform be denoted by $G^*(s)$. The $g(y)$ is given by the following equation:

$$g(y) = pu(y - d) + (1 - p)f(y),$$

where $u(y - d)$ is the unit impulse function, and

$$f(y) = \begin{cases} \lambda\, e^{-\lambda(d-y)} + e^{-\lambda d}u(y), & 0 \le y \le d \\ \\ 0, & \text{otherwise} \end{cases}$$

Let us now deal with the probability p. From the state description above, it is obvious that p is the time percentage the system serves a message already present (without the preprocessed part), which equals λ multiplied by the new average service time d'. Thus, we can first calculate p and then d'.

$$p = d'\lambda = \lambda \left[pd + (1 - p)\int_{0^-}^{d} yf(y)dy \right], \quad d' = \begin{cases} \dfrac{d - \dfrac{1}{\lambda}\left(1 - e^{-\lambda d}\right)}{e^{-\lambda d}}, & 0 < \lambda \le \dfrac{1}{d} \\ 0 & , \lambda = 0 \end{cases}$$

We obtain the second moment of the new service time $\overline{Y^2}$ by applying one of the following formulas:

$$\overline{Y^2} = \int_{0}^{d} y^2 g(y)dy \ \text{ or } \ \frac{d^{(2)} G^*(s)}{d s^2}\Bigg|_{s=0} = (-1)^2 \overline{Y^2},$$

$$\overline{Y^2} = \lambda\, d'd^2 + (1 - \lambda\, d')\left(d^2 - \frac{2}{\lambda^2}\left(d\lambda - 1 + e^{-\lambda d}\right)\right)$$

In the calculation of the waiting time, we must pay attention to the fact that when a new message arrives at the system, the number of messages waiting in the queue and their service times are independently distributed. The service times are then equal to d for all waiting messages without preprocessing, since there would be no idle period for preprocessing between subsequent messages. Hence, this leads to the following, when taking expectations:

$$E\{W_i'\} = E\{R_i'\} + E\left\{\sum_{j=i-N_i}^{i-1} E\{X_j = d | N_i' \neq 0\}\right\}$$

$$= E\{R_i'\} + dE\{N_i'\}$$

where we denote [14]

W_i': The waiting time in queue of the i-th message.

R_i': The residual service time seen by the i-th message.

X_j: The service time of the j-th message.

N_i' :   The number of messages found waiting in queue by the i-th message.

Taking the limit as $i \rightarrow \infty$ we obtain

$$W' = R' + dN_Q' = R' + d\lambda\, W = \frac{R'}{(1 - d\lambda)}$$

The mean residual time can be obtained as usual for M/G/1-systems: $R' = \lambda \overline{Y^2}/2$. Now, we can proceed with our performance analysis as we do when analyzing M/G/1 queueing systems. The delay T without and T′ with preprocessing are given by the following equations. We obtain these by means of the Pollaczek-Khinchin mean-value formula [6] and by means of the formula for the waiting time W', respectively:

$$T = d + \frac{\lambda d^2}{2(1 - d\lambda)}, \quad T' = d' + \frac{\lambda \overline{Y^2}}{2(1 - d\lambda)}$$

The calculation of the performance benefit in terms of mean values leads to the following result:

$$T - T' = (d - d') + \frac{\lambda\left(d^2 - \overline{Y^2}\right)}{2(1 - d\lambda)} = d$$

This last result leads to a simplified formula for T' as follows:

$$\boxed{T' = \frac{\lambda d^2}{2(1 - d\lambda)}}$$

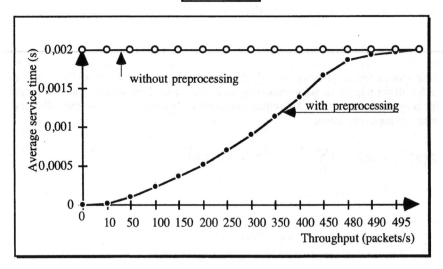

Fig. 4. The average service time with and without preprocessing as a function of the throughput.

Example. The Fig. 4 and 5 show the performance benefit we achieve when applying preprocessing for various utilization values and for $d = 2$ ms. As we expect for $\rho = 0$, the new average response time is zero and for $\rho = 1$ we have no performance benefit. However, for utilizations $\rho \neq 1$ we can achieve a delay reduction with preprocessing (which equals the preprocessable part of the service time d), e.g., for $\rho = 0,6$ of ca. 60%, for $\rho = 0,86$ of ca. 25% and for $\rho = 0,96$ of ca. 8%.

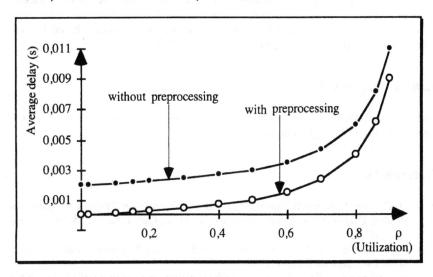

Fig. 5. The average delay with and without preprocessing as a function of the utilization

3.2 Message Segmenting

By communicating long messages and employing encryption in one of the application oriented layers, we can achieve a performance improvement when segmenting the messages in small data units. As an analogon consider packet versus message switching [10]. Associated with the segmenting is additional overhead which must be considered to determine the length of the data units. The performance benefit results from the fact that, while the last part of a message can stil be in service in the bottleneck component (i.e., cryptographic function of the sender), other parts can be taken into service by the subsequent system components (i.e., in the intermediate nodes or in the destination.)

3.3 Message Compression

Also, compression may be used in combination with message segmenting to further improve the performance measures when communicating long messages. The possible benefit is obvious and its analysis straightforward.

4 Conclusion

In this paper we introduced queueing theory in the performance study of secure data networks, and showed and quantified the tradeoff between security and performance. In order to improve the performance of secure communication protocols we discussed and partially analyzed optimization concepts. Preprocessing, message segmenting and compression functions may be employed to significantly improve the delay character istics of secure communication. Compression functionality is foreseen in the presentation layer but preprocessing and message segmenting mechanisms should be considered in secure protocols of application oriented layers.

Acknowledgements

I wish to thank Prof. W. Zorn and H. Schickle for their useful comments and Michelle Specht and Rosi Charitopoulou for text corrections.

References

1. D. Chaum: Security Without Identification: Transaction Systems to Make Big Brother Obsolete, Communications of the ACM, Oct. 1985, V. 28, No. 10, pp. 1030-1044.
2. D. W. Davies, W. L. Price: Security for Computer Networks, John Willey & Sons, Inc., Second Edition, 1989.
3. D. Gollmann, T. Beth, F. Damm: Authentication services in distributed systems, Computers & Security, 12 (1993), pp. 753-764.
4. M. J. Johnson: Using high-performance networks to enable computational aerosciences applications, Proc. of the IFIP WG6.1/WG6.4 Third International Workshop on Protocols for High-Speed Networks, Stockholm, Sweden, 13-15 May, 1992, pp. 137-152.
5. R. R. Jueneman: Analysis of Certain Aspects of Output Feedback Mode, Proc. of CRYPTO 1982, Advances in Cryptology, Plenum Press 1983, pp. 99-127.
6. L. Kleinrock: Queueing Systems, Volume I: Theory, John Willey & Sons, Inc. 1975.
7. A. Pfitzmann, M. Waidner: Networks without User Observability, Computers & Security, 6 (1987), pp. 158-166.
8. W. Stallings: SNMP, SNMPv2 and CMIP: the practical guide to network management standards, Addison-Wesley Publishing Company, Inc., 1993.
9. J. J. Tardo, K. Alagappan: SPX: Global Authentication Using Public Key Certificates, Proc. 1991 IEEE Computer Society Symposium on Research in Security and Privacy, May 20-22, 1991, pp. 232-244.
10. A. S. Tanenbaum: Computer Networks, Prentice-Hall International Editions, Second Edition, 1989.
11. ISO 7498-2: Security Architecture.
12. CCITT 509: Authentication Framework.
13. ANS CO+RE Systems, Inc.: Interlock 2.1 and ANSKeyRing, (18.08.1993).
14. D. Bertsekas, R. Gallager: Data Netwotks, Prentice-Hall International Editions, 1987.

High Assurance Software

Non-interference through Determinism

A. W. Roscoe   J. C. P. Woodcock   L. Wulf

Oxford University Computing Laboratory
Parks Road, Wolfson Building, Oxford OX1 3QD, UK

Abstract. The standard approach to the specification of a secure system is to present a (usually state-based) abstract security model separately from the specification of the system's functional requirements, and establishing a correspondence between the two specifications. This complex treatment has resulted in development methods distinct from those usually advocated for general applications.
We provide a novel and intellectually satisfying formulation of security properties in a process algebraic framework, and show that these are preserved under refinement. We relate the results to a more familiar state-based (Z) specification methodology. There are efficient algorithms for verifying our security properties using model checking.

Keywords
Security, Non-interference, Formal methods, Process algebra,
Determinism, Automatic verification

1 Introduction

Security requirements of a computer system are regarded as critical properties that demand the availability of mechanisms which control or protect programs and data. Three issues in particular are related to the area of computer security: (i) *confidentiality* (*secrecy*), the problem of protecting information from unauthorised disclosure; (ii) *integrity*, the protection of information from unauthorised modification or destruction; and (iii) *denial of service*, the avoidance of major reduction in system performance.

It is possible to regard these security concerns as properties of *information flow* within the system and base a specification of security on the absence of undesired flows. The notion of *non-interference* captures the idea that no information can flow from one user to another if the system view of the second is completely unaffected by actions of the first. We introduce a novel characterisation of non-interference based on the notion of deterministic views. This elegant formulation of non-interference has, unlike others described in the literature, the property of preserving security requirements under refinement.

The development of a secure system entails the construction of an abstract security model in addition to the specification of the system's functional requirements. The model is intended to capture abstractly the complete set of security requirements, which are derived from the system's (possibly informal) security policy, and which form part of the total system requirements. Depending on the level of rigour required during development, it is necessary to either informally establish or formally prove a correspondence between the functional specification and the abstract model.

The construction of the security model has been attempted [Col94, Jon92] with the same methods as functional specifications, such as the Z notation [Spi92]. We suggest that there are good reasons to employ a process algebraic notation for this purpose. Firstly, it is not the individual operations of the system, but the system as a whole that is to satisfy critical properties. Secondly, insecurity is introduced not by a single operation in isolation but by certain sequences of operations. And thirdly, it turns out to be possible to express non-interference constraints directly on a process representation of the system, thus eliminating the need for constructing a separate abstract model.

We therefore propose a process-algebraic approach (based on CSP [Hoa85]) to the specification of security properties. In particular the property of a process being *deterministic* is fundamental to the conditions we introduce for non-interference. This property can be verified using standard algorithms on finite-state systems, such as those implemented in the CSP model checker FDR[1] [Ros94a].

This paper is organised as follows. The following section defines the non-interference conditions and illustrates some of their properties. The conditions are generalised to systems with multiple users. Section 3 presents a functional specification of a file systems that is intended to maintain confidential information. A systematic way of mapping this specification into process algebra is given in section 4, and the particular conditions for non-interference in the process model are clearly stated. The security flaw of the system is detected by automatic verification in section 5, and it is shown how the system can be made secure. Finally, we present our conclusions in section 6.

2 Non-interference and Determinism

There have been a number of CSP formulations of non-interference, such as Jacob's use of inference functions [Jac90]. None of these approaches is based on the notion of determinism, which has only recently been recognised as the fundamental concept underlying the various definitions of non-interference [Ros94b]. This section will introduce some formal definitions of non-interference and analyse their properties.

2.1 Notation and Conventions

We will employ the failures-divergences model of CSP, in which a process is characterised by its failures and its divergences. We use the following notation to refer to various observations of a process P.

---

[1]FDR (Failures Divergence Refinement) is a product of Formal Systems (Europe) Ltd., 3 Alfred St., Oxford OX1 3EH, UK.

$\alpha(P)$	alphabet	set of events process P can engage in
TRACES(P)	traces	set of finite sequences of events P can engage in
FAILS(P)	failures	set of pairs (s, X) such that P can refuse events X after trace s
DIVS(P)	divergences	set of traces after which P may behave chaotically

The semantics of the *failures-divergences model* of CSP is detailed in (e. g.) [Hoa85]. Of particular relevance below will be the concealment and interleaving operators whose formal semantics are given in the Appendix. Informally, $P \setminus A$ is a process that behaves like P except that occurrences of events in set A are concealed. A concealed event occurs automatically and instantaneously as soon as it can, without being observed or controlled by the environment of the process. The $|||$ interleaving operator models asynchronous composition of processes: $P \ ||| \ Q$ is a process whose trace forms an arbitrary interleaving of events from processes P and Q. An event can be refused by the composition only if both component processes refuse it.

We will interpret some processes U_i as users interacting with another process P called the system. A user U of P is defined by its interface to the system. For the moment, it is assumed that the system has only two users U_H and U_L, with $\alpha(P) = H \cup L$ and $H \cap L = \varnothing$. This latter condition of disjoint set of actions available to the users is convenient since it prohibits direct communication between users by synchronisation.

These simplifying assumptions will be relaxed in section 2.5 where the non-interference conditions will be generalised to multi-user systems.

2.2 Abstracting Events

In a system with two users U_H and U_L we will typically want one user (U_L) to be completely unaware of what the other (U_H) does. In other words, the system view of U_L should be unaffected by the presence or absence of events user U_H might engage in. If this is the case, we say that there is no flow of information from U_H to U_L, or that U_H is non-interfering with U_L.

In a sense, it is necessary to abstract away from the actual or potential behaviour of U_H and ensure that this abstraction cannot affect how the system appears to U_L. There are several ways this abstraction may be captured, e.g. by concealing or obscuring U_H's actions. In CSP, the concealment of events is expressed using the $\setminus$ hiding operator, and the obscuring of events may be achieved using $|||$ interleaving.

It is well-known that concealment and interleaving of events may introduce non-determinism [Hoa85, pp. 113 and 120]. A non-deterministic system may, under the same conditions, behave differently towards its environment, due to some internal, uncontrollable choice. Though this choice cannot be observed directly, its external effects can, and thus provide clues on abstracted activities. The result of this abstraction will be that U_H's actions become choices which, though not visibly directly to U_L, may resolve non-determinism that is. The absence of non-determinism under abstraction of U_H's behaviour guarantees the absence of undesired information flow towards U_L.

The notion of determinism is formally defined as follows. A process P is *deterministic* if it is free of divergence, and if it never has a choice whether to refuse an event it can engage in.

$$P \text{ det} \iff \text{DIVS}(P) = \varnothing \wedge (tr^\frown\langle a \rangle \in \text{TRACES}(P) \Rightarrow (tr, \{a\}) \notin \text{FAILS}(P))$$

A process lacking this property is *non-deterministic*; under identical environmental conditions it may behave differently in an unpredictable fashion.

2.3 Non-interference Conditions

The conditions we propose are all based on the absence of non-determinism after the abstraction of "high-security" events, and are justified in detail in [Ros94b]. Concealment is the simplest method of abstracting from events in CSP which can serve as a first attempt to define the notion of non-interference.

Definition 1. A system P is said to be *eagerly secure* with respect to H if concealment of H events does not introduce non-determinism, i.e.

$$\text{E-Sec}_H(P) \iff (P \setminus H) \text{ det}$$

The terminology will become clear later on. Another way of abstracting events in CSP is not by concealing but by obscuring their occurrence. This can be achieved using another process

$$RUN_H = x : H \rightarrow RUN_H$$

and combining it with the original system P by interleaving as $P \,|||\, RUN_H$.

This process can never refuse an H event since RUN_H is always prepared to contribute one in arbitrary places. An outside observer will not be able to tell whether such an action came originally from P or from RUN_H. As above, we postulate that abstraction by interleaving does not introduce non-determinism.

Definition 2. A system P is said to be *lazily secure* with respect to H if obscuring H events by interleaving does not introduce non-determinism, i.e.

$$\text{L-Sec}_H(P) \iff (P \,|||\, RUN_H) \text{ det}$$

Example 1. Consider the system P with $H = \{h_1, h_2\}$ and $L = \{l\}$ defined

$$P = (h_1 \rightarrow l \rightarrow P) \,\square\, (h_2 \rightarrow l \rightarrow P)$$

The system repeatedly offers a choice of a single H event followed by action l. Concealing H permits U_L to engage in l whenever desired independently of the (hidden) choice between h_1 and h_2. Hence U_L's view of $P \setminus H$ is deterministic and $\text{E-Sec}_H(P)$ holds. We may doubt, however, whether the system should really be regarded as secure because the availability of l depends on the previous occurrence of an H action. The lazy condition does not make the assumption that H actions occur so quickly such that no refusal to communicate l may be recognised by U_L. System P therefore fails to be lazily secure, reflecting a dependence of U_L's system view on activity of the other user. $\square$

The terminology of the conditions reflects the semantics of the operators involved. The \ concealment operator is defined in a way such that hidden (internal) actions occur instantly. Abstraction of events by concealment is eager in the sense that the events cannot be prevented or delayed by the environment.

This situation contrasts with the usual interpretation of communications between interacting processes. The standard interpretation of the occurrence of an event is that the process and its environment have agreed on the action; it cannot occur without mutual consent. The agreement of U_H to engage in H events cannot be assumed to be immediately forthcoming. Abstraction by interleaving $P \;|||\; RUN_H$ does not force events from P to happen, it simply prevents an observer from knowing whether they came from P or from RUN_H. This lack of urgency explains why this is lazy abstraction. $P \;|||\; RUN_H$ can only be deterministic if the set of L events available before and after any H event of P are the same, since if the same event is communicated by RUN_H the state of P does not change. Lazy abstraction is thus sensitive not only to the effects of different actions by U_H, but also to the choice between action and inaction.

The possibility of infinite sequences of H actions give rise to the danger that a system implementation will prefer them forever, thereby denying U_L the opportunity to communicate—which would be a clear breach of security. The eager security condition, which entails the assumption that H actions are never delayed, is necessarily sensitive to this possibility as $P \setminus H$ introduces divergence.[2]

Example 2. Let $H = \{d_1, d_2, s_1, s_2\}$ and $L = \{l_1, l_2\}$. In the system

$$Q = (l_1 \rightarrow l_2 \rightarrow P)$$
$$\square\, (d_1 \rightarrow s_1 \rightarrow P)$$
$$\square\, (d_2 \rightarrow s_2 \rightarrow P)$$

there is the possibility of an infinite sequence of H actions. This potentially endless delay of U_L's request is flagged by the eager condition since $Q \setminus H$ diverges, so Q is not eagerly secure. The system also fails the lazy condition since event l_1 will be removed from the interface when U_H engages in either d_1 or d_2. Thus U_H will delay the system by communicating d_1 or d_2 until a further s action is taken. User U_L will recognise that the system refuses a request l_1 before U_H's request is complete. $\quad\square$

Whether the lack of lazy security in Example 2 should be regarded as a security breach depends on the nature of events $\{s_1, s_2\}$. If these are events which occur instantaneously—such as a system message appearing on the user's screen— then they are indistinguishable to U_L from the ordinary internal actions of Q. As long as these "signal" events are guaranteed to occur instantaneously there will be no refusal of a request by U_L at the interface to the system.

The H events can therefore be divided into two categories: signal events S which are guaranteed to occur instantly, and events D which cannot occur without the agreement of U_H and may thus be delayed. In many systems, delayable

---

[2] The lazy condition (where H actions may be subject to delay) assumes that the implementation is sufficiently fair to avoid this insecurity.

events take the form of inputs whereas the signals appear as output communications to the environment (including users).

Since S events resemble internal system actions we can abstract from them by hiding while we still use interleaving for ordinary events such as $\{d_1, d_2\}$ above. The combination of the two forms of abstraction results in a *mixed* non-interference condition.

Definition 3. A system P whose H events can be partitioned into delay events D and signal events S satisfies $\textbf{M-Sec}_{(D,S)}(P)$ if $(P \setminus S) \mathbin{|||} RUN_D$ is deterministic.

2.4 Properties of Conditions

From the eager and lazy conditions based on the notion of determinism it is possible to derive conditions involving only observations of the process concerned. Eager security can be paraphrased as stating that nothing which is observed in L after trace tr will allow the H events which happened during tr to be inferred.

Proposition 4. *If system P satisfies $\textbf{E-Sec}_H(P)$, then $P \setminus H$ is free of divergence, and for any two traces $tr, tr' \in \textsc{Traces}(P)$,*

$$tr \upharpoonright L = tr' \upharpoonright L \;\Rightarrow\; (P/tr) \setminus H =_{FD} (P/tr') \setminus H$$

A corresponding consequence can be derived from the definition of lazy security.

Proposition 5. *If system P satisfies $\textbf{L-Sec}_H(P)$, then P is free of divergence, and for any two traces $tr, tr' \in \textsc{Traces}(P)$,*

$$tr \upharpoonright L = tr' \upharpoonright L \;\Rightarrow\; (P/tr) \mathbin{|||} RUN_H =_{FD} (P/tr') \mathbin{|||} RUN_H$$

The approach of postulating determinism after abstraction of high-security events can be generalised by analysing various models of U_H. The framework in which this can be done is provided by the condition

$$(P \mathbin{\|[H]\|} U) \setminus H \ \textbf{det} \tag{1}$$

for a suitably chosen process U which has to synchronise with P on every event in H. Process U can be regarded as a model of user U_H.

The user with the widest range of behaviour is one whose actions are unpredictable and uncontrollable. Such activity is represented in CSP by a process $CHAOS$ defined as

$$CHAOS_H = STOP \sqcap (x : H \to CHAOS_H)$$

displaying the most non-deterministic behaviour which is free of divergence. A system with such a non-deterministic user will lack interference only in the case of both eager and lazy security.

Proposition 6. *A system P satisfies $\textbf{E-Sec}_H(P)$ and $\textbf{L-Sec}_H(P)$ if, and only if, the process $(P \mathbin{\|[H]\|} CHAOS_H) \setminus H$ is deterministic.*

It is shown in [Ros94b] that all three non-interference conditions (eager, lazy, and mixed) can in fact be expressed in the form of (1). For eager security, the model for user U_H is simply identical to RUN_H since $P \,\|[\, H \,]\|\, RUN_H = P$ for all processes P.

Corresponding formulations for lazy and mixed security require a more powerful model of CSP. In the infinite traces model [Ros93] the failures-divergences representation of a process is augmented with its set of infinite traces. The model of user U_H required for lazy security is a process $FINITE_H$ which behaves just like $CHAOS_H$ but without ever engaging in an infinite trace. This restriction prohibits the occurrence of infinite H sequences resulting in divergence under concealment.

Proposition 7. *Eager, lazy, and mixed security can be all be expressed in the general form of (1) as follows.*

$$\textbf{E-Sec}_H(P) \;\Leftrightarrow\; (P \,\|[\, H \,]\|\, RUN_H) \setminus H \;\textbf{det}$$

$$\textbf{L-Sec}_H(P) \;\Leftrightarrow\; (P \,\|[\, H \,]\|\, FINITE_H) \setminus H \;\textbf{det}$$

$$\textbf{M-Sec}_{(D,S)}(P) \;\Leftrightarrow\; (P \,\|[\, H \,]\|\, (RUN_S \,\|\|\, FINITE_D)) \setminus H \;\textbf{det}$$

These various 'users' suggest a more general approach to security specification: for a particular context, choose a process U which characterises all possible behaviours of U_H under which it is expected that confidentiality will be maintained. Usually this will be all its behaviours, but it is possible to imagine other circumstances, for example if the system P represents a mail system where it is allowable for a high-security user to send a message to a low-security one, we might expect to maintain confidentiality so long as no such messages are sent. (This type of property is known as *conditional* non-interference.)

The more non-deterministic the abstract model U the stronger is the equivalent security condition. When a more deterministic process is substituted for U, the properties of CSP refinement guarantee the preservation of non-interference.

More precisely, if P is a system component in context C, then refinement of P – replacing it with a less non-deterministic component – preserves determinism of the original system:

$$C(P) \;\textbf{det}\; \wedge \; P \sqsubseteq P' \;\Rightarrow\; C(P') \;\textbf{det}$$

It is equally a consequence of this fact that refining P preserves the determinism of $(P \,\|[\, H \,]\|\, U) \setminus H$, and that therefore each of our non-interference properties is preserved under refinement. This is a result which may be exploited in system development or maintenance.

Proposition 8. *Eager, lazy, and mixed security are preserved under refinement:*

$$\textbf{E-Sec}_H(C(P)) \wedge \; P \sqsubseteq P' \;\Rightarrow\; \textbf{E-Sec}_H(C(P'))$$

$$\textbf{L-Sec}_H(C(P)) \wedge \; P \sqsubseteq P' \;\Rightarrow\; \textbf{L-Sec}_H(C(P'))$$

$$\textbf{M-Sec}_{(D,S)}(C(P)) \wedge \; P \sqsubseteq P' \;\Rightarrow\; \textbf{M-Sec}_{(D,S)}(C(P'))$$

A number of additional results concerning the composition and decomposition of secure systems may be derived; see [Ros94b]. One such result is that a system P may be decomposed into two non-interacting parts if it is lazily secure with respect to two disjoint alphabets.

Proposition 9. *Let A, B be disjoint alphabets.* **L-Sec**$_A(P)$ *and* **L-Sec**$_B(P)$ *hold of a system if, and only if, there are two deterministic processes P_A with $\alpha(P_A) = A$ and P_B with $\alpha(P_B) = B$ such that $P = P_A \parallel P_B$.*

Further properties of our non-interference conditions as well as the proofs of the propositions in this section may be found in [Ros94b].

2.5 Generalisation

We will now generalise the determinism conditions for multi-user systems. If F is the system whose non-interference properties we attempt to establish, the system model can be described as

$$SYSTEM = Users \parallel F \quad \text{where} \quad Users = \big\|\big\|_{i>0} U_i$$

It is assumed that there is a security classification associated with each user. Let $CLASS$ be the partially ordered set of these classifications. The total function $cl : Users \rightarrow CLASS$ assigns one classification to each user process. A further assumption is $\alpha(U_i) \cap \alpha(U_j) = \varnothing$ whenever $cl(U_i) \neq cl(U_j)$.

The function $above : CLASS \rightarrow \mathbb{P}\alpha(SYSTEM)$ is used to define the set of events that should be hidden from a user operating on a particular level of classification, which is given by

$$above(c) = \alpha(SYSTEM) - above^{-1}(c)$$

where

$$above^{-1}(c) = \bigcup\{\alpha(U_i) \mid cl(U_i) \leq c\}$$

The non-interference conditions of section 2.3 hold for a multi-user system if they hold on each security level of the system.

Definition 10. A multi-user system P is eagerly and (respectively) lazily-secure if,

$$\forall\, c_i \in CLASS \bullet \textbf{E-Sec}_{H_j}(P)\,, \text{ and}$$

$$\forall\, c_i \in CLASS \bullet \textbf{L-Sec}_{H_j}(P)$$

where $H_j = above(c_i)$.

In a realistic system it is typically the mixed non-interference condition that requires verification on each security level, as will be illustrated in the following case study.

3 A "Secure" File System

This and the following section will illustrate the framework in which our non-interference conditions can be applied. The example is that of a file system in which confidential data is to be maintained.

It is widely accepted that a formal specification can increase the level of assurance that a system will meet its security requirements [Gas88]. In fact governmental standards for the development of secure systems mandate the use of formal methods and proof. The Z notation [Spi92] is particularly suited for this task since (i) it has a well-defined semantics; (ii) it has been successfully employed in industrial scale software development; and (iii) it has become increasingly popular for the specification and verification of secure systems [Col94, Jon92].

We begin the specification of the file system by introducing some basic types. The set of users of the system is represented by type $USER$, each of which holds an associated security classification from the set $CLASS$. FID represents the set of file identifiers, and $DATA$ refers to the set of possible data that may be stored in a file. This type contains a special value $NULL$ representing invalid data. These are the basic types we will use

$$[USER, CLASS, FID, DATA]$$

There is a security classification associated with each user. We use a global function cl to obtain the appropriate class by supplying it with a user identification. It is declared as a *total* function; there cannot be users without classification.

$$|\quad cl : USER \rightarrow CLASS$$

3.1 File Model

Each file has the structure[3]

$$\begin{array}{|l}\hline \_File _____ \\ class : CLASS \\ data : DATA \\ \hline \end{array}$$

where the *class* component relates to the level of security of the stored *data*. Each file initialised with the level of clearance at which the file is created.

$$\begin{array}{|l}\hline \_Init _____ \\ File' \\ clear? : CLASS \\ \hline class' = clear? \\ data' = NULL \\ \hline \end{array}$$

---

[3] In Z, formal notation is separated from informal descriptions by so-called schema boxes. A schema contains a number of declarations and, if there are any constraints on these declarations, a separating line followed by appropriate predicates. Schemas are used to represent structured state as well as operations on structures.

We follow a standard convention of decorating inputs with ?, outputs with !, and states after completion of the operation with a prime $'$. Unprimed variables or schemas refer to states before the operation.

Two operations are provided on files: reading stored data, and writing new data, provided the file access is carried out with the appropriate clearance. Reading is permitted only when the operation is carried out with appropriate access permission $clear? \geq class$, in which case stored data is output as $data!$. The notation $\Xi File$ indicates that reading a file does not change its state.

```
┌─ Rd0 ──────────────────────────────────────────────
│ Ξ File
│ clear? : CLASS
│ data! = data
│ ────────────────────────────────────────────────
│ clear? ≥ class
│ data! = data
└────────────────────────────────────────────────────
```

Storing new data in a file is carried out with a $Wr0$ operation which is permitted only if the user clearance is equal to the file classification. The $\Delta File$ schema component indicates that writing data changes the file state; the input data $new?$ is stored in the $data$ component of $File$.

```
┌─ Wr0 ──────────────────────────────────────────────
│ ΔFile
│ clear? : CLASS
│ new? : DATA
│ ────────────────────────────────────────────────
│ clear? = class = class'
│ data' = new?
└────────────────────────────────────────────────────
```

To indicate the success or failure of an operation, we define the system's response as type

$$RESP ::= ok \mid fail$$

Each operation on a file is accompanied by an indication of whether it has succeeded. The output message is defined by the (horizontal) schemas

$$Success \; \widehat{=} \; [resp! : RESP \mid resp! = ok]$$
$$Failure \; \widehat{=} \; [resp! : RESP \mid resp! = fail]$$

We do not give the user any indication of whether a failure was caused by a functional error or a security breach, in order to avoid a potential channel of information flow.

If a request for file access is carried out without valid clearance the operation fails, and the file status remains unchanged ($\Xi File$). The case of invalid read access is described as

```
┌─ NoRdAccess ──────────────────────
│ Ξ File
│ Failure
│ clear? : CLASS
│ data! : DATA
├───────────────────────────────────
│ clear? < class
│ data! = NULL
└───────────────────────────────────
```

The corresponding error condition for writing is

```
┌─ NoWrAccess ──────────────────────
│ Ξ File
│ Failure
│ clear? : CLASS
├───────────────────────────────────
│ clear? ≠ class
└───────────────────────────────────
```

The total read and write operations are Rd and Wr specified as

$$Rd \;\;\widehat{=}\;\; (Rd0 \wedge Success) \vee NoRdAccess$$

$$Wr \;\;\widehat{=}\;\; (Wr0 \wedge Success) \vee NoWrAccess$$

If the request is carried out with appropriate clearance the system reports with *ok*, otherwise the user just receives a *fail* message and the file remains unaltered.

3.2 File System

Our file system is given by

```
┌─ FileSystem ──────────────────────
│ files : FID ↦ File
└───────────────────────────────────
```

Component *files* is declared as a partial function from file identifiers to files. This means that no two files can have the same name. The system initially contains no files:

$$FInit \;\widehat{=}\; [FileSystem' \mid files' = \varnothing]$$

In addition to the initialisation occurring when a file is created at the system level, we want the operations of reading and writing a file to be available at the system interface. This is a achieved by *promoting* the schemas *Init*, *Rd*, and *Wr* with the aid of two "framing" schemas:

```
┌─ Φ1 ──────────────────────────────
│ Δ FileSystem
│ file? : FID
│ user? : USER
├───────────────────────────────────
│ clear? = cl(user?)
│ files' = files ⊕ {file? ↦ θFile'}
└───────────────────────────────────
```

$$\boxed{\begin{array}{l} \Phi 2 \\ \hline \Phi 1 \\ \hline file? \in \operatorname{dom} files \\ \theta File = files(file?) \end{array}}$$

The promoted operations will require both a file name (*file?*) and a user identification (*user?*) as input. The user's classification is then the clearance at which the file operation is carried out. The three operations available at the interface are

$$
\begin{aligned}
Create0 &\;\widehat{=}\; \exists\, File' \bullet (\Phi 1 \wedge Init) \\
Read0 &\;\widehat{=}\; \exists\, \Delta File \bullet (\Phi 2 \wedge Rd) \\
Write0 &\;\widehat{=}\; \exists\, \Delta File \bullet (\Phi 2 \wedge Wr)
\end{aligned}
$$

It is necessary to ensure that no operation is carried out on files which do not exist. This error condition can occur if the user supplies an invalid file identifier.

$$\boxed{\begin{array}{l} UnknownFile \\ \hline \Xi FileSystem \\ Failure \\ file? : FID \\ \hline file? \notin \operatorname{dom} files \end{array}}$$

Similarly, a request for file creation cannot succeed if the suggested name has already been used for another file.

$$\boxed{\begin{array}{l} FileExists \\ \hline \Xi FileSystem \\ Failure \\ file? : FID \\ \hline file? \in \operatorname{dom} files \end{array}}$$

The total operations available at the file system interface are then given by

$$
\begin{aligned}
Create &\;\widehat{=}\; (Create0 \wedge Success) \vee FileExists \\
Read &\;\widehat{=}\; Read0 \vee UnknownFile \\
Write &\;\widehat{=}\; Write0 \vee UnknownFile
\end{aligned}
$$

We suggest that a security analysis is best carried out on a process algebraic representation of the system. This representation may be regarded as a security model [Gas88] which can in fact be derived by translation. It is therefore unnecessary to engage in an error-prone attempt to prove a correspondence between model and specification. In the coming section we map the functional specification of the file system into CSP and state the non-interference conditions that require verification.

4 Z into CSP

The Z specification may be translated into CSP according to the technique described in [Woo94]. The theoretical basis for this work may be found in [WM90].

First we interpret the Z specification as an action system [BKS83] whose state is specified by *File*. It has two actions corresponding to the operations *Rd* and *Wr*. However, each of these operations also has an output, and we must be careful to separate the two parts of the operation and associate an action with each, since we cannot regard input and output as happening simultaneously. When a user has invoked an operation, but has not consumed its output, then the system will do nothing else while that output is pending. When no output is pending, all operation actions are enabled.

This interpretation of a Z specification is informal (albeit systematic), but it does correspond to the intuitive meaning given to Z specifications (see [Spi92], for example).

Consider the *Wr* operation. We must separate it into two parts: the first part consumes the input and then stores its output in the state; the second part waits for the opportunity of delivering its output. Define a new free type that is either a response or nothing:

$$RESP_+ ::= nullresp \mid outresp \langle\!\langle RESP \rangle\!\rangle$$

and augment the state of a file with a component that contains the pending output (if it exists)

$$
\begin{array}{|l}
\hline
\_File_+ _____ \\
File \\
wrpend : RESP_+ \\
\hline
\end{array}
$$

The first part of the operation is as follows

$$
\begin{array}{|l}
\hline
\_Wr_+ _____ \\
\Delta File_+ \\
clear? : CLASS \\
new? : DATA \\
\hline
wrpend = nullresp \\
\exists\, resp! : RESP \mid wrpend' = outresp(resp!) \bullet Wr \\
\hline
\end{array}
$$

and the second part is

$$
\begin{array}{|l}
\hline
\_Wr_- _____ \\
\Delta File_+ \\
\Xi File \\
resp! : RESP \\
\hline
wrpend \neq nullresp \\
resp! = outresp^\sim(wrpend) \\
wrpend' = nullresp \\
\hline
\end{array}
$$

We can prove that the only change we are making to Wr by splitting into two is to delay its output:

$$\vdash Wr = \exists\, wrpend, wrpend' : RESP_+ \bullet Wr_+ \,\fatsemi\, Wr_-$$

According to [Woo94], we can now translate our specification of the write operation into two actions.

$$wr?clear?new \wedge wrpend = nullresp \rightarrow Wr_+$$

$$wrout!(outresp^\sim(wrpend)) \wedge wrpend \neq nullresp \rightarrow wrpend := nullresp$$

Thus, upon receipt of the communication of a clearance and some new data, then, providing that there is no write-output pending, the Wr_+ operation is performed. Output may be transmitted whenever it is pending.

We can make similar transformations for the other operations.

The actions may now be embedded in a CSP-framework process. We now have a CSP process which is formally equivalent to the *File* abstract data type.

$$File = init?class \rightarrow File(class, NULL, (nullresp, nulldata), nullresp)$$

$File(class, data, rdpend, wrpend) =$
    if $rdpend = nullresp \wedge wrpend = nullresp$
    then
        $rd?clear \rightarrow$
            if $clear \geq class$
            then $File(class, data, (outresp(ok), outdata(data)), wrpend)$
            else $File(class, data, (outresp(fail), outdata(NULL)), wrpend)$
        $\square\ wr?clear?new \rightarrow$
            if $clear = class$
            then $File(class, new, rdpend, outresp(ok))$
            else $File(class, data, rdpend, outresp(fail))$
    else
        if $rdpend \neq nullresp$
        then $rdout!outresp^\sim(rdpend)$
            $\rightarrow File(class, data, (nullresp, nulldata), wrpend)$
        else $wrout!outresp^\sim(wrpend)$
            $\rightarrow File(class, data, rdpend, nullresp)$

The *File* process may now be transformed using the laws of CSP, and, if desired, the state variables containing the pending outputs elided.

In [Woo94], the connection is made between the technique of promotion in Z, and the use of subordination or the means of sharing through interleaving. In this way, the file system can be created as a system of CSP processes.

The structure of the resulting CSP implementation is illustrated in Figure 1. *FILES* will be a shared pool of files accessible through the interface *FSYS*. Each file has an associated name and classification, and may contain arbitrary data. The process *File* models a file waiting to be initialised.

$$File = init?file?class \rightarrow File(file, class, NULL)$$

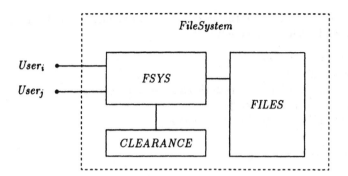

Fig. 1. The file system implemented by communicating processes.

A file after initialisation may be read or written to.

$$File(file, class, data) \ = \ Rd(file, class, data) \ \Box \ Wr(file, class, data)$$

The read operation is implemented by process Rd as

$Rd(file, class, data) = rd.file?clear \rightarrow$
  if $clear \geq class$
  then $rdout.file!ok!data \rightarrow File(file, class, data)$
  else $rdout.file!fail!NULL \rightarrow File(file, class, data)$

Storing new data in a file is realised with process

$Wr(file, class, data) = wr.file?clear?new \rightarrow$
  if $clear = class$
  then $wrout.file!ok \rightarrow File(file, class, new)$
  else $wrout.file!fail \rightarrow File(file, class, data)$

The total pool of files is given by

$$FILES \ = \ \big|\big|\big|_{0 \leq i < n} File$$

4.1 The System Interface

It is not possible to conjoin $FILES$ with the set of user processes directly because users must be protected from a number of functional errors, such as reading a file which does not exist. To this purpose, we will provide a system interface process $FSYS$ which manages access to the individual files.

$$\alpha(FSYS) = \{create, createout, read, readout, write, writeout,$$
$$init, rd, rdout, wr, wrout, clear\}$$

$FSYS$ holds state variable $files$, the set of current file names

$$FSYS(files) \ = \ Create(files) \ \Box \ Read(files) \ \Box \ Write(files)$$

The three services available at the interface are implemented with processes *Create*, *Read*, and *Write* respectively.

$Create(files) = create?user?file \rightarrow$
    if $file \notin files$
    then $clear.user?class \rightarrow init!file!class \rightarrow createout.user!ok$
        $\rightarrow FSYS(files \cup \{file\})$
    else $createout.user!fail \rightarrow FSYS(files)$

$Read(files) = read?user?file \rightarrow$
    if $file \in files$
    then $clear.user?class \rightarrow rd.file!class \rightarrow rdout.file?resp?result$
        $\rightarrow readout.user.file!resp!result \rightarrow FSYS(files)$
    else $readout.user.file!fail!NULL \rightarrow FSYS(files)$

$Write(files) = write?user?file?new \rightarrow$
    if $file \in files$
    then $clear.user?class \rightarrow wr.file!class!new \rightarrow wrout.file?resp$
        $\rightarrow writeout.user.file!resp \rightarrow FSYS(files)$
    else $writeout.user.file!fail \rightarrow FSYS(files)$

Process *CLEARANCE* provides the appropriate classification of a user when required.

$$CLEARANCE = (\Box\ clear.u!(cl(u)) \rightarrow CLEARANCE) \quad \text{for all } u \in USER$$

The complete file system is given by parallel composition of the interface process, the file pool, and the clearance process, with intermediate channels concealed.

$$FileSystem = (FSYS(\varnothing) \parallel FILES \parallel CLEARANCE)$$
$$\setminus \{init, rd, rdout, wr, wrout, clear\}$$

4.2 Security Specification

Any particular instance of the file system can be subjected to the security conditions presented in section 2. We will consider the case of three users with the following classifications.

USER	CLASS
Lisa	3 (highest)
Mari	2
Nina	1 (lowest)

It is convenient to partition the events at the system interface into "delay" and "signal" events on each level of user classification (except the top level).

$H2d = \{\ create.user.file, read.user.file, write.user.file.data \mid user \in \{Lisa\}\ \}$
$H2s = \{\ createout.user.resp, readout.user.file.resp.data,$
    $writeout.user.file.resp \mid user \in \{Lisa\}\ \}$

$H1d = \{\, create.user.file, read.user.file, write.user.file.data$
$\qquad |\; user \in \{Lisa, Mari\}\,\}$
$H1s = \{\, createout.user.resp, readout.user.file.resp.data,$
$\qquad writeout.user.file.resp \mid user \in \{Lisa, Mari\}\,\}$

The file system satisfies **E-Sec**(*FileSystem*) if

$(FileSystem \setminus (H2d \cup H2s))$ **det** $\land (FileSystem \setminus (H1d \cup H1s))$ **det**

The file system is lazily secure if

$(FileSystem \;|||\; RUN_{(H2d \cup H2s)})$ **det** $\land (FileSystem \;|||\; RUN_{(H1d \cup H1s)})$ **det**

The file system satisfies the mixed security property if

$((FileSystem \setminus H2s) \;|||\; RUN_{H2d})$ **det** $\land$
$((FileSystem \setminus H1s) \;|||\; RUN_{H1d})$ **det**

It turns out that none of these conditions is met – i. e. that the system contains undesired information flows. Since it may not be obvious that the conditions fail to hold (and why not), we employ a verification tool.

5 Automated Verification

The effort of formulating the eager/lazy/mixed non-interference conditions would be futile without a method of verifying them. Luckily, the absence of non-determinism on which the conditions are based can be automatically verified using standard algorithms on finite-state systems. We show that the CSP proof tool FDR can be used to complete the security analysis.

5.1 FDR

The FDR tool [Ros94a] has been originally designed to verify behavioural CSP specifications, in particular refinement relations between processes. These refinement checking capabilities are employed to decide whether a given process is deterministic using the following algorithm:

1. Search through the state space of P, resolving all non-determinism that is encountered. In a "stable" state (in which internal progress is impossible) a single representative for each available action is selected, whereas in a state where internal actions are possible we chose one of these arbitrarily. This search either finds a divergence of P (in which case it is clearly non-deterministic) or yields a deterministic process Q that refines the original P.
2. Use the refinement checker to confirm whether $Q \sqsubseteq P$. The check succeeds if, and only if, P is deterministic.

The algorithm is justified by the fact that the deterministic processes are maximal in the failures-divergences model of CSP, and are therefore incomparable. Thus, for some arbitrary deterministic refinement Q of P,

P **det** $\Leftrightarrow P =_{FD} Q$

5.2 Making the File System Secure

Checking the security specification of section 4.2 using FDR confirms that the file system is neither eagerly nor lazily secure. The reasons for this lie in the basic structure of the system interface: a menu of services is offered to users with various classifications, and a choice of service by a particular user is followed by a system response on the same security level.

This structure resembles that of the (much simpler) process Q of Example 2 which was already observed to be insecure under the eager and lazy conditions. As was motivated there, these conditions are inappropriate for a system structured like Q or *FileSystem*, and it becomes necessary to partition events into delay and signal events in order to apply the mixed condition.

However **M-Sec**(*FileSystem*) fails to hold as well, which must be of serious concern to the system designers. A check using FDR shows the reason for this to be the possible failure of a request to create a file. The file system was specified to prohibit the existence of two files with the same name. This feature is a security flaw since a user who attempts to create a file (with identifier *id* say) and fails has learned that a file named *id* of higher classification exists. This clear breach of non-interference is reflected in the failure of the mixed condition.

The question remains how the flaw can be overcome. One idea may be to change the *Create* operation so that a request of file creation always succeeds. This approach is probably unsatisfactory if creation of a file which already exists results in stored data to be lost. A more promising approach is to somehow associate classifications with file identifiers in order to guarantee that files on different security levels have different names.

A simple way of implementing this is to provide pairwise disjoint sets of identifiers for the different levels. For the system in section 4 one might consider partitioning the set *FID* into three sets (say)

$$FID_1 = \{a, b\}, \ FID_2 = \{c, d\}, \ FID_3 = \{e, f\}$$

so that for all $i \in CLASS$

$$FID = \bigcup FID_i$$

Doing so entails the re-definition of the *Create* operation which now needs to confirm whether the use of a particular identifier is valid with regard to the user's classification:

> $Create(files) = create?user?file \rightarrow$
> $\quad$ **if** $file \notin files$
> $\quad$ **then** $clear.user?class \rightarrow$
> $\quad\quad$ **if** $file \in FID_{class}$
> $\quad\quad$ **then** $init!file!class \rightarrow createout.user!ok \rightarrow FSYS(files \cup \{file\})$
> $\quad\quad$ **else** $createout.user!fail \rightarrow FSYS(files)$
> $\quad$ **else** $createout.user!fail \rightarrow FSYS(files)$

Verification of the mixed security condition now shows that **M-Sec**(*FileSystem*) does indeed hold, *provided* that the number of files available through the system is equal to or exceeds the combined total of identifiers for all levels of classification. So if

$$FILES = \big|\big|\big|_{0 \leq i < n} File$$

we require $n \geq size(FID)$. Without the proviso the file system does not pass the mixed condition, again because an attempt of file creation may fail. This time the security breach is caused by the potential exhaustion of the pool of available files.

6   Conclusion

This paper presents process algebraic specifications as a practical framework for the development of systems with security constraints. The approach is illustrated with an example of a file system intended to maintain secret data, but in fact our results apply equally to systems with security concerns other than confidentiality. This is a consequence of defining general non-interference conditions which require the system view of particular users to be unaffected by the actions taken by others.

Our non-interference conditions are based on the notion of deterministic views. This elegant characterisation of secure systems has only recently been recognised as the fundamental concept underlying various definitions of non-interference, such as those surveyed in [Gra92]. Although these alternative definitions are cast in rather different notation without employing determinism, Roscoe [Ros94b] demonstrates that many are either straightforward consequence of, or closely related to, the conditions for eager, lazy, and mixed security. For example our lazy property $\textbf{L-Sec}_H(L)$ corresponds precisely both to Graham-Cumming's own non-interference property and those of Allen [All91] and Ryan [Rya91] for systems whose overall behaviour is deterministic (as opposed to the abstractions used in formulating our properties). A significant advantage of our conditions in comparison to others is the preservation of non-interference under refinement, thus eliminating the potential compromise of security during development. A detailed discussion of this phenomenon, and an explanation of why it is desirable, may be found in [Ros94b].

The general framework envisaged for the development of secure systems falls into two parts: functional specifications of the system using state-based notations as for general applications, followed by an analysis of non-interference properties of a process-algebraic representation of the system. The main advantage of this method is in avoiding the complex treatment of establishing a correspondence between the specification and a separate generic security model. In contrast, the mapping of the specification into process algebra can in many cases be carried out by direct translation (tool support for this task is, however, at present not available). Process algebras such as CSP based on possible sequences (traces) of events provide an ideal notation for non-interference analysis since they naturally incorporate the notion of (non-)determinism, thus permitting the application of the conditions of section 2. These conditions can then be automatically verified using a currently available proof tool.

Initial experience with the CSP model checker FDR [Ros94a] shows that a security analysis as illustrated in section 5 can be carried out within minutes. This result propounds the hope that the verification approach will scale up to systems of realistic size. The size of problem we can deal with will benefit from the proposed development [Ros94a] of FDR to incorporate *implicit* model-checking techniques such as the hierarchical compression of intermediate state-spaces. Verification speed will further increase by the exploitation of behavioural independence of processes from particular values of data communicated. This property of *data-independence* [RMacC94] has already shown promise in significant reduction of state spaces as well as the induction of properties of arbitrary data types based on finite checks.

Future work is required to formalise the mapping of state-based specifications to process descriptions. The techniques of [WM90, Woo94] still have to be extended to be applicable to specifications with complex semantics, and utilised to provide tool support for the translation into process algebra. We intend to apply these techniques and the framework outlined in this paper in a case study of a large-scale secure system. A further avenue of research is to explore potential applications of our determinism-based conditions for non-interference on systems with critical requirements other than security, such as in the areas of safety-critical systems, fault tolerance, and feature independence.

References

[All91] P.G. Allen. "A comparison of non-interference and non-deducibility using CSP", *Proc. 1991 IEEE Computer Security Workshop*, pp 43-54. IEEE Computer Society Press 1991.

[BKS83] R-J. R. Back, R. Kurki-Suonio. "Decentralization of process nets with centralized control", *Proc 2nd Annual Symposium on Principles of Distributed Computing*, Montreal, 1983.

[Col94] R. Collinson. "Proving Critical Properties of Functional Specifications", *Proc FME'94 Symposium*, Springer-Verlag LNCS, Barcelona, October 1994.

[Gas88] M. Gasser. *Building a Secure Computer System*, Van Nostrand Reinhold, 1988.

[Gra92] J. Graham-Cumming. *The Formal Development of Secure Systems*, Oxford University DPhil Thesis, 1992.

[Hoa85] C. A. R. Hoare. *Communicating Sequential Processes*, Prentice Hall 1985.

[Jac90] J. L. Jacob. "Specifying Security Properties", in C. A. R. Hoare (ed), *Developments in Concurrency and Communication*, ACM Press, 1990.

[Jon92] R. B. Jones. "Methods and Tools for the Verification of Critical Properties", in C. B. Jones, R. C. Shaw, T. Denvir (eds) *Proc 5th Refinement Workshop*, Springer Verlag, London, 1992.

[Ros93] A. W. Roscoe. "Unbounded Non-determinism in CSP", *Journal of Logic and Computation* **3**, 1993.

[Ros94a] A. W. Roscoe. "Model Checking CSP", in A. W. Roscoe (ed) *A Classical Mind*, Prentice Hall 1994.

[Ros94b] A. W. Roscoe. "CSP and Determinism in Security Modelling", in preparation.

[RMacC94] A. W. Roscoe, H. MacCarthy. "Verifying a replicated database: A case study in model-checking CSP", submitted for publication.

[Rya91] P. Y. A. Ryan. "A CSPformulation of non-interference", *Cipher*, pp 19-27. IEEE Computer Society Press, 1991.

[Spi92] J.M. Spivey, *The Z Notation: A Reference Manual* (2nd ed.), Prentice-Hall International, 1992.

[WM90] J. C. P. Woodcock, C. Morgan. "Refinement of State-based Concurrent Systems", *Proc VDM Symposium 1990*, LNCS 428, Springer Verlag.

[Woo94] J. C. P. Woodcock. "CSP Interpretations of Z Specifications", in preparation.

A CSP Reference

In the failures-divergences model of CSP, two processes are regarded as equal if they agree in their failures and their divergences:

$$P =_{FD} Q \iff \text{FAILS}(P) = \text{FAILS}(Q) \land \text{DIVS}(P) = \text{DIVS}(Q)$$

When a process Q is more deterministic than another process P we say that P is refined by Q. This relation is written $P \sqsubseteq Q$ and formally defined by

$$P \sqsubseteq Q \iff \text{FAILS}(P) \supseteq \text{FAILS}(Q) \land \text{DIVS}(P) \supseteq \text{DIVS}(Q)$$

The semantics of the hiding operator in the failures-divergences model is given by

$$
\begin{aligned}
\text{DIVS}(P \setminus A) = &\{ (s \setminus A)\hat{}t \mid s \in \text{DIVS}(P) \} \cup \\
&\{ (s \setminus A)\hat{}t \mid (\forall n \in \mathbb{N} \bullet (\exists u \in A^* \bullet \#u > n \land s\hat{}u \in \text{TRACES}(P))) \} \\
\text{FAILS}(P \setminus A) = &\{ (u, X) \mid u \in \text{DIVS}(P \setminus A) \} \cup \\
&\{ (s \setminus A, X) \mid (s, X \cup A) \in \text{FAILS}(P) \}
\end{aligned}
$$

The semantics of ||| interleaving is defined as

$$
\begin{aligned}
\text{DIVS}(P \;|||\; Q) = \{ u \mid &\; \exists s, t \bullet u \text{ interleaves } (s, t) \land \\
&(s \in \text{DIVS}(P) \land t \in \text{TRACES}(Q)) \lor \\
&(s \in \text{TRACES}(P) \land t \in \text{DIVS}(Q)) \} \\
\text{FAILS}(P \;|||\; Q) = \{ (u, X) \mid &\; u \in \text{DIVS}(P \;|||\; Q) \} \cup \\
\{ (u, X) \mid &\; \exists s, t \bullet u \text{ interleaves } (s, t) \land \\
&(s, X) \in \text{FAILS}(P) \land (t, X) \in \text{FAILS}(Q) \}
\end{aligned}
$$

Compile-time detection of information flow in sequential programs

Jean-Pierre Banâtre
Ciarán Bryce
Daniel Le Métayer
IRISA
Campus de Beaulieu
35042 Rennes Cedex, France
e-mail: *jpbanatre/bryce/lemetayer@irisa.fr*

Abstract. We give a formal definition of the notion of information flow for a simple guarded command language. We propose an axiomatisation of security properties based on this notion of information flow and we prove its soundness with respect to the operational semantics of the language. We then identify the sources of non determinism in proofs and we derive in successive steps an inference algorithm which is both sound and complete with respect to the inference system.

Keywords: formal verification, program analysis, verification tools, computer security, information flow.

1   Introduction

The context of the work described in this paper is the application of formal methods to the verification of information flow properties in programs. In contrast with most previous contributions in this area we put emphasis on the design of mechanical tools. Rather than considering a general (and undecidable) logic in which the development of proofs requires some interaction with the user, we start with a restricted language of properties which allows us to derive an automatic proof checker. The proof checking method is akin to the program analysis techniques used in modern optimising compilers [2]. Such a tool must satisfy two crucial properties in order to be useful for checking security properties:

– Its correctness must be established.
– It must be reasonably efficient.

These goals are achieved in several stages. We first provide a formal definition of the notion of information flow embodying the intuitive idea that information does not flow from a variable x to a variable y if variations in the original value of x cannot produce any variation in the final value of y. We define an *information flow logic* and we prove its correctness with respect to the operational semantics of the language. We identify the sources of non determinism in proofs which use this logic and we successively refine the proof system into a correct and complete algorithm for information flow analysis. The techniques used to transform the original proof system into an algorithmic version are akin to methods used to get a syntax-directed version of type inference systems including weakening rules [10].

The rest of the paper is organised in the following way. Section 2 introduces our guarded command language with its operational semantics and our definition of information flow. We propose an information flow logic SS_1 and we state its correctness with respect to the semantics of the language. In section 3 we present more deterministic versions of the original system (SS_2 and SS_3). The basic idea is that SS_2 avoids the use of a specific weakening rule and SS_3 derives at each step the most precise property provable in SS_2 (or the conjunction of all the properties derivable in SS_2). We state the soundness and a form of completeness of the new system (with respect to the information flow logic SS_1). SS_3 still contains a source of non determinism in the rule for the repetitive command. We consequently propose a fourth system SS_4 in section 4 which can be seen as a property transformer. In section 5, we show that properties can be represented as graphs for an efficient implementation. The iteration itself can be replaced by a simple graph transformation. A property can be extracted from a graph using a path finding algorithm. Section 6 provides insights on the extension to more realistic language features including parallelism and pointer manipulation and section 7 reviews related work. Space considerations prevent us from providing details about the proofs here. The interested reader can find a complete treatment in [5].

2 An inference system for security properties

We consider a simple guarded command language whose syntax is defined as follows:

Program	::= Decl $\prec$; Decl $\succ$; Stmt	*program*
Decl	::= **var** v	*declarations*
Stmt	::= (p, Comm)	*statements*
Comm	::= v := E | **skip** | Stmt; Stmt | Alt | Rep	*commands*
Alt	::= [guard → Stmt$\prec$; □ guard → Stmt$\succ$]	*alternative*
Rep	::= *[guard → Stmt$\prec$; □ guard → Stmt$\succ$]	*repetitive*
guard	::= B	*guard*

where $\prec\succ$ stands for zero or more repetitions of the enclosed syntactical units, 'v' stands for a variable or a list of variables, 'E' for an integer expression and 'B' for a boolean expression. Commands are associated with program points p. All program points are assumed to be different and p_0 and p_x stand for respectively the entry point and the exit point of the program. We omit program points in the text of the programs but they are used to state certain properties. The alternative and repetitive commands consist of one or more guard branch pairs. A guard is a boolean expression. A guard is *passable* if it evaluates to true.

When an alternative command is executed, a branch whose guard is passable is chosen. If more than one guard is passable, then any one of the corresponding branches can be executed. If no guard is passable then the command fails and the program terminates. On each iteration of the repetitive command, a branch whose guard is passable is executed. If more than one guard is passable, then like for the alternative, any one of the branches is chosen. When no guard is passable, the command terminates and the program continues. The structural operational semantics of this language is defined in Figure 1. The rules are expressed in terms of rewritings of configurations. A configuration is either a pair $< S, \sigma >$, where S is a statement and σ a state, or a state σ. The latter is a terminal configuration.

$$< y := exp, \sigma > \;\to\; \sigma[val(exp, \sigma)/y]$$

$$< t[i] := exp, \sigma > \;\to\; \sigma[t[i \leftarrow val(exp, \sigma)]/t]$$

$$< \mathbf{skip}, \sigma > \;\to\; \sigma$$

$$\frac{< S_1, \sigma > \;\to\; < S_1', \sigma' >}{< S_1; S_2, \sigma > \;\to\; < S_1'; S_2, \sigma' >}$$

$$\frac{< S_1, \sigma > \;\to\; \sigma'}{< S_1; S_2, \sigma > \;\to\; < S_2, \sigma' >}$$

$$\frac{< S_1, \sigma > \;\to\; abort}{< S_1; S_2, \sigma > \;\to\; abort}$$

$$\frac{< C_i, \sigma > \;\to\; true}{< [C_1 \to S_1 \square C_2 \to S_2 \square ...... \square C_n \to S_n], \sigma > \;\to\; < S_i, \sigma >}$$

$$\frac{< C_i, \sigma > \;\to\; abort}{< [C_1 \to S_1 \square C_2 \to S_2 \square ...... \square C_n \to S_n], \sigma > \;\to\; abort}$$

$$\frac{\forall i. < C_i, \sigma > \;\to\; false}{< [C_1 \to S_1 \square C_2 \to S_2 \square ...... \square C_n \to S_n], \sigma > \;\to\; abort}$$

$$\frac{< C_i, \sigma > \;\to\; true}{\substack{< *[C_1 \to S_1 \square C_2 \to S_2 \square ...... \square C_n \to S_n], \sigma > \;\to\; \\ < S_i; *[C_1 \to S_1 \square C_2 \to S_2 \square ...... \square C_n \to S_n], \sigma >}}$$

$$\frac{< C_i, \sigma > \;\to\; abort}{< *[C_1 \to S_1 \square C_2 \to S_2 \square ...... \square C_n \to S_n], \sigma > \;\to\; abort}$$

$$\frac{\forall i. < C_i, \sigma > \;\to\; false}{< *[C_1 \to S_1 \square C_2 \to S_2 \square ...... \square C_n \to S_n], \sigma > \;\to\; \sigma}$$

Fig. 1. Operational semantics

Let us now turn to the problem of defining the information flow for this language. There are two classes of information flows in programs. An assignment command causes a **direct** flow of information from the variables appearing on the right hand side of the $(:=)$ operator to the variable on the left hand side. This is because the information in each of the right hand side operands can influence value of the left hand side variable [6]. The information that was in the destination variable is lost.

Conditional commands introduce a new class of flows [8]. The fact that a command is conditionally executed signals information to an observer concerning the value of the command guard. Consider the following program segment. e is some expression:

$$x := e;$$
$$a := 0;$$
$$b := 0;$$
$$[\, x = 0 \rightarrow a := 1$$
$$\square\ x \neq 0 \rightarrow b := 1\,]$$

In this program segment, the values of **both** a and b after execution indicate whether x was zero or not. This is an example of an implicit flow [8] or what we more generally refer to as an **indirect** flow.

We note IF_p the set of indirect information flow variables at a particular program point p. IF_p can be defined syntactically as the set of variables occurring in embedding guards.

We need some way of representing the set of variables which may have flown to, or influenced, a variable v. We call this set the **security variable** of v, denoted $\bar{v}$. We define $\overline{IF_p}$ as:

$$\overline{IF_p} = \{x \mid x \in \bar{v} \text{ and } v \in IF_p\}$$

Our inference system for the proof of information flow properties is described in Figure 2.

An array assignment $t[i] := e$ is treated as $t := exp(t, i, e)$. The last rule in Figure 2 is called the consequence rule or the *weakening rule*. We use the notation $\vdash_1 \{P\}\ S\ \{Q\}$ to denote the fact that $\{P\}\ S\ \{Q\}$ is provable in SS_1.

We define a correspondence relation between properties and the semantics of statements and we use it to state the correctness of the information flow logic of Figure 2.

Definition

$$C(P, S) =$$
$$(P \Rightarrow x \notin \bar{y}) \quad \Rightarrow$$
$$\forall \sigma, v. \text{ such that } < S, \sigma > \downarrow \text{ and } < S, \sigma[v/x] > \downarrow$$
$$\{v' \mid < S, \sigma > \xrightarrow{*} \sigma', \ \sigma'(y) = v'\} =$$
$$\{v'' \mid < S, \sigma[v/x] > \xrightarrow{*} \sigma'', \ \sigma''(y) = v''\}$$

Proposition 1 (correctness of SS_1).

$$\forall S, P. \text{ if } \vdash_1 \{Init\}S\{P\} \text{ then } C(P, S)$$

$$\{P[\bar{y} \leftarrow \bigcup_i \overline{x_i} \cup \overline{IF_p}]\} \; y := exp(x_1, x_2, \ldots, x_n) \; \{P\}$$

$$\{P\}\mathbf{skip}\{P\}$$

$$\frac{\{P\}S1\{Q\}, \{Q\}S2\{R\}}{\{P\}S1; S2\{R\}}$$

$$\frac{\forall i = 1..n \{P\}S_i\{Q\}}{\{P\}[C_1 \rightarrow S_1 \square C_2 \rightarrow S_2 \square \ldots \square C_n \rightarrow S_n]\{Q\}}$$

$$\frac{\forall i = 1..n \{P\}S_i\{P\}}{\{P\} * [C_1 \rightarrow S_1 \square C_2 \rightarrow S_2 \square \ldots \square C_n \rightarrow S_n]\{P\}}$$

$$\frac{P \Rightarrow P', \; \{P'\} \, S \, \{Q'\}, \; Q' \Rightarrow Q}{\{P\} \, S \, \{Q\}}$$

Fig. 2. System SS_1

Init is defined as $\forall x, y \; x \neq y. \; x \notin \bar{y}$. It represents the standard (minimal) initial property. $S[v/x]$ is the same as S except that variable x is assigned value v. $< S, \sigma >\downarrow$ stands for $\exists \sigma' \neq abort. \; < S, \sigma > \xrightarrow{*} \sigma'$ which means that the program may terminate successfully. The above definition characterises our notion of information flow. If $P \Rightarrow x \notin \bar{y}$ holds, then the value of x before executing S cannot have any effect on the possible values possessed by y after the execution of S. In other words, no information can flow from x to y in S. The condition $< S, \sigma >\downarrow$ and $< S, \sigma[v/x] >\downarrow$ is required because the execution of S may terminate or not depending on the original value of x.

The correctness of SS_1 can be proven by induction on the structure of terms as a consequence of a more general property [5].

Let us now consider, as an example, a library decryption program. The program has three inputs and two outputs. The input consists of a string of encrypted text, or *cipher*, a key for decryption and a unit rate which the user is charged for each character decrypted. The variable *cipher* is an array of characters. A character is decrypted by applying it to an expression D with the *key* parameter. To save computing resources, some characters may not have been encrypted. The user pays twice the price for every encrypted character that goes through the decryption program. The boolean expression *encrypted()* determines if the character passed is encrypted or not. The outputs are the decrypted text, or *clear*, and the charge for the decryption. We assume that *clear* is output to the user and that *charge* is output to the library owner. To be usable, the user must trust the program not to secretly leak the clear text or the key to the library owner via the charges output. Such a leakage is termed a *covert channel* in [14]. The proof system described in Figure 2 allows us to prove the following property:

$$\vdash_1 \{Init\}\ Library\ \{(clear \notin \overline{charge})\ and\ (key \notin \overline{charge})\}$$

that is, the charge output may not receive a flow of information from the *clear* variable or from the *key* input. We show in section 5 that this property can in fact be proven mechanically.

```
var: i, charge, key, unit;
array: clear, cipher;
cipher := ≺ message to be decrypted ≻;
unit := ≺ unit rate constant ≻;
charge := unit;
i := 0;
*[ cipher[i] ≠ null_constant →
        [ encrypted(cipher[i]) → clear[i] := D(cipher[i], key);
                                        charge := charge + 2*unit;
        □ not encrypted(cipher[i]) → clear[i] := cipher[i];
                                        charge := charge + unit;
        ];
        i := i + 1
]
```

Fig. 3. Library decryption program

3 A more deterministic system

We consider now the problem of mechanising the proof of security properties. As suggested above, the sort of properties we are interested in are of the form $x \notin \overline{y}$. The language of properties is:

$$P ::= x \notin \overline{y} \mid P_1 \wedge P_2$$

where $\wedge$ represents the logical "and" connective.

The system SS_1 presented in section 2 is not suggestive of an algorithm for several reasons:

- The relationship between the input and the output property of the rule for assignment is not one to one.
- The weakening rule can be applied at any time in a proof.

The combination of the weakening rule with the rule for the repetitive command in particular requires some insight. In general this amounts to guessing the appropriate invariant for the loop. There are two possible ways of proving a property of the form $\{P\}$ *Prog* $\{Q\}$: one can either start with P and try to find a postcondition implying Q or start with Q and derive a precondition implied by P. These techniques are called respectively *forwards analysis* and *backwards analysis*. The method we present here for deriving security properties belongs to the forwards analysis category. Let us note however that the inference system SS_1 is not biased towards one technique or the other and we can apply the same idea to derive a backwards analysis. In order to reduce the amount of non determinism we first distribute the weakening rule over the remaining rules, getting system SS_2 presented in Figure 4.

$$\frac{P \Rightarrow P'[\bar{y} \leftarrow \bigcup_i \overline{x_i} \cup \overline{IF_p}], \quad P' \Rightarrow Q}{\{P\} \, y := exp(x_1, x_2, ..., x_n) \, \{Q\}}$$

$$\frac{P \Rightarrow P'}{\{P\}\mathbf{skip}\{P'\}}$$

$$\frac{P \Rightarrow P', \quad \{P'\}S1\{Q'\}, \, Q' \Rightarrow Q", \quad \{Q"\}S2\{R'\}, \quad R' \Rightarrow R}{\{P\}S1; S2\{R\}}$$

$$\frac{P \Rightarrow P', \quad \forall i = 1..n\{P'\}S_i\{Q'\}, \quad Q' \Rightarrow Q}{\{P\}[C_1 \rightarrow S_1 \Box C_2 \rightarrow S_2 \Box ......\Box C_n \rightarrow S_n]\{Q\}}$$

$$\frac{P \Rightarrow P', \quad \forall i = 1..n\{P'\}S_i\{P'\}, \quad P' \Rightarrow Q}{\{P\} * [C_1 \rightarrow S_1 \Box C_2 \rightarrow S_2 \Box ......\Box C_n \rightarrow S_n]\{Q\}}$$

Fig. 4. System SS_2

The soundness of SS_2 is obvious and its completeness follows from the transitivity of implication:

Proposition 2 (soundness and completeness of SS_2).

$$\forall S, P, Q. \quad \vdash_1 \{P\} \, S \, \{Q\} \textbf{ if and only if } \vdash_2 \{P\} \, S \, \{Q\}$$

This first transformation still yields a highly non deterministic proof procedure but it paves the way for the next refinement. Let us first note that the new system SS_2 is syntax directed. In order to derive an algorithm from SS_2 we want to factor out all the possible proofs of a program into a single *most precise* proof. This proof should associate with any property P the greatest property Q (in the sense of set inclusion) such that $\vdash_2 \{P\}\, S\, \{Q\}$. This requirement allows us to get rid of most of the uses of $\Rightarrow$ in the rules (but not all of them) and imposes a new rule for the assignment command. The new system SS_3 is described in Figure 5.

$$\{R\}\ y := exp(x_1, x_2, \ldots, x_n)\ \{T_y(R)\}$$

$$\{P\}\mathbf{skip}\{P\}$$

$$\frac{\{P\}S1\{Q\}, \{Q\}S2\{R\}}{\{P\}S1; S2\{R\}}$$

$$\frac{\forall i = 1..n\{P\}S_i\{Q_i\}}{\{P\}[C_1 \rightarrow S_1 \square C_2 \rightarrow S_2 \square \ldots \square C_n \rightarrow S_n]\{\bigsqcup_i Q_i\}}$$

$$\frac{P \Rightarrow P',\quad \forall i = 1..n\{P'\}S_i\{Q_i\},\quad \bigsqcup_i Q_i \Rightarrow P'}{\{P\} * [C_1 \rightarrow S_1 \square C_2 \rightarrow S_2 \square \ldots \square C_n \rightarrow S_n]\{\bigsqcup_i Q_i\}}$$

with:

$$R^y = \bigwedge_{z \neq y} \{(x \notin \bar{z}) \mid R \Rightarrow (x \notin \bar{z})\}$$
$$T_y(R) = R^y \bigwedge_i \{(y_i \notin \bar{y}) \mid \forall j \in [1, \ldots, n].\ R \Rightarrow (y_i \notin \bar{x_j})\ and$$
$$\forall v \in IF_p.\ R \Rightarrow (y_i \notin \bar{v})\}$$
$$\bigsqcup_i Q_i = \bigwedge\{(x \notin \bar{y}) \mid \forall i \in [1, \ldots, n], Q_i \Rightarrow (x \notin \bar{y})\}$$

Fig. 5. System SS_3

The intuition behind the new rule for the assignment command is that $T_y(R)$ represents the conjunction of all the properties $x \notin \bar{z}$ derivable from the input property R. R_y is the restriction of R to properties of the form $(x \notin \bar{z})$ with $z \neq y$. $\bigsqcup$ is the approximation in our language of properties of the logical "or" connective ($\vee$). It is expressed in terms of sets as an intersection. For instance:

$$((x \notin \bar{y}) \wedge (z \notin \bar{t})) \bigsqcup ((x \notin \bar{t}) \wedge (z \notin \bar{t})) = (z \notin \bar{t})$$

It is easy to see that

$$(Q_1 \vee Q_2) \Rightarrow (Q_1 \bigsqcup Q_2)$$

This approximation is required because the "or" connective does not belong to our language of properties. The language could be extended with $\vee$ but it makes the treatment more complex and it does not seem to allow the derivation of more useful information.

We cannot get rid of the implication in a straightforward way in the rule for the repetitive command because:

$$P \Rightarrow P' \quad and \quad \{P'\}S_i\{P'\}$$

does **not** imply

$$\{P\}S_i\{P\}$$

In order to prove a property of the repetitive command an appropriate invariant P' has to be discovered. We show in the next section how the maximal invariant can be computed iteratively.

The following properties state respectively the soundness and the completeness of SS_3 with respect to SS_2.

Proposition 3 (soundness of SS_3).

$$\forall S, P, Q. \ \textbf{if} \ \vdash_3 \ \{P\} \ S \ \{Q\} \ \textbf{then} \ \vdash_2 \ \{P\} \ S \ \{Q\}$$

Proposition 4 (completeness of SS_3).

$$\forall S, P, Q. \ \textbf{if} \ \vdash_2 \ \{P\} \ S \ \{Q\} \ \textbf{then} \ \exists Q'. \ \vdash_3 \ \{P\} \ S \ \{Q'\} \ Q' \Rightarrow Q$$

Both properties are proved by induction on the structure of commands [5].

4 Mechanical analysis of the repetitive command

In order to be able to treat the repetitive statement mechanically we must be able to compute a property P' such that

$$P \Rightarrow P'$$

and

$$\forall i = 1..n\{P'\}S_i\{Q_i\} \ and \ \bigsqcup_i Q_i \Rightarrow P'$$

Furthermore it must be the greatest of these properties in order to retain completeness. We compute this property using an iterative technique akin to the method used for finding least fixed points in abstract interpretation [1]. Figure 6 presents SS_4 which is a refinement of SS_3 with an effective rule for the repetitive statement.

The following properties show that SS_4 is the expression, in the form of an inference system, of a terminating, correct and complete algorithm.

$$\{R\} \; y := exp(x_1, x_2, ..., x_n) \; \{T_y(R)\}$$

$$\{P\}\mathrm{skip}\{P\}$$

$$\frac{\{P\}S1\{Q\}, \; \{Q\}S2\{R\}}{\{P\}S1; S2\{R\}}$$

$$\frac{\forall i = 1..n\{P\}S_i\{Q_i\}}{\{P\}[C_1 \rightarrow S_1 \square C_2 \rightarrow S_2 \square ......\square C_n \rightarrow S_n]\{\bigsqcup_i Q_i\}}$$

$$\frac{\forall i = 1..n\{P^0\}S_i\{Q_i^0\}, \quad Q^0 = \bigsqcup_i Q_i^0, \quad Q^0 \not\Rightarrow P^0, \quad P^1 = P^0 \bigsqcup Q^0}{\forall i = 1..n\{P^1\}S_i\{Q_i^1\}, \quad Q^1 = \bigsqcup_i Q_i^1, \quad Q^1 \not\Rightarrow P^1, \quad P^2 = P^1 \bigsqcup Q^1}$$

$$\vdots$$

$$\frac{\forall i = 1..n\{P^{n-1}\}S_i\{Q_i^{n-1}\}, \quad Q^{n-1} = \bigsqcup_i Q_i^{n-1}, \quad Q^{n-1} \Rightarrow P^{n-1}, \quad P^n = Q^{n-1}}{\{P^0\} * [C_1 \rightarrow S_1 \square C_2 \rightarrow S_2 \square ......\square C_n \rightarrow S_n]\{P^n\}}$$

Fig. 6. System SS_4

Proposition 5 (termination of SS_4).

$$\forall S, P, \quad \exists Q. \vdash_4 \{P\} \, S \, \{Q\} \; and \; Q \; is \; unique$$

Proposition 6 (soundness of SS_4).

$$\forall S, P, Q. \; \textbf{if} \vdash_4 \{P\} \, S \, \{Q\} \; \textbf{then} \; \vdash_3 \{P\} \, S \, \{Q\}$$

Proposition 7 (completeness of SS_4).

$$\forall S, P, Q. \; \textbf{if} \vdash_3 \{P\} \, S \, \{Q\} \; \textbf{then} \; \exists Q'. \; \vdash_4 \{P\} \, S \, \{Q'\} \; Q' \Rightarrow Q$$

The three properties are proven by induction on the structure of commands [5].

5 Inference as transformations on graphs

A conjunctive property P can alternatively be represented as a set of pairs of variables:

$$\{(y, x) \, | \, P \Rightarrow x \notin \bar{y}\}$$

For instance $z \notin \bar{t} \wedge t \notin \bar{u}$ is represented as $\{(t, z), (u, t)\}$. We present in Figure 7 a new version of SS_4 expressed in the form of an algorithm T_5 taking as arguments a property P represented as a set and a program $Prog$ and returning the property Q such that $\vdash_4 \{P\} \, Prog \, \{Q\}$.

$$T_5(P, (y := exp(x_1, x_2, ..., x_n))) \ = \ T_y(P)$$

$$T_5(P, \mathbf{skip}) \ = \ P$$

$$\frac{T_5(P, S1) \ = \ Q, \ \ T_5(Q, S2) \ = \ R}{T_5(P, S1; S2) \ = \ R}$$

$$\frac{\forall i = 1..n \ \ T_5(P, S_i) \ = \ Q_i}{T_5(P, [C_1 \rightarrow S_1 \Box C_2 \rightarrow S_2 \Box ......\Box C_n \rightarrow S_n]) \ = \ \bigcap_i Q_i}$$

$$\frac{\forall i = 1..n \ \ T_5(P^0, S_i) \ = \ Q_i^0, \ \ Q^0 \ = \ \bigcap_i Q_i^0, \ \ Q^0 \ \not\supset \ P^0, \ \ P^1 \ = \ P^0 \bigcap Q^0}{\forall i = 1..n \ \ T_5(P^1, S_i) \ = \ Q_i^1, \ \ Q^1 \ = \ \bigcap_i Q_i^1, \ \ Q^1 \ \not\supset \ P^1, \ \ P^2 \ = \ P^1 \bigcap Q^1}$$

$$\vdots$$

$$\frac{\forall i = 1..n \ \ T_5(P^{n-1}, S_i) \ = \ Q_i^{n-1}, \ \ Q^{n-1} = \bigcap_i Q_i^{n-1}, \ \ Q^{n-1} \supset P^{n-1}, \ \ P^n = Q^{n-1}}{T_5(P^0, *[C_1 \rightarrow S_1 \Box C_2 \rightarrow S_2 \Box ......\Box C_n \rightarrow S_n]) \ = \ P^n}$$

with:

$$R^y = \{(z, x) \in R \mid z \neq y\}$$
$$T_y(R) \ = \ R^y \bigcup \{(y, y_i) \mid \ \forall j \ \in [1, \ldots, n]. \ (x_j, y_i) \in R$$
$$and \ \forall v \ \in \ IF_p. \ (v, y_i) \in R\}$$

Fig. 7. System SS_5

The proof of the equivalence of SS_4 and SS_5 is obvious. In terms of sets, $\bigsqcup$ is implemented as set intersection($\bigcap$) and $\Rightarrow$ corresponds to the superset relation ($\supset$).

Proposition 8 (correctness and completeness of T_5).

$$\forall S, P, Q. \ \ \vdash_4 \ \{P\} \ S \ \{Q\} \ \textbf{if and only if} \ \ T_5(P, S) \ = \ Q$$

The representation of properties as sets of pairs leads to a very expensive implementation of the rule for assignment involving a quadratic number of tests in sets R and IF_p. We propose instead to represent properties as accessibility graphs. We consider directed graphs defined as pairs of a set of nodes and a set of arcs:

$$\begin{aligned} G &::= (N, A) \\ N &::= \{n\} \\ n &::= V^p \\ A &::= \{a\} \\ a &::= (n_1, n_2) \end{aligned}$$

V^p is the set of the variables of the program subscripted by program points. The property represented by a graph G at program point p is given by the function H defined as follows:

$$H(p, G) = \{(y, x) \mid Nopath(G, x^0, y^p)\}$$

$Nopath(G, x^0, y^p)$ returns $True$ is there is no path from node x^0 to node y^p in the graph G. We have now to show how the operations on properties required by T_5 are implemented in terms of graphs. Since the set of nodes of the graphs manipulated by our algorithm is constant it is convenient to introduce the following notation:

$$\text{if } G = (N, A) \text{ then } G + A' = (N, A \cup A')$$

Furthermore the symbol $+$ is overloaded to operate on two graphs (no ambiguity can arise from this overloading):

$$\text{if } G = (N, A) \text{ and } G' = (N, A') \text{ then } G + G' = (N, A \cup A')$$

The final version of our algorithm is described in Figure 8 (variables v are implicitly quantified over the whole set of variables of the program).

$T_6(G, p, (q, (y := exp(x_1, x_2, .., x_n)))) = G + \{(x_i^p, y^q) \mid i = 1..n\} + \{(z^p, z^q) \mid z \neq y\}$
$$+ \{(z^r, y^q) \mid z_r \in IF_q\}$$

$$T_6(G, p(q, \mathbf{skip})) = G$$

$$\frac{T_6(G, p, (q_1, S1)) = G_1, \quad T_6(G_1, q_1, (q_2, S2)) = G_2}{T_6(G, p, (q, (q_1, S1); (q_2, S2))) = G_2 + \{(v^{q_2}, v^q)\}}$$

$$\frac{\forall i = 1..n \quad T_6(G, p, (q_i, S_i)) = G_i}{T_6(G, p, (q, [C_1 \rightarrow (q_1, S_1) \square C_2 \rightarrow (q_2, S_2) \square ... \square C_n \rightarrow (q_n, S_n)])) = +_i G_i + \{(v^{q_i}, v^q)\}}$$

$$\frac{\forall i = 1..n \quad T_6(G^0, p, (q_i, S_i)) = G_i^0, \quad G^1 = +_i G_i^0 + \{(v^{q_i}, v^q)\} + \{(v^q, v^p)\}}{T_6(G^0, p, (q, *[C_1 \rightarrow (q_1, S_1) \square C_2 \rightarrow (q_2, S_2) \square ...... \square C_n \rightarrow (q_n, S_n)])) = G^1}$$

Fig. 8. System SS_6

T_6 takes three arguments: a graph G, a program point p and a statement $S \in Stmt$. The program point characterises a statement "preceding" the current statement in the (execution of) the program. The program is analysed with the input program point p^0 as argument. Program points are made explicit in the statements because they play a crucial rôle at this stage. The rule for assignment can be explained as follows. An arc is added to the graph from each occurrence of variables x_i at the preceding program point p to y at the current program point q, and from each variable in the set of indirect flow to y. Other variables are not modified and an arc is added from their occurrence at point p to their occurrence at point q. In the rules for the alternative command and the repetitive command the operation $+$ is used to implement $\bigcap$. This comes from the fact that graphs record accessibility when sets contain negative information of the form $x \notin \overline{y}$.

The correctness of this last algorithm is stated as follows:

Proposition 9 (correctness of T_6).

$$\forall S, P, Q, G, p, q. \ \ H(p, G) = P \ \ and \ \ T_5(P, S) = Q \ \ \Rightarrow$$

$$H(q, T_6(G, p, (q, S))) = Q$$

This property can be proved by induction on the structure of expressions [5].

It should be clear that some straightforward optimisations can be applied to this algorithm. First it is not necessary to keep one occurrence of variable per program point in the graph. As can be noticed from the rule for assignment, most of these variables would just receive one arc from the previous occurrence of the variable. All these useless arcs can be short-circuited and the only nodes kept into the graph are occurrences of x^p where p is an assignment to x or an alternative (or repetitive) statement with several assigments to x. Also a naïve implementation of the rules for the alternative and the repetitive statements would lead to duplications of the graph. The monotonicity of T_6 allows us to get rid of this duplication. Instead the graph can be constructed iteratively as follows:

$$\frac{G_0 = G, \ \ \forall i = 1..n \ \ T_6(G_{i-1}, p, (q_i, S_i)) \ = \ G_i}{T_6(G, p, (q, [C_1 \rightarrow (q_1, S_1) \square C_2 \rightarrow (q_2, S_2) \square ...... \square C_n \rightarrow (q_n, S_n)])) \ = \ G_n + \{(v^{q_n}, v^q)\}}$$

Let us now return to the library decryption program to illustrate the algorithm. Figure 9 is a new presentation of the program making some program points explicit (we do not include all of them for the sake of readability).

Figure 10 presents the main steps of the application of T_6 to this program. We note P_i the command associated with p_i and we consider only the arc component of the graph. We avoid the introduction of useless nodes and arcs as described above. As a consequence, only 14 nodes are necessary for this program. Figure 11 shows the graph returned by the algorithm. Applying the *Nopath* function to this graph, we can derive the property mentioned in section 2 (p_4 is the exit program point for *charge*):

$$(clear \notin \overline{charge}) \ and \ (key \notin \overline{charge})$$

```
var: i, charge, key, unit;
array: clear, cipher;
cipher := ≺ message to be decrypted ≻;
unit := ≺ unit rate constant ≻;
(p₁,charge := unit;
i := 0);
(p₂,*[ cipher[i] ≠ null_constant →
        (p₃,(p₄,[ encrypted(cipher[i]) → (p₅,(p₆,clear[i] := D(cipher[i], key));
                                            (p₇,charge := charge + 2*unit));
                □ not encrypted(cipher[i]) → (p₈,(p₉,clear[i] := cipher[i]);
                                            (p₁₀,charge := charge + unit));
        ]);
        (p₁₁,i := i + 1))
])
```

Fig. 9. Library decryption program

$$
\begin{aligned}
T_6(\emptyset, p_0, P_1) = G_1 \quad G_1 &= \{(unit^0, charge^1)\} \\
T_6(G_1, p_1, P_6) = G_2 \quad G_2 &= G_1 + \{(cipher^0, clear^6), (key^0, clear^6), (i^1, clear^6), \\
&\quad (clear^0, clear^6)\} \\
T_6(G_2, p_6, P_7) = G_3 \quad G_3 &= G_2 + \{(charge^1, charge^7), (unit^0, charge^7), \\
&\quad (i^1, charge^7), (cipher^0, charge^7)\} \\
T_6(G_3, p_1, P_9) = G_4 \quad G_4 &= G_3 + \{(cipher^0, clear^9), (i^1, clear^9), (clear^0, clear^9)\}\} \\
T_6(G_4, p_9, P_{10}) = G_5 \quad G_5 &= G_4 + \{(charge^1, charge^{10}), (unit^0, charge^{10}), \\
&\quad (i^1, charge^{10}), (cipher^0, charge^{10})\} \\
T_6(G_5, p_1, P_4) = G_6 \quad G_6 &= G_5 + \{(charge^7, charge^4), (charge^{10}, charge^4), \\
&\quad (clear^6, clear^4), (clear^9, clear^4)\} \\
T_6(G_6, p_1, P_2) = G_7 \quad G_7 &= G_6 + \{(charge^4, charge^1), (clear^4, clear^0)\}
\end{aligned}
$$

Fig. 10. Analysis of the library decryption program

6 Extensions

There are three main directions in which we plan to extend this work in order to be able to cope with more realistic languages:

- The introduction of pointer manipulation operators.
- The treatment of less structured control flow.
- The extension to a parallel language.

We consider each in turn.

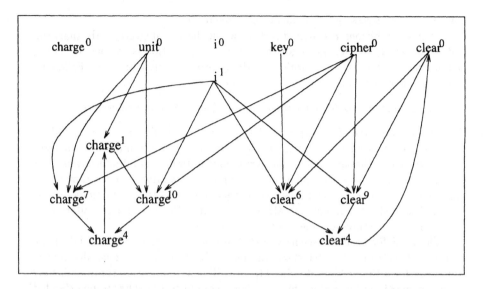

Fig. 11. Result of the analysis of the library decryption program

The addition of general pointers in a language complicates most program analyses because it introduces the well-known problem of *aliasing*. Aliasing occurs during program execution when two or more names exist for the same location [15]. Let us take a small example in the context of information flow to illustrate the problem.

$$
\begin{aligned}
&\textbf{int } i,\ j,\ k,\ *p \\
&p := \&i; \\
&i := j; \\
&k := *p;
\end{aligned}
$$

The variable p is assigned the location of i. As a consequence, an information flow from i to p must be accounted for. Furthermore the assignment of j to i introduces a new (and hidden) flow of information between j and p and the assignment of $*p$ to k creates a flow from i to k. The semantics of the language and the definition of information flow (section 2) must be adapted to take into account the fact that a variable can have access to the value (or part of) of another variable through dereferences. As far as the proof checking algorithm is concerned, the first solution is to complement the method presented in this paper with a pointer aliasing analysis. Various techniques have been proposed in the literature to tackle this problem [15, 16]. These techniques are more or less accurate (and expensive) depending on the level of indirection which is considered. The rule for assignment can be enhanced to take this new form of flow into account:

$$
T_6'(G, p, (q,\ (y := exp(x_1, x_2, ..., x_n)))) = G + \{(x_i^p, y^q) \mid i = 1..n\} + \{(z^p, z^q) \mid z \neq y\}
$$

$$
+ \{(z^r, y^q) \mid z_r \in IF_q\} \quad + \{(y^q, z^t) \mid Alias(y^q, c.z^t)\}
$$

where c is an access chain (sequence of dereferences).

A more ambitious research direction would be to integrate both analysers into a single, more efficient, algorithm. A possible solution is to consider *object names* rather than simple variables in the information flow analysis. Following [16], object names can be defined as follows:

$$object\_name = variable \mid *.object\_name \mid object\_name.field\_of\_structure$$

The introduction of less structured sequential control flow does not introduce deep technical problems into our analysis. It may however make the analyser more expensive (the same situtation occurs in traditional data flow analysis). For instance we can deal with explicit *goto* commands by adding new assignments at the join nodes of the control flow graph (very much like the ϕ-functions in SSA forms [7]). Such assignments are already implicit in the rules for the alternative and repetitive commands (see Figure 8 for instance).

The need for ensuring security properties becomes especially crucial in the context of distributed systems. We are currently studying the generalisation of our work for a full version of CSP [11]. In CSP, communication commands may occur in guards and in statements. The notion of indirect flow has to be extended to take such communications into account. The semantics of CSP introduces two main technical difficulties for a correct treatment of control flow:

- Indirect control flow can occur even in the absence of rendez-vous (when such a rendez-vous would have been made possible by a different execution of a guarded command).
- The non termination of a process can influence the values of the variables of the processes it might have communicated with.

As an example of how indirect flows can occur in the absence of a rendez-vous, consider the following program segment. Suppose that y of process $P1$ is either 1 or 0. Whatever, the value of y, at the end of process $P1$, x will equal y. The reason for this is that, if $y = 0$ in process P1, then P1 passes the value 1 to b of process P2 which then passes 0 back to x. Conversely, if y is 1 in P1, then P1 signals 0 to process P3 which signals 1 to P2's b which in turn passes this value back to x.

```
[
  P1::                      P2::                  P3::
  [var x,y;                 [var a,b;             [var s ;
  y := e();                 [ P1 ? b → b:=b-1 □   P1 ? s;
  [ y=0 → P2 ! 1 □             P3 ? b → skip ]    P2 ! 1
  y≠0 → skip ]              a := b;               ]
  P3 ! 0;                   P1 ! a
  P2 ? x                    ] ‖
  ] ‖
]
```

Our solution consists of associating each program point p_i with a *control flow variable* c_i containing all the variables which may influence the fact that the execution of the program reaches that point. When a communication occurs between $p_1 : P_2 \ ! \ v$ and $p_2 : P_1 \ ? \ x$, the control flow c_1 at point p_1 is added to the security variable $\overline{x}$. Furthermore both control flows c_1 and c_2 become $c_1 \cup c_2$. As far as algorithmic aspects are concerned, communications introduce a new source of non determinism in the proof. The traditional technique consists in carrying out the proof of each process independently before checking a *cooperation condition* on the individual rules. The first phase places little constraints on communication commands and appropriate properties have to be guessed in order to derive proofs that satisfy the cooperation conditions. Our graph algorithm can be extended in a natural way to simulate this reasoning. The set of nodes includes control flow variables and the required arcs are added between matching communication commands. The important property allowing us to retain the simplicity of the algorithm described here is the fact that we derive for each point of the program the strongest property provable at this point. As a consequence the graph can still be built incrementally avoiding the need for an iterative process.

7 Related work

Language based information flow control mechanisms have traditionally used *security levels* [8, 3]. Each variable is assigned a level denoting the sensitivity of the information it contains. After an operation, the level of the variable which received the information flow must be no less than the level of the flow source variables. However, the security level approach severely restricts the range of policies that one might like to support. A flow mechanism should log the variables that have flown to each variable rather than the level of the data. Jones and Lipton's *surveillance set* mechanism [12] is in this spirit and has some similarities with the mechanism proposed here.

In [18], McLean describes a unified framework for showing that a software module specification is *non-interfering* and that the module code satisfies this specification. Non-interference is a security property which states that a user's output cannot be affected by the input of any user with a higher security level. McLean's approach is based on the trace method for software module specification [17]. This method defines a module's semantics as the set of legal module traces (sequences of module procedure calls), the values returned by the traces terminating in a function call and a trace equivalence. Non-interference can be proved from the module's trace semantics. The author then defines a simple sequential procedural based programming language and gives the semantics of the language in trace form. This method is attractive because it allows the non-interference proof to be conducted at the abstract level of functional specifications. Program security is then established as a consequence of the functional correctness. In contrast with our approach however, no attempt is made to conduct proofs in a mechanical (or even systematic) way.

The main contribution of this paper is to provide a formally based and effective tool for checking security properties of sequential programs. To our knowledge there have been surprisingly few attempts to achieve these goals so far. Most of the approaches described in the literature either lead to manual verification techniques [3] or rely on informal correctness proofs [9]. The closest work in the spirit of the contribution presented here is [19]. They derive a flow control algorithm as an abstract interpretation of the denotational semantics of the programming language. The programmer associates each variable with a security class (such as *unclassified, classified, secret, ...*). Security classes correspond to particular abstract semantics domains forming a lattice of properties and the analysis computes abstract values to check the security constraints. In contrast with this approach, we do not require security classes to be associated with variables but we check that the value of one particular variable cannot flow into another variable. We have shown in [4] that this approach provides more flexibility in the choice of a particular security policy. Our algorithm could in fact be applied to synthesise the weakest constraints on the security classes of the variables of an unannotated program. These two options can be compared with the choice between explicit typing and type synthesis in strongly typed programming languages.

References

1. Abramsky (S.) and Hankin (C. L.), "Abstract interpretation of declarative languages", Ellis Horwood, 1987.
2. Aho (A. V.), Sethi (R.) and Ullman (J. D.), "Compilers: Principles, Techniques and Tools", Addison Wesley, Reading, Mass, 1986.
3. Andrews (G.R.), Reitman (R.P.), "An Axiomatic Approach to Information Flow in Programs", in *ACM Transactions on Programming Languages and Systems*, volume 2 (1), January 1980, pages 504-513.
4. Banâtre (J.-P.) and C. Bryce, (C.), "A security proof system for networks of communicating processes", Irisa research report, no 744, June 1993.
5. Banâtre (J.-P.) and C. Bryce, (C.), and Le Métayer (D.), "Mechanical proof of security properties", Irisa research report, no 825, May 1994.
6. Cohen (E.), "Information Transmission in Computational Systems", in *Proceedings ACM Symposium on Operating System Principles*, 1977, pages 133-139.
7. Cytron (R.), Ferrante (J.), Rosen (B. K.) and Wegman (M. N.), "Efficiently computing Static Single Assignment form and the control dependence graph", in *ACM Transactions on Programming Languages and Systems*, Vol. 13, No 4, October 1991, pages 451-490.
8. Denning (D.E.), *Secure Information Flow in Computer Systems*, Phd Thesis, Purdue University, May 1975.
9. Denning (D.E.), Denning (P.J.), "Certification of Programs for Secure Information Flow", in *Communications of the ACM*, volume 20 (7), July 1977, pages 504-513.
10. Hankin (C. L.) and Le Métayer (D.), "Deriving Algorithms from Type Inference Systems: Application to Strictness Analysis", in *Proceedings ACM POPL*, 1994, pages 202-212.
11. Hoare (C.A.R.), *Communicating Sequential Processes*, Prentice-Hall London, 1985.

12. Jones (A.), Lipton (R.), "The Enforcement of Security Policies for Computations", in *Proceedings of the 5th Symposium on Operating System Principles*, November 1975, pages 197-206.

13. Kennedy K. W., "A Survey of Data Flow Analysis Techniques", in *Program Flow Analysis*, S. S. Muchnik and N. D. Jones, Eds, Prentice-Hall, Englewood Cliffs, NJ, 1981.

14. Lampson (B.), "A note on the Confinement Problem", in *Communications of the ACM*, volume 16 (10), October 1973, pages 613-615.

15. Landi (W.) and Ryder (B. G.), "Pointer-induced aliasing: a problem classification", in *Proceedings ACM POPL*, 1991, pages 93-103.

16. Landi (W.) and Ryder (B. G.), "A safe approximate algorithm for interprocedural pointer aliasing", in *Proceedings ACM Programming Language Design and Implementation*, 1992, pages 235-248.

17. McLean (J.), "A Formal Method for the Abstract Specification of Software", in *Journal of the ACM*, 31, July 1984, pages 600-627.

18. McLean (J.), "Proving Non-interference and Functional Correctness Using Traces", in *Journal of Computer Security*, 1(1), Spring 1992, pages 37-57.

19. Mizuno (M.), Schmidt (D.), "A Security Control Flow Control Algorithm and Its Denotational Semantics Correctness Proof", *Journal on the Formal Aspects of Computing*, 4 (6A), november 1992, pages 722-754.

Security Through Type Analysis

C O'Halloran and C T Sennett

Systems Engineering and High Integrity Systems Division
DRA Malvern
Worcs WR14 3PS
UK
email: colin@green.dra.hmg.gb, C.T.Sennett@green.dra.hmg.gb

Abstract. The objective of the work reported in this paper is to develop very low cost techniques for demonstrating that the trusted software for a secure system has the security properties claimed for it. The approach also supports integrity properties. The approach is based on type checking, which ensures that operations cannot be called with arguments they should not handle. This paper presents an informal technical description of the work with respect to a particular case study. An outline of the type checking algorithm is given in an appendix.

Keywords: Types, formal techniques, secure computer systems, security evaluation.

1 Introduction

This paper reports a new approach to establishing the security properties of a system, based on software analysis and type checking. The approach is motivated by the perception that current practice is leading to systems which are unusable, slow and costly to develop and maintain. At the heart of these troubles is the reference monitor concept: security is seen as being concerned with controlling access to objects according to clearances and labels, to be enforced by a reference monitor, which is software executing within an isolated hardware protection regime. This very simple view leads to performance problems, as all accesses to objects must be mediated by the reference monitor, and to usability problems as a result of the very simple controls which can be implemented in a centralised piece of software.

In addition to these usability problems, the reference monitor concept leads to a large cost of ownership because of the difficulty of disentangling the reference monitor from the operating system which it uses. The basic operating system primitives, above which the reference monitor runs, tend to execute with more privilege and could corrupt the reference monitor. To gain assurance that the security mechanisms work correctly it becomes necessary to evaluate all the security relevant code, now including the basic operating system primitives. This leads to the need to evaluate megabytes of code which is costly, and the inability to change the system while maintaining the evaluation status.

The desire for increased flexibility leads almost inexorably to the need for protection mechanisms based on software rather than hardware. Clearly there are many mechanisms such as data hiding, type checking and the use of modules which are highly relevant to security and potentially offer much more flexible protection than can be provided in hardware. In addition, being implemented at compile time, they have little or no run time overhead. However, just because these mechanisms are implemented by compilers and, in the case of languages such as C, can be subverted by the programmers, there is an integrity issue. How trustworthy can software be if the protection is derived from compilers, which are large and complicated programs? The approach we are developing uses an analysis technique, based on type checking, and applied to compiler output, to give an independent check of the integrity mechanisms in the compiler and it is hoped that this would lead to a technique for guaranteeing security without the need to centralise all the security checking code.

The need to maintain and update software components fits naturally within this type of software checking regime. What is required is that security properties should be broken down into the conditions which each individual software component must satisfy, in order to provide security for the system as a whole. These conditions must be expressed in terms of the software interfaces in order to give a test which can be applied during maintenance and it is hoped that this information, namely the software interface specification, can be used to drive the analysis process.

It should be emphasised that the work described here is very much ongoing. The analysis method is being specified formally and is at a fairly detailed level of development. The means of actually specifying interfaces to capture security properties has not been completed and to some extent is dependent on the analysis method. Nevertheless, the paper gives an overall view of the whole process and includes a case study to illustrate how it is expected to work.

2   Security Properties

Security in a system is achieved by a mixture of functional and non-functional properties. The functional properties are concerned with the correct operation of the security checking mechanisms while the non-functional ones are concerned with the absence of by-pass and side effects.

Functional properties are demonstrated by formal verification, but this will rely at some point on the integrity of the implementation language and the compiler which implements it. The desire to have a reliable basis for compilation has led to previous work with Ada [1, 2], but the desire to use commercial components leads to the necessity to establish integrity in software written using C. In either case one would like a check that what had been verified in the source language could be relied on in the machine code, but with C there is an additional problem in that the programmer is not forbidden in the language from misusing pointers in a way which would render the verification invalid and which could corrupt other software. The analysis method supports this integrity check, not the verification which precedes it.

Non-functional security properties are often simply a question of capability: for example, the users should not be able to use the system management functions or it should not be possible to log in from a remote computer. These are naturally provided in a system which constrains the code only to use the interfaces explicitly provided. This works for static properties where it can be checked that one module simply cannot call another module providing the capability which it is required to control. However, the absence of by-pass is usually specified in behavioural terms as constraints on the sequence of operations allowed. One of the problems of specifying security is that the condition for an operation to be legitimate or not is dependent on what has gone before. The desire for flexible security controls means that these constraints can be quite complicated and so the interface descriptions must be able to reflect this.

2.1 Rely and guarantee conditions

If a system is composed of software components, they can be evaluated separately if the properties they rely upon can be determined. These rely conditions on the environment are "preconditions" under which the component will guarantee to exhibit some property. The guarantee condition is analogous to a post condition.

Rely and guarantee conditions were originally formulated to reason about safety properties of shared memory. They have been proposed as a means of proving confidentiality, but because of their origin are probably more suited to demonstrating absence of bypass of security mechanisms.

Absence of bypass of security mechanisms is the non-functional property required to demonstrate security. In behavioural terms, this is a safety property because absence of bypass can be shown when no illegal operations are used. The legality of an operation will depend upon what operations have occurred and thus absence of bypass is about demonstrating certain traces (that is, sequences of operations) are not present, which is a safety property.

A rely condition will be an assumption about traces which the environment is allowed to perform. A guarantee condition will be a promise to the environment to perform only certain traces. Put another way a rely condition states that the environment will not do anything to bypass the security mechanisms. A guarantee condition makes a promise to the environment not to bypass the security mechanisms.

A software component can be slotted into a system if the other components guarantee the behaviours the component is relying upon and it guarantees the behaviours the rest of the system is relying on. In this way components can be maintained and upgraded while still maintaining the property of absence of bypass.

2.2 Information flow

One of the problems with controlling the information held in a computer system is that information is itself a nebulous entity. Although it is useful to think of files and records being held by a computer system, they are actually just bits in a machine which can be duplicated and moved with great speed and ease by a program. The exploitation of indirect means of communication within a system is called using covert channels.

The problem of covert channels arises because the very mechanisms used to protect data can be used to communicate that data to unauthorized individuals. The covert channel problem, although a real threat, has been given undue prominence in recent years leading to over restrictive security properties which impair the functionality of the system.

The absence of covert channels looks at first sight like absence of bypass which it has been shown is an absence of illegal operations, assuming the integrity of the legal operations. Unfortunately covert channels arise from the legitimate use of legal operations. This means that the elimination of covert channels would eliminate useful and sometimes vital functions of the system: for an example, see [3].

To address confidentiality, it first has to be defined. In their seminal paper [4], Goguen and Messeguer gave a formalization of a confidentiality property in terms of observations of a system. The intuitive idea behind the formalism was that if a "low" observer cannot detect any change in the behaviour of a system when a "high" user is removed from the system, then that system protects the confidentiality of the "high" user. The "high" user is said to *non-interfere* with the "low" user; that is there is nothing the high user can do to communicate, covertly or otherwise, with the low user.

The idea of using observations to define confidentiality has been developed by Jacob [5] to give a formal meaning to the amount of confidentiality required. This is formalised over the trace model of CSP [6] and defines the degree of confidentiality to be the set of traces which can be inferred given full knowledge of the CSP process and a local observation. The smaller the inference set, the more certain a local observer is that a particular trace of the process has occurred. The bigger the inference set, the more secure a process is for that local observation.

The concept of using inference from a local observation of a system can be used to define a specification language for confidentiality requirements, [7, 9]. To show that a system satisfies such a specification it is necessary to show that it is meaningful to view the system as a process which engages in events. This means that the integrity of the events, or operations, which make up the traces of the system have to be ensured.

2.3 Type checking

The flow specifications give constraints on the sequence of events a given process can engage in. In a process description simple events have no specific meaning, they are just markers for the start, or end, of an operation or even the whole operation. Events which have values associated with them carry more information about how they can be interpreted but they are still fairly abstract. In both cases there is an obligation to demonstrate a correspondence between software operations and the events they implement.

Type checking is one way of demonstrating this correspondence. Types give a meaning to the events of a process and allows a consistency check for a software interface against a process description. The types of values input from the environment can be used in type checking the software hidden by the interface in order to establish its integrity. Values which are output to the environment have a type which is determined by type checking the software hidden by the interface. This link between process events and operations on the interfaces of a software component are as yet unformalised.

Type checking in itself may provide one way of separating events and therefore could demonstrate the satisfaction of a flow specification. This would be the case for example if objects were given types according to their classification and separately typed procedures for handling them were provided. This possibility is unlikely to be generally useful as the flow properties are dynamic and specify constraints on sequences of operations. It is necessary for example, to make the results of a file opening operation depend upon the results of previous operations.

Such dynamic behaviour requires the storage of additional information to record the history and this information needs to be bound into the objects being controlled. Typically a file needs its classification, a process its clearance and user identity. Correct manipulation of this historical data is a functional property necessary for security. The functionality is usually trivial, but it could be established by verification if necessary. The non-functional property of lack of by-pass is that data can only be altered by the security checking code and it is this property which can be achieved by type checking.

Our approach is to treat such encapsulated objects as the implementation of an abstract data type. If the using code has correctly treated such objects as abstract, it should always have dealt with them as a whole. An abstract object can be used, assigned, provided as a parameter to a procedure and delivered as a result, but the internals of the object cannot be inspected or altered.

3   Software analysis and type checking

To summarise, our approach is to use flow specifications which are sufficiently flexible to capture the complexities of real requirements; to break these down into specifications for individual software components; to relate these specifications to the software interfaces using functional control of abstract objects; to provide lack of bypass at the source code level using the structuring and type checking properties of languages (and any other means relevant at that level); and to replace the hardware protection by an integrity check on the compiler. This is clearly a large scale programme, and one would expect to use many different techniques, particularly at the language level. We have concentrated on the last problem, the demonstration of the integrity of the compilation process, as the one on which the others are built.

3.1 The integrity problem

A compiler transforms a source language into machine code: the integrity requirement is that the semantics of the source language are respected by the executing machine code. Basically, there are three issues:

- The mapping of operations into corresponding machine code operations (such as arithmetic and logic).
- The mapping of identifiers and objects in the source code to machine memory.
- The mapping of program structure into corresponding machine code structures (conditional statements and loops into corresponding machine code statements and jump instructions).

The third is clearly the most difficult as the mapping is not by any means one-to-one, nor is the same mapping used in the same syntactic situation. However, from the integrity point of view, one is concerned about the usage of objects defined in an interface. What is required is that the code which uses objects in the interface should not, by virtue of operations on its own identifiers, corrupt the interface. For this aspect, the first two elements are important.

The complication in these elements arises from the following sources:

- The machine operations are not defined on the natural numbers, but on several different formats (single length, double length, characters, floating point) which not only have different sizes, but also must be aligned at particular positions within memory.
- Machine manipulation of objects is usually in terms of pointer arithmetic. Pointers are not constrained to point to one particular type of data structure.
- A given memory location may hold, at one location, a value of one size at one time and a value of another size at different time, depending on the dynamic conditions of execution.

These last two points are particularly important for the compilation of languages such as C where pointer manipulation, and the use of unconstrained unions, are features of the language, rather than being introduced by the compilation process.

Rather than analyse machine code, we have chosen to use the TenDRA portability technology [8] and analyse its distribution format (TDF). TDF is a compiler output language (that is, the output from a compiler front end) which is capable of representing all the commonly used languages and can be translated into all the commonly used machines. The production of TDF corresponds to the code generation phase of compilation. Checking at this particular stage of the process has a number of advantages:

- Because it can be installed on a number of different machines and architectures, the TDF must make explicit all the interfaces. A correctly installed unit of TDF code cannot use any other unit, or make use of the machines operating system, except through the interface mechanism provided. This allows both the checking of the interfaces actually used and their replacement, at installation time, with equivalent interface components of equivalent functionality but with extra dynamic checking.
- The architecture neutrality ensures that one checking tool will suffice for several different machines.
- The checking process can add more TDF code to implement dynamic checks.

Type checking at the TDF interfaces allows the software object to be checked against typed events in a process description of the software object. This means that the alphabet of a process can be compared with the typed operations of a software object, this constitutes a static compliance check. Comparing the dynamic behaviour of a software object against a process is a more difficult task which is not addressed by this work.

In designing a checking process for TDF, the first obvious candidate is to use simple static type checking. This can establish things like the fact that an integer in an interface is only operated on by integer operations and a procedure is only called, not operated on by any other operation.

The integrity of the memory is rather more difficult to establish. Memory is accessed by taking the contents of a pointer, or assigning to a pointer. Pointer values are either given by an original allocation or derived from original pointers by pointer arithmetic. This involves the symbolic addition of offsets given in terms of alignments and the sizes of primitive objects. In checking the integrity of this process, the typing is being applied not so much to the pointers themselves as to the memory being pointed at. Pointer arithmetic constrains memory to have objects of certain sizes at certain points while assignment achieves the typing of memory at the position currently being pointed at. Type checking within this context is naturally done by inference.

3.2 Type checking

The actual layout of memory is going to be a compiler choice, rather than being specified by the user. What is required is that when an object is accessed in an interface, sufficient space is allowed to store it: this space must not be infringed by other objects internal to the using code. The type checking therefore has to deduce the layout being adopted by the compiler and make sure that that is being used consistently and that it respects the integrity of the objects imported from or exported to the interface. The method chosen for this is a system of type inference which is rather analogous to polymorphic type checking in the language ML. Here the memory is treated as polymorphic and the inferences establish the particular instantiation chosen by the compiler. As a by product of this approach, there is no problem in dealing with polymorphic procedures.

The actual type checking process for memory is almost statically determined. Apart from pointers to arrays, which correspond to original allocations, pointers will be used for accessing structures or equivalent operations. Pointer arithmetic within the structure will be determined by the layout of the structure itself, which must be a static quantity. Pointer arithmetic can therefore usually be evaluated statically and used to check the memory layout without the need for a dynamic check. The situation is rather analogous to a type system containing integer ranges rather than integers (for example, those for Ada or Pascal). In these languages it is often possible to check the types statically because the construction (a loop for example) will ensure the controlled variable will not go out of bounds.

The existence of unconstrained unions does unfortunately almost inevitably lead to dynamic checks. Within C, it is possible to construct a pointer and access from it at one time an integer, at another a floating point number. Provided the program previously stored an integer in the one case and a floating point number in the other there is no problem. Clearly, two consecutive accesses like this cannot be correct; assignment statements may satisfy them, but where the two cases are combined in a conditional, there is a dynamic condition to be propagated back to where the assignments were originally done. This part of the checking process is therefore rather like a weakest precondition calculation. In favourable situations it might be possible to simplify the well-typing condition to true. This might be the case for checking output from an Algol 68 compiler, which is strongly typed, achieved by the compiler outputting dynamic code to keep track of the current types holding for a union. Compiler generated code for these situations ought to be small, regular, and easily verifiable. Output from a compiler for a statically typed language, such as Algol 60, should not generate any well typing conditions at all. Where the user is in control of the dynamic conditions for the types, as in C, the conditions might be more complicated.

Thus the process actually chosen to demonstrate the integrity of the compilation is a combination of static type checking, type inference and a weakest precondition calculation for the dynamic checks. It should be emphasised that this checks the integrity of the compilation process. In particular, if aliasing is allowed in the language (as in Ada or C) this will not be detected. But if aliasing is forbidden in the language (as in the Ada subset SPARK) the checking process will guarantee that it does not occur through a fault in the compiler.

4 The File Transfer Case Study

Two case studies are being undertaken within the programme: one concerned with file exchange, which demonstrates a very simple application of the approach; and one concerned with the use of X-Windows which is very much more complicated. The way in which the approach might be applied will be described for the file transfer case. We have not yet completed either the decomposition of the security properties or the analysis of the software.

4.1   Background

Interoperability is an increasingly important concern with secure systems. A straightforward application of standard security practice would treat the two interoperable systems as a whole and attempt to work out an appropriate security policy and assurance level for the combined system.

This approach goes against the philosophy of building a total system from smaller simpler parts and is rarely a practical proposition. The individual systems will have different security requirements, management, and capabilities for evolution. The combined system will have a large population of users with conflicting functional as well as security requirements which will be difficult, if not impossible, to satisfy.

In practice the degree of interoperability required is usually quite small, and considerably less than the full functionality of a system. By restricting the interoperability to the minimum necessary to meet the requirements, it is possible to design a system which presents little possibility for misuse and it becomes tractable to demonstrate this.

The transfer of files is often all that is required. We shall assume a very simple situation in which a high security multi-level system needs to send files to a low security dedicated system. The direction of transfer (from high to low) is not just a question of choosing a perverse example. In real life information (commands, for example) often have to be exported to less classified environments. One of the problems with current systems is that these real life requirements are being disallowed by inappropriate security policies. With this sort of requirement, a one way filter is inappropriate and the solution often proposed is to isolate the high computer by means of a guard computer, which provides a facility by means of which a watch officer can inspect all information flowing through the guard. Unfortunately, no amount of verification of the software in the guard is going to reduce the vulnerability of the watch officer blinking or not realising the significance of what is being displayed on his screen. A guard computer is nearly always applying an inappropriate check at an inappropriate place. Instead the flexibility allowed by the checking approach allows an appropriate check to be applied, without the need for a guard or a watch officer.

4.2   The file transfer security requirement

There are many possible scenarios for file transfer and it is possible to design appropriate security policies for most of them. We shall take the simplest possible in which files are sent from the high security computer to the low security computer (called A and B respectively) as a result of actions on A. That is files are pushed from A rather than pulled from B. In this case, an adequate security policy, that is, one which countered the potential threats to the system, might consist of the following four requirements:

1. No file whose security is greater than the level of B may be sent to B.
2. Files only pass to B as a result of the action of an identifiable user on A.

3. Only B receives files from A.

4. Only file transfer from A to B happens on A.

The first of these is a functional requirement, while the other three, being essentially concerned with bypass, are non-functional.

These requirements statements are easily linked to the threat. The first ensures that the handling requirements are respected, while the second allow the action to be audited and counter Trojan horse attack in A's untrusted software. The third and fourth counter attacks via the network. Clearly a selection of security requirements can be made according to the threat situation of the system. Note however that the second requirement can only be implemented on A.

4.3   The implementation

The implementation is shown in figure 1:

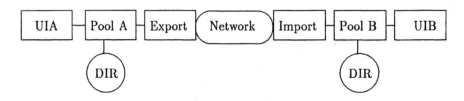

Fig. 1. File transfer diagram

The various components of this implementation are as follows:

UIA   The user interface on machine A. This allows the user to access files and give them to PoolA for sending to B.

PoolA This checks the classification of files presented by UIA and if allowed invokes FileExport to send to B.

FileExport This obeys the file transfer protocol at the instigation of PoolA.

Network Carries out the data transfers between A and B.

FileImport Carries out the receiving end of file transfer.

PoolB Temporary store for files received.

UIB   User interface for storing the files received from A.

To implement the security requirements given above, only the network and the components on A need to be trusted. Their rely and guarantee conditions are as follows:

Network	**Guarantees:** A may only exchange data with B.
	Relies on: Encryption
FileExport	**Guarantees:** Provides file transfer facility only to PoolA.
	Relies on: Unique binding of network interface.
PoolA	**Guarantees:** Provides checked file transfer facility only to UIA.
	Relies on: Unique binding of FileExport interface.
UIA	**Guarantees:** File transfer only takes place as a result of user interaction. Whatever auditing and inspection functions needed.
	Relies on: The trusted path mechanism (probably another unique binding).

These have been chosen so that these trusted modules may be constructed from untrusted software together with a small amount of encapsulating code. The details clearly depend upon the features of the component, but one would expect to use the encapsulation of files with labels in PoolA.

Note that the rely conditions tend to invoke lower level mechanisms, such as encryption in the case of the network and configuration management in the case of those components relying on unique bindings of modules. It is not yet clear how to manage these conditions (for example, whether to formalise them, whether to store in a rule based fashion or simply in a database) in order to make the argument for security clear.

5 Conclusions

Making secure systems which actually work and which have defences appropriate to the attacks which might be made on them needs a significantly different approach from the access control and reference monitor approach which is commonly adopted. First of all, security policies need to take into account operational needs to transfer information from high security environments to low security environments. There is no operational point in having a system which only accepts information and gives nothing in return. This means policies must contain dynamic conditional elements.

These policies inevitably lead to security functionality being present in and enforced by software. This is true even of current reference monitor based systems. It is simply not possible to build a system in which all the security is concentrated in one place. This makes it highly desirable to be able to decompose security requirements so that the particular security requirements of a software component can be identified and checked during maintenance of the component.

In this decomposition process it is important to recognise that security has both functional and non-functional elements. The non-functional elements are usually associated with lack of side effects and bypass of the security mechanisms. The functional elements are relatively easily traced whereas the non-functional elements are not. Another important factor is that the decomposition usually involves change of representation as the design is implemented in high level language and the language is compiled into machine code. At these changes of representation, the issue is not just one of tracing the old requirement to the new representation, but is also one of identifying the new hazards posed by the particular implementation decisions chosen. Appropriate counters to these hazards (such as configuration management and encryption) must be chosen and used effectively.

The particular hazards at the compilation stage are associated with lack of integrity in the translation process and errors in system construction. At the moment, the only counter to these hazards is to use a reliable compiler. An additional check, associated with the interfaces to a software component, would be highly desirable. This paper has described what such a check might be and how it might fit into the whole process of showing how a system satisfies its security requirements. This check, based on the application of type checking to compiler output, would allow a much more extensive use of software mechanisms to be made and would also allow for the incorporation of commercial or otherwise adopted software.

The checking process unfortunately cannot be entirely carried out at compile time: the elements which cannot be resolved may either be incorporated as dynamic checks or used as a measure of the quality of the software. It is possible that the checking process may be too strict for typical applications: further work will be necessary to resolve this issue.

References

1. B. A. Wichmann, *Insecurities in the Ada programming language*, NPL report DITC 137/89, National Physical Laboratory, Teddington 1989.
2. K. A. Nyberg, *The annotated Ada reference manual (2nd edition)*, Grebyn corporation, 1992.
3. C.O'Halloran, *BOOTS, a secure CCIS.*, DRA, Malvern Report 92002 1992.
4. J.A. Goguen and J. Meseguer, *Security policies and security models*, Proceedings 1982 IEEE Symposium on Security and Privacy, Oakland.
5. J. Jacob, *Specifying Security Properties*, in *Developments in Concurrency and Communication* C. A. R. Hoare, editor. The Proceedings of the Year of Programming Institute in Concurrent Programming), Addison Wesley, 1990
6. C.A.R. Hoare, *Communicating sequential processes*, Prentice Hall 1985.
7. C.O'Halloran, *A Calculus of Information Flow (specifying confidentiality requirements)*, DRA, Malvern Report 92001 1992.
8. *TDF Specification*, available from Dr. N. Peeling, N101, DRA Malvern, St. Andrews Rd., Malvern, Worcs. WR14 3PS, UK.
9. C.O'Halloran, *Category theory and information flow applied to computer security*, DPhil thesis, Oxford University 1993.

Appendix

A An outline of the checking algorithm

A.1 Static type checking

As discussed in the main body of the paper, the checking algorithm consists of three parts: simple static type checking, a type inference system and a well-typing dynamic condition generator. These parts are interwoven in the algorithm, but are described here separately. For static type checking, three things are necessary: the representation of the types, the abstract syntax of the language and the set of well typing rules which say how to give a type to the constructions in the language. The representation of the types is given by a sequence of Σ where:

$[\Pi, \mathit{Identifier}]$

$$
\begin{aligned}
\Sigma ::= \ & \mathit{Integer} \langle\!\langle \mathit{Variety} \rangle\!\rangle \\
| \ & \mathit{Floating} \langle\!\langle \mathit{Variety} \rangle\!\rangle \\
| \ & \mathit{Bitfield} \langle\!\langle \mathit{Variety} \rangle\!\rangle \\
| \ & \mathit{Offset} \\
| \ & \mathit{Pointer} \langle\!\langle \Pi \times \mathit{offset} \rangle\!\rangle \\
| \ & \mathit{Union} \langle\!\langle \Pi \rangle\!\rangle \\
| \ & \mathit{Proc} \langle\!\langle \Pi \rangle\!\rangle \\
| \ & \mathit{Named} \langle\!\langle \mathit{Identifier} \times \mathrm{seq}\ \Sigma \rangle\!\rangle \\
| \ & \mathit{Top} \\
| \ & \mathit{Bottom}
\end{aligned}
$$

Note that this is a simplification of the datatype actually being used as it omits parts necessary to take into account the alignment of items. The *Integer*, *Floating* and *Bitfield* constructors represent machine integers, floating point numbers and bit strings in various lengths. An *Offset* is the type given to values which can be added to pointers while *Pointer*, *Union* and *Proc* are used to represent values which are pointers, which can have several types, or which can only be called respectively. The *Named* constructor is used to implement the abstract data type concept and the *Top* and *Bottom* constructors are used to give top and bottom elements for forming LUB and GLB of types.

Missing from this datatype is any constructor corresponding to structure or cartesian product. In its place is the fact that a sequence of Σ (or rather a sequence of aligned Σs) is used for the types of expressions and memory. This allows for the free manipulation of pointers and the use of part structures, apart from the specific structure indicated by the *Named* types.

For pointers, unions and procedures it is necessary to know the type of what is being pointed at, the potential types for the union, and the potential types for the procedures. These are given using Π values, which should be treated as instance variables. Two pointers are assumed to have different types unless the Π values are the same, in which case it will be known that they have been derived from the same original pointer. Associated with each pointer Π-value there will be a sequence of aligned Σs corresponding to what has been inferred about the memory as a result of the usage of the pointer. The *offset* value, used in the construction of the pointer type, gives where in memory the pointer is currently pointing.

In a similar way, the Π-values associated with the union and procedure constructors allow information to be obtained from an environment about the conditions under which a union value has one of the types available to it and the type of a procedure value.

The abstract syntax of the language is given by the abstract syntax of TDF insofar as it applies to expressions and statements: both aspects of the language are contained within one very extensive data type called *EXP* which has well over a hundred constructors, corresponding to the various operations (arithmetic, assignment, conditional etc) which are available.

The checking process constructs a schema value:

$$
\begin{array}{|l}
\_\text{Exp} _____ \\
\hline
e : exp \\
\omega : \Omega \\
\hline
\end{array}
$$

where Ω is the Z type for the sequence of aligned Σ and *exp* is an abstraction of *EXP* needed for the calculation of well typing conditions. The signature of the checking function for TDF expressions is therefore given by

$$
\mid \quad check_{EXP} : EXP \times Env \rightarrowtail Exp \times Env
$$

That is, the checking function evaluates an *EXP* to an *Exp* within an environment, and may change the environment.

This function is defined by cases over the constructors of *EXP*: a typical example is the integer addition constructor which has two EXP arguments (and an error treatment argument). The two arguments should evaluate to integers of the same variety and this is the type of the result delivered.

A.2   Type inference

Type inference is used to deduce the layout of memory. The environment keeps the relation between the Π values used in the pointer types and what is known about the memory in the form of a sequence of aligned Σs. The inferences about the memory are made as a result of checking sub-expressions and working out their types. The use of Π values and the environment ensures that when an inference is made about a sub-expression it is propagated to the other elements of the expression.

A typical operation which allows inferences to be made adds an offset to a pointer. The offset is represented by a sequence of aligned shapes where the *Shape* datatype represents the size of objects. With some simplifications, this is given by:

$$
\begin{aligned}
Shape ::= \; & int\_s \langle\!\langle Variety \rangle\!\rangle \\
\mid \; & float\_s \langle\!\langle Variety \rangle\!\rangle \\
\mid \; & bit\_s \langle\!\langle Variety \rangle\!\rangle \\
\mid \; & point\_s \\
\mid \; & offset\_s \\
\mid \; & proc\_s \\
\mid \; & union\_s \langle\!\langle \mathsf{F} \; offset \rangle\!\rangle
\end{aligned}
$$

The sequence of shapes which make up the offset, is clearly related to the sequence of Σs which make up memory. If the memory is longer than the offset then each of the shapes must correspond with the Σs. If the offset is longer than the memory, then the operation allows us to infer what the memory should be. New Σs are created corresponding to each of the shapes: where pointers, unions or procedures are involved, new Π values must be created.

To capture the effect of assignment on pointers, it is necessary to work backwards (that is, work out the pre-condition for well-typing). Consider an assignment such as

$$x := E;$$

where E is some expression. The type of E must be compatible with that of **x**: it might actually depend on **x**. However, what **x** points to after the assignment might not be the same as what it is pointing to before. This will only be the case if the assignment is in the path of a loop, so it is at the loop heads that expressions and pointers are unified, which in effect constrains the type of pointers to be invariant if they are used for assignment within the scope of a loop.

A.3 Dynamic type checking

This is required whenever the programmer uses unions, that is, where the same area of memory is used for objects of differing types. In order to calculate the well-typing condition, it is necessary to associate a condition with each of the possible types of a union and for each programme element, propagate this weakest pre-condition backwards. Given variables r, i and u of type (pointer to) floating, integer and a union respectively, a code sequence like

$$r := u; \ i := u;$$

is clearly incorrect. The two arms of a conditional may, however, use a union in two different ways. In the case of

$$\text{if } G \text{ then } r := u \text{ else } i := u;$$

where G is some boolean expression, the weakest precondition for well-typing is G for u floating, not G for u integer. This is often written as a predicate:

$$u\%Floating \wedge G \vee u\%Integer \wedge \neg G$$

Conditions of this form can be simplified at assignment. For example, the weakest precondition of u := 3; with respect to this condition is $\neg G$.

Key Management I

Designing Secure Key Exchange Protocols[*]

Colin Boyd and Wenbo Mao

Communications Research Group,
Electrical Engineering Laboratories,
University of Manchester,
Manchester M13 9PL, UK
Email: Colin.Boyd@man.ac.uk

Abstract. Protocols for authentication and key exchange have proved difficult to develop correctly despite their apparent simplicity in terms of the length and number of messages involved. A number of formal techniques have been developed to help analyse such protocols and have been useful in detecting errors. Nevertheless it is still difficult to be certain that a particular protocol is correct.

This paper explores a different approach; instead of analysing existing protocols the aim is to design protocols to be secure in the first place. A methodology is developed for designing key exchange protocols in a restricted way such that they must be correct according to a defined security criterion. The protocols are defined abstractly with the cryptographic operations specified only according to their basic functions. This allows the protocols to be made concrete in a variety of ways. A number of concrete protocols are presented, some of which appear novel and, at the same time, efficient in comparison with existing ones.

Keywords: Cryptographic protocols, key management, authentication.

1 Introduction

The difficulty of correctly designing secure cryptographic protocols for authentication and key exchange has become widely recognised in recent years. As a result a number of formal techniques have been developed to enable analysis of such protocols [3, 7, 22, 13, 11]. These methods have proved successful at finding problems with existing protocols, sometimes previously unrecognised ones. Unquestionably formal analysis techniques have helped to further understanding in how protocols work, or fail to work, by providing a language in which to mathematically describe and argue about them. Despite these successes, there remains a great deal of doubt as to whether any of the existing techniques is sufficient to provide a proof that a given protocol is sound [15, 23, 2, 8]. The situation seems to have a fair analogy in testing for computer programs; rigorous testing allows many bugs to be found but will not provide a proof of correctness.

---

[*] This work is funded by the UK Science and Engineering Research Council under research grant GR/G19787.

The experience gained in correct design of computer programs provides a lesson for correct protocol design. It is now well understood that to develop a correct program the best method is to design it formally in an abstract way and then to proceed towards a concrete implementation [10]. The difficulty of proving that an existing program is correct is usually far greater. In this light it seems obvious that we should develop techniques to design protocols that are guaranteed to be correct in the first place, rather than design them with *ad hoc* techniques and try to remove any bugs by formal analysis afterwards [8].

This paper describes a technique to design key exchange protocols which are guaranteed to be correct in the sense that a specified security criterion will not be violated if protocol principals act correctly. The technique is developed from basic cryptographic properties that can be expected to be held by a variety of cryptographic algorithms. Protocols can be developed abstractly and any particular type of algorithm that possesses the required property can then be used in a concrete implementation. Building on previous work [1] protocols may be classified according to what secure channels initially exist.

The idea of the technique is to restrict attention to protocol messages which contain a small number of elements which have a well defined purpose and meaning. This implies that only a restricted set of protocols can emerge as a product of the technique. Nevertheless, comparison with existing protocols indicates that the protocols developed are both efficient and flexible enough to accommodate most reasonable requirements.

The remainder of the paper is organised as follows. In the next section the model of security is explained using some mathematical formalism. The security criterion appropriate for this model is defined and it is shown that if principals act according to a set of simple security assumptions then the security criterion will not be violated. These assumptions are then used as guidance to develop the basic format of messages. Generic protocols with this message format are suggested which can be made concrete in a particular design. Section 3 includes protocols suitable for common situations designed using the technique. These include user-to-user protocols, protocols using a trusted third party and conference protocols. Concrete implementations of the protocols are suggested and compared with existing protocols. The final section examines limitations of the technique and possible further developments.

2   The Model of Security

In this paper the only issue to be addressed is that of secure key exchange. Protocols aimed solely at authentication are not addressed. There are at least two reasons for this. One is in order to concentrate on a single achievable goal. Another is that there is some difficulty in agreeing exactly what is meant by authentication in a general sense. Nonetheless authentication plays a crucial part in key exchange protocols, but here it is clearer exactly what is required. It will be assumed that a successful run of a protocol should achieve the following goals for a participating user.

1. The user should possess a new key for use with a set of users $\mathcal{U}$.
2. The new key should not be known by any non-trusted user except those in $\mathcal{U}$.

It will be assumed that the new key is a shared symmetric key for use in a single session, but existing keys used during the protocol may be symmetric or asymmetric. The above goals are uncontroversial but it is frequently desired to include further goals. For example it may be desired that the user should know that all the users in $\mathcal{U}$ are in possession of the new key. This can be achieved by further mechanisms if desired and may properly be seen as distinct from the mechanism to enable key exchange. Note that $\mathcal{U}$ will often be a single user but there is no reason to make this distinction in the model and not doing so allows the inclusion of conference key protocols.

A large variety of key exchange protocols exist. It is not at all obvious why there are so many nor what the differences are between them. Some of the issues that may be important in the design of a particular protocol are as follows.

- A specific set of goals may be desired for the protocol. These will always include those expressed above. Others may be achieved subsequently. The protocols designed in this paper may be extended to achieve further goals.
- There may be constraints on the order in which messages are sent and the channels available to send them on. For various practical reasons communications channels may not exist between every pair of principals and there may be reasons why one principal or another must initiate communications. In the protocols of this paper the physical path a message takes is of no importance. The ordering of messages is also irrelevant except that in some cases certain messages cannot be formed until others are received.
- Different principals may have different computational capabilities. In particular only some principals may be competent to generate good keys. The type of cryptographic algorithm available, particularly public key algorithms, may also be restricted. The two most common situations are where a user generates a key intended for use with one other user, and where a trusted party generates a key for one or more users. These are the two cases covered in this paper. Variations allow any type of cryptographic algorithm to be used as long as the basic requirements for secure communications [1] are satisfied.

Despite the flexibility of the protocols proposed below, they appear economical in comparison with most existing key exchange protocols. This results from deciding exactly which message components are required and which of these should be processed cryptographically. If it is felt desirable to avoid special cryptographic opportunities for attack, such as *known plaintext attacks* [4], further processing may be used.

2.1 Cryptographic keys and secure channels

The secure channels available in a particular architecture can be described in terms of the cryptographic keys known to the participants. This information alone is sufficient to decide whether it is possible to arrange for secure communications between every pair of users [1]. The model described here uses a similar idea; it is mathematically very simple relying on just a few sets and functions between them. Two fundamental sets are assumed whose structure is outside the concern of the model. The set *User* consists of principals in the system who will participate in protocols; it is of no concern to the model how different users are named. The set *Key* contains all keys that are available for use with the cryptosystems of interest in the system. The length and value of any key is of no concern. The cryptographic information stored by each user is modelled as a set of ordered pairs connecting a key and a user[2].

$$LocalSecret : User \rightarrow (Key \leftrightarrow User)$$

For example if user A associates key k with user B then this is modelled as

$$(k, B) \in LocalSecret(A)$$

The set *Key* can be thought of as partitioned into three subsets *Private*, *Public* and *Shared*. These accommodate the difference between conventional symmetric (or shared-key) cryptography and asymmetric (or public-key) cryptography. The *dual* is defined for every key; for a shared key the dual is the key itself but for a public key the dual is the corresponding private key and *vice versa*. A user who associates a shared key with one or more other users must know the value of that key. However a user who associates a private key with a user will know only the dual public key.

Consider now what it means for the system to be secure from the viewpoint of an individual user *Alice*. There are two operations that Alice may perform using the keys that she knows about.

1. Alice may use a key to send a confidential message to another user. This will be achieved by encrypting the message using a cryptographic algorithm which allows only those users in possession of the decrypting key to recover the message. In the case of a shared key it is necessary that all those users who possess this key are known to Alice. It does not matter, from the security viewpoint, if some of the users in Alice's list do *not* in reality possess the key. In the case of a public key it is necessary that all those users who possess the dual private key are known to Alice. As long as this is the case Alice will not be surprised by who gets her message.

2. Alice may use a key to authenticate a message received by her. It can be verified that in this case also she will not be surprised by who sent the message as long the same condition holds. That is, Alice must know all users who possess the private, or shared, key required to form the authenticated message.

In order to model this security condition a global notion of which users may be in possession of which keys is required. This is a set of ordered pairs as follows.

---

[2] The notation $A \leftrightarrow B$ denotes the set of relations between the set A and the set B

$$GlobalSecret : Key \leftrightarrow User$$

Keys are issued by authorised principals and we will assume, for simplicity that there is a single principal, called the *server* who does this. The set *GlobalSecret* does not conform to any real system variable but is an abstract modelling device. The set records all the keys k which have been issued by the server and which are good, in the sense that k is known to user U implies $(k, U) \in GlobalSecret$. In a practical interpretation, the *GlobalSecret* set includes all key encrypting keys shared between the server and each user, and all session keys which have not expired. Of course no user is able to decide with certainty which keys are good (and so in the *GlobalSecret* set) and which are not. In practice each user will have to believe that newly generated keys received from the server are still good, and hence will be in the set. For the moment we will ignore this issue.

The above notion of security may now be defined in terms of these sets. For a particular key k used by Alice there will be a set of users in her set *LocalSecret* (that is *LocalSecret(Alice)*) which she associates with that k (or its dual if it is a public key). All users U with (k, U) in *GlobalSecret* should be contained within this set known to Alice. This can be defined in one equation as follows.

Security Criterion (for Alice)

$$\forall k \in \text{dom}(LocalSecret(Alice)) \bullet GlobalSecret(k) \subseteq LocalSecret(Alice)(k)$$

All this says is that for those keys which Alice has in her list, she has all those names against it which are in the *GlobalSecret* set. Note that it is an implicit assumption in this equation that the only keys in Alice's list are also in the global list; in other words, only good keys are in her list.

The method of protocol design in this paper is to only allow messages which leave this condition true. The server always generates and sends a *new* key which therefore (formally) does not exist in the *LocalSecret* of any user. A user's *LocalSecret* set is only updated when a key is received from the server. Messages contain information on who else has been sent the key and hence who is linked with that key in *GlobalSecret*. Users ensure that keys received from the server are new and can therefore be assumed to exist in the global set. We may summarise the assumptions required to maintain security as follows.

Security Assumptions

1. The trusted server generates a new key k each time it is activated.
2. The new key is sent to only those users in $GlobalSecret(k)$.
3. A recipient only accepts a key k if it is in the *GlobalSecret* set.
4. Each key k is received together with the set of users in $GlobalSecret(k)$. The new keys and the set of users are added to the *LocalSecret* set of the recipient.

Theorem 1 *With the above security assumptions, if Alice starts in a secure state then she remains in a secure state after receiving a new key.*

The proof of this theorem is immediate. Key generation and distribution does not affect Alice's security criterion since it involves a new key which cannot be in the domain of her local secrets. When she receives a new key she adds it to her *LocalSecret* set and maps it to the set of all users which it is mapped to in *GlobalSecret*. Thus the security criterion is automatically maintained.

In the next subsection, the problem is addressed of how Alice can be confident that the received key is in the global set.

2.2 Abstract Protocol Messages

The cryptographic keys known to system users result in a set of secure channels between pairs of users [1]. These channels provide confidentiality of data (the sender knows who will receive the message) or authentication of data (the recipient knows who has sent the message) or both. A useful notation for use of these channels is as follows.

$$A \xrightarrow{c} B : M$$

This means that A sends the message M on a confidentiality channel to B. Note that this is an action of the process representing A and implies no action for the process of B which may or may not receive such a message.

$$B \xleftarrow{a} A : M$$

Similarly this means that B receives a message M on an authentication channel from A. This is an action involving only the process of B. However, B may correctly deduce that at some time in the past M was formed by someone in possession of the key of A. This notation is now used to represent the abstract processes involved in the protocols.

In order to convey a symmetric key from one user to another (key exchange) a confidentiality and an authentication channel must both exist [1]. Such channels may need to be set up as part of the protocol. Cases where these do not initially exist will be discussed below. The format of messages used to convey keys can be derived by examining the required properties. An authorised principal S will pass a key k to a recipient A only over a confidentiality channel. This is necessary for security assumption 2.

$$S \xrightarrow{c} A : k$$

In the model we regard the generation and sending of the key k to the set $\mathcal{R}$ of all recipients to be a single state change and this is recorded as a corresponding update to the *GlobalSecret* set.

$$GlobalSecret' = GlobalSecret \cup \bigcup_{U \in \mathcal{R}} \{(k, U)\}$$

An authorised principal will only accept a key k from the server if it is received in an authenticated message. In order for the recipient to be confident that the key is indeed in the *GlobalSecret* set (security assumption 3) she must have some way of knowing that it is newly generated. For this purpose it must include a liveness indicator, or *nonce*, N which ensures that the message (and hence the key) is a new one. The key must be accompanied by a set $\mathcal{R}$ of the names of all users who are associated with k in *GlobalSecret*, in other words, the names of all users who have been sent k.

$$A \xleftarrow{a} S : k, \mathcal{R}, N$$

In the model this means that the recipient Alice must update her *LocalSecret* by adding all the pairs (k, U) for all users U in $\mathcal{R}$ (security assumption 4).

$$LocalSecret'(Alice) = LocalSecret(Alice) \cup \bigcup_{U \in \mathcal{R}} \{(k, U)\}$$

If these procedures for the sending and receiving of messages are followed by all authorised users then the security criterion is maintained. This is simply a re-interpretation of the theorem from the last subsection. Note that it is not necessary to consider what attacks may be mounted against the system. What we know is that if the authorised principals act correctly and the security channels provide the stated properties, then the security criterion will be maintained regardless of the actions of an attacker.

2.3 Concrete Protocol Messages

In a concrete protocol the conditions for both the sender and the recipient must be satisfied together. This can be done by sending messages using channels which provide both confidentiality and authentication at the same time. This is the way that protocols have usually been designed in the past. However there is no need for this restriction as long as the key is always sent along a confidentiality channel. The reason that this can be useful is that authenticated messages are very often not authenticated as plaintext, but after processing by a oneway hash function [19]. Such a oneway function may be regarded as providing a confidentiality channel to the empty set of users - there is no key to recover the message. However the oneway function is sufficient to provide specific authentication channels.

In order to describe concrete protocols some notation to record cryptographic transformations is required. This is achieved through three different kinds of brackets to distinguish between transformations which provide confidentiality, those which provide authentication, and those which provide both.

- $[M]_k$ **confidentiality**: the message M cannot be recovered from the transformed data without knowledge of k.
  Typical transformations providing such a property are the Data Encryption Standard (DES) in one of its usual modes for data encryption [18], encryption using the public key of an asymmetric cryptosystem [17], or the unconditionally secure one time pad [20].

– $[M]_k$ **authentication**: the transformed data may not be formed from the message M without knowledge of k.

Typical transformations providing this property are a Message Authentication Code (MAC) such as may be formed using the Data Encryption Standard (DES) [18], encryption using the private key of an asymmetric cryptosystem [17], or an unconditionally secure authentication code [21].

– $\{M\}_k$ **confidentiality and authentication**: both the above properties hold. Transformations providing both properties will typically have distinct elements dedicated to each property. A typical examples would be concatenation of a digest of the message using a oneway hash function [19] prior to DES encryption. Another example is a digital signature scheme followed by encryption with the public key of the recipient, but here the key k must be identified with two separate keys and the transformation may usually be considered as two distinct operations.

Using this notation the two general formats for key exchange messages are as follows.

1.

$$\{k, \mathcal{R}, N\}_{k_S}$$

where k_S is a key associated by the recipient with an authorised user and is suitable for use to provide both confidentiality to the recipient and authentication from the sender. As above, $\mathcal{R}$ is a set of recipient names and N is a nonce. This is a typical key exchange message in existing protocols. Unfortunately the requirement of both authentication and confidentiality properties is often not made explicit and this can lead to attacks [12].

2.

$$[k]_{k_A}, [h(k, \mathcal{R}, N)]_{k_S}$$

where k_A is a key associated by the sender with an authorised user and is suitable to provide confidentiality and k_S is a key associated by the recipient with an authorised user and is suitable for use to provide authentication. This is not a typical format for key exchange messages in existing protocols. Nevertheless it has significant potential advantages over the first format. Firstly, it allows flexibility in choice of cryptographic algorithms; for example the unconditionally secure one time pad may be efficiently used for confidentiality. Secondly, it will often be more efficient than the first format, by limiting cryptographic transformations only to those fields where they are required. In some situations this latter advantage will be accompanied by a very small field size for the secure messages.

2.4 Nonces and Channel Inversion

So far it has been assumed that both confidentiality and authentication channels exist from the sender S to the recipient of the key A. Although a common situation this need not always be the case initially and it may be necessary to invert existing secure channels. This can be done efficiently as part of the protocol. In order for key exchange to be possible the initial state must include either $S \xrightarrow{c} A$ or $S \xleftarrow{a} A$ and also either $A \xleftarrow{a} S$ or $A \xrightarrow{c} S$ [1].

Suppose, for example, that $A \xrightarrow{c} S$ exists initially but not the desired $A \xleftarrow{a} S$. Then the new channel $A \xleftarrow{a} S$ may be formed by sending a key using $A \xrightarrow{c} S$.

$$A \xrightarrow{c} S : k_A$$

As long as k_A is a key suitable for use for authentication then it may be used by S to authenticate a new key passed back to A. There is no reason why this mechanism should not be used with a subset of those users involved in the protocol. Similarly the channel $A \xrightarrow{c} S$ may be converted to $A \xleftarrow{a} S$ by passing a public key for confidentiality over the channel $A \xleftarrow{a} S$. An example of this is to send a Diffie-Hellman [5] key exchange message, just in the one direction, which establishes a confidentiality channel in the other direction.

It has also been assumed up to now that the sender of the key is able to include a nonce in the message to show that the key is new. Nonces may be classified into the three types: timestamps, counters and random challenges. The first two may be assumed to be known to the sender without any information from the recipient. The third requires a previous protocol message which is the challenge sent from key recipient to key sender. All types are equally applicable to the model. Selection and use of appropriate nonces is complex in practice [8] and is outside the scope of this paper.

3 Design of Protocols

In this section the design rules developed in the previous section will be brought together to design a number of concrete protocols.

3.1 User to User Protocols

The basic protocol using the first format is a single message as follows, specified in the traditional manner indicating only a successful message exchange.

1. $A \rightarrow B : \{k, A, B, N\}_{k_{AB}}$

Here k_{AB} is a key already shared by A and B which is suitable to provide both confidentiality and authentication. N is a nonce which is initially predictable by A, so is a timestamp or a sequence number. A implicitly sends the key to itself and hence updates its own *LocalSecret* when it sends such a message. The recipient updates its *LocalSecret* when it receives a message of the correct format, otherwise rejects it. The variation of this protocol using a random challenge as a nonce is only trivially different.

1. $B \rightarrow A : N$

2. $A \rightarrow B : \{k, A, B, N\}_{k_{AB}}$

The second type of message has its basic form as follows.

1. $A \rightarrow B : [k]_{k_B}, [h(k, A, B, N)]_{k_A}$

Here k_B (which may be public or shared) and k_A (which may be private or shared) are keys already known by A with k_B suitable to provide confidentiality to B and k_A suitable to provide authentication from A to B. Again it is assumed that the nonce N is predictable to B and a trivial variation allows B to issue a random challenge.

1. $B \rightarrow A : N$
2. $A \rightarrow B : [k]_{k_B}, [h(k, A, B, N)]_{k_A}$

Further variations on these two types of protocols cover the cases where the initial channels are not $A \xrightarrow{c} B$ and $B \xleftarrow{a} A$ and so require channel inversion. For example the following protocol is suitable when k_{BA} is a key initially known by B (perhaps a public key) and suitable for providing confidentiality to A.

1. $B \rightarrow A : [k_A]_{k_{BA}}$
2. $A \rightarrow B : [k]_{k_B}, [h(k, A, B, N)]_{k_A}$

3.2 Protocols using a Trusted Party

These protocols make use of a trusted server S which sends a key to principals A and B for use with each other. The basic protocols of the first type is as follows.

1. $S \rightarrow A : \{k, A, B, N\}_{k_{SA}}$
2. $S \rightarrow B : \{k, A, B, N\}_{k_{SB}}$

Here k_{SB} and k_{SB} are keys already shared by S and A, and by S and B respectively, which are suitable to provide both confidentiality and authentication. The basic protocol of the second type is this.

1. $S \rightarrow A : [k]_{k_A}, [h(k, A, B, N)]_{k_{SA}}$
2. $S \rightarrow B : [k]_{k_B}, [h(k, A, B, N)]_{k_{SB}}$

Here k_A, k_B (which may be public or shared) and k_{SA}, k_{SB} (which may be private or shared) are keys already known by S with k_A and k_B suitable to provide confidentiality to A and B respectively, and k_{SA} and k_{SB} suitable to provide authentication from S to A and B respectively.

A practical implementation will require further messages to enable principals to place messages received in context. In addition, of course, specific algorithms will need to be chosen which are believed to be either confidentiality or authentication functions or both. A particularly simple way to authenticate a hashed value is to include a secret key in the elements to be hashed.

$$[h(X)]_k = h(k, X)$$

This relies on the assumption that it is not possible to form the value $h(k, X)$ from X without knowledge of k. While this is a reasonable looking assumption, it does not follow from the usual definition of a one-way hash function and so must be explicitly stated. Using such a function an implementation might be as follows.

1. $A \rightarrow B : A, N_a$
2. $B \rightarrow S : A, N_a, B, N_b$
3. $S \rightarrow B : [k]_{k_{AS}}, h(k_{SA}, k, A, B, N_a), [k]_{k_{BS}}, h(k_{SB}, k, A, B, N_b)$
4. $B \rightarrow A : [k]_{k_{BS}}, h(k_{SB}, k, A, B, N_b)$

Here k_{SA} and k_{SB} are keys shared by S with A and B respectively. It is perfectly acceptable to have $k_{SA} = k_{AS}$ but it may be preferred to let k_{AS} be different, for example to be used from a one-time pad to give unconditional secrecy to the keys. This is done with maximum efficiency by applying only to the key bits.

The above protocol specification is finally in a form suitable for comparison with usual key exchange protocols. A similar implementational version can be given to all the above protocols by a choice of suitable algorithms, hints for principals, and physical paths for the messages.

3.3 A Conference Key Protocol

Since it was at no time assumed that the set of recipients $\mathcal{R}$ in the abstract protocols only had two users, the above protocols generalise naturally to allow conference key distribution. These protocols again make use of a trusted server S which sends a key to principals in the set $\mathcal{U} = \{U_1, U_2, \ldots, U_N\}$ for use with each other. The basic protocol of the first type consists of the following message sent to each U_i.

1. $S \rightarrow U_i : \{k, \mathcal{U}, N\}_{k_{SU_i}}$

As usual the k_{SU_i} are keys already shared by S and U_i suitable to provide both confidentiality and authentication. The basic protocol of the second type is the following message sent to each U_i.

1. $S \rightarrow U_i : [k]_{k_{U_i}}, [h(k, \mathcal{U}, N)]_{k_{S_i}}$

As usual k_{U_i} and k_{S_i} are keys already known by S (which may be public, private or shared) with k_{U_i} suitable to provide confidentiality to U_i and k_{S_i} suitable to provide authentication from S to U_i.

4 Discussion

The technique of this paper appears to be the first attempt to enable design of key exchange protocols which allows flexible choice of cryptographic algorithms relying only on their fundamental properties. An advantage of the current technique is that algorithms may be chosen appropriate to the implementation. If desired these can be unconditionally secure, or they may be a standard mode of operation for a block cipher.

Although the motivating idea has been to produce protocols which are known to be secure in terms of the defined model, it is interesting to make a comparison with existing protocols. Protocols of the first type, with combined authentication and confidentiality algorithms, are similar to a number already existing in the literature. Those using a trusted server and two other principals can be compared with those of Otway and Rees [16] and Needham and Schroeder [14]. The new protocol is similar to these but is more efficient both in terms of lengths of messages and use of encryption as well as checking required by the server. Conference key generalisations do not appear to have been discussed in the literature.

Protocols of the second type, with separate confidentiality and authentication algorithms, are by contrast not at all common in the literature. Perhaps the closest are some variations of the Diffie-Hellman key exchange protocol [6] which are again specific to a particular algorithm. These protocols have the potential to be particularly efficient in terms of lengths of messages and use of encryption and are also particularly flexible for selection of algorithms.

Despite its generality in a number of directions, the technique has a number of limitations at present and there is considerable potential for extensions. In particular:

- it has been a clear assumption that all legitimate principals act correctly. However, it seems clear that the local security of one user is not affected by the actions of any other users which are not trusted in the distribution process. It should be possible to model the effect of untrustworthy behaviour of one principal on other principals.
- more complex protocols involving distributed servers to allow authorisation [9] and delegation of rights will require a considerable further development.

References

1. C.A.Boyd, *Security Architectures using Formal Methods*, IEEE Journal on Selected Areas on Communications, June 1993, pp.694-701.
2. C.A.Boyd and W.Mao, *On a Limitation of BAN logic*, Proceedings of Eurocrypt 93, Springer-Verlag 1993.
3. M.Burrows, M.Abadi, and R.Needham, *A Logic of Authentication*, ACM Transactions on Computer Systems, Vol 8,1, February 1990, pp 18-36.
4. D.W.Davies and W.L.Price, *Security for Computer Networks*, John Wiley and Sons, 1989.
5. W.Diffie and M.E.Hellman, *New Directions in Cryptography*, IEEE Transaction on Information Theory, IT-22, pp.644-654, 1976.
6. W.Diffie, P.C.VanOorschot and M.Wiener, *Authentication and Authenticated Key Exchanges*, Designs, Codes and Cryptography, 2, pp.107-125 (1992).

7. L.Gong, R.Needham & R.Yahalom, *Reasoning about Belief in Cryptographic Protocols* Proceedings of the 1990 IEEE Computer Society Symposium on Security and Privacy, pp. 234-248, IEEE Computer Society Press, 1990.

8. L.Gong, *Variations on the Themes of Message Freshness and Replay*, IEEE Security Foundations Workshop, pp.131-136, 1993.

9. L.Gong, *Increasing Availability and Security of an Authentication Service*, IEEE Journal on Selected Areas on Communications, June 1993, pp.657-662.

10. C.B.Jones, *Systematic Software Development Using VDM*, Prentice-Hall, 1986.

11. W.Mao and C.A.Boyd *Towards Formal Analysis of Security Protocols*, IEEE Security Foundations Workshop, pp.147-158, IEEE Press, 1993.

12. W.Mao and C.A.Boyd, *On the use of Encryption in Cryptographic Protocols*, Proceedings of 4th IMA Conference on Coding and Cryptography, *to appear.*

13. C.Meadows, *A System for the Specification and Analysis of Key Management Protocols*, Proceedings of the 1991 IEEE Computer Society Symposium on Security and Privacy, pp. 182-195, IEEE Computer Society Press, 1991.

14. R.M.Needham & M.D.Schroeder, *Using Encryption for Authentication in Large Networks of Computers*, Communications of the ACM, 21,12, December 1978, 993-999.

15. D.M.Nessett, *A Critique of the Burrows, Abadi and Needham Logic*, ACM Operating Systems Review, 24,2,pp.35-38,1990.

16. Dave Otway & Owen Rees, *Efficient and Timely Mutual Authentication* ACM Operating Systems Review, 21,1,pp.8-10, 1987.

17. R.Rivest, A.Shamir & L.Adleman, *A Method for Obtaining Digital Signatures and Public Key Cryptosystems*, Communications of the ACM, 21,pp.120-126,1978.

18. M.E.Smid and D.K.Branstad, *The Data Encryption Standard: Past and Future*, Proceedings of the IEEE, 76,5,pp.550-559, 1988.

19. R.L.Rivest, *The MD4 Message Digest Algorithm*, Advances in Cryptology - CRYPTO '90, Springer-Verlag, 1991.

20. C.E.Shannon, *Communication Theory of Secrecy Systems*, Bell Systems Technical Journal, pp.656-715, 1949.

21. G.J.Simmons, *A Survey of Information Authentication*, in Contemporary Cryptology, G.J.Simmons Ed., pp.379-419, IEEE Press, 1992.

22. E.Snekkenes, *Exploring the BAN Approach to Protocol Analysis*, Computer Security Foundations Workshop, pp.171-181, IEEE Press, 1991.

23. P.Syverson, *The Use of Logic in the Analysis of Cryptographic Protocols*, IEEE Symposium on Security and Privacy, pp.156-170, 1991.

Robust and Secure Password and Key Change Method

Ralf Hauser[1], Philippe Janson[1], Refik Molva[2],
Gene Tsudik[1], Els Van Herreweghen[1]

[1] IBM Research Laboratory, CH-8803 Rüschlikon, Switzerland.
{rah,pj,gts,evh}@zurich.ibm.com
[2] EURECOM Institute, Sophia Antipolis, 06560 Valbonne, France.
molva@eurecom.fr

Abstract. This paper discusses issues and idiosyncrasies associated with changing passwords and keys in distributed computer systems. Current approaches are often complicated and fail to provide the desired level of security and fault tolerance. A novel and very simple approach to changing passwords/keys is presented and analyzed. It provides a means for human users and service programs to change passwords and keys in a robust and secure fashion.

1 Introduction: Changing One's Password

Much effort has recently gone into securing user access to computer systems over insecure communication lines from untrusted (or partially-trusted) workstations and other end-user devices. In a distributed and dynamic network environment, solutions are often based on the use of a highly-secure and trusted entity called an Authentication Server (AS). An AS processes authentication requests by acting as a trustworthy intermediary. As such, the AS has access to and control over the authenticating secrets of all its principals, be they human users or service programs. (Hereafter, we use the term *principal* to refer to both human users and service programs.)

Typically, a principal's password is a fairly long-term secret, i.e., most principals are not required to change their passwords more often than, say, once a month. When a principal wishes to change its password, an appropriately authenticated exchange with the AS must take place. Obviously, any such exchange must meet some basic security requirements such as resistance to guessing attacks and replays of change-password requests. Another desirable feature is the *correctness* of the change-password protocol. We say that a change-password protocol is correct if it provides a guarantee of state synchronization between the two parties involved (AS and principal) in the presence of possible crashes and network failures.

This last issue is not directly relevant to the protocol security and is thus frequently overlooked or not given enough consideration. However, it has to do with the robustness and usability of the protocol which is, in the end, an issue of great importance to the end-users.

Supposing that a principal would like to change its password from K_{old} to K_{new}, six outcomes of the password change protocol are possible:

	Principal believes its secret is	AS believes principal's secret is
1	K_{new}	K_{new}
2	K_{old}	K_{old}
3	K_{old}	K_{new}
4	K_{new}	K_{old}
5	K_{old}	K_{unk}
6	K_{new}	K_{unk}

The first two outcomes are considered normal and desirable. In the first case, a successful password change takes place, i.e., the AS records the new password and the principal receives the change confirmation. In the second case, the new password is rejected for some reason and the principal is informed.

The rest of the cases represent anomalous situations and must be avoided at all costs. Case 3 may occur when a change acknowledgement is lost or when the AS crashes after making a change but before sending out the acknowledgement. The next situation (case 4) may take place if the acknowledgement is somehow spoofed, i.e., an adversary is able to compose a fake confirmation message.[3] Case 5 is the result of an adversary successfully manipulating the protocol is such a way that the AS changes the principal's key to some value (K_{unk}) unknown to or, at least, not intended by, the principal. In fact, case 5 can occur without any activity on the part of the principal; the adversary may simply concoct the entire protocol. Finally, case 6 is very similar to case 5 except that here the principal is actually trying to run the protocol and the adversary not only succeeds in *convincing* the AS to change the principal's password to some K_{unk}, but also manages to convince the principal that the AS accepted K_{new}.

In the rest of this paper we review the current state-of-the-art (exemplified by Kerberos) and go on to develop a protocol that is at the same time simple, robust and secure. The protocol is explicitly constructed to handle anomalous behavior (i.e., events that can lead to cases 3-6 above) of the network and arbitrary failures of the components involved.

2 The *Kerberos* Approach

One of the most popular network security solutions in use today is the Kerberos Authentication and Key Distribution Server originated at MIT[2] and later integrated in the OSF DCE product[3]. Among its multitude of features, Kerberos

---

[3] We do not consider the case when an AS fails to make the change but acknowledges it nonetheless.

includes a change password (CPW) protocol implemented by the kpasswd command which is part of the standard Kerberos distribution package. The actual protocol varies slightly between successive versions of Kerberos. The CPW protocol for Kerberos versions 4 and 5, is illustrated in Fig. 2.

The general course of events in Kerberos CPW protocols is as follows (unless noted otherwise, the following description applies to both versions):

1. Initially, the requesting principal engages in an authentication exchange with the AS to obtain credentials for the Admin server. An Admin server, in Kerberos parlance, is a logically distinct entity which is responsible for the maintenance of all information about principals. (In practice, Admin server is almost always co-located with an AS).

   This initial exchange with the AS requires the principal to provide its current password. The credentials obtained consist of a temporary key K_{cpw} to be shared with the Admin server and a special CHANGEPW ticket (T_{cpw}) with a reasonably short lifetime, typically set to one minute.

2. The second part of the protocol consists of an exchange between the principal and the Admin server. In the course of this exchange, the principal authenticates itself to Admin and sends along the new password, encrypted with the shared key K_{cpw}. In the version 5 protocol, a complete mutual authentication between principal and Admin takes place before the principal sends its encrypted password; while in the version 4 protocol, the same message carries the principal's authentication and the (encrypted) new password.

3 Discussion

The Kerberos CPW protocol is, essentially, capability-based. The capability is embodied in the CHANGEPW ticket which gives the principal the right to change its password. It *does not* restrict the number of times a principal may do so using the same capability. Thus, in general, a principal can use the same ticket multiple times (of course, as long as the ticket does not expire.) This feature is not a drawback in and of itself but it separates two important events that should ideally go hand-in-hand:

- The verification of the previous state of the principal (i.e., making sure that the principal knows the old key/password)

     and

- The verification of the new state of the principal (i.e., making sure that the new password is actually supplied by the true principal and is acceptable to the Admin server) plus the actual database change.

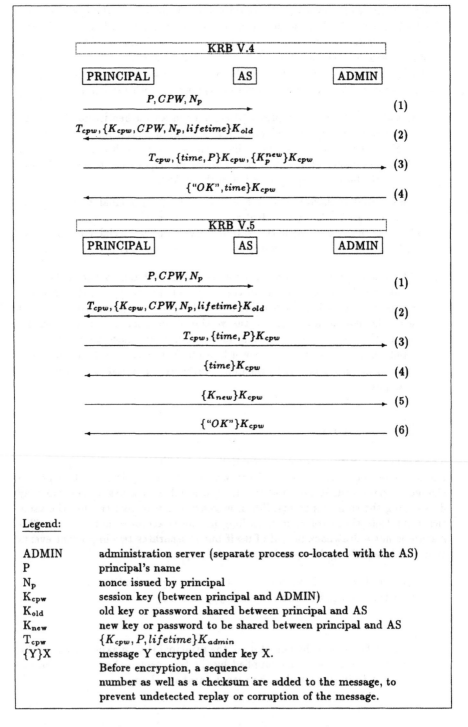

Fig. 1. The Kerberos CPW protocols

As is typical with capability-based approaches, revocation is very difficult if not impossible and is the source of many problems. Of course, a capability tightly bound by time (i.e., one minute in Kerberos) is not as dangerous, but on the other hand, the usual approach of using black-lists to provide for revocation is also not very effective because the assembly and distribution of such a list already might take a significant fraction of this short time.

The existence of the capability-like CHANGEPW ticket itself is dangerous because Kerberos stores its tickets in special cache files on disk. Within the lifetime of a CHANGEPW ticket (which is by default a minute) a trojan horse program could create an additional message changing the password to a value unknown to the principal but known to an adversary controlling the trojan horse. A similar problem could occur if the principal left the terminal unattended just after changing the password. Then, an adversary could walk by and, on the victim's behalf, run kpasswd. Since there can still be a valid CHANGEPW ticket cached locally, kpasswd could bypass prompting the principal (actually, the adversary) for the old password and use the CHANGEPW ticket to change the principal's password to anything the adversary chooses. It should be noted, that, in practice, the Kerberos kpasswd command promptly destroys the CHANGEPW ticket upon the completion of the protocol so that the described attack is mainly theoretical.

More often than not, a principal wanting to change its password already obtained a Ticket-Granting-Ticket (TGT) from the AS by going through the initial login procedure. Therefore, a principal already has a strong key that can be used to protect all subsequent communication from, among other things, password-guessing attacks. The Kerberos approach doesn't take advantage of this. Consequently, the initial message (request for CHANGEPW ticket) in the Kerberos protocol is susceptible to password-guessing attacks in case when pre-authentication is used. Also in the case when the pre-authentication feature is not used, the reply from the AS is still susceptible to password-guessing attacks (since the password-derived key K_{old} is used to distribute K_{cpw} in CHANGEPW ticket.)

Another concern with the Kerberos approach is the number of protocol messages involved. As mentioned earlier, fault tolerance is of utmost importance when it comes to changing one's password. Therefore it is beneficial to minimize the number of protocol exchanges. In Kerberos, four (in version 4) or six (in version 5) messages are neeeded between the AS/Admin and the principal's end-system. This is a direct consequence of the Kerberos AS and the Admin server being logically distinct entities: the principal has to first authenticate itself to the AS before requesting the actual password change from Admin. As will be described below, it is possible and desirable to reduce the number of messages to just two, by authenticating the CPW request directly with the principal's password (or key) instead of a short-term key.

Perhaps one of the main issues is that in case of a loss of one of the (4 or 6) protocol messages, no algorithm is given to allow for automatic recovery without resorting to off-line means. In particular, if the last (number 4 or 6 depending on the version) protocol message is lost or if the Admin server crashes right before sending out the last message, the protocol terminates in a state without automatic recovery. In other words, one has to resort to extra-protocol means such as trying to log in anew with, say, the old key and, if that fails, with the new key. Alternatively, one can try to change password once again and hope that the change has not gone through.

Despite the above criticism, Kerberos provides a reasonably workable and secure solution. However, there are several undesirable characteristics where improvement is possible:

- Too many protocol messages

- Vulnerability to password-guessing attacks

- No provisions for *graceful* recovery in case of message loss and/or component failures.

The protocol presented in the next section addresses these issues.

4 Solution

NOTE: For the sake of uniformity, the term *key* is used in reference to both passwords and keys.

Our approach addresses the following requirements:

- The change request should contain authentication of the sender. In case when the request originates with a human user at a remote workstation, the user must provide old (current) password in order to prevent fraudulent password changes when a workstation is left unattended.

- The request itself must be authenticated, i.e. the AS must be able to establish the integrity of the new key (K_{new}) defined in the request.

- The AS has to confirm the outcome of the password change to the requesting principal. The acknowledgement itself must be authenticated.

- The AS must be able to identify retransmissions of previously processed requests and to issue acknowledgments for such retransmissions. This is necessary whenever the original acknowledgement is lost and the principal resubmits the change request. (There is no danger in that as long as the acknowledgements remain identical.)

- An adversary should not be able to gather any useful information from replaying a *stale* request message. This should hold even in the event that the principal makes a serious error of reusing passwords.

4.1 Assumptions

The following assumptions are made hereafter:

1. The principal does not start "believing" in K_{new} until successful completion of the CPW protocol. Of course, K_{new} is also not used if a negative acknowledgement rejecting K_{new} is received (e.g., because it is trivial, predictable, or otherwise unacceptable to the AS.)

2. If the CPW protocol does not terminate normally, the principal is capable of remembering the new and old password until the next attempt, i.e., the resumption of CPW protocol. In other words, if something abnormal takes place and the protocol does not complete, the principal does not **abandon** the change; instead the procedure is re-tried at some later time.

3. The AS needs to be no more than *single-state*. In other words, it only has to remember one (current) password per principal and does not have to keep any password history. Furthermore, it has a fairly accurate clock. Fairly accurate means that it is accurate with respect to the frequency of CPWs which happen infrequently, i.e., daily, weekly or monthly, but not every minute or hour.

4. The hosts or workstations (where CPW requests originate) also possess fairly accurate clocks. If not, the principal's wristwatch or wall-clock readings are good enough.

5. It is not taken for granted that the principal shares a strong key with the AS. (Such a key could be obtained during initial login by the principal, and cached locally). However, if such a strong key ($K_{s,o}$) is present, it may be used to increase the security of the change-password protocol.

4.2 Basics

The basic idea of the protocol is to construct an atomic "flip-flop" request in such a way that a change-key request from principal P to change its key (password) from K_{old} to K_{new} can be verified and honored by the AS **independent** of whether the AS knows only K_{old} or only K_{new}. In other words, the AS is able to recognize, authenticate and acknowledge a retransmission of the CPW request, even after having discarded K_{old} and replaced it with K_{new}. This feature enables the AS and P to resynchronize even in case a positive acknowledgment from the AS is lost or the AS has crashed at an inopportune moment.

If the initial request goes unacknowledged, the principal simply retransmits the request. In this case, the AS knows either K_{old} or K_{new} depending on whether it was the request or the acknowledgement that was lost. In any case, the flip-flop construction of the request enables the AS to process the request message correctly regardless of the current state.

As soon as the AS receives a well-formed authentic request, it replies with an acknowledgement. If the AS receives the same request again, the acknowledgement must have been lost, thus the database is left untouched and another acknowledgement (the exact copy of the original one) is re-generated.

The result of this simple protocol is that there may be a temporary uncertainty on the side of the principal as to the current state of the AS, but this requires no action by the principal beyond retransmitting the original request. The principal may do so ad nauseum but, eventually, when communication is re-established, the first acknowledgement re-synchronizes the two sides.

4.3 Protocol Description

The actual protocol is depicted in Fig. 2. It consists of only two messages. In the first message (REQ_CPW), P transmits two tickets to the AS: a ticket $T(K_{new})K_{old}$ containing the new key K_{new}, and sealed with K_{old}; and a "sanity check" ticket $T(K_{old})K_{new}$ sealed with K_{new}, and containing K_{old}. The ticket expressions are similar to those used in the KryptoKnight Authentication and Key Distribution Service [8]. (See also [6, 7, 5].)

If the request is well-formed and authentic, AS replies with an authenticated acknowledgment REP_CPW which can take on two flavors: ACK (*accept*) or NACK (*reject*). The AS generates a NACK if only if K_{new} is not acceptable for some reason (e.g., predictable password). However, K_{new} must still satisfy the "flip-flop" property of the REQ_CPW. In other words, AS replies (be it with an ACK or a NACK) only if REQ_CPW is genuine.

4.3.1 Details of the REQ_CPW Message.

As shown in the ticket expression of $T(K_{old})K_{new}$ in Fig. 2, the function "g" provides for asymmetry between the two tickets in such a way that an adversary cannot swap the two tickets and convince a server to switch back to the old key. We note that "g" must be asymmetric, otherwise manipulation of the plaintext N2 (e.g. reciprocal value or XOR with $N1$) would re-enable the above swapping attack.

With the above requirement in mind, one possibility is g=(x+1). Another one is $g=\{N2\}K_{new}$.

If the principal already obtained a strong key K_{sso} (perhaps during the initial login) then "g" could depend on K_{sso}. For example we can set $g=\{N2\}K_{sso}$. This increases the resistance of the protocol against password guessing attacks (since an adversary would have to break K_{sso} before attacking K_{old} and/or K_{new}).

The first nonce N1 is chosen at random. In contrast, N2 is set to the current time. This does not require synchronized clocks because the maximum workstation clock-skew is assumed to be smaller than the frequency of key changes. An adversary could still set a workstation's clock to some random time in the

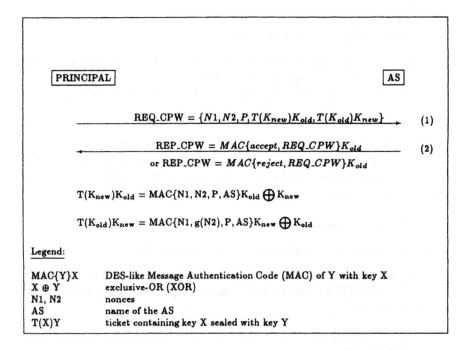

Fig. 2. Secure and fault-tolerant CPW protocol

future. The AS would reject the REQ_CPW because of the wrong timestamp, but the adversary could replay it later when the timestamp becomes *ripe*. However, according to the second assumption (in Section 4.1), the principal does not abandon the change but retries at a later time. Eventually, a re-try will be acknowledged by the AS.

All in all, two items provide for AS-principal synchronization: K_{old} and N2 which represents a timestamp.

4.3.2 Processing REQ_CPW.

1. Having received a REQ_CPW, the AS first extracts K'_{new} from $T(K_{new})K_{old}$, using K_{as} – the principal's key currently in the database. (Assuming, so far, that $K_{as} = K_{old}$.)

2. Then, using K'_{new}, the AS extracts K'_{old} from $T(K_{old})K_{new}$.

3. If $K'_{old} = K_{as}$, the AS is assured that it still has the principal's old key and K'_{new} is the new key intended. AS then stores K_{new} in the database

and sends back a positive acknowledgement, i.e., REP_CPW(accept) the format of which is described below.

4. If $K'_{old} <> K_{as}$, the message could still be a re-try from a principal who didn't receive the original REP_CPW(accept) message for a successful key-change. In this case, K_{as} would already be the same as K_{new}.

   (a) Using K_{as}, the AS extracts K'_{old} from $T(K_{old})K_{new}$.

   (b) Using K'_{old}, the AS extracts K'_{new} from $T(K_{new})K_{old}$.

   (c) If $K'_{new} = K_{as}$, the AS is assured that it already has the new key stored in the database; it then generates REP_CPW(accept) for requesting principal.

4.3.3 Acknowledgements.

Acknowledgments for the following cases must be provided:

 - key successfully changed to K_{new} as a result of either this or some previous REQ_CPW. (In the latter case, the present REQ_CPW is a retransmission.)

 - K_{new} is unacceptable but REQ_CPW is well-formed, i.e., its token structure is correct.

The acknowledgement message has the following form:

REP_CPW = token(K_{old}) containing [accept/reject, REQ_CPW]

This token is an integrity check of the above two components of REP_CPW. An incorrect or malformed REQ_CPW is one where:

 - K_{old}/K_{new} do not satisfy the "flip-flop" structure described above,

   or

 - the timestamp represented by N2 is unacceptable, i.e., outside the limits of maximum acceptable clock skew.

Malformed (not authentic) REQ_CPWs are not acknowledged at all. A cleartext error message is a possible alternative. However, any kind of authenticated acknowledgment in response to an incorrect REQ_CPW is out of the question. This is because doing so would require using the principal's current stored key which would present an opportunity for a known plaintext attack (the AS would become an *oracle*, see [4]). Therefore, the mechanism on the principal's side must at least provide for an error message which after a certain number of unanswered REQ_CPW (timeout) checks for the general availability of the AS and suggests resorting to off-line means for re-synchronization.

Obviously, the acknowledgment (REP_CPW) must be protected. If it is not protected by a strong integrity check, an adversary could trap the original REQ_CPW, prevent it from reaching the AS and convince the principal that the change has taken place. The key used to protect REP_CPW can be any of: K_{new}, K_{old} or K_{sso}. However, if K_{sso} is used, the previous flow, REQ_CPW, must additionally contain the ticket with K_{sso}. One problem with using K_{new} is when the AS rejects K_{new} for some reason (e.g., weak key) it cannot very well use the same key it just rejected to compute the integrity check. Therefore, K_{old} must be used in this case. Alternatively, for the sake of uniformity and simplicity, K_{old} can be used in all cases (i.e., ACK or NACK).

5 Some Remarks on the Security of the Proposed Protocol

In addition to the threats already addressed in the protocol description above, the following possible attack on the protocol must be considered: if the adversary eavesdrops on a REQ_CPW, the "flip-flop" feature allows for an off-line key-search attack. This attack is possible because the very same structure of REQ_CPW that allows the AS to verify K_{new} and K_{old} allows the adversary to verify its guesses by iterating through the key space.

If the function "g" involves K_{sso}, the adversary must additionally eavesdrop on the initial login flows containing a ticket sealed with K_{old}. Therefore, this attack is not applicable since the adversary could verify its password guesses directly on any other subsequent message security of which depends on the initial SSO without needing REQ_CPW at all. If "g" does not depend on K_{sso}, the threat remains valid. However, the initial login (SSO) protocol is still the weakest point for the following reasons:

- *unassisted login* without smartcards or similar devices is at least as vulnerable as the present protocol.

- principals log in much more often than they change passwords thus affording much greater opportunity for adversaries.

6 Protocol Correctness

In this section we analyze the correctness of the proposed protocol.

6.1 Assumptions

To aid in our analysis, the following assumptions are made:

- **Assumption 1:** The principal generates a different key at every execution of the change password protocol. Therefore the password history has no cycles. An execution of CPW means a protocol run until successful completion or synchronization by out-of-band means.

- **Assumption 2:**
  Each message will be received after a finite number of retransmission attempts.

- **Assumption 3:**
  To simplify the proof of correctness, we will assume that the AS only sends positive acknowledgments (*rejected* requests are not acknowledged).

6.2   Idealized Protocol

Before we proceed to the formal analysis we need an idealized and formal representation of the protocol.

Idealized representation of the protocol:
The protocol consists of two communicating state machines U and AS depicted in Fig. 3, that respectively represent the behavior of the change password program on the principal's side and the behaviour of the AS in response to the presented change password protocol.

Notation:

- Since each key generated by the principal is different from all the ones that were previously generated (Assumption 1), the keys form a *totally ordered set*
$$K = \{K_0, K_1, K2, ..\}$$
  whereby K_i is generated before K_j if $i < j$ or, equivalently, K_i is the last key generated before K_{i+1}.

- U_i is the *stable state* of U characterized by the knowledge of K_i as the current key.

- U_i' is the *transient state* of U corresponding to the transition from state U_i to state U_{i+1}.

- AS_i is the state of AS characterized by the knowledge of K_i as the current key representing the principal.

- !m represents the sending of message m.

- ?m represents the receipt of message m.

- := denotes the assignment operation.

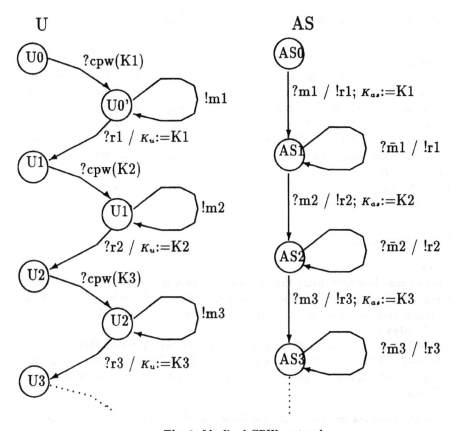

Fig. 3. Idealized CPW protocol

- K_u is the state variable of U that represents the current key.

- K_{as} is the state variable of AS that represents the current key.

- $cpw(K_i)$ is the command entered by the principal that triggers a password change operation on U. The old password is K_i and the new one is K_{i+1}.

- m_i is the REQ_CPW message where $K_{old} = K_i$ and $K_{new} = K_{i+1}$

- $\bar{m}_i$ is the REQ_CPW message, a retransmission from the AS's point of view, where $K_{new} = K_{i+1}$ and K_{old} can take any value.

- r_i is the positive (*accept*) response to m_i.

6.3 Properties of the Idealized Protocol

Owing to its message structure, the protocol has the following properties:

Property 1:

AS_i can correctly determine the transition (the loop or the transition to the next state) to be executed because AS_i can always tell apart m_i from m_{i+1}. When AS_i receives a message m, it can identify the message as m_i if $K_{old} = K_{as}$ and as m_{i+1} if $K_{new} = K_{as}$. This property is based on Assumption 1 and on the structure of REQ_CPW's which distinguishes the "new" key from the "old" one. In other words, K_{new} can never be mistaken for K_{old} and vice versa.

Property 2:

With the knowledge of K_i, AS_i can always extract the new key K_{i+1} (K_{new}) contained in message m_{i+1}.

6.4 Analysis

Goal:

Now we can show that, using this protocol, the principal and the AS will always (eventually) agree on the same key and that there will never be a deadlock situation even in the presence of message losses and replay attacks.

Basic Idea :

We will first show the single step correctness of the protocol, that is, if the principal and the AS both are in a state where both "know" the same key, and the principal triggers the password change protocol, then the following events take place:

- the protocol terminates after a finite period of time.

- after the termination of the protocol, both the principal and the AS will have replaced the old key with the new key provided by the principal.

Initial Equilibrium:

A complete proof of the protocol correctness requires that the system start in a *good* initial state, i.e., the combination of the states of the principal and the AS when both are *initialized* with the same key.

Single step correctness:

Let's assume that U is in state U_i, that AS in state AS_i, that they both consider K_i as the current key and that the principal enters cpw(K_{i+1}),

- **the protocol terminates:** because of Assumption 2 there will eventually be a pair of messages m_{i+1} and r_{i+1} that will be received (by AS and principal, respectively) after a finite number of retransmissions. After protocol termination U will reach state U_{i+1} and AS the state AS_{i+1}. Any transition of U to a state other than U_{i+1} and any transition of AS to a state other than AS_{i+1} are excluded because of Property 1.

- **after protocol termination U and AS will have replaced the old key with the key provided by the principal:** The value of K_u in state U_{i+1} can only be K_{i+1} since this is assured by the good behaviour of the program independently of the communication between U and AS. By definition m_{i+1} contains K_{i+1} in the position of the new key and by virtue of property 2 AS_i can extract K_{i+1} from m_{i+1} and assign its value to K_{a_s}. Thus AS also knows K_{i+1} in state AS_{i+1}.

The correctness proof is still valid when we take into account the effect of a *crash* on the side of either the principal or the AS. If the principal's end-system crashes in a transient state U_i' between state U_i and U_{i+1} the principal needs only to restart the protocol by entering $\text{cpw}(K_{i+1})$ ($K_{old} = K_i$ and $K_{new} = K_{i+1}$) in order to properly terminate the single step execution of the protocol. If the AS crashes, assuming that its non-volatile memory is crash-proof (otherwise there would be no recovery at all), and if the duration of the crash and recovery is comparable to a period of retransmissions from the principal's point of view, the crash has the same effect as the loss of a message and the protocol has been shown correct in the presence of failures and message losses. If the crash and recovery takes a very long time, the change password command will abort and the principal must restart from state U_i as in the case of the crash at the principal's side, but this is still considered to be only *one* protocol run and the principal must stick to $K_{new} = K_{i+1}$ since the server might have updated the password database before the crash.

7 Summary

The proposed protocol is based on a single and atomic challenge/response exchange. The possibility of atomic re-tries provides for a level of robustness and security that is not possible with current protocols. The advantages of the proposed key change mechanism can be summarized as follows:

1. The protocol is resistant to replay attacks due to the asymmetric flip-flop property of the token construction in REQ_CPW.

2. Unlike traditional authentication protocols, the messages in CPW do not need to contain an explicit challenge (timestamp or nonce) to demonstrate their freshness and to counter replay attacks. This property is a result of the logical temporal order provided by the sequence of keys and the robustness of the protocol messages. Because of the inherent strong synchronization on keys that the protocol provides, replay detection can be based on the sequencing of keys.

3. The protocol offers protection against walk-by-attacks whereby a previously authenticated principal leaves the workstation unattended.

4. Optionally, the protocol can permit recycling of keys without being susceptible to replay. By using a timestamp as one of the "nonces", the key sequence can be roughly anchored in time without requiring secure time-services. This is because the timestamp has to be *fresh* only with respect to the relatively low frequency of password changes.

5. The protocol can be resumed after a system crash on the side of either the AS or the requesting principal.

6. Last, but not least, the protocol is compact both in number of messages and individual message sizes, and it requires very few cryptographic computations.

References

1. National Bureau of Standards, *Federal Information Processing Standards*, National Bureau of Standards, Publication 46, 1977.

2. J. G. Steiner, B. C. Neuman, J. I. Schiller, *Kerberos: An authentication service for open network systems*, Usenix Conference Proceedings, Dallas, Texas, pp. 191-202, February 1988.

3. Open Software Foundation, *DCE User's Reference Manual*, Cambridge, Massachusetts, 1992.

4. S. M. Bellovin, M. Merrit, *Limitations of the Kerberos Authentication System*, Computer Communication Review, vol. 20(5), pp. 119-132, October 1990.

5. G. Tsudik, E. Van Herreweghen, *On Simple and Secure Key Distribution*, Proceedings of 1993 ACM Conference on Computer and Communications Security, November 1993.

6. R. Bird, I. Gopal, A. Herzberg, P. Janson, S. Kutten, R. Molva, M. Yung, *Systematic Design of a Family of Attack-Resistant Authentication Protocols* , IEEE JSAC Special Issue on Secure Communications, July 1993.

7. R. Bird, I. Gopal, A. Herzberg, P. Janson, S. Kutten, R. Molva, M. Yung, *A Modular Family of Secure Protocols for Authentication and Key Distribution* (DRAFT) in submission to IEEE Transactions on Communications, August 1993.

8. R. Molva, G. Tsudik, E. Van Herreweghen, S. Zatti, *KryptoKnight Authentication and Key Distribution Service*, Proceedings of ESORICS 92, October 1992.

Authentication

Beacon Based Authentication

Azad Jiwa   Jennifer Seberry (FIMA)   Yuliang Zheng

Centre for Computer Security Research,
University of Wollongong.
Wollongong, NSW 2522, Australia.
Telephone: +61 42 21 4327 Fax: +61 42 21 4329
Email: azad/j.seberry/y.zheng/@uow.edu.au

Abstract.
Reliable authentication of communicating entities is essential for achieving security in a distributed computing environment. The design of such systems as Kerberos, SPX and more recently KryptoKnight and Kuperee, have largely been successful in addressing the problem. The common element with these implementations is the need for a trusted third-party authentication service. This essentially requires a great deal of trust to be invested in the authentication server which adds a level of complexity and reduces system flexibility.

The use of a Beacon to promote trust between communicating parties was first suggested by M. Rabin in "Transactions protected by beacons," *Journal of Computer and System Sciences*, Vol 27, pp 256-267, 1983. In this paper we revive Rabin's ideas which have been largely overlooked in the past decade. In particular we present a novel approach to the authentication problem based on a service called *Beacon* which continuously broadcasts certified nonces. We argue that this approach considerably simplifies the solution to the authentication problem and we illustrate the impact of such a service by "Beaconizing" the well know Needham and Schroeder protocol. The modified protocol would be suitable for deployment at upper layers of the communication stack.

Term Index: Beacon, Authentication, Network Security, Information Security, Security Protocol.

1   Introduction

In the past thirty years the rapid evolution of electronic data communication has been breath taking. This growth and reliance on electronic communication has increased concern about data privacy and integrity. Much effort is currently being devoted to providing security services for a variety of communication environments. Authentication is universally acknowledged as being essential for secure communications in a distributed system.

Informally, authentication is the capability of the recipient of a communication to be able to verify that the message did come from the alleged sender. As a further requirement, it is usual to expect such systems to perform verification over an open insecure network. This requirement constrains the authentication system in the following manner:

- Reliance must not be placed in the physical security of all hosts in the distributed system.
- It should be assumed that packets traveling along the network can be read, modified and inserted with little effort by an adversary.
- Trust cannot be based on the senders' address.
- Trust cannot be based on the senders' operating system security.

Currently, the dominant authentication protocols employed in a client-server environment use a broker to arbitrate between principals who wish to communicate. In such a scheme, a principal must first contact the broker to obtain credentials which can be trusted by its communicating partner. The protocol will typically rely on an exchange of cryptographic messages and the participant's knowledge of some secret. Well known examples of such systems are Kerberos [16, 7, 2], SPX [17], KryptoKnight [8] and Kuperee [6].

In this paper we present a novel approach to the authentication problem for a distributed computer system using a public key cryptographic system and we introduce a new service called *Beacon* which has been inspired by Rabin [12]. A Beacon broadcasts, at regular intervals, certified nonces which are accessible to all hosts within the network. In section 3 we give a brief description of Rabin's use of Beacons. In section 4 the approach taken in this paper is described.

As a means of contrasting the Beacon based approach to authentication with the more established authentication protocols, in section 5 we "beaconize" the very well known Needham and Schroeder public key protocol. We assume that the reader is familiar with the basic philosophy of Needham and Schroeder. For a complete description of the protocol we would direct the reader to [9].

In section 6 we discuss the advantages of the beaconized approach. The paper finally closes in section 7 with some concluding remarks.

2 Conventions

Throughout this paper certain terms are used which may appear to be ambiguous or new to readers. In the following section the use of these terms, in the context of this document, are stated. This should avoid any difficulty caused by their being used differently elsewhere.

2.1 Terminology

A *host* is a computer with a unique address which is connected to a computer network.

The *user* is the human being who is using some services provided by the network. All programs in the system are initiated by users. The main purpose of authentication is to verify the identity of the users within a network.

A *client* is a program which runs on behalf of a user in order to request some service that is available on a remote host. Since the client runs on a user's behalf, it assumes the user identity and privileges. Any action taken by a client is said to have been carried out by the user.

The *server* is a program which provides a service to a client on the network. It is usually installed by the system administrator and runs on behalf of the system. A server remains active in a network for much longer than a client and thus is given an identity. Each server is therefore registered with the system, in a similar manner to a user, and must prove its identity before a client will accept it.

Any communicating network entity, that is client or server, can be referred to as a *principal*.

A *realm* is organized in a hierarchical structure and has a strong analogy to *domains* in Internet. A single authentication server, be it a Beacon or Third-party Authenticator, is responsible for all local principals. This collection of network entities, the authentication server and its clients, are referred to as a realm. A client who wishes to obtain some service from a server within the same realm would use the service to prove its identity.

2.2 Cryptographic Requirements

The Beacon based system relies on a public key (or asymmetric) cryptographic system. Many such systems have been designed and examples of such schemes can be found in [19, 15]. For the purpose of our discussion the system's cryptographic requirements can be simplified and kept generic.

A public key system differs from a secret key (or symmetric) system in that each principal in the distributed system has a pair of keys. The calculation of this private and public key pair, given the initial conditions, is easy. However, it would be infeasible for an adversary who knows a public key to calculate the secret key or the initial conditions. Each principal has a private key which is kept secret and is only known to that principal. The corresponding public key is made available to all other principals. In the remainder of this paper "$\{\}_Z$" means encipher with key Z. The private and public key pair will be denoted as "X" and "Y" respectively and subscripts will be used to identify the associated principal. Thus the Beacon would have a key pair X_{BN}, Y_{BN}, the principal, Alice, would have the pair X_A, Y_A while Bob would have X_B, Y_B.

The advantage of a public key system is that it supports secrecy, authentication, and integrity. Communication secrecy is supported by the transformations:

$$M = \{\{M\}_{Y_B}\}_{X_B}$$

That is, suppose Alice wishes to send a secret message, M, to Bob. Then Alice must have access to Bob's public key and encipher the message, thus:

$$C = \{M\}_{Y_B}$$

Alice sends Bob the cryptographic string C. On receipt Bob is able to employ his private key to decipher the message.

$$\{C\}_{X_B} = \{\{M\}_{Y_B}\}_{X_B} = M$$

The encryption and decryption processes are easy using the appropriate keys. However, it would be infeasible for an adversary to decipher C without the private key X_B, ensuring secrecy. Now, since Y_B is publicly known, Bob has no way of being certain of the sender's identity. Thus authenticity has not been assured using this method.

Authentication, using a public key system, is satisfied by the following transformation.

$$M = \{\{M\}_{X_A}\}_{Y_A}$$

Alice is able to "sign" her message to Bob by using her private key, X_A:

$$C = \{M\}_{X_A}$$

Bob is able to verify that the message could have only come from Alice by deciphering the message using Alice's public key, Y_A, thus:

$$\{C\}_{Y_A} = \{\{M\}_{X_A}\}_{Y_A} = M$$

If the message is plain-text, Bob knows that C has in fact not been altered. However, if the message, or any portion of the message, is a random string then it may be difficult for Bob to ascertain that the message has not been altered merely by examining it. For this reason it is more usual for Alice to employ a suitable one-way hashing function (eg. [14, 18]) to produce a Message Digest (MD). Alice would sign the MD with her private key and append it to the message. On receiving the message, Bob is able to reproduce the MD in order to confirm that the message is from Alice and that it has not been altered. Finally, all three can be employed by Alice to communicate securely with Bob thus:

$$C = \{M, \{MD\}_{X_A}\}_{Y_B}$$

3 Rabin's Approach Using Beacons

The use of a Beacon as a security service within a distributed computer system was first suggested by M. Rabin [12]. He defined a Beacon as emitting, at regular intervals, a random integer sealed using a suitable cryptographic signature system. The integer would be selected randomly and uniformly within the range 1 to N, where N is publicly known. With this basic concept he proposed two protocols based on a probabilistic approach, one for the signing of contracts and the second for information disclosure. In the following section Rabin's use of Beacons is illustrated by briefly outlining the contract signing protocol. For a full account, the reader is referred to the original paper.

Consider, Alice and Bob have negotiated a contract over a computer network and are ready to exchange signed copies. It is not possible for them to meet and they wish to use the network to make the exchange electronically. We can assume that the contracts can be signed by a suitable electronic signature scheme. The problem addressed by Rabin was, if Alice signs and sends the contract to Bob, then Alice is committed, but Bob is not. Bob could take the opportunity to look for a better deal, leaving Alice vulnerable. A similar argument can be made about Bob.

In Rabin's protocol we can assume the following initial conditions:

- Each of the participants has an asymmetric cryptographic key pair which can be used for signing messages and verifying signatures. The Beacon has the private and public key pair X_{BN}, Y_{BN}, Alice's keys are X_A, Y_A and Bob's are X_B, Y_B. The public keys, Y_{BN}, Y_A and Y_B are widely known and are available to the participants. Each participant's private key has been kept secret and is known only to its owner.
- The Beacon broadcasts a token, T every Δ seconds and the next broadcast will be at time $t + \Delta$. The T has the following form:

$$T = \{t, i\}_{X_{BN}}$$

where t is the time at which the token was emitted and i is a randomly selected integer between 1 and N. The value of N is publicly known. The Beacon seals the token using its private key X_{BN}.

- Alice and Bob have agreed to the contract name, C, such that:

$$C = h(contract)$$

where a suitable hash function h is applied to the text of the contract and the obtained result is used to denote the contract.

- Alice and Bob have agreed and signed preliminary agreements. We will refer to these agreements signed by Alice and Bob as P_A and P_B respectively. The text of P_A is as follows:
{*If Bob can produce (C, T) signed by Alice and T signed by the Beacon for some token T, then I, Alice will be committed to the contract as of the time t mentioned in the token T.* }$_{X_A}$

Bob signs a similar contract with the name Alice and Bob exchanged. Since this agreement does not bind either party to the contract, it reasonable to assume that this initial exchange will pass off without incident.

The protocol for the exchange of contracts requires that both parties follow a timed sequence. The exchange is aborted if one party fails to transmit the specified message within the allocated time. The exchange takes place in the time between Beacon broadcasts. This time Δ is divided in six equal segment. The protocol is as follows:

1.	$t \geq time \leq t + \frac{1}{6}\Delta$	Alice $\Rightarrow$ Bob: P_A
2.		Bob $\Rightarrow$ Alice: P_B
3.	$t + \frac{1}{6}\Delta \geq time \leq t + \frac{1}{3}\Delta$	Alice $\Rightarrow$ Bob: i_A
4.	$t + \frac{1}{3}\Delta \geq time \leq t + \frac{1}{2}\Delta$	Bob $\Rightarrow$ Alice: i_B
5.		$i = i_A + i_B \bmod N$
6.	$t + \frac{1}{2}\Delta \geq time \leq t + \frac{2}{3}\Delta$	Alice $\Rightarrow$ Bob: $\{C, i, t + \Delta\}_{X_A}$
7.		Bob $\Rightarrow$ Alice: $\{C, i, t + \Delta\}_{X_B}$

Within the first segment (steps 1 and 2) the two parties are required to exchange the preliminary contract. In the next two segments both Alice and Bob exchange random numbers which each has generated independently, that is i_A and i_B. Each party is then able to calculate i. Finally, (steps 6 and 7) the two parties sign and exchange the messages which could bind them to the contract. These messages contain the contract name, C, and possibly the next token. If neither party has cheated and the next token emitted by the Beacon contains i, then both parties are committed to the contract at the same time. If the next emitted token does not contain i, then neither party is committed and steps 3 to 7 have to be repeated. Rabin showed that in such an exchange there is a probability of $1/N$ that one of the parties could cheat successfully.

4 Beacons

Rabin's novel ideas on the use of beacons have been largely overlooked by the research community during the past decade. We revive these ideas by transferring them to the authentication problem. The following is a more detailed description of the concept, feasibility and implementation of a Beacon.

A Beacon, within the context of this paper, is a service which is provided by a secure host in a computer network. The Beacon broadcasts, at regular intervals, a nonce encapsulated within a certified token. The emitted token would be accessible to all hosts on the network and each host maintains a short list of fresh tokens. The additional load caused by this service would be small as each host is only required to listen for a short and relatively infrequent message.

4.1 Token

The token has the following form:

$$N_i, time, life, \{MD\}_{X_{BN}}$$

where:

N_i → is a freshly generated nonce.
$time$ → is the time at which the token was emitted.
$life$ → is the time after which the token will not be valid.
MD → is the message digest.
X_{BN} → is the Beacon's secret encryption key which is used to certify the token.

Each host which receives the token is able to verify its validity by decrypting the MD using the Beacon's public key. The MD ensures that the token has not been tampered with. Since the token is signed with the Beacon's secret key it is reasonable to assume the token originated from the Beacon. Each host is able to maintain, on behalf of its principals, a short list of currently valid tokens. Thus these tokens are available to all principals to use in the authentication process.

4.2   Network Synchronization

There is reliance within a Beacon based system that each principal has access to a stable clock and that these clocks are to some extent synchronized. Since the life of a token can be relatively long, say an hour, differences of a few seconds between the hosts can be tolerated. In this section we examine the Internet's Network Time Protocol (NTP) to show that in fact it is feasible to have much closer synchronization between communication hosts.

Any attempt to synchronize communicating entities requires access to an accurate standard. Since 1972 the time standard for the world has been based on International Atomic Time which is currently maintained to an accuracy of a few parts in 10^{12} [1]. Many countries operate standard time and frequency broadcast stations which collectively cover most areas of the world.

The network time protocol (NTP) is an Internet standard protocol [13] which is used to maintain a network of time servers, accessible over normal Internet paths. Even though transmission delays over Internet can vary widely, due to fluctuations in traffic loads and dynamic message routing, NTP acts to provide global synchronization. NTP is built on Internet's User Datagram Protocol (UDP) [11] which provides a connectionless transport mechanism.

The NTP system consists of a network of primary and an estimated total of over 2000 secondary time servers. Primary time servers are directly synchronized by reference source, usually a timecode receiver, or a calibrated atomic clock. Secondary time servers are synchronized by either a primary server or another secondary time servers. Due to the wide dispersal of these servers, access is available using some thousands of routes over hundreds of networks, making the system very reliable.

In a typical configuration used at the University of Illinois and the University of Delaware, the institutions operate three campus servers. These servers are synchronized using two primary servers and each other. The three campus servers in turn provide synchronization for department servers which then deliver time to remaining hosts. In such a configuration, several hundred synchronization milliseconds-seconds would not be uncommon.

4.3   Creating a Beacon

As stated above, a Beacon is a service which, at regular intervals, emits a token which can be authenticated. The emitted token must be accessible to all hosts on the network and each host is required to maintain a short list of fresh tokens. Since the broadcast is short and relatively infrequent, implementation is quite feasible in either software or hardware. Algorithm 1 shows the functionality.

Algorithm 1 *Beacon()*
1. $t = clock + \Delta$
2. $N_i = G()$
3. $MD_i = h(t, life, N_i)$
4. $T = t, life, N_i, \{MD_i\}_{X_{BN}}$
5. while $(clock < t)$ wait
6. broadcast(T)
7. goto(1)

end

The algorithm begins by setting, t, the time for the next broadcast. Next, the token is constructed prior to broadcasting (steps 2 to 4). The cryptographically strong pseudo-random generator, $G()$, is used to create a nonce N_i. The final component required to create the token is the message digest (MD). The one-way hash function, h, is employed to compress the bit string created by the concatenation of the broadcast time, t, the token life, l and the nonce N_i. The output, which is of a fixed length, is used as the MD. The token, T consists of the MD, MD_i, signed with the Beacon's private key and the other three fields. The token is broadcast at time t (steps 5 and 6). The algorithm is then repeated (step 7).

4.4   One-time Token

It is generally accepted that the beneficial features of a public key cryptosystem are bought at the expense of speed. At present it is not feasible to use a public key system for bulk encryption. In practice, however, it is quite desirable to create a hybrid system in which a public key system is used for authentication and distribution of a session key. The session key would then be used by the two principals to communicate securely using a symmetric key system.

With a Beacon based system, a "one-time token" can be used to simplify the process. By one-time token it is meant that a token emitted by the Beacon can be used only once to obtain service from a particular server; much like an admission ticket to a theatre. Once the token has been presented, it is marked and will not be accepted by that server on any subsequent occasion. The process of marking tokens is much easier for the server than maintaining a database of prior requests. The use of one-time tokens eliminates the possibility of a replay attack and thus simplifies the process.

To illustrate the process consider a very simple case. Alice wishes to communicate securely with Bob. In this case Bob can be thought of as being the server and Alice the client. Assume, for simplicity, that Alice and Bob communicated yesterday and they are both certain that each knows the other's public key. Such an occurrence is not uncommon in a distributed system since most principals communicate within a small group and a cache is commonly used to store commonly used keys. The process has two steps:

1. Alice $\Rightarrow$ Bob: Alice,N_i, $\{K_{A,B}\}_{Y_B}$, $\{MD\}_{X_A}$

   Alice initiates the exchange by sending Bob a message which contains her name, the nonce N_i, and a session key $K_{A,B}$. The session key is created by Alice, and will be used with a symmetric cryptographic system to secure subsequent messages. Since the session key is the secret in the message, it is the only part that is enciphered with Bob's public key, Y_B. The nonce, N_i, is selected at random by Alice from the list of active tokens and ensures message freshness. The message integrity is protected using a MD which is signed by Alice.

2. Bob $\Rightarrow$ Alice: $\{N_i\}_{K_{A,B}}$

   Bob, having received the request for communication, can confirm that the message did come from Alice and that it has not been altered. The freshness of the message is guaranteed by the use of a nonce, N_i, which was recently broadcast by the Beacon. Since the nonce can be used only once there is of course a finite probability that the nonce chosen by the Alice from the active list has already been presented to Bob by someone else. In such a case the request would be rejected and Alice would have to re-apply with another nonce. The probability of such a collision occurring is dependent on factors such as network load, token frequency and token life. In practical applications the additional load caused by this effect should be minimal.

   Having received a session key which he can trust, Bob completes the protocol by authenticating himself to Alice. He enciphers the nonce with a session key and sends it to Alice. Since only Bob could have obtained session key, the message proves Bob's identity.

5 Beaconizing the Needham and Schroeder Protocol

The Needham and Schroeder (NS) protocol [9] is arguably one of the best known authentication and key distribution protocols. It has been the basis of a number of systems which use the nonce to prove freshness. In 1981 Denning and Sacco [5] pointed out a weakness in the NS protocol and suggested the use of time-stamped certificates to guard against a replay attack. Since that time authentication protocols have been divided into two groups, one preferring the use of nonces and the other preferring time-stamps.

In this section we briefly outline the NS protocol using asymmetric keys. Next we will describe the weakness pointed out by Denning and Sacco and their solution to the problem. For a complete description the reader is directed to the original papers [9] and [5]. We will then modify the NS protocol to take advantage of a Beacon. We will show that the modified protocol simplifies the solution to the authentication problem and has advantages over both the NS protocol and modified protocol suggested by Denning and Sacco.

5.1 Needham and Schroeder Protocol

The NS protocol requires a trusted authentication server (AS) to establish trust between two principals wishing to communicate. Each principal within a realm which is dominated by a particular AS, is required to register his or her public key with that AS. To establish trust between principals, the AS must have the trust of all principals within its realm, to maintain and distribute these keys reliably.

The NS protocol can be divided in to distinct sections. The following illustrates the two protocol sections.

Public Key Distribution Protocol
Consider the situation where Alice wishes to communicate with Bob but is not certain of his public key. Thus she must apply to the AS to obtain Bob's public key. The steps required are as follows:

1. Alice $\Rightarrow$ AS: Alice,Bob
   Alice sends a message to the AS requesting the public key. The requesting message is in clear text and is the names of both principals.
2. AS $\Rightarrow$ Alice: $\{Bob, Y_B\}_{X_{AS}}$
   The AS responds with a message containing the requested public key and is signed with the AS's private key. The message contains the name of the key's owner which allows Alice to verify that the reply contains the correct key.

This exchange does not by itself provide any assurance that the request was initiated by Alice nor of the freshness of the AS's reply.

Connection Protocol

Assuming that both Alice and Bob are able to obtain any required keys from the AS, the following are the steps required for them to authenticate each other in order to establish a conversation. Alice is the initiator.

1. Alice $\Rightarrow$ Bob: $\{N_A, \text{Alice}\}_{Y_B}$

   Alice is able initiate the authentication process by sending Bob a message which contains a nonce, N_A, and her identity. The message is enciphered with Bob's public key, Y_B, which means only Bob will be able to access N_A.

2. Bob $\Rightarrow$ Alice: $\{N_A, N_B\}_{Y_A}$

   On receiving the message, Bob obtains the nonce N_A. However, Bob cannot be certain of freshness nor of the identity of the actual sender. To verify identity and guard against a replay attack, Bob generates a nonce, N_B, and sends it to Alice. Bob also proves his identity to Alice by including N_A in the reply. The message to Alice is encrypted with Alice's public key.

3. Alice $\Rightarrow$ Bob: $\{N_B\}_{Y_B}$

   As a final step in this authentication process, Alice proves her identity to Bob by returning N_B.

5.2   Denning and Sacco's Modification

In [5] Denning and Sacco analyzed the protocol and pointed out that it is only secure while there hasn't been a key compromise. The solution suggested by Denning and Sacco uses time stamped certificates. The form of these certificates is as follows:

$$\{P, Y_P, T\}_{X_{AS}}$$

where:

P	$\rightarrow$ is the principal's identification.
Y_P	$\rightarrow$ is the public key belonging to principal P.
T	$\rightarrow$ is the time at which the certificate was issued.
X_{AS}	$\rightarrow$ is the AS's private key which is used to sign the certificate.

The Denning and Sacco modified protocol combines the authentication and key distribution into a single process. That is, if the principals are able to obtain public keys reliably and message freshness can be guaranteed, then the communicating principals are able to use the features of their public key cryptographic system to authenticate messages. The steps of the modified protocol are as follows:

1. Alice $\Rightarrow$ AS: Alice,Bob

   As before, Alice sends a request for two certificates, one containing Bob's public key and the other containing Alice's public key.

2. AS $\Rightarrow$ Alice: C_A, C_B

   The AS responds with a message containing two signed certificates. C_A contains Alice's public key and C_B contains Bob's.

3. Alice $\Rightarrow$ Bob: C_A, C_B

   Alice initiates the conversation with Bob by sending the certificates. Since the certificates are signed by the AS and contain a time-stamp to prove freshness, Bob is able to trust them.

In [5] Denning and Sacco point out that in order for Alice to obtain the certificates and deliver them to Bob, the certificates must have a lifetime. By this it is meant that the certificates must be valid for a duration of time. The length of the certificate lifetime would depend on factors such as the synchronization discrepancy between hosts and communication delays. During this period the protocol is vulnerable to a replay attack. Thus if the certificate lifetime is kept short, the protocol reduces the likelihood of a replay attack, but does not eliminate it.

Another feature of the modified protocol is that principals are no longer able to cache commonly used keys. Since the certificate lifetime must be kept short to minimize the risk of a replay attack, the AS must initiate all conversations.

5.3 A Beacon Based Approach

We now introduce a Beacon to the distributed system and modify the NS protocol to take advantage of the new service. As in the unmodified NS protocol, the beaconized protocol can be divided into two sections. The first enables a principal to obtain another's public key. The second, the connection protocol, is used by a principal to initiate a conversation. We end this section by modifying the connection protocol to include the distribution of a symmetric session key. Once again we will use the over worked principals, Alice and Bob, to demonstrate the protocol features.

Public Key Distribution Protocol

The following are the steps required for Alice to obtain Bob's public key.

1. Alice $\Rightarrow$ AS: Alice,Bob

   Alice sends a message to the AS stating her name is Alice and requesting Bob's public key. The message is in plain-text and only contains the two identities.

2. AS $\Rightarrow$ Alice: Bob, $Y_B, N_i, \{MD\}_{X_{AS}}$

   Since the reply to Alice contains no secret information, the message is not enciphered. As in the NS protocol the message contains the requested public key and the name of the key's owner. This ensures that the request made by Alice has not been altered. The nonce, N_i, is picked randomly by the Beacon from the list of active tokens and is used to guarantee that this message is not a replay. The message integrity is ensured by the MD which is signed by the AS.

Since the Beacon based system uses the concept of a "one-time token", if N_i has previously been presented to Alice, then it would have been marked and consequently the AS's reply would be rejected. In such circumstances, Alice would have to reinitated the request. The probability of such a collision occurring, in a practical application, is quite low.

Connection Protocol

Assuming that both Alice and Bob are able to obtain the required keys, the following is the step required for Alice to initiate a conversation.

1. Alice $\Rightarrow$ Bob: Alice,N_j, $\{MD\}_{X_A}$

   Alice initiates the exchange by sending Bob a message which contains her name and the nonce, N_j. The nonce is selected at random by Alice from the list of active tokens and is used to ensures message freshness. The message integrity is protected using a MD which is signed by Alice. Since the message contains no secret information it is not encrypted with Bob's public key.

If N_j has previously been presented to Bob, then it would have been marked and the request for connection would be rejected. In such an event Bob would reply with an error message and Alice would select another nonce and reinitiate the request.

Distribution of a Symmetric key.

At present it is not feasible to use a public key system for bulk encryption. Thus, it is quite desirable to create a hybrid system in which a public key system is used for authentication and distribution of a session key. The session key would then be used by the two principals to communicate securely using a symmetric key system. We now modify the protocol to allow the two principals, Alice and Bob, to share a session key.

1. Alice $\Rightarrow$ Bob: Alice,N_k, $\{K_{A,B}\}_{Y_B}$, $\{MD\}_{X_A}$

   Alice would initiate such an exchange by sending Bob a message containing her name, the nonce N_k, and the session key, $K_{A,B}$. Once again N_k is used to ensure freshness. Since the session key is the only secret in the message, it is the only part that is enciphered with Bob's public key, Y_B. The message integrity is protected using a MD which is signed by Alice.

5.4 Attacks on the Modified Protocol

The attacks that can be launched against the beaconized protocol can be broken up in to six categories. In the following section the effects of these are discussed in turn.

- In a *masquerade* attack, an adversary attempts to impersonate one of the principals in the system. Since the principal's secret key is used to prove its identity, for such an attack to succeed an adversary would require knowledge of such a key. If a principal's secret key were to be compromised, it is possible that an adversary could masquerade as that principal while the problem was undetected and before a new key was distributed. However, unlike the case of the NS protocol, an adversary is unable to block the distribution of new keys.

- By *eavesdropping* (or monitoring) network traffic, an adversary hopes to gain some advantage or learn some secret. Since the public key protocol does not require the transmission of any secret information, such an attack cannot succeed. In the case of the hybrid system, the session key is enciphered. Thus an adversary would require knowledge of the deciphering key.

- The goal of a *replay* attack is to gain some advantage or secret knowledge by retransmitting a message which was intercepted earlier. There are three distinct areas in which a replay attack could be attempted. They are:

  1. The token transmitted by the Beacon. The purpose of this message is to broadcast a unique token to all hosts on the network. Since the token has a finite life, if an expired token were retransmitted, the message would simply be discarded. Replaying the message before the token expires gains no advantage for the adversary as the duplicate token would be detected and thus discarded.

  2. The second attempt could be made against the public key distribution portion of the protocol. The protocol consists of two message. The effect of replaying these would be:

     • The protocol is initiated by a principal request another principal's public key. The request is in plain-text and is directed to the AS. Since the information is public and service is freely available, the adversary can gain nothing new.

     • The reply from the AS contains the requested public key. Since the message is unique; in that it contains the name of the recipient, a one-time nonce and is signed by the sender, a replayed message would be detected.

  3. The final message that could be replayed is the request for connection. This message is also unique, thus a replayed message would be detected and the attack would fail.

- A *modification* attack is an attempt to change the contents of packets as they travel across the computer network. For such an attack to succeed the change must be undetected. Such an attack would be futile because the recipient of a message is always able to detect any changes.

- An attempt to *delay* authentication messages would cause the token to expire and prevent the principal from completing the authentication process. Such an attack would have the same results as "denial of service".

- A *denial of service* attack could be launched by an adversary who is able to hinder communications in some manner. Detection and countering of such an attack is best dealt with by other means, such as statistical monitoring of the network.

6   Discussion on Advantages

At present there are two dominant approaches to guaranteeing message freshness within authentication schemes; the method favored by Needham and Schroeder

requires that principals generate and exchange nonces. The second method which
has been suggested by Denning and Sacco makes use of a timestamp within
certificates that are fabricated by the authentication server. In this section we
discuss the five main advantages gained by the use of a beaconized approach.
We will compare our approach with these well known protocols.

- The Needham and Schroeder (NS) protocol has been the basis for a number of systems. The approach taken by them requires principals, wishing to
  establish a conversation, to engage in a three step message exchange. The
  purpose of this exchange is to ascertain the identity of the other principal
  and to guard against a replay attack. The distribution of public keys is provided by a trusted authentication server, AS. In the worst case, where both
  principals require the services of the AS to obtain public keys, the protocol
  requires a total of seven messages to be exchanged.

  In Denning and Sacco's modified protocol (DS) principals are required to obtain certificates from the authentication server. One benefit of this approach
  is that the number of messages required to initiate a conversation is reduced
  to three.

  The beaconized protocol allows principals with cached keys to initiate a con-
  version with a single message. The procedure for a principal to acquire the
  public key of a communicating partner requires two steps.

- In [5], Denning and Sacco pointed out that the NS protocol is vulnerable to
  a replay attack in the event that a principal's key is compromised. To over
  come this difficulty, they suggested the use of time-stamped certificates. The
  resulting protocol requires a principal who wishes to initiate a conversation,
  to contact the AS to obtain two certificates; one for each principal. Each
  certificate has a finite life and contains a public key. During the period between the certificate being issued and expiring, the DS protocol is also is
  vulnerable to a replay attack. Kerberos [16, 7, 2] is the best known implementation of timestamp certificates and uses the symmetric key version of
  the DS protocol [5]. In practice the duration of an authenticator within Kerberos is typically five minutes [3]. The DS protocol does not eliminate the
  possibility of a replay attack, but reduces it.

  The beaconize protocol's use of one-time token eliminates the possibility of
  a replay attack without the increased steps that are suggested within the NS
  protocol.

- Another feature of the DS protocol is that principals are no longer able to
  cache commonly used keys. The beaconized approach, like the NS protocol,
  allows principals to cache commonly used keys which results in the reduction
  of network traffic and load on the authentication server.

- Within the DS protocol the certificate lifetime must be kept short to minimize the risk of a replay attack, the AS must initiate most (if not all) attempts to communicate. Consequently, a greater amount of trust is invested

in the AS and the realm now has a single point of failure.

The beaconized approach reduces the role of the AS to simply being a distributor of public keys which was suggested in the original NS protocol.

— In response to the criticism made in [5] Needham and Schroeder suggested a modification to their original protocol [10]. The revised NS protocol guards against the redistribution of a compromised key by requiring the principals to include a nonce in their communications with the authentication server. The purpose of this nonce is to reassure each principal that the message received from the authentication server is fresh. This revision adds a small amount of load to principals engaged in initiating a conversation.

In contrast the beaconized approach does not require each principal to have the ability to generate nonces. It would be fair to say that this advantage is offset within the overall system by the additional load caused by the introduction of a Beacon. However, within a practical environment there are likely to be principals of varying abilities and it would be preferable if the generation of good quality nonces was provided by a single service.

7 Concluding Remarks

In this paper we have attempted to revive Rabin's ideas regarding beacons and have shown that the use of Beacons can simplify authentication in a distributed system.

The fundamental difference between our approach and that more traditionally taken is the use of a Beacon to deliver a "one-time token" to each host. This simplifies the authentication process by taking advantage of the features of a public key cryptographic system. In contrast to the modification proposed by Denning and Sacco, the beaconized approach eliminates the possibility of a replay attack, allows principals to cache commonly used keys and preserves the role of the AS as a distributor of public keys.

8 Acknowledgment

We would like to thank Thomas Hardjono and Anish Mathuria for their interest and support. We would also like to thank the anonymous referees for their helpful comments and pointing out the use of Beacons in [4].

This work has been supported in part by the Australian Research Council (ARC) under the reference number A49232172 and the University of Wollongong Computer Security Technical and Social Issues research program. The second author has received additional funding from the ARC under the reference numbers A49130102 and A49131885.

References

1. D. W. Allan, J. E. Grey, and H. E. Machlan. The national bureau of standards atomic time scale: generation, stability, accuracy and accessibility. In *Time and Frequency Theory and Fundamentals*, pages 205–231, 1974.

2. E. Balkovich, S. R. Lerman, and R. P. Parmelee. Computers in higher education: The Athena experience. *Communications of the ACM*, 28:1214–1224, 1985.

3. S. M. Bellovin and M. Merritt. Limitations of the kerberos authentication system. *Computer Communications Review*, 20(5):119–132, 1990.

4. Josh Benaloh and Dwight Tuinstra. Receipt-free secret-ballot election. In *Proceedings of the STOC'94*, pages 544–553, Montreal, Quebec, Canada, May 1994.

5. D. E. Denning and G. M. Sacco. Time-stamps in key distribution protocols. *Communications of the ACM*, 24(8):533–536, Aug 1981.

6. Thomas Hardjono, Yuliang Zheng, and Jennifer Seberry. Kuperee: An approach to authentication using public keys. In M. Medina and N. Borenstein, editors, *Proceedings of the ULPAA'94 International Conference on Upper Layer Protocols, Architectures and Applications*, pages 61–72, Barcelona, June 1994.

7. J. T. Kohl. The evolution of the kerberos authentication service. In *Proceeding of the Spring 1991 European Conference, Tromsø, Norway*, 1983.

8. Refik Molva, Gene Tsudik, Els Van Herreweghen, and Stefano Zatti. KryptoKnight Authentication and Key Distribution System. In Y. Deswarte, G. Eizenberg, and J.-J. Quisquater, editors, *Computer Security - ESORICS 92*, number 648 in Lecture Notes in Computer Science, pages 155–174. Springer-Verlag, 1992.

9. R. Needham and M. Schroeder. Using encryption for authentication in large networks of computers. *Communications of the ACM*, 21(12):993–999, 1978.

10. R. M. Needham and M. D. Schroeder. Authentication revisited. *ACM Operating Systems Review*, 21(1):7, January 1987.

11. J. Postel. User datagram protocol. *Request for Comments (RFC) 768*, 1980.

12. M. O. Rabin. Transactions protected by beacons. *Journal of Computer and System Sciences*, 27:256–267, 1983.

13. Network Working Group Report. Network time protocol specification and implementation. *Request for Comments (RFC) 1119*, 1989.

14. R. Rivest. The MD5 message digest algorithm. Request for Comments, RFC 1321, 1992.

15. R.L. Rivest, A. Shamir, and L. Adleman. A method for obtaining digital signatures and public-key cryptosystems. *Communications of the ACM*, 21(2):120–126, 1978.

16. J. G. Steiner, C. Neuman, and J. I. Schiller. Kerberos: an authentication service for open network systems. In *Proceedings of the 1988 USENIX Winter Conference Dallas, TX*, pages 191–202, 1988.

17. J. J. Tardo and K. Alagappan. SPX: Global authentication using public key certificates. In *IEEE Symposium on Research on Security and Privacy*, pages 232–244. IEEE, 1991.

18. Y. Zheng, J. Pieprzyk, and J. Seberry. HAVAL - A one-way hashing algorithm with variable length of output. Abstracts of AUSCRYPT'92, Gold Coast, Australia, December 1992.

19. Y. Zheng and J. Seberry. Immunizing public key cryptosystems against chosen ciphertext attacks. *IEEE Journal on Selected Areas in Communications*, 11(5):715–724, 1993.

Authentication via Multi-Service Tickets in the *Kuperee* Server

(Extended Abstract)

Thomas Hardjono[1,2] and Jennifer Seberry[1]

[1] Centre for Computer Security Research, University of Wollongong,
Wollongong, NSW 2522, Australia
[2] Department of Computing and Information Systems,
University of Western Sydney at Macarthur, Campbelltown, NSW 2560, Australia

Abstract. The subject of this paper is the authentication services as found in the *Kuperee*[3] server. The authentication protocol is based on the Zheng-Seberry public key cryptosystem, and makes use of the distinct features of the cryptosystem. Although couched in the terminology of Kerberos, the protocol has subtle features, such as the *binding* together of two entities by a third entity, leading to the need of equal co-operation by the two entities in order to complete the authentication procedure. Another important feature is the use of a *multi-service* ticket to access multiple services offered by different servers. This removes the need of the Client to consult the Trusted Authority each time it needs a service from a Server. In addition, this allows an increased level of parallelism in which several Servers may be concurrently executing applications on behalf of a single Client. The scheme is also extendible to cover a more global scenario in which several realms exist, each under the care of a trusted authority. Finally, the algorithms that implement the scheme are presented in terms of the underlying cryptosystem. Although the scheme currently employs a public key cryptosystem, future developments of the server may combine private key cryptosystems to enhance performance.

1 Introduction

In the last two decades an explosion of interest have been shown in the use of cryptographic techniques to provide some solutions to the problems of information security. Previously, the study of these techniques was confined only to within the military and intelligence communities, with the primary non-government application being in the banking sector. However, more recently these techniques have been widely recognized and appreciated as being crucial to security and they have been incorporated into the more general computing and information systems environments. Specialized architectures providing for specific security services have found realization within the client-server paradigm.

---

[3] *Kuperee* is a mythical enormous black kangaroo in the Dreamtime Myths of the Australian Aboriginal people. It moves at a high speed, and leaves havoc and terror wherever it goes.

The two types of servers that have emerged corresponding to the two approaches in cryptographic techniques are *Authentication Servers*, which embody private-key cryptosystems, and *Certification Servers*, which rely on public-key cryptosystems. Both types of servers provide for services relating to the secrecy of communications and interactions between entities, and for the authentication of one entity by another. The development of these servers represent the bridging stage from systems with little integrated security features to systems with security as one of their major design considerations. With most of the secure systems being expensive and less compatible with existing systems, the notion of a bridging server that provide for secrecy and authentication is an attractive one.

In the past few years a number of systems for authentication services have been developed, among others the *Kerberos* authentication service [1, 2, 3] within Project Athena at MIT [4], *SPX* [5, 6] as part of the DEC's Distributed Systems Security Architecture (DSSA) [6] and *Sesame* [7, 8, 9] within ECMA's standard for security framework.

Kerberos adopts the private (shared) key approach, and is a trusted third-party authentication service developed from the Needham-Schroeder protocol [10] which has subsequently been improved and shown to be reliable [11, 12]. The Kerberos authentication service provides a trusted intermediary between a *User* or *Client* that requires services from a *Server*. It authenticates the User or Client by way of a shared private key, and it provides a way for the Server to authenticate the User or Client when it request the services of the Server.

Due to the use of private key cryptography, the Kerberos authentication service requires a key to be shared between the User or Client and the trusted authorities in the system, namely the *Key Distribution Center* (KDC) and the *Ticket Granting Server* (TGS) [3]. This, however, requires a great amount of trust to be placed on the implementation of the trusted authorities, since their compromise results in possible masquerade by the attacker of the User or Client whose private key are stored with these trusted authorities [13].

In this paper we discuss the authentication service provided by the *Kuperee* server. The authentication protocol is based on the Zheng-Seberry public key cryptosystem [14], and makes use of the distinct features of the cryptosystem. In general, the use of a public key cryptosystem provides an advantage in terms of the trust level expected from a server [15]. That is, a server based on a public key cryptosystem would hold certified public keys of Users and/or Clients, and thus the compromise of the server does not lead to the compromise of the corresponding secret keys.

Although couched in the terminology of Kerberos, *Kuperee* has a number of subtle features, such as the *binding* together of two entities by a third entity, leading to the need of equal co-operation by the two entities in order to complete the authentication procedure. That is, a Ticket Granting Server has the ability to bind together a Client and the Server that is providing the Client with some services. In this case the Server cannot proceed without the cooperation of the Client in the form of the client submitting a cryptographic *authenticator* to the server. The authenticator in this case is not an enciphered piece of information (as in Kerberos), but rather it is a cryptographic component that contributes to the successful authentication by the Server. This paper also focuses on a feature of the scheme in which one *multi-service* ticket can be used by a Client to access multiple Servers, thereby reducing the need of the Client to continually prompt the TGS for service tickets. This allows an increased level of parallelism in which several Servers may be concurrently executing applications on behalf of a single Client. The scheme is also extendible to cover a more global scenario in which several realms exist, each under the care of a Trusted Authority.

Although we initially model our approach on Kerberos and employ its language in our discussions, we by no means limit ourselves to the use of the underlying cryptosystem following the steps of Kerberos. The underlying public key cryptosystem has more to offer and future developments of Kuperee will address more efficient ways to achieve authentication than currently presented in this paper. Efforts such as in *SPX* [5] clearly show that better performance and security may be achieved by combining suitable implementations of both public key and private key cryptosystems.

In the next section (Section 2) for the sake of clarity we briefly summarize the Kerberos authentication service (version 5) as described in [3]. Readers unfamiliar with Kerberos are directed to [1, 3] for more details on its implementation. In Section 3 we present our approach using the public key cryptosystem of [14]. This is continued in Section 4 by the description of our method to generate a multi-service ticket for multiple services. The algorithms that implement our approach are then given in Section 5. The flexibility of our approach is further illustrated in Section 6 by inter-realm authentication in a hierarchically organized realms or domains, each managed by a TGS. Section 7 briefly discusses the security level achieved by our solution, while the paper is finally closed in Section 8 by some concluding remarks.

2 Kerberos authentication service

In the Kerberos authentication system [1, 3] the entities that interact with the authentication service are called *principals*. The term can be used for Users, Clients or Servers. Commonly, a user directs a Client (eg. a program) on a machine to request a service provided by a Server on a remote machine. The Server itself is usually a process on the remote machine, and different services are usually taken to be available on differing remote machines. Kerberos employs two types of credentials to achieve authentications, namely the *tickets* of the form

$$\{s, c, addr, timestamp, lifetime, K_{s,c}\}$$

and the *authenticators* of the form

$$\{c, addr, timestamp\}$$

which is enciphered using a key common to the issuer and the recipient. Here the ticket consists of the Server and Client identities, followed by the Client's network address, a unique timestamp, the lifetime of the ticket and finally by the common key to be shared between the Server and the Client [1]. In this example, the ticket contains the key $K_{s,c}$ shared between the Client c and the Server s. The Server is trusted to generate such shared keys and when the ticket is to be given to a Client c then it must be enciphered using the Client's key K_c. In the remainder of the paper we will employ the notation used for Kerberos in [1, 3] with respect to the encipherment/decipherment operation. That is, the operation "$\{\}_K$" means that the contents within the braces "$\{\}$" are enciphered/deciphered using the key K (Section 5 gives the precise algorithms for the encipherment/decipherment operations).

In brief, the interactions within the authentication service consists of the Client requesting the Key Distribution Center (KDC) for a *ticket-granting ticket* to be submitted by the Client to the Ticket Granting Server (TGS). The TGS then issues the Client with a *service ticket* which has a shorter lifetime compared to the ticket-granting ticket. The service ticket is then used by the Client to request the services of the Server which is mentioned in the ticket. These two stages are also referred to as the credential-initialization and client-server authentication protocols respectively in [13].

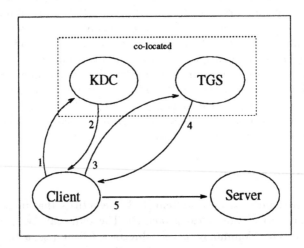

Fig. 1. Obtaining a service ticket (after [3])

The actions of the Kerberos authentication service following the description of [3] is given in the following (Figure 1).

1. Client $\rightarrow$ KDC: c, tgs
2. KDC $\rightarrow$ Client: $\{K_{c,tgs}\}_{K_c}, \{T_{c,tgs}\}_{K_{tgs}}$
3. Client $\rightarrow$ TGS: $\{A_c\}_{K_{c,tgs}}, \{T_{c,tgs}\}_{K_{tgs}}, s$
4. TGS $\rightarrow$ Client: $\{K_{c,s}\}_{K_{c,tgs}}, \{T_{c,s}\}_{K_s}$
5. Client $\rightarrow$ Server: $\{A_c\}_{K_{c,s}}, \{T_{c,s}\}_{K_s}$

6. Server $\rightarrow$ Client: $\{timestamp + 1\}_{K_{c,s}}$

In step 1 the Client c requests the Key Distribution Center (KDC) for an initial ticket and credentials to be presented to the Ticket Granting Server (TGS).

In step 2 the KDC generates a *session* key $K_{c,tgs}$ that will be shared between the Client and the TGS. A copy of this key is enciphered using the Client's key K_c to guarantee that the Client can obtain it securely. The ticket-granting ticket $T_{c,tgs}$ to be presented to the TGS by the Client already contains a copy of the session key $K_{c,tgs}$. Hence, both the Client and the TGS can later communicate securely using this session key shared between them. Note that the ticket is enciphered using the TGS's private key K_{tgs} known only to the KDC and the TGS.

In step 3 the Client then creates an authenticator A_c to be read only by the TGS (hence enciphered using $K_{c,tgs}$) and presents it to the TGS together with the ticket $\{T_{c,tgs}\}_{K_{tgs}}$ which the Client obtained from the KDC.

On receiving the authenticator and ticket-granting ticket from the Client, the TGS deciphers and authenticates the ticket (step 4). The TGS then generates another session key $K_{c,s}$ to be shared between the Client c and the Server s. The TGS also creates a service ticket destined for the Server. This ticket $T_{c,s}$ contains a copy of the new session key, and its lifetime is shorter than the lifetime of the initial ticket $T_{c,tgs}$. The TGS knows the private key of every Server s, and ticket is made exclusively for the eyes of the Server by enciphering it using K_s. A copy of the session key $K_{c,s}$ (hidden by enciphering it using $K_{c,tgs}$) accompanies the ticket to the Client.

In step 5, the Client enciphers the authenticator A_c using the session key $K_{c,s}$ which it will share with the Server s. This is then sent to the Server s together with the ticket obtained from the TGS. The Client may request the Server to prove its identity which can be achieved by the Server incrementing the timestamp value by one, and enciphering the result using the session key shared between the Server and the Client (step 6).

3 Public key approach

In this section we propose an approach based on public key cryptography. Our approach is founded on the public key cryptosystem of [14], and some of its constructs that are necessary for the current discussion will be presented in the following. The algorithms that implement the cryptosystem are deferred until Section 5 in order to simplify discussion.

In the public key cryptosystem of [14] a secret key is chosen randomly and uniformly from the integers in $[1, p-1]$, where the prime p is public and is used to generate the multiplicative group $GF(p)^*$ of the finite field $GF(p)$. The generator of this multiplicative group is denoted as g and it is a publicly known value. This usage of g and p is inspired by notable works of [16] and [17]. The corresponding public key is then produced by using the secret key as the exponent of g modulo p. In the remainder of this paper all exponentiations are assumed to be done over the underlying groups.

For the current usage of the cryptosystem, assume that the secret and public key pairs of the principals are as follows. The KDC has the pair $(X_{kdc}, Y_{kdc} \equiv g^{X_{kdc}})$, the Client has $(x_c, y_c \equiv g^{x_c})$, the TGS has $(X_{tgs}, Y_{tgs} \equiv g^{X_{tgs}})$, while the Server has $(X_s, Y_s \equiv g^{X_s})$. The keys Y_{kdc}, y_c, Y_{tgs} and Y_s are known to the public as in other systems based on public key cryptography.

Each session secret and public key pair is denoted by $(k, K \equiv g^k)$, and their subscripts indicates which principals employ the key pair. Hence, the pair $(k_{c,tgs}, K_{c,tgs})$ is used for interactions between the Client and the TGS. In our case the tickets to be employed do not contain any keys, hence their form are:

$$\{s, c, addr, timestamp, lifetime\}$$

3.1 Getting an initial ticket

1. Client $\rightarrow$ KDC: c, tgs
2. KDC $\rightarrow$ Client: $K_{c,tgs}$, $C_{c,tgs}$

The KDC first generates the session key pair $(k_{c,tgs}, K_{c,tgs})$ to be used between the Client and the TGS.
The cryptogram $C_{c,tgs}$ is the ticket-granting ticket $T_{c,tgs}$ being enciphered as:

$$C_{c,tgs} \equiv \{T_{c,tgs}\}_{r_{c,tgs}}$$

where

$$r_{c,tgs} \equiv (y_c \, Y_{tgs})^{X_{kdc} + k_{c,tgs}} \qquad (1)$$

3. Client $\rightarrow$ TGS: $A_{c,tgs}$, $K_{c,tgs}$, $C_{c,tgs}$, s

On receiving the enciphered ticket $C_{c,tgs}$ together with its accompanying session public key $K_{c,tgs}$ the Client computes a *Authenticator* $A_{c,tgs}$:

$$A_{c,tgs} \equiv (Y_{kdc} \, K_{c,tgs})^{x_c} \qquad (2)$$

The authenticator, the received session public key and enciphered ticket-granting ticket, and the identity of the destination Server s are then delivered to the TGS.
The TGS employs the session public key $K_{c,tgs}$ to compute its *Decryptor* $D_{tgs,c}$ as:

$$D_{tgs,c} \equiv (Y_{kdc} \, K_{c,tgs})^{X_{tgs}} \qquad (3)$$

This is then used to recreate the key $r_{c,tgs}$ that was used by the KDC to encipher the ticket:

$$r_{c,tgs} \equiv A_{c,tgs} \, D_{tgs,c}$$

The resulting key $r_{c,tgs}$ is then used to recover the ticket $T_{c,tgs}$.

3.2   Getting a service ticket

In order to obtain the services of the Server the Client must obtain a service ticket from the TGS to be presented to the Server. We continue the procedure in the following steps.

4. TGS $\to$ Client: $K_{c,s}$, $C_{c,s}$

   In order to encipher the service ticket $T_{c,s}$ the TGS must generate the session key pair $(k_{c,s}, K_{c,s})$ which is used as follows:

   $$C_{c,s} \equiv \{T_{c,s} \| k_{c,s}\}_{r_{c,s}}$$

   where

   $$r_{c,s} \equiv (y_c \, Y_s)^{X_{tgs} + k_{c,s}}$$

   resulting in the cryptogram $C_{c,s}$.
   The cryptogram $C_{c,s}$ and the session public key $K_{c,s}$ are then delivered to the Client.

5. Client $\to$ Server: $A_{c,s}$, $K_{c,s}$, $C_{c,s}$

   As when dealing with the TGS, the Client must compute the authenticator $A_{c,s}$ indicating its desire to use the service provided by the Server:

   $$A_{c,s} \equiv (Y_{tgs} \, K_{c,s})^{x_c}$$

   This authenticator, the received session public key and enciphered service ticket are then presented to the Server whenever the Client requires the service.
   On first being presented with the (enciphered) service ticket, the Server must compute its corresponding decryptor

   $$D_{s,c} \equiv (Y_{tgs} \, K_{c,s})^{X_s}$$

   The Server is then able to recreate the session key $r_{c,s}$ as:

   $$r_{c,s} \equiv A_{c,s} \, D_{s,c}$$

   to be used to obtain $\{T_{c,s} \| k_{c,s}\}$.

6. Server $\to$ Client: $\{timestamp + 1\}_{r_{s,c}}$

   If required, the Server may respond to the Client's request of proving the Server's identity. This can be done by the Server reusing the key $k_{c,s}$ that was enciphered together with the service ticket $T_{c,s}$. The key is reused to create $r_{s,c}$ as:

   $$r_{s,c} \equiv (y_c)^{X_s + k_{c,s}}$$

   to encipher $\{timestamp + 1\}$.
   The Client can recreate the key $r_{s,c}$ as:

   $$r_{s,c} \equiv (K_{c,s} \, Y_s)^{x_c}$$

   which is then used to recover and check $\{timestamp + 1\}$.

4 Multi-service ticket

One interesting feature in Kuperee deriving from its usage of the public key cryptosystem of [14] is its ability to present Clients with one service-ticket which can be used with several Servers (Figure 2) This removes the need of the Client to consult the TGS each time it needs a service from a Server. In addition, this allows an increased level of parallelism in which several Servers may be concurrently executing applications on behalf of a single Client. The level of dependence of the Client on the TGS is also reduced since such multi-service tickets maybe given a longer life-time, hence reducing the impact on the system when the TGS is temporarily unavailable.

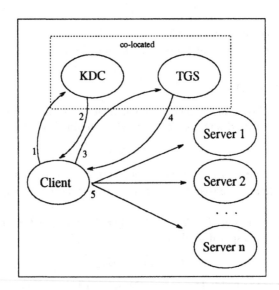

Fig. 2. Obtaining a multi-service ticket

In this section the creation and use of the multi-service tickets is discussed. First, the TGS must be notified by the Client about the q Servers $s_1, s_2, \ldots, s_q$ that the Client wishes to access. We can repeat the last two steps (ie. steps 4 and 5) as follows:

M3. Client $\rightarrow$ TGS: $A_{c,tgs}$, $K_{c,tgs}$, $C_{c,tgs}$, $m = (s_1, s_2, \ldots, s_q)$
M4. TGS $\rightarrow$ Client: $K_{c,m}$, $C_{c,m}$ $(R_{c,s_1}, R_{c,s_2}, \ldots, R_{c,s_q})$

The TGS prepares the service ticket $T_{c,m}$, generates the key pair $(k_{c,m}, K_{c,m})$ and enciphers the ticket into $C_{c,m}$:

$$C_{c,m} \equiv \{T_{c,m} || k_{c,m}\}_{r_{c,m}}$$

where

$$r_{c,m} \equiv (y_c \, Y_{s_1} \, Y_{s_2} \cdots Y_{s_q})^{X_{tgs} + k_{c,m}}$$

The TGS must also computer q number of *selectors* $R_{c,s_1}, R_{c,s_2}, \ldots, R_{c,s_q}$ which will be used by the Client to choose among the q specified Servers $s_1, s_2, \ldots, s_q$. These selectors are computed as:

$$R_{c,s_1} = (Y_{s_2} Y_{s_3} \cdots Y_{s_q})^{X_{tgs}+k_{c,m}}$$
$$R_{c,s_2} = (Y_{s_1} Y_{s_3} \cdots Y_{s_q})^{X_{tgs}+k_{c,m}}$$
$$\vdots \qquad\qquad \vdots$$
$$R_{c,s_q} = (Y_{s_1} Y_{s_2} \cdots Y_{s_{q-1}})^{X_{tgs}+k_{c,m}}$$

The cryptogram $C_{c,m}$, the session public key $K_{c,m}$ and the selectors are then delivered to the client.

M5. Client $\rightarrow$ Server s_v: $A_{c,m}$, $K_{c,m}$, $C_{c,m}$, R_{c,s_v}

As in the single-service case, the Client must compute its authenticator to be delivered to the Server. Thus,

$$A_{c,m} \equiv (Y_{tgs} K_{c,m})^{x_c}$$

However, in this multi-service case, the Client must select the Server from which it requires service. Assuming that the Client requires service from Server s_v $(1 \leq v \leq q)$, then the Client must employ the selector R_{c,s_v}.
This authenticator $A_{c,m}$, the received session public key $K_{c,m}$, the enciphered service ticket $C_{c,m}$ and the selector R_{c,s_v} must then be presented to the Server s_v.
On first being presented with the (enciphered) service ticket, the Server s_v must compute its corresponding decryptor

$$D_{m,c} \equiv (Y_{tgs} K_{c,m})^{X_{s_v}}$$

The Server is then able to recreate the enciphering key $r_{c,m}$ as:

$$r_{c,m} \equiv A_{c,m} D_{m,c} R_{c,s_v}$$

to be used to decipher the service ticket $C_{c,m}$.

5 Algorithms

As described briefly in Section 3, our approach is based on the public key cryptosystem of [14]. In this section we provide further notations for the cryptosystem and present the algorithm for the encipherment and decipherment of tickets based on a modified version of the original cryptosystem of [14]. The algorithms expresses only the encipherment (decipherment) of the plaintext (ciphertext) tickets, and do not incorporate the steps taken by the KDC, Client, TGS and the Server. Hence, the reader is encouraged to read them in conjunction with the steps provided in Sections 3.2 and 3.1.

5.1 Notation

The following notation is taken directly from [14]. The cryptosystem of [14] employs a n-bit prime p (public) and a generator g (public) of the multiplicative group $GF(p)^*$ of the finite field $GF(p)$. Here n is a security parameter which is greater that 512 bits, while the prime p must be chosen such that $p-1$ has a large prime factor. Concatenation of string are denoted using the "$||$" symbol and the bit-wise XOR operations of two strings is symbolized using "$\oplus$". The notation $w_{[i\cdots j]}$ $(i \leq j)$ is used to indicate the substring obtained by taking the bits of string w from the i-th bit (w_i) to the j-th bit (w_j).

The action of choosing an element x randomly and uniformly from set S is denoted by $x \in_R S$. G is a cryptographically strong pseudo-random string generator based on the difficulty of computing discrete logarithms in finite fields [14]. G stretches an n-bit input string into an output string whose length can be an arbitrary polynomial in n. This generator produces $O(\log n)$ bits output at each exponentiation. All messages to be encrypted are chosen from the set $\Sigma^{P(n)}$, where $P(n)$ is an arbitrary polynomial with $P(n) \geq n$ and where padding can be used for messages of length less than n bits. The polynomial $\ell = \ell(n)$ specifies the length of tags. The function h is a one-way hash function compressing input strings into ℓ-bit output strings. In the remainder of this paper all exponentiations are assumed to be done over the underlying groups. The reader is directed to [14] for a comprehensive discussion on the constructs of the family of cryptosystems.

5.2 Getting initial and service tickets

In the process of getting an initial ticket the Clients asks the KDC to prepare the ticket to be submitted by the Client to the TGS. The KDC first performs $k_{c,tgs} \in_R [1, p-1]$ followed by the calculation $K_{c,tgs} \equiv g^{k_{c,tgs}}$. The KDC then enciphers the ticket $T_{c,tgs}$ using the key $r_{c,tgs}$ by invoking $Encipher$ (Algorithm 1) with the input parameters $(p, g, r_{c,tgs}, T_{c,tgs})$ resulting in the output $C_{c,tgs}$.

Algorithm 1 $Encipher(p, g, r, T)$
1. $z = G(r)_{[1\cdots(P(n)+\ell(n))]}$.
2. $t = h(T \oplus r)$.
3. $m = (T||t)$.
4. $C = z \oplus m$.
5. output (C).

end

The KDC then sends the resulting ciphertext $C_{c,tgs}$ and the session public key $K_{c,tgs}$ to the Client who proceeds to compute $A_{c,tgs}$. These values are then submitted by the Client to the TGS who tries to decipher $C_{c,tgs}$. This is done by the

TGS first computing $D_{tgs,c}$ and using it and the received values as input to *Decipher* (Algorithm 2). That is, the TGS inputs $(p, g, A_{c,tgs}, K_{c,tgs}, C_{c,tgs}, D_{tgs,c})$ and receives the output $T_{c,tgs}$.

Algorithm 2 *Decipher*(p, g, A, K, C, D)

1. $r' = A\,D$.
2. $z' = G(r')_{[1\cdots(P(n)+\ell(n))]}$.
3. $m = z' \oplus C$.
4. $T' = m_{[1\cdots P(n)]}$.
5. $t' = m_{[(P(n)+1)\cdots(P(n)+\ell(n))]}$.
6. if $h(T' \oplus r') = t'$ then
      output (T')
   else
      output $(\varnothing)$.

end

The same procedure is followed by the TGS in enciphering the ticket to be submitted by the Client to the Server. The minor difference in this case is that the TGS appends a response key $k_{c,s}$ (ie. the secret half of the session key) to the ticket $T_{c,s}$. This addition does not affect the algorithms and their security in any way. Hence, the TGS invokes *Encipher* (Algorithm 1) with the input parameters $(p, g, r_{c,s}, (T_{c,s}||k_{c,s}))$ resulting in the output $C_{c,s}$. The Server deciphers $C_{c,s}$ into $(T_{c,s}||k_{c,s})$ using *Decipher* (Algorithm 2) with input values $(p, g, A_{c,s}, K_{c,s}, C_{c,s}, D_{s,c})$.

6 Hierarchical inter-realm authentication

The integration of security into distributed systems has introduced the need to manage the information pertaining to the security functions in the distributed system. The most common and important need is that of providing a method to manage cryptographic keys of the components in the distributed system. One approach that may be adopted is that of organizing the components into a hierarchy consisting of a number of domains or realms, each being managed by an independent trusted authority (eg. TGS). This approach has the advantage of the localized distribution of new keys, hence reducing the replication of keys across the entire distributed system.

Within the context of our discussion a domain or realm can consist of Clients, Servers, a local managing TGS and of other TGSs that manage their own realms. In this manner, the components are organized into a hierarchy based on the TGSs, with each TGS managing a certain number of Clients, Servers and other

TGSs. A Client within a realm may request service from a Server in the same domain in the manner previously discussed. However, it is also natural for a Client to request service from a "foreign" Server which is located in a different realm on another part of the hierarchy. In this section we address inter-realm authentication together with some accompanying issues. Our approach is general enough to be applicable to a number of areas, one being the X.500 Directory Services [18].

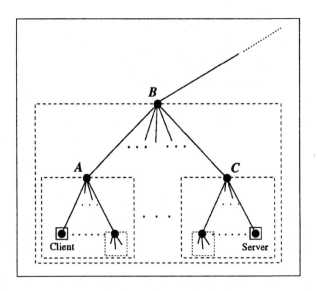

Fig. 3. A hierarchy of TGSs

In our usage, a hierarchy is assumed to be a directed acyclic graph and each node in the hierarchy is assumed to have only one parent node. An example of such a hierarchy that will be used in the following discussions is given in Figure 3. In Figure 3 the Client is located in the domain or realm under the jurisdiction of the TGS A. The Client requires the service provided by a Server which is located within the realm of TGS C. In this case the TGS A must enroll the aid of its parent TGS B to forward the Client's request to TGS node C. Two general arrangements of the keys of the nodes in the hierarchy will be considered in the following. Note that the terms "TGS" and "node" will be used interchangeably to simplify discussion. In our example, we assume that the TGSs A, B and C have the key pairs (X_{tgsa}, Y_{tgsa}), (X_{tgsb}, Y_{tgsb}) and (X_{tgsc}, Y_{tgsc}) respectively.

6.1 Localized keys

One possible arrangement of keys in the hierarchy is based on their maintenance on a per realm basis. That is, in this arrangement a TGS node holds the public key of only its parent node and all its children nodes. This arrangement is similar to the arrangement of directories in [19]. Using Figure 3 as an example, TGS node B has the public key of its parent and of TGS nodes A and C. However, B does not have the public keys of the descendants of TGS nodes A and C. In this situation the TGS node A must refer the Client to node A's parent, namely node B. The node B, not knowing the public key of the Server must then refer the Client to B's child node C. Since node C is the trusted authority of the realm in which the Server resides, node C knows the public key of the Server and thus can forward the Client's request to the Server. These steps are shown in the following (Figure 4). Note that in essence, the Client must interact with every TGS node between its own TGS node (A) and the common ancestor node (B), and between the common ancestor node and the destination's TGS node (C). The deeper the Client is located in the hierarchy from the common ancestor, the more interactions it has to perform in order to reach the destination.

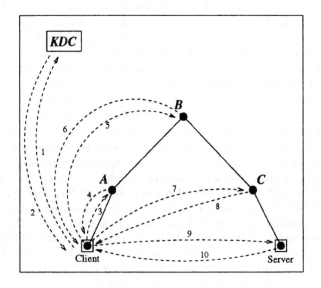

Fig. 4. Authentication with localized keys

1. Client → KDC: $c, tgsa$
2. KDC → Client: $K_{c,tgsa}, C_{c,tgsa}$
3. Client → TGS A: $A_{c,tgsa}, K_{c,tgsa}, C_{c,tgsa}, s$
4. TGS A → Client: $K_{c,tgsb}, C_{c,tgsb}$
5. Client → TGS B: $A_{c,tgsb}, K_{c,tgsb}, C_{c,tgsb}, s$
6. TGS B → Client: $K_{c,tgsc}, C_{c,tgsc}$
7. Client → TGS C: $A_{c,tgsc}, K_{c,tgsc}, C_{c,tgsc}, s$
8. TGS C → Client: $K_{c,s}, C_{c,s}$
9. Client → Server: $A_{c,s}, K_{c,s}, C_{c,s}$
10. Server → Client: $\{timestamp + 1\}_{r_{s,c}}$

6.2 Globalized keys

Another possible arrangement of keys in the hierarchy is a more globalized one, in which a node knows not only the public key of all its descendant nodes, but also the public key of all its ancestor nodes (bearing in mind that a node only has one parent). Here a node does not have the public keys of any of its sibling nodes nor that of their descendants. Although such a configuration is costly in terms of the number of messages to be delivered when a node generates a new public key, the gains occur during the interaction with nodes located in other realms. Note that in our approach the public keys are not distributed in a fully globalized manner. That is, since a node does not have the public keys of its siblings, it must request the aid of its parent when dealing with such siblings. However, the steps used in our approach can be modified in a straight-forward manner to suit cases in which a node has a copy of the public key of every other node in the hierarchy.

Returning to our scenario where a Client requires the services offered by a foreign Server, the TGS in the Client's realm has more flexibility in issuing the enciphered ticket. Hence, with a TGS node knowing the public keys of all its ancestors, the node can find a common ancestor between itself and the TGS who manages the realm in which the Server resides. Looking back at Figure 3, the TGS node A (managing the Client's realm) and the TGS node C (managing the Server's realm) have a common ancestor (parent) in the TGS node B.

In this case, the TGS node A must prepare the enciphered ticket to be decipherable by the common ancestor (node B). This common ancestor node B must then locate the desired Server and re-encipher the ticket in such a way that it is decipherable by the Server with the necessary approval of the TGS within the Server's realm. That is, the ticket must be decipherable by the Server with the approval of the TGS node C in the form of node C sending a decryptor for the ticket to the Server. Note that only TGS A and C are involved with the common ancestor B, eventhough both TGSs A and C may have many other ancestors between them and TGS B respectively. Hence, in such a globalized key approach only a maximum of three TGSs (A, B and C) are invoked independent of the depth of the two TGS nodes (A and C) from their common ancestor (B). This scenario is expressed in the following steps (Figure 5).

1. Client $\rightarrow$ KDC: $c, tgsa$
2. KDC $\rightarrow$ Client: $K_{c,tgsa}, C_{c,tgsa}$
3. Client $\rightarrow$ TGS A: $A_{c,tgsa}, K_{c,tgsa}, C_{c,tgsa}, s$
4. TGS A $\rightarrow$ TGS B: $K_{c,tgsb}, C_{c,tgsb}$
   Here

$$C_{c,tgsb} \equiv \{T_{c,tgsb}\}_{r_{c,tgsb}}$$

   where

$$r_{c,tgsb} \equiv (y_c \, Y_{tgsb})^{X_{tgsa} + k_{c,tgsb}}$$

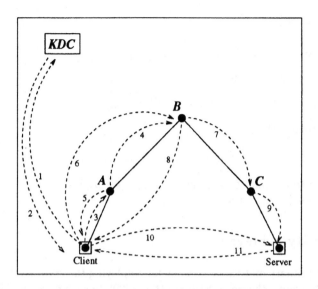

Fig. 5. Authentication with globalized keys

5. TGS $A \to$ Client: $K_{c,tgsb}$
6. Client $\to$ TGS B: $A_{c,tgsa}$
   where

$$A_{c,tgsa} \equiv (Y_{tgsa} K_{c,tgsb})^{x_c}$$

7. TGS $B \to$ TGS C: $K_{c,tgscs}, C_{c,tgscs}$
   The TGS B computes

$$D_{tgsb,tgsa} \equiv (Y_{tgsa} K_{c,tgsb})^{X_{tgsb}}$$

   and recreates the key

$$r_{c,tgsb} \equiv A_{c,tgsa} D_{tgsb,tgsa}$$

   in order to decipher $C_{c,tgsb}$ into $T_{c,tgsb}$.
   TGS B then renames the ticket into $T_{c,tgscs}$ and enciphers it as

$$C_{c,tgscs} \equiv \{T_{c,tgscs}||k_{c,tgscs}\}_{r_{c,tgscs}}$$

   where

$$r_{c,tgscs} \equiv (y_c Y_{tgsc} Y_s)^{X_{tgsb}+k_{c,tgscs}}$$

8. TGS $B \to$ Client: $K_{c,tgscs}$
9. TGS $C \to$ Server: $K_{c,tgscs}, C_{c,tgscs}, D_{tgsc,tgsb}$
   where

$$D_{tgsc,tgsb} \equiv (Y_{tgsb} K_{c,tgscs})^{X_{tgsc}}$$

10. Client $\rightarrow$ Server: $A_{c,tgsb}$
where

$$A_{c,tgsb} \equiv (Y_{tgsb} K_{c,tgscs})^{x_c}$$

The Server then computes

$$D_{s,tgsb} \equiv (Y_{tgsb} K_{c,tgscs})^{X_s}$$

and recreates the key

$$r_{c,tgscs} \equiv A_{c,tgsb} D_{tgsc,tgsb} D_{s,tgsb}$$

in order to decipher $C_{c,tgscs}$ into $\{T_{c,tgscs} \| k_{c,tgscs}\}$

11. Server $\rightarrow$ Client: $\{timestamp + 1\}_{r_{s,c}}$

7 Security achieved

One of the primary motivating reasons for employing the cryptosystem of [14] is its strength against chosen ciphertext attacks [20]. In such an attack the attacker has access to the deciphering algorithm and can feed the algorithm with any input ciphertext in order to obtain its corresponding original plaintext. From these matching instances the attacker can then obtain information to finally cryptanalyze and break a given ciphertext.

The cryptosystem is promising because it has been show in [14] to be secure, not only against chosen ciphertext attacks, but further against *adaptively* chosen ciphertext attacks. In this type of attacks the attacker is permitted to select the input ciphertext which are *correlated* to the target ciphertext. Hence, the attacker continues to have access to the enciphering algorithm even after the attacker has the target ciphertext. Clearly, the attacker is not permitted to feed the target ciphertext into the deciphering algorithm.

In our mode of usage of the cryptosystem, the weakest point in the scheme is equivalent to solving instances of the discrete logarithm problem [21]. More specifically, in attempting to obtain any secret key that participated in the creation of an authenticator, a descriptor or a selector the attacker is faced with solving a discrete logarithm problem. In attempting to obtain the plaintext ticket from any given ciphertext, the attacker must break the cryptosystem.

8 Conclusion

In this paper we have discussed the authentication services as found in the *Kuperee*. Kuperee is based on the recent public key cryptosystem of [14], which has been shown to be secure against the adaptatively chosen ciphertext attacks. The protocol has subtle features, such as the *binding* together of two entities by a third entity, leading to the need of equal co-operation by the two entities in order to complete the authentication procedure. Furthermore, it allows a Client to use a *multi-service* ticket to access multiple services offered by different Servers.

This removes the need of the Client to consult the TGS each time it needs a service from a Server. In addition, this allows an increased level of parallelism in which several Servers may be concurrently executing applications on behalf of a single Client. Hierarchical inter-realm authentication has been illustrated by way of two protocols based on the localized and globalized arrangement of keys. In general public key cryptography provides the advantage of one-to-one secure and authentic communications between entities in the system, something which is not immediately available to approaches based on private key cryptography. Our selection of the cryptosystem of [14] is motivated not only by its high level of security, but also by the ease at which session key compositions can be created. The use of public key cryptography also has the advantage in that the trusted authorities can be implemented with less trust since they only maintain the publicly-known keys [13]. This offers considerable benefit over systems such as Kerberos which are based on private key cryptography, since in these systems the compromise of a trusted authority leads to the capture of all the private keys of entities which are held by the trusted authority. The protocols in the current work represents a step towards solutions based on the mixture of private key and public key cryptography (such as in [5]), combining the advantages of both philosophies.

Acknowledgements We thank our colleagues, Azad Jiwa, Yuliang Zheng and Anish Mathuria for their interest, comments and support in this project. This work has been supported in part by the Australian Research Council (ARC) under the reference number A49232172 and the University of Wollongong Computer Security Technical and Social Issues research program. The second author has received additional funding from the ARC under the reference numbers A49130102 and A49131885.

References

1. J. G. Steiner, C. Neuman, and J. I. Schiller, "*Kerberos*: an authentication service for open network systems," in *Proceedings of the 1988 USENIX Winter Conference*, (Dallas, TX), pp. 191–202, 1988.
2. S. M. Bellovin and M. Merritt, "Limitations of the Kerberos authentication system," *Computer Communications Review*, vol. 20, no. 5, pp. 119–132, 1990.
3. J. T. Kohl, "The evolution of the *kerberos* authentication service," in *Proceedings of the Spring 1991 EurOpen Conference*, (Tromsø, Norway), 1991.
4. E. Balkovich, S. R. Lerman, and R. P. Parmelee, "Computing in higher education: The Athena experience," *Communications of the ACM*, vol. 28, pp. 1214–1224, November 1985.
5. J. J. Tardo and K. Alagappan, "SPX: Global authentication using public-key certificates," in *Proceedings of the 1991 IEEE Symposium on Research in Security and Privacy*, (Oakland, CA), pp. 232–244, IEEE Computer Society, 1991.
6. M. Gasser, A. Goldstein, C. Kaufman, and B. Lampson, "The Digital Distributed Systems Security Architecture," in *Proceedings of the 12th National Computer Security Conference*, (Baltimore, MD), pp. 305–319, NIST/NCSC, October 1989.

7. R. Cole, "A model for security in distributed systems," *Computers & Security*, vol. 9, no. 4, pp. 319–330, 1990.

8. T. A. Parker, "A secure European system for applications in a multi-vendor environment (the SESAME project)," in *Information Security: An Integrated Approach* (J. E. Ettinger, ed.), ch. 11, pp. 139–156, Chapmal & Hall, 1993.

9. P. Kaijser, T. Parker, and D. Pinkas, "SESAME: The solution to security for open distributed systems," *Computer Communications*, vol. 17, no. 4, pp. 501–518, 1994.

10. R. M. Needham and M. D. Schroeder, "Using encryption for authentication in a large network of computers," *Communications of the ACM*, vol. 21, no. 12, pp. 993–999, 1978.

11. D. E. Denning and G. M. Sacco, "Timestamps in key distribution protocols," *Communications of the ACM*, vol. 24, no. 8, pp. 533–536, 1981.

12. R. M. Needham and M. D. Schroeder, "Authentication revisited," *Operating Systems Review*, vol. 21, no. 1, p. 7, 1987.

13. T. Y. C. Woo and S. S. Lam, "Authentication for distributed systems," *IEEE Computer*, vol. 25, pp. 39–52, January 1992.

14. Y. Zheng and J. Seberry, "Immunizing public key cryptosystems against chosen ciphertext attacks," *IEEE Journal on Selected Areas in Communications*, vol. 11, no. 5, pp. 715–724, 1993.

15. L. Gong, "Increasing availability and security of an authentication service," *IEEE Journal on Selected Areas in Communications*, vol. 11, no. 5, pp. 657–662, 1993.

16. W. Diffie and M. E. Hellman, "New directions in cryptography," *IEEE Transactions on Information Theory*, vol. IT-22, no. 6, pp. 644–654, 1976.

17. T. El Gamal, "A public key cryptosystem and a signature scheme based on discrete logarithms," *IEEE Transactions on Information Theory*, vol. IT-31, no. 4, pp. 469–472, 1985.

18. ISO/IEC, "Information Processing Systems - Open Systems Interconnection - The Directory - Information Model," 1989. ISO/IEC 9594-1.

19. A. D. Birrell, B. W. Lampson, R. M. Needham, and M. D. Schroeder, "A global authentication service without global trust," in *Proceedings of the 1986 IEEE Symposium on Security and Privacy*, (Oakland, CA), pp. 156–172, IEEE Computer Society, 1986.

20. J. Seberry and J. Pieprzyk, *Cryptography: An Introduction to Computer Security*. Sydney: Prentice Hall, 1989.

21. M. R. Garey and D. S. Johnson, *Computers and Intractability: A Guide to the Theory of NP Completeness*. New York: W. H. Freeman, 1979.

Oblivious Signatures

Lidong Chen

Aarhus University, Denmark

Abstract. Two special digital signature schemes, oblivious signatures, are proposed. In the first, the recipient can choose one and only one of n keys to get a message signed without revealing to the signer with which key the message is signed. In the second, the recipient can choose one and only one of n messages to be signed without revealing to the signer on which message the signature is made.

Key words: oblivious signatures

1 Introduction

A digital signature scheme is a protocol of a signer and a recipient (see [DH76]). In a public key system, the protocol has a secret key as a secret auxiliary input of the signer. By executing the protocol, the recipient gets a message m signed. The signature $\sigma(m)$ can be verified with a corresponding public key.

In some of cryptology schemes, digital signatures are used as subroutines of the scheme. In order to protect the privacy of the recipient of a signature, in a certain stage, the information about with which key the recipient wants to get the message signed or which message the recipient wants to be signed should not be revealed. Blind signature (see [Ch82]) is a beautiful solution for this kind of problems. But sometimes it requires more restrictive for users' choice.

This note proposes a special kind of digital signature schemes: oblivious signatures. This name is from the fact that, theoretically, it can be implemented by an oblivious transfer (see [Ra81], [Cr87]). The signature schemes here are more efficient. We will consider two oblivious signature schemes.

The first scheme could be considered a complement of group signature (see [ChHe91]). The scheme is a multiparty protocol. The participants are a group of signers $S_1, S_2, ..., S_n$ and a recipient R. There are n pairs of public and secret keys involved. Each signer has one of the secret keys as a secret auxiliary input. The scheme has the following characteristics.

- By executing the protocol, the recipient can get a message signed with one of n keys which is chosen by himself and is called accepted key in this executing.
- The signers, even the holder of accepted key, can not find out with which key the signature is got by the recipient.
- If it is necessary, the recipient can show that he has got a signature with one of n keys without revealing with which special one.

One example of application of the oblivious signature with n keys is that in order to access a database, the user must pay certain amount of money to get a permit which is possibly a signature from the manager of the database. But the information about which database interests the user is sensitive. So he can choose n databases which he is eligible to access. By executing oblivious signing protocol with the managers, he can get the permit for only one of n databases without revealing which one.

The second scheme involves a signer S and a recipient R. This oblivious signature scheme has n messages as a part of common input. The scheme has the following characteristics.

- By executing the protocol, the recipient can choose only one of n messages to get signed.
- The signer cannot find out on which message the recipient has got the signature.
- If it is necessary, the recipient can show that he has got a signature of one of n messages without revealing which special one.

Such an oblivious signature can be used to protect the privacy of users. For example, the user will buy a software from the seller. The software can be used if and only if it is signed by the seller. But the information about which software interests the user may be sensitive in some stage. So the user can choose n softwares and get one and only one signed by the seller without revealing which one.

Both oblivious signatures can be converted to designated confirmer signatures (see [Cha94]) such that

- only the recipient is able to convincingly show the signature afterwards.

2 Basic Protocol and Its Divertibility

2.1 Basic protocol

First we consider the basic three move protocol proposed in [ChaPe92]. Suppose p is a prime, q is the largest prime factor of $p - 1$, and g is a generator of G_q, the multiplying group of order q. The participants of the protocol are a prover $\mathcal{P}$ and a verifier $\mathcal{V}$.

The common input for $\mathcal{P}$ and $\mathcal{V}$ is

$$(g, h, m, z),$$

and the secret auxiliary input for $\mathcal{P}$ is

$$x = \log_g h.$$

We call (g, h) the public key and x the secret key of the protocol.

For given $h, m, z \in G_q$, the protocol is a proof of knowledge of $x = \log_g h$ and $\log_g h = \log_m z$.

The whole process is shown in Figure 1.

$$\begin{array}{cc}
\mathsf{P} & \mathsf{V} \\
(x = \log_g h) & (g, h)
\end{array}$$

$$t \in_{\mathcal{R}} \mathbb{Z}_q^*$$
$$a \leftarrow g^t$$
$$b \leftarrow m^t$$

$$\xrightarrow{\quad (a, b) \quad}$$

$$c \in_{\mathcal{R}} \mathbb{Z}_q^*$$

$$\xleftarrow{\quad c \quad}$$

$$r \leftarrow t + cx$$

$$\xrightarrow{\quad r \quad}$$

$$g^r \stackrel{?}{=} ah^c$$
$$m^r \stackrel{?}{=} bz^c$$

Fig. 1. $\mathcal{P}$ proves that $\log_g h = \log_m z$

2.2 The signature based on basic protocol

If the basic three move protocol is a proof of knowledge, then a class of signature schemes can be established. This kind of signature scheme is first proposed by Fiat and Shamir (see [FS87]). So it is called Fiat-Shamir style signature in the literature.

Let $\mathcal{H}$ be a hash function. The signature based on the basic protocol on message m with secret key

$$x = \log_g h$$

is

$$\sigma_{(g,h)}(m) = (z, a, b, r).$$

It is correct if $c = \mathcal{H}(m, z, a, b)$ and

$$g^r = ah^c \qquad \text{and} \qquad m^r = bz^c.$$

Remark. Here we suppose that the message m is in G_q. If it is not the case, a hash function will be used to map the message to G_q.

The signature is secure, if the basic protocol is witness hiding (see [FS90]) and the hash function $\mathcal{H}$ satisfies the following assumption.

Assumption 1 $\mathcal{H}$ *has the property that if the basic protocol is a proof of knowledge, then it is as difficult to convince a verifier, who chooses $c = \mathcal{H}(m, z, a, b)$, as a verifier who chooses c at random.*

2.3 Divertibility

The basic protocol has a very important property: the verifier, without the secret key as an auxiliary input, can divert the protocol to a third party when executing the protocol with the prover. This property is called divertibility (see [CheDaPe94]). The protocol is shown in Figure 2. For a history reason, we will call the middle one warden (see [Sim84]) denoted as $\mathcal{W}$.

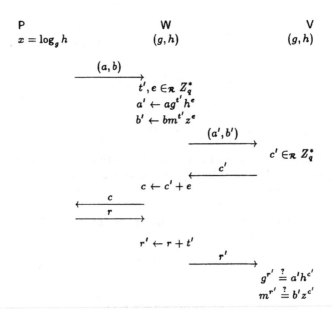

$$
\begin{array}{lll}
\mathsf{P} & \mathsf{W} & \mathsf{V} \\
x = \log_g h & (g,h) & (g,h)
\end{array}
$$

$(a,b) \longrightarrow$

$t', e \in_{\mathcal{R}} Z_q^*$
$a' \leftarrow ag^{t'}h^e$
$b' \leftarrow bm^{t'}z^e$

$(a',b') \longrightarrow$

$c' \in_{\mathcal{R}} Z_q^*$

$\longleftarrow c'$

$c \leftarrow c' + e$

$\longleftarrow c$

$\longrightarrow r$

$r' \leftarrow r + t'$

$\longrightarrow r'$

$g^{r'} \overset{?}{=} a'h^{c'}$
$m^{r'} \overset{?}{=} b'z^{c'}$

Fig. 2. Divertibility of the basic protocol

¿From Figure 2, it is easy to see that the warden $\mathcal{W}$ can play the role of prover to execute the protocol with the verifier $\mathcal{V}$. Furthermore, neither $\mathcal{P}$ nor $\mathcal{V}$ can perceive what the warden has done. This property will be used to construct the oblivious signatures in the following sections.

3 Oblivious Signature with n Keys

3.1 Divertibility for different secret keys

In the previous section, we have seen a possibility to divert the basic protocol to a third party, in which both $\mathcal{P}$ and $\mathcal{W}$ prove the same secret key $x = \log_g h$. In this section, we will introduce another possibility to divert the basic protocol.

Suppose the input to $\mathcal{P}$ and $\mathcal{W}$ is

$$(g, h, m, z),$$

when $\mathcal{W}$ diverts it to $\mathcal{V}$, the common input to $\mathcal{W}$ and $\mathcal{V}$ is

$$(g, k, m, w),$$

where $k = h^y$ and $w = z^y$. $\mathcal{P}$ has secret input x and $\mathcal{W}$ chooses y by himself. In this protocol, $\mathcal{P}$ and $\mathcal{W}$ prove knowledge of different secret keys, $\log_g h$ and $\log_g k$ respectively. The divertibility is shown in Figure 3.

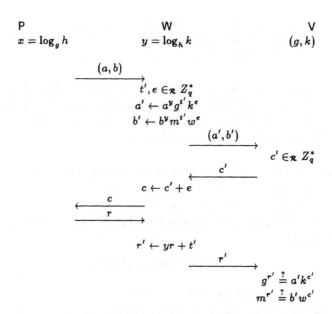

Fig. 3. Divertibility for different secret keys

If, instead of getting the random challenge c' from $\mathcal{V}$, $\mathcal{W}$ computes c' as a value of a hash function

$$c' = \mathcal{H}(m, w, a', b'),$$

then $\mathcal{W}$ gets a signature with the secret key $\log_g k$ as defined in Section 2.2.

3.2   Oblivious signing protocol (I)

The oblivious signature is a kind of random signature defined as follows.

Definition 1. (Random signature (I)) A random signature on a message m with the public key (g, h) and a random element $k \in Z_p^* - \{1\}$ is defined as

$$\Gamma_{(g,h)}(k, m) = \{\sigma_{(g,k)}(m), \sigma_{(h,k)}(m)\},$$

where $\sigma_{(g,h)}(m)$ and $\sigma_{(h,k)}(m)$ are defined in Section 2.2.

Here we will not specify the hash functions used in the signatures. We only suppose that the hash functions are given and with the property stated in Assumption 1.

It is clear that by executing the basic protocol with $\mathcal{P}$, $\mathcal{W}$ can get a random signature on m with the public key (g, h) and a random element k.

Definition 2. (Oblivious signature (I)) Suppose Ω is a group of signers (public-secret keys). An oblivious signature on message m from Ω is a random signature $\Gamma_{(g,h_i)}(k, m)$ for some public key (g, h_i) in Ω.

Suppose that the public key for signer S_i is (g, h_i) and secret key is $x_i = \log_g h_i$, $i = 1, 2, ..., n$. In order to get the random signature on the message m with one of the secret keys, say, $\log_g h_1$, R chooses $y \in_R Z_q^*$ and computes $k = h_1^y$. The signing process goes as follows.

1. R starts the protocol by broadcasting the message m.
2. Each S_i computes $z_i = m^{x_i}$ and sends z_i to R.
3. S_i sends (a_i, b_i) to R, $i = 1, 2, ..., n$.
4. R chooses $t, e \in_R Z_q^*$ and computes $a = a_1^y g^t h_1^{ye}$ and $b = b_1^y m^t z_1^{ye}$.
5. R broadcasts

$$c = \mathcal{H}(m, z, a, b) + e.$$

6. S_i sends r_i for the challenge c to R, $i = 1, 2, ..., n$.
7. R verifies r_i's. If all of them are correct, he computes $r = yr_1 + t$, otherwise halts.

By executing the protocol above R gets

$$\sigma_{(g,k)}(m) = (w, a, b, r),$$

where $w = z_1^y$. He can compute $\sigma_{(h_1,k)}(m)$ by himself. So he gets a random signature $\Gamma_{(g,h_1)}(k, m)$.

Remark. In fact, we can suppose either that n different signers hold different keys or only one signer holds all n keys.

3.3 Security of oblivious signature (I)

In this section, we suppose that the signature scheme defined in Section 2.2 is secure with the definition of [GMR88]. The security for the signer is partly based on a limitation of divertibility of the basic protocol. In [CheDaPe94], similar kind of limitation has been proved. However it is weaker than what we need here to prove the security of the oblivious signature (I).

First we must extend the divertibility stated in Section 2.3.

Suppose a warden W executes the basic protocol with $\mathcal{P}_i$, $i = 1, 2, \ldots, n$, with common input (g, h_i, m_i, z_i) parallely. The rule for W is that he can only send to all the $\mathcal{P}_i$'s a same challenge c. At the same time, he can divert the protocol to a verifier with some common input, say, (g, h, z, m). The limitation is that W, with limited computational power, cannot divert it to two verifiers $\mathcal{V}_1$ and $\mathcal{V}_2$ parallely. We will state this limitation as a conjecture.

Conjecture 1 *By executing the basic protocol in Section 2 parallely with $\mathcal{P}_i$, $i = 1, 2, \ldots, n$ with the restriction that only a same challenge c can be sent to all $\mathcal{P}_i$'s, any warden W with limited computational power cannot divert the basic protocol to two independent verifiers $\mathcal{V}_1$ and $\mathcal{V}_2$ with the input (g, h, m, z) and (g, h', m', z') separately with nonnegligible probability unless he knows one of $\log_g h$ and $\log_g h'$.*

This conjecture can only be proved when the challenge set is a subset E of Z_q^* in the basic protocol such that

$$|E| < k^c,$$

for some $c > 0$, where k is the length of input.

Theorem 3. *By executing protocol in Section 3.2, the recipient, with limited computational power, cannot get more than one oblivious signature.*

Proof. In order to get two signatures from one execution of the protocol in Section 3.2, R must work as the warden to divert the protocol to two independent verifiers if we suppose that the hash function is a random oracle as in Assumption 1, which is impossible by the conjecture. □

Sometimes, it is necessary to be sure that R does get a random signature with one of the keys. This can be done by requiring R to prove that he knows one of $\log_{h_i} k$, $i = 1, 2, \ldots, n$ for $\sigma_{(g,k)}(m)$ without revealing which one by the protocol proposed by Schoenmakers (see [Sch93]).

The next theorem is about the security for the recipient.

Theorem 4. *From the transcripts of the protocol in Section 3.2, and from the signer's proof that he has got the message signed by one of the n keys, it cannot be recognized with which key the recipient got the signature even with unlimited computational power.*

Proof. Suppose that $\log_g h_i = x_i$ is held by S_i, $i = 1, 2, ..., n$. R chooses k as a random element in the protocol. For any i, $k = h_i^{y_i}$ and $\log_g k = x_i y_i$. If $a_i = g^{s_i}$, $b_i = m^{s_i}$, $i = 1, 2, ..., n$, and $a = g^s$, $b = m^s$, then denoting $s - s_i y_i = t_i$, $r = y_i r_i + t_i = c(x_i y_i) + s$, $i = 1, 2, ..., n$. Since the proof that the signer knows one of $\log_{h_i} k$, $i = 1, 2, ..., n$, is witness hiding, from $\sigma_{(g,k)}(m)$ and the transcripts of the protocol, no Shannon information about which key has been chosen by R is revealed. □

Remark. By a small change of the protocol in Figure 3, the protocol can be diverted to a blind message $m' = m^{v_1} g^{v_2}$. In this case, both key and message are blinded. The oblivious signatures are untraceable even though they are shown afterwards.

4 Oblivious signature on n messages

4.1 Divertibility for different messages

In order to describe the oblivious signature scheme on n messages, we first introduce the divertibility of the basic protocol for different messages. In this case, the common input for $(\mathcal{P}, \mathcal{W})$ is

$$(g, h, m, z),$$

and for $(\mathcal{W}, \mathcal{V})$ is

$$(g, h, m', z'),$$

where

$$m' = m^y g^s$$

for some y, s, $y \neq 0$, which $\mathcal{W}$ knows. In this protocol, $\mathcal{P}$ and $\mathcal{W}$ prove the same secret key $\log_g h$ but for different m and m'. The protocol is shown in Figure 4.

If for some y, s, $m' = m^y g^s$ is also a message, with $c' = \mathcal{H}(m', z', a', b')$, $\mathcal{W}$ can get a blind signature on message m' by executing the basic protocol. However we cannot use a blind signature to construct an oblivious signature on n messages since in this case, the recipient is not necessarily to get one of n predetermined messages signed. Instead, he may construct some other message on which the signer is not going to offer the signature.

4.2 Oblivious signing protocol (II)

In order to restrict the recipient getting one of the given messages signed, we assume the signature scheme stated in Section 2.2 is on a hash value of the message $\mathcal{H}_1(m)$. The hash function $\mathcal{H}_1$ satisfies the following assumption.

Assumption 2 *Assume that $\mathcal{H}_1$ is a hash function on message space $\mathcal{M}$. $\mathcal{H}_1$ has the property that for any polynomial time Turing machine M, by choosing the input $m \in \mathcal{M}$ randomly, M cannot output $m' \in \mathcal{M}$, $m' \neq m$, and y, s such that*

$$\mathcal{H}_1(m)^y g^s = \mathcal{H}_1(m')$$

with nonnegligible probability.

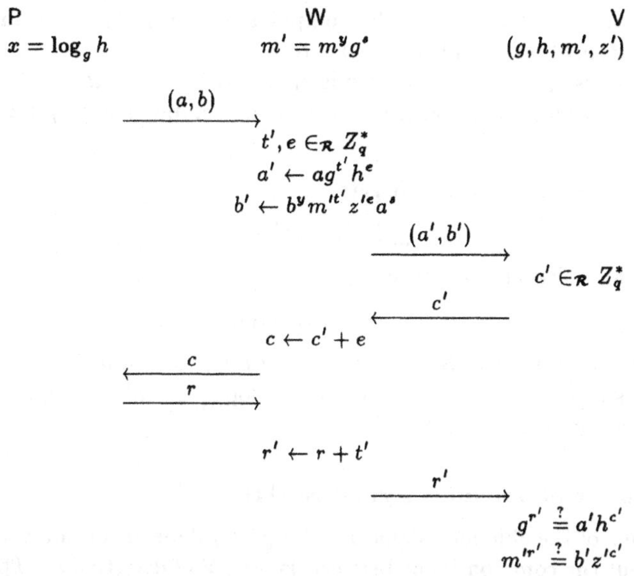

$$P \qquad\qquad W \qquad\qquad\qquad V$$
$$x = \log_g h \qquad m' = m^y g^s \qquad\qquad (g, h, m', z')$$

$$\xrightarrow{\quad (a, b) \quad}$$

$$t', e \in_R Z_q^*$$
$$a' \leftarrow a g^{t'} h^e$$
$$b' \leftarrow b^y m'^{t'} z'^e a^s$$

$$\xrightarrow{\quad (a', b') \quad}$$

$$c' \in_R Z_q^*$$

$$\xleftarrow{\quad c' \quad}$$

$$c \leftarrow c' + e$$

$$\xleftarrow{\quad c \quad}$$

$$\xrightarrow{\quad r \quad}$$

$$r' \leftarrow r + t'$$

$$\xrightarrow{\quad r' \quad}$$

$$g^{r'} \overset{?}{=} a' h^{c'}$$
$$m'^{r'} \overset{?}{=} b' z'^{c'}$$

Fig. 4. Divertibility for different messages

For oblivious signature on n messages, we use another kind of random signature which is defined as follows.

Definition 5. (Random signature (II)) A random signature on a message m with the public key (g, h) and a random element $m' \in Z_p^* - \{1\}$ is defined as

$$\Sigma_{(g,h)}(m', m) = (\sigma_{(g,h)}(m'), \sigma_{(\mathcal{H}_1(m), m')}(m)),$$

where $\sigma_{(g,h)}(m')$ and $\sigma_{(\mathcal{H}_1(m), m')}(m)$ are defined in Section 2.2.

Definition 6. (Oblivious signature (II)) Suppose $\mathcal{H}_1$ is a hash function. An oblivious signature on message $m_1, m_2, ..., m_n$ with public key (g, h) and secret key $x = \log_g h$ is a random signature $\Sigma_{(g,h)}(m', m_i)$ on one of m_i's.

The recipient can get it by executing the following protocol with the signer. Without loss of generality, we assume that R would like to get the signature on m_1. He chooses y at random and computes $m' = \mathcal{H}_1(m_1)^y$.

1. The recipient R starts the protocol by sending n messages $m_1, m_2, ..., m_n$ to the signer S.
2. S computes $z_i = \mathcal{H}_1(m_i)^x$, and sends z_i, $i = 1, 2, ..., n$ to R.
3. S chooses $t_i \in_R Z_q^*$, computes $a_i = g^{t_i}$, $b_i = \mathcal{H}_1(m_i)^{t_i}$, and sends (a_i, b_i), $i = 1, 2, ..., n$ to R.

4. R chooses t, e in Z_q^* randomly, computes $a = a_1 g^t h^e$, $b = b_1^y m'^t z_1^{ye}$, $c' = \mathcal{H}(m', z_1^y, a, b)$, and sends $c = c' + e$ to S.
5. S computes $r_i = xc + t_i$, and sends r_i, $i = 1, 2, ..., n$ to R.
6. R verifies r_i's. If all of them are correct, he computes $r = r_1 + t$. Otherwise halts.

By executing the protocol, R gets

$$\sigma_{(g,h)}(m') = (z_1^y, a, b, r).$$

So he gets an oblivious signature

$$\Sigma_{(g,h)}(m', m_1).$$

In order to prove that R has got a signature of one of n messages, he shows $\sigma_{(g,h)}(m')$ and proves that he knows one of $\log_{\mathcal{H}_1(m_i)} m'$, $i = 1, 2, ..., n$, by the witness hidding protocol in [Sch93].

4.3 Security of oblivious signature (II)

The security of the oblivious signature (II) partly depends on some kind of limitation about the common input between $\mathcal{W}$ and $\mathcal{V}$ of divertibility. The following conjecture has been used in the literature (see [Bran94a]).

Conjecture 2 *For any polynomial time warden $\mathcal{W}$, if the basic protocol with input (g, h, m, z) can be diverted to $\mathcal{V}$ by $\mathcal{W}$ for input (g, h, m', z'), then either $\mathcal{W}$ knows the secret key $x = \log_g h$, or $m' = m^y g^s$ for some y, s, $y \neq 0$, that $\mathcal{W}$ knows.*

There is no formal proof for this, even though it is believed to be true and no counterexample has been found. A proof of the conjecture appears to require an assumption which is seemingly stronger than the discrete logarithm assumption.

Theorem 7. *By executing the protocol in Section 4.2, the recipient, with limited computational power, can get at most one of $m_1, m_2, ..., m_n$ signed.*

Proof. By Assumption 2 about the hash function $\mathcal{H}_1$ and Conjecture 2, it is impossible to get a signature on message $m \neq m_i$, $i = 1, 2, ..., n$ by executing the protocol in Section 4.2. By Assumption 1 and Conjecture 1, R cannot get more than one signature in executing the protocol in Section 4.2 once. □

The privacy of the recipient is clear.

Theorem 8. *From the transcript of protocol in Section 4.2, and from the proof that the recipient has got a signature on one of n messages, it cannot be recognized on which message the recipient has got the signature even with unlimited computational power.*

Proof. In executing the protocol, all the messages of R are blinded by random factors. Even with unlimited computational power, it is impossible to find out on which message R will get the signature. Also the proof that R knows one of $\log_{\mathcal{H}_1(m_i)} m'$, $i = 1, 2, \ldots, n$, is witness hiding. So no Shannon information about on which message R will get signature is revealed. □

5 Oblivious Signature with the Recipient as a Confirmer

The oblivious signature defined in Section 3 and Section 4 are digital signatures. It is not only recipient but also anyone who has got a copy of signature can convince the verifiers. If the signature is bought by a recipient, then sometimes he will not lost his privilege of convincing the correctness of the signature. Chaum proposed a kind of signature called *designated confirmer signatures* (see [Cha94]). After the recipient gets the signature, instead of the signer, some designated confirmer can convince the verifier that this is a correct signature with signer's key.

In this section, the oblivious signature will be constructed as the signature which can only be confirmed by the recipient.

In order to make the oblivious signatures with n keys as designated confirmer signatures, the oblivious signature on message m with public key (g, h_i) will be

$$\sigma_{(g,k)}(m)$$

for random factor $k = h_i^y$ together with a proof of the knowledge

$$\log_{h_i} k.$$

For the oblivious signatures on n messages, the oblivious signature is

$$\sigma_{(g,h)}(m')$$

where $m' = \mathcal{H}_1(m_i)^y$ together with a proof of the knowledge

$$\log_{\mathcal{H}_1(m_i)} m'.$$

After getting an oblivious signature, the recipient is the only one who can show its correctness.

6 Conclusion and Open Problems

A class of oblivious signature schemes can be established based on divertibility of a three move basic protocol. The security of oblivious signatures partly depends on some limitations of divertibility of the protocol. The proof of the limitations is an open problem.

The oblivious signature can be constructed based on almost all known Fiat-Shamir style signature which is based on three move proof of knowledge without special difficulties. Another open problem is how to construct the oblivious signature by RSA signature scheme.

References

[Bran94a] S. Brands. Untraceable Off-line Cash in Wallet with Observers. In *Advances in Cryptology – Proceedings of CRYPTO 93*. Lecture Notes in Computer Science #773, Springer-Verlag, 1994, pp. 302–318.

[Ch82] D. Chaum. Blind Signatures for Untraceable Payments. In *Advances in Cryptology - Proceedings of Crypto '82*, Plenum Press, 1983, pp. 199–203.

[Cha94] D. Chaum. Designated confirmer signatures. In *Advances in Cryptology - proceedings of EUROCRYPT'94*,

[ChHe91] D. Chaum, E. van Heyst. Group Signatures. In *Advances in Cryptology - proceedings of EUROCRYPT 91*, Lecture Notes in Computer Science, pages 257-265. Springer-Verlag, 1991.

[ChaPe92] D. Chaum and T. P. Pedersen. Wallet Databases with observers. In *Advances in Cryptology - proceedings of CRYPTO 92*, Lecture Notes in Computer Science, pages 89 – 105. Springer-Verlag, 1993.

[CheDaPe94] L. Chen, I. Damgaard and T. P. Pedersen. Parallel divertibility of proofs of knowledge. In *Advances in Cryptology - proceedings of EUROCRYPT 94*,

[Cr87] C. Crepeau Equivalence between two flavours of oblivious transfer. In *Advances in Cryptology - proceedings of CRYPTO 87*, Lecture Notes in Computer Science, pages 350 – 354. Springer-Verlag, 1988.

[DH76] W. Diffie and M. E. Hellman New Directions in Cryptography. In *IEEE Trans. Inform.*, IT-22(6):644–654, November, 1976.

[FS87] A. Fiat and A. Shamir. How to prove yourself: Practical solutions to identification and signature problems. In *Advances in Cryptology - proceedings of EUROCRYPT 86*, Lecture Notes in Computer Science, pages 186 – 194. Springer-Verlag, 1987.

[FS90] U. Feige and A. Shamir. Witness Indistinguishable and Witness Hiding Protocols. In *Proceedings of the 22nd Annual ACM Symposium on the Theory of Computing*, pages 416 – 426, 1990.

[GMR88] S. Goldwasser, S. Micali, and R. L. Rivest. A Digital Signature Scheme Secure Against Adaptive Chosen Message Attack. *SIAM Journal on Computing*, 17(2):281 – 308, April 1988.

[Ra81] M. Rabin. How to exchange secrets by oblivious transfer Tech. Memo TR-81, Aiken Computation Laboratory, Harvard University,1981.

[Sch93] B. Schoenmakers. Efficient Proofs of Or. Manuscript, 1993.

[Sim84] G. J. Simmons. The Prisoner's Problem and the Subliminal Problems. In *Advances in Cryptology - proceedings of CRYPTO 83*, Plenum Press, pages 51–67. 1984.

Key Management II

Key Management 11

A Calculus for Secure Channel Establishment in Open Networks

Ueli M. Maurer

Pierre E. Schmid

Inst. for Theoretical Computer Science
ETH Zürich
CH-8092 Zürich, Switzerland

Omnisec AG
Trockenloostrasse 91
CH-8105 Regensdorf, Switzerland

Abstract. This paper presents a calculus of channel security properties which allows to analyze and compare protocols for establishing secure channels in an insecure open network at a high level of abstraction. A channel is characterized by its direction, time of availability and its security properties. Cryptographic primitives and trust relations are interpreted as transformations for channel security properties, and cryptographic protocols can be viewed as combinations of such transformations. A protocol thus allows to transform a set of secure channels established during an initial setup phase, together with a set of insecure channels available during operation of the system, into the set of secure channels specified by the security requirements. The necessary and sufficient requirements for establishing a secure channel between two entities are characterized in terms of secure channels to be made available during the initial setup phase and in terms of trust relations between users and/or between users and trusted authorities.

Keywords. Network security, Key management, Cryptography, Security transformations, Formal models.

1. Introduction

The importance of security in large distributed systems has long been identified and addressed by academic and industrial research (e.g., see [1, 2, 4, 6, 7, 16, 17]), and several solutions and products have been proposed [13, 9, 8, 15, 18]. In the coming years, these concepts will most likely be introduced and used on a large scale in government, commercial and academic networks. While the cryptographic technology (both private-key and public-key mechanisms) is available, the key management and in particular the trust management presents non-trivial problems. It remains to be evaluated for which application scenarios approaches based on on-line servers [13, 9], centralized and hierarchical certification authorities [15, 19] or decentralized key certification [18] are best suited. These approaches vary dramatically with respect to the required communication, user responsibility and trust relations, and it is one of the goals of this paper to compare them in a formal framework.

The process of establishing security in a distributed system can be viewed as a two-phase process: During an *initialization phase*, communication channels with security properties (e.g. trusted couriers, personal registration at a trusted center, mutual authentication by speaker identification on a voice channel, etc.) are available for setting up security parameters like shared secret encryption keys and authenticated or certified public keys. During the later *communication phase*, entities (users or applications) can typically communicate only over insecure channels. The purpose of applying cryptographic techniques can be viewed as the tranfer of the security properties of initially available channels to the insecure channels available in the communication phase, thus making the latter secure.

The purpose of this paper is to provide a straight-forward formalism for illustrating and comparing the various approaches to security in distributed open systems. The emphasis of our approach is on the simplicity and expressive power of the model. Unlike many previous formal treatments of security and authentication in distributed systems [2, 5, 14, 17], it is not intended to be applied for the design or the security verification of protocols. On the other hand, it allows to illustrate in a simple manner the minimal requirements for achieving security between two users in a distributed system, the timing constraints on the involved communication channels, the complete duality between authenticity and confidentiality and the distinguishing features between secret-key and public-key cryptography.

While cryptography is sometimes believed to solve all security problems in open systems, our model allows to demonstrate in a simple manner that cryptography cannot "create" security. The design of a cryptographic protocol can rather be seen as the problem of finding an initialization scenario that is practical and realistic in terms of the initially required secure channels and in terms of inherent assumptions such as a person's or autority's trustworthyness, and from which the desired security goal for the communication phase can be derived by cryptographic transformations. The minimal requirements for achieving security between two users in a distributed system are characterized in terms of secure channels to be made available in an initial setup phase and in terms of necessary trust relations between users and/or between users and trusted authorities. Several types of protocols are reviewed within the presented framework, but it is not a goal of this paper to develop new protocols. We do not distinguish in this paper between different types and degrees of trust [17], but our model could be extended in this directions.

The paper is organized as follows. Section 2 describes a classification of channel security properties and Section 3 provides a complete list of cryptographic transformations of such channel security properties. Sections 6 and 4 discuss the necessary and sufficient condition for establishing a secure channel between two users in an open network, with and without exploiting trust relations, respectively, and security transformations based on trust relations are introduced in Section 5. In Section 7, several approaches to bootstrapping security in an open network are discussed and compared.

2. Classification of channel security properties

A communication channel can be viewed as a means for transporting a message from a source (the channel input) to a destination (the channel output). The duality of source and destination of a message or, equivalently, the duality of input and output of a channel, is reflected in the duality of the two fundamental security goals for messages (or channels). A channel provides *confidentiality* if its output is exclusively accessible to a specified receiver and this fact is known to the potential senders on the channel. Similarly, a channel provides *authenticity* if its input is exclusively accessible to a specified sender and this fact is known to the receivers.

Confidentiality and authenticity are independent and dual security properties. One can be available without the other. Hence channels can be classified into four different types according to whether they provide none, either or both of these security properties.

Channels are denoted by the symbol $\longrightarrow$ and allow to transmit, at a given time, a message of unspecified length from an input to an output. The symbol $\bullet$ attached to the channel symbol $\longrightarrow$ will indicate that the user at the corresponding end of the channel has exclusive access to the channel. The symbols for the four types of channels from an entity A to an entity B, as well as for a bidirectional secure channel, are:

$A \longrightarrow B$ channel that provides no security.

$A \longrightarrow\!\!\bullet B$ provides confidentiality but not authenticity.

$A \bullet\!\!\longrightarrow B$ provides authenticity but not confidentiality.

$A \bullet\!\!\longrightarrow\!\!\bullet B$ provides both confidentiality and authenticity.

$A \bullet\!\!\longleftrightarrow\!\!\bullet B$ bidirectional secure channel between A and B.

An illustrative real-world example of a $\longrightarrow\!\!\bullet$ channel is a mailbox for which only a designated person possesses a key. Someone putting a letter into the mailbox is assured of the message's confidentiality, but the recipient has no direct means for authenticating the sender. A more realistic example will be discussed in Section 8. Examples of $\bullet\!\!\longrightarrow$ channels are a bulletin board that is physically protected by a glass cover and a lock (with the key available only to a designated sender), and an insecure telephone line combined with reliable speaker identification. Examples of a $\bullet\!\!\longrightarrow\!\!\bullet$ channel are a trusted courier, an optical fiber (under certain assumptions) or an insecure channel protected by encryption.

Extending our classification of channels, a parameter above the channel symbol $\longrightarrow$ will indicate the time when such a channel is available. The symbols $\overset{t}{\longrightarrow}$, $\overset{t}{\bullet\!\!\longrightarrow}$, $\overset{t}{\longrightarrow\!\!\bullet}$ and $\overset{t}{\bullet\!\!\longrightarrow\!\!\bullet}$ will denote channels that are available at time t. For example, the availability of a trusted courier from A to B at time t is denoted as $A \overset{t}{\bullet\!\!\longrightarrow\!\!\bullet} B$. If this channel is used to send a secret key which can thereafter be used to encrypt and authenticate messages exchanged between A and B, an insecure channel $A \xrightarrow{t'} B$ from A to B available at some later time t' can thus be converted into a secure channel from A to B available at time t', denoted $A \bullet\!\xrightarrow{t'}\!\bullet B$.

In many derivations in the paper we will also need to consider channels that allow to send a message at a certain time t_2, but only a message that has been fixed at an earlier time $t_1 < t_2$. For the various types of security properties, such channels will be denoted by $A \xrightarrow{t_2[t_1]} B$, $A \bullet\!\xrightarrow{t_2[t_1]} B$, $A \xrightarrow{t_2[t_1]}\!\bullet B$ and $A \bullet\!\xrightarrow{t_2[t_1]}\!\bullet B$, where the notation $t_2[t_1]$ implies that $t_2 > t_1$ and where the bracketed time can be omitted when $t_1 = t_2$. For example, a $A \bullet\!\xrightarrow{t_2[t_1]} B$ could result when A gets a certificate from a trusted authority on her public key at time t_1, which she sends to B at time t_2. Assuming that B can validate the certificate, the channel is authenticated, but note that the message (A's public key) had to be known and fixed at time t_1.

We have the following trivial channel transformations: If a $A \xrightarrow{t_2[t_1]} B$ channel is available then so is a $A \xrightarrow{t_2[t_1']} B$ channel for all $t_1' \le t_1$; this is also true for the other types of channels. Hence we have for instance

$$\left.\begin{array}{c} A \xrightarrow{t_2[t_1]} B \\ t_1' \le t_1 \end{array}\right\} \quad \Longrightarrow \quad A \xrightarrow{t_2[t_1']} B$$

Furthermore, the symbol $\bullet$ can trivially be dropped when it is not needed in a transformation. For instance,

$$A \bullet\!\xrightarrow{t}\!\bullet B \quad \Longrightarrow \quad A \bullet\!\xrightarrow{t} B \tag{1}$$

If channels are available from A to B and from B to C at some times t_2 and t_4, respectively (where possibly the messages must be fixed at earlier times t_1 and t_3, respectively), then B can relay a message from A to C provided that $t_3 > t_2$. Formally we write:

$$\left.\begin{array}{c} A \xrightarrow{t_2[t_1]} B \\ B \xrightarrow{t_4[t_3]} C \\ t_3 > t_2 \end{array}\right\} \quad \Longrightarrow \quad A \xrightarrow{t_4[t_1]} C \tag{2}$$

Note that the message on the resulting channel from A to C must be fixed by A at time t_1 while it is received by C only at time t_4.

Of course, for the $A \xrightarrow{t_4[t_1]} C$ channel to be reliable, B must be reliable. However, unlike trust, reliability is not explicitly represented in our model because our goal is to achieve security in an insecure but reasonably reliable open network. If the channels from A to B and from B to C both either provided confidentiality or authenticity or both, then so would the channel from A to C, but only if B can be trusted by A and C. Such transformations based on trust relations will be discussed in Section 5.

A typical security goal for an open network is that every pair (U_i, U_j) of users can communicate securely at any time. In our formalism, a $U_i \xleftrightarrow{\;t\;} U_j$ channel is required for all $i \neq j$ and for all $t > t_0$ where t_0 is some sufficiently early system setup time. In an open system where insecure channels can be assumed to be available at all times, one way for achieving this goal is for two users to agree on a bilateral secret key for use in a symmetric cryptosystem.

3. Basic cryptographic security transformations

The purpose of this section is to present a systematic discussion of the well-known cryptographic primitives (symmetric encryption, public-key cryptosystem and digital signature schemes) by interpreting them as transformations of channel security properties.

3.1. Symmetric encryption and message authentication codes

It is often assumed that a symmetric cryptosystem provides implicit message authentication: the fact that a message is encrypted with a certain key "proves" that the sender knows the key. However, it should be pointed out that this can only be true under the assumption that plaintext is sufficiently redundant and hence that meaningless messages can be distinguished from valid messages. Moreover, certain types of ciphers (e.g. additive stream ciphers) provide no implicit message authentication because single bits in the ciphertext, and hence in the plaintext, can be flipped selectively. This problem can be solved by appending to a given message a cryptographic hash value of the message. In the sequel we therefore assume without loss of generality that a symmetric cipher provides both confidentiality and authenticity.

The basic security transformation provided by a symmetric cipher is to transfer the security of a channel available at some time t_2 to an insecure channel available at some later time t_4. The times t_1 and t_3 are included for the sake of generality and will be used later, but the reader can here and in the sequel just as well assume that $t_2 = t_1$ and $t_4 = t_3$.

$$\left. \begin{array}{c} A \xbullet{\;t_2[t_1]\;} B \\ A \xrightarrow{\;t_4[t_3]\;} B \\ t_4 \geq t_2 \end{array} \right\} \quad \Longrightarrow \quad A \xbullet{\;t_4[t_3]\;} B \qquad (3)$$

If the insecure channel is from B to A rather than from A to B, then so is the resulting secure channel:

$$\left. \begin{array}{c} A \xbullet{\;t_2[t_1]\;} B \\ A \xleftarrow{\;t_4[t_3]\;} B \\ t_3 > t_2 \end{array} \right\} \quad \Longrightarrow \quad A \xbulletleft{\;t_4[t_3]\;} B \qquad (4)$$

It is interesting to notice that a symmetric cryptosystem can also be used to transfer confidentiality without authenticity:

$$
\left.\begin{array}{l}
A \xrightarrow{t_2[t_1]}\bullet B \\
A \xrightarrow{t_4[t_3]} B \\
t_4 \geq t_2
\end{array}\right\} \quad \Longrightarrow \quad A \xrightarrow{t_4[t_3]}\bullet B \tag{5}
$$

A can use the confidential $A \xrightarrow{t_2[t_1]}\bullet B$ channel for transferring a (not authenticated) cipher key. Messages encrypted with this key can only be decrypted by B who can check that the message was sent by the same person who previously sent the secret key. However, the $A \xrightarrow{t_2[t_1]}\bullet B$ channel provides no authenticity and hence nor does the $A \xrightarrow{t_4[t_3]}\bullet B$ channel. On the other hand, if the second channel provides authenticity, then so does the resulting channel:

$$
\left.\begin{array}{l}
A \xrightarrow{t_2[t_1]}\bullet B \\
A \bullet\!\xrightarrow{t_4[t_3]} B \\
t_4 \geq t_2
\end{array}\right\} \quad \Longrightarrow \quad A \bullet\!\xrightarrow{t_4[t_3]}\bullet B \tag{6}
$$

While a symmetric cryptosystem allows to transfer confidentiality without authenticity (transformation (5)), it is important to note that it does not allow to transfer authenticity without confidentiality. The latter is achieved only by digital signatures and can be seen as a (the) major achievement of public-key cryptography. On the other hand, a symmetric cryptosystem can be used to convert a confidential channel into an authenticated channel. If A sends a secret key to B over the confidential channel, then A can later recognize messages encrypted with this key as authentic from B. However, since B cannot verify that A is indeed the sender of the secret key, the confidentiality of encrypted messages is not guaranteed. If B receives several (not authenticated) secret keys he can authenticate a message for each key separately.

$$
\left.\begin{array}{l}
A \xrightarrow{t_2[t_1]}\bullet B \\
A \xleftarrow{t_4[t_3]} B \\
t_3 > t_2
\end{array}\right\} \quad \Longrightarrow \quad A \xleftarrow{t_4[t_3]}\bullet B \tag{7}
$$

If the second channel provides confidentiality, then so does the resulting channel:

$$
\left.\begin{array}{l}
A \xrightarrow{t_2[t_1]}\bullet B \\
A \bullet\!\xleftarrow{t_4[t_3]} B \\
t_3 > t_2
\end{array}\right\} \quad \Longrightarrow \quad A \bullet\!\xleftarrow{t_4[t_3]}\bullet B \tag{8}
$$

Note that the timing constraint in (4), (7) and (8) is different from that in (3), (5) and (6) because B can send the reply only after receiving the message from A. Transformations (7) and (8) can also be achieved by using a message authentication code (MAC) which provides explicit symmetric authentication of messages that need not be confidential.

3.2. Public-key cryptosystems

The basic transformation provided by an (asymmetric) public-key cryptosystem is to transform the authenticity of a channel into confidentiality of a channel available at some later time:

$$
\left.
\begin{array}{l}
A \overset{t_2[t_1]}{\bullet\longrightarrow} B \\[4pt]
A \overset{t_4[t_3]}{\longleftarrow} B \\[4pt]
t_3 > t_2
\end{array}
\right\}
\quad \Longrightarrow \quad
A \overset{t_4[t_3]}{\bullet\longleftarrow} B
\tag{9}
$$

If the second channel provides authenticity then so does the resulting channel:

$$
\left.
\begin{array}{l}
A \overset{t_2[t_1]}{\bullet\longrightarrow} B \\[4pt]
A \overset{t_4[t_3]}{\longleftarrow\bullet} B \\[4pt]
t_3 > t_2
\end{array}
\right\}
\quad \Longrightarrow \quad
A \overset{t_4[t_3]}{\bullet\longleftarrow\bullet} B
\tag{10}
$$

It should be pointed out that a public-key distribution system as defined by Diffie and Hellman [3], if combined with a symmetric cryptosystem, is equivalent to a public-key cryptosystem in the sense that it provides exactly the same transformations (9) and (10).

A comparison of transformations (7) and (9) suggests that a public-key cryptosystem is in some sense the dual of a symmetric message authentication code (MAC).

3.3. Digital signature schemes

The set of transformations considered so far is not complete. The missing one, namely to transfer the authenticity of a channel to an insecure channel available at some later time, is provided by a digital signature scheme:

$$
\left.
\begin{array}{l}
A \overset{t_2[t_1]}{\bullet\longrightarrow} B \\[4pt]
A \overset{t_4[t_3]}{\longrightarrow} B \\[4pt]
t_4 > t_2
\end{array}
\right\}
\quad \Longrightarrow \quad
A \overset{t_4[t_3]}{\bullet\longrightarrow} B
\tag{11}
$$

If the second channel is confidential, then so is the resulting channel:

$$
\left.
\begin{array}{l}
A \overset{t_2[t_1]}{\bullet\longrightarrow} B \\[4pt]
A \overset{t_4[t_3]}{\longrightarrow\bullet} B \\[4pt]
t_4 > t_2
\end{array}
\right\}
\quad \Longrightarrow \quad
A \overset{t_4[t_3]}{\bullet\longrightarrow\bullet} B
\tag{12}
$$

Of course the $A \overset{t_2[t_1]}{\bullet\longrightarrow} B$ channel is not "consumed" by the transformation. Thus for instance if $t_2 > t_4$ one could use the $A \overset{t_2[t_1]}{\bullet\longrightarrow} B$ channel directly without applying digital signatures. Notice the different timing constraints when compared to transformations (9) and (10). A comparison of transformations (5) and (11) demonstrates that a digital signature scheme is in some sense the dual of a symmetric cryptosystem.

4. The necessary and sufficient condition for a secure channel $A \bullet\!\!\longleftrightarrow\!\!\bullet B$ between two users

The transformations discussed in the previous section can be interpreted as methods for moving or replacing channel symbols ($\longrightarrow$) while keeping the security symbols $\bullet$ in place and attached to the corresponding users. For example, transformation (3) can be interpreted as replacing the channel $\overset{t_2[t_1]}{\longrightarrow}$ in $A \bullet\!\!\overset{t_2[t_1]}{\longrightarrow}\!\!\bullet B$ with the channel $\overset{t_4[t_3]}{\longrightarrow}$ while keeping the $\bullet$'s in place. This allows to transfer the security from an initially available secure channel to a later available insecure channel.

It is important to notice that a security symbol $\bullet$ is attached to the corresponding user rather than to the corresponding channel. Channels can be replaced by cryptography, as mentioned above, but it is obvious that $\bullet$'s cannot be "created" or moved from one user to another by cryptographic transformations. In other words, the fact that a user is exclusive in a certain sense cannot be transferred to another user. Hence security symbols $\bullet$ must be created by noncryptographic means such as authentication based on a passport or on speaker identification. This observation appears to be impossible to prove and is therefore stated as an axiom.

Axiom. *There exists no cryptographic transformation allowing to "create" a $\bullet$ or to move a $\bullet$ from one user to another.*

A typical security goal for an open network is that every pair of users (e.g., A and B), can communicate securely, i.e., over a $A \bullet\!\!\longleftrightarrow\!\!\bullet B$ cannel, at any time. Of course, a necessary condition is that they be able to communicate at all, i.e., that there exists a channel $A \overset{t}{\longleftrightarrow} B$ at any time t later than some initial system setup time. For the remainder of this section we focus our attention on security transformations rather than the availability of communication channels and therefore make the following assumption, which can in some sense be interpreted as a characterization of a reliable open networks. The assumption will be dropped again in Section 7.

Assumption 1. *Insecure channels ($\longleftrightarrow$) between every pair of users are always available.*

Theorem 1. *Under Assumption 1 it is a sufficient condition for achieving a secure channel between A and B from time t_0 on ($A \bullet\!\!\overset{t}{\longleftrightarrow}\!\!\bullet B$ for $t \geq t_0$) that one of the following four preconditions is satisfied for some $t_2 < t_0$ and $t_4 < t_0$:*

$$\{A \bullet\!\!\overset{t_2[t_1]}{\longrightarrow} B \text{ and } A \overset{t_4[t_3]}{\longrightarrow}\!\!\bullet B\}$$
$$or \quad \{A \bullet\!\!\overset{t_2[t_1]}{\longrightarrow} B \text{ and } A \overset{t_4[t_3]}{\longleftarrow}\!\!\bullet B\}$$
$$or \quad \{A \bullet\!\!\overset{t_2[t_1]}{\longleftarrow} B \text{ and } A \overset{t_4[t_3]}{\longrightarrow}\!\!\bullet B\}$$
$$or \quad \{A \bullet\!\!\overset{t_2[t_1]}{\longleftarrow} B \text{ and } A \overset{t_4[t_3]}{\longleftarrow}\!\!\bullet B\}$$

Assuming the above axiom, this condition is also necessary.

Proof sketch. It is easy to verify that for every precondition there exists a transformation or a sequence of transformations for creating a secure channel. For instance, every confidential channel can be transformed into an authenticated channel by application of transformation (7) and the obtained scenario consisting of two complementary authenticated channels can be transformed into a secure channel by transformation (10). Now transformations (3) and (4) can be applied to complete the proof.

Remarks. It need not be assumed that $t_4 > t_2$. The precondition $A \overset{t}{\bullet\!\!-\!\!\bullet} B$ (e.g. a trusted courier) implies the first precondition with $t_2 = t_4 = t$. It is interesting to note that conventional symmetric cryptography allows to achieve the security transformation of Theorem 1 if and only if the first (in time) of the two available channels is a confidential one. If the first of the two available channels is authentic but not confidential, then public-key cryptography is required. This observation demonstrates the significance of the discovery of public-key cryptography by Diffie and Hellman [3], especially in view of the fact that in many practical scenarios there exist authenticated channels (e.g., partner identification on telephone channels) that are not confidential.

5. Security transformations based on trust

The necessary condition of Theorem 1 is pessimistic because it states that in order to establish security in an open system, some secure channel(s) must exist between every pair of users at some time. The only solution to this quadratic (in the number of users) growth of the key distribution problem is to involve a trusted user or authority which can serve as a relay for authenticated or confidential messages. Trust is a fundamental ingredient for secure communications in open networks. Various types and degrees of trust can be distinguished (e.g., see [17]), but for the sake of simplicity of the model, such a distinction will not be made in this paper, although our model could be extended in this direction.

If a user B trusts another user or authority T to send only authenticated information (i.e., T is trusted to properly authenticate its sources of information as well as not to fraudulently distribute inaccurate information), T can connect two authenticated channels $A \overset{t_2[t_1]}{\bullet\!\!\longrightarrow} T$ and $T \overset{t_4[t_3]}{\bullet\!\!\longrightarrow} B$ to result in an authenticated channel from A to B, provided that $t_3 > t_2$, i.e., provided that the message on the $T \overset{t_4[t_3]}{\bullet\!\!\longrightarrow} B$ channel need not be fixed before the first message is received by T on the $A \overset{t_2[t_1]}{\bullet\!\!\longrightarrow} T$ channel:

$$\left. \begin{array}{c} A \overset{t_2[t_1]}{\bullet\!\!\longrightarrow} T \\ T \overset{t_4[t_3]}{\bullet\!\!\longrightarrow} B \\ t_3 > t_2 \\ B \text{ trusts } T \end{array} \right\} \implies A \overset{t_4[t_1]}{\bullet\!\!\longrightarrow} B \qquad (13)$$

This transformation is a generalization of transformation (2). Note that A need not trust T.

If a user A trusts another user or authority T to treat secret information confidentially and to send it only to entities approved by A, then T can connect two confidential channels, provided that $t_3 > t_2$:

$$\left. \begin{array}{l} A \xrightarrow{t_2[t_1]}\!\!\bullet\, T \\ T \xrightarrow{t_4[t_3]}\!\!\bullet\, B \\ t_3 > t_2 \\ A \ trusts \ T \end{array} \right\} \quad \Longrightarrow \quad T \xrightarrow{t_4[t_1]}\!\!\bullet\, B \tag{14}$$

The following transformation, which corresponds to the classical secret key distribution by a trusted authority, cannot be derived by combining previously described transformations. It requires additionally that A and B trust T to generate a random session key.

$$\left. \begin{array}{l} T \,\bullet\!\!\xrightarrow{t_2[t_1]}\!\!\bullet\, A \\ T \,\bullet\!\!\xrightarrow{t_4[t_3]}\!\!\bullet\, B \\ A \xrightarrow{t_5} B \\ t_5 > t_2, t_5 \geq t_4 \\ A \ and \ B \ trust \ T \end{array} \right\} \quad \Longrightarrow \quad A \,\bullet\!\!\xrightarrow{t_5}\!\!\bullet\, B \tag{15}$$

A crucial application of digital signatures (transformation (11)) is for achieving transformation (13) even when $t_3 < t_2$. Of course, no communication can take place from A to B in this case. However, if we assume the existence of an insecure channel $T \xrightarrow{t} B$ from T to B at some time $t > t_2$, then we can use transformation (11) to obtain a channel $T \,\bullet\!\!\xrightarrow{t} B$ and hence by application of (13) a channel $A \,\bullet\!\!\xrightarrow{t[t_1]} B$. The drawback of this approach is that T must participate actively in the communication from A to B.

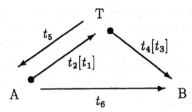

Figure 1. Connecting two authenticated channels by a trusted party T.

Therefore, a more realistic scenario, which corresponds to the well-known certification of public keys by a trusted user or authority, is shown in Figure 1, where we assume the existence of insecure channels $T \xrightarrow{t_5} A$ and $A \xrightarrow{t_6} B$. Here the interaction between A and T is independent of the message sent by T over the $T \,\bullet\!\!\xrightarrow{t_4[t_3]} B$ channel to B.

If $t_6 > t_5$ we can apply transformation (2) to obtain

$$\left.\begin{array}{c} T \xrightarrow{t_5} A \\ A \xrightarrow{t_6} B \\ t_6 > t_5 \end{array}\right\} \xRightarrow{(2)} \quad T \xrightarrow{t_6[t_5]} B$$

Now transformation (11) for digital signatures yields

$$\left.\begin{array}{c} T \xbullet\xrightarrow{t_4[t_3]} B \\ T \xrightarrow{t_6[t_5]} B \\ t_6 > t_4 \end{array}\right\} \xRightarrow{(11)} \quad T \xbullet\xrightarrow{t_6[t_5]} B$$

If B trusts T and if $t_5 > t_2$ we can now apply transformation (13) to obtain

$$\left.\begin{array}{c} A \xbullet\xrightarrow{t_2[t_1]} T \\ T \xbullet\xrightarrow{t_6[t_5]} B \\ t_5 > t_2 \\ B \ trusts \ T \end{array}\right\} \xRightarrow{(13)} \quad A \xbullet\xrightarrow{t_6[t_1]} B$$

which together with transformation (11) for digital signatures gives the desired result, an authenticated channel from A to B:

$$\left.\begin{array}{c} A \xbullet\xrightarrow{t_6[t_1]} B \\ A \xrightarrow{t_6} B \end{array}\right\} \xRightarrow{(11)} \quad A \xbullet\xrightarrow{t_6} B$$

Since we assumed that $t_3 > t_2$, the applications of transformations (2) and (13) are unavoidable. Hence the above derivation illustrates that an authenticated channel $A \xbullet\xrightarrow{t_6} B$ can be achieved if and only if $t_2 < t_5 < t_6$ and only if B trusts T. Two applications of a digital signature scheme are required, first by T for certifying A's public key and secondly by A to authenticate actual messages. In this model of public-key certification, user A serves as a relay from T to B for his own public key certificate. When a $A \xleftarrow{t_7} B$ channel is available for some $t_7 > t_6$ and the goal of the transformations is to achieve a confidential $A \xbullet\xleftarrow{t_7} B$ channel, this could be achieved by replacing the last transformation by

$$\left.\begin{array}{c} A \xbullet\xrightarrow{t_6[t_1]} B \\ A \xleftarrow{t_7} B \\ t_7 > t_6 \end{array}\right\} \xRightarrow{(9)} \quad A \xbullet\xleftarrow{t_7} B$$

6. The necessary and sufficient condition for security in an open network

The following theorem follows from the above sequence of transformations, from Theorem 1 and from the fact that confidential channels can be transformed into authenticated channels by transformation (7).

Theorem 2. *Under Assumption 1 it is a sufficient condition for achieving an authenticated channel from A to B from time t_0 on ($A \xrightarrow{\;t\;} B$ for $t \geq t_0$) that there exists a connected path of channels from A to B such that*

(1) every channel in the path is available at some time earlier than t_0 and has a • attached to that end of the channel which is closer to A and
(2) user B trusts every intermediate user on the path.

Assuming the above axiom the condition is also necessary.

Corollary 3. *Under Assumption 1 it is a sufficient condition for achieving a secure channel between A and B from time t_0 on ($A \xleftrightarrow{\;t\;} B$ for $t \geq t_0$) that there exist two paths of channels according to Theorem 2, one from A to B and one from B to A. Assuming the above axiom the condition is also necessary.*

Example: Consider the somewhat artificial scenario of Figure 2: Assume that T_1, T_2 and T_3 are trusted by A and B, that the channels are available at the indicated times and that insecure channels are freely available. In order to determine the earliest time after which A and B can communicate securely, one has to find two paths as required by Corollary 3 with the smallest possible maximal path time on the paths. In this example there exist two paths from A to B, namely $A - T_3 - B$ and $A - T_1 - T_3 - B$, and one path from B to A, namely $B - T_2 - T_1 - T_3 - A$. Hence the earliest time for secure communication between A and B is $\max(t_2, t_3, t_4, t_6, t_7, \min(t_2, \max(t_1, t_3)))$.

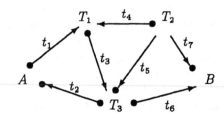

Figure 2. A security bootstrapping scenario.

7. Protocols for bootstrapping security in open networks

In the previous section we have demonstrated the theoretical limitations to establishing security in an open network. This section is devoted to reviewing within our framework some previously proposed protocols for establishing a secure channels between two users.

7.1. Protocols based on symmetric cryptography

Assume that every user shares a secret key with a trusted party T. In other words, there exist channels $T \xrightarrow{\;t_1\;} A$ and $T \xrightarrow{\;t_2\;} B$ for some time instances t_1 and

t_2. From the point of view of the required (insecure) communication channels, the simplest protocol exploits transformation (15), requiring only communication between A and B, not involving T. While this approach is used in military and diplomatic applications, it is of course completely impractical in large networks because the communication on the two channels $T \bullet\xrightarrow{t_1}\bullet A$ and $T \bullet\xrightarrow{t_2}\bullet B$ is necessarily correlated. In other words, T must generate a secret key for every pair of users and send each user the approriate secret keys (for communication with the other users) over the secure channel (e.g. by a trusted courier).

7.1.1. Message or session key relaying by a trusted server

The correlation between the secure channels available during the setup phase can be avoided at the expense of requiring T to be *on-line*. This also allows the encryption key generation to take place only when needed (session keys). The most simple such protocol, involving transformations (8), (13) and (14), is when T serves as a relay for messages. If A wants to send a message to B, he or she encrypts it with the secret key shared with T and sends it to T using a channel $A \longrightarrow T$, who decrypts and reencrypts it with the secret key shared with B, and sends the result to B using a $T \longrightarrow B$ channel.

A more reasonable protocol additionally requiring direct interaction between A and B is the so-called wide-mouthed-frog protocol proposed by Burrows [2]. Here, T merely relays a session key generated by A for communication between A and B, and all subsequent encrypted communication between A and B happens over a $A \longleftrightarrow B$ channel.

7.1.2. Session key distribution by a trusted server

The following type of protocol is used in Kerberos [13] and in KryptoKnight [9] and has the advantage that it does not require users to be capable of generating "good" encryption keys. Otway and Rees [11] have proposed a similar protocol with a different sequence of interactions with the trusted server T. Figure 3 illustrates the scenario in which T agrees on a bilateral secret key with every user during an initialization phase (in our example at time t_1 with A and at time t_2 with B).

When A wants to communicate with B she asks T to provide a session key. T sends the encrypted session key to A, together with the same session key encrypted for B (i.e., with the key shared by T and B). A can then initiate a communication with B by sending the encrypted session key.

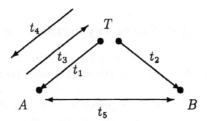

Figure 3. Session key distribution by a trusted server T.

The sequence of transformations used for obtaining a secure channel $A \overset{t_5}{\bullet\!\!-\!\!\bullet} B$ is as follows: If $t_5 > t_4$ then the channels $T \overset{t_4}{\longrightarrow} A$ and $A \overset{t_5}{\longrightarrow} B$ can be connected by transformation (2):

$$\left.\begin{array}{c} T \overset{t_4}{\longrightarrow} A \\ A \overset{t_5}{\longrightarrow} B \\ t_5 > t_4 \end{array}\right\} \quad \overset{(2)}{\Longrightarrow} \quad T \overset{t_5[t_4]}{\longrightarrow} B$$

Now transformation (3) applied to channels $T \overset{t_5[t_4]}{\longrightarrow} B$ and $T \overset{t_2}{\bullet\!\!-\!\!\bullet} B$ gives

$$\left.\begin{array}{c} T \overset{t_2}{\bullet\!\!-\!\!\bullet} B \\ T \overset{t_5[t_4]}{\longrightarrow} B \\ t_5 \geq t_2 \end{array}\right\} \quad \overset{(3)}{\Longrightarrow} \quad T \overset{t_5[t_4]}{\bullet\!\!-\!\!\bullet} B$$

Channels $T \overset{t_1}{\bullet\!\!-\!\!\bullet} A$ and $T \overset{t_4}{\longrightarrow} A$ are combined by another application of (3):

$$\left.\begin{array}{c} T \overset{t_1}{\bullet\!\!-\!\!\bullet} A \\ T \overset{t_4}{\longrightarrow} A \\ t_4 > t_1 \end{array}\right\} \quad \overset{(3)}{\Longrightarrow} \quad T \overset{t_4}{\bullet\!\!-\!\!\bullet} A$$

Now $T \overset{t_4}{\bullet\!\!-\!\!\bullet} A$, $T \overset{t_5[t_4]}{\bullet\!\!-\!\!\bullet} B$ and $A \overset{t_5}{\longrightarrow} B$ can be used for key distribution according to (15):

$$\left.\begin{array}{c} T \overset{t_4}{\bullet\!\!-\!\!\bullet} A \\ T \overset{t_5[t_4]}{\bullet\!\!-\!\!\bullet} B \\ A \overset{t_5}{\longrightarrow} B \\ t_5 > t_4 \\ A \text{ and } B \text{ both trust } T \end{array}\right\} \quad \overset{(15)}{\Longrightarrow} \quad A \overset{t_5}{\bullet\!\!-\!\!\bullet} B$$

It may be desirable for A to generate the session key herself. In this case, a modified version of the above protocol in which $A \overset{t_3}{\bullet\!\!-\!\!\bullet} T$ is created from $T \overset{t_1}{\bullet\!\!-\!\!\bullet} A$ and $A \overset{t_3}{\longrightarrow} T$ by application of (4), $A \overset{t_5[t_3]}{\bullet\!\!-\!\!\bullet} B$ is created from $A \overset{t_3}{\bullet\!\!-\!\!\bullet} T$ and $T \overset{t_5[t_4]}{\bullet\!\!-\!\!\bullet} B$ by application of (13) and (14), and $A \overset{t_5}{\bullet\!\!-\!\!\bullet} B$ is created from $A \overset{t_5[t_3]}{\bullet\!\!-\!\!\bullet} B$ and $A \overset{t_5}{\longrightarrow} B$ by application of (3). This sequence of transformations requires that $t_1 < t_3 < t_4 < t_5$.

7.2. Protocols based on public key certification

The major drawback of the protocols described in the previous section (and of all protocols based solely on symmetric cryptography) is that either a trusted authority T must be available on-line or the initial secure communications between different users and T must be correlated. This problem of relying on an authority for every session can be solved by using certified public keys as mentioned in Section 4. However, in a very large network such as the Internet, several trusted authorities are required to make the system practical, i.e., to provide all the paths of channels required by Corollary 3.

7.2.1. Hierarchical public key certification

The certification authorities can be organized in a hierarchy as suggested in [19], in which each authority can certify the public key of lower-level authorities. Of course, cross-certification links can be introduced when needed [19].

A simple scenario with a two-level hierarchy is shown in Figure 4: T_1 is a system-wide authority which certifies public keys of regional authorities (T_2 and T_3). A and B get certificates for their public keys from T_2 and T_3, respectively. Such a certification step consists of sending the public key, over an authenticated channel, to the higher-level authority and receiving from it over another authenticated channel the certified public key together with the public keys and certificates of all authorities on the path to T_1. Typically, it is realized by a personal registration with mutual identification. It should be pointed out that a user's public key may consist of two components, the public keys for a digital signature scheme and for a public-key cryptosystem or public-key distribution system. One public key suffices if the RSA system [12] is used.

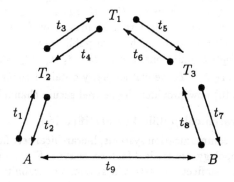

Figure 4. Hierarchical public key certification.

A formal derivation using security transformations demonstrates the constraints on the timing of the channels required to achieve a secure channel between A and B. It further illustrates the fact that all authorities on the path between A and B must be trusted by both A and B. The sequence of transformations leading to an authenticated channel $A \overset{t_9}{\bullet\!\!-\!\!\to} B$ from A to B is shown in Figure 5.

$$\left.\begin{array}{l} T_2 \xrightarrow{t_2} A \\ A \xrightarrow{t_9} B \\ t_9 > t_2 \end{array}\right\} \xRightarrow{(1),(2)} T_2 \xrightarrow{t_9[t_2]} B \qquad \left.\begin{array}{l} T_2 \xrightarrow{t_3} T_1 \\ T_1 \xrightarrow{t_9[t_4]} B \\ t_4 > t_3 \\ B \text{ trust } T_1 \end{array}\right\} \xRightarrow{(13)} T_2 \xrightarrow{t_9[t_3]} B$$

$$\left.\begin{array}{l} T_1 \xrightarrow{t_4} T_2 \\ T_2 \xrightarrow{t_9[t_2]} B \\ t_2 > t_4 \end{array}\right\} \xRightarrow{(1),(2)} T_1 \xrightarrow{t_9[t_4]} B \qquad \left.\begin{array}{l} T_2 \xrightarrow{t_9[t_3]} B \\ T_2 \xrightarrow{t_9[t_2]} B \end{array}\right\} \xRightarrow{(11)} T_2 \xrightarrow{t_9[t_2]} B$$

$$\left.\begin{array}{l} T_1 \xrightarrow{t_5} T_3 \\ T_3 \xrightarrow{t_7} B \\ t_7 > t_5 \\ B \text{ trusts } T_3 \end{array}\right\} \xRightarrow{(13)} T_1 \xrightarrow{t_7[t_5]} B \qquad \left.\begin{array}{l} A \xrightarrow{t_1} T_2 \\ T_2 \xrightarrow{t_9[t_2]} B \\ t_2 > t_1 \\ B \text{ trust } T_2 \end{array}\right\} \xRightarrow{(13)} A \xrightarrow{t_9[t_1]} B$$

$$\left.\begin{array}{l} T_1 \xrightarrow{t_7[t_5]} B \\ T_1 \xrightarrow{t_9[t_4]} B \\ t_9 > t_7 \end{array}\right\} \xRightarrow{(11)} T_1 \xrightarrow{t_9[t_4]} B \qquad \left.\begin{array}{l} A \xrightarrow{t_9[t_1]} B \\ A \xrightarrow{t_9} B \end{array}\right\} \xRightarrow{(11)} A \xrightarrow{t_9} B$$

Figure 5. Exploiting the certification hierarchy of Figure 4.

Note that this sequence of transformations requires that $t_1 < t_2$, $t_3 < t_4$, $t_5 < t_7$ and $t_4 < t_2 < t_9$ as well as that B trusts T_1, T_2 and T_3. The condition $t_4 < t_2 < t_9$ follows from the fact that T_2 must provide A with T_1's public key as well as with T_1's certificate for his own public key.

For the symmetric conditions $t_8 < t_7$, $t_6 < t_5$, $t_4 < t_2$ and $t_5 < t_7 < t_9$ and if also A trusts T_1, T_2 and T_3 we can similarly obtain a channel $B \xrightarrow{t_9} A$. Hence transformation (10) now provides the desired secure channel: $A \xleftrightarrow{t_9} B$.

7.2.2 Non-hierarchical public key certification

In very large communication systems, hierarchical certification schemes with a tree-shaped topology are critical for two reasons. First, a single failure of one of the authorities suffices to destroy a system's operability. Second, and more importantly, both users must trust *every* authority on the certification path, i.e., a certification path can be at most as strong as its weakest link. A user's trust in an authority T_i is in most cases based on the fact that some higher-level authority once trusted T_i. In other words, a user need not only trust the honesty of the authority T at the root of the tree but, also T's ability to judge the trustworthyness of authorities it either certifies or distributes the public-key of, which again must be trusted to judge the trustworthyness of further authorities, and so on. Trust management is therefore one of the fundamental research areas in distributed system security (e.g., see [17]).

The situation is comparable to that in other large organizations such as a company or government organization: Although the president hires as executive vice-presidents people he or she considers highly capable and trustworthy, who do the same for hiring second-level managers, etc., it is nevertheless unavoidable that the company ends up having some incapable and non-trustworthy employees. The major difference compared to a certification hierarchy is that in the latter, not a single failure can be tolerated, i.e., a single dishonest authority in the path can destroy the system's security. Note that the $X.509$ framework allows for cross-certification between arbitrary intermediate authorities, thus relaxing the described problem.

However, it appears crucial in very large networks that not only the communication links, but also the certification paths be highly redundant. Zimmermann's Pretty Good Privacy (PGP) software [18] allows for a very flexible use of certificates, leaving the responsibility completely in the hands of the users. This approach exploits Theorem 2 and Corollary 3 in their full generality. However, a more general approach allowing to fully express and exploit various degrees of trust and combine certificates of varying trust levels is needed.

8. Exploiting $\longrightarrow\!\!\bullet$ channels

The theorems in Sections 4 and 6 illustrate the complete duality between authenticity and confidentiality. While authenticated channels without confidentiality ($\bullet\!\!\longrightarrow$) are used routinely in open systems, the theorems in Sections 4 and 6 suggest that confidential channels without authenticity ($\longrightarrow\!\!\bullet$) could be used equally well. It remains an interesting open question whether such channels exist in a practical application scenario.

To illustrate that such channels need not be unrealistic, consider for instance a user B with several accounts on various machines on a large network with cryptographically protected channels between his terminal and these machines. It may be reasonable to assume that an eavesdropper could simultaneously access messages sent by another user A to a few of these machines, but that he is unable to access all the messages sent to these machines at a given time. In such a scenario, a $A \longrightarrow\!\!\bullet B$ channel to be exploited in one of the transformations (5), (6), (7), (8), (12) and (14) could for instance be established by A by dividing a secret key S into various pieces such that all pieces are required to obtain any information about S, and sending (without authenticity, and preferably from accounts on different machines) the individual pieces to B's mailboxes on the various machines. If B can do the same symmetrically, these confidential channels could replace the authenticated channels needed for public-key certification. This technique may be particularly attractive for establishing secure channels with trusted authorities.

References

1. A. Birell, B. Lampson, R. Needham and M. Schroeder, A global authentication service without global trust, *Proc. IEEE Symposium on Research in Security and Privacy*, 1986, pp. 223–230.
2. M. Burrows, M. Abadi and R. Needham, A logic of authentication, *ACM Transactions on Computer Systems*, Vol. 8, No. 1, 1990, pp. 18–36.

3. W. Diffie and M.E. Hellman, New directions in cryptography, *IEEE Transactions on Information Theory*, Vol. 22, No. 6, 1976, pp. 644–654.
4. M. Gasser, A. Goldstein, C. Kaufman and B. Lampson, The Digital distributed system security architecture, *Proc. 12th National Computer Security Conference*, NIST/NCSC, Baltimore, 1989, pp. 305–319.
5. J. Glasgow, G. MacEwen and P. Panangaden, A logic for reasoning about security, *ACM Transactions on Computer Systems*, Vol. 10, No. 3, 1992, pp. 226–264.
6. V.D. Gligor, S.-W. Luan and J.N. Pato, On inter-realm authentication in large distributed systems, *Proc. IEEE Conference on security and privacy*, 1992, pp. 2–17.
7. B. Lampson, M. Abadi, M. Burrows and E. Wobber, Authentication in distributed systems: theory and practice, Proc. 13th ACM Symp. on Operating Systems Principles, 1991, pp. 165–182.
8. J. Linn, Privacy enhancement for internet electronic mail: Part I, Message encipherment and authentication procedures, Internet RFC 1421, Feb. 1993.
9. R. Molva, G. Tsudik, E. Van Herreweghen and S. Zatti, "KryptoKnight Authentication and Key Distribution System", *Proc. 1992 European Symposium on Research in Computer Security (ESORICS 92)*, Toulouse (Nov.92).
10. R.M. Needham and M.D. Schroeder, Using encryption for authentication in large networks of computers, *Communications of the ACM*, Vol. 21, 1978, pp. 993–999.
11. D. Otway and O. Rees, Efficient and timely mutual authentication, *Operating systems review*, Vol. 21, No. 1, 1987, pp. 8–10.
12. R.L. Rivest, A. Shamir, and L. Adleman, A method for obtaining digital signatures and public-key cryptosystems, *Communications of the ACM*, Vol. 21, No. 2, 1978, pp. 120–126.
13. J.G. Steiner, C. Neuman and J.I. Schiller, Kerberos: An authentication service for open network systems, Proceedings of *Winter USENIX 1988*, Dallas, Texas.
14. P. Syverson and C. Meadows, A logical language for specifying cryptographic protocols requirements, *Proc. IEEE Conf. on Research in Security and Privacy*, 1993, pp. 165–180.
15. J.J. Tardo and K. Alagappan, SPX: Global authentication using public key certificates, *Proc. IEEE Conf. on Research in Security and Privacy*, 1991, pp. 232–244.
16. V. Voydock and S. Kent, Security mechanisms in high-level network protocols, *ACM Computing Surveys*, Vol. 15, No. 2, 1983, pp. 135–171.
17. R. Yahalom, B. Klein and T. Beth, Trust relationships in secure systems – a distributed autentication perspective, *Proc. IEEE Conf. on Research in Security and Privacy*, 1993, pp. 150–164.
18. P. Zimmermann, PGP User's Guide, Dec. 1992, available on the Internet.
19. ISO/IEC International Standard 9594-8, Information technology – open systems interconnection – the directory, Part 8: Authentication framework, 1990.

On Strengthening Authentication Protocols to Foil Cryptanalysis*

Wenbo Mao   and   Colin Boyd

Communications Research Laboratory
Department of Electrical Engineering
University of Manchester
Manchester M13 9PL, UK
Email: wenbo@comms.ee.man.ac.uk

Abstract. Cryptographic protocols have usually been designed at an abstract level without concern for the cryptographic algorithms used in implementation. In this paper it is shown that the abstract protocol definition can have an important effect on the ability of an attacker to mount a successful attack on an implementation. In particular, it will be determined whether an adversary is able to generate corresponding pairs of plaintext and ciphertext to use as a lever in compromising secret keys. The ideas are illustrated by analysis of two well-known authentication systems which have been used in practice. They are Kerberos and KryptoKnight. It is shown that for the Kerberos protocol, an adversary can acquire at will an unlimited number of known plaintext-ciphertext pairs. Similarly, an adversary in the KryptoKnight system can acquire an unlimited number of data pairs which, by a less direct means, can be seen to be cryptanalytically equivalent to known plaintext-ciphertext pairs. We propose new protocols, using key derivation techniques, which achieve the same end goals as these others without this undesirable feature.

1   Introduction

In recent years great advances have been made in understanding how to design cryptographic protocols for entity authentication and secure message exchange. Various techniques have been proposed (e.g., [19, 20, 12, 13, 10, 4]) and thereafter security flaws or weaknesses were discovered. To repeatedly find and fix problems in the published authentication mechanisms is an active research topic. Meanwhile, systems based on these mechanisms have been implemented; two well-known systems are Kerberos [17, 14] and KryptoKnight [18]. Naturally, these implementations should also be frequently examined and debugged in accordance with discoveries of the problems in the underlying mechanisms.

In applications of distributed computation which crucially require secure communication, entity authentication establishes a secure channel between communication parties remotely situated in a hostile environment. In the techniques

* This work is funded by the UK Engineering and Physical Sciences Research Council under research grant GR/G19787.

mentioned above, this task is achieved through the use of a trusted authentication server and as a special case, the server itself can be one of the communication parties. It is always assumed that a secure channel already exists between a client principal and the server. Let this existing channel be referred to as a *long-term channel*, which is established through some expensive method in a higher level of the security hierarchy. It must be understood that the security essence of a long-term channel is its low bandwidth: its usage must be limited only to establish other channels of higher bandwidth. In other words, authentication protocols are meant to use a secure long-term channel to transmit or to agree a *small* amount of secrets (usually, a cryptographic key) which may serve as a new secure channel (called a *session channel*) along which information can be transmitted with a smaller delay. Notice that a channel with a high bandwidth is vulnerable to temptations in terms of cryptanalysis; it therefore should a limited lifetime. Whenever needed, communication parties should run an authentication protocol to create a new session channel.

It is thus clear that the reason for maintaining the low bandwidth of a long-term channel is in order to foil cryptanalysis passively and/or actively targeted on it. Only by taking this into account does the required and assumed long lifetime of a long-term channel make sense. In public-key cryptographic techniques there is also a need for thoughtful use of a long-term channel. For instance, in the case of the RSA algorithm [21], a long-term channel between a pair of principals can be identified with the private keys of each party; such a key is matched to the public key which is *certified* to the principal. This viewpoint should be considered when the RSA algorithm is used to "bootstrap" a conventional encryption scheme.

In this paper, we keep in mind the working principle of entity authentication mechanisms discussed above while we investigate the existing techniques. We focus on two implemented systems, Kerberos (Section 2) and KryptoKnight (Section 3). These two systems will be shown to allow an adversary to acquire at will an unlimited number of known plaintext-ciphertext pairs. So viewed by the adversary, long-term channels of these systems are actually used at a *very high* bandwidth, even higher than that of any session channel. This is inconsistent with respect to the working principle of authentication mechanisms. Our investigation will result in some insight into how an authentication mechanism should be designed to fulfill the intended purpose of entity authentication. In Section 4, we will demonstrate our idea by presenting remedies for the problem, using an idea of "one-time" channel derivation, which achieves the same end goals as these others without the undesirable feature revealed. In addition we will see another good feature possessed in one of our remedy techniques: *perfect forward secrecy* [8], which means that loss of a long-term key should not lead to loss of any session key which has been established by the lost key. We will also discuss the possibility of extending our techniques to conventional authentication protocols. Finally, Section 5 forms our conclusion.

The remainder of this section is devoted to a brief overview of cryptanalysis threats that we will be discussing throughout the paper. Further details may be found in various texts such as the recent book by Schneier [22].

1.1   An Overview of Cryptanalysis Threats

In conventional cryptography the sender and recipient of a message share a key, which is known to no other principals, that allows each of them to encrypt or decrypt messages. It is inevitable that an attacker will be able to record and analyse a large amount of the encrypted ciphertext transmitted between the two parties with the aim of extracting the plaintext or analysing the key used. The cryptographic algorithm employed should be designed so that this is not possible for an attacker using the resources anticipated.

However, resistance to such a *ciphertext only* attack is not sufficient to guarantee security. It may be anticipated that the attacker will be able to obtain portions of ciphertext for which he also knows the corresponding plaintext. These are known as *plaintext-ciphertext pairs*. A *known plaintext* attack, which attempts to find the shared key from a number of plaintext-ciphertext pairs, is considerably harder to defeat. An even sterner case is the *chosen plaintext* attack, in which the attacker is able to choose plaintext portions and see their encrypted versions. Recent advances in cryptanalysis [3] have shown that resilience to known and chosen plaintext attacks is not so easy to achieve as had been previously thought. It is particularly worth noticing that authentication protocols which apply a *challenge-response* technique, if not carefully designed, can be abused to form a substantial amount of plaintext-ciphertext pairs. In Section 2 we will see that the authentication system Kerberos, which implements the techniques of a category of published authentication protocols, allows an attacker to obtain an unlimited amount of plaintext-ciphertext pairs to be used to undermine the long-term channel between a server and a client.

Another type of cryptographic function is a *one-way hash function*. Such a function has a one-way property which means that it is easy to compute hashed values in the direction from domain to range but computationally infeasible, given almost any hashed value, to find any input it could have come from. Typically such functions map long strings onto much shorter ones. An attractive feature due to the unequal sizes of domain and range is that plaintext-ciphertext pairs generated on the channel are of little use for an opponent. The idea of using one-way hash functions as the basis of cryptographic protocols appeared quite early in the literature, e.g., Evan *et al.* [9], Merkle [16] and Gong [10]. Subsequently the idea has been employed in the authentication and key exchange system KryptoKnight [18]. However, in Section 3 we will see that owing to an undesirable design feature, an attacker can force the domain and the range of the one-way function implemented in the system to have the same size and at the same time obtain an unlimited amount of plaintext-ciphertext pairs. Normal cryptanalysis techniques can then be applied to undermine the long-term channel.

Having explained the threat scenario, it is attractive if we can *guarantee* that a long-term channel will never be used to provide plaintext-ciphertext pairs. Such a technique will be presented in this paper.

2 Kerberos

Kerberos is based on the Needham-Schroeder protocol, but makes use of times-tamps as nonces to remove the problem pointed out by Denning and Sacco [6]. In Kerberos, basic message exchanges between a network client A and an authentication server S have the following form:

1. $A \to S :$ *request*
2. $S \to A :$ *reply*

In this presentation, the line $X \to Y : Z$ describes a message communication directed from principal X to principal Y; Z represents the transmitted message. Requests from clients are always sent in plaintext and replies from the server are organised messages called *tickets*. A ticket is a record that helps a client to authenticate a service. A slightly simplified form of ticket can be written as below (cf., Kerberos version 5 [14]):

$ticket =$ version-number, addresses, names, *encrypted-part*

where the *encrypted-part* is as below:

$encrypted\text{-}part = \{$flag-bits, session-key, address, names, timestamps, lifetimes, host-addresses, authorization-data $\}_{K_{AS}}$

The notation $\{M\}_K$ denotes a ciphertext generated from a (symmetric) crypto-algorithm which uses M as input data and K as encryption key. In the above example, the key K_{AS} is the secret key shared between the client principal A and the server principal S; it is the basis of the long-term channel existing between these two principals.

We see that in the encrypted part of a Kerberos ticket the messages are non-secret data except for the session key. To an external adversary, the principal addresses and names are fully known, and timestamps and lifetimes have easily guessable formats. To an internal adversary, such as the third party principal, B, with whom A intends to share a session key by initiating an authentication run, all data in the encrypted part of a ticket are fully known. (In this paper, B is always viewed as a potential enemy.) We observe that the encryption algorithms used by Kerberos (they will be discussed below) treat these data as secrets. We regard such a treatment to be unwise. In so doing, each run of the protocol will generate plaintext-ciphertext pairs for an adversary to analyse the long-term secret key shared between the server and a client principal. We now explain why in the case of Kerberos, the effect of the cryptanalysis may not be ignored.

In Kerberos, a request from a client principal to the server is sent in plaintext. Thus the adversary's action is not limited only to passive monitoring of the normal runs of the protocol on the network traffic, which can only allow him to obtain a trivially small amount of plaintext-ciphertext pairs. The opponent can in fact masquerade as A and send an *unlimited number* of plaintext requests to S, who presumably is a node in the computer network and will prompt the opponent by supplying tickets, i.e., plaintext-ciphertext pairs, onto the network.

In the encrypted part of a ticket, known data follow a session key which varies in every ticket returned from the server. Thus in the case of using a chained encryption algorithm (in Kerberos V5, the encryption algorithm used is cipher block chaining (CBC), see Section 6.3 of [14]), the constant known plaintexts will be "garbled" by the feedback of the previous ciphertext output. We now look at how such a garbling will help the adversary to obtain a large amount of plaintext-ciphertext pairs. The output of a block cipher using CBC mode is a sequence of n-bit cipher blocks which are chained together in that each cipher block is dependent not only on the current input plaintext block, but also on the previous output cipher block. Let $P_1, P_2, \cdots, P_m$ be plaintext blocks to be input to CBC algorithm and $C_1, C_2, \cdots, C_m$ be ciphertext blocks output from the algorithm. Then the encryption procedure to generate a block of ciphertext is as below:

$$C_i = eK(P_i \oplus C_{i-1})$$

where $eK()$ denotes an encryption algorithm keyed by K and $\oplus$ denotes the addition, bitwise modulo 2. So $P_i \oplus C_{i-1}$ and C_i form a plaintext-ciphertext pair. Now let P_1 be the session key which varies in every ticket returned from the server. Then it is easy to see that $C_1, C_2, \cdots$ vary in every ticket. The consequence of this garbling is: simply repeating a constant request, the opponent will be guaranteed to obtain varied plaintext-ciphertext pairs with which he can build a dictionary. Notice that the correct use of CBC requires each encryption calculation be initialised by a new "initial vector" (IV); these varied IV's can also play the role of the session keys.

It seems there is a simple cure for the problem that we have revealed: the server should record the requests from clients; if numerous requests from a principal are detected within a short period of time, the service should be denied. However, this then allows a denial of service attack with which a malicious person can cheat the server to stop serving innocent clients. A denial of service attack of this kind can only be prevented if such an attack as the above is allowed.

From our analysis so far it is apparent that the Kerberos authentication system can be abused by an opponent to obtain an *arbitrary* amount of plaintext-ciphertext pairs. It is not hard to imagine that by performing the attack in a short period of time, the amount of *pairs* gathered by the opponent can exceed the quantity of ciphertexts of a session. This forms rather a strange situation: a session key which generates a *smaller* amount of *ciphertext-only* data is stipulated to have a short lifetime while a key which can generate a *larger* amount of *plaintext-ciphertext pairs* is, on the contrary, to be used in a much longer period of time. Considering that cryptographic keys in modern encryption algorithms (such as DES) have a fixed format, it cannot be that some keys are unconditionally stronger than others. The stipulated difference in lifetimes of the keys is due to the consideration of different types of data to be encrypted. Unfortunately, in the case of Kerberos, this reasonable stipulation turns out to be a dangerous practice.

3 KryptoKnight

KryptoKnight is an authentication system developed by Molva *et al.* [18]. Its technical basis is similar to that of a protocol that Gong devised [10]. In the treatment of non-secret data, KryptoKnight is extremely different from Kerberos where a substantial amount of non-secret data are encrypted against access. In KryptoKnight, non-secret data are sent in plaintext. The integrity of these data is protected by using the one-way property of a cryptographic transformation. Such a treatment shows a better understanding of authentication mechanisms, i.e., the required property of cryptographic services for authentication is one-way transformation, rather than secret concealment. In the previous section we have seen that to conceal non-secret data against access is not a good practice. Authentication applying the one-way property has many other advantages over applying the secret-concealment property [15].

In the message exchange for key distribution, KryptoKnight uses the image of a one-way transformation, namely, a mechanism called a message authentication code (MAC), as a key to conceal a distributed session key in the fashion of the one-time pad. Below is such an exchange where a client principal A requires the authentication server S to generate and send to her a session key K to be shared with a third party B.

1. $A \rightarrow S : A, B, N_A$
2. $S \rightarrow A : N_S, N_A, B, T, MAC_{K_{AS}}(N_A \oplus B, N_S, N_A \oplus S, T) \oplus K$

In the above messages, N_A is a nonce chosen by A for verifying the timeliness of the message replied from the server, N_S is the nonce generated by the server and T is a lifetime stating the expiration time of the distributed session key K. The one-way transformation is denoted by $MAC_{K_{AS}}(\cdot)$; it is keyed by the long-term key K_{AS} shared between A and S. Notice that because of the one-way property of the MAC mechanism, the long string of plaintext input and the short string of the MAC (64 bits, see [18]) in message line 2 do not form useful pairs for an adversary. Furthermore, the MAC is concealed by the session key so it is not available to an external adversary on the network. Therefore, the attacking scenario that applies to Kerberos does not apply to KryptoKnight.

However, this clever design does not stop an internal opponent who has a long-term channel with the server. Assume that B is such a person. The message line 1 sent in plaintext means that B can masquerade as A, at the same time playing his own role. By fixing (or carefully choosing) N_A, he can obtain an unlimited number of MAC's which we put in the following set:

$$\{MAC_{K_{AS}}(N_A \oplus B, N_S, N_A \oplus S, T) \mid N_S \text{ known to } B\}$$

Notice that among the data input to these MAC's only N_S is a variable, or a real input value; the rest of the data are constants. Therefore we can rewrite the above set as the following one:

$$\{MAC'_{K_{AS}}(N_S) \mid N_S \text{ known to } B\}$$

In fact, elements in this set can be viewed as outputs from a block encryption algorithm which transforms one block of nonces, i.e., N_S, into one block of ciphers with the same block size. A more appropriate name for such a transformation should be ECB, the electronic code book mode of operation on a block cipher algorithm. Algorithmically, we can see little difference between a MAC with one-block length of input string and an ECB with the same input string. Now that both N_S and $MAC'_{K_{AS}}(N_S)$ are 64-bit blocks (see [18]), they form a perfect plaintext-ciphertext pair. B can build a dictionary of such pairs for undermining the long-term channel between A and S.

Similar to the scenario of the denial of service attack toward Kerberos that we discussed in the previous section, it is not a good solution to stop serving B when numerous malicious requests are detected. A desirable solution should be some mechanism designed in the protocol which does not prevent malicious action but instead prevents achieving the intended goal of such a malicious action. For instance, it will be attractive if no plaintext-ciphertext pairs will be produced against the long-term channel through sending a large amount of malicious requests onto the network. Such a technique will be devised in the next section.

4 Two Remedies for KryptoKnight

Kerberos and KryptoKnight apply encryption techniques in two extremely different manners. Kerberos overuses the secret-concealment property of crypto-algorithms; it unnecessarily, even harmfully, protects the confidentiality of non-secret data. KryptoKnight, on the other extreme end, underuses that property; lack of a secret transmitted along the long-term channel (the session key distributed in KryptoKnight is not a secret to an internal attacker as the third party) makes the channel too exposed. Naturally, we should consider a balance between these two extreme situations. Our remedies are to design some secrets to be passed through the long-term channel. Such a secret is protected by, and protects, the long-term key. Two remedies for KryptoKnight using this idea are given below.

4.1 Remedy Scheme 1

In the first remedy, the needed secret is a nonce N'_S replied from the server. The original protocol will be revised into the following version:

1. $A \rightarrow S : A, B, N_A$
2. $S \rightarrow A : \{N'_S\}_{K_{AS}}, N_S, B, T, MAC_{K_{AS} \oplus N'_S}(N_A \oplus B, N_S, N_A \oplus S, T) \oplus K$

In this specification, the usage of the identifiers is the same as in the original KryptoKnight, except the extra nonce N'_S, which is generated by the server for each run. The server sends it to A under the protection of the long-term key K_{AS} with an appropriate encryption algorithm (e.g., DES ECB). Thus, N'_S is a secret between A and S. By adding this secret, bitwise modulo 2, to the long-term key K_{AS}, a "one-time" channel is formed and used to create a "one-time" MAC for each run. Thus, if B performs the same attack that we have described in the previous section, then each attacking run will give him *one* plaintext-ciphertext pair against a "*one-time*" channel.

Finally, it is not difficult to see that in this revision, except that we have eliminated the attacking scenario revealed in Section 3, the security essence of the original KryptoKnight has not been changed and this can be analysed analogously to that of the original KryptoKnight [18].

4.2 Remedy Scheme 2

In the second remedy, the needed secret is derived from the Diffie-Hellman exponential key exchange technique [7]. Briefly, A and S each pick random exponents R_A and R_S. Assuming they agree on a common base α and modulus p, A computes $N_A = \alpha^{R_A} \bmod p$ and S computes $N_S = \alpha^{R_S} \bmod p$. The N_A and N_S are used in the same way as these two identifiers are in KryptoKnight.

Now A, knowing R_A and $\alpha^{R_S} \bmod p$, can compute

$$(\alpha^{R_S})^{R_A} \bmod p = \alpha^{R_S R_A} \bmod p$$

Similarly, S can compute

$$(\alpha^{R_A})^{R_S} \bmod p = \alpha^{R_A R_S} \bmod p$$

So A and S agree a secret

$$Y = \alpha^{R_S R_A} \bmod p = \alpha^{R_A R_S} \bmod p$$

The value Y will be used as the needed secret which is exclusively shared between A and the server.

A message exchange for key distribution to realise this idea is given below.

1. $A \rightarrow S : A, B, N_A$
2. $S \rightarrow A : N_S, N_S', B, T, MAC_{K_{AS} \oplus Y}(N_A \oplus B, N_S, N_A \oplus S, T) \oplus K$

The protocol presentation is almost identical to KryptoKnight. In the message returned from S, a one-time channel is used to create the MAC. This channel is formed by adding, bitwise modulo 2, the secret Y to the long-term key K_{AS}. It is one-time because even if N_A is a replay of an old message, the server will always generate a new N_S, and so Y is fresh. Now let B perform the same attack that we have described in Section 3. As above, each attacking run will give him *one* plaintext-ciphertext pair against a *one-time* channel. So no plaintext-ciphertext pair will be generated by this protocol against the long-term channel based on K_{AS}. In order to form a dictionary against the long-term channel, B faces the well-known difficulty of computing a large amount of discrete logarithms.

The challenge-response mechanism of the original KryptoKnight based on the exchange of freshness identifiers N_A and N_S is maintained, because now these two identifiers are essentially fresh and random as long as R_A and R_S are. N_S is now no longer related to N_A as it is in the KryptoKnight protocol. For message integrity and authentication purpose, the value N_S' is now a cipher of N_S under the session key K, i.e., $N_S' = \{N_S\}_K$. The security essence of the original KryptoKnight will not be changed due to this revision and can be analysed analogously to that of the original KryptoKnight [18].

A good property possessed by this version of the remedy for KryptoKnight can be referred to as *perfect forward secrecy*. An authenticated key exchange protocol provides perfect forward secrecy [8] if disclosure of long-term secret keying material does not compromise the secrecy of the exchanged keys from earlier runs. Here in the revised KryptoKnight, the secrecy of the session keys established in the history of a long-term key depends on the various one-time secrets agreed between A and S. The secrecy will not be damaged as long as these one-time secrets have been properly disposed of. This property is inherited from the use of the Diffie-Hellman technique for derivation of the one-time secrets.

4.3 Discussion

The first remedy scheme given in Section 4.1 effectively eliminates the potential attack revealed in Section 3 which allows an adversary to accumulate an arbitrary amount of plaintext-ciphertext pairs against a long-term key. The remedy strengthens the original KryptoKnight in terms of disallowing algorithmic cryptanalysis methods based on numerous chosen or known plaintext-ciphertext pairs. However, we should point out that if the cryptanalysis technique is simply key-space search by brute force, then that remedy does not strengthen the original protocol. This is because the computing time needed for searching a key for the first remedy protocol and that for the original KryptoKnight only differ a polynomial function of the key size (it is reasonable to view the computing time as a function of the key size). For instance, guessing a candidate key K_{AS}, we can obtain a candidate nonce N_S' in the remedy protocol by a step of decryption which takes a polynomial time; then we can further test whether $K_{AS} \oplus N_S'$ is a correct keying value to have been used for creating the MAC, and this test is the basic computation of any key-searching algorithm. Now that the time for key search is an exponential function of the key size, the polynomial difference due to the remedy will not count.

In the second remedy scheme, due to the use of the Diffie-Hellman exponential key derivation technique, the key searching problem now faces computing discrete logarithms. The difficulty of this problem will depend on the size of the prime p used. For a properly chosen large prime, the best known algorithm to date has a sub-exponential complexity [5]; no polynomial time algorithm is known. However, it should be noted that there is a trade-off between the extra security gained and the consequent increase in system complexity.

There are various techniques for distributing or agreeing session keys, but the entity authentication steps that are inevitably needed in these techniques are often very similar. In practice these are mainly achieved by using shared secret keys or passwords in a conventional fashion (see e.g., [8, 11] for non-conventional key agreeing ideas with conventional authentication methods). Similar to the problem found in KryptoKnight, the authentication parts of these techniques are found to have weaknesses for allowing cryptanalysis of shared keys or passwords. Our techniques proposed in this paper show a practical idea for preventing potential algorithmic cryptanalysis threats based on gathering numerous chosen or known plaintext-ciphertext pairs. In addition, the discussion supplied here points out that cryptanalysis threats in terms of brute-force key search needs to be countered by extra system complexities. Some authors [1, 2] have considered methods against brute-force searching for passwords; the remedy scheme 2 can be viewed as a different approach to a similar goal.

4.4 Applicability of the Strengthening Technique to Conventional Authentication protocols

Finally, we point out that the techniques supplied in this paper can be applied to strengthening conventional authentication and key distribution protocols which employ authentication servers. Here we show an example based on using the remedy scheme 2.

The weakness that we have discussed on Kerberos in Section 2 generally applies to conventional protocols. For instance, in the case of the Otway-Rees protocol [20] below:

1. $A \rightarrow B : M, A, B, \{N_A, M, A, B\}_{K_{AS}}$
2. $B \rightarrow S : M, A, B, \{N_A, M, A, B\}_{K_{AS}}, \{N_B, M, A, B\}_{K_{BS}}$
3. $S \rightarrow B : M, \{N_A, K_{AB}\}_{K_{AS}}, \{N_B, K_{AB}\}_{K_{BS}}$
4. $B \rightarrow A : M, \{N_A, K_{AB}\}_{K_{AS}}$

an opponent can repeat sending messages specified in the first line on to the network (he can do so by varying M and using any garbage for the cipher chunk), and B will thereby prompt messages specified in the second line. This malicious action results in an accumulation of chosen plaintext-ciphertext pairs in the same way as the attack on Kerberos explained above.

To make an example of a wide application of our technique, we suggest strengthening the Otway-Rees protocol into the following version:

1. $A \rightarrow B : M, A, B, N_A$
2. $B \rightarrow S : M, A, B, N_A, N_B$
3. $S \rightarrow B : M, N_{SA}, \{B, N_A, K_{AB}\}_{K_{AS} \oplus Y_A}, N_{SB}, \{A, N_B, K_{AB}\}_{K_{BS} \oplus Y_B}$
4. $B \rightarrow A : M, N_{SA}, \{B, N_A, K_{AB}\}_{K_{AS} \oplus Y_A}$

where

$$Y_A = \alpha^{R_{SA} R_A} \bmod p = N_{SA}^{R_A} \bmod p = N_A^{R_{SA}} \bmod p$$

and

$$Y_B = \alpha^{R_{SB} R_B} \bmod p = N_{SB}^{R_B} \bmod p = N_B^{R_{SB}} \bmod p$$

and α, p are appropriate elements in the Diffie-Hellman key-agreement technique.

5 Conclusion

Protocols need to be designed to take account of their implementation as well as their abstract security properties. We have shown how well known protocols allow attackers to obtain unnecessary assistance in obtaining plaintext-ciphertext pairs for use in cryptanalysis. Finally we have illustrated that simple steps may be taken to prevent such attacks which have very little computational cost to the legitimate users.

Acknowledgements

We would like to thank Paul Van Oorschot for helpful comments and suggestions on a draft of this paper which lead to the use of the Diffie-Hellman exponential key derivation technique.

References

1. R.J. Anderson and R.M.A. Lomas. On fortifying key negotiation schemes with poorly chosen passwords. Computer Laboratory, University of Cambridge (obtained from personal contact), 1994.
2. S.M. Bellovin and M. Merritt. Encrypted key exchange: Password-based protocols secure against dictionary attacks. In *Proceedings of the 1992 IEEE Symposium on Research in Security and Privacy*, 1992.
3. E. Biham and A. Shamir. *Differential Cryptanalysis of the Data Encryption Standard*. Springer Verlag, 1993.
4. R. Bird, I. Gopal, A. Herzberg, P. Janson, S. Kutten, R. Molva, and M. Yung. Systematic design of two-party authentication protocols. In *Crypto '91, LNCS*, 1991.
5. E.F. Brickell and A.M. Odlyzko. *Cryptanalysis, A Survey of Recent Results*, pages 501–540. IEEE Press, 1992.
6. D.E. Denning and G.M. Sacco. Timestamps in key distribution protocols. *C.ACM*, 24(8):533–536, August 1981.
7. W. Diffie and M.E. Hellman. New directions in cryptography. *IEEE Trans. Info. Theory*, IT-22(6):644–654, 1976.
8. W. Diffie, P.C. Van Oorschot, and M. Wiener. Authentication and authenticated key exchanges. *Designs, Codes and Cryptography*, 2:107–125, 1992.
9. E. Evan, W. Kantrowitz, and E. Weiss. A user authentication scheme not requiring secrecy in the computer. *C.ACM*, 17:437–442, 1974.
10. L. Gong. Using one-way function for authentication. *Computer Communication Review*, 19(5):8–11, 1989.
11. L. Gong. Authentication, key distribution, and secure broadcast in computer networks using no encryption or decryption. Technical Report SRI-CSL-94-08, SRI International, 1994.
12. ISO/IEC. N 739, DIS 9798-2, information technology - security techniques - entity authentication mechanisms - part 2: Entity authentication using symmetric techniques, 1993-08-13.

13. ISO/IEC. CD 11770-2: Key management, part 2: Key management mechanisms using symmetric techniques, 1993-10-03.

14. J. Kohl and C. Neuman. The Kerberos network authentication service (v5). Internet Archive RFC 1510, September 1993.

15. W. Mao and C. Boyd. Development of authentication protocols: Some misconceptions and a new approach. In *Computer Security Foundations Workshop VII*. IEEE Computer Society Press, 1994.

16. R.C. Merkle. Secure communications over insecure channels. *C.ACM*, 21:294–299, 1978.

17. S.P. Miller, C. Neuman, J.I. Schiller, and J.H. Saltzer. Kerberos authentication and authorization system. Project Athena Technical Plan Section E.2.1, 1987.

18. R. Molva, G. Tsudik, E. van Herreweghen, and S. Zatti. Kryptoknight authentication and key distribution system. In *ESORICS '92, LNCS 648*, pages 155–174, 1992.

19. R.M. Needham and M.D. Schroeder. Using encryption for authentication in large networks of computers. *C.ACM*, 21(12):993–999, 1978.

20. D. Otway and O. Rees. Efficient and timely mutual authentication. *Operating Systems Review*, Vol 21(1):8–10, 1987.

21. R.L. Rivest, A. Shamir, and L. Adleman. A method for obtaining digital signatures and public-key cryptosystems. *C.ACM*, 21:120–126, 1976.

22. B. Schneier. *Applied Cryptography*. John Wiley & Sons, 1994.

Digital Payment

An Efficient Electronic Payment System Protecting Privacy

Jan L. Camenisch[1], Jean-Marc Piveteau[2], Markus A. Stadler[1]

[1] Institute for Theoretical Computer Science
ETH Zurich
CH-8092 Zurich, Switzerland
Email: {camenisch, stadler}@inf.ethz.ch

[2] UBILAB
Union Bank of Switzerland
Bahnhofstrasse 45
CH-8021 Zurich, Switzerland
Email: piveteau@ubilab.ubs.ch

Abstract. Previously proposed anonymous electronic payment systems have the drawback that the bank has to maintain large databases, which is a handicap for the realization of such systems. In this paper, we present a practical anonymous payment system that significantly reduces the size of such databases. It uses the concept of anonymous accounts and offers anonymity as an add-on feature to existing EFTPOS systems.

Keywords: electronic payment systems, privacy, cryptography

1 Introduction

The number of private and corporate financial transactions that are done electronically is growing rapidly. From a user's point of view security, efficiency, and flexibility are the main advantages of existing or emerging electronic payment systems. However, most of the systems used commercially do not combine a high level of security with privacy protection, although several theoretical proposals for secure anonymous payment systems have been published [1, 2, 4, 5, 6, 7, 8, 9, 10, 11, 12, 13, 14]. While the market needs are not clearly established, governments and organizations like banks usually consider anonymity as an obstruction to the system security surveillance, and they prefer to protect users' privacy by legal and administrative steps. Furthermore, two technical characteristics shared by all of these theoretical proposals of secure payment systems protecting privacy compromise their realization:

- they present implementation difficulties, often related to the maintenance and the consultation of large databases necessary to prevent frauds;

---

[1] The first and the third author are jointly supported by the Swiss Federal Commission for the Advancement of Scientific Research (KWF), and the Union Bank of Switzerland.

— they are incompatible with existing electronic payment systems; this implies that their introduction would necessitate a complete redesign of currently used systems.

A secure electronic payment system protecting privacy can be seen as a protocol involving a customer, a shop and a bank. Both the customer and the shop have an account with the bank. One can distinguish between *on-line* payment systems, where all parties, the customer, the shop, and the bank, need to be connected on-line (at least once), and *off-line* payment systems, where each interaction during the protocol requires two communicating parties only. On-line systems have already been proposed for electronic coins [4, 6], and have been generalized to electronic cheques [7]. However, their applicability is significantly limited by the very large size of the database consulted on-line by the bank in order to prevent frauds (e.g. double-spending of an electronic coin). Off-line schemes have been proposed as an alternative. They do not present the drawback of the previous on-line schemes, since the bank consults its database after, and not during the payment. However, the published off-line systems do not prevent double-spending, but only allow to detect it and then to reveal the identity of the cheater.

In this paper, we propose a practical and efficient secure payment system protecting the customer's privacy. As for the majority of such systems, it is essentially based on the concept of blind signature [3]. Our protocol describes an on-line system which presents similar advantages as [4, 6, 7]. However, the database stored by the bank for preventing double-spending is significantly smaller, and its on-line consultation should not represent a handicap for concrete realization anymore[3]. Furthermore, our system is compatible with currently used electronic payment systems, i.e. it could be implemented as an added-value service offered by a bank to its customers.

2 Basic Concepts

The underlying model of an electronic payment system consists of three interacting entities: a bank B, a customer C, and a shop S. Both customer C and shop S have an account with the bank B. An electronic payment system consists of protocols that allow customer C to make a payment to the shop S. Although payment systems differ significantly from each other, it is often possible to identify three phases: a *withdrawal phase* involving the bank B and the customer C, a *payment phase* involving the customer C and the shop S, and a *deposit phase* involving the shop S and the bank B.

Customer, shop and bank have different security requirements. A shop, receiving a payment, wants to be sure that the bank will accept to credit its account with the paid amount. The bank wants to make sure that for each account credited, another account has been debited (i.e. the bank does not want anybody to

---

[3] In fact, the records consulted on-line are comparable to those used in existing on-line EFTPOS (=Electronic Funds Transfer at the Point Of Sale) systems.

to create money or to spend the same money more than once). Finally, a customer needs to be assured that money withdrawn from his or her account will be accepted for a payment; furthermore, he or she may desire privacy protection.

Time of Transactions

This model leads to a classification of payment systems according to the sequential ordering of the three phases. Let t_w (t_p, t_d) denote the time of the withdrawal (payment, deposit). Since the bank will not allow to deposit money which has not been withdrawn previously (assuming that the bank gives no credit), we have $t_w \leq t_d$, and a deposit will only be possible after a payment: $t_p \leq t_d$. With these conditions the three phases can take place in six orders. For most of these there are existing or proposed payment systems:

$$t_p = t_w = t_d \text{ EFTPOS}$$
$$t_p < t_w = t_d \text{ cheque}$$
$$t_w < t_p = t_d \text{ on-line digital cash protecting privacy}^4$$
$$t_p = t_w < t_d$$
$$t_w < t_p < t_d \text{ off-line digital cash protecting privacy}^5$$
$$t_p < t_w < t_d$$

Some of the security requirements mentioned above strongly depend on the order of these phases. For instance, the prevention of multiple spending of money is not a problem if the withdrawal takes place during the payment, i.e. $t_w = t_p$, because the shop can be sure that the customer's account has been debited for the payment. However this condition seems to be incompatible with any form of privacy protection if the bank knows the identifier of the customer during withdrawal (which seems necessary because the customer's account is debited): the shop could always tell the bank the exact time t_p which allows the bank to recover the customer's identity assuming that all withdrawals have been stored.

For this reason, all published payment systems protecting privacy have introduced a delay between withdrawal and payment. But such a delay could facilitate multiple spending of money. One way to solve this problem is that the bank stores all previously spent coins. However this implies the maintenance of large databases.

Anonymity, Untraceability and Privacy

Anonymity and untraceability are often used as synonyms. We prefer to make a difference between these terms, grasping in this way different levels of protection. Each customer is characterized by an identifier (e.g. name, account number, social security number). A customer is said to be *anonymous* if his or her identifier cannot be linked to the sent messages. However, it may be feasible to link the

---

[4] See [2, 4, 6, 7].

[5] See [1, 5, 8, 10, 11, 12, 13, 14].

different messages transmitted by the same customer. An anonymous customer is said to be *untraceable* if no message can be linked not only to the customer's identifier, but also to any previously sent messages; so *untraceability* is stronger than *anonymity*. A system providing either anonymity or untraceability is said to *protect privacy*.

Blind Signature Scheme

A blind signature scheme is a tuple $(Bl(\cdot, \cdot), Sig(\cdot), Ex(\cdot, \cdot), Ver(\cdot, \cdot))$. For a message m and a random value ρ, $Bl(\rho, m)$ is the blinded message, $\sigma' = Sig(Bl(\rho, m))$ is the blind signature and $\sigma = Ex(\rho, Sig(Bl(\rho, m)))$ is the 'real' signature extracted from σ' using ρ. The variable ρ, called *blinding factor*, is chosen at random to prevent the signer from learning m and to guarantee that $Bl(\rho, m)$ and σ' are not linkable to m and σ. The predicate $Ver(\cdot, \cdot)$ is used to check the validity of the signature:

$$\forall \rho, \forall m: \qquad Ver(m, Ex(\rho, (Sig(Bl(\rho, m))))) = 1$$

3 Secure Payment System with Anonymous Accounts

The basic idea of our proposal is to conceal the customer's identity during the withdrawal phase. This is achieved by introducing anonymous accounts[6]. The bank B is responsible for the maintenance of two types of accounts: personal accounts and anonymous accounts. Personal accounts are normal bank accounts associated with a customer's identifier, whereas the identity of the owner of an anonymous account is unknown. The main part of our new system is a set of protocols which allows a customer to anonymously transfer money between accounts. Payments are done on-line by debiting the payer's account and simultaneously paying the same amount into the payee's account. If the payer uses an anonymous account, his or her identity cannot be linked to the payment.

Let us now describe our payment system in detail. The system parameters are a one-way hash function $\mathcal{H}$ and a set of blind signature schemes $\{(Bl_v, Sig_v, Ex_v, Ver_v)\}$. Each signature scheme is used to associate a transaction with a certain value v, e.g. the use of Sig_{100} would indicate a transaction worth hundred dollars.

For the opening of anonymous accounts and for the anonymous transfer of money, two new phases are required: the *anonymous account opening phase* and the *anonymous deposit phase*[7]. The payment and deposit phases merge into the *transaction phase*.

---

[6] Anonymous accounts have also been introduced in [1] and [2], but they do not share the same characteristics as in our protocol.

[7] Here deposit means a deposit to the customers anonymous account and not to the shop's account.

Anonymous Account Opening Phase

To open an anonymous account, the customer C proceeds as follows:

1. C contacts the bank B without showing his or her actual identifier (therefore B does not know anything about the true identity of C during this phase). B opens a new anonymous account A with account number acc_A, secret parameter k_A, and a counter cnt_{AB}. B sets $cnt_{AB} = 0$.
2. B sends acc_A and k_A to C.
3. C stores acc_A, k_A and initializes a counter $cnt_{AC} = 0$.

Withdrawal Phase

In order to transfer v dollars from his or her personal account to the anonymous account acc_A, C first withdraws v dollars as follows:

1. C proves his or her identity to B, randomly selects r and ρ, computes the message $m = \mathcal{H}(acc_A, cnt_{AC}, r)$, and sends the blinded message $m' = Bl_v(\rho, m)$ together with v to B.
2. B debits C's personal account with v dollars, and returns the blinded signature $\sigma' = Sig_v(m')$.
3. C extracts the valid signature $\sigma_v = Ex_v(\rho, \sigma')$ of m.
4. C increments cnt_{AC} by one.

The signed message $m = \mathcal{H}(acc_A, cnt_{AC}, r)$ may be seen as an anonymous coin (like a metal coin). The fact that the message contains acc_A prevents anybody from paying the same anonymous coin into different anonymous accounts. This offers simultaneously a protection against loss or theft of anonymous coins. The counters cnt_{AC} and cnt_{AB} guarantee that the customer cannot deposit the same coin more than once in the same account.

Anonymous Deposit Phase

1. C sends acc_A, r, v and σ_v to B.
2. B computes $m = \mathcal{H}(acc_A, cnt_{AB}, r)$, using cnt_{AB} stored in the account data of account A, and checks the validity of the signature σ_v.
3. B pays v dollars into acc_A.
4. B increments cnt_{AB} by one.

To guarantee the acceptance of all deposits it is necessary that the anonymous electronic coins are deposited in the same order as they have been withdrawn, i.e. the customer has to deposit the coin containing the current value of cnt_{AB}.

Transaction Phase

We assume that the three parties communicate on-line, i.e. every communication between any two of them is heard by the third, and that C has to pay p dollars to the shop S.

1. C is identified by B through the knowledge of k_A as the owner of the anonymous account acc_A.
2. B debits acc_A with p dollars.
3. B pays p dollars into S's account.

The shop S who hears on-line the conversation between B and C knows that the requested payment has taken place, and the transaction between C and S can be completed.

Note that the protocol of the withdrawal phase can easily be modified to transfer money from an anonymous account to another.

It has often been argued that on-line systems are unpractical for technical reasons. This is true if searching in a large database has to be realized on-line. However, using current telecommunication technology, the connection itself between three entities, even if one of them (the bank B) is involved in each transaction, does not present an unsolvable problem. In fact, many existing EFTPOS systems use an on-line link between a bank (or a clearing center), a shop and a customer[8].

Our payment system assures the customer's anonymity, but not untraceability if the same anonymous account is used for several transactions. Complete untraceability is provided if every anonymous account is used only once.

4   Related Work

Let us compare our proposal with some previously proposed on-line payment systems.

The first secure anonymous payment system was described by Chaum in [4]. Let us recall the essential idea of this scheme:

1. **Withdrawal:** B provides C with a signature of a blinded coin. C extracts a valid signature of the coin.
2. **Payment and Deposit:** C presents the signed coin to S, which sends it directly to B, and B consults on-line a database to check whether the coin has not been spent up to now.

A blinded coin in [4] is comparable to a anonymous account used only once (to provide perfect untraceability) in our scheme. Both are indeed anonymous pieces of information used to credit the shop's account. However, there is an

---

[8] Note that in EFTPOS systems the connection is established between the bank and the shop, so the connection itself does not give information about the customer.

essential difference: in our proposal, the account number is chosen by the bank B during the anonymous account opening phase, while in [4] the generation of a blinded coin preceding the withdrawal does not necessitate the intervention of the bank.

This apparently subtle difference has an important practical consequence: our scheme requires the bank B to maintain only a list of open anonymous accounts, which can be interpreted (if the accounts are used only once) as a record of coins which have already been debited from some (personal) account, but have not been spent yet. Such a database can be expected to have a reasonable size.

Several variations on this first scheme have been presented in [6]. One of them, providing untraceability for a payer with a designated payee, presents similarities with the part of our proposal where the customer transfers money from his or her personal account to an anonymous account. However, the fact that in this part of our scheme the payer and the payee, corresponding to the same person, trust each other (what could not be assumed in [6]) allows to prevent a double deposit by introducing a sequence number. This considerably reduces the amount of data to be stored. Such a simple method would not be adequate in the general case [6].

In [2] Bürk and Pfitzmann proposed a payment system using so called standard values. A standard value may be seen as an anonymous account upon which a predefined value has been deposited. The owner of a standard value is known to the bank by a pseudonym. Payments are done by transferring the ownership of a standard value: the bank replaces the pseudonym of the payer (who was registered as the owner of the standard value) by the pseudonym of the payee (who is the new owner of the standard value). Such a payment is anonymous, but it is possible for the bank to link two transactions where the payee of the first transaction is the payer of the second. As suggested in [2], this problem could be solved using techniques described in [4] to change a pseudonym, but further modifications seem to be necessary in order to prevent double-spending. In our proposal, this problem is solved by the way money is transferred anonymously from one account to another.

5 Conclusions

The version of our system providing perfect untraceability, even if it appears to be more practical than previous proposals with similar characteristics, is not completely satisfactory since each transaction requires the opening of a new anonymous account. We believe that our scheme is particularly suited for a customer requiring anonymity (and not untraceability), because of its relative simplicity and its high flexibility. From a practical point of view, it is interesting to observe that the use of anonymous accounts allows intermediary levels of privacy protection, between the simple anonymity and the complete untraceability. It suffices indeed for the customer to have different anonymous accounts with the bank. Whenever he or she desires that two transactions remain unlinkable, two different anonymous accounts must be used.

Furthermore, the following facts might support the acceptance of this anonymous payment system:

- It is compatible with existing EFTPOS systems, since for the majority of them, a link to the bank (or a clearing center) is created when the customer is visiting the shop. This means that the three parties actually communicate on-line during the transaction. Furthermore, from the shop's viewpoint, it does not matter whether the customer is using a personal account or an anonymous account. A realization of this scheme would therefore neither require a modification of the communication system itself, nor the replacement of the shop's installation.
- It considers anonymity as an added-value service which may be requested by the customer. Its management (e.g. charging) is simplified by the fact that the payee does not have to modify its behaviour for an anonymous transaction.

Acknowledgment

The authors would like to thank U. Maurer and H.P. Frei for their support and the anonymous referee for valuable remarks.

References

1. S. Brands: Untraceable Off-line Cash in Wallets with Observers, *Advances in Cryptology, Crypto '93*, LNCS 773, Springer-Verlag, pp.302-318.
2. H. Bürk, A. Pfitzmann: Digital Payment Systems Enabling Security and Unobservability, *Computer & Security, 8 (1989)*, pp. 399-416
3. D. Chaum: Blind Signature Systems, *Advances in Cryptology, Crypto '83*, Plenum, p. 153.
4. D. Chaum: Security Without Identification: Transaction Systems to Make Big Brother Obsolete, Communications of the ACM, 28 (1985), pp. 1030-1044.
5. D. Chaum, A. Fiat, M. Naor: Untraceable Electronic Cash, *Advances in Cryptology, Crypto '88*, LNCS 403, Springer-Verlag, pp. 319-327.
6. D. Chaum: Privacy Protected Payment, SMART CARD 2000, Elsevier Science Publishers B.V. (North-Holland), 1989, pp. 69-93.
7. D. Chaum: Online Cash Checks, *Advances in Cryptology, Eurocrypt '89*, LNCS 434, Springer-Verlag, pp. 289-293.
8. D. Chaum, B. den Boer, E. van Heyst, S. Mjølsnes, A. Steenbeek: Efficient Offline Electronic Checks, *Advances in Cryptology, Eurocrypt '89*, LNCS 434, Springer-Verlag, 294-301.
9. D. Chaum, T. Pedersen: Wallet databases with observers, *Advances in Cryptology, Crypto '92*, LNCS 740, Springer-Verlag, pp. 89-105.
10. A. De Santis, G. Persiano: Communication Efficient Zero-Knowledge Proofs of Knowledge (with Applications to Electronic Cash), *Proceedings of STACS '92*, LNCS 577, Springer-Verlag, pp. 449-460.
11. N. Ferguson: Single Term Off-line Coins, *Advances in Cryptology, Eurocrypt '93*, LNCS 765, Springer-Verlag, pp. 318-328.

12. M. Franklin, M. Yung: Towards Provably Secure Efficient Electronic Cash, Columbia University, Dept. of Computer Science, TR CUSC-018-92, April 24, 1992.
13. T. Okamoto, K. Ohta: Disposable Zero-Knowledge Authentication and Their Application to Untraceable Electronic Cash, *Advances in Cryptology, Crypto '89*, LNCS 435, Springer-Verlag, pp. 134-149.
14. T. Okamoto, K. Ohta: Universal Electronic Cash, *Advances in Cryptology, Crypto '91*, LNCS 576, Springer-Verlag, pp. 324-337.

The ESPRIT Project **CAFE**
— High Security Digital Payment Systems —[†]

Jean-Paul Boly[1], Antoon Bosselaers[2], Ronald Cramer[3], Rolf Michelsen[4],
Stig Mjølsnes[4], Frank Muller[1], Torben Pedersen[5], Birgit Pfitzmann[6],
Peter de Rooij[1], Berry Schoenmakers[3], Matthias Schunter[6], Luc Vallée[7],
Michael Waidner[6,8]

Abstract. CAFE ("Conditional Access for Europe") is an ongoing project in the European Community's ESPRIT program. The goal of CAFE is to develop innovative systems for conditional access, and in particular, digital payment systems. An important aspect of CAFE is high security of all parties concerned, with the least possible requirements that they are forced to trust other parties (so-called multi-party security). This should give legal certainty to everybody at all times. Moreover, both the electronic money issuer and the individual users are less dependent on the tamper-resistance of devices than in usual digital payment systems. Since CAFE aims at the market of small everyday payments that is currently dominated by cash, payments are offline, and privacy is an important issue.

The basic devices used in CAFE are so-called electronic wallets, whose outlook is quite similar to pocket calculators or PDAs (Personal Digital Assistant). Particular advantages of the electronic wallets are that PINs can be entered directly, so that fake-terminal attacks are prevented. Other features are:

- Loss tolerance: If a user loses an electronic wallet, or the wallet breaks or is stolen, the user can be given the money back, although it is a prepaid payment system.
- Different currencies.
- Open architecture and system.

The aim is to demonstrate a set of the systems developed in one or more field trials at the end of the project. Note that these will be real hardware systems, suitable for mass production.

This paper concentrates on the basic techniques used in the CAFE protocols.

Keywords: Security in Applications (Financial); Security Versus other Requirements (Performance, Fault Tolerance).

[†] A preliminary version of this paper was presented at Securicom '94, Paris, June 1994 [BBCM 94].
[1] PTT Research, P.O. Box 421, NL-2260 AK Leidschendam, the Netherlands
[2] Katholieke Universiteit Leuven, Dept. Elektrotechniek E.S.A.T., Kardinaal Mercierlaan 94, B-3001 Heverlee, Belgium
[3] CWI, Kruislaan 413, NL-1098 SJ Amsterdam, the Netherlands
[4] SINTEF-DELAB, O.S. Bragstads Plass, N-7034 Trondheim, Norway
[5] Aarhus Universitet, Matematisk Institut, Ny Munkegade, DK-8000 Aarhus C, Denmark
[6] Universität Hildesheim, Institut für Informatik, Postfach 101363, D-31113 Hildesheim, Germany
[7] SEPT, 42 rue des Coutures, BP 6243, F-14066 Caen Cedex, France
[8] Universität Karlsruhe, Institut für Rechnerentwurf und Fehlertoleranz, Postfach, D-76128 Karlsruhe, Germany

1 The Project

1.1 Goals and Participants

CAFE ("Conditional Access for Europe") is a project in the European Community's program ESPRIT (Project 7023). Work on CAFE began in December 1992 and will probably be finished in December 1995. The consortium consists of groups for social and market studies (Cardware, Institut für Sozialforschung), software and hardware producers (DigiCash, Gemplus, Ingenico, Siemens), and designers of secure cryptographic protocols (CWI Amsterdam, PTT Research (NL), SEPT, Sintef Delab Trondheim, Universities of Århus, Hildesheim, and Leuven). The project coordinator is David Chaum for CWI.

The goal of CAFE is to develop innovative systems for conditional access, i.e., digital systems that administer certain rights of their users. The rights may be digital forms of passports, access to confidential data, entry to buildings, or — the most important example for CAFE — digital payment systems. A **digital payment system** is an information technology system for transferring money between its users. The market demands and the legal requirements of the member states of the European community on such systems are continuously studied by evaluations of existing comparable systems and by interviews with their users and experts from bank, consumer organizations, administrations, etc.

Within the project, the systems will actually be built, so that a realistic field trial can be carried out in the last year of the project.

1.2 Devices

The basic device for CAFE is an **electronic wallet.** This is a small portable computer, similar to a pocket calculator or a PDA (Personal Digital Assistant). It has its own battery, keyboard, and display, and its own means of communicating with other devices. In CAFE, the communication means will be an infrared channel. Every user of the system owns and uses her own wallet, which administers her rights and guarantees her security.

Particular advantages of the electronic wallets are that PINs can be entered directly, so that fake-terminal attacks are prevented. Furthermore, the users themselves agree on the amount paid by their device. This feature was considered very important by users in the surveys: They liked the secure feeling of not having to give their wallets into the hands of someone else, e.g., in a shop (which they would not do with their normal wallets containing cash either). They would also like to be able to look up their previous payments on the wallet.

In an application, there might be different types of wallets for users with different preferences. Compatibility is no problem because of the infrared communication. Luxury versions could combine the CAFE functions with those of a universal PDA, a mobile phone, or a notebook computer. Basic versions just contain the CAFE functions, and their keyboard only consists of a few buttons.

1.3 Basic Functionality

The basic CAFE system will be a prepaid offline payment system.

- **"Prepaid"** means that a user must buy so-called electronic money from an electronic money issuer and load it into her wallet before she can make payments.

- **"Offline"** means that no contact to a central database, usually at an electronic money issuer, is needed during a payment. The alternative, online payments, is far too costly for low-value payments because of the communication and the processing at the electronic money issuer.

This basic system is primarily intended for **payments** from wallets to POS (point-of-sale) terminals. Hence it allows just one transfer of the electronic money. This means that the payee must **deposit** the electronic money with an electronic money issuer before he can use it for his own payments (although he can, of course, locally verify that the electronic money is genuine, similar to traveler cheques).

Withdrawals of electronic money, i.e., loading it into an electronic wallet, are online transactions (usually against a debit to a normal bank account). They can be carried out from public ATM-like machines or from home terminals.

1.4 Additional Features

The basic CAFE system has the following additional features:

- **Different currencies**: It is both possible to store different currencies in the wallet and to exchange them during a payment.

- **Loss and fault tolerance**: If a user loses an electronic wallet, or the wallet breaks or gets stolen, the user can be given the money back (although it is a prepaid payment system!).

The basic CAFE system is an **open system** in many respects:

- Like cash, it is designed as a universal payment system: A user should be able to pay for arbitrary services by arbitrary service providers with her wallet. Examples are shopping, telephone, and public transport.

- Interoperability between any number of electronic money issuers is guaranteed (i.e., payments between clients of different electronic money issuers are possible). New electronic money issuers can join afterwards, and they can select some options according to their wishes.

- Only certain protocols are fixed, and not precise soft- and hardware components. Hence CAFE is open for new hardware platforms and can be integrated into other systems. The contactless communication is particularly useful here, and the system can also be used for payments over networks.

- No restrictions on the payers and payees need to be made, since the basic payment system is prepaid and of high security.

- Simple wallets can be cheap in mass production, and the use of both wallets and POS terminals can be simple. (The absolutely minimal version of a wallet displays the required amount to its user, and the user actively confirms that by pressing an "ok"-button on the wallet.) Thus from a practical point of view, too, nobody is excluded from the system.

2   The Special Security Goals of CAFE

The most important difference between the CAFE systems and other universal digital offline payment systems is in the very high security standards of CAFE. In this section, we explain the goals, and in the following section, we sketch the technical measures that make it possible to achieve all these goals simultaneously.

2.1   Multi-Party Security

Most existing digital payment systems are designed as systems with **one-sided security**: All participants have to rely on the trustworthiness of a single party, usually an electronic money issuer.

For payment systems, however, one-sided security is unsuitable, since it cannot offer legal certainty to any of the parties. For instance, let us consider ATMs (automatic teller machines): When a client uses her bank card at an ATM, her security is completely dependent on the trustworthiness of the bank: Everything she knows, the bank knows, too. Hence everything she can do, a dishonest bank insider can do, too. (There is nothing like a withdrawal order signed by the client that the bank had to store as a proof of transaction in conventional payment systems.) No court can decide whether a withdrawal was made by the client or such a fraudulent bank insider. Thus *neither* of the two parties "bank" and "client" has legal certainty about how a court would decide, and thus security from fraud by the other party.

Even if one accepts that at least some banks, as institutions, are more trustworthy than most clients, it does not change the situation: In this case, one would decide for the bank if it could prove by its internal security measures that insider fraud is impossible. However, it is currently highly improbable that any bank could show this to a satisfactory degree. On the one hand, many cases of insider fraud in spite of seemingly strong security measures have been reported [Ande 93, Neum 92]. On the other hand, the group of relevant insiders is just incalculably large: It comprises not only the bank employees, but also all those institutions and their employees who ever had anything to do with the design, production, installation, and maintenance of the hard- and software of the payment system.

If, on the other hand, courts would decide against the bank when in doubt, the banks would be completely insecure from dishonest clients.

To avoid such undecidable situations, the CAFE systems are designed as systems with **multi-party security** [Chau 85, PWP 90]: All security requirements of a party are guaranteed without forcing this party to trust other parties. In particular, mutual trust between parties with conflicting interests (like client and bank in the example) is not assumed. Ideally, a party only has to trust itself and the jurisdiction (and even the decision of a court can be verified). Multi-party security is beneficial for all parties:

- It increases legal certainty, since no undecidable situations as with one-sided security can occur. There is always enough evidence for an unambiguous decision.

- It decreases the security bottleneck of insider attacks.

- It makes the system more acceptable for potential users and is therefore a PR argument for the electronic money issuers.

Multi-party security has some implications on the design and manufacturing process as such (apart from the implications on the protocols described below):

- All designs (soft- and hardware) that are crucial for the security of a party must be available to this party for inspection. Hence secret algorithms are ruled out for CAFE (unless for internal procedures of the electronic money issuers).

- It must be ensured that parties can trust their own devices. Since most users can neither produce nor inspect their own wallets, there must be a sufficient number of competent and independent authorities that verify both the design and the devices themselves. The latter means that they verifies samples of the wallets as they are handed to the users, not near the manufacturer. Sufficient means that one can expect each user to trust at least one authority. Possible authorities are state-owned certification agencies, technical control boards like the German TÜV, and consumer organizations.

2.2   Data Protection

The CAFE payment systems are intended as mass systems for everyday use. Thus they should be particularly suited for frequent low-value payments, e.g., during the daily shopping, phone calls, and the use of public transport.

If one used, for instance, a credit card for each such payment, the credit card company would obtain an extensive profile of the user's behaviour. It would know where the user goes shopping at what time of the day (and maybe even what she buys), at what time she phones, where she goes by bus, etc. From the point of view of privacy, this is highly undesirable.

If one uses cash instead, the payer is **untraceable**: The coins used do not identify her, neither towards the payee nor towards the bank. Moreover, different payments of the same user are **unlinkable**, because one cannot see from two coins whether they were paid by the same person or not.

This form of untraceability is also desired for the users of the CAFE systems:

- In the basic CAFE system, the payee will be perfectly untraceable, i.e., neither the payee nor an electronic money issuer will learn the identity of the payer from the payment itself, and different payments are unlinkable [Chau 85].

- Just as with cash, this does not exclude that the payer is identified by other means, whether unintentionally or deliberately, e.g., by a cryptologic identification protocol.

In particular, one can fix an upper limit for the amounts that can be paid without identification. However, if all the security measures of the basic CAFE protocols are taken, this limit can be rather high, e.g., 2500 ECU, since the security of the electronic money issuer is independent of it.

Moreover, it will be useful to have an earlier limit beyond which payments must be online (e.g., 500 ECU), but are still untraceable, because that increases security for the electronic money issuers more, and does not infringe privacy.

- For payees, *no* untraceability is required. The reason is that the main use of CAFE will be purchases of goods or services from providers who are known to the payers anyway.

- In contrast to payments, withdrawals and deposits of electronic money are traceable, i.e., the client is identified towards an electronic money issuer.

The assumptions for privacy are the same as with the multi-party security against fraud: A user should not need to trust other parties for her untraceability.

Improved privacy is obviously beneficial to users, but also for electronic money issuers: On the one hand, it increases the acceptability of the system in the public and can therefore be a PR argument. On the other hand, it reduces the electronic money issuers' problem of keeping sensitive client data confidential, since there are not so many.

2.3 Loss and Fault Tolerance

For users, loss tolerance may be the most important special feature of the basic CAFE system. If a payer loses her wallet, or if it stops working or gets stolen, then with a usual prepaid system, she would lose all the money stored in the wallet. Loss tolerance means that she gets her money back.

3 Techniques

The most basic question is: how can one combine security for the electronic money issuer with offline payments, and moreover privacy and little trust in tamper-resistance? The question arises because electronic money is, after all, just bit strings. Hence even if a system is secure in the sense that users cannot produce new electronic money, i.e., new valid-looking bit strings, anybody who has seen such a bit string can copy it arbitrarily often and try to spend it more than once.

The optimal solution is as follows:

- As long as certain devices are tamper-resistant, it is completely impossible to spend electronic money more than once. This is called **strong integrity** for the electronic money issuers.

- Even if the tamper-resistance is *broken*, users who spend electronic money more than once are identified, and the fraud can be proved to them. (The only risk is then that the payer has disappeared or cannot pay the money back.)

- However, users need not trust those tamper-resistant devices (which must be provided by the electronic money issuers, whose security they protect, and whose interior the users naturally cannot verify) to protect their own security and privacy, too.

Note that online systems can achieve even more, namely that an attempt to spend electronic money more than once can be detected immediately by contact with a central database. This is why one usually fixes an upper limit on offline payments. Such online systems exist with full privacy [Chau 85, Chau 89, PWP 90].

We now consider the techniques used in such a solution one by one.

3.1   A Standard Measure: Digital Signatures Throughout

One standard measure that must be applied in many places in a payment system with multi-party security is digital signatures [DiHe 76, GoMR 88]. Such schemes simulate handwritten signatures for digital messages and are indispensable for systems with multi-party security.

Although we assume that most readers know what digital signature schemes are and some important constructions, such as RSA and the Schnorr scheme [RSA 78, Schn 91], so that we do not go into details, it has to be stressed that symmetric authentication schemes (often called MAC, *Message Authentication Code*, and based, e.g., on DES) are unsuitable as replacements for handwritten signatures as a matter of principle: The person who "signs" and the person who "tests" have the same keys, and thus a third party, such as a court, can never decide which of the two produced a certain authenticated message. Thus the recipient of an authenticated message cannot use it as credible evidence against the sender.

Note that every message of legal significance must be signed in a payment system to provide legal certainty. In particular, the wallet must send a signed order to withdraw electronic money to the electronic money issuer, and payees must get signed receipts for deposited money. Furthermore, the initialization of wallets must ensure that secrets used for generating signatures are not known to any other party.

3.2   Tamper-Resistant Devices: Guardians

The tamper-resistant devices that protect the electronic money issuers against double-spending of electronic money must be in the wallets of the payers: Since payments are off-line, this is the only place where any attempt to spend the same money twice can be noticed. However, since the users are not supposed to trust the same devices, they are not "the wallets" themselves. Hence they are called **guardians**. In CAFE, the guardian is a smartcard chip with a crypto processor that is placed inside a wallet [Weik 93, GuUQ 92]. The guardian can either be fixed in the wallet or mounted on a smartcard, so that it can be exchanged — the CAFE protocols work with both these hardware platforms. In the field trial of CAFE, the guardian will have a Siemens crypto processor [BaPe 94].

How Wallets and Guardians Work Together

Since the owner of the wallet is not supposed to trust the electronic money issuer's guardian inside it, the guardian is not allowed to communicate with other devices on its own: It is only allowed to communicate via the wallet, and the wallet checks and suitably modifies the messages the guardian sends and receives.

This scenario where a wallet protects the interests of a user, and a guardian inside protects the interests of an electronic money issuer (or other service provider) was first presented in [Chau 92, ChPe 93, CrPe 94].

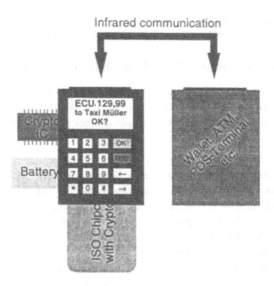

Figure 1   One hardware platform for a wallet-and-guardian protocol: The wallet is the bigger device with the keyboard and display; the guardian has been mounted on a smartcard and is inserted into the wallet. The guardian can only communicate directly with the wallet, and the wallet takes over the communication with the outside world via its infrared link.

How Guardians Protect the Electronic Money Issuer

The guardian can protect the electronic money issuer, because no transaction will be possible without its cooperation. In particular, no payment is accepted unless the guardian gives its okay, and for each unit of electronic money, the guardian gives its okay only once. The okay is something like a signature by the guardian, but a very restricted version from which neither the payee nor the electronic money issuer can derive which guardian made it, nor any other information about the payer. Details can be seen below when more about the protocols has been described.

3.3 Fall-Back Security: Cryptologic Protection

In this subsection, we describe the ideas for the fall-back security that is still guaranteed even if a user *breaks* the guardian. Breaking usually means reading out secret data, such as the keys the guardian uses to give its okay to transactions. Note that it does not matter if the guardian is destroyed in this process, because the user could build new fake guardians with the same secret information, and those would give their okay to incorrect transactions.

Of course, everybody hopes that smartcard chips will resist such attacks, but finally, it depends on the resources of a particular attacker. Hence the CAFE protocols provide a fall-back service for the electronic money issuer, where even in the unfortunate case where a guardian is broken, a user who uses this guardian to spend more money than allowed will be identified, and the identity of the user whose guardian was used for this fraud can be proved. (Note that it is necessary for multi-party security that the identity is not just found out, but proved, so that such a case could be handled in court.)

Since this protection for the electronic money issuer is not by tamper-resistant devices, it must be by **cryptologic protocols**.

Such payment systems where honest users have privacy, while double-spenders are identified, were first described in [ChFN 90]. More efficient variants were developed in, e.g., [FrYu 93, Bran 93, Ferg 94, Bran 94]. They are called **electronic offline coin** systems. Originally, they are all for a scenario with user-owned wallets only, without guardians. This is natural, since even in our scenario, we only need these protocols when the guardians are broken and thus no more protections for the electronic money issuer than the user's wallet.

We will now explain these protocols, starting with the basic primitives and working upwards until guardians are added again.

The Cryptologic Primitive: Blind Signatures

Payments where payers are untraceable all rely on **blind signature** schemes [Chau 85]. Here, signing is a protocol between two parties, the signer and the recipient. As a result of the protocol, the recipient obtains a message with a signature from the signer. The message, however, is *unknown* to the signer (thus "blind"), but the signer may be guaranteed that it has a certain form. Efficient constructions of blind signatures exist for RSA [Chau 85, Ferg 94] and the Schnorr signature scheme [ChPe 93].

The typical use of blind signatures in payment systems is as follows [Chau 85]: Electronic money is represented by messages of a certain form, which are signed by the electronic money issuer. Such signed messages are called *electronic coins*. The message signed is called the *coin number*. During withdrawal, the electronic money issuer's device makes a blind signature on a message unknown to the issuer, but of appropriate form. Thus the client obtains one electronic coin (and only one!), but the electronic money issuer does not know what it looks like. Hence, when a payee later deposits this electronic coin, the electronic money issuer cannot recognize it and therefore does not know which payer went shopping at this payee. This makes the payment untraceable (among all payments with electronic coins of the same denomination).

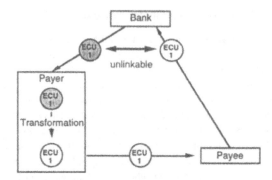

Figure 2   Basic payment system with blind signatures

"Off-Line Coins"

As describe so far, the system with blind signatures was only suitable for online payments: It guarantees that clients cannot produce new coins, but to guarantee that each coin is only spent once, a central database of spent coins (for coins from a certain electronic money issuer and issue period) must be queried.

The idea for off-line payments in [ChFN 90] is as follows: The identity of the payer is encoded into the coin number. (The blind signature protocol can guarantee, by something like a zero-knowledge proof, that the coin number is of a certain form, and this encoding of the identity will be the form required.) When a coin is used in a payment, the payer must divulge parts of the coding of the identity to the payee. If the same coin were used in two payments, the payer would have to divulge two different parts of the coding (with very high probability). Now the coding is constructed in such a way that from two parts, the identity can be found out, whereas one part alone does not give any information about the identity.

A simple version of such a coding, used in [ChFN 90], is that the identity I is encrypted perfectly with a one-time pad P, and the coin explicitly contains two parts. In one of them, the encrypted identity, $I \oplus P$, is contained, and in the other, the key P. Each part is further hidden with a commitment scheme, i.e., an encryption scheme with the following additional property: Nobody can find two keys such that the same ciphertext can be decrypted as two different messages with these two keys. Thus our coin number is constructed from two commitments $C(I \oplus P)$ and $C(P)$. In one payment, the payer will have to open one of the commitments, and the content will be either only $I \oplus P$ or only P, which does not say anything about the identity. If, however, the other part has to be opened in another payment, the identity is found out.

In order to detect such cheating payers, each electronic money issuer must store all deposited coins for a certain time and search for pairs. This can be done in parallel with the usual clearing between different issuers.

This should give an idea how this sort of system works — describing the full system is beyond the scope of this paper. Note that in the basic form we presented, the probability that the payee is found out would only be $1/2$ in two payments, and a payer and a payee together could cheat. All this is taken care of in the full system. Much more efficient versions were described in [FrYu 93, Bran 93, Ferg 94, Bran 94].

Furthermore, some additional signatures are hidden in the payment protocols: On the one hand, the wallet signs to whom it pays a coin (thus, only the intended payee can deposit the coin). On the other hand, if the pure identity were contained in a coin, it would prove nothing if one found it out — anybody could have constructed such a coin. Instead, there is a kind of signature hidden that only the payer could have constructed.

The CAFE protocols are based on the system from [Bran 93, Bran 94], but with some modifications.

Adding a Guardian

If the "off-line coin" systems are combined with a guardian, the guardian prevents that an electronic coin is spent twice, as long as it is unbroken. To do this, the coins are not given to the wallet alone in a withdrawal. Instead, one part is held by the wallet, and another part by the guardian. These parts together form the secret key needed to sign the spending of a coin. The electronic money issuer can ensure that the guardian is in fact involved by requiring something like a signature of the guardian that it holds a part of this secret key, where the key is identified by a one-way image.

All this is more complicated because the messages from the wallet to the electronic money issuer are not allowed to carry any secret information, i.e., the wallet must ensure that there is no covert channel between the guardian and the electronic money issuer. Hence all the messages are transformed in transit. The first such protocols were described in [Chau 92, ChPe 93, Bran 93, Ferg1 94, Bran 94].

Efficiency Improvements

So far, we described a system that resembled cash coins in the following respect, too: An amount to be paid will usually be paid with a combination of electronic coins of certain fixed denominations. This is the solution with optimal security and privacy in the long run, but for current smartcard chips it is a bit hard. Moreover, one has the problem of change, which is non-trivial in a system which distinguishes payers (clients with wallets) and payees (POS terminals).

Hence CAFE uses a mixture of several additional measures. Two related approaches are known from [OkOh 92, Ferg1 94]: One can construct coins that can be split into smaller amounts if necessary (e.g., an 8-ECU coin into one 4-ECU coin and two 2-ECU coins), or coins that can be spent more than once (e.g., one would pay 8 ECU for a 1-ECU coin that the guardian and the cryptologic measures allow to spend 8 times). These measures reduce the unlinkability of payments, but not the integrity.

A different measures is known from [BoCh 90]. It corresponds to the use of cheques instead of coins in the following sense: The amount is only entered to the "electronic coin" and signed during the payment. Now the guardian has to keep a counter of the money that is still there, and it will only play its part in signing during payments if the cheque is written out up to this amount. This measure decreases the cryptologic fall-back security for the electronic money issuer in case the guardian is broken.

3.4   Loss and Fault Tolerance

For users, loss tolerance may be the most important special feature of the basic CAFE system. With a usual prepaid system, a payer who lost her wallet would lose all the money stored in the wallet. The same would happen if the wallet stopped working or got stolen. Loss tolerance means that she gets her money back.

The basic idea for loss tolerance is to keep a backup of the user's electronic money somewhere outside the wallet [WaPf 90, WaPf 91]. This backup must not infringe the privacy of the payer, hence it must be on a backup card of the user or in encrypted form at her electronic money issuer. If a user loses her wallet, the backup is evaluated in cooperation of the user and the electronic money issuer: The electronic money is reconstructed, and that part of it that has not yet been spent is credited to the user's account. What has been spent (usually between the last withdrawal and the loss) can be detected by comparing the reconstructed electronic money with the deposits. Note that the backups do not infringe the security of the electronic money issuer either: The user cannot use the copy of the electronic money in payments, since there is no guardian to give its okay to such a transaction.

In the optimal case, a user gets all the lost money back. One factor limit loss tolerance, however:

- If a lost or stolen wallet can be used *without* user identification, such as a PIN, the owner cannot get the money back that the finder or thief of the wallet spends. (But if the wallet was just broken, the money can be given back.) To limit this loss, one has to limit the amount that can be spent without intermediate entry of a PIN.

For this purpose, CAFE will offer optional payment PINs. (Withdrawals are protected with PINs anyway.) The users are urged to choose their payment PIN different from their withdrawal PIN, because payment PINs are more likely to be observed. If a user cannot remember two PINs, it is still better to have an easy to remember payment PIN or to write it down somewhere than to have none at all. (The withdrawal PIN, in contrast, must be kept more secure.)

The use of the payment PINs will be very flexible: They can be used either during a payment or for unlocking a certain amount *before* one or more payments. This is useful since the payment itself may have to be done in a hurry or in a place where the PIN could be observed too easily. The user can also lock the amount again.

Apart from tolerating losses or faults of complete wallets, the system also tolerates interruptions of individual transactions, either because the communication is interrupted or because one of the devices breaks down or loses power during this transaction (unintentionally or deliberately).

3.5   Phone Ticks

The basic CAFE protocols contain special measures for paying phone ticks, i.e., many payments of very small amounts to the same payee in very fast succession. Since there is no reason to require unlinkability of the payments of the individual ticks, they are all parts of the same coin in a special way.

4 Outlook

Until mid 1994, the end of the first half of the project, the work on CAFE concentrated on market and social studies, the design of the basic CAFE system, and preparations for the actual implementation. A software package demonstrating the CAFE features is already available*.

The second half of the project starts with the implementation, in particular of the hardware components. In particular, Gemplus wallets and smartcard(chip)s with Siemens crypto processors will be used. Then a field trial can follow. It will be accompanied by studies of user reactions.

In parallel, the time will be used for further developments in the design of the basic CAFE system and the development of other conditional access systems on the basis of CAFE wallets and guardians.

Acknowledgment

This presentation of the project (by the secure protocols group) is based on [Waid 94, WaWe 94]. We also thank the other partners in the project for their share of the work.

References

Ande 93   Ross Anderson: Why Cryptosystems Fail; 1st ACM Conference on Computer and Communications Security, acm Press, New York 1993, 215-227.

BaPe 94   Peter Bauer, Heribert Peuckert: Chipkarten mit Kryptographie erschließen neue Anwendungsfelder; Siemens-Zeitschrift Special, FuE, Frühjahr 1994, 17-20.

BBCM 94   Jean-Paul Boly, Antoon Bosselaers, Ronald Cramer, Rolf Michelsen, Stig Mjølsnes, Frank Muller, Torben Pedersen, Birgit Pfitzmann, Peter de Rooij, Berry Schoenmakers, Matthias Schunter, Luc Vallée, Michael Waidner: Digital Payment Systems in the ESPRIT Project CAFE; Proc. of Securicom '94, Paris, June 1994.

BoCh 90   Jurjen Bos, David Chaum: SmartCash: a Practical Electronic Payment System; Centrum voor Wiskunde en Informatica, Computer Science/Departement of Algorithmics and Architecture, Report CS-R9035, August 1990.

Bran 93   Stefan Brands: An Efficient Off-line Electronic Cash System Based On The Representation Problem; Centrum voor Wiskunde en Informatica, Computer Science/Departement of Algorithmics and Architecture, Report CS-R9323, March 1993.

Bran 94   Stefan Brands: Untraceable Off-line Cash in Wallets with Observers; Crypto '93, LNCS 773, Springer-Verlag, Berlin 1994, 302-318.

Chau 85   David Chaum: Security without Identification: Transaction Systems to make Big Brother Obsolete; Communications of the ACM 28/10 (1985) 1030-1044.

Chau 89   David Chaum: Privacy Protected Payments – Unconditional Payer and/or Payee Untraceability; SMART CARD 2000: The Future of IC Cards, Proceedings of the IFIP WG 11.6 International Conference; Laxenburg (Austria), 19.-20. 10. 1987, North-Holland, Amsterdam 1989, 69-93.

Chau 92   David Chaum: Achieving Electronic Privacy; Scientific American (August 1992) 96-101.

ChFN 90   David Chaum, Amos Fiat, Moni Naor: Untraceable Electronic Cash; Crypto '88, LNCS 403, Springer-Verlag, Berlin 1990, 319-327.

ChPe 93   David Chaum, Torben Pryds Pedersen: Wallet Databases with Observers; Crypto '92, LNCS 740, Springer Verlag, Berlin 1993, 89-105.

---

*   Please contact Ray Hirschfeld, CWI, Phone +31 20 592 4049, e-mail cafe@cwi.nl.

CrPe 94   Ronald J. F. Cramer, Torben Pryds Pedersen: Improved Privacy in Wallets with Observers
           (Extended Abstract); Eurocrypt '93, LNCS 765, Springer-Verlag, Berlin 1994, 329-343.

DiHe 76   Whitfield Diffie, Martin E. Hellman: New Directions in Cryptography; IEEE Transactions on
           Information Theory 22/6 (1976) 644-654.

Ferg 94   Niels Ferguson: Single Term Off-Line Coins; Eurocrypt '93, LNCS 765, Springer-Verlag,
           Berlin 1994, 318-328.

Ferg1 94   Niels Ferguson: Extensions of Single-Term Coins; Crypto '93, LNCS 773, Springer-Verlag,
           Berlin 1994, 292-301.

FrYu 93   Matthew Franklin, Moti Yung: Secure and Efficient Off-Line Digital Money; 20th International
           Colloquium on Automata, Languages and Programming (ICALP), LNCS 700, Springer-Verlag,
           Heidelberg 1993, 265-276.

GoMR 88   Shafi Goldwasser, Silvio Micali, Ronald L. Rivest: A Digital Signature Scheme Secure
           Against Adaptive Chosen-Message Attacks; SIAM J. Comput. 17/2 (1988) 281-308.

GuUQ 92   Louis Claude Guillou, Michel Ugon, Jean-Jacques Quisquater: The Smart Card: A Standardized
           Security Device Dedicated to Public Cryptology; Gustavus J. Simmons: Contemporary
           Cryptology – The Science of Information Integrity; IEEE Press, Hoes Lane 1992, 561-613.

Neum 92   Peter G. Neumann: Inside Risks: Fraud by computers; Communications of the ACM 35/8
           (1992), 154.

OkOh 92   Tatsuaki Okamoto, Kazuo Ohta: Universal Electronic Cash; Crypto '91, LNCS 576, Springer
           Verlag, Berlin 1992, 324-337.

PWP 90   Birgit Pfitzmann, Michael Waidner, Andreas Pfitzmann: Rechtssicherheit trotz Anonymität in
           offenen digitalen Systemen; Datenschutz und Datensicherung DuD 14/5-6 (1990) 243-253, 305-
           315.

RSA 78   R. L. Rivest, A. Shamir, L. Adleman: A Method for Obtaining Digital Signatures and Public-
           Key Cryptosystems; Communications of the ACM 21/2 (1978) 120-126, reprinted: 26/1 (1983)
           96-99.

Schn 91   C.P. Schnorr: Efficient Signature Generation by Smart Cards; Journal of Cryptology 4/3 (1991)
           161-174.

Waid 94   Michael Waidner: CAFE – Conditional Access for Europe; 4. GMD-SmartCard Workshop, 8.-
           9. Februar 1994, GMD Darmstadt; Multicard '94, Berlin, 23.-25. Februar 1994.

WaPf 90   Michael Waidner, Birgit Pfitzmann: Loss-Tolerance for Electronic Wallets; Proceedings 20th
           International Symposium on Fault-Tolerant Computing (FTCS 20), Newcastle upon Tyne
           (UK), 140-147.

WaPf 91   Michael Waidner, Birgit Pfitzmann: Loss-tolerant electronic wallet; David Chaum (ed.): Smart
           Card 2000, Selected Papers from the Second International Smart Card 2000 Conference, North-
           Holland, Amsterdam 1991, 127-150.

WaWe 94   Michael Waidner, Arnd Weber: Europäisches Industrie- und Forschungskonsortium entwickelt
           neuartiges Zahlungsverfahren; will be published in: Datenschutz-Berater, 1994.

Weik 93   Franz Weikmann: Chipkarten – Entwicklungsstand und weitere Perspektiven; PIK, Praxis der
           Informationsverarbeitung und Kommunikation 16/1 (1993) 28-34.

Liability and Computer Security: Nine Principles

Ross J Anderson
Cambridge University Computer Laboratory
Email: rja14@cl.cam.ac.uk

Abstract. The conventional wisdom is that security priorities should be set by risk analysis. However, reality is subtly different: many computer security systems are at least as much about shedding liability as about minimising risk. Banks use computer security mechanisms to transfer liability to their customers; companies use them to transfer liability to their insurers, or (via the public prosecutor) to the taxpayer; and they are also used to shift the blame to other departments ("we did everything that GCHQ/the internal auditors told us to"). We derive nine principles which might help designers avoid the most common pitfalls.

Introduction

In the conventional model of technology, there is a smooth progression from research through development and engineering to a product. After this is fielded, the experience gained from its use provides feedback to the research team, and helps drive the next generation of products:

$$\text{RESEARCH} \rightarrow \text{DEVELOPMENT} \rightarrow \text{ENGINEERING} \rightarrow \text{PRODUCT}$$

This cycle is well known, and typically takes about ten years. However, the product's failure modes may not be immediately apparent, and may even be deliberately concealed; in this case it may be several more years before litigation comes into the cycle. This is what happened with the asbestos and tobacco industries; many other examples could be given.

$$\text{RESEARCH} \rightarrow \text{DEVELOPMENT} \rightarrow \text{ENGINEERING} \rightarrow \text{PRODUCT} \rightarrow \text{LITIGATION}$$

Now many computer security systems and products are designed to achieve some particular legal result. Digital signatures, for example, are often recommended on the grounds that they are the only way in which an electronic document can be made acceptable to the courts. It may therefore be of interest that some of the first court cases involving cryptographic evidence have recently been decided, and in this paper we try to distil some of the practical wisdom which can be gleaned from them.

Civilian Uses of Cryptography

Cryptography was originally a preserve of governments; military and diplomatic organisations used it to keep messages secret. Recently, however, cryptographic mechanisms have been incorporated in a wide range of commercial systems. Automatic teller machines (ATMs) were the pioneers, and much of commercial cryptology was developed in the late 1970's and early 1980's in order to tackle the real or perceived security problems of ATM systems [MM].

This technology has since been applied to many other systems, such as lottery terminals, prepayment electricity meters, satellite and cable TV decoders, burglar alarms, membership cards, access control devices and road toll tokens. Most of these devices use cryptography to make the substitution of bogus tokens more difficult, and thus protect revenue or assets; with millions of them being sold every year, it was inevitable that the courts would sooner or later have to assess the evidence they can provide, and this is now starting to happen.

Since early 1992, we have advised in a number of cases involving disputed withdrawals from ATMs. These now include five criminal and three civil cases in Britain, two civil cases in Norway, and one civil and one criminal case in the USA. Since ATMs have been in use the longest, and are an obvious target of crime, it is not surprising that the first real legal tests of cryptographic evidence should have arisen in this way.

All our cases had a common theme of reliance by one side on claims about cryptography and computer security; in many cases the bank involved said that since its PINs were generated and verified in secure cryptographic hardware, they could not be known to any member of its staff and thus any disputed withdrawals must be the customer's fault.

However, these cases have shown that such sweeping claims do not work, and in the process have undermined some of the assumptions made by commercial computer security designers for the past fifteen years.

At the engineering level, they provided the first detailed threat model for commercial computer security systems; they showed that almost all frauds are due to blunders in application design, implementation and operation [A1]: the main threat is not the cleverness of the attacker, but the stupidity of the system builder. At the technical level, we should be much more concerned with robustness [A2], and we have shown how robustness properties can be successfully incorporated into fielded systems in [A3].

However, there is another lesson to be learned from the "phantom withdrawal" cases, which will be our concern here. This is that many security systems are really about liability rather than risk; and failure to understand this has led to many computer security systems turning out to be useless.

Using Cryptography in Evidence

We will first look at evidence; here it is well established that a defendant has the right to examine every link in the chain of evidence against him.

- One of the first cases was R v Hendy at Plymouth Crown Court. One of Norma Hendy's colleagues had a phantom withdrawal from her bank account, and as the staff at this company used to take turns going to the cash machine for each other, the victim's PIN was well known. Of the many suspects, Norma was arrested and charged for no good reason other than that the victim's purse had been in her car all day (even although this fact was widely known and the car was unlocked).
  She denied the charge vigorously; and the bank said in its evidence that the alleged withdrawal could not possibly have been made except with the card and PIN issued to the victim. This was untrue, as both theft by bank staff using extra cards, and card forgery by outsiders were known to affect this bank's customers. We therefore demanded disclosure of the bank's security manuals, audit reports and so on; the bank refused, and Norma was acquitted.
- Almost exactly the same happened in the case R v De Mott at Great Yarmouth. Philip De Mott was a taxi driver, who was accused of stealing £50 from a colleague after she had had a phantom withdrawal. His employers did not believe that he could be guilty, and applied for his bail terms to allow him to keep working for them. Again, the bank claimed that its systems were secure; again, when the evidence was demanded, it backed down and the case collapsed.

Now even the banks admit an error rate of 1 in 34,000 for ATM systems [M], and it follows that a country like Britain with 10^9 ATM transactions a year will have 30,000 phantom withdrawals and other miscellaneous malfunctions; if 10,000 of these are noticed by the victims, and the banks deny liability, then perhaps a few hundred cases will be referred to the police. Even though the police often 'file and forget' difficult cases (especially where small sums are involved and there has been no physical injury to anyone), it is not surprising that we have seen a handful of dubious prosecutions each year.

Thankfully, there now exists a solid defence. This is to demand that the Crown Prosecution Service provide a full set of the bank's security and quality documentation, including security policies and standards, crypto key management procedures and logs, audit and insurance inspectors' reports, test and bug reports, ATM balancing records and logs, and details of all customer complaints in the last seven years. The UK courts have so far upheld the rights of both criminal defendants [RS] and civil plaintiffs [MB] to this material, despite outraged protest from the banks. It is our experience that when this disclosure is granted in time, then it is highly likely that the bank will withdraw its cooperation and the case will collapse.

Of course, this defence works whether or not the defendant is actually guilty, and the organised crime squad at Scotland Yard has expressed concern that the inability of banks to support computer records could seriously hinder police operations.

In a recent trial in Bristol, for example, two men who were accused of conspiring to defraud a bank by card forgery threatened to call a banking industry expert to say that the crimes they had planned could not possibly have succeeded [RLN]. If this had been believed, then they might well have been acquitted; it is not an offence to conspire to do something which is physically impossible.

However, a journalist from a Sunday newspaper helped us to destroy this ingenious defence; after we had told her the principle of the proposed attack (but not any details), she managed to successfully alter an ATM card issued by that bank, and thus discredit the defence expert [L]. Indeed, the information we gave her was available in a document which circulated widely in the UK prison system [S] and of which the defence expert should have been aware.

Thus the first (and probably most important) lesson is this:

> **Principle 1:** Security systems which are to provide evidence must be designed and certified on the assumption that they will be examined in detail by a hostile expert.

This should have been obvious to anybody who stopped to think about the matter, yet for many years nobody in the industry (including the author) did so. Thanks to the difficulty of getting legal aid to cover expert witnesses' fees, it is only recently that such cases have started to be well fought.

These contests could have wider implications, as many banking sector crypto suppliers also sell equipment to governments. Have their military clients stopped to assess the damage which could be done if a mafioso's lawyers, embroiled in a dispute over a banking transaction, raid the design lab at six in the morning and, armed with a court order, take away all the schematics and source code they can find? Pleading national security does not work - in a recent case, lawyers staged just such a dawn raid against Britain's biggest defence electronics firm, in order to find out how many PCs were running unlicensed software.

Using the Right Threat Model

Another problem is that many designers fail to realise that most security failures occur as a result application and management blunders, and rather than concentrating on producing a well engineered system they may instead pin their faith on some particular 'silver bullet'. This might be some new cryptographic algorithm or protocol, a delivery mechanism such as a smartcard, or a set of standards such as ITSEC.

This is illustrated by a current ATM dispute in Norway. Norwegian banks spent millions on issuing all their customers with smartcards, and are now as certain as British banks (at least in public) that no debit can appear on a customer's account without the actual card and PIN issued to the customer being used. Yet a number of phantom withdrawals around the University of Trondheim have undermined their position.

In these cases, cards were stolen from offices on campus and used in ATMs and shops in the town; among the victims are highly credible witnesses who are quite certain that their PINs could not have been compromised. The banks refused to pay up, and have been backed up by the central bank and the local banking ombudsman; yet the disputed transactions (about which the bank was so certain) violated the card cycle limits. Although only NOK 5000 should have been available from ATMs and NOK 6000 from eftpos, the thief managed somehow to withdraw NOK 18000 (the extra NOK 7000 was refunded without any explanation) [BN].

This problem with the card cycle limit makes it clear that there was a problem with the application software. Now the victim cannot reasonably be expected to establish whether this problem lies in the card, in the reader, in the network, in the settlement system, or in the bank branch; it might even lie in the manual procedures for card and PIN issue or in some subtle combination. What is known is that blunders are common in the design of large systems, and many examples of unexpected application programming and management failures were noted in our technical survey of ATM crime [A1] [A2].

This survey showed that the real threat model for payment systems is that blunders get exploited in an opportunistic way. Although military intelligence agencies may have the experts and the money to carry out technical attacks on algorithms and operating systems, most crime is basically opportunist, and most criminals are both unskilled and undercapitalised; thus most of their opportunities come from the victim's mistakes. This threat model has since been further confirmed by a study of attacks on prepayment electricity meter systems [AS]; here too, security failures resulted from blunders in design and management, which some subscribers found ways to exploit.

Principle 2: Expect the real problems to come from blunders in the application design and in the way the system is operated.

Security Goals

It may seem by now that disputed transaction cases will be lost by whichever party has to bear the burden of proof. Where the customer says, "I didn't make that withdrawal", and the bank says "You did so", then what is the court to do? If the victim is supposed to find exactly where the fault lies in the bank's system, then it is very unlikely that she will succeed. If, on the other hand, the bank is asked to establish the security of its systems, then how can this be done in the face of hostile experts?

Here it is instructive to compare the practice in Britain with that in the United States. British banks claim that their systems are infallible, in that it is not possible for an ATM debit to appear on someone's account unless the card and PIN issued to him had been used in that ATM. People who complain are therefore routinely told that they must be lying, or mistaken, or the victim of fraud by a friend or relative (in which case they must be negligent). There has recently been a cosmetic change, with the introduction of a new code of banking practice; in this, the banks say that the onus is now on them. However, when confronted with a phantom withdrawal, they consider this onus to be discharged by a statement that their computer systems were working and that no known frauds were taking place at the relevant time and place.

The US is totally different; there, in the landmark court case Judd v Citibank [JC], Dorothy Judd claimed that she had not made a number of ATM withdrawals which Citibank had debited to her account; Citibank claimed that she must have done. The judge ruled that Citibank was wrong in law to claim that its systems were infallible, as this placed 'an unmeetable burden of proof' on the plaintiff. Since then, if a US bank customer disputes an electronic debit, the bank must refund the money within 30 days, unless it can prove that the claim is an attempted fraud.

British bankers claim that such a policy would be utterly disastrous; if they paid up whenever a customer complained, there would be an avalanche of fraudulent claims of fraud. But US bankers are more relaxed; their practical experience is that the annual loss due to customer misrepresentation is only about $15,000 per bank [W1], and this will not justify any serious computer security programme. In areas like New York and Los Angeles where risks are higher, banks use ATM cameras to resolve disputes.

Another unexpected finding was the relationship between risk and security investment. One might expect that as US banks are liable for fraudulent transactions, they would spend more on security than British banks do; but our research showed that precisely the reverse is the case: while UK banks and building societies now use hardware security modules to manage PINs, most US banks just encrypt PINs in software.

Thus we conclude that the real function of these hardware security modules is due diligence rather than security. British bankers want to be able to point to their security modules when fighting customer claims, while US bankers, who can only get the advertised security benefit from these devices, generally do not see any point in buying them. Given that the British strategy did not work - no-one has yet been able to construct systems which bear hostile examination - it is quite unclear that these devices add any real value at all.

Now, one of the principles of good protocol engineering is that one should never use encryption without understanding what it is for (keeping a key secret, binding two values together, ...) [AN]. This generalises naturally to the following:

> **Principle 3:** Before setting out to build a computer security system, make sure you understand what its real purpose is (especially if this differs from its advertised purpose).

Where there is a hidden purpose, designers should be aware of a possible problem with the rules of evidence. In the USA, computer records are usually only admissible if they are made in the normal course of business; so using the computer for an abnormal purpose can render its output useless [W2]. In the UK, too, a court has thrown out ATM evidence which was obtained by a nonstandard manipulation of the system [RS].

Shifting the Blame

The most common reason for a system to have a real purpose which differs substantially from its advertised purpose is, of course, when the system owner wishes to avoid the blame when things go wrong.

In the software industry, for example, it is standard practice to offer an installation service, whereby the vendor will send a technician to install the latest upgrade for a substantial fee. Most users save the money by installing the upgrades themselves - and in so doing lose much of their ability to sue the vendor if their files get corrupted. It is also standard practice that bespoke software houses get clients to sign off every tiny specification change before it is coded and implemented - and again, this is not so much for change control and security purposes, but to make it much harder for the poor client to sue.

Things become even more problematic when one of the parties to a dispute can use market power, legal intimidation or political influence to shed liability. There are many examples of this:

1. We recently helped to evaluate the security of a burglar alarm system which is used to protect bank vaults in over a dozen countries. The vendor had claimed for years that the alarm signaling was encrypted; in Europe, this is a requirement for class 4 risks (over $10m) and recommended for class 3 risks ($250,000 to $10m) [B1]. We found that the few manipulations performed to disguise the data could not in fairness be called 'encryption' - they could not be expected to withstand even an amateur attack. The vendor's response was to try and intimidate our client into suppressing the report

2. We have mentioned some of the tricks that software houses employ; and within organisations, similar strategies are commonplace. One can expect that managers will implement just enough computer security to avoid blame for any disaster; if possible, they will ask for guidance from the internal auditors, or some other staff function, in order to diffuse the liability

3. If there is no internal scapegoat, a company may hire consultants to draw up a security specification. Members of the academic security community

often complain that so many lucrative consulting contracts go to large, well-known consultancy firms, who often do not possess their technical skills; the dynamics of blame shifting may provide an insight into the relative merits of fame and competence when purchasing security consultancy services

4. If liability cannot be transferred to the state, to suppliers, to another department, or to consultants, then managers may attempt to transfer it to customers - especially if the business is a monopoly or cartel. Utilities are notorious for refusing to entertain disputes about billing system errors; and many banking disputes also fall into this category.

> **Principle 4:** Understand how liability is transferred by any system you build or rely on.

The Limitations of Legal Process

In the world of academic cryptography, it is common to assume that the law works with the precision and reliability of the theory of numbers. Conference papers often say things like "and so Alice raises X to the power Y, and presents it to the judge, who sees that it is equal to Z and sends Bob to jail".

Would that the world were that simple! Even if we have a robust system with a well designed and thoroughly tested application, we are still not home and dry; and conversely, if we suffer as a result of an insecure application built by someone else, we cannot rely on beating them in court.

Lawyers are well aware that the use of technical evidence, and in particular of computer evidence, is fraught with difficulty. Most judges have a background in the humanities rather than the sciences, and may be more than normally technophobic; even where these feelings are dutifully suppressed, experienced and otherwise intelligent men can find it impossible to understand simple evidence. The author has observed this phenomenon at a number of computer trials from 1986 down to the present, and has often felt that no-one else in court had any idea what was going on. Specialist computer lawyers confirm that this feeling is not uncommon in their practice.

Consider the recent case of R v Munden, in which one of our local police constables came home from holiday to find his bank account empty, asked for a statement, found six withdrawals for a total of £460 which he did not recall making, and complained to his bank. It responded by having him prosecuted for attempting to obtain money by deception. It came out during the trial [RM] that the bank's system had been implemented and managed in a rather ramshackle way, which is probably not untypical of the small data processing departments which service most medium sized commercial firms.

– The bank had no security management or quality assurance function. The software development methodology was 'code-and-fix', and the production code was changed as often as twice a week.

- No external assessment, whether by auditors or insurance inspectors, was produced; the manager who gave technical evidence was the same man who had originally designed and written the system twenty years before, and still ran it. He claimed that bugs could not cause disputed transaction, as his system was written in assembler, and thus all bugs caused abends. He was not aware of the existence of TCSEC or ITSEC; but nonetheless claimed that as ACF2 was used to control access, it was not possible for any systems programmer to get hold of the encryption keys which were embedded in application code.
- The disputed transactions were never properly investigated; he had just looked at the mainframe logs and not found anything which seemed wrong (and even this was only done once the trial was underway, under pressure from defence lawyers). In fact, there were another 150-200 transactions under dispute with other clients, none of which had been investigated.

It was widely felt to be shocking that, even after all this came to light, the policeman was still convicted [E]; one may hope that the conviction is overturned on appeal.

The larger pattern here is that when a new technology is introduced, the first few cases may be decided the wrong way. This is especially the case with the criminal law, as most defendants in criminal trials rely on the legal aid system, and this has a number of well documented weaknesses [HBP]. Prosecutors can expect a series of successes against poorly defended suspects, followed at last by a defeat which may define the law (and in so doing upset an entire industry's ways of working).

It seems likely that the ATM disputes will follow the same pattern. One of the first ATM related prosecutions in the UK, that of Janet Bagwell [A1], led to a notorious miscarriage of justice: there, an innocent girl admitted theft on advice for her solicitor that her chances of a successful defence were slim, and it later turned out that the disputed transaction had been the bank's fault all along. More recently, in the Hendy and De Mott cases mentioned above, the defendants had access to expert advice in time, and were acquitted; in the Munden case, the author was only brought in as the defence expert while the trial was underway, and even then the bank has shown clear public signs of remorse that the prosecution was ever brought.

A number of changes in the law have been proposed, but not all of them will be for the better. One of the main motives for change is the large number of convictions for serious crimes, such as murder and terrorism, which have recently been overturned. Many of them involved doubtful forensic evidence, and legal aid restrictions prevent most defendants from challenging this effectively.

Also, in the area of financial crime, the inability of juries to deal with complex fraud cases has led to debate on whether 'special' juries, selected from professional people, should be reintroduced in the City. Thus the problems of computer evidence are part of a much wider problem: progress makes for increasing specialisation, and without specialist knowledge being available to all parties, there are many ways in which the legal system can come adrift.

All this has led to one of the main campaigners on this issue, Michael Mansfield QC, to call for a move to the French system of examining magistrates [C1]. However, this would mean a single expert being appointed by the court, and it seems likely that such experts would be like the defendants' expert in the Bristol case (or the Home Office explosives expert in the recent IRA cases) - a man with eminent qualifications, but unable to see faults in the systems which he had spent years helping to develop.

A final problem is that even when judicial practices do finally stabilise, they may not converge. In the USA, for example, the definition of a signature varies widely. Depending on the context, one may need an original autograph signature, or a fax may do, or a tape recording, or a stamp, or even a typewritten name [W2]. Even the passage of time is not guaranteed to sort things out: in some jurisdictions, contracts are signed at the bottom, while in others they must be initialled on every page as well; this is a throwback to nineteenth century disputes on whether typewritten documents were too easy to forge, and their fallout has persisted for a century, despite causing problems for international trade.

It is thus foolish to assume that digital signatures will end up being accepted equally in all countries, or even for all purposes in any one country. Our next principle is therefore:

> **Principle 5:** The judicial treatment of new kinds of technical evidence may take years to stabilise, and may not converge to anything consistent.

This is well enough known to lawyers, but is usually ignored by the security community - perhaps because the remedy is to prefer mechanisms which are easy for a layman to understand. Security cameras are unproblematic; yet we would not look forward to being the first litigant to try and adduce a zero knowledge proof in evidence.

Legislation

Strange computer judgments have on occasion alarmed lawmakers into attempts to rectify matters by legislation. For example, in the case of R v Gold & Schifreen [RGS], two 'hackers' had played havoc with British Telecom's electronic mail service by sending messages 'from' Prince Philip 'to' people they didn't like announcing the award of honours; this greatly upset the Establishment and they were charged with forgery (of British Telecom's engineering password). They were convicted in the first instance, but eventually freed on appeal by Lord Lane, on the grounds that information (unlike material goods) cannot be stolen or forged. This was proclaimed by the press (and by the computer security industry) to be a hackers' charter, and the ensuing panic in parliament led to the Computer Misuse Act.

This act makes 'hacking' a specific criminal offence, and thus tries to transfer some of the costs of access control from system owners to the Crown Prosecution Service. Whether it actually does anything useful is open to dispute: on the one hand firms have to take considerable precautions if they want to use it against errant employees [A5] [C2]; and on the other hand it has led to surprising convictions, such as that of a software writer who used the old established technique of putting a timelock in his code to enforce payment [C3]. Similar laws have been passed in a number of jurisdictions, and similar problems have arisen.

But even if the state possessed the competence to frame good laws on computer issues, its motives are often dubious. Powerful lobby groups get legislation to transfer their costs to the public purse; and governments have often tried to rewrite the rules to make life easier for their signals intelligence people, without thinking through the consequences for other computer users.

For example, the South African government decreed in 1986 that all users of civilian cryptology had to provide copies of their algorithms and keys to the military. Bankers approached the authorities and said that this was a welcome development; managing keys for automatic teller machines was a nuisance and the military were welcome to the job; but of course, whenever a machine was short, they would be sent the bill. At this the military backed down quickly.

More recently, the NIST public key initiative [C4] proposes that the US government will certify all the public keys in use in that country. They seem to have learned from the South African experience, in that they propose a statutory legal exemption for key management agencies; but it remains to be seen how many users will trust a key management system which they will not be able to sue when things go wrong.

Given all these problems, our next principle is inevitable:

> **Principle 6:** Computer security legislation is highly likely to suffer from the law of unexpected consequences.

Standards

Another tack taken by some governments is to try and establish a system of security standards. These are often designed to give a legal advantage to systems which use some particular technology. For example, to facilitate CREST (the Bank of England's new share dealing system), the Treasury proposes to amend English law so that the existence of a digital signature on a stock transfer order will create 'an equitable interest by way of tenancy in common in the ... securities pending registration' [HMT].

On a more general note, some people are beginning to see a TCSEC C2 evaluation as the 'gold standard' of commercial computer security. This might lead in time to a situation where someone who had not used a C2 product might be considered negligent, and someone who had used one might hope that the burden of proof had passed to someone else. However, in the Munden case, the bank did indeed use an evaluated product - ACF2 was one of the first products to gain the C2 rating - yet this evaluation was not only irrelevant to the case, but not even known to the bank.

The situation can be even worse when standards are promulgated which have flaws, or which conflict with each other. The problems with X.509 [BAN], the controversy over ISO 11166 [R], and the debate about the relative merits of RSA and DSA, are well enough known to; it may be that some of the things said by eminent people about DSA in the heat of the debate in 1992 [B2] will be exhumed in years to come and brandished by a jubilant defence lawyer.

In any case, it is well known that standards are used as pawns in battles for market share, and a standard which appears to be safe and well established today might be subject to a fierce challenge in a few years' time - again, the RSA versus DSA debate is a useful example here.

For all these reasons, it is imprudent to expect that the standards industry will ultimately provide an effort-free solution to all the legal problems which can affect security systems. Standards are much less stable than laws should be, and are often founded on much baser and more fickle motives.

> **Principle 7:** Don't rely on engineering standards to solve legal problems.

A related point is that although the courts often rely on industry practice when determining which of two parties has been negligent, existing computer security standards do not help much. After all, they mostly have to do with operating system level features, while the industry practices themselves tend to be expressed in application detail - precisely where the security problems arise. The legal authority flows from the industrial practice to the application, not the other way around.

It is pure hubris for the security technical community to think that court cases should be decided by considering the merits of various encryption schemes. Of course, it is always conceivable that some future dispute will involve mutual allegations of insecurity between two EDI trading partners, and that competing expert evidence will be heard on which of two authentication schemes is easier to circumvent. However, where there is a conflict of experts, the courts tend to disregard both of them and decide the case on other evidence.

This other evidence then has to be interpreted in line with normal practice, whatever that may be. Is it usual for a Dutch banker to issue a guarantee in the form of a telex, or of a letter with two signatures? Should an Indian scrap metal purchaser draw a letter of credit to be made payable against a faxed copy of an inspection certificate, or should he stipulate the production of the original document? These are the sort of questions on which real cases turn, and they are usually decided by reference to the actual practice in a given trade.

Understanding this could have saved British and Norwegian bankers a lot of security expenditure, legal fees and public embarrassment; for in traditional banking, the onus is on the bank to show that it made each debit in accordance with the customer's mandate.

Principle 8: Security goals and assumptions should be based on industry practice in the application area, not on general 'computer' concepts.

Liability and Insurance

The above sections may have given the reader the impression that managing the liability aspects of computer security systems is just beyond most companies. This does not mean that the problem should be accepted as intractable, but rather that it should be passed to a specialist - the insurer.

As insurers become more aware of the computer related element in their risks, it is likely that they will acquire much more clout in setting security standards. This is already happening at the top end of the market: banks who wish to insure against computer fraud usually need to have their systems inspected by a firm approved by the insurer.

The present system could be improved [A4] - in particular the inspections, which focus on operational controls, should be broadened to include application reviews. However, this is a detail; certification is bound to spread down to smaller risks, and, under current business conditions, it could economically be introduced for risks of the order of $250,000. It is surely only a matter of time before insurance driven computer security standards affect not just businesses and wealthy individuals, but most of us [N1].

Just as my insurance policy may now specify 'a five-lever mortise deadlock', so the policy I buy in ten years' time is likely to insist that I use accounting software from an approved product list, and certify that I manage its security features in accordance with the manual, if my practice is to be covered against loss of data and various kinds of crime.

Insurance-based certification will not mean hardening systems to military levels, but rather finding one or more levels of assurance at which insurance business can be conducted profitably. The protection must be cheap enough that insurance can be sold, yet good enough to keep the level of claims under control.

Insurance-based security will bring many other benefits, such as arbitration; any dispute I have with you will be resolved between my insurer and your insurer, as with most motor insurance claims, thus saving the bills (and the follies) of lawyers. Insurance companies are also better able to deal with government meddling; they can lobby for offensive legislation to be repealed, or just decline to cover any system whose keys are kept on a government server, unless the government provides a full indemnity.

A liability based approach can also settle a number of intellectual disputes, such as the old question of trust. What is 'trust'? At present, the US DoD 'functional' definition states that a trusted component is one which, if it breaks, can compromise system security, while Needham's alternative 'organisational' definition [N2] states that a trusted component is one which my employer allows me to trust (if it breaks and the system security is compromised as a result, I do not get fired).

From the liability point of view, of course, a component which can be trusted is one such that, if it breaks and compromises my system security, I do not lose an unpredictable amount of money. In other words:

> **Principle 9:** A trusted component or system is one which you can insure.

References

[A1]	RJ Anderson, "Why Cryptosystems Fail", in *Proceedings of the 1st ACM Conference on Computer and Communications Security* (1993) pp 215 - 227
[A2]	RJ Anderson, "Why Cryptosystems Fail", in *Communications of the ACM*, November 1994
[A3]	RJ Anderson, "Making Smartcard Systems Robust", to appear in *Cardis 94*
[A4]	RJ Anderson, "Liability, Trust and Security Standards", in *Proceedings of the 1994 Cambridge Workshop on Security Protocols* (Springer, to appear)
[A5]	J Austen, "Computer Crime: ignorance or apathy?", in *The Computer Bulletin v 5 no 5* (Oct 93) pp 23 - 24
[AN]	M Abadi, RM Needham, '*Prudent Engineering Practice for Cryptographic Protocols*', DEC SRC Technical Report no 125 (1994).
[AS]	RJ Anderson, S Bezuidenhout, "On the Security of Prepayment Metering Systems" (*to appear*)
[B1]	KM Banks, Kluwer Security Bulletin, 4 Oct 93
[B2]	DJ Bidzos, Letter to Congress, September 20 1991; published in usenet newsgroup `comp.risks` **12.37**
[BAN]	M Burrows, M Abadi, RM Needham, "A Logic of Authentication", in *Proceedings of the Royal Society of London A* v 426 (1989) pp 233 - 271
[BN]	Behne v Den Norske Bank, Bankklagenemnda, Sak nr: 92457/93111
[C1]	S Clark, "When justice lacks all conviction", in *The Sunday Times* (31 July 1994) section 4 page 7
[C2]	T Corbitt, "The Computer Misuse Act", in *Computer Fraud and Security Bulletin* (Feb 94) pp 13 - 17
[C3]	A Collins, "Court decides software time-locks are illegal", in *Computer Weekly* (19 August 93) p 1
[C4]	S Chokhani, "Public Key Infrastructure Study (PKI)", in *Proceedings of the first ISOC Symposium on Network and Distributed System Security* (1994) p 45
[E]	B Ellis, "Prosecuted for complaint over cash machine", in *The Sunday Times*, 27th March 1994, section 5 page 1

[HBP]   M McConville, J Hodgson, A Pavlovic, *'Standing Accused: The Organisation and Practices of Criminal Defence Lawyers in Britain'*, OUP (1994) reviewed by David Pannick QC in The Times, 16 August 1994, p 33

[HMT]   HM Treasury, *'CREST - The Legal Issues'*, March 1994

[ITSEC]   *'Information Technology Security Evaluation Criteria'*, June 1991, EC document COM(90) 314

[J]   RB Jack (chairman), *'Banking services: law and practice report by the Review Committee'*, HMSO, London, 1989

[JC]   Dorothy Judd v Citibank, *435 NYS, 2d series, pp 210 - 212, 107 Misc.2d 526*

[L]   B Lewis, "How to rob a bank the cashcard way", in *Sunday Telegraph* 25th April 1992 p 5

[M]   S McConnell, "Barclays defends its cash machines", in *The Times*, 7 November 1992

[MB]   McConville & others v Barclays Bank & others, Queen's Bench Division 1992 ORB no. 812

[MM]   CH Meyer and SM Matyas, *'Cryptography: A New Dimension in Computer Data Security'*, John Wiley and Sons 1982.

[N1]   RM Needham, "Insurance and protection of data", *preprint*

[N2]   RM Needham, comment at 1993 Cambridge formal methods workshop

[R]   RA Rueppel, "Criticism of ISO CD 11166 banking - key management by means of asymmetric algorithms", in *Proceedings of 3rd Symposium on State and Progress of Research in Cryptography*, Fondazione Ugo Bordoni (1993) pp 191 - 198

[RGS]   R v Gold and Schifreen, Southwark Crown Court, 1986

[RLN]   R v Lock and North, Bristol Crown Court, 1993

[RM]   R v Munden, Mildenhall Magistrates' Court, 8-11 February 1994

[RS]   R v Small, Norwich Crown Court, 1994

[S]   A Stone, "ATM cards & fraud", *manuscript 1993*

[TCSEC]   *'Trusted Computer System Evaluation Criteria'*, US Department of Defense, 5200.28-STD, December 1985

[W1]   MA Wright, "Security Controls in ATM Systems", in *Computer Fraud and Security Bulletin*, November 1991, pp 11 - 14

[W2]   B Wright, *'The Law of Electronic Commerce'*, Little, brown & Co, 1994

Distributed Systems

Implementing Secure Dependencies over a Network by Designing a Distributed Security SubSystem

Bruno d'AUSBOURG

CERT - ONERA
Département d'Etudes et de Recherches en Informatique
2, Avenue E. Belin - B.P. 4025
31055 Toulouse - Cedex- FRANCE
email: ausbourg@tls-cs.cert.fr

It was recently argued that the presence of covert channels should no longer be taken for granted in multilevel secure systems. Until today, multilevel security seems to have been an ideal to approach and not a requirement to meet. The question is: is it possible to design a practical multilevel system offering full security? Based on which architecture? The approach described in this paper reflects some results of a research project which suggests some ideas to answer this question. We have chosen the distributed architecture of a secure LAN as an application framework. In particular we show how controls exerted on dependencies permit to control exhaustively the elementary flows of information. The enforced rules govern both the observation and the handling of data over the whole system. They are achieved by means of some hardware mechanisms that submit the access of hosts to the medium to a secure medium access control protocol. We evaluate how secure dependencies used to ensure confidentiality in such an architecture may also be used to answer some other needs with respect to other attributes of security.

1 Introduction

Many systems were designed in order to protect confidentiality of data and processes. This can be done by building multilevel architectures of machines and networks. These architectures tolerate the existence of covert channels, because standards consider that covert channels are inevitable. Proctor and Neumann in [14] argued that the presence of covert channels should no longer be taken for granted in multilevel secure systems. Indeed, applications should not tolerate any compromise of multilevel security, not even through covert channels of low bandwidths. They argued also that systems with multilevel processors seem to be either impractical or insecure. They suggest to redirect research and development efforts towards developing multilevel disk drives and multilevel network interface units for use with only single level processors in building multilevel distributed systems.

This position may be debated, but the asked question is interesting. Until today, multilevel security seems to have been an ideal to approach and not a requirement to meet. The question is: is it possible to design a practical multilevel system offering full security? Based on which architecture?

The approach described in this paper reflects some results of a research project[1] which suggests some ideas to answer this question. This project aims at building a system architecture (machine and LAN) that offers a high degree of protection both for storage, processing and communication of user data. This protection is based on an exhaustive control of information flows, including timing flows, and ensuring there is no place for covert channels. We have chosen the distributed architecture of a secure LAN as an application framework.

2 Related works

Randell and Rushby described a secure distributed system in [15]. This system was designed to offer multilevel file system services over a network. The security was founded on an interpretation of the Bell and La Padula model [3] and enforced by use of cryptographic techniques to enforce separation between levels and to ensure confidentiality or integrity of files and file servers. The security was located in trusted network interface units (TNIUs), trusted terminal interface units (TTIUs) and a trusted multilevel station running a security kernel. This approach relied on securing application services over a network.

It was developped and extended through the DSS project ([17] and [18]) at DRA Malvern: the architecture of the Distributed Secure System is close to our own architecture. But the mechanisms chosen to enforce separation are not the same.

Other approaches tend to locate security controls inside various protocol layers and to protect connections established between entities over a network. The Trusted Network Architecture [10] is based on secure data channels over which only authorized subjects can send, inspect or modify the data stream. This is achieved through the use of mechanisms including encryption, checksums and nonces. Network communication that bypasses these secure data channel is not possible.

More commercial approaches [6] tried to devise secure networks. The Verdix secure LAN, for example, also founds the multilevel security it enforces on the Bell and La Padula model. A network security centre manages and controls all the operations and connections exerted by trusted network interface units. Protection and separation between connections is logical, and is based on the use of cryptographic techniques. The Boeing Secure LAN also consists of trusted interface units. The secure network server attaches labels to datagrams and provides mandatory access control decisions based on the value of the labels. The Sun MLS OS is an extension of SunOS to provide mandatory access control. It requires source hosts to label packets and destination hosts to check labels on received packets.

All these approaches were developed in order to protect confidentiality in systems. They are founded on the use of labels and of cryptographic methods to separate levels. But they do not prevent some illicit information flows. In particular, they are not involved in managing the allocation of resources among levels. And resource allocation or management is the reason for most of the covert channels in

---

1. This project was supported by DGA in France.

systems. In this case, cryptographic methods and labelling of packets are inefficient. Of course, if network lines are vulnerable, encryption can help to preserve the confidentiality and integrity of data transmitted by the network.

But if the system does not carefully manage the allocation of resources among levels, user communicating at low levels could detect and perceive the activity at higher levels. And encrypting messages does nothing to eliminate these covert channels. Achieving an efficient control of information flows, able to separate system domains in a quite secure manner, can eliminate them. Our goal is to devise such a "secure system".

3 Causal Dependencies and Security

3.1 Causal dependencies

A system may be described as a set of points (o,t). A point references an object o at a time or date t. This introduction of time is necessary because time can be observed in the system, for example: durations of operations.

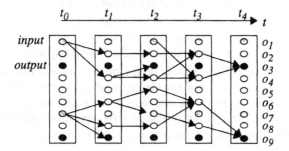

Fig. 1 Causal dependencies inside a system

So, one can act on the value of the object o, at the instant t, or one can act on the instant t at which the object o is given a particular value. In the first case, the object o can be used to transmit some information if any semantics can be assigned to its value and a storage channel is involved here; in the second case, time is used and therefore, a timing channel is involved if any semantics can be assigned to the observed instant values.

Some of these points are *input* points, others are *output* points, and the last ones are *internal* points. These points evolve with time and this evolving is due to the elementary transitions made by the system. An elementary transition can modify a point: then, at instant t, it sets a new value v for the object o of the point. This instant t and the new value v functionally depend on previous points.

This *functional dependency* on *previous* points is named *causal* dependency[1]. The causal dependency of (o,t) on (o',t') with $t' < t$ is denoted by $(o',t') \rightarrow (o,t)$. Informally, by (o,t) "causally depends on" $(o't')$ we mean that the point $(o't')$ is used to generate the point (o,t). An interesting discussion of McLean in [11] illustrates the need to take account of these dependencies when addressing information flows. The assumption made here may seem too strong with respect to this discussion. But it is useful because it permits to build sufficient conditions for security.

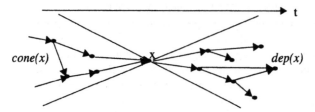

Fig. 2 Cones of causality and of dependencies

The transitive closure of the relation "→" (denoted "→*") at (o,t) defines the *causality cone* of (o,t), in short:

$$cone(o,t) = \{(o',t') / (o',t') \rightarrow^* (o,t)\}.$$

Conversely, we denote the *dependency cone* the set $dep(o,t)$ of points which causally depend on (o,t):

$$dep(o,t)= \{(o',t') / (o,t) \rightarrow^* (o',t')\};$$

A relation between the sets *cone* and *dep* is given by:

$$y \in dep(x) \Leftrightarrow x \in cone(y)$$

where x and y denote two points (o,t) and $(o't')$ of the system.

These causal dependencies make up the structure of information flows inside the system. If a subject s has any knowledge about the internal functioning of the system, then he is able to know the internal scheme of causal dependencies. So, by observing any output point x_o, he is able to infer any information in $cone(x_o)$. In particular $cone(x_o)$ may include input points x_i which contain some input data of the system.

Conversely, by altering an input point x_i, s can alter any point in $dep(x_i)$ and in particular an output point $x_o \in dep(x_i)$.

In particular, if a subject s can observe a set O_s of output points x_o in the system, we denote by Obs_s the set of all points that s can observe in the system:

$$Obs_s = \bigcup_{x_o \in O_s} cone(x_o)$$

Similarly, if a subject s can alter a set A_s of input points x_i in the system, we denote by Alt_s the set of all points that s can alter and

$$Alt_s = \bigcup_{x_i \in A_s} dep(x_i)$$

3.2 Security

The aimed security must control both observation and alteration over the system. In a first part, we address only the observation problem, and its related property of confidentiality. Informally, the system must ensure that causal dependencies enforce secure internal information flows.

Obs_s contains the points that a subject s in the system is able to observe in the system. The set R_s contains the points that the subject s has the right to observe in accordance with the security policy. So, we say in accordance with [5] that the system is secure if a subject s can observe the only objects he has the right to observe:

$$Obs_s \subseteq R_s \qquad (1)$$

When the security policy which is used to define the rights of subjects is the multilevel security policy, a classification level $l(x)$ is assigned to points x and a clearance level $l(s)$ is assigned to subjects s and the set $R(s)$ may be defined quite naturally by:

$$R(s) = \{x \,/\, l(x) \leq l(s)\}$$

3.3 Security conditions

Two conditions are *sufficient* in order to guarantee the security defined by *(1)*. Firstly, an interface rule expresses conditions on the classification level of an output point x_0 and on the clearance level of the subject s who can observe this point:

$$\forall s, \, x_0 \in O_s \Rightarrow l(s) \geq l(x_0) \qquad (2)$$

The second condition requires a monotonic increasing of levels over causal dependencies. If values of levels increase with sensitivity of points:

$$\forall x, \, \forall y, \, x \rightarrow y \Rightarrow l(x) \leq l(y) \qquad (3)$$

Cone-Lemma. If condition *(3)* is enforced then

$$x \in cone(y) \Rightarrow l(x) \leq l(y) \qquad (4)$$

Proof. We take the depth of the cone into account. We define $cone_n(y)$ the cone of y of depth n: so, $\forall x \in cone_n(y)$ there is a string of n points $x = x_n \rightarrow x_{n-1} \rightarrow ... \rightarrow x_1 \rightarrow y$. We want to prove that $\forall n \, x \in cone_n(y) \Rightarrow l(x) \leq l(y)$. This is done by induction on n. If $n=1$ then $x \rightarrow y$ and by *(3)* we have $l(x) \leq l(y)$.

For a depth of $n+1$, $x = x_{n+1} \rightarrow x_n \rightarrow x_{n-1} \rightarrow ... \rightarrow x_1 \rightarrow y$. And $l(x_n) \leq l(y)$ by induction assumption. Then $x \rightarrow x_n$ and by *(3)* $l(x) \leq l(x_n) \leq l(y)$. ∎

Fact 1. If Conditions *(2)* and *(3)* are enforced in a system then the system is secure.

Proof. We must show that *(2)* + *(3)* $\Rightarrow$ *(1)*.
If $x \in Obs_s$ then $x \in O_s$ or $\exists y \in O_s \,/\, x \in cone(y)$. If $x \in O_s$, then by *(2)*, $l(x) \leq l(s)$.. In the other case $\exists y \in O_s \,/\, x \in cone(y)$, and then $l(x) \leq l(y) \leq l(s)$ by *(2)* and Cone-Lemma. So $x \in R_s$. ∎

With respect to confidentiality, the both rules *(2)* and *(4)* ensure that for any subject s who has the right to observe an output point x_0, the observation of x_0 will give to s only information he has the right to observe. So the definition of security given by *(1)* is satisfied.

The rule *(3)* defines *secure* dependencies. It gives the semantics of an internal control which can be exerted on each system transition when a relation of causal dependency is involved. This control on levels is sufficient to guarantee the security of the whole system. It enforces the exhaustive control of information flows. This control of information flows (including its temporal aspects embedded in the definition of points) is achieved by making sure each transition and each elementary transfer of information from input points until system points which can be observed directly by a user. An other equivalent formulation of this last condition may be expressed as

$$\forall x, \forall y, \, l(x) > l(y) \Rightarrow \neg \, [x \rightarrow y]$$

When $x = (o,t')$ and $y = (o,t)$ and $t' < t$, this means that the level value of the object o may be downgraded, but both points before and after downgrading must not depend one on the other. In other words, this change on the value of the classification level of the object o may be done, but the value of the object o must also be erased, for example, in order (o,t) after downgrading does not causally depend on (o,t') before downgrading.

4 Interpretation

4.1 Choice of the hardware layer as context of interpretation

These rules must be instantiated in the framework of a real system to be used as a reference for building a secure system. This can be done by making an interpretation of the model in the context of one among the various abstract layers of a real system. The choice has been made to perform this interpretation in the most concrete system layer: the hardware layer. This approach offers two main advantages.

Firstly, the hardware layer manages only elementary objects whose granularity is the smallest in the system. So, by defining exhaustively all the observable objects inside this layer and by defining security controls on elementary operations that can be exerted on these objects, all the operations done on more abstract objects in the system will be submitted to these controls. Indeed, these more abstracts objects are built from elementary concrete objects and are accessed through combinations of elementary operations on these concrete objects. For example, assume that memory cells and disk blocks can be observed and that controls are enforced consequently on read and write operations. Then we can state that the use of files, in upper layers of the system, are constrained by these elementary controls: if write operations are prohibited on memory cells and blocks implementing a file f, neither f nor data structures associated to f (as file descriptor nodes) can be used by open or write operations on f to store any new information.

Secondly, this layer has few types of objects and subjects. So, the expression of controls is simplified and their enforcement may be done exhaustively. Let us detail this fact.

4.2 Security conditions in network interface units

Network interface units U connecting stations to a comunication medium constitute the system architecture. These units access the medium according to the CSMA/CD Medium Access Control protocol, as defined by IEEE 802.3. We denote by M the *Medium* managed by the Physical Layer. In particular, this layer offers two elementary signals (*Carrier Sense, Collision Detection*) and B which contains the bit value carried by M.

The active entities, which are the *subjects* inside this hardware layer, are only the network interface units U. These units have one input *delay* value , that is chosen externally as a uniformly distributed random value in a finite range. They can be represented by two data cells: the bit value b it has to deposit on M or it has sampled from M and d that contains a delay value to spend before transmitting.

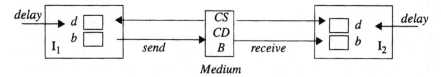

Fig. 3 The system architecture

In the same way, the *objects* are the internal cells b and *delay* of U and the communication medium M (including CS,CD and B). A level is assigned to all objects and subjects. The cells b and *delay* in U are doted with the level $l(U)$ and all objects in M share the same level $l(M)$. The elementary transitions include the elementary *send* and *receive* operations made by U between its own cells and M.

The *receive* operation, as expressed in the CSMA/CD protocol, consists in permanently listening to signals CS and to the bit value B carried by M. This operation produces a new value for b and the following dependencies are involved:

$$\{CS,B\} \to b$$

Condition-receive. In this case, the rule *(3)* applied to the *receive* operation produces:

$$l(M) \leq l(U)$$

The *send* operation is less simple. Firstly, the decision by U to deposit a bit value upon M is taken by listening to M and watching at signals CS and CD. The transmission of the b value may be delayed according to the delay value stored in d when CD indicates that a collision occured. When transmitting the bit b, a new value is assigned to the M components. So

$$\{CS,CD\} \cup \{delay\} \to \{d\}$$
$$\{b,d\} \to \{CS,CD,B\}$$

Condition-send. The rule *(3)* applied to these dependencies produces

$$l(M) \leq l(U) \leq l(M) \Rightarrow l(M) = l(U)$$

4.3 Management of level objects

Levels are themselves objects in the system. So they are also submitted to the control of dependencies. A classification level is assigned to them: we have chosen to give the value "*Low*" to the level of a level object.Then, the fact that an information is secret is not itself a secret. That is not a doctrine, but only a work assumption that we made in order to simplify.

Being submitted to the control of dependencies, the rule *(3)* must be applied to levels and then, given a level l_i:

$$x \rightarrow l_i \Rightarrow l(x) \leq l(l_i) \Rightarrow l(x) = Low$$

In other words, the value of a level and the instant at which this level gets a given value only depend on low level information. This condition is sometimes difficult to enforce, for example, when the value of a level decreases from a *high* to a *low* value. This change of the level value must have been planned and declared at low level.

In our system architecture, the value of the level of M , and time at which this level takes a given value must be generated from *Low* level points. Then, the value of the level of the medium and the time spent to this level are stated at *Low* level. Therefore, the use of M is time sliced between levels. And slices are declared or computed at *Low* level. A *High* process never acts on the value of a level (by maintainig it or by changing it).

Similarly, the level of U must be declared at low level. And the time spent by U at this given level is also declared in advance at *Low* level. So at the beginning, U is at *Low* level. If a user wants to use the host and U at a level *High*, this user (and not a process running on the untrusted host) must firstly declare at *Low* level (not *High*) that he requires to use the unit U at level *High* during time *t*, in order to achieve communications at level *High*. This can be viewed as a constraint for the user. In fact, it is no more inconvenient than doing a login procedure. Of course, it is sometimes difficult to estimate exactly the amount of time that he will need. But experiments on the architecture that was developped on these principles show that light overestimations do not degrade performances tragically [16].

4.4 Security SubSystem: S^3

Because they are simple, the controls expressed in *Condition-receive* an *Condition-send* can be enforced in U by a subset of hardware features which are driven by a subset of software. These two subsets constitute the *Security SubSystem* or S^3 of the system. This S^3, so called by ITSEC [8] in Europe, is in fact the TCB, as formalized in the Orange Book [12] and later the Red Book [13], of the interface unit U and acts as a reference monitor.

Fact 2. If Condition-receive and Condition-send are enforced in U by S^3 then the system is secure.

Proof. The system is secure if condition *(4)* is always satisfied. The points that a user (or a process) can observe in an interface U_i are b_i and d_i. From 4.2 and 4.3 we can state that

$$cone\ (b_i, d_i) \supseteq \{CS, CD, B\} \cup delay_i \cup l(U_i) \cup l(M)\ and$$
$$cone\ (CS, CD, B) \supseteq l(M) \cup [\{b_j, d_j, delay_j\} \cup l(U_j)]\ \forall j,\ U_j\ sending$$

Then,

$$cone\ (b_i, d_i) = \{CS, CD, B\} \cup delay_i \cup \{l(U_i),\ l(M)\} \cup [\{b_j, d_j, delay_j\} \cup l(U_j)]\ \forall j,\ U_j\ sending$$

And

$$l(CS) = l(CD) = l(B) = l(M);$$
$$l(delay_i) = l(b_i) = l(d_i) = l(U_i);$$
$$l(b_j) = l(d_j) = l(delay_j) = l(U_j) = l(M) \text{ because } U_j \text{ is sending}$$
$$l(l(M)) = l(l(U_i) = l(l(U_j)) = Low$$
$$l(M) \leq l(Ui) \text{ from condition-receive and condition-send}$$

So,

$$x \in cone(b_i, d_i) \Rightarrow l(x) \leq l(Ui) \blacksquare$$

The S^3 functionning ensures that values of points observed in U_i and time t at which these points take these values depend only on information that are allowed to be observed. Some modulations on values or durations of elementary *send* and *receive* operations can be observed in U_i: these modulations may be created in order to generate information flows, but these flows are inefficient and do not strike a blow at the security, thanks to the controls done by local S^3.

5 Implementation of a Distributed S^3 over a LAN

5.1 Security conditions enforced in a local S^3

The *local S^3* is in charge of enforcing the controls defined by the two send and receive conditions and regulating the access of these interface units to the communication medium according to these. This local S^3 keeps values of levels for the interface unit and for M. It grants or denies to the interface unit the access right to M according to those values of levels.

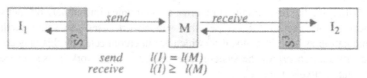

send $l(I) = l(M)$
receive $l(I) \geq l(M)$

Fig. 4 Rules to access the medium in a network interface unit

In fact, it can intervene by hardware on elementary operations exerted in order to deposit or sample information on M. So, for the interface unit, the ability to send or receive at any instant t is given by its own level and the level of the medium. An interface unit equipped with its local S^3 constitutes a Trusted Network Interface Unit or TNIU.

5.2 Trusted paths to local S^3

There is a need for building a trusted path between users and local S^3 of the network interface unit. The mechanism of a Secure Interface Device (SID) is used and permits to implement the principle of reservation of resources in advance. It is shown in Fig. 5 . A quite simple dialogue between users and local S^3 permits:

- to declare the value of the current level of the connected host for the next session and the required duration for this session; this fixes the level of the interface unit and the time needed for exchanges at this level;

• to initialize then the local S^3 functioning in accordance with these declarations.

Single level host SID

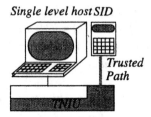

Fig. 5 Trusted Path

This is insufficient. Indeed, the local S^3 must be able to require a level for the medium in accordance with the reservations made by the user, and to know its current level value. A real security subnetwork is needed.

5.3 Security Subnetwork

Exchanges between hosts running at various current levels may occur only if the level of the medium can change. In fact, this value is time sliced in accordance with rules defined in 4.3: this slicing is based on level reservations which are produced and emitted at low level by user through the trusted path.

Then, two conditions must be satisfied. Firstly, the value assigned to the level of the medium must be known by every local S^3. Secondly, the time slicing of this value must be enforced in a synchronous way over the LAN.

Satisfying the first condition requires a communication subnetwork between all the local S^3. In fact, in this case, this subnetwork uses the same medium of communication as hosts. The local S^3 which are interconnected by this way constitute the *security subnetwork* of the system. This security subnetwork is used to exchange security data between local S^3.

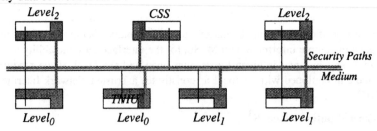

Fig. 6 Security Subnetwork

A *centralized security station* (or *CSS*) manages the data of security for the network. In particular, it manages levels which are assigned to interface units and to the communication medium according to reservations made by hosts and users through the SID and emitted to CSS by local S^3. It broadcasts also these data to all the local S^3 over the security subnetwork.

Satisfying the second condition requires the existence of a protocol in charge of regulating the exchanges of security data. It is also in charge of ensuring that the time slicing of the medium level is known by all the local S^3 in a synchronous manner. So, the rules which are used to access the medium in order to exchange security data are not the same as the rules used by hosts in order to exchange user data. These rules constitute the *Security Medium Access Control (SMAC)* protocol.

6 SMAC protocol and multilevel LAN

6.1 The SMAC Protocol

It enforces time slicing for the level of the medium according to reservations made to the CSS. It manages also the exchange of security data under the authority of the CSS. These data include particularly reservation data emitted from local S^3 and level settings for the medium which are emitted from the CSS. In few words, the SMAC protocol is reservation based.

It manages two functioning modes for the interface unit: a user mode and a security mode. In the security mode, only local S^3 can use the medium M to exchange security data with CSS. In user mode, operations to send and receive user data can be performed by the interface units according to values of their own level and of the level of M. The CSS computes time slices for sessions of exchanges in user mode which correspond to various values assigned to the level of M. These values are set in accordance with reservations previously received. At the end of a slice, the interface unit always returns to the security mode. In security mode, the CSS may ask to local S^3 if reservations are pending. If yes, local S^3 may answer by giving the content of their pending reservations. The protocol for this dialogue is a synchronous one. The CSS fixes a transmission slot for each local S^3 to answer and each local S^3 may answer during its reserved slot. The CSS broadcasts then a new value for the level of the medium and a new session in user mode is started. In user mode, a Medium Access Control (MAC) protocol arbitrates the access to the medium between units which are allowed to access it: this protocol is CSMA/CD is in our case.

The SMAC protocol is similar to protocols used in the real time world where requirements on the amount of delay between the time a packet is ready and the time it is received at destination are stringent. In these protocols, some sources must reserve transmission slots before they can begin transmission [19].

6.2 Architecture of the interface unit

So, this protocol leads to a quite simple architecture for secure interface units. Two components make up them.

The first component is a classical one which enforces a standard MAC protocol. In our case, this protocol is CSMA/CD. This component achieves the *send* and *receive* requests issued by upper communication layers in hosts. These two operations are achieved by activating the *Rec* and *Send₁* modules in accordance with the CSAM/CD protocol.

The second component enforces the operations of the local S^3. Four functions are needed: they are achieved by activation of four modules. The *Rec* module is similar to the *Rec* module of the CSMA/CD component: it listens to the medium and recovers frames from it. The *Send$_0$* module enforces sending operation for the local S^3. But these operations are done in a synchronous way by getting transmission slots computed by the CSS. So this module is quite much simpler than the *Send$_1$* asynchronous module of the CSMA/CD component. Then the *Int* interpretation module achieves the interpretation of security commands emitted by the CSS (*set_level_medium*, *set_level_niu...*) or by the user through the Trusted Path and its SID (*reserv_level*). The last *Inhib* module drives the physical connection of the CSMA/CD component to the medium. It inhibits *Rec* or *Send$_1$* accesses to the medium according to values of the medium level and of the interface level.

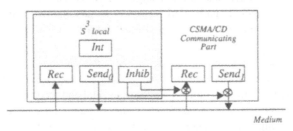

Fig. 7 SMAC interface unit

These are all elementary modules, whose functions are simple and not complex. So the local S^3 is in fact a much lighter component than the CSMA/CD component. It can be connected with an existing standard CSMA/CD component.

6.3 DS^3 and multilevel LAN

The CSS, the local S^3 and the medium which is accessed in accordance with the rules of the SMAC protocol constitute the *Distributed S^3* of the LAN (or DS^3). The DS^3 and the local S^3 cooperate in enforcing the control of information flows in the more concrete layer of the system: the hardware layer. In particular, this control is enforced by programming the local S^3. This programming is done in security mode by exchanging security frames between the trusted CSS and local S^3. So, these exchanges are isolated from the behaviouring of the untrusted interface components

A multilevel station, built above the same principles (more details in[4]) may be added to ensure a secure sharing of data between levels. Because such a station is able to manage multilevel data structures and processes, it permits to monolevel stations to access data through levels in a quite secure manner.

The global architecture of such a system constitutes a secure LAN which is said to have a multilevel functioning mode. Such an architecture satisfies the required security property: all information flows, including timing flows, are controlled exhaustively.

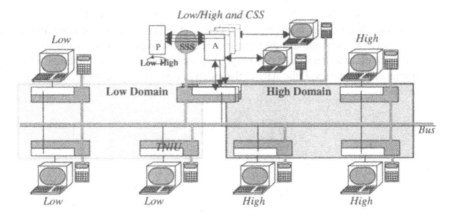

Fig. 8 Multilevel LAN architecture with two levels

It is obvious that this architecture is insufficient if the communication medium is vulnerable: that is not the addressed problem in this paper. Cryptographic techniques may be added to preserve the confidentiality and integrity of messages transmitted over the network. These techniques may rely on cryptographic devices and functions which can be driven by the Distributed S^3 (local S^3 and CSS). They can be viewed as an external protection layer, by opposite to the internal protection layer described here.

7 Discussion

Such an architecture enforces the rules of multilevel security. The DS^3 aim at controlling internal information flows which are involved when communications are achieved over the medium by ensuring that the involved causal dependencies are secure. This control of information flows may be used in order to enforce confidentiality, integrity and availability properties.

7.1 With respect to confidentiality

Let x_{low} and y_{high} two points that belong to two different domains D_{low} and D_{high} in the system. These domains may be defined, when multilevel security is the applied security policy, by $D_l = \{x / l_c(x) = l\}$ with $l(x)$ the confidentiality level of x and $D_{high} \cap D_{low} = \emptyset$. The cone-lemma ensures that:

$$cone(x_{low}) \subseteq D_{low} \tag{5}$$

$$cone(y_{high}) \subseteq D_{low} \cup D_{high} \tag{6}$$

These conditions ensure that the observation of any point in D_{low} will reveal no information about points in D_{high}. But points of D_{high} may be built from points of D_{low}. The only allowed flows of information are from *low* to *high*. It is a classical result in confidentiality. In this case, all information flows are controlled.

By managing levels of interface units and of the medium, the SMAC protocol permits the local S^3 to authorize or not any send or receive accesses of interface units to the medium. The enforced rules authorize an interface unit to send data to the medium when both levels of the interface and of the medium are the same. In this case, the state of the medium at a given time depends on the previous state and operations of interface units at the same level only. This fact implements the condition (5) and in particular, at *Low* level, the state of the medium depend only on points at the same *Low* level.

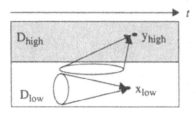

Fig. 9 Graphical translation of confidentiality properties

Conversely, the enforced rules authorize an interface unit to receive data from the medium when the level of the interface dominates (*high*) the level of the medium (*low*). So a point y_{high} in the interface may depend on the state of the medium and it was showed that this state of the medium only depends on points at the same level. This state is a point x_{low} in D_{low} and $x_{low} \in cone(y_{high})$. This fact is in accordance with the condition (6).

The definition of points includes objects and timing components. The conditions (5) and (6) with respect to timing components are ensured by the time slicing enforced by the SMAC protocol on the level of the medium. Slices are computed on a *Low* level information basis, from reservations. So, for example, durations assigned to send or receive operations exerted by an interface unit depend on: firstly, durations of time slices which are assigned to each level of the medium, and secondly, on the state of the medium. We have showed that both depend on points whose level is dominated by the level of the interface.

7.2 With respect to integrity

When integrity is the addressed property, the same approach can be used. The set Alt_s contains the points that a user, or more generally a subject s is able to alter and the set R_s contains the points the subject s has the right to alter in accordance with the security policy. So, the definition of the security given in (1) is the same here: the system is secure if a subject s can act only on the objects he has the right to act:

$$A_s \subseteq R_s \qquad (7)$$

The set R_s is also given by

$$R_s = \{x \mid l_i(x) \leq l_i(s)\}$$

where $l_i(s)$ denotes the clearance of the user in integrity and $l_i(x)$ is the integrity level of point x. The interface rule expresses conditions on the integrity level of an input point x_i and the clearance level of the subject s who can alter this point:

$$\forall s, \, x_i \in A_s \Rightarrow l_i(s) \geq l_i(x_i) \qquad (8)$$

The second condition requires monotonic decreasing of levels over causal dependencies. If values of levels increase with integrity of points:

$$\forall x, \forall y, x \to y \Rightarrow l_i(x) \geq l_i(y) \qquad (9)$$

Dep-Lemma. If condition *(3)* is enforced

$$x \in dep(y) \Rightarrow l_i(y) \geq l_i(x)$$

Proof. The proof is trivially similar to the proof of cone-lemma. ■

Fact 3. If in a system Conditions *(2)* and *(3)* are enforced then the system is secure.

Proof. We must show that *(2)* and *(2)* $\Rightarrow$ *(7)*. If $x \in Alt_s$ then $x \in A_s$ or $\exists y \in A_s / x \in dep(y)$. If $x \in A_s$, then by *(2)* , $l_i(x) \leq l_i(s)$.. In the other case $\exists y \in A_s / x \in dep(y)$, and then $l_i(x) \leq l_i(y) \leq l_i(s)$ by *(2)* and Dep-Lemma. So x is in R_s. ■

With respect to integrity, the both rules *(2)* and *(3)* ensure that any subject s who has the right to alter an input point x_i is allowed to alter any point of $dep(x_i)$. So the alteration of x_i by s will have an impact only on points that s has the right to alter.

A convention on levels can be chosen: a level l is a pair (l_c, l_i) where l_c denotes a confidentiality level and l_i is an integrity level and a comparison rule on levels may be:

$$(l_1 \leq l_2) \Leftrightarrow (l_{c1}, l_{i1}) \leq (l_{c2}, l_{i2}) \Leftrightarrow (l_{c1} \leq l_{c2}) \wedge (l_{i1} \geq l_{i2})$$

With such a convention, the confidentiality conditions *(3)* can be extended with condition *(3)* in a simple way by using a level l for integrity and confidentiality:

$$\forall x, \forall y, x \to y \Rightarrow l(x) \leq l(y) \qquad (10)$$

Then the send and receive conditions can be expressed in the same way for both confidentiality and integrity.

Let x_{low} and y_{high} two points that belong to two different domains of integrity D_{low} and D_{high} in the system. These domains may be defined by $D_l = \{x / l_i(x) = l\}$ if $l_i(x)$ is the integrity level of x and $D_{high} \cap D_{low} = \varnothing$. So D_{low} denotes a domain of low integrity and D_{high} denotes a domain of high integrity. Referring to the rule *(3)* , then $dep(x_{low})$ and $dep(y_{high})$ are sets of points in the system and the rules ensure that

$$dep(x_{low}) \subseteq D_{low} \qquad (11)$$
$$dep(y_{high}) \subseteq D_{low} \cup D_{high} \qquad (12)$$

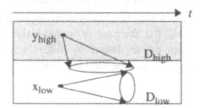

Fig. 10 Graphical translation of integrity properties

The condition *(11)* express that the alteration of any point in D_{low} will alter no information about points in D_{high}. So the only allowed flows of information are from *high* to *low* (condition *(12)*). This is in accordance with classical results as expressed by Biba [2] for example.

This is achieved in the context of the multilevel LAN by enforcing the same mechanisms of control as for confidentiality. Each communicating host and interface unit belongs to an integrity domain, and every elementary transfer of information is submitted to this control of information flows.

By defining integrity domains and by controlling flows between these domains according to the previous rules, we ensure there is no way, at a low integrity domain, to use any input covert channel in order to insert corrupted instructions or data in a high integrity domain.

These results may be applied to isolate and minimize functions which are vital to run a critical process inside. Criticality levels may be defined; they reflect the degree of criticality of functions or data with respect to the system objective. So a *High* critical domain is fully protected from eventually malicious operations exerted from a *Low* critical domain. This scheme is interesting in a security point of view, but also for cost considerations. Indeed, it permits to minimize the *High* critical domain by including in it the only really critical functions and data. Techniques used during the development of such a system and during its running in order to ensure dependability properties may be reduced by limiting them to the only critical domain.

7.3 With respect to availability

A particular case of the integrity property which was previously described offers some kind of availability. Indeed, the SMAC protocol which is used to share the communication medium of the multilevel LAN tends to separate domains of integrity/criticality and to regulate flows between these domains according to multilevel rules.

In particular, the time slicing exerted on the level of the medium coupled with the ability assigned to the interface units of sending or receiving according to time slices make impossible for an interface at a *Low* integrity level to disrupt the use of the communication medium by interfaces at a *High* level of integrity. When communications occur at a given level, there is no way for interface units at an other level to get any send access to the medium.

So the availability of services inside the domain of *High* integrity can not be countered by malicious processes at a *Low* level of integrity or by a crash or a bad functioning occurring on an host at a lower level of integrity.

So, some mechanisms may be employed to ensure high availability inside the high integrity domain itself. But their use is limited inside this domain only, and the availability property is not put in danger by lower integrity levels, thanks to the separation enforced by the DS^3 and the SMAC protocol.

8 Conclusion

Techniques and mechanisms suggested here were firstly designed and developed in order to protect the confidentiality of data, processes and communications over a LAN. This protection is based on a control of dependencies that enforces an exhaustive control of information flows. It relies upon a distributed security subsystem composed of a particularly restricted subset of hardware mechanisms: they are in charge of ensuring that accesses of interface units to the medium are done in accordance with multilevel rules. This leads to share the medium in a particular way which defines a secure medium access control (or SMAC) protocol. This protocol may be viewed as an extension of an existing MAC protocol, as CSMA/CD.

This logical separation, achieved by means of this protocol, may be also used in order to separate integrity levels. In particular, the extremely strong control of information flows which is enforced can isolate some domain where a high level of integrity may be needed drastically. This domain is then protected from other domains of low integrity that can not corrupt its behaviour: in particular they can not enforce any communication channel to send malicious data or pieces of code. Such levels of integrity can be used in critical applications to protect some vital functions. As a particular case of the application of control of dependencies to integrity, some needs in availability may be answered also. The separation between high integrity and low integrity domains ensure that any (malicious or not) failure in a low integrity domain will not disrupt the good functioning inside a high integrity domain.

This whole security protects efficiently all the information that needs to be protected, and only this information. We feel that this approach is well adapted to the real world, where in fact, few informations and functions necessitate to be protected. So, such a system does not penalize the use and processing of most of the data which belong to an unprotected domain. Rather, it makes lighter the amount of protected processing by reserving it to the only data which necessitate it.

A real system is actually under development upon these principles. Some mechanisms and functions of distributed operating systems are beeing built above this basic architecture. They implement classical distributed operating services, but, taking account of the underlying architecture and of its multilevel functioning, they implement also new multilevel distributed operating services: sharing files between hosts running at different levels, or accessing remote files, running processes on remote hosts. Then the challenge is no longer building a secure distributed operating system but to building some distributed operating services upon a secure architecture, and taking advantage of its security features.

9 References

1. P. Bieber, F. Cuppens, "A logical view of secure dependencies." In *Journal of Computer Security*, Vol. 1, Nr. 1, IOS Press, 1992

2. K. J. Biba, "Integrity Considerations for Secure Computer Systems", Technical Report ESD-TR-76-372, ESD/AFSC, Hanscom AFB, Bedford, Mass., 1977. Also MITRE MTR-3153.

3. D. E. Bell and L. J. Padula "Secure Computer Systems: Unified Exposition and Multics Interpretation", MTR-2997, MITRE Corporation, Bedford, Mass. (1975).

4. B. d'Ausbourg and J.H. Llareus, "M^{2}S: A machine for multilevel security", *in Proceedings of ESORICS92*, Toulouse, France, 1992

5. G.Eizenberg, "Mandatory policy: secure system model". In AFCET,editor, *European Workshop on Computer Security*, Paris,1989.

6. G.King "A survey of commercially available secure LAN product" , *in Proc. Int. IEEE Conf. on Computer Security Applications*, Tucson, Arizona, December 1989

7. ISO 7498-2, Organization for Standardization, Information Processing Systems - Open System Interconnection Reference Model - Security Architecture, 1988

8. Information Technology Security Evaluation Criteria, Harmonized Criteria of France, Germany, the Netherlaands, and the United Kingdom, 1990

9. H.L Johnson et al. "Integrity and Assurance of service Protection in a large, multipurpose, critical System" , *In Proceedings of the 15th National Computer Security Conference, Baltimore,* MD, October 1992

10. E.S. Lee, B. Thomson, Peter I.P. Boulton and M. Stumm "An architecture for a Trusted Network" *European Symposium on Research in Computer Security, ESORICS90*, Toulouse, France, 1990

11. J. McLean, "Security Models and Information Flow" *,IEEE Symposium on Security and Privacy, Oakland,* 1990.

12. NCSC. Department of Defense. Trusted Computer Systems Evaluation Criteria. Technical report DoD 5200.28-STD, National Computer Security Center, Fort Meade, MD, December 1985

13. National Computer Security Center Trusted Network Interpretation of the Trusted Computer System Evaluation Criteria, NCSC-TG-005, July 1987

14. N. E. Proctor and P. G. Neumann "Architectural implications of covert channels", *In Proceedings of the 15th National Computer Security Conference, Baltimore,* MD, October 1992

15. J.M. Rushby and B. Randell, "A Distributed Secure System" Computer vol 16 no 7, IEEE, July 1983

16. P.Siron and B.d'Ausbourg "A Secure Medium Access Control Protocol: Security versus Performances" *in Proceedings of ESORICS 94*, Brighton, UK, November 1994.

17. J. Wood and D.H. Barnes "A Practical Distributed System" *in Proceedings of the International Conference on System Security, London,* October 1985

18. J. Wood "A practical Distributed System" in *Proceedings of the Second International Conference on Secure Communication Systems*, IEE, London, October 1986

19. R. Yavatkar, P. Pai and R. Finkel "A reservation based CSMA Protocol for Integrated Manufacturing networks", *Tecn. Rep. 216-92, Department of Comp. Sc., Univeristy of Kentucky,* Lexington, KY

A Secure Medium Access Control Protocol: Security versus Performances

Pierre SIRON, Bruno d'AUSBOURG

CERT-ONERA
Département d'Etudes et de Recherches en Informatique
2 avenue E.Belin
B.P. 4025
31055 Toulouse cedex FRANCE
email: (siron,ausbourg} @tls-cs.cert.fr

Abstract. Many systems were built in order to protect confidentiality of data and processes. This can be done by using multilevel architectures of machines and networks. But these architectures tolerate the existence of covert channels.We designed an architecture of a distributed security subsystem in order to avoid them, basing it on the use of secure dependencies. Controls exerted on dependencies can control exhaustively elementary flows of information. These controls are achieved by means of some hardware mechanisms which govern the access of hosts to the medium according to secure medium access control protocol (or SMAC). This approach implements in a straightforward manner some multilevel security conditions that ensure a very high degree of protection. We wanted to measure the real cost of introducing security inside a MAC protocol, by comparing under simulation the performances of the SMAC protocol with some other standard but insecure MAC protocols.

1 Introduction

This paper is the second in the series documents describing how one can build a security subsystem in order to implement secure dependencies over a distributed architecture over a LAN. This document builds on the more fundamental issues outlined in the first paper (see [4]) and assumes that the reader is familiar with the basic concepts of the approach. We strongly urge the uninitiated to refer to the above paper before proceeding to read any further.

In brief, we followed the approach[1] described in [4] basing it on using secure dependencies as defined by [1]. The idea is that controls which are exerted on dependencies can control exhaustively elementary flows of information. These controls are achieved by means of some hardware mechanisms which regulate the access of hosts to the medium according to a secure medium access control protocol (or SMAC).

This approach implements, in a straightforward manner, some multilevel security

---

1. This project was supported by DGA in France

conditions that ensure a very high degree of protection. But it may be argued·that introducing any security controls inside a communication protocol is an unacceptable approach because performances may be degraded. So, we wanted to measure the real cost of introducing security inside a MAC protocol, by comparing performances of the SMAC protocol with some other standard but insecure MAC protocols.

The first part of the paper reminds of the approach and explains the choices of implementation that we made with respect to the required security. The second part describes the SMAC protocol and the third part shows some simulation results that seem very interesting because they thwart some too commonly accepted ideas.

2 Overview of the security approach

The enforced security is based on controlling dependencies that are involved in elementary operations over a LAN architecture. This control aims at authorizing only *secure* dependencies in the system with respect to the security policy.

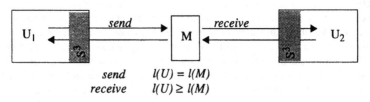

$$\begin{array}{ll} send & l(U) = l(M) \\ receive & l(U) \geq l(M) \end{array}$$

Fig. 1 Rules to access the medium in a network interface unit

In our case, the policy in question is the multilevel security policy, and then levels are assigned to the communication medium and to the network interface units (NIU). Dependencies that are involved in sending or receiving operations are secure if the two conditions on levels as illustrated on Fig. 1 are always satisfied.

The enforcement of these rules is performed by local security subsystems (or S^3) in every NIU. Send and receive operations on the medium can be performed by NIUs only when security conditions are verified. It follows that bidirectional exchanges can occur only between NIUs at the same level l, when this level l is assigned to the medium. Globally, levels are managed and assigned to the medium and to NIUs by a Centralized Security Station or CSS. Each local S^3 must be able to know the level value of the medium and of its own NIU.

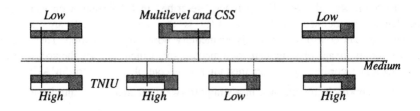

Fig. 2 Multilevel LAN

The enforcement of the access rules to the medium and the need to exchange security data between CSS and local S^3 in NIUs have an impact on the Medium Access Control entities in each NIU. The MAC protocol must be adapted in order to take these constraints into account.

This adapting process has been performed in the framework of a distributed architecture. In fact this protocol operates over a LAN architecture as described by Fig. 2 . Stations are connected to the medium through Trusted NIUs (or TNIUs) that are composed by the NIUs and their own local S^3. CSS is the security manager of the LAN. A multilevel station can be used to enforce the sharing of data between processes at different running levels. This secure multilevel station[3] can be used to implement the CSS functions.

Secure MAC or SMAC is the adapted MAC protocol we devised to regulate accesses of NIUs to the medium in accordance with the security rules.

3 The SMAC protocol

3.1 Global functioning: user and security modes

This protocol is in charge of regulating the access of network interface unit to the medium. But this access must be done in a secure way.

In particular, SMAC takes account of the time slicing that is exerted on the level of the medium. It manages also the exchanges of security data under the authority of the CSS. These data include particularly reservation data emitted from *local S^3* and level settings for the medium which are emitted from the *CSS*.

SMAC manages two functioning modes of the interface unit: a *user* mode and a *security* mode. In the security mode, only *local S^3* can use the medium M to exchange security data with the *CSS*. In user mode, send and receive operations can be performed by the interface units according to values of their own level and of the level of M. The CSS computes time slices for sessions of exchanges in user mode; each session corresponds to a value assigned to the level of M. These values are set in accordance with reservations previously received. At the end of a slice, the interface unit always returns to the security mode. In security mode, the *CSS* may ask to *local S^3* if reservations are pending. If yes, *local S^3* may answer by giving the content of their pending reservations. The protocol for this dialogue is a synchronous one. The *CSS* fixes a transmission slot for each local S^3 to answer and each local S^3 may answer during its reserved slot. The CSS broadcasts then a new value for the level of the medium and a new session in user mode is started. In user mode, a Medium Access Control (MAC) protocol arbitrates the access to the medium between units which are allowed to access it: this protocol is CSMA/CD in our case.

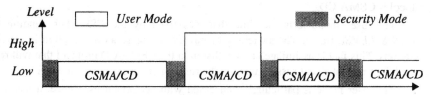

Fig. 3 Alternating modes of functioning

The SMAC protocol is similar to protocols used in the real time world where requirements on the amount of delay between the time a packet is ready and the time it is received at destination are stringent. In these protocols, some sources must reserve transmission slots before they can begin transmission [12].

3.2 Security mode

This mode of functioning is dedicated to the *Distributed Security Subsystem* or DS^3. Only the local S^3 on the network interface units and the *CSS* are allowed to access the medium that is used to implement the security subnetwork. In the first version of SMAC, the master of exchanges is the *CSS*; it can perform various security operations. Mainly:

- It can ask to several *local S^3* (or to all of them) if pending reservations of levels were requested by the user on the host. This is done by broadcasting a *GET_REQUESTS* frame to these *local S^3*. This frame contains a slot number that is assigned to each *local S^3* and that can be used to emit a pending request to the *CSS*.

- It can accept or reject a reservation request. This is done by sending a *ACK_LEVEL* or *NACK_LEVEL* frame to the *local S^3* that emitted the request. When receiving the *ACK_LEVEL* frame, the *local S^3* sets the level of the interface unit to the requested value of this level and sets a watchdog to the value of duration assigned by the user to the functioning of the interface at this level.

- It can change the current level of the medium by broadcasting a *SET_BUS_LEVEL* frame to all the *local S^3*. A duration value is embedded in the frame: this value gives the duration that is assigned to the next session of exchanges at the new current level. This value is kept by all the *local S^3*: they use it to set a watchdog. When this frame is received, the *local S^3* enter the user mode, and the network interface units are set in accordance to their own level and the new current level. A new session of exchanges can start. When the watchdog indicates that time has elapsed, the *local S^3* enters the security mode.

3.3 User mode

This mode of functioning is dedicated to the network interface units. They can perform send or receive operations in accordance with settings done by the *local S^3* with respect to the values of the levels assigned to the interface and to the medium. The enforced MAC protocol is CSMA/CD.

This user mode lasts the time that was fixed by the *CSS* when sending the *SET_BUS_LEVEL* frame. The switching of modes can cause an interruption in sending operations. This fact is assimilated to a collision in the CSMA/CD protocol that will retry to send the frame at a next session that will be running at the same current level.

This user mode is particularly concerned with performances. Hence, it has to be submitted to performance evaluation measures.

4 Performance evaluation

We carried out a performance evaluation of the SMAC protocol. This effort had several main objectives:

- To estimate the cost of security, in particular by comparing the secure protocol and the standard but not secure CSMA-CD protocol. We could hope for a performance advantage, due to the partitioning of the users into several communicating classes (one per security level).
- To calculate some parameters for the SMAC protocol: for example the time to assign to each security level in the communication medium multiplexing (the *slot time*).
- To examine the overall performance of the network concerning contention (number of collisions) and effective utilization.

Before performing any experiments on a real system, we chose to proceed to exhaustive simulations. The following sections describe the simulation environment, the simulation model, the performed experiments, the first results of our evaluation and the work that remains to do.

4.1 Simulation environment

The quality of a simulation depends partially on the software tools which are used. The list of requirements may be long [10]: reliability, readability, adaptability, portability, efficiency. These requirements are more or less achieved easily if software is well structured. Commercial products meet them, but we chose to use the MIT Network Simulator NETSIM (cf. [7]) for two main reasons:

- NETSIM is available by ftp.
- NETSIM was used in several research projects (cf. [9]) and in particular in a study [12] that is close to this one, an extension to the CSMA-CD protocol to support real-time traffic.

NETSIM is a discrete-event simulator. It can simulate anything that can be modelled by a network of components that send messages to one another. The components schedule events in order to make appear the evolving of the simulation. The model being simulated and the action of components are determined entirely by the code that controls the components, and not by the framework of the simulator. A new code must be written to develop a new component: data structures and action functions are written in C language in accordance with a given frame.

The program provides the user with the means to display (XWindow system) the topology of the network and the parameters of the simulation, to modify them, and to save and load the various configurations. It allows also a user to control the simulation process, to log various events and to produce statistics.

4.2 Simulation model

A simulation requires models that can be viewed as simplified representations of complex processes. By definition, they do not express the full behaviour of processes but they capture the most significant phenomena that may affect the predicted results.

272

We limited the models to the exchanges of packets rather than elementary exchanges of bits. The granularity of simulation is then greater, but that is not really a problem, because exchanges of packets are always performed in accordance with the security rules. Therefore the simulation time is shorter and more acceptable and the model is closer to the user point of view. We simulated also the collisions between concurrent communications.

The main problem was to simulate the SMAC protocol but also the standard CSMA-CD protocol. NETSIM contains a detailed implementation of this last protocol developed at the University of Washington (cf. [6]) and many other components of the local network world.

The components that were used with minimal changes only were:

- UWETLINK: It models the passive Ethernet cable with its physical characteristics such as propagation delay, channel contention, and delivery of packets to the destination interface.
- HOST: Implements the standard CSMA-CD protocol at the Medium Access Sublayer (MAC), connected to UWETLINK.
- TCP: Is an implementation of the TCP protocol (Transmission Control Protocol) and is connected to an HOST component. This TCP component includes the latest version of TCP enhancements including the slow-start congestion avoidance and retransmission timer estimation algorithms [11].
- USER: The supplier and consumer of data for the TCP module.
- PSOURCE:A simple Poisson traffic source, directly connected to an HOST.
- SINK: A packet sink.

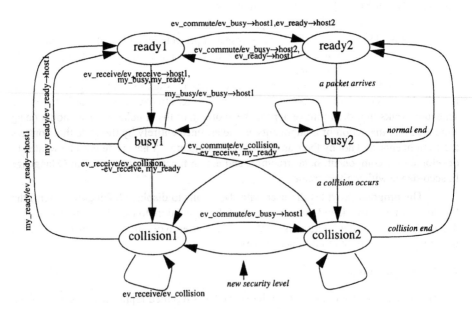

Fig. 4 SUWETLINK automaton

Let us detail the UWETLINK component, that was mainly modified in order to model the SMAC protocol. In this close shot, the events manipulated by the simulator are of two types:

- The external events (for the communication between the components):

- EV_RECEIVE: A packet reception signal.
- EV_READY: Component ready signal.
- EV_BUSY: Component busy signal.
- EV_COLLISION: A collision has occurred.

- And the private events:

- MY_BUSY: A packet is sent.
- MY_READY: End of the sending.

The automaton, that was simplified for understanding needs, is shown on the left side of the Fig. 4 . The EV_RECEIVE reception in the ready state will cause at a given time a EV_RECEIVE reception for the next host, and the MY_BUSY and MY_READY sending for internal purposes. The MY_BUSY reception indicates the end of the collision detection period, and the component notifies the other hosts of the channel acquirement (EV_BUSY event). A second EV_RECEIVE reception announces a collision case, and implies to send EV_COLLISION and to remove the sent EV_RECEIVE. At the MY_READY event reception, the channel becomes free and the EV_READY signal is the opposite of the EV_BUSY one.

To simulate the SMAC protocol, the most significant problem is to represent the temporal multiplexing of the network, and therefore to develop a new component, called SUWETLINK (S for Secure). The new automaton corresponds to the whole Fig. 4 for two security levels. The states are now subscribed by the security level and a new event, denoted by EV_COMMUTE, indicates the context switches. The trick is to consider the busy state of the HOST component either as the standard state (an host is emitting) or as a state where the medium is at a different security level and where the communications are prohibited. A switch during a communication interrupts it, and, in order to simplify, this is considered as a new case of collision (outside the usual collision detection period).

Fig. 5 and Fig. 6 visualize the simulated worlds. It was not necessary to calibrate the components. The key point here was to compare the CSMA-CD and SMAC protocols with models of the same complexity.

4.3 Workload model

The numbers of subscribers and security levels vary in the simulated worlds, but also the simulation workload, which consists of two classes: the strong and the weak workload models.

Strong workload

Simultaneous file transfer sessions, and consequently TCP and USER components, are used. An example is given in Fig. 5 : user1 sends a file to user2, 3 to 4, 5 to 6 and 7 to 8, and each users pair belongs to a different security level. For a file size of 20000 bytes, the results show a network utilization between 60 and 70%.

274

These worlds are rather realistic if we consider that the algorithms of the TCP components are close to the real implementations

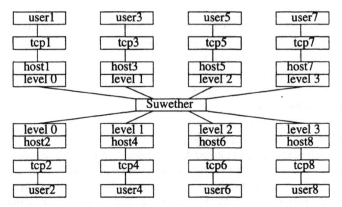

Fig. 5 TCP communication (20000 bytes, 8 points, 4 levels) example: the simulated world.

Weak workload

Packets generators use a Poisson distribution and send data to simple sinks. These worlds can model interactive sessions. An example is given Fig. 6 where two security levels are defined. It illustrates a network utilization less than 5%.

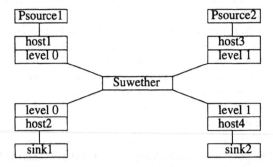

Fig. 6 Weak workload communication (4 points, 2 levels) example: the simulated world.

4.4 Performance measures

Among many results that were produced, we emphasized two parameters in the case of strong workload:

- Simulation time: It is the simulated time since the instant 0 until the instant of the last file transfer session. In this paper all the transfers have the same beginning and the same length, so the simulation time depends on the effective network utilization and the global number of packets, that may vary in function of the retransmissions and the TCP optimizations.
- Collisions: We measured the total number of collisions for each experiment, which includes usual collisions between packets and security level switching collisions.

In the case of the weak workloads the simulation time is an input, and in this time sources and sinks are running, Therefore the main performance measurement is the mean packet transfer time: this value is the difference between the reception by the sink and the emission by the source.

4.5 Experimental results

Only two significant results among the first experiments are showed in this paper. Parameters are standard: for example the maximal packet length is 1024 bytes, and the network data rate is 10 Mbits/s (Ethernet). Experiments were repeated with several security slots (the duration where the medium security level is constant): 1, 2, 3, 4, 5 and 10 ms. The null value can be considered as the standard protocol.

The results in Fig. 7 correspond to the strong workloads (TCP world). These curves are noteworthy, the SMAC protocol is more efficient than the CSMA-CD protocol in saturated and well-balanced worlds where the problem is to share the bandwidth.

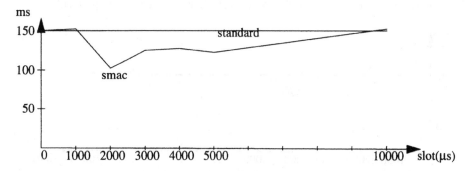

Fig. 7 TCP communication (20000 bytes, 8 points, 4 levels) example: the simulation time.

The network efficiency depends on the packet retransmission rate (and depends also on the number of dropped packets in the case of multiple checks). The number of collisions is a good indicator and this number is decreasing (see Fig. 8). This constitutes the main reason for the better performance of the CSMA-CD protocol.

We expected this result because there is no interference between communications of different security levels due to the security conditions that are enforced. Nevertheless the switching of security level introduces new collisions, when the commutation occurs during a packet transmission. But, globally. we observed on the simulator, that the number of collisions is lower.

The number of collisions is higher for 3 ms than for 2 ms (idem for 3 ms vs 5ms) and this fact could appear amazing. The explanation is in the fitting between the slot time and the effective time to transmit one, two, three,... packets. In the first case the commutation occurs rather when the host is processing, and there is no collision. In the second case the commutation occurs more often when the host is sending a packet.

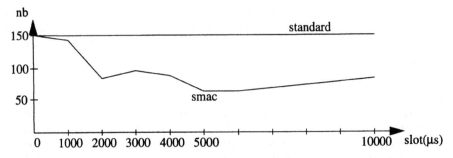

Fig. 8 TCP communication (20000 bytes, 8 points, 4 levels) example: the number of collisions.

We observed the same kind of results with various numbers of hosts and there is often a gain in performances when the security levels are more numerous. The Fig. 9 gives results for the same world but with two security levels. If we compare the SMAC protocol curves in the two cases, the simulation time is generally greater. For slot = 4ms, the simulation time equals 118ms for SMAC and 152ms for the standard protocol.

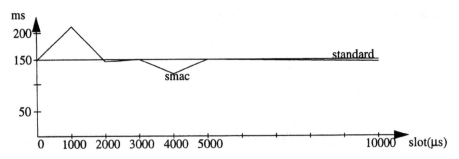

Fig. 9 TCP communication (20000 bytes, 8 points, **2 levels**) example: the simulation time.

As expected the number of collisions (Fig. 10) is greater, because there are now more users of the same security level, which compete for the channel possession. For slot = 2ms, we obtain 84 collisions for 4 levels and 153 collisions for 2 levels. The optimal value to assign to the slot duration is not easy to find, it varies all along the experiments.

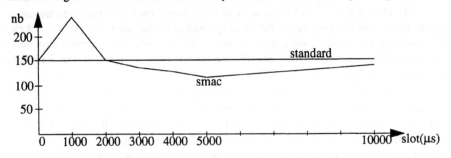

Fig. 10 TCP communication (20000 bytes, 8 points, **2 levels**) example: the number of collisions.

For the weak workloads (Fig. 11) the results are less favourable. The mean packet transfer time is steadily growing with the security slot and the number of levels. On the given example the host must wait every two times for the good slot to succeed in the packet transmission. Nevertheless the transfer times remains transparent to the user.

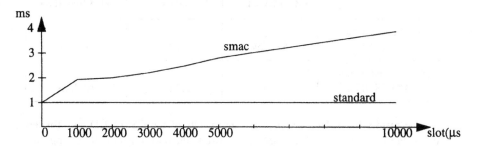

Fig. 11 Weak workload communication (4 points, 2 levels) example: the mean transfer time.

The weak workload explains the very little number of collisions (Fig. 12) in the standard case. For the SMAC protocol the collisions come from the security level switching. The mean transfer time is 1 ms, we have about 1200 packets in this test, and we can verify that the collision rate is about 1/2 for slot=1ms.

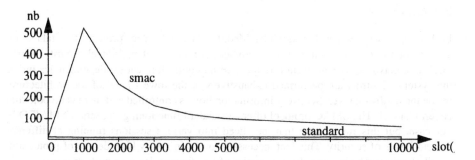

Fig. 12 Weak workload communication (4 points, 2 levels) example: the number of collisions.

We could here develop simplified formulae, that well describe the expected results. With the events traces, this is a kind of validation of the simulator.

4.6 Comparison with a tokenring network

NETSIM has a component that simulates a tokenring network. It was interesting to use it, although we did not verify in details its modelization nor we calibrated it.

The following table shows results for the standard CSMA-CD, the secure SMAC and the standard Tokenring protocols. The simulated worlds include 8 points. The number of security levels is 2 and the security slot is fixed to 2 ms. The strong workload corresponds to 4 file transfers of 100 kbytes.

Table 1: Performance results

	CSMA-CD	SMAC	TOKENRING
simulation time TCP	539 ms	482 ms	465 ms
mean transfer time POISSON	1 ms	2.7 ms	10.2 ms

The results for SMAC are between the results of the CSMA-CD and Tokenring protocols. For the strong workload, SMAC is close to the best protocol: Tokenring. In this case the data transfers are well scheduled by the circulation of a token on a ring. We can do an analogy to the switches of the security levels.

For the weak workload, SMAC is closer to CSMA-CD. This result allows us to differently appreciate the results of the previous paragraph. SMAC seems to keep the advantage of Ethernet, and the waiting time for the good security level seems lower than the waiting time for the token.

5 Conclusion

In this paper, we described a particular Medium Access Control protocol that takes into account of the enforcement of some sufficient conditions of multilevel security over a local area network. The protection is founded on controlling causal dependencies inside the system. Controls are performed exhaustively at the lowest level of the architecture: inside the hardware layer. So, every information flow is controlled and there is no potential covert channel. The SMAC protocol offers a standard functioning to users, CSMA/CD in our case, but this functioning may be sliced into various sessions running at different current levels of security. This fact, necessary to obtain a very high degree of protection, may be criticized by arguing that these rules of functioning decrease performances.

Several lessons were learned from the results of simulation that were reported here. Firstly, when the network is used at a single public level, it functions in a standard way and the rules to access the medium are in accordance with the CSMA/CD protocol. When the network is used in a multilevel functioning mode, two cases may occur.

The first case consists in a good use of the multilevel features: the network is effectively used to exchanges data (files for example) at different levels. This case was modelled by the strong workload world. In this case, there is a gain of throughput, because SMAC organizes the accesses to the medium. The second case consists in a bad use of the multilevel features: the network is used in a sporadic manner at different levels. This case was modelled by the weak workload world. In this case, there is effectively a transfer time growing. But the results of comparison with the Token Ring protocol, for example, show that the advantage of CSMA/CD in case of weak loads is not lost with SMAC. So, extending CSMA/CD with SMAC in order to get secure exchanges over a network may produce an increase of performances in the best case, and preserves the benefits of CSMA/CD over other protocols in the worst case.

We emphasize the reuse of the original TCP and HOST (CSMA-CD) components. We added only the security level parameter to them. This is also a good point before a real implementation. It is probably a good thing to obtain good performances with components that ignore the underlying multiplexing (the delay retransmission computation and the round trip time estimation of a packet could be no more appropriate).

Of course, a lot of work remains to do to complete these first results: in particular to accumulate the simulation experiments. But they constitute an encouragement for designers of secure systems because they make appearing that security and performances are not necessary antagonistic.

6 References

1. P. Bieber, F. Cuppens: A logical view of secure dependencies. In *Journal of Computer Security*, Vol. 1, Nr. 1, IOS Press, 1992

2. D. E. Bell and L. J. Padula: Secure Computer Systems: Unified Exposition and Multics Interpretation, MTR-2997, MITRE Corporation, Bedford, Mass. (1975).

3. B. d'Ausbourg and J.H. Llareus: M^2S: A machine for multilevel security, *European Symposium on Research in Computer Security, ESORICS92*, Toulouse, France, 1992

4. B. d'Ausbourg: Implementing Secure Dependencies over a Network by designing a Distributed Security SubSystem, *ESORICS94*, Brighton, UK,1994

5. G.Eizenberg: Mandatory policy: secure system model. In AFCET,editor, *European Workshop on Computer Security*, Paris,1989.

6. H. Golde: University of Washington version of MIT Network Simulator. October 1991. (available by anonymous FTP from june.cs.washington.edu).

7. A. Heybey: MIT Network simulator. *MIT Laboratory for Computer Science*, 1988.

8. G.King: A survey of commercially available secure LAN product, *in Proc. Int. IEEE Conf. on Computer Security Applications*, Tucson, Arizona, December 1989

9. MIT: NETSIM mailing list, info-netsim@lcs.mit.edu.

10. G.R. Sherman: The quality of a scientific simulation in *SIMULETTER vol 15 , n 3,* July 1984.

11. Van Jacobson: Congestion avoidance and control. *in Proc. of ACM SIGCOMM'88 Symposium*. pp. 314-329, August 1988.

12. R. Yavatkar, P. Pai and R. Finkel: A reservation based CSMA Protocol for Integrated Manufacturing networks, *Tecn. Rep. 216-92, Department of Comp. Sc., Univeristy of Kentucky,* Lexington, KY.

Distributed file system over a multilevel secure architecture problems and solutions

Christel CALAS

CERT-ONERA
Département d'Etudes et de Recherches en Informatique
2 av. Edouard Belin
BP 4025
31055 Toulouse Cedex FRANCE
email: calas@tls-cs.cert.fr

Abstract. This paper presents the principles of a distributed and secure file system. It relies on M^2S machines and a secure network which control dependencies and avoid any storage and temporal covert channel. It describes how, from NFS (Network File System) principles, we adapt the organization and the structures to obtain practical services despite constraining controls performed by the hardware. Finally it proves that it is possible to obtain a practical distributed file system, with usable features without any compromise on security enforcement.

Keywords. Security, Distributed file system, Multilevel security, M^2S machine, secure LAN.

1 Introduction

Distributed environment is today an important feature to provide in a multiple host system. Particularly it is very efficient to offer distributed processing and remote access to information from any station connected to the system: many distributed systems and operating systems were built to that end. But well known techniques in classical environments become difficult to enforce when a high degree of security is required. Indeed distribution and security make a strange mixture where security, performances and access possibilities seem to be incompatible.

This paper aims at presenting a distributed file system that enforces the security of its data according to the multilevel security policy. It is based on using a particular machine called M^2S (*Machine for Multilevel Security*) [2] and a network assuring secure communication between hosts. The security of M^2S and of the network relies on the interpretation of the *causality* security model [3]. This model is based on controls of dependencies between objects maintained inside the system (*cell memory, driver ports, ...*). These controls enforce the security but entail constraints on the operating system, the file system and the applications running upon them. These constraints are not imposed to obtain security like *"You must do that or else security would be broken"* but rather *"Services are always secure and if you do not do that, your service could not run"*.

This enforcement of security requires an adaptation of usual functions and structures to obtain practical services. We illustrate this fact through a distributed file system example. As depicted in [2] or [6] security and distribution entail new problems both of security and functionalities and we explain how to resolve them and show that it could be realized in a simpler manner.

We first present hardware components and the local file system constructed on M^2S inside an adapted Unix operating system [1]. Then we depict the distributed file system principles and structure through a description of its actors and its organization. We discuss problems ensuing from this organization and propose solutions and finally we describe examples of the utilization of this MLS distributed file system.

2 Secure basis

2.1 M^2S: A Machine for Multilevel Security

M^2S is a secure machine built at CERT[1]-ONERA[2] which enforces multilevel security of its processes and its data avoiding any storage and timing covert channel. Its principles are depicted on Fig. 1. Its architecture is composed of two processors: one classical processor MC68020 and a MC68010 that is called the *security processor*. This security processor controls the dependencies between objects by controlling the accesses requested by the classical processor to memory cells and to device ports. The security processor plus some simple software constitute the *Security SubSystem* (SSS) of M^2S. A UNIX operating system has been developed over this machine and classical kernel has been modified to take account of the special functionalities of M^2S. It offers multilevel services as multilevel processing and multilevel file system through special calls and a multiplexed organization which are described more precisely in [1,2].

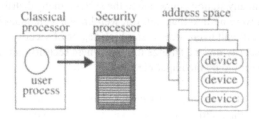

Fig. 1. M^2S security enforcement: Classical and security processors

---

1. Centre d'Etudes et de Recherches de Toulouse.
2. Office National d'Etudes et de Recherches Aéronautiques.

2.2 Secure LAN (Local Area Network)

Several M^2S machines can communicate through an Ethernet local network. The SSS has been extended in order to control the accesses of the classical processor to the communicator. As in case of local accesses, the SSS controls the dependencies between the processor, the bus and the buffer data. It allows the communications only when the communicators and the bus are at the same level. Moreover the SSS assures the timing and the level multiplexing of the bus in order to control the sharing of the network. This controls entails that:

- A l process may exchange information only with l processes.

3 Processing

Processes can run concurrently at different levels on M^2S machine. The SSS controls direct and indirect transmissions of information from high to low levels. Each machine is able to run processes up to a level corresponding to the maximum clearance assigned to the site. Processes are created either at login time by the login process or during sessions by user processes. Creating and killing processes can be done in accordance with the security rules due to the M^2S functioning:

- Processes at l level *(l > Unclassified)* may only create l children.

- Unclassified processes may create children at any l level managed by their host *(l ≥ Unclassified)*.

Having many hosts running multilevel processes and a secure LAN able to provide secure communications, multilevel distributed processing can be enforced.

4 Multilevel file system

Multilevel data are maintained on M^2S, inside multilevel, single-level files and directories. Multilevel files store data at different levels inside a single object [1]. The Unix kernel constructed upon M^2S provides the user with a multilevel tree-organized structure inside which files can be collected as depicted on Fig. 2. This structure and the associated services constitute the multilevel file system of a machine where the SSS controls the elementary flows. This fact necessitate to manage the underlying structures *(buffer, disk blocks, ...)* in order to be in accordance with these security controls. The following rules describe the perception of these controls at the user point of view:

- classified l files can be created only inside directories with same l level.

- classified l directories can be created both in unclassified or l directories.

- creation or deletion of a file or of a directory inside a given l directory can be made only by a process running at this l level.

Users handle the file system structure through classical Unix services (*open, read, write, close, cp, mv, ...*) and some new ones (*smkdir, sopen, ...*) that handle the multilevel objects.

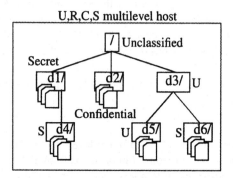

Fig. 2. Example of a multilevel tree in a multilevel file system.

5 Multilevel distributed file system

Consider a distributed environment composed of several sites and a communication channel. The sites maintain files and run processes for users. Every user can run its programs on any of these machines and so needs a common configuration that can be shared by these hosts. With respect to the file system, the distributed environment aims at providing the ability of accessing files of any sites from any machine.

But new problems appear in distributed systems: concurrent accesses, replication, cache coherency management due to remote location of resources and due to the entailed communications. Furthermore many others problems come from the controls enforced by the SSS. It is not problems of enforcement of security but rather problems of functionalities to provide in this secure and distributed environment.

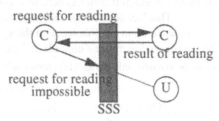

Fig. 3. Reading a remote file is forbidden by the SSS from high to low level

A classical problem occurs when a high level process attempts to read a low file maintained on a remote host at low level. It is a legal operation from a multilevel security point of view but it poses a serious problem in a distributed environment. Indeed in a single-host system, read operations are exerted on passive objects whereas they are realized through exchange of messages in a distributed system. These exchanges occur between process requestor and a file manager process running on the remote site. We saw in 2.2 that the secure network allows only the exchanges at equal level. So it prevents the exchanges from high process to low process and the reading of a low remote file from a high process cannot be processed.

In [2] the authors present some solutions to resolve this problem. They suggest either to put the file manager in the SSS or to downgrade the read request or yet to construct multiple managers. Finally they chose the second solution for SDOS (*Secure Distributed Operating System*) consisting in downgrading read requests under the user control. On the contrary we chose to implement *multilevel managers*. It is a better solution for our point of view since, first, we need to maintain the SSS as light as possible avoiding to increase its size with unnecessary code and second, we prefer avoiding any downgrading mechanism which is a very constraining technique.

Knowing the controls enforced by the SSS we have chosen a structure and an implementation of a distributed file system which offer the bigger set of functionalities.

5.1 Overview

The system comprises at least one M^2S machine which offer multilevel processing and storage. It is characterized by a maximum level called *clearance* corresponding to the maximum level it can handle. A multilevel machine accepts logins at any level lower or equal than its maximum clearance so that a Secret multilevel site, for instance, is designed as a *[Unclassified, Restricted, Confidential, Secret]* machine. Let us remark that a multilevel machine can manage every level dominated by its clearance so it always manages the Unclassified level. This level is essential to construct multilevel services like multilevel managers. If it is necessary, several M^2S can be used in the distributed system.

The distributed environment contains also single-level sites characterized by their level *[level]*, providing single-level processing and storage. Single-level machines could be any kind of machines but they must be connected to the network through a TNIU (Trusted Network Interface Unit) controlling their accesses to the network. To obtain a correct functioning, this SSS must use the same protocol as M^2S.

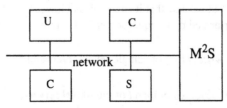

Fig. 4. Exemple of a hardware configuration of the distributed system

The last hardware component of the distributed environment is the secure network assuring the multilevel communications in a secure way. The goal of a multilevel file system is to offer some degree of sharing among the files stored on various machines in a practical manner. Now let us look at the principles of this sharing.

5.2 Principles

The sharing of files is based on a client/server paradigm. Servers handle locally files and offer services to remote clients for accessing them (*read, write, create, delete, ...*). Servers and clients may run both on single-level and multilevel sites so that there are single-level and multilevel servers. Multilevel servers run only on multilevel sites whereas single-level servers run both on multilevel and single-level machines. A multilevel server is composed of one process by levels. Each process runs the same piece of code. A multilevel server is characterized by the maximum level of processes which compose it and it contains a process for every level lower than this maximum level. A process of a l multilevel server manages files at l level but can also read files maintained by processes at level lower or equal than l and belonging to the same multilevel server. So these files are accessible from high clients through high server intermediary. Fig. 6 shows an example of Confidential multilevel server and Confidential single-level one.

Fig. 5. Multilevel and single-level servers maintain files

Clients are always single processes at a given level running on a single-level or multilevel sites. They realize user processing and contact remote server when it is necessary.

Fig. 6. Clients

A client at *l* level can only converse with a process at l level and so operates on files with l classification but we saw that it can read also lower files through reading operations that can be performed by its equal server in the multilevel server. To sum up a client with *l* level can:

- access (*read, write*) *l* files of *l* single-level servers and of *l'* (l'≥l) multilevel servers.

- read files with level lower than *l* of multilevel servers.

From these rules we now present how clients contact servers and reference a file.

5.3 Mount-points

Accesses to remote files can be performed through direct addressing. When a user needs to realize an operation on a file he calls a special service and gives the name of the file and the address of the server maintaining it. This address must reference a process at the same level than the user or else the access will be rejected. This technique is simple but very constraining because it supposes than users know file location precisely at any time.

We prefer a more transparent technique based on the use of *mount-p*. Locally, clients keep mount-p tied up with remote files and perform access to these mount-p rather than to the files. A client does not know the real location of the file and only handles mount-p which can viewed as a pipe between this client and the file maintained by a server. A mount-p is one end of the pipe where clients see the remote file. Reading the pipe returns the file content and writing into the pipe modifies the file content. So pipe seems like the file for the user client.

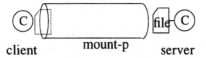

client   mount-p   server

Fig. 7. Mount-p acts as a pipe pointed on a remote file

Mount-points are created either by clients themselves or by the kernel running on the client machine. As any other objects, mount-p have a level of classification. This level is defined by the classification of the process which creates them. It defines the set of operations that can be realized on them by a given process according to the security rules. The level of mount-p is equal to the level of the creating process and higher or equal than the file level.

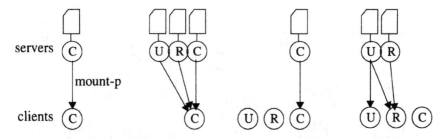

Fig. 8. Mount-pointsbetween single-level, multilevel, clients and servers hosts.

A mount-p pointing on a lower file is called an *inter-level mount-p*. An inter-level mount-p is an ambiguous object since it has a classification offering to realize some operations which cannot affect real file. One example is a C mount-p pointing to an U file. C processes can read, write, delete the mount-p but can only read the bound file. Fig. 8

depicts examples of every kind of mount-p that can be built with single-level and multilevel client and server sites. Mount-points are figured as arrows that point the client. An arrow between a client and a server figures all the mount-p between the client and files maintained by this server. Therefore they denote access possibilities and not only mount-p constructed effectively.

5.4 File system structure

We present now the implementation of the mount-p abstract structure in the distributed system. We chose a transparent naming scheme and a tree organization like the UNIX one. Every host maintains a local tree-structured file system inside which users (*or system*) can place mount-p. Mount-p creation is called *mount* operation. Mount-points do not reference files but directories and look like regular local directories. Their creation is done explicitly by indicating the remote host and the local name of the directory being bound (*see mount procedure*). On the other hand, we saw that usage is made transparently through the classical primitives and therefore a user can ignore the real kind of mount-p when it did not create the mount-p itself. Mount-p name is chosen by the creator and any string accepted by classical UNIX file system is allowed for this name.

In a tree-structured file system every directory but root, is stored in another one called its *parent*. There are rules which restrict mount-p creations and define the level of parent according to the remote directory level. These rules come from both security constraints and implementation choices.

- Mount-p created by a process with *l* level can only be inserted in *l* parent.

- Processes of a site with *ml* maximum level can mount mount-p only pointing on directories with parent lower than *ml*. Indeed the directories must be visible to be mounted.

- Mount-p on *l* directory can be created in any directory with level higher or equal than *l*.

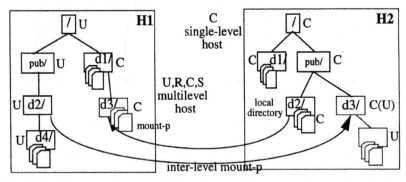

Fig. 9. Example of file system organization. Mount-points are stored as any other directories.

Fig. 9 presents an example of such a distributed file system containing a [U,R,C,S] multilevel host *H1* and a [C] single-level site *H2*. Each one contains local directories, files and mount-p to remote directories. On *H2* "*cd /pub/d3/d4*" is a valid command and can be followed by an execution of "*cat f1*" if *f1* is a file of */pub/d2/d4* on *H1*.

It shows also an example of inter-level mount-p through *d3/* on *H2* site. This mount-p has a Confidential classification but points on an Unclassified directory. Confidential is the real classification but operations are performed on the real Unclassified directory so that its behaviour (*result of operations*) always appears to *H2* processes as the behaviour of an Unclassified entity. Whatever the destruction or modification operations intended on this mount-p they concern only local structure on H2 and not real directory on H1.

Clients and servers constitute the heart of the system. They communicate through the secure network using an extension of TCP/IP and the protocol *SMAC* (*Secure Medium Access Control*) regulating operation requests and data exchanges.

5.5 Server

The role of servers is to maintain files, directories and to offer services in order to manage them from remote processes. There is only one server by host and it is the only way to offer directory access to a remote site. Therefore files of a serverless host could not be accessed remotely.

Servers receive requests from clients describing the directory operations requested (*change directory, file creation, file destruction, file transfer*) then realize the service and send the response. They use the local file system of the host on which they rely to provide the realization of the operations. They perform the communication with clients and control the creation of mount-p established on one of their own directories. These controls prevent a mount operation on an inexistent directory and avoid so unnecessary mount-p creation on client side.

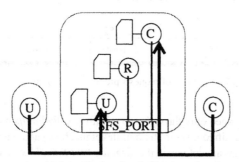

Fig. 10. Port numbers are multiplexed by level and clients reach only processes at their level

Servers could be single-level or multilevel according to type of their host and the kind of clients they must be able to serve. In the distributed system presented here, there is only one multilevel server which run on the M^{2}S machine. Clients at l level contact servers at l level. The multilevel server is composed of processes running at different levels and waiting connections on the same TCP port number. This port is called *SF-S_PORT* and it is reserved in every machine for the file system server. So from the address of a machine, a process is able to reach its file system server by connecting to *address:SFS_PORT*.

Port numbers are multiplexed by level so that connections to port *SFS_PORT* wake up the server having the same level as the requestor. The multilevel server is initialized from Unclassified level which is always processed in multilevel machine. Its creation is made by Unclassified process which creates the other classified processes composing the server. This initialization is made at boot time in the *initfs()* procedure. Every process of the multilevel server binds itself to the *SFS_PORT* port number and waits for client requests on this port. Monolevel servers are identical to multilevel ones except that they are single process.

Servers of the file system are stateless as NFS servers so that they do not keep any information on client mount-p, connections and requests. Therefore clients must indicate the whole information necessary to perform an operation inside every request. The advantage of stateless servers is that they can crash and later rejoin the system without any drawbacks than the lack of service during their malfunction. So global state is conserved and does not need to be restored.

Client requests have all the same structure presented on Fig. 11. They contain the identification of the operation requested *(opid)*, the local path *(local path)* of the file or the directory on which the operation must be intended by the server and finally the length and the data necessary to provide the operation (*name file in file creation, offset in the file and so on*). Every operation corresponds exactly to one local service and *localpath* is directly used by the server to perform the operation through call of the local file system. Servers receive the result of the local execution and send it to the client. Error report is generated when the operation fails.

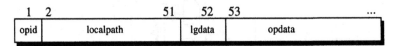

Fig. 11. Structure of requests provided by a client to a server

Servers are managed only through one primitive called *initfs()* which is executed at boot time (at Unclassified level in the multilevel machine) and realizes server creation. Server characteristics are defined in the local file *"/SFS.INIT"* which describes if a server must be created on this host, its type (*multilevel or single-level*) and its level. Of course these informations are restricted by the abilities of the site to manage the levels. For instance a Secret multilevel server becomes a Confidential single-level server on a

Confidential single-level site and on the other hand, single-level server may be created on a multilevel site in order to restrict the remote accesses to one given level.

5.6 Client

Clients are the second components of the multilevel distributed file system. A user process intending an operation on a mount-p becomes a client of the corresponding server. Ideally, this transformation is transparent to the user but in fact it could be perceptible through the difference in response time between a local and a remote response due to the communication duration. Cache mechanisms can be used to improve the response time in the better case where file content is in the local buffer. [4] presents the security problem due to the cache utilization and we discuss it in section 5.7.

Mount-points are the only means to reach remote files and directories. They maintain the correspondence between a virtual local directory (*the mount-p*) and the real remote directory attached to it. This correspondence is only maintained on a client site. In the following text we will use the word mount-p instead of the corresponding virtual local directory. From transparency principle, user processes use mount-p as any other local directory both in commands and file system calls. References to these mount-p are then transformed on remote communications with the server handling the real directory.

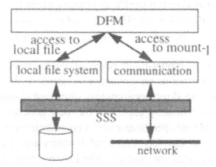

Fig. 12. The Distributed File system Manager switches user accesses either to local file system or to a server

These conversions are performed by the *DFM (Distributed File Manager)* which is a special module located over the local file system. Any call to file system reaches the DFM which switches it either to local file system or to communication layer. DFM uses an extension of classical inodes to determine the type of directory referenced and find its real address. Precisely extensions concern *inode mode* field which can take the new value *MODE_REMOTE* indicating a mount-p to a remote directory. The *r_localpath* field receives the localpath of the mounted directory (*real name on server host*), *r_level* keeps the level of this directory and *r_server_level* contains the type of server (*single-level or multilevel*) and its level. The two last fields are used to anticipate errors returned by the SSS when a process intents a forbidden access. Remember that these fields are not used in any way to enforce security but only to gain time in avoiding requests which will be anyway not accepted by the SSS.

```
struct inode_DFM
            {
            Struct inode inode_l;
            char        r_localpath[LG_LOCAL_PATH];
            int         r_level;
            int         r_server_level;
            }
```

For example at current level *current_level* it is not necessary to intent an access on an host at level *r_server_level* lower than *current_level (current_level > r_server_level)*. As we saw in 5.4, mount-p on single-level host have not necessarily the same level as the remote directory and *r_level* is used to avoid request impossible to realize on the real directory *(destruction or modification for example)*. *r_level* is also used by DFM to display correct information in *ls* command for example where level of a mount-p takes *r_level* value and not the real level of the mount-p. So users have all the information to understand the result of their operations *(modification rejection for example)*.

Consider now the DFM primitives *mount, umount, lmount* and *initfs* managing the mount-p. For every one we present its syntax and a description of its functionalities. The syntax is the same as classical UNIX description where [...] denotes an optional parameter and <...> contains the description of a real parameter.

• mount [-f] <machine>:<remote directory> <mount-pname>

mount creates a new mount-p, in place of the existent local directory named *<mount-p name>*, which points on *<remote directory>* of the *<machine>* site. From this creation, the <remote directory> content *(files and directories)* is transparently present in the directory <mount-p name> of the local host and can be manipulated as any other directories. *Mount* operations entail a communication with the corresponding server which verifies the existence of its local directory and sends an acknowledgment or an error both when it does not exist and when none server can be reached at current level. The server sends the new location of the directory afetr a file system reorganisation. Optional parameter -f forces the mount-p creation even when an error occurs. It is usable when the corresponding server has not yet be initialized. Mount-p creation performs a directory modification so that DFM allows creation *(due to SSS controls)* only when it takes place in a directory having same level than the process intending it. Therefore mount-p take the level of their creator and never the level of their bound remote directory.

• umount <mount-p name>

umount deletes a mount-p. It entails a modification of parent directory and must be executed at parent level. Only the mount-p is concerned by this command and in any way the remote directory bound with it.

• lmount

lists the whole mount-p mounted on the host with real directory names and levels associated. It is useful for administrator users intending debug procedures.

• initfs [-g]

We saw this primitive in 5.5 for server initialization but it concerns also the client part to initialize the initial tree-structure at boot time. It reads a setup multilevel file called *"/TFS.INIT"* containing the description (*mount-p name - remote directories*) of the initial structure, at every level managed by the host. On the multilevel site an Unclassified boot process creates a process for every level managed by the host. Each one of these processes realizes the mount operations at its level and then dies. Option -*g* executes a global initialization. In global initialization the system uses a remote *"/TFS.INIT"* called *global file*, rather than the local *"/TFS.INIT"*. This global file is stored on a host called *global host* (classically the M^2S machine) whose identification is given in *GLOBAL_SERVER* variable. Each initialization process contacts the process of that global server and requests the content of the setup file. Then it realizes the mount operations and dies. Of course multilevel server must be present on *GLOBAL_SERVER* host or else local file will be used. *Initfs* execution must be integrated in the boot procedure.

5.7 Problem discussion

Transparency is a requirement that is difficult to meet in a distributed and secure environment because of the set of complex actions executed inside a simple operation. For example reading a file implies a connection to the server and exchange of part of its content. It takes a not inconsiderable time to execute these sub operations and then reading a file becomes a slow service. Therefore caches can be maintained on the client hosts.

But in [2, 5] authors explain that there is a possibility of timing covert channels in using these caches since they modulate the time of file access. Assume that a high process is reading a low file for the first time on a machine. This operation creates a cache on the machine. Then a low process intents a read on the same low file. The response time depends on the cache existence an so on high process actions. So there is a timing covert channel.

In the system presented in this paper, this timing covert channel is inexistent because either cache is a low memory and so high process cannot place the file content in it or it is a high buffer and low process cannot read it. In both cases the same cache may not be used by processes running at different level.

Fig. 13 shows a functionality problem specific to a multilevel system: the problem of Tantalus mount-p. Tantalus mount-p are directories visible to high processes but inaccessible for them.

This problem appears when a low process on the multilevel host creates a mount-p to a low directory maintained in a low single-level site. The example shows an Unclassified mount-p which points a directory stored on an Unclassified single-level site *H2*. Being an Unclassified mount-p, it is visible for high processes. U clients of *H1* contact [U] server of *H2* to realize operations on the directory. Any other high clients of *H1* cannot contact this server and so cannot access to the remote directory whereas they see the Unclassified mount-p.

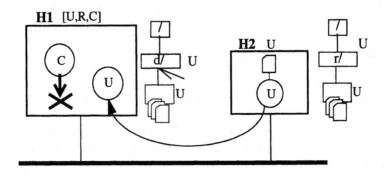

Fig. 13. Tantalus mount-p: processes see them but cannot reach.

It is the Tantalus mount-p problem. We have at least two solutions to solve this problem. Either to reject all creations of mount-p on a site whose levels are not managed by the server or to allow this problem but offering a manner to console frustrated processes. We chose the latter solution which is based on the multiplexing of inodes in memory.

When a process realizes a directory operation, the DFM loads in memory the inode of the directory. This inode is stored in memory inside the *in-core inode table*. This table is multiplexed by levels and the inode is stored in the table classified at the process level. In a mount operation, the information about the remote directory pointed by this mount-p are stored in this table (see structure of inode_DFM in 5.6). Therefore processes classified at various level can create mount-p with the same name (in place of the same directory) but which point various remote directories. These mount-p are called *multiplexed mount-p*.

Fig. 14 depicts its principles based on inodes table multiplexed by levels in memory and on a searching procedure *namei()* running at current level. When a process intends to access to a directory *(mount-p) d/* it calls a file system service and furnishes the name of this directory. *Namei()* is then executed to find the inode associated with the given name. This function realizes its research in the in-core inode table classified at the current level and so reaches the directory stored at this current level.

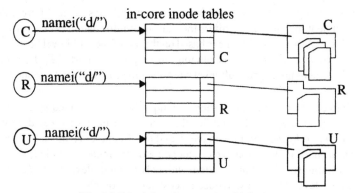

Fig. 14. Principles of mount-p multiplexing

The advantages of this functionning is that low mount-p will be visible only to low processes and not to high ones (and conversely) hiding the Tantalus mount-p problem. Low process can also perform a copy of this file from the single level site to its multi-level host. Rather than to impose a rigid solution, the freedom is given to users to organize clients, servers and mount-p in order to avoid such a problem.

The multiplexed mount-p can also be used to assure a multiplexed service. Fig. 15 shows an example of such a utilization. In this example, U and C users need to run a program which displays the list of books classified at their level. Each list is maintained by a server and the program accesses to them in the same directory (*mount-p*) *"BOOKS"* whatever the level. Transparency is so given between level and multiplexed service is assured.

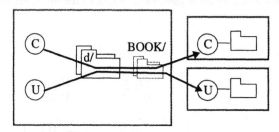

Fig. 15. Mount-pmultiplexing can provide transparent multiplexed services

6 Sharing

The following text describes the real possibilities of sharing provided by this file system. If we consider an environment composed only of single-level sites (*at identical levels*) this system offers the same functionalities as the *NFS* protocol. But advantages came in an heterogeneous system where users, files and sites run at different levels. In this environment mount-p usage offers the sharing of information between various levels. The classical sharing technique is based on the use of the multilevel host M^2S maintaining shared files and of clients running on single-level hosts [2]. Low processes modify file content inside the multilevel site and high processes read it when they need.

The implementation of this sharing technique in the distributed system presented here, relies on the usage of the multilevel server and of mount-p created on the client hosts (*low and high*) and pointing on the shared file. Remark that this organization provide the sharing of information even if client hosts are single-level. So it is possible to construct a multilevel distributed system with only one multilevel host (*the server*) and several single-level sites and so reduce its cost and its complexity.

Multiplexed mount-p are a new functionality offered by this system. On one hand there are several single-level hosts running servers and on the other hand users on the multilevel site which access transparently to the site running at their level. This construction is very important to assure the perfect transparency necessary to run a program from any level. The multiplexing technique can be used either on the data files or directly on the programs.

In any case, the users (*or an organizer*) are in charge of constructing the system and of placing the files in order to offer the sharing of data in a practical way. Indeed if a user decides to maintain a file inside a single-level site, the system will be never able to offer accesses from another level. But, on the other hand, it offers the possibilities of publishing a file by copying it in a mount-p pointed on a server. The file will be so placed on the server and will be accessible by any client handling a mount-p on this server. Therefore and only if they decide it, the users are the possibility to allow access on their files. But whatever the organization chosen by the users, the security is always assured.

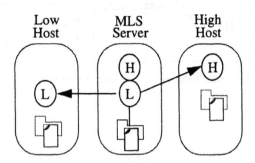

Fig. 16. Example of MLS server

7 Summary

Distribution functionalities and security are often difficult to mix. They seem to be antagonistic and pose problems to any designer of distributed file system. Generally compromises must be made and some lacks of security are commonly accepted. In this project compromises are made on functionalities and not on security. Indeed, this project aims at assuring the functionality of a practical distributed file system over secure basis and not the security of a distributed file system. We showed that despite the controls enforced by the hardware, it is possible to construct a practical system offering the classical services and many new ones (*multiplexed views*). Of course it entails some problems but we saw that solutions could always be constructed and that they are quite simple.

Further, we would discuss about other kind of security as discretionary policies. Client/server is a practical paradigm to realize controls on user accesses since the servers handle the whole accesses intended on one of their files. It would be so the main actor of this security. It would be also interesting to study how we could use process migration to realize accesses impossible directly or yet redundant servers.

8 References

1. B. d'Ausbourg, C. Calas
   "Unix services for multilevel storage and communications over a LAN"- Proceeding of the Winter 93 USENIX Technical Conference, San Diego, 1993

2. B. d'Ausbourg, J-H. Llareus
   "M2S: A Machine for Multilevel Security"- Proceeding of Esorics'92, Toulouse, November 23-25, 1992

3. P. Bieber, F. Cuppens
   "A Logical view of Secure Dependencies"- Journal of Computer Security, Vol 1,Nr 1, 1992

4. Thomas A. Casey Jr., Stephen T. Vinter, D.G. Weber,
   R. Varadarajan,D. Rosenthal
   "A Secure Distributed Operating System"- Proceeding of IEEE Symposium on Security and Privacy, Oakland, April 18-21, 1988.

5. Glenn H. MacEwen, Bruce Burwell, Zhuo-Jun Lu
   "Multi-Level Security Based on Physical Distribution"- Proceeding of IEEE Symposium on Security and Privacy, Oakland, 1984.

6. Richard E. Smith
   "MLS File Service for Network Data Sharing"- Proceeding of Computer Security Applications Conference, Orlando December 6-10, 1993

Access Controls

On the Expressive Power of the Unary Transformation Model

Ravi S. Sandhu and Srinivas Ganta

Center for Secure Information Systems
&
Department of Information and Software Systems Engineering
George Mason University, Fairfax, Va 22030-4444, USA
sandhu@isse.gmu.edu, gsriniva@isse.gmu.edu

Abstract. The Transformation Model (TRM) was recently introduced [10] in the literature by Sandhu and Ganta. TRM is based on the concept of *transformation of rights*. The propagation of access rights in TRM is authorized entirely by existing rights for the object in question. It has been demonstrated in the earlier work that TRM is useful for expressing various kinds of consistency, confidentiality, and integrity controls.

In our previous work [10], a special case of TRM named Binary Transformation Model (BTRM) was defined. We proved that BTRM is equivalent in expressive power to TRM. This result indicates that it suffices to allow testing for only two cells of the matrix.

In this paper we study the relationship between TRM and the Unary Transformation Model (UTRM). In UTRM, individual commands are restricted to testing for only one cell of the matrix (whereas individual TRM commands can test for multiple cells of the matrix). Contrary to our initial conjecture (of [10]), we found that TRM and UTRM are formally equivalent in terms of expressive power. The implications of this result on safety analysis is also discussed in this paper.

Keywords: Access Control, Access Rights, Authorization, Client-Server Architecture, Expressive Power.

1 Introduction

In this paper we analyze the expressive power of a family of access control models called transformation models [10]. These models are based on the concept of *transformation of rights*, which simply implies that the possession of rights for an object by subjects allows those subjects to obtain and lose rights for that object and also grant and revoke the rights (for that object) to other subjects. Hence, in these models, the propagation of access rights is authorized entirely by the existing rights for the object in question. (More generally, propagation could also be authorized by the existing rights for the source and destination subjects, for example, in models such as HRU [4] and TAM [8].) The concept of transformation of rights allows us to express a large variety of practical security policies encompassing various kinds of consistency, confidentiality and integrity controls.

The concept of transformation of access rights was introduced by Sandhu in [7]. Based on it the monotonic transform model [7] and its non-monotonic extension (NMT) [9] were proposed. The simplicity and expressive power of NMT is demonstrated in [9] by means of a number of examples. It was recently discovered by the authors that NMT cannot adequately implement the document release example given in [9]. The reason behind this is the limited testing power of NMT. This led us to the formulation of the Transformation Model (TRM). TRM substantially generalizes NMT.

TRM does have good expressive power (which NMT lacks). TRM can also be implemented efficiently [10] in a distributed environment using a typical client-server architecture. This is due to the fact that the propagation of access rights in TRM is authorized entirely by existing rights for the object in question. In typical implementations these rights would be represented in an access control list (ACL), stored with the object. The server responsible for managing that object will have immediate access to all the information (i.e., the ACL) required to make access control decisions with respect to that object. Moreover, the effect of propagation commands is also confined only to the ACL of that object.

The Binary Transformation Model (BTRM) was defined in [10]. BTRM is a simpler version of TRM in which testing can involve up to two cells of the matrix. It has been proven in [10] that BTRM is formally equivalent to TRM. (Two models are said to be equivalent in expressive power, if for every system in one model, there is an equivalent system in the other, and vice versa. For the purpose of this paper, we simplify the definition of equivalence of two systems to intuitively mean that two systems are equivalent if and only if both of them enforce the same policy). This also implies that it suffices to have systems that test for two cells of the matrix.

In this paper we study the relationship between TRM and the Unary Transformation Model (UTRM) defined in [10]. In UTRM the commands are authorized by checking for rights in a single cell of the access matrix. It has been conjectured in [10] that UTRM does not have the adequate expressive power to enforce simple policies like the document release example. On the contrary, we prove in this paper that UTRM is equivalent to TRM in terms of expressive power and hence UTRM can also enforce all the policies enforced by TRM (including the document release example). The equivalence of TRM and UTRM helps in concluding that the safety results of UTRM are in no way better than that of TRM.

The rest of the paper is organized as follows. Section 2 gives a brief background of the Transformation Model (TRM). It also describes two models, UTRM and BTRM, which are restricted cases of TRM. In section 3 we first briefly describe the discussion of [10], which conjectured that UTRM is not adequate enough to express the document release example. We then prove that this is not the case by proving formally that UTRM is equivalent to TRM. We also discuss in section 3, the implications of this result on safety analysis. Finally, section 4 concludes the paper.

2 Background

In this section, we review the definition of the Transformation Model (TRM), which was introduced in [10]. Our review is necessarily brief. The motivation for developing TRM, and its relation to other access control models are discussed at length in [10]. Following the review of TRM we briefly review the definitions of UTRM and BTRM.

2.1 The Transformation Model

TRM is an access control model in which authorization for propagation of access rights is entirely based on existing rights for the object in question. As discussed in the introduction this leads to an efficient implementation of TRM in a distributed environment using a simple client-server architecture. The expressiveness of TRM is indicated in [10] by enforcing various kinds of consistency, confidentiality, and integrity controls.

The protection state in TRM can be viewed in terms of the familiar access matrix. There is a row for each subject in the system and a column for each object. In TRM, the subjects and objects are disjoint. TRM does not define any access rights for operations on subjects, which are assumed to be completely autonomous entities. The $[X, Y]$ cell contains rights which subject X possesses for object Y.

TRM consists of a small number of basic constructs and a language for specifying the commands which cause changes in the protection state. For each command, we have to specify the authorization required to execute that command, as well as the effect of the command on the protection state. We generally call such a specification an *authorization scheme* (or simply scheme) [8].

A scheme in the TRM is defined by specifying the following components.

1. A set of access rights R.
2. Disjoint sets of subject and object types, TS and TO, respectively.
3. A collection of three classes of state changing commands: *transformation commands, create commands*, and *destroy commands*. Each individual command specifies the authorization for its execution, and the changes in the protection state effected by it.

The scheme is defined by the security administrator when the system is first set up and thereafter remains fixed. It should be kept in mind that TRM treats the security administrator as an external entity, rather than as another subject in the system. Each component of the scheme is discussed in turn below.

The Typed Access Matrix Model (TAM) [8] and TRM are strongly related. They differ in state changing commands. In TRM, propagation of access rights is authorized entirely by existing rights for the object in question, whereas in TAM this authorization can involve testing rights for multiple objects. TRM commands can only modify one column at a time, where as TAM can modify multiple columns of the matrix. TRM does allow testing for absence of rights, while the original definition of TAM in [8] does not allow for such testing. If TAM is augmented with testing for absence of rights (as in [1]), it is then a generalization of TRM.

Rights

Each system has a set of rights, R. R is not specified in the model but varies from system to system. Generally R is expected to include the usual rights such as *own, read, write, append* and *execute*. However, this is not required by the model. We also expect R to generally include more complex rights, such as *review, pat-ok, grade-it, release, credit, debit,* etc. The meaning of these rights will be explained wherever they are used in our examples.

The access rights serve two purposes. First, the presence of a right, such as r, in the $[S, O]$ cell of the access matrix may authorize S to perform, say, the read operation on O. Secondly, the presence of a right, say o, or the absence of right o, in $[S, O]$ may authorize S to perform some operation which changes the access matrix, e.g., by entering r in $[S', O]$. The focus of TRM is on this second purpose of rights, i.e., the authorization by which the access matrix itself gets changed.

Types of Subjects and Objects

The notion of type is fundamental to TRM. All subjects and objects are assumed to be strongly typed. Strong typing requires that each subject or object is created to be of a particular type which thereafter does not change. The advantage of strong typing is that it groups together subjects and objects into classes (i.e., types) so that instances of the same type have the same properties with respect to the authorization scheme.

Strong typing is analogous to tranquility in the Bell-LaPadula style of security models [2], whereby security labels on subjects and objects cannot be changed. The adverse consequences of unrestrained non-tranquility are well known [3, 5, 6]. Similarly, non-tranquility with respect to types has adverse consequences for the safety problem [8].

TRM requires that a disjoint set of subject types, TS, and object types, TO, be specified in a scheme. For example, we might have TS={*user, security-officer*} and TO={*user-files, system-files*}, with the significance of these types indicated by their names.

State Changing Commands

The protection state of the system is changed by means of TRM commands. The security administrator defines a finite set of commands when the system is specified. There are three types of state changing commands in the TRM, each of which is defined below.

Transformation Commands

We reiterate that every command in TRM has a condition which is on a single object and the primitive operations comprising the command are only on that object. In all the commands the last parameter in the command is the object which is being manipulated, and the first parameter is the subject who initiates the command.

A *transformation command* has the following format:

> **command** $\alpha(S_1 : s_1, S_2 : s_2, \ldots, S_k : s_k, O : o_i)$
>   **if** *predicate* **then**
> $op_1; op_2; \ldots; op_n$
> **end**

The first line of the command states that α is the name of the command and $S_1, S_2, \ldots, S_k, O$ are the formal parameters. The formal parameters $S_1, S_2, \ldots, S_k$ are subjects and of types $s_1, s_2, \ldots, s_k$. The **only** object formal parameter O is of type o_i and is the last parameter in the command.

The second line of the command α is the predicate and is called the *condition* of the command. The predicate consists of a boolean expression composed of the following terms connected by the usual boolean operators (such as $\land$ and $\lor$):

$$r_i \in [S, O] \text{ or } r_i \notin [S, O]$$

Here r_i is a right in R, S can be substituted with any of the formal subject parameters $S_1, S_2, \ldots, S_n$; and O is the sole object parameter. Simply speaking the predicate tests for the presence and absence of some rights for subjects on object O. Given below are some examples of TRM predicates:

1. $approve \in [S_1, O] \land prepare \notin [S_2, O]$
2. $prepare \in [S, O] \land assign \in [S_1, O] \land creator \notin [S, O]$
3. $own \in [S, O] \lor write \in [S, O]$
4. $r_1 \in [S_1, O] \land (r_2 \in [S_1, O] \lor r_1 \in [S_2, O]) \land r_3 \in [S_2, O] \land r \in [S_3, O]$

If the condition is omitted, the command is said to be an *unconditional command*, otherwise it is said to be a *conditional command*.

The third line of the command consisting of sequence of operations $op_1; op_2; \ldots; op_n$ is called the *body* of α. Each op_i is one of the following two primitive operations:

- **enter** r **into** $[S, O]$
- **delete** r **from** $[S, O]$

Here again, r_i is a right in R, S can be substituted with any of the formal subject parameters $S_1, S_2, \ldots, S_n$; and O is the sole object parameter. It is important to note that all the operations enter or delete rights for subjects on object O alone.

The **enter** operation enters a right $r \in R$ into an existing cell of the access matrix. The contents of the cell are treated as a set for this purpose, i.e., if the right is already present, the cell is not changed. The **delete** operation has the opposite effect of **enter**. It (possibly) removes a right from a cell of the access matrix. Since each cell is treated as a set, **delete** has no effect if the deleted right does not already exist in the cell. The **enter** operation is said to be *monotonic* because it only adds and does not remove from the access matrix. Because **delete** removes from the access matrix it is said to be a *non-monotonic* operation.

A command is invoked by substituting actual parameters of the appropriate types for the formal parameters. The condition part of the command is evaluated with respect to its actual parameters. The body is executed only if the condition evaluates to true.

Some examples of transformation commands are given below.

command *transfer-ownership* $(S_1 : s, S_2 : s, O : o)$
   if *own* $\in [S_1, O]$ **then**
   enter *own* in $[S_2, O]$
   delete *own* from $[S_1, O]$
end

command *grade* $(S_1 : professor, S_2 : student, O : project)$
   if *own* $\in [S_2, O] \wedge grade \in [S_1, O]$ **then**
   enter *good* in $[S_2, O]$
   delete *grade* from $[S_1, O]$
end

command *issue-check* $(S_1 : clerk, O : voucher)$
   if *prepare* $\notin [S_1, O] \wedge approve \notin [S_1, O]$ **then**
   enter *issue* in $[S_1, O]$
end

Command *transfer-ownership* transfers the ownership of a file from one subject to another. In the command *grade*, the professor gives right *good* to the students project. In command *issue-check*, a clerk gets an *issue* right only if he/she is not the one who prepared and approved it.

Create Commands

A *create command* is an unconditional command. The creator of an object gets some rights for the created object like *own, read*, etc., as specified in the body of the command. No subject other than the creator will get rights to the created object in the create command. Subjects other than the creator can subsequently acquire rights for the object via transformation commands. In short, the effect of a create command is to introduce a new column in the matrix with some new rights for the subject who created it.

A typical create command is given below.

command $create(S_1 : s_1, O : o_i)$
    create object O
    enter own in $[S_1, O]$
end

In the general case the body of the command may enter any set of rights in the $[S_1, O]$ cell.

A create command is necessarily an unconditional command as the command cannot check for rights on an object which does not exist, and TRM commands do not allow testing for rights on objects other than the object which is being created. The create object operation requires that the object being created have an unique identity different from all other objects. A create command is monotonic.

Destroy Commands

A *destroy command* is in general, a conditional command. The effect of a destroy command on the matrix will be removal of the corresponding column from the access matrix. A typical destroy command is given below.

command $destroy(S_1 : s_1, O : o_i)$
    if $own \in [S_1, O]$ **then**
    destroy object O
end

In this case the condition ensures that only the owner can destroy the object. More generally, deletion can be authorized by some combination of rights possessed by the destroyer. A destroy command is non-monotonic.

Summary of TRM

To summarize, a system is specified in TRM by defining the following finite components.

1. A set of rights R.
2. A set of disjoint subject and object types TS and TO respectively.
3. A set of state-changing transformation, creation and destroy commands.
4. The initial state.

We say that the rights, types and commands define the system *scheme*. Note that once the system scheme is specified by the security administrator it remains fixed thereafter for the life of the system. The system state, however, changes with time.

2.2   The Unary Transformation Model (UTRM)

The Unary Transformation Model is a simpler version of TRM in which testing in a command can be on only one cell of the matrix. A UTRM predicate consists of a boolean expression composed of the following terms:

$$r_i \in [S_j, O] \text{ or } r_i \notin [S_j, O]$$

where r_i is a right in R and S_j can be any one of the formal subject parameters, but all the terms in the expression must have the same S_j. In other words, the predicate tests for the presence and absence of rights for a single subject S_j on object O. Usually S_j will be the first parameter in the command, since that is the one who initiates the command.

UTRM generalizes the model called NMT (for Non-Monotonic Transform) [9]. The transformation commands in NMT, viz., grant transformation and internal transformation, are easily expressed as UTRM commands (as they test for rights in one cell of the matrix). NMT is a restricted version of UTRM as the state changing commands in NMT test only one cell and modify at most two cells.

2.3   The Binary Transformation Model (BTRM)

The Binary Transformation Model is also a simpler version of TRM in which testing in a command can involve up to two cells of the matrix. A BTRM predicate consists of a boolean expression composed of the following terms:

$$r_i \in [S_j, O] \text{ or } r_i \notin [S_j, O]$$

where r_i is a right in R and S_j can be any one of the formal subject parameters, but the expression can have at most two different S_j's from the given parameters. In other words, the predicate tests for the presence and absence of rights for at most two subjects (on object O). One of the S_j's will typically be the first parameter which is the initiator of the command.

3   Expressive Power of UTRM

In this section we first briefly look at the discussion given in [10], which conjectured that UTRM cannot adequately enforce the document release example. We then prove that the conjecture is wrong by formally proving that UTRM is equivalent to TRM. The equivalence of TRM and UTRM indicates that UTRM can enforce all the policies enforced by TRM (including the document release example). We also discuss the implications of the equivalence result on safety analysis.

3.1 Document Release Example

In this subsection we will take a brief look at the discussion given in [10] which conjectured that UTRM cannot adequately enforce the document release example.

Consider the document release example discussed in [9]. In this example, a scientist creates a document and hence gets *own, read* and *write* rights to it. After preparing the document for publication, the scientist asks for a review from a patent officer. In the process, the scientist loses the *write* right to the document, since it is clearly undesirable for a document to be edited during or after a (successful) review. After review of the document, the patent officer grants the scientist an approval. It is reasonable to disallow further attempts to review the document after an approval is granted. Thus the *review* right for the document is lost as approval is granted. After obtaining approval from the patent officer, the scientist can publish the document by getting a *release* right for the document. (The problem discussed in [9] also requires approval by a security officer prior to document release, but that aspect of the problem is not germane to the discussion here.)

To express this policy, we employ the following rights and types:

- R = {*own, read, write, review, pat-ok, pat-reject, release*}
- TS = {*sci, po*}, TO = {*doc*}

The *own, read,* and *write* rights have their usual meaning. The other rights correspond to stages in the approval process. The right *review* lets a patent officer review a document; *pat-ok* is the right that is returned if the patent review is satisfactory otherwise *pat-reject* is returned; and *release* authorizes release of the document. Subject types *sci* and *po* are abbreviations for scientists and patent officers respectively, and there is a single object type *doc*.

The following TRM (or more precisely BTRM) commands enforce the desired policy:

```
command create-doc(S : sci, O : doc)
    create object O
    enter own in [S, O]
    enter read in [S, O]
    enter write in [S, O]
end
command rqst-review(S : sci, P : po, O : doc)
if own ∈ [S, O]∧ write ∈ [S, O] then
    enter review in [P, O]
    delete write from [S, O]
end
command get-approval(S : sci, P : po, O : doc)
if review ∈ [P, O] ∧ own ∈ [S, O] then
    enter pat-ok in [S, O]
    delete review from [P, O]
end
```

command *get-rejection(S : sci, P : po, O : doc)*
if *review* ∈ [P, O] ∧ *own* ∈ [S, O] **then**
    enter *pat-reject* in [S, O]
    delete *review* from [P, O]
end
command *release-doc(S : sci, O : doc)*
if *pat-ok* ∈ [S, O] **then**
    enter *release* in [S, O]
    delete *pat-ok* from [S, O]
end
command *revise-doc(S : sci, O : doc)*
if *pat-reject* ∈ [S, O] **then**
    enter *write* in [S, O]
    delete *pat-reject* from [S, O]
end

The scientist creates a document using the command *create-doc*. After preparing the document the scientist asks the patent officer to review it through command *rqst-review*. The scientist gets approval to release through command *get-approval* or a rejection via *get-rejection*. In the former case the scientist gets the *release* permission by means of the command *release-doc*. In the latter case the scientist gets the *write* permission by means of the command *revise-doc* so as to revise the document if appropriate.

We now discuss why UTRM cannot adequately express the document release example. All the commands, except *get-approval* and *get-rejection*, are UTRM commands. The commands *get-approval* and *get-rejection* are BTRM commands as they test two cells.

The *get-approval* command tests for rights in two cells of the matrix. More specifically, it tests if the patent officer has the *review* right for the document and if the scientist is the owner of the document. If this condition is satisfied the command gives the right, *pat-ok*, to the owner.

If the *get-approval* command does not test for the *own* right, then the command might give the *pat-ok* right to some other scientist who is not a owner. The system will then halt in an unwanted state as the scientist who creates the document cannot get the *release* right for it. This is due to the fact that the scientist cannot request a second review prior to receiving a response for the first one (this is achieved by conditioning the request for review on presence of the *write* right, which is then removed until a rejection is received). At the same time, the patent officer can give the *pat-ok* only once to one scientist (as the patent officer loses the *review* right in this process). Therefore if the patent officer gives the right *pat-ok* to a scientist who is not owner, the actual owner cannot get the *release* right and the system halts in an unwanted state.

If the *get-approval* command does not test for the *review* right then a patent officer can grant *pat-ok* for documents which the scientist can still write. Moreover, this can be done whether or not a request for review has been made. The danger of this approach is obvious. But then the required policy cannot be conveniently enforced by UTRM. Note that similar considerations apply to the *get-rejection* command.

In short, to enforce the document release example, it appears that there is a need for commands which test for two cells of the matrix. Since UTRM (and NMT lack) such commands, they cannot conveniently express the document release example.

The discussion above (of [10]) argues informally that UTRM is inadequate to express the document release example. On the contrary, we formally prove in the next subsection, the equivalence of UTRM and TRM, which implies that UTRM can also enforce all the policies enforced by TRM (including the document release example).

3.2 Equivalence of TRM and UTRM

We now analyze the relative expressive power of TRM and UTRM. TRM and UTRM are said to be equivalent in expressive power, if for every scheme in TRM, there is an equivalent scheme in UTRM, and vice versa. For the purpose of this paper, we simplify the definition of equivalence of two systems to intuitively mean that two systems are equivalent if and only if both of them enforce the same policy.

Recall that UTRM is a restricted version of TRM. It is the same as TRM except that the testing in a command can only be on a single cell. It has been proven in [10] that TRM is equivalent to BTRM with just three parameters. Thus to prove the equivalence of TRM and UTRM, it is sufficient to show that for every BTRM scheme with three parameters, there exists an equivalent UTRM scheme.

We will now show how any given BTRM command can be simulated by multiple UTRM commands. The Boolean condition of any BTRM command, say Y, can be converted into the familiar *disjunctive normal form* which consists of a disjunction (i.e., $\vee$) of *minterms*. Each minterm is a conjunction (i.e., $\wedge$) of primitive terms of the form $r_i \in [S_i, O]$ or $r_i \notin [S_i, O]$. The command Y can then be factored into multiple commands, each of which has one minterm as its condition and the original body of Y as its body. Hence, we can assume without loss of generality that the predicate of every BTRM command consists of a conjunction of primitive terms.

We will illustrate the construction by simulating a BTRM command X (which has three parameters) of the following format.

> **command** $X(S_1 : t_1, S_2 : t_2, O : o)$
> **if** $P_1 \wedge P_2$ **then**
>   **operations** in $[S_1, O]$
>   **operations** in $[S_2, O]$
> **end**

In the above command, each P_i is itself composed of a conjunction of terms $r_j \in [S_i, O]$ or $r_j \notin [S_i, O]$, where $r_j \in \mathrm{R}$. Intuitively P_i tests for the presence

	$O:o$			$O:o$
$S_1 : t_1$	α_1	$Lock : lock$		L
$S_2 : t_1$	α_2	$S_1 : s_1$		α_1
$S_3 : t_2$	α_3	$S_2 : s_2$		α_2
...		...		
$S_n : t_x$	α_n	$S_n : s_n$		α_n

(a) Initial state of BTRM   (b) Initial state of UTRM

Fig. 1. UTRM simulation of command X

of, and absence of some rights in the single cell $[S_i, O]$. In the body of command X, the phrase "**operations** in $[S_i, O]$" denotes a sequence of enter and delete (or possibly empty) operations in the $[S_i, O]$ cell. Note that the types t_1 and t_2 need not be distinct. The formal parameters S_1, S_2 must of course be distinct, but the actual parameters used on a particular invocation of this command may have repeated parameters as allowed by parameter types. For ease of exposition, we will initially assume that the actual parameters S_1 and S_2 are distinct. The simulation of a BTRM command with repeated parameters, will be explained at the end of this section.

We now consider how the BTRM command X can be simulated by several UTRM commands. As X tests two cells, it is obvious that the simulation of X cannot be a single UTRM command. Since UTRM can test for only one cell, the simulation of X must be done by multiple commands in the UTRM system. The key to doing this successfully is to prevent other UTRM commands from interfering with the simulation of the given BTRM command, X. The simplest way to do this is to ensure that BTRM commands can be executed in the UTRM simulation only one at a time. To do this we need to synchronize the execution of successive BTRM commands in the UTRM simulation.

This synchronization is achieved by introducing an extra subject called $Lock$ of type $lock$, and an extra right, L. The role of $Lock$ is to sequentialize the execution of simulation of BTRM commands in the UTRM system. The type $lock$ is assumed, without loss of generality, to be distinct from any type in the given BTRM system.

Also the initial state of the UTRM system is modified in such a way that every subject of the BTRM system is given a different type. This assumption is acceptable within the framework of these models, because the number of subjects in the system is static (as there is no creation and destruction of subjects in Transformation Models). If the initial state of the BTRM system resembles figure 1(a), then in our construction the initial state of the UTRM system resembles figure 1(b). The α_i's are sets of rights in the indicated cell.

The UTRM simulation of X proceeds in five phases as indicated in figure 2 and 3. In these figures we show only the relevant portion of the access matrix, and only those rights introduced specifically for the UTRM simulation. Hence, for clarity of the diagram, we do not show the α_i's rights, but these are intended to be present. Since the focus in TRM is on a single object, the matrix reduces to a single column for that object.

The objective of the first phase is to make sure that no other UTRM command corresponding to another BTRM command can execute (on object O) until the simulation of X is complete. The first phase also ensures that the actual parameters of the UTRM commands are tied to the actual parameters of the BTRM command. In the second phase, if P_1 part of the condition of X is true, then that fact is indicated to all the subjects in the system. If P_1 is false, the second phase indicates the failure of the condition of X by entering right $cleanX$ in $[Lock, O]$. In the third phase, if the condition of X is true, then the body of X is partly executed. If the condition of X is false, the third phase also indicates the failure of the condition of X. In the fourth phase, the rest of the body of X is executed. And finally the fifth phase removes all the additional bookkeeping rights and also indicates that the simulation of X is complete. Each of the phases and the commands used are explained briefly below.

The UTRM command X-1-$invocation$ corresponds to phase I. It checks for right L in $[Lock, O]$, and if present deletes it, to make sure that no other UTRM command (simulating some other BTRM command) can execute (on object O) until the simulation of X is complete. It also makes sure that the actual parameters of X are used in the simulation by entering rights p_1, p_2 in cells $[S_1, O]$ and $[S_2, O]$ respectively. It also enters the right X in cells $[S_1, O], [S_2, O]$ to indicate that the simulation of X is currently in progress. The matrix, after the execution of command X-1-$invocation$ resembles figure 2(a). To simulate X, we need a different X-i-$invocation$ command for each distinct combination of a subject of type t_1 and a subject of type t_2. For example, if there are m subjects of type t_1 and n subjects of type t_2 in the BTRM system, then in phase I, the simulation of command X requires mn commands in the UTRM system. Phase I command simulating X with actual parameters corresponding to types s_1 and s_2 respectively is given below.

command X-1-$invocation(S_1 : s_1, S_2 : s_2, Lock : L, O : o)$
if $L \in [Lock, O]$ **then**
    delete L from $[Lock, O]$
    enter p_1 in $[S_1, O]$
    enter p_2 in $[S_2, O]$
    enter X in $[S_1, O]$
    enter X in $[S_2, O]$
end

In phase II, the commands test if the P_1 part of the condition of X is true. If so, the command X-2-$successful$ gives the right P_1^* to all the subjects (to indicate that P_1 is true). The matrix at the end of successful phase II, resembles figure 2(b). If P_1 is false, the command X-2-$fail$ enters the right $cleanX$ in $[Lock, O]$ to indicate that the condition of command X is false. The right $cleanX$ in $[lock, O]$ also indicates that simulation has reached the final phase. In this case, the matrix at the end of failed phase II, resembles figure 3(a). It is important

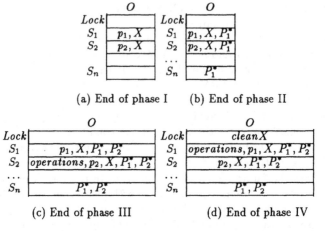

(a) End of phase I   (b) End of phase II

(c) End of phase III   (d) End of phase IV

Fig. 2. UTRM simulation of the authorized BTRM command X

(a) End of phase II   (b) End of phase III

Fig. 3. UTRM simulation of unauthorized BTRM command X

to note that in phase II, only one of *X-2-fail* or *X-2-successful* can execute. To simulate X, we need a different *X-2-successful* command for each subject of type t_1 and a different *X-2-fail* command for each subject of type t_1. Phase II commands simulating X with actual parameters corresponding to types s_1 and s_2 respectively, are given below.

command *X-2-successful*$(S_1 : s_1, S_2 : s_2, S_3 : s_3, \ldots, S_n : s_n, Lock : L, O :$
$o)$
if $p_1 \in [S_1, O] \wedge P_1 \wedge X \in [S_1, O]$ **then**
    enter P_1^* **in** $[S_1, O]$
    . . .
    enter P_1^* **in** $[S_n, O]$
end
command *X-2-fail*$(S_1 : s_1, Lock : L, O : o)$
if $p_1 \in [S_1, O] \wedge \neg P_1 \wedge X \in [S_1, O]$ **then**
    enter $cleanX$ **in** $[Lock, O]$
end

Note that these are valid UTRM commands because all tests in the condition part are in the $[S_1, O]$ cell.

In phase III, the rest of the condition of X is tested in *X-3-successful*. If the condition is true, part of the body of X is executed. The matrix at the end of successful phase III, resembles figure 2(c). If the condition is not true, the command *X-3-fail* enters the right *cleanX* in $[Lock, O]$ to indicate that the simulation of X has failed. In this case the matrix at the end of phase III, resembles figure 3(b). It is important to note that in phase III, only one of *X-3-fail* or *X-3-successful* can execute. Here also to simulate X, we need a different *X-3-successful* command for each subject of type t_2 and a different *X-3-fail* command for each subject of type t_2. Phase III commands simulating X with actual parameters corresponding to types s_1 and s_2 respectively, are given below.

command *X-3-successful*($S_1 : s_1, S_2 : s_2, \ldots, S_n : s_n, Lock : L, O : o$)
if $p_2 \in [S_2, O] \wedge P_1^* \in [S_2, O] \wedge P_2 \wedge X \in [S_2, O]$ **then**
    operations in $[S_2, O]$
    enter P_2^* in $[S_1, O]$
    . . .
    enter P_2^* in $[S_n, O]$
end
command *X-3-fail*($S_2 : s_2, Lock : L, O : o$)
if $p_2 \in [S_2, O] \wedge \neg P_2 \wedge X \in [S_2, O]$ **then**
    enter *cleanX* in $[Lock, O]$
end

In the fourth phase, the rest of the body of X is executed. Also right *cleanX* is entered in $[lock, O]$ also indicate that simulation has reached the final phase. It is also important to note that the phase IV command is executed only if the commands executed in phases II and III are successful commands. The matrix at the end of phase IV resembles figure 2(d). Here also to simulate X, we need a different *X-4-successful* command for each subject of type t_1. Phase IV commands simulating X with actual parameters corresponding to types s_1 and s_2 respectively, are given below.

command *X-4-successful*($S_1 : s_1, Lock : L, O : o$)
if $p_1 \in [S_1, O] \wedge P_2^* \in [S_1, O] \wedge X \in [S_1, O]$ **then**
    operations in $[S_1, O]$
    enter *cleanX* in $[Lock, O]$
end

In the final phase, all the bookkeeping rights $R^* = \{p_1, p_2, X, P_1^*, P_2^*, cleanX\}$ are deleted. Also right L is entered back into $[Lock, O]$ to indicate that the simulation of X is complete and the simulation of some other BTRM command (on object O) can now begin. The matrix after the final phase, resembles figure 1(b). The phase V command to simulate X is given below.

command X-5-complete$(S_1 : s_1, S_2 : s_2, S_3 : s_3, \ldots, S_n : S_n, Lock : L, O : o)$
if $cleanX \in [Lock, O]$ **then**
    delete R^* **from** $[S_1, O]$

    $\ldots$

    delete R^* **from** $[S_n, O]$
    delete $cleanX$ **from** $[Lock, O]$
    enter L **in** $[Lock, O]$
end

The important thing to be noted from our construction is that once the UTRM simulation of command X proceeds with some actual parameters in phase I, then in all other phases, the commands execute with the same parameters.

We have shown how a BTRM command X, can be simulated by UTRM commands. The command X has actual parameters (S_1, S_2) which are distinct (as they are of types t_1 and t_2). A BTRM command can also have actual parameters which are repeated. This is possible if the command has two parameters of the same type. Our construction can be easily extended to simulate such commands. For example, if the BTRM command X has both the subject parameters of type t_1, then the following type of commands are needed **along** with the five phases of commands explained before. The command X-1-invocation-repeated will make sure that the two actual subject parameters of X are same and the command X-repeated-done does the necessary operations (if the two actual subject parameters of X are same). If there are m subjects of type t_1 in the BTRM system, then we need to give m X-1-invocation-repeated commands and m X-repeated-done commands. The UTRM commands simulating X with repeated actual parameters corresponding to type s_1 are given below.

command X-1-invocation-repeated$(S_1 : s_1, Lock; L, O : o)$
if $L \in [Lock, O]$ **then**
    delete L **from** $[Lock, O]$
    enter p_1 **in** $[S_1, O]$
    enter p_2 **in** $[S_1, O]$
    enter X **in** $[S_1, O]$
end
command X-repeated-done$(S_1 : s_1, Lock; L, O : o)$
if $X \in [Lock, O] \wedge p_1 \in [S_1, O] \wedge p_2 \in [S_1, O] \wedge P_1 \wedge P_2$ **then**
    operations in $[S_1, O]$
    enter $cleanX$ **in** $[Lock, O]$
end

A proof sketch for the correctness of the construction is given below.

Theorem 1. *For every BTRM system β_1, the construction outlined above produces an equivalent UTRM system β_2.*

Proof Sketch: It is easy to see that any reachable state in β_1 can be reached in β_2 by simulating each BTRM command by UTRM commands, as discussed above. Conversely any reachable state in β_2, with $L \in [LOCK, O]$, will correspond to a reachable state in β_1. A reachable state in β_2, with $L \notin [LOCK, O]$ and which passes phase III, will correspond to a state in β_1 where one BTRM command has been partially completed. A state in β_2, with $L \notin [LOCK, O]$ and which fails the testing phase, will then lead β_2 to a previous state where $L \in [LOCK, O]$, which is reachable in β_1. Our construction also ensures that once the UTRM simulation passes the first phase, then the simulation proceeds with the same actual parameters of the first phase. Hence the above construction proves the equivalence of TRM and UTRM. A formal inductive proof can be easily given, but is omitted for lack of space.

Discussion

The construction given in this section illustrates that TRM and UTRM are equivalent in terms of expressive power. (The discussion of [10] given earlier in this section indicates that this result is not obvious). The construction also indicates how the document release example can be enforced in UTRM (as the document release example given in this section has BTRM commands, and our construction gives multiple UTRM commands to simulate those BTRM commands. The UTRM system obtained from our construction also assumes that all the subjects are each of a different type). The UTRM scheme to enforce the document release example is not given in this paper due to lack of space. We can also extend the construction given in this paper to prove that NMT augmented with testing for absence of rights is equivalent to TRM. We have omitted it due to lack of space.

The equivalence of TRM and UTRM would imply that the safety results of UTRM are not any better than TRM. As TRM does not have any efficient non-monotonic safety results, neither would UTRM. This leads to the fact that it is difficult to have a model which can express some simple policies and at the same time have efficient non-monotonic safety results.

4 Conclusion

In this paper we have shown that the Transformation Model (TRM) [10] and the Unary Transformation Model (UTRM) [10] are formally equivalent in expressive power. The equivalence of TRM and UTRM would imply that the safety results of UTRM are not any better than TRM. The fact that TRM does not yet have any efficient non-monotonic safety results indicates that it is difficult to have a model which can express some simple policies and at the same time have efficient non-monotonic safety results.

Acknowledgement

The work of both authors is partially supported by National Science Foundation grant CCR-9202270 and by the National Security Agency contract MDA904-92-C-5141. We are grateful to Dorothy Darnauer, Nathaniel Macon, Howard

Stainer, and Mike Ware for their support and encouragement in making this work possible.

References

1. Ammann, P.E. and Sandhu, R.S. "Implementing Transaction Control Expressions by Checking for Absence of Access Rights." *Proc. Eighth Annual Computer Security Applications Conference*, San Antonio, Texas, December 1992.

2. Bell, D.E. and LaPadula, L.J. "Secure Computer Systems: Unified Exposition and Multics Interpretation." MTR-2997, Mitre, Bedford, Massachusetts (1975).

3. Denning, D.E. "A Lattice Model of Secure Information Flow." *Communications of ACM* 19(5):236-243 (1976).

4. Harrison, M.H., Ruzzo, W.L. and Ullman, J.D. "Protection in Operating Systems." *Communications of ACM* 19(8), 1976, pages 461-471.

5. McLean, J. "A Comment on the 'Basic Security Theorem' of Bell and LaPadula." *Information Processing Letters* 20(2):67-70 (1985).

6. McLean, J. "Specifying and Modeling Computer Security." *IEEE Computer* 23(1):9-16 (1990).

7. Sandhu, R.S. "Transformation of Access Rights." *Proc. IEEE Symposium on Security and Privacy*, Oakland, California, May 1989, pages 259-268.

8. Sandhu, R.S. "The Typed Access Matrix Model" *IEEE Symposium on Research in Security and Privacy*, Oakland, CA. 1992, pages 122-136.

9. Sandhu, R.S. and Suri, G.S. "Non-monotonic Transformations of Access Rights." *Proc. IEEE Symposium on Research in Security and Privacy*, Oakland, California, May 1992, pages 148-161.

10. Sandhu, R.S. and Srinivas Ganta. "On the Minimality of Testing for Rights in Transformation Models." *Proc. IEEE Symposium on Research in Security and Privacy*, Oakland, California, May 16-18, 1994, pages 230-241.

Privilege Graph: an Extension to
the Typed Access Matrix Model

Marc Dacier, Yves Deswarte

LAAS-CNRS & INRIA
7, avenue du Colonel Roche
31077 Toulouse, France
(dacier@laas.fr, deswarte@laas.fr)

Abstract. In this paper, an extension to the TAM model is proposed to deal efficiently with authorization schemes involving sets of privileges. This new formalism provides a technique to analyse the safety problem for this kind of schemes and can be useful to identify which privilege transfers can lead to unsafe protection states. Further extensions are suggested towards quantitative evaluation of operational security and intrusion detection.

1   Introduction

The problem of controlled sharing of information in multi-user computing systems has been the subject of a large literature for more than 20 years. Many solutions have been advanced. Among them, the various access control based models are the most widely-known. The key abstractions they handle are those of subjects, objects and access rights. They also make use of two other concepts: the *protection state* and the *authorization scheme* [14]. A protection state is defined by the sets of rights held by each individual subject. The authorization scheme is defined by a set of rules that lets the protection state evolve by the autonomous activity of the subjects.

The primary goal of these models is to offer an efficient resolution of the so-called *safety problem* defined by Harrison, Ruzzo and Ullman in [7]. It consists in identifying states[1] that violate the security constraints and that are reachable given a initial state and an authorization scheme. Their model, the *HRU* model, possesses a very broad expressive power but appears to be inefficient in most practical cases. As a consequence, other models have been suggested. Lipton and Snyder, in [11], set a model forth that can solve the safety problem in linear time but at a price of poor expressiveness. To fill the gap, various solutions have been proposed (*SPM* [12], *ESPM* [1], *NMT* [13], ...), the most promising of which are *TAM* [14] and *ATAM* [2]. These models are expressive enough — as claimed by the authors — to model most security policies of practical interest and still offer strong safety properties.

In this paper, we focus on a specific class of authorization schemes where a user can grant a, possibly large, set of rights to other users. Such authorization schemes are quite common in most real-world situation and, therefore, are worth considering. Two

---

1.   In the rest of the paper, we use indifferently "state" for "protection state".

different solutions to the safety problem in that case, using the *TAM* formalism, are discussed. It follows that *TAM* can effectively solve that specific class of safety problems but in a non optimal way regarding ease of use and algorithmic complexity. Hence, we propose to enhance *TAM* with a complementary formalism based on a graph of sets of privileges[2] . This approach is presented as well as its main advantages and limitations. Furthermore, we indicate two other possible applications of our formalism, namely in the context of intrusion detection techniques and in the context of quantitative evaluation of computing systems security.

The paper's organization is as follows. Section 2 briefly summarizes previous works, highlighting the connections between them. Section 3 presents a specific authorization scheme using *TAM* formalism and, taking a simple example, gives three different solutions to the safety problem. Section 4 suggests a more efficient approach to solve that specific problem, based on a privilege graph. Section 5 justifies the authorization scheme used in Section 2 and 3 by giving real-world examples of such a scheme. Section 6 describes three possible applications of our approach and Section 7 gives a conclusion.

2   Background

Access controls models originate in Lampson's famous access matrix model [9] but Harrison, Ruzzo and Ullman were the first in [7] to formalize the *safety problem* in their *HRU* model. Their results are deceptive in the sense that they prove that, using *HRU*, the general safety problem is not decidable. In response to these negative results, other approaches have been suggested. One of them is the *take-grant* model [3, 10, 11, 17, 18]. In [11], Lypton and Snyder described an algorithm that can solve the safety problem, for this model, in linear time. Sadly, efficiency is acquired at the price of expressiveness. Indeed, in this model, it is not possible to restrict the granting of rights. One is allowed to grant all the rights one holds to someone else or none of them. Therefore, as noted in [17], the model appears to be disappointingly weak when applied to typical protection problems. More recently, work has been carried out to relax some of the assumptions of this model [4, 6, 19, 20] but, still, it remains ill-adapted for practical applications.

In [12], Sandhu defined the *Schematic Protection Model* (*SPM*) whose intent is to fill the gap in expressive power between the *take-grant* and the *HRU* models. However, attempts to prove the equivalence of *SPM* to monotonic *HRU* have remained unsuccessful and another model *ESPM* (*Extended SPM*) had to be designed for that purpose [1].

---

2.   In order to be consistent with previous work we use the same convention as in [14]: "We view *privilege* as a primitive undefined concept. For the most part, privileges can be treated as synonymous with access rights. However, there are privileges such as security level, type or rôle, which are usually represented as attributes of subjects and objects rather than as access rights".

Later, Sandhu proposed the *Typed Access Matrix* model (*TAM*), a refinement of the *HRU* model in which he introduces strong typing [14]. A *TAM* model is characterized by a finite set $\mathcal{R}$ of rights, a finite set $\mathcal{T}$ of objects types, and a set $\mathcal{T}_s$ of subjects types ($\mathcal{T}_s \subseteq \mathcal{T}$). These sets are used to define the protection state by means of a typed access matrix. The authorization scheme consists of $\mathcal{R}$, $\mathcal{T}$ and a finite collection of commands.

> **command** $\alpha(X_1 : t_1, X_2 : t_2, ..., X_k : t_k)$
>   **if** $r_1 \in [X_{s_1}, X_{o_1}] \wedge r_2 \in [X_{s_2}, X_{o_2}] \wedge r_m \in [X_{s_m}, X_{o_m}]$
>   **then** $op_1; op_2; ... ; op_n$

Table 1. Format of a TAM command

A *TAM* command has the format shown in Table 1 where α is the *name* of the command; $X_1, X_2,..., X_k$ are *formal parameters* whose types are respectively $t_1, t_2,...,t_k$; $r_1, r_2,..., r_m$ are rights; and $s_1, s_2,..., s_m$ and $o_1, o_2,..., o_m$ are integers between 1 and k. Each op_i is one of the *primitive operations* shown in Table 2, in which $z \in \mathcal{R}$ and s and o are integers between 1 and k.

enter z **into** $[X_s, X_o]$	**create subject** X_s of type t_s	**create object** X_o of type t_o
delete z **from** $[X_s, X_o]$	**destroy subject** X_s of type t_s	**destroy object** X_o of type t_o

Table 2. The six primitive operations of TAM.

In the same paper [14], Sandhu demonstrates that it is possible in many practical cases to make safety tractable without loss of expressive power. An algorithm is described to compute the *maximal state*, i.e., a state where no rule can be applied any more. In [2], an augmented version of *TAM* has been proposed which allows to test for absence of rights. The aim of *ATAM* is to easily allow separation of duties in the definition of the authorization scheme. It has been proved in [15] that both models are formally equivalent in their expressive power.

This result highlights two points: i) TAM is a general model and, therefore, can be used as a reference, ii) ATAM existence shows the usefulness of enriching TAM when dealing with some specific authorization schemes.

To conclude with our historical review, it is worth mentioning that, in [13], the problem of non-monotonic transfer of rights has been considered. The model proposed (*NMT*) exhibits some promising results, though no formal proof of its expressiveness is given. Moreover, even if safety is shown to be decidable for *NMT*, yet the decision procedure has exponential complexity.

3 The problem of granting sets of rights

3.1 A simple example

As indicated in Section 2, the expressive power of the *take-grant* model is very restricted. In this model, a grant action can focus neither on a given object, nor on a given right. One is only allowed to grant a given subject every rights in one's possession on every object. On the contrary, *TAM* commands are such that they allow the granting of one right on one object to one subject. In real-world situations, the problem of granting sets of privileges appears to be quite common and seems to require an expressiveness virtually located between the expressive power of these two models. This is the reason why it can be interesting to consider the ability of *TAM* to deal efficiently with such authorization schemes.

In the following, we will focus on some of these schemes which are characterized by empty intersections between the granted privileges and those checked in the conditional parts of the commands. Such schemes present interesting properties to solve the safety problem, namely the absence of cycles[3].

Throughout this paper, we use a simple example where the set T of types is defined as $T = \{user, file_1, file_2, file_3\}$ and the set R of rights as $R = \{e,o,r,w\}$ (where the letters stand for the mnemonics of *"execute"*, *"own"*, *"read"* and *"write"* respectively). Table 3 gives the initial protection state for this example[4].

	$f : file_1$	$g : file_2$	$h : file_3$	$i : file_3$
$a : user$	e,o,r,w			
$b : user$	e	r,w	r	
$c : user$		e,o,r,w	o,r,w	r

Table 3. A simple Typed Access Matrix

The authorization scheme we consider consists of two rules:

Rule 1:   If a user U_1 owns a file F of type $file_1$ and if a user U_2 can execute that file F, then U_2 can grant U_1 all the *read* rights that U_2 holds on files of type $file_3$.

Rule 2:   if a user U_1 can write into a file F of type $file_2$ and if a user U_2 owns that file F, then U_2 can grant U_1 all *read* and *write* rights that U_2 holds on files of type $file_3$

Section 5 explains this choice by showing that these rules are representative of real-world problems. Based on these protection state and authorization scheme, we consider in the next subsections the two following basic safety problems:

Q1: Can the system reach a state where the user a can gain the r right on i ?

Q2: Can the system reach a state where the user a can gain the w right on h ?

3.2   First Solution: Direct Application of TAM

The most obvious way to model this authorization scheme, using TAM formalism, is by defining the three following commands:

command $R_1(U_1: user, U_2: user, F_1: file_1, F_2: file_3)$
     if $o \in [U_1,F_1] \wedge e \in [U_2,F_1] \wedge r \in [U_2,F_2]$
         then enter r **into** $[U_1, F_2]$

This first command expresses the first rule of our authorization scheme.

---

3.   As discussed in Section 4.4, performance reasons can impose another constraint to the authorization scheme: there should be small mutual intersections between granted privilege sets.

4.   Empty rows and empty columns are not represented for the sake of conciseness.

command $R_{2read}(U_1: user, U_2: user, F_1: file_2, F_2: file_3)$
   if $w \in [U_1,F_1] \wedge o \in [U_2,F_1] \wedge r \in [U_2,F_2]$
      then enter r **into** $[U_1, F_2]$

command $R_{2write}(U_1: user, U_2: user, F_1: file_2, F_2: file_3)$
   if $w \in [U_1,F_1] \wedge o \in [U_2,F_1] \wedge w \in [U_2,F_2]$
      then enter w **into** $[U_1, F_2]$

These last two commands express the second rule of our authorization scheme. Table 4 represents the maximal state of this system. Obtaining this maximal state can be achieved in different ways. Here is an example of one sequence of command applications that reaches it: $R_1(a,b,f,h)$ - $R_{2read}(b,c,g,i)$ - $R_{2write}(b,c,g,h)$ - $R_1(a,b,f,i)$. Four command applications are required. Resolving the safety problem is straightforward with this method: a simple inspection of the matrix leads us to answer the question Q1 positively and Q2 negatively.

	$f: file_1$	$g: file_2$	$h: file_3$	$i: file_3$
$a: user$	e,o,r,w		r	r
$b: user$	e	r,w	r,w	r
$c: user$		e,o,r,w	o,r,w	r

Table 4. Maximal state for the first solution

It is important to note that the number of command applications is directly proportional to the number of files of type $file_3$. This can be highlighted by a rough generalization of our example. Consider an authorization scheme defined by the only rule R_1; consider a protection state with n users $(U_1, U_2,..., U_n)$, each of them having the r right on m different files of type $file_3$. Suppose also the existence of n-1 files of type $file_1$ $(F_1,F_2,...,F_{n-1})$ such that: $\forall j, (1 \leq j \leq n-1)$ $o \in [U_j,F_j] \wedge e \in [U_{j+1},F_j]$. In this case, the maximal state can be reached by applying m times the command R_1 with U_n and U_{n-1} as parameters, $2m$ times with U_{n-1} and $U_{n-2},...,$ $(n-1)m$ times with U_1 and U_2. Thus, the amount of command applications required to build the maximal state in this case is equal to:

$$m + (m + m) + ... + (m + ... + m) = m \times (1 + ... + n - 1) = \frac{m \times n \times (n - 1)}{2}$$

Hence, in this case, we need $O(mn^2)$ command applications to reach the maximal state. It is shown in the next Subsection, that one could easily take profit of the richness of TAM to find a much more efficient modelization.

3.3   Second solution: Introducing ad-hoc privileges

The number of applications could remain constant, whatever is the number of $file_3$ present in the system, thanks to the definition of two *ad-hoc* privileges tr and tw, where tr (resp. tw) stands for the mnemonic of "*take read*" (resp. "*take write*"). Hence, we can express the same authorization scheme with only two rules:

command $R'_1(U_1: user, U_2: user, F_1: file_1)$
   if $o \in [U_1,F_1] \wedge e \in [U_2,F_1]$
      then enter tr **into** $[U_1, U_2]$

command $R'_2(U_1: user, U_2: user, F_1: file_2)$
    if $w \in [U_1, F_1] \wedge o \in [U_2, F_1]$
        then enter tr **into** $[U_1, U_2]$; **enter** tw **into** $[U_1, U_2]$

Table 5 shows the maximal state obtained by applying $R'_1(a,b,f)$ and $R'_2(b,c,g)$ to the protection state defined in Table 3.

	b	c	$f : file_1$	$g : file2$	$h : file_3$	$i : file_3$
a : user	tr		e,o,r,w			
b : user		tr,tw	e	r,w	r	
c : user				e,o,r,w	r,w	r

Table 5. Maximal State with the tr and tw privileges.

It was shown in the previous section that the rough generalization of our example required $O(mn^2)$ to build the maximal state. Now, with this solution, it would require only n-1 command applications but the answer cannot be found directly in the matrix as before. The privileges tr and tw have semantics that must be considered to answer that question.

Actually, these privileges act like pointers. We note that introducing special rights which have such rôle is nothing new in a *TAM* model. This is the trick used by Sandhu and Ganta in [15] to show that *TAM* and *ATAM* are formally equivalent in their expressive power. In our case, a recursive function *get_answer* will be used to solve the safety problem. Its algorithm[5] is given below:

function *get_answer*(U_1: user, F: object, R: right)
if $R \in [U_1, F]$
        then   **answer is** *YES*
        elsif $(R = r)$
            then foreach (U: user **such that** $tr \in [U_1, U]$) {*get_answer*(U, F, R)};
        end if;
        elsif $(R = w)$
            then foreach (U: user **such that** $tw \in [U_1, U]$) {*get_answer*(U, F, R)};
        end if;
end if

Hence, *get_answer*(a,i,r) will first search in the matrix if a has the right r on i. If not, it looks for a pointer to another subject who would hold this right or who would have another pointer to a third subject, etc. In this particular case, getting the answer requires five inspections[6] of the matrix for the question Q1 and three[7] for Q2. It is important to note that these results are independent of the number of files of type $file_3$ and linear with respect to the number of users (to compare with $O(mn^2)$ of the rough generalization).

---

5.   The function *get_answer* returns *YES* if the answer is positive. It returns nothing if the answer is negative. This is a simplified version of the algorithm. A complete one should take care of the existence of possible cycles.
6.   **Q1**: $r \notin [a,i] \Rightarrow tr \in [a,b] \Rightarrow r \notin [b,i] \Rightarrow tr \in [b,c] \Rightarrow r \in [c,i] \Rightarrow$ *YES*
7.   **Q2**: $w \notin [a,h] \Rightarrow tw \notin [a,b] \Rightarrow tw \notin [a,c] \Rightarrow$ *NO*

Of course, the astute reader has noticed that this example has been designed on purpose. In fact, this solution is directly proportional to the *number of pointers*. If we consider a protection state with many users, none of them having the right to read *"i"*, this solution is clearly worse than the first one. Indeed, it will probably impose us to follow a long list of pointers to eventually reach a negative conclusion that could have been immediately derived with the first method! However, it will be shown in Section 5 that our example is representative of many common, yet specific, real-world situations. In these cases, the second solution is better than the first one.

3.4   Discussion

As can be seen, the introduction of ad-hoc privileges in a given TAM model can improve dramatically its efficiency in some given situations. Unfortunately, this requires at least a new right for each class of set of privileges that can be granted. Each new right definition induces the rewriting of the *get_answer* algorithm in order to take the new pointer's semantics into account. Such task could rapidly become cumbersome with the growth of the set of commands. This solution looks promising but it suffers from its lack of modularity.

As a result of this comment, one could be tempted to define a new approach using only one kind of pointer towards new virtual users created on purpose. For instance, to represent that the user b grants to a all his r rights on objects of type $file_3$, one could create a new user β, give him all the r rights that b possesses on objects of type $file_3$ and introduce in $[a,\beta]$ a pointer called, for example, *take_set*. However, such solution is not easy to implement with TAM. The two following scenarios highlight this point:

1)   Once β created, suppose that b acquires a new right r on an object of type $file_3$, then β's privileges must be updated ! Thus, we must define rules to take care of every change in b's privileges.

2)   Once β created, b acquires all the r and w rights on all objects of type $file_3$ that c has. Therefore, a new user γ is created (with all the r and w rights on all objects of type $file_3$ that c has) and the right *take_set* has to be inserted in $[b,\gamma]$. How should this update be taken in consideration for the update of β ? If we put a *take_set* right into $[\beta,\gamma]$ then a, by transitivity, will gain the w rights of c, which is not correct ! It is clear, therefore, that the required update rules are not easy to define. Actually, this approach suffers from the same lack of modularity that the one explained hereabove.

If we could *define* β rather than *create* it, as we do by putting access rights in matrix cells, then the problem, explained in the first scenario, would disappear because no update would be necessary any more. Indeed, its definition would be independent of the evolution of the privileges of b.

Furthermore, if we have such formal definition of β, then we can also get rid of the second problem by integrating the update commands into the usual commands. This is explained into the next section where we propose an extension to TAM that offers such formal definitions of sets of privileges.

4   The Privilege Graph.

4.1   Definitions

It is important to note that our formalism is not aimed at replacing *TAM* which has proved to be very powerful in many situations but rather as an efficient complementary notation. Our solution is based on a directed graph, the nodes of which are sets of triples $(U, O, \Sigma_{\mathcal{R}})$ where U is a subject, O an object and $\Sigma_{\mathcal{R}}$ a set of rights $(\Sigma_{\mathcal{R}} \subseteq \mathcal{R})$. For each type θ $(\theta \in \mathcal{T})$, we define Σ_{θ} as the set of all objects of type θ. We define $\Sigma_{\mathcal{T}}$ as a union of sets: $\Sigma_{\mathcal{T}} = \bigcup_{\theta \in \mathcal{T}} \Sigma_{\theta}$.

Nodes do represent sets of privileges on sets of objects. A node is not supposed to correspond to any row in any access matrix. It defines a set of privileges that can be granted to other users. For instance, suppose that a rule specifies that the user b can grant all the read rights he has on every file of type $file_3$. The application of this rule will create a node defined as: $N = \{(b,O,r) | O \in \Sigma_{file_3} \wedge r \in [b,O]\}$. This node represents a subset of the privileges that b effectively holds in the access matrix when the rule is applied but this subset is not "frozen". Indeed, such a definition could take "new" rights into account, i. e. rights entered into the matrix for b by some rule application after the creation of the node. This is possible because the content of the node is characterized by a formal definition rather than by the enumeration of its contents.

For each user U, we define $\mathcal{M}_U$ as the maximal set of privileges that U could get. This set can be identified with the row corresponding to U in the classical maximal state, defined in Section 3.2. Formally[8] :

$$\forall U \qquad \mathcal{M}_U = \{(U,O,\Sigma_{\mathcal{R}}) | O \in \Sigma_{\mathcal{T}} \wedge \left(\Sigma_{\mathcal{R}} = \left(\mathcal{R} \cap [U,O]^*\right)\right) \wedge \Sigma_{\mathcal{R}} \neq \varnothing\} .$$

It is important to note that we do not define any node that corresponds to that definition. Actually, as explained below, we never have to compute this maximal state.

The existence of a directed edge in the graph from a node N_1 to a node N_2 implies that $\forall U, U \in \Sigma_{users}, \mathcal{M}_U \supseteq \mathcal{N}_1 \Rightarrow \mathcal{M}_U \supseteq \mathcal{N}_2$. Roughly speaking, the existence of an edge from a node N_1 to a node N_2 means that, every user who can acquire N_1, can acquire N_2. The formal definition is not used in practice because, as already mentioned, we do not want to compute $\mathcal{M}_U$.

Edges and nodes are created by successive applications of the rules that compose the authorization scheme. Therefore, we add two primitive operations to *TAM:* *make_node* and *make_edge*. The operation *make_node* (resp. *make_edge*) will create a node in the graph (resp. an edge) only if this node (resp. edge) does not already exist.

4.2   Construction

We have already mentioned that we do not have to compute $\mathcal{M}_U$ at any time. Indeed, with this method, solving the safety problem is reduced to finding a path in a digraph. This is highlighted by the following protocol:

1)   For each subject U in the initial protection state, create a node defined as follows $\mathcal{N}_U = \{(U,O, \Sigma_{\mathcal{R}}) | O \in \Sigma_{\mathcal{T}} \wedge (\Sigma_{\mathcal{R}} = (\mathcal{R} \cap [U,O])) \wedge \Sigma_{\mathcal{R}} \neq \varnothing\} .$

---

8.   The notation $[U,O]^*$, instead of $[U,O]$, indicates that we do refer to the matrix representing the maximal state.

At any time, this definition represents the privileges present in the matrix for this user[9].

2) Apply the commands up to reach a maximal state[10]. The maximal state, in this case, is characterized by the matrix and by the graph. Both are needed to define the final protection state.

3) Reformulate the safety problem in terms of two conflicting sets of nodes and find if a path exists between these two sets.

Each step of this process is better understood by showing how it is achieved in our running example. Therefore, we need to define new commands to characterize our authorization scheme:

command $R''_1(U_1: user, U_2: user, F_1: file_1, \mathcal{N}_1: node, \mathcal{N}_2: node)$
    if $o \in [U_1,F_1] \wedge e \in [U_2,F_1] \wedge \{(U_1,O,r)|O \in \Sigma_{file_3} \wedge r \in [U_1,O]\} \subseteq \mathcal{N}_1$
        then   **make_node** $\mathcal{N}_2 = \{(U_2,O,r)|O \in \Sigma_{file_3} \wedge r \in [U_2,O]\}$
            make_edge from $\mathcal{N}_1$ **to** $\mathcal{N}_2$
    end if

Compared to command R'_1, we see that R''_1 contains a third test in its conditional part:

1) $o \in [U_1,F_1] \wedge e \in [U_2,F_1]$ deals with the authorization scheme itself (identical to R'_1).

2) $\{(U_1,O,r)|O \in \Sigma_{file_3} \wedge r \in [U_1,O]\} \subseteq \mathcal{N}_1$ identifies in the graph the node to which the primitive operation *make_edge* will be applied. The rule will be applied for each node that satisfies this definition. As a result, for a given triple (U_1,U_2,F_1), this rule will create one node N_2 but several links could be created, originating from various nodes N_1 to N_2.

Keeping the same principles in mind, we define two new rules R''_{2read} and R''_{2write} to implement the second rule. Namely:

command $R''_{2read}(U_1: user, U_2: user, F_1: file_2, \mathcal{N}_1: node, \mathcal{N}_2: node)$
    if $w \in [U_1,F_1] \wedge o \in [U_2,F_1] \wedge \{(U_1,O,r)|O \in \Sigma_{file_3} \wedge r \in [U_1,O]\} \subseteq \mathcal{N}_1$
        then
            make_node $\mathcal{N}_2 = \{(U_2,O,r)|O \in \Sigma_{file_3} \wedge r \in [U_2,O]\}$
            make_edge from $\mathcal{N}_1$ **to** $\mathcal{N}_2$
    end if

command $R''_{2write}(U_1: user, U_2: user, F_1: file_2, \mathcal{N}_1: node, \mathcal{N}_2: node)$
    if $w \in [U_1,F_1] \wedge o \in [U_2,F_1] \wedge \{(U_1,O,w)|O \in \Sigma_{file_3} \wedge w \in [U_2,O]\} \subseteq \mathcal{N}_1$
        then
            make_node $\mathcal{N}_2 = \{(U_2,O,w)|O \in \Sigma_{file_3} \wedge w \in [U_2,O]\}$
            make_edge from $\mathcal{N}_1$ **to** $\mathcal{N}_2$
    end if

---

9. $\mathcal{N}_U$ is identical to $\mathcal{M}_U$ if and only if there is no edge originating from $\mathcal{N}_U$. In general, this is not true and we have $\mathcal{N}_U \subseteq \mathcal{M}_U$.

10. The task of constructing the graph is finite because the number of nodes is at most a linear combination of the number of cells in the maximal state matrix of Section 3.2 — the size of which is finite [14].

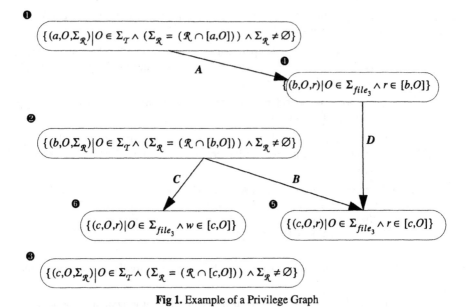

Fig 1. Example of a Privilege Graph

In the first step, we create the nodes **❶**, **❷**, and **❸**. They refer to the protection state of Table 3. In the second step, we can apply, for instance, the following sequence of command applications that leads to a maximal state: $R''_1(a,b,f,❶,❹)$ - $R''_{2read}(b,c,g,❷,❺) - R''_{2write}(b,c,g,❷,❻)$, $R''_{2read}(b,c,g,❶,❺)$. This is represented in the graph of Fig. 1 which could have been obtained with any other sequence. The third step is detailed in the next subsection.

4.3   Resolution of the safety problem

To solve the question Q1 of our safety problem, we run the following steps:

1) Check in the matrix if a has *read* access to i; if the answer is no, go to the next step.

2) Identify in the matrix the subjects who have *read* access to i; the only subject with that right in our example is c.

3) Identify in the graph every node which contains the triple (c,i,r); both nodes **❸** and **❺** have this property in our example.

4) If a path can be found between the node representing the set of privileges of a (**❶**) and one of the nodes identified in step 3, then, we know that a can read i; in this case the existence of the path between **❶** and **❺** (arcs A and D) implies a positive answer to the question.

For the question Q2, the same scheme leads us to deduce a negative answer because no path exists, neither between the nodes **❶** and **❻**, nor between **❶** and **❸**.

4.4   Discussion

We have already mentioned that this method was only efficient for specific authorization schemes. The conditions under which our method is worth being used are recalled hereafter:

1) Sets of granted privileges should not contain access rights on objects checked in the conditional parts of the commands. This ensures that the conditional part can be evaluated by the sole inspection of the matrix, without looking at the graph (of course, the node identification still requires inspection of the graph). In our example, for instance, we grant privileges on objects of type $file_3$ but the conditions always checks files of type $file_1$ or $file_2$. If this was not the case, the expression of the condition, though possible, would be cumbersome and require to check for the existence of some well-defined node in a specific path. It is clear that the complexity of this process would impede the usefulness of this solution.

2) Sets of granted privileges should have small mutual intersections. Clearly, the best situation consists of distinct sets of privileges. This will minimize the number of edges created.

3) If the safety problem is made of a conjunction of n questions, such as $(r \in [a,i]) \wedge (w \in [a,i])$, then its solution is found as the conjunction of the n answers to each individual question. In this case, $(true \wedge false)$ returns $false$.

The following example highlights the algorithmic complexity of the method when these two requirements are satisfied. Consider the initial access matrix represented in Table 8 and the command R_e.

	$x : file_1$	$y : file_1$	$z : file_1$	$u : file_2$	$v : file_2$	$w : file_2$
a: user	e,o,r,w			e,o,r,w		
b: user		e,o,r,w			e,o,r,w	
c: user			e,o,r,w	o,r,w		e,o,r,w

Table 6. A simple Typed Access Matrix

command $R_e(U_1: user, U_2: user, F_1: file_1, F_2: file_2)$
   if $o \in [U_1,F_1] \wedge e \in [U_1,F_2]$
      then enter e **into** $[U_2, F_2]$

Suppose also the existence of a rule R_r (resp. R_w) equivalent to R_e where the right e has been replaced by the right r (resp. w).

In terms of privileges sets, we can rewrite[11] this authorization scheme as:

---

11. Actually, one such rule must be written for each subset of the set $\{e,r,w\}$. They determine the definition of N_1 but are equivalent for the primitive operations involved.

command $R'_e(U_1: user, U_2: user, F_1: file_1, \mathcal{N}_1: node, \mathcal{N}_2: node)$
   if $o \in [U_1, F_1] \wedge \{(U_2, O, \Sigma_{\mathcal{R}}) | O \in \Sigma_{file_2} \wedge (\Sigma_{\mathcal{R}} = \{e\} \cap [U_2, O]) \wedge \Sigma_{\mathcal{R}} \neq \emptyset\} \subseteq \mathcal{N}_1$
   then
      make_node $\mathcal{N}_2 = \{(U_1, O, \Sigma_{\mathcal{R}}) | O \in \Sigma_{file_2} \wedge (\Sigma_{\mathcal{R}} = (\{e, r, w\} \cap [U_1, O])) \wedge \Sigma_{\mathcal{R}} \neq \emptyset\}$
      make_edge from $\mathcal{N}_1$ **to** $\mathcal{N}_2$
   end if

In this case, the two above requirements are satisfied: i) objects involved in the condition are distinct from those granted and ii) the sets of privileges granted are distinct.

Hence, suppose that we have n users. Each user has the o right on at least one object of type $file_1$. Furthermore, each user has r rights that can be granted on m objects of type $file_2$. Then, in this case, TAM requires $n \times r \times m \times (n-1)$ rule applications to reach a maximal state. With the privilege graph, it requires $n \times r \times (n-1+n-1)$. Thus, when the requirements are satisfied, the complexity is reduced by a factor approximately equal to $m/2$. Furthermore, in general, we will have $m >> n$. Of course, if the requirements are not satisfied, the best trade-off must be found between pure TAM and pure privilege graph, based on complexity evaluation. This evaluation can only be made with full knowledge of the access matrix and of the rules.

In order to show the usefulness of the method, we show hereafter real-world examples where the requirements are satisfied, and where, therefore, the use of privilege graph must be preferred to TAM.

5 Real World Examples

In this section, we wish to stress that the authorization scheme presented in Section 3 is not artificial; it is representative of privilege transfer features that can be found in most real life systems. To show this, we consider three examples based on Unix™: a .xinitrc file, a .rhosts file and setuid files.

5.1 The .xinitrc File

When running, the X Window System initializer looks for a specific file in the user's home directory, called .xinitrc, to run as a shell script to start up client programs. Daily practice shows that novice users can encounter some difficulty to configure correctly this file. If a novice user trusts another user, more expert in X than himself, he may prefer use the expert's configuration file rather than bother to understand all the commands and options. To do so, an easy solution is to establish a symbolic link between his own .xinitrc file and the expert's file[12]. Then, if the so-called expert enhances his set-up file, the novice will enjoy the result as well.

From a security point of view, this can also be a good solution. Indeed, if the novice chooses inappropriate options or commands, this file will turn out as a trapdoor, letting his data unprotected. Using the expert's file — who should be aware of the vulnerabilities — his data security is enhanced. Of course, he is at the mercy of this

---

12. ln -s ~expert/.xinitrc ~novice/.xinitrc

expert who can introduce a Trojan horse in his configuration file, and then acquire most of the novice's privileges[13] . This is exactly what the first rule of our authorization scheme wanted to characterize in its conditional part: the expert owns the .xinitrc file executed by the novice.

5.2   The . rhosts File

To log in a Unix system, a password is required. However, there is a mechanism in Unix that allows remote trusted users to access local system without supplying a password. This functionality is implemented by the .rhosts file which enables to bypass the standard password-based authentication: if in John's home directory there is a .rhosts file which contains Fred's username, then Fred, when logged in another machine, can establish a remote connection to John's machine and be identified as John on this machine, without typing John's password. Once again, this allows John to grant Fred almost all his privileges. This feature is frequently used, for instance if John wishes Fred to take care of any urgent work during his vacations, without giving him his own password. Another advantage of this feature is to enable remote login without transmitting a password on the network where it would be vulnerable to wire tapping.

If such a file exists, any user who has *write* access to John's .rhosts can get this set of privileges. This is an example of the second rule of our authorization scheme: a user who can write in John's .rhosts can read and write the same files as John[14] .

5.3   Setuid Files

In Unix, every process holds the same privileges as the user for whom the process is run. However, it is possible to let a process get the privileges of the owner of the program rather than the privileges of the user initiating the process. This is particularly useful when an operation needs more privileges than held by the user. An example of this is the program /bin/passwd that changes user passwords: every user must be able to change his own password but this operation requires to write in a protected file, usually the /etc/passwd file, to which no user has write access except the superuser; to do so, /bin/passwd uses the setuid facility to run with superuser privileges on behalf of less privileged users. This functionality has many other applications, all of them being examples of grants of sets of privileges by the owner of the program to the user of the program. As long as these setuid programs are correct and no low privileged user can create or modify such programs, the security is satisfactory. Indeed, this feature strengthens security since, without this feature, users should be granted more privileges constantly. But if a setuid-program owner trusts another user and gives him write access to his program, he is at the mercy of this user. Such behaviour is another example of the second rule of the authorization scheme given in Section 3.1.

---

13. Actually, the expert cannot acquire all the novice's privileges since, for instance, without knowing the novice's password he will not be able to change it. Other specific privileges could be denied to the expert due to the fact that, for instance, he is not physically located at the same place than the novice, etc.

14. It is clearly a very bad idea to grant another user write access to your   . rhosts file but this is another problem! Preventive and/or corrective actions are beyond the scope of this paper.

6   Potential Applications of the Privilege Graph

6.1   Practical Solutions to the Safety Problem

It has already been explained at length how the *privilege graph* formalism could be used to analyse in an efficient way the safety problem. But to know whether an unsafe state is reachable is not enough: we wish to know what can be done to prevent to reach this state, i.e., which modification of the protection state can solve the problem. The graph enables to identify which paths are conflicting with the security constraints. In our experiments, this feature has proved to be helpful to solve conflicts.

6.2   Quantitative Evaluation of Security

The safety problem accepts only a boolean answer: either an unsafe state is reachable or not. There is no information on how easily or how fast the unsafe state can be reached. Yet, in most practical systems, attacks and intrusions are more or less easy and fast according to the configuration of the system. For instance, it can be more or less difficult to guess a user's password. In the safety problem, either you consider that passwords are guessable and then the system is unsafe, or that no password can be guessed and then ignore that indeed some of them can be guessed by chance or by brute force[15].

With the privilege graph, it can be envisaged to assign a weight to each edge corresponding to the likelihood associated to this privilege transfer; for instance, if an edge represents the possibility to guess user A's password, the corresponding weight can be lower if A's password is in a dictionary than if it had been carefully chosen. Moreover, it is possible to consider that successful attacks are represented in the graph as paths between potential attackers' privileges (e.g., non-users, or ftp users) and potential targets' privileges (e.g., superuser). The system security can then be assessed not only by the existence or absence of such a path, but also by the length of this path and the weights on the traversed edges. This approach could lead to a quantitative evaluation of the operational security but, firstly, open theoretical problems have to be solved, as discussed in [5].

6.3   Intrusion Detection

Intrusion detection is another potential application of the privilege graph: if it is possible to correlate the user's behaviour observed by an intrusion detection system with a progress in the privilege graph towards a potential target, alarms of different levels can be triggered according to the likelihood to reach the target. This approach is similar to the pattern-oriented model proposed by [16]. It is probably possible to integrate the privilege graph analysis in sophisticated intrusion detection tools such as NIDES [8], e. g., in the resolver module, to help in detecting malicious activities carried on by a hacker impersonating other users by using their privileges. The graph could be used to correlate various suspicious activities that, if considered separately, would not

---

15.   Of course, intermediate considerations could be that low privileged users' passwords are guessable and superuser's password is not, but this does not change the problem.

bring enough evidence to detect an intruder. Also, their correlation could highlight on the graph that some possible attack is progressing along a path leading to a target.

7 Conclusions

In this paper, a graphical extension to the TAM model has been proposed to represent authorization schemes based on privilege transfers. This formalism provides an efficient technique to analyse the safety problem and can be useful to identify which privilege transfers can lead to an unsafe state. Further extensions are suggested towards quantitative evaluation of operational security and intrusion detection.

It is our claim that this formalism is flexible enough to represent real world systems such as Unix systems. Indeed, it is possible to build a privilege graph by means of an automatic tool analysing the permissions in the Unix file system. In this case, nodes are privileges held by users or groups and edges are elementary privilege transfers corresponding to Unix operations on permissions. A prototype of such a tool has been implemented and experimented successfully [5].

8 Acknowledgments

Thanks are due to Mohamed Kaâniche and Jean-Claude Laprie for useful discussions that have led to the writing of this paper. The authors also want to thank the anonymous referees for their valuable comments. Finally, the authors acknowledge several insightful comments from Catherine Meadows and Gerard Eizenberg which enabled significant improvements of this paper.

This work has been partially supported by ESPRIT Basic Research Action Project n°6362: Predictable Dependable Computing Systems (*PDCS2*) and by the ESPRIT Basic Research Network of Excellence in Distributed Computing Systems Architectures - (*CaberNet*).

References

1. Amman, P. E. and Sandhu, R. S. "Extending the Creation Operation in the Schematic Protection Model," *Proc. Sixth Annual Computer Security Applications Conference*, 1990, pp. 340-348.

2. Amman, P. E. and Sandhu, R. S. "Implementing Transaction Control Expressions by Checking for Absence of Access Rights," *Proc. Eighth Annual Computer Security Applications Conference*, San Antonio (Texas, USA), December 1992, pp. 131-140.

3. Bishop, M. and Snyder, L. "The Transfer of Information and Authority in a Protection System," *Proc. of the Seventh Symposium on Operating Systems Principles*, Pacific Grove, California (USA), December 10-12, 1979, SIGOPS (ACM), pp. 45-54.

4. Biskup, J. "Some Variants of the Take-Grant Protection System", *Information Processing Letters*, 19, 1984, pp. 151-156.

5. Dacier, M., Deswarte, Y. and Kaâniche, M. "A Framework for Security Assessment of Insecure Systems," Predictably Dependable Computing Systems (PDCS-2), *First Year Report,* ESPRIT Project 6362, September 1993, pp. 561-578.

6. Dacier, M. "A Petri Net Representation of the Take-Grant Model," *Proc. of the 6th. Computer Security Foundations Workshop,* Franconia (USA), June 15-17, 1993, pp. 99-108.

7. Harrison, M. A., Ruzzo, W. L. and Ullman, J. D. "Protection in Operating Systems," *Communications of the ACM,* 19(8), August 1976, pp. 461-470.

8. Jagannathan, R., Lunt, T., Gilham, F., Tamaru, A., Jalali, C., Neumann, P., Anderson, D., Garvey, T. and Lowrance, J., Requirements Specification: Next-Generation Intrusion Detection Expert System (NIDES), SRI Project 3131 - Requirement Specifications (A001, A002, A003, A004, A006), September 3, 1992.

9. Lampson, B. W. "Protection", *ACM Operating Systems Review,* 8(1), 1974, pp. 18-24.

10. Landwehr, C. E. "Formal Models for Computer Security", *ACM Computing Surveys,* 13(3), 1981, pp. 247-278.

11. Lypton, R. J. and Snyder, L. "A Linear Time Algorithm for Deciding Subject Security," *Communications of the ACM,* ACM, 24(3), July 1977, pp. 455-464.

12. Sandhu, R.S. "The Schematic Protection Model: Its Definition and Analysis of Acyclic Attenuation Schemes," *Journal of the ACM,* No. 2, 1988, pp. 404-432.

13. Sandhu, R. S. and Suri, G. S. "Non-monotonic Transformation of Access Rights," *Proc. 1992 IEEE Symposium on Research in Security and Privacy,* May 4-6, 1992, pp. 148-161.

14. Sandhu, R. S. "The Typed Access Matrix Model," *Proc. 1992 IEEE Symposium on Research in Security and Privacy,* May 4-6, 1992, pp. 122-136.

15. Sandhu, R. S. and Ganta, S. "On Testing for Absence of Rights in Access Control Models," *Proc. of the Computer Security Foundations Workshop VI,* IEEE Computer Society Press, Franconia (NH,USA), June 15-17, 1993, pp. 109-118.

16. Shieh, S. W. and Gligor, V. D. "A Pattern-Oriented Intrusion-Detection Model and Its Application", *Proc. 1991 IEEE Symposium on Research in Security and Privacy,* Oakland (USA), May 20-22, 1991, pp. 327-342.

17. Snyder, L. "On the Synthesis and Analysis of Protection Systems," *Proc. of the Sixth Symposium on Operating Systems Principles,* Purdue University (USA), November 16-18, 1977, SIGOPS (ACM), 11(5), pp 141-150.

18. Snyder, L. "Formal Models of Capability-Based Protection Systems", *IEEE Transactions on Computers,* C-30(3), 1981, pp.172-181.

19. Snyder, L. "Theft and Conspiracy in the Take-Grant Protection Model", *Journal of Computer and System Sciences,* 23, 1981, pp. 333-347.

20. von Solms, S. H. and de Villiers, D. P. "Protection Graph Rewriting Grammars and the Take-Grant Security Model", *Quæstiones Informaticæ,* 6(1), 1988, pp.15-18.

A Consideration of the Modes of Operation for Secure Systems

C L Robinson and S R Wiseman

Secure Information Systems Group
Defence Research Agency
Malvern
Worcestershire, WR14 3PS, UK

email: harrold@dra.hmg.gb or wiseman@dra.hmg.gb

Abstract. Secure systems are often characterised by a 'mode of operation'. This acts as a shorthand for the degree of risk to the information on the system and the minimum security functionality required as a countermeasure. This paper examines the UK definitions of these modes and proposes a model of a system which can be used to capture the distinctions between them. The variations of possible secure system functionality within each mode are then discussed. Some new definitions, which are orthogonal to the modes of operation, are proposed which can be used to resolve ambiguities.

Keywords. Security Mode of Operation, Dedicated, System High, Compartmented, Multi-Level, System Model, Z Notation

1 Introduction

Within the UK, secure systems are often characterised by a 'mode of operation'. This acts as a shorthand for the degree of risk to information on the system and the minimum security functionality required as a countermeasure. There are currently four UK modes of operation: Dedicated; System High; Compartmented and Multi-Level. The CESG Glossary [1] provides definitions of these modes as particular combinations of user need-to-know, formal clearances and security functionality. Similar terms and definitions are used in the US [2].

Any definition relating to a secure system requires a precise understanding of the boundary of a system and its users. Such an understanding was relatively straightforward when systems were large standalone mainframes located in computer rooms. However, in the age of desktop computers and networks the boundary of the system and the identification of its users becomes more problematical. This difficulty does appear to be recognised, since the definitions of the UK modes have been clarified with subsequent issues of the glossary. Similar problems with the US definitions are discussed in [3].

The main problem with the definitions of the modes of operation is that they are not sufficiently detailed enough to give a complete picture of a system. Systems which have the same mode of operation can have different security functionality requirements. Thus, the use of the mode of operation alone as a shorthand to describe a system can potentially lead to misunderstandings. This paper proposes additional sets of terms to characterise the 'boundary mode', 'output class mode' and 'output need-to-know mode' of a system. The intention is that the definitions can provide a framework to assist in the identification of appropriate security requirements for individual projects.

The definitions in this paper are firmly based upon an abstract mathematical model of a system. This model has been used to explore the distinctions between the different modes of operation and how they relate to the system boundary and to justify the proposed new definitions. Therefore, in this paper the purpose of the model is to explore the different ways in which secure systems may be used in military environments. The model is at a high level of abstraction, without many of the details of system functionality or security mechanisms. This use of a model is therefore different to the commonly quoted models of operating system security mechanisms, due to Bell and LaPadula [4].

In order to avoid ambiguity, the Z notation [5] is used to precisely define the system model and definitions. The notation is based on standard set theory, and a brief explanation of the symbols used is given as Annex A. However, the overview of the model and English commentary to the formal specifications should be sufficient to gain an appreciation of the model, the distinctions between the different modes of operation and the proposed new definitions.

The structure of this paper is as follows: Section 2 considers the standard UK definitions of the modes of operation and identifies the concepts which are required to model them; Section 3 describes the model of a system, which is then specified formally in Section 4; Section 5 defines the four modes of operation for secure systems, and for completeness an additional mode that corresponds to an insecure system; Section 6 discusses these formal definitions and proposes some orthogonal criteria which can be used to distinguish particular types of system within the mode categories; Finally, Section 7 draws some conclusions.

2 Identification of Model Elements

The following definitions are directly taken from the official UK glossary of computer security terminology [1].

DEDICATED. "A mode of operation in which all the users of a system are cleared for, need to know about and have access to all the data handled by it. Hence, the system does not enforce national security rules or need-to-know and little or no technical security functionality is required."

SYSTEM HIGH. "A mode of operation in which all the users are cleared for, and have formal access approval for, all the information handled by it, but not all of whom actually need to know about all of the data. In this mode of operation DAC will normally be applied".

COMPARTMENTED. "A mode of operation in which all the users of a system are cleared for all the data handled by the system; and who only need to have, and are only given, access to some of the data by means of MAC."

MULTILEVEL. "A mode of operation in which a computer system (or network·of computer systems) handles data at various classifications etc., but for which there are users not cleared for all that data whose access is restricted appropriately. Hence, the system (or network) is relied upon to enforce the national security rules."

Thus, it can be seen that the basic concepts in the model will need to be user clearances, data classifications and need-to-know requirements.

The definitions for System High and Compartmented modes are similar. Indeed, the Compartmented mode has only relatively recently been introduced into UK terminology, although it appears to have been used in the US for some time. The distinction between the two modes is in the type of security functionality used to control the user's need-to-know. In a System High mode, need-to-know is controlled by Discretionary Access Control (DAC) mechanisms, whereas in a Compartmented mode Mandatory Access Control (MAC) mechanisms are used.

Thus, the model will need to distinguish between systems with no technical security functionality (i.e. for Dedicated Mode) and between those with DAC or MAC functionality. The model also needs to distinguish between MAC functionality which is used to control need-to-know (i.e. for Compartmented Mode) and MAC based on clearances (i.e. for Multi-Level Mode).

The standard definitions for MAC and DAC, for example in [1], are not sufficiently precise to clearly explain the intended differences between the System High and Compartmented modes of operation. However, the mode definitions suggest that the difference relates to the strength of the mechanism. With DAC functionality, there would appear to be the potential for users to be given access to information for which they do not have a need-to-know. Obviously, to operate in this mode, the system risk assessment must have determined that this did not represent a significant threat.

It is assumed that in a System High Mode, the discretion of the users of a system can be trusted. Therefore, a reasonable interpretation of the difference between MAC and DAC for need-to-know relates to the trustworthiness of software. In other words, software acting on behalf of a user might misuse discretionary controls but cannot step outside of the bounds imposed by mandatory controls. Precise definitions for the different types of access control are proposed in [6].

Therefore, the model of a system includes the notion of software proxies. These are the active agents working for the human users within the computer system. The model distinguishes between software which can be trusted only to alter a discretionary control with the authority of the user, and software which cannot be so trusted.

The technical security controls within a system are not modelled at the same level of abstraction as in the Bell and LaPadula models of [4]. Instead, they are modelled by identifying the possible handling restrictions applied to outputs. This is based on the modelling approach of Goguen and Meseguer [7]. In a system with no technical security controls all the output has to be treated at the level of the highest possible security class on the system. Alternatively, in a system with technical security functionality, i.e. MAC or DAC, to control the flows of information within the system, output can be labelled more accurately.

3 An Overview of the Model

This section gives an overview of the proposed model of a system. This model is subsequently used to explore the modes of operation and propose further definitions. The purpose of the model is to define a generalised secure system, and therefore many of the details of realistic implementations are omitted. Further, the model permits cases which may not be required in particular environments. However, it is not considered to be sensible to complicate the model by explicitly excluding some situations.

Figure 1 below depicts the elements of the model and their relationship to each other and the system boundary. The elements of the model are described in the following text, and then precise definitions are given in the formal model of section 4.

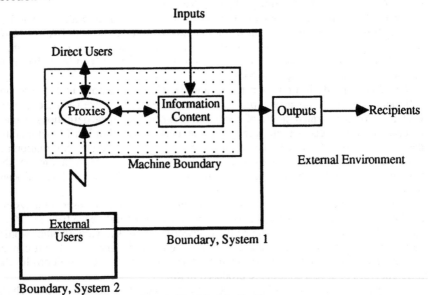

Fig. 1. The Model of a System

3.1 Information and its Security Class and Need-to-Know

A system contains information. This comprises input from other systems and input from the users of the system, together with information generated as a result of calculations and associations made within the machine. All the information in a system has an inherent security class and need-to-know requirement associated with it. The need-to-know for information is abstractly represented by the set of people who need-to-know the information in order to effectively carry out their job function.

A system may not contain information at all possible security classes. Neither do the need-to-know sets for a particular system necessarily contain all combinations of people. This is because a system generally exists in an environment which can restrict what is entered into the system. The functionality of a system can also limit the security classes and need-to-knows for the information it can create.

The inherent need-to-know of information in a system can include people who are not users of the machine. However, someone has to have a need-to-know for each item of information, either in the system or output from it (see below). In other words, the model does not consider something to be information if no one needs to know it.

However, the model does not restrict the inherent need-to-know for information to the users of the machine. Instead, the need-to-know in the model represents all the people who need to have access to the information in some form. Thus, the model permits there to be information in a system for which no user has a need-to-know.

3.2 Users

A system has at least one authorised user. The users are the people who influence the contents of the system. They are the people who enter and manipulate information on the system via the functionality of the machine. The users are outside of the machine boundary and interact with the contents via software proxies within the machine boundary.

A distinction is made between the direct and external users. Direct users are under the direct control of the system management, and will generally access the system via its physical components, such as screens and keyboards. The external users access the system via an interconnection, and will be the direct users of a different system. A particular person could be both an external and a direct user of a system, for example if they were able to logon both at a connected workstation and remotely from another system.

The reason for the distinction between direct and external users relates to the positioning of a system boundary when many computers from different management domains are interconnected. However, the exact positioning of the boundary is not important to the model. What is important is that all the people who can influence the information in the system are identified by the two sets.

3.3 Outputs and Recipients

A system produces outputs, although there may be some information on a system which is never output. An output is something, either paper-based or electronic, which enters the environment outside of the direct control of the system. Within the external environment there are people who are the potential recipients of the outputs. These people could also be users of the system. The difference between a recipient and a user is that the former cannot influence the information, but only receive it.

A system has to 'trust' its external environment to ensure that its outputs are handled appropriately. To assist the external environment, a system will label its outputs with respect to the minimum security clearance and need-to-know requirements.

3.4 Clearances and User Need-to-Knows

The authorised users may have different formal clearances, and there may also be users of a system who hold no formal clearance. However, every user of the system has to have a need-to-know for some item of information on the system. This represents the obvious requirement that people should only be given access to a computerised system if they have a need to do so. Therefore, this definition rules out people hacking into a system across a network, and thus the model requires that a system has appropriate identification and authentication measures in place.

It is less obvious that it is reasonable for there to be information on the system for which no user is formally cleared. For example, it is possible to postulate a messaging system where highly classified information is transported by users not cleared to access the information. They obviously need-to-know some aspect of the information, such that it exists and the address it is intended for, but do not need-to-know or be cleared for the contents.

In addition, UK Security Policy contains an "Occasional Access" rule. This permits a person with insufficient formal clearance to be given access to a limited amount of information above their clearance because they have a genuine need-to-know that information in order to effectively carry out their duties. Therefore, the model of an electronic system should not rule out this case.

However, although the system model permits otherwise, in practice it would be expected that there will always be a user who is actually formally cleared for all information on a system, such as system security administrators. In this case the interesting point is that they need to be formally cleared in order to manage the system, but do not in fact have a genuine need-to-know for the information they are managing. Thus, the managers represent the dual of the Occasional Access rule. In effect the need for a system manager who is able to access all the information on the system arises from the implementation of the system and is not a system requirement. Therefore, from an abstract viewpoint the system managers could be considered as an implementation detail.

3.5 Software Proxies and Confidence

Although software acts as a user's proxy within the machine, the user does not necessarily have complete confidence that their wishes are being faithfully carried out. This is because software is generally not well specified and is frequently accepted and used when it contains errors. It can thus exhibit surprising or unexpected behaviour. Where this is the case the user will have a fairly low level of confidence that their wishes are being carried out.

On the other hand, using a Trusted Path to invoke a security critical function gives the user a great deal of confidence that their wishes are being carried out. This is because additional effort has been expended in the specification, design, testing and evaluation of the software and its means of invocation. Thus, in a system there will be differing degrees of confidence in the software proxies which act on behalf of the human users.

Control over need-to-know is achieved through human discretion, actioned via software proxies within the machine boundary. Therefore, the model associates with each software proxy which is capable of altering need-to-know controls, a degree of confidence that it only does so with the authority of the responsible person.

3.6 Security Policy

A secure system is always 'no flows down' with respect to security classes. Thus CONFIDENTIAL information may be output labelled CONFIDENTIAL, SECRET, etc., but cannot be labelled UNCLASSIFIED.

A system may contain technical security functionality which is able to maintain separation between the different classes of information on the system and monitor the flows of classified information around the system. Where this is the case, information can be output labelled at its inherent security class. Such functionality is generally referred to as MAC.

Other systems may not contain security functionality capable of maintaining accurate labels within the system. When this is the case, all the outputs must be labelled at the level of the highest security class on the system. Otherwise the system might not be 'no flows down'.

No information flow property is given for need-to-know. Thus, no constraints are placed on the possible output labels with respect to need-to-know for the information on the system. Appropriate control is achieved for need-to-know by applying human judgement and discretion.

3.7 Summary

To summarise, a system contains information at various security classes and with various need-to-know requirements. The information is accessed by its users via software proxies, and there are varying degrees of confidence in the trustworthiness of this software. A system loses direct control over its outputs. It therefore applies security markings in order that the recipients of output can be limited to those with adequate clearance or need-to-know. A formal specification is given in section 4.

4 The Formal Model

This section specifies the model of a system using the Z notation [5] along with a brief English commentary that explains the intended interpretation of the mathematics. The meaning of the Z symbols used is included as Annex A.

Computerised systems are used by people. Thus a set is introduced to represent all the possible people of interest. This set includes the users, i.e. the people who are able to influence the state of the computer system, and the people who receive the outputs from the system.

    [PERSON]

However, the users cannot directly manipulate the information within a computer, but must use software to act on their behalf. Thus, the model identifies a set of software agents, or proxies.

    [PROXY]

Although software acts as a user's proxy within the computer, the user does not necessarily have complete confidence that their wishes are being faithfully carried out. For the purposes of this model a set is introduced to represent the various degrees of confidence that people could have in software. The confidence levels are partially ordered by a relation called ≥ (dominates), which defines which degrees of confidence are 'better' than others.

```
[ CONFIDENCE ]

│ _ ≥ _ : partial_order CONFIDENCE
```

One particular confidence is important to the modes of operation, although the system model permits there to be other confidences. This confidence is called NTKfaithful and is the point at which the people start to believe that the software carries out their wishes with respect to need-to-know (NTK) controls. Thus software with a confidence which dominates NTKfaithful is trusted not to misuse the discretion of the human user with respect to the need-to-know controls. Software whose confidence level does not dominate NTKfaithful is not so trusted.

```
│ NTKfaithful : CONFIDENCE
```

Secure systems manipulate classified information, and thus a set of security classes is defined. Note that a security class encompasses categories and caveats in addition to a hierarchical component, as defined in [1]. Thus, security classes can encompass certain need-to-know controls such as codewords. The security classes are partially ordered by a relation called ≥ (dominates). A least upper bound function is given for security classes, but the definition is omitted for clarity.

```
[ CLASS ]

│ _ ≥ _ : partial_order CLASS
│ LUB : ℙ CLASS → CLASS
├──────────────────────────────
│ ...
```

A system is characterised by the non-empty set of identities for its users and the non-empty set of clearances which they hold. At the level of abstraction used in this model, it is not necessary to directly relate users to clearances. A distinction is made between the direct users, who are under the control of the system management, and external users, who access the system via an interconnection. Not all the authorised users of a system need to hold a formal clearance.

```
┌─ USERS ─────────────────────────────────────────┐
│ DirectNames, ExternalNames : ℙ PERSON            │
│ DirectClearances, ExternalClearances : ℙ CLASS   │
├──────────────────────────────────────────────────┤
│ DirectNames ∪ ExternalNames ≠ {}                 │
│ DirectClearances ∪ ExternalClearances ≠ {}       │
└──────────────────────────────────────────────────┘
```

Additional sets of people and clearances are identified in the model. These represent the identities of all the people who may potentially receive outputs from the system, either paper-based or electronic, and their clearances.

```
┌─ RECIPIENTS ─────────────────────────────────────────────┐
│  RecipientNames  :  ℙ PERSON                              │
│  RecipientClearances  :  ℙ CLASS                          │
├──────────────────────────────────────────────────────────┤
│  RecipientClearances ≠ {} ⇒ RecipientNames ≠ {}          │
│                                                           │
└──────────────────────────────────────────────────────────┘
```

The security classes and need-to-know for information on the system (section 3.1) and the labelling of output from a system (section 3.6) are both captured in the Z specification using functions called OutputClasses and OutputNTKs.

The domain of the OutputClasses function models the inherent security classes for the information contained within the system. For each possible security class within the system, the OutputClasses function gives the set of possible output security labels. OutputClasses is restricted to ensure that the system is 'no flows down'. In other words, for each security class on the system, all the possible output labels must be at least as high.

The distinction between no technical security functionality within the system and functionality to separate different classes is also captured. The CLASS_CONTROLS schema states that either information can be output at its inherent security class, i.e. separation is maintained, or alternatively all the outputs must be labelled at the level of the highest security class within the system.

```
┌─ CLASS_CONTROLS ─────────────────────────────────────────┐
│  OutputClasses  :  CLASS ⇸ ℙ CLASS                        │
├──────────────────────────────────────────────────────────┤
│  OutputClasses ≠ {}                                       │
│  ∀ c : dom OutputClasses  •                               │
│     ∀ l : OutputClasses( c )  •  l ≥ c                    │
│  ( ∀ c : dom OutputClasses  •  c ∈ OutputClasses( c )     │
│    ∨ rng OutputClasses = {{ LUB (dom OutputClasses) }} )  │
│                                                           │
└──────────────────────────────────────────────────────────┘
```

Similarly, the domain of the OutputNTKs function models the sets of people who need to know the various pieces of information within the system. For each possible need-to-know set within the system, the OutputNTKs function gives the set of possible output security labels. However, no information flow restrictions are defined for need-to-know labelling.

```
┌─ NTK_CONTROLS ─────────────────────────────────────┐
│  OutputNTKs : IP₁ PERSON ⇸ IP IP₁ PERSON            │
│                                                     │
├─────────────────────────────────────────────────── │
│  OutputNTKs ≠ {}                                    │
│                                                     │
└─────────────────────────────────────────────────── ┘
```

Note that a possible interpretation of the abstract type $\mathbb{P}_1$ PERSON could be an Access Control List, although other interpretations, such as all the people who are cleared into a particular codeword, are not ruled out by the model. Alternatively, certain codewords could be modelled by security classes.

The final element of the formal model is a function to capture the level of confidence in the trustworthiness of the particular software proxies with respect to the need-to-know controls. The domain of this function represents all the software proxies within the system which have the ability to alter the need-to-know controls. For each, the function gives the level of confidence that they carry out the human user's wishes. An empty set for this function is intended to capture the case where the system contains no technical need-to-know controls.

```
┌─ SOFTWARE ─────────────────────────────────────────┐
│  NTKProxyConfidence : PROXY ⇸ CONFIDENCE            │
│                                                     │
└─────────────────────────────────────────────────── ┘
```

Thus, in this model a system is defined by: its users; the recipients of output; the security classes of information it contains and how it labels its outputs; the need-to-know for information and how this is labelled on output, together with the confidence that software does not misuse any need-to-know controls.

```
┌─ SYSTEM ───────────────────────────────────────────┐
│  USERS                                              │
│  RECIPIENTS                                         │
│  CLASS_CONTROLS                                     │
│  NTK_CONTROLS                                       │
│  SOFTWARE                                           │
│                                                     │
├─────────────────────────────────────────────────── │
│  ∀ u : DirectNames ∪ ExternalNames ·                │
│     ∃ ntk : dom OutputNTKs · u ∈ ntk                │
│                                                     │
└─────────────────────────────────────────────────── ┘
```

5 Definition of Security Modes of Operation

Returning to the glossary definitions of the modes of operation, given in Section 2, it can be seen that they require four criteria with which to partition the model of a system.

i) Whether all the users (both direct and external) are cleared for all of the information on the system.
ii) Whether all the users have a need-to-know for all of the information on the system.
iii) The kind of technical security mechanisms which are used for need-to-know.
iv) Whether the system contains security functionality which can ensure that information is accurately labelled on output with a security class.

A Dedicated system is distinguished from all the other modes of operation by the fact that all the users are both formally cleared and have a need-to-know for all of the information on the system. Consequently, a Dedicated system is secure whether or not it contains technical security functionality for need-to-know or security classes.

```
┌─ Dedicated ──────────────────────────────────────────────────┐
│ SYSTEM                                                         │
├────────────────────────────────────────────────────────────  │
│ (DirectClearances ∪ ExternalClearances) ×                     │
│    (dom OutputClasses) ⊆ _ ≀ _                                │
│ ∀ ntk : dom OutputNTKs ·                                      │
│    DirectNames ∪ ExternalNames ⊆ ntk                          │
└────────────────────────────────────────────────────────────  ┘
```

For a System High mode of operation all the users are formally cleared, but do not have a need to know for all of the information. In other words, there must exist at least one need-to-know grouping of information on the system which does not include at least one of the users. However, the main distinguishing feature of the System High mode is that the need-to-know controls are vulnerable to misuse by the software acting on behalf of the users. This is expressed by stating that at least one software proxy capable of altering the need-to-know controls, is not trusted to always faithfully carry out the user's wishes.

```
┌─ SystemHigh ─────────────────────────────────────────────────┐
│ SYSTEM                                                         │
├────────────────────────────────────────────────────────────  │
│ (DirectClearances ∪ ExternalClearances) ×                     │
│    (dom OutputClasses) ⊆ _ ≀ _                                │
│ ∃ ntk :dom OutputNTKs ·                                       │
│    ¬( DirectNames ∪ ExternalNames ⊆ ntk )                     │
│ ∃ c : rng NTKProxyConfidence · ¬( c ≀ NTKfaithful )           │
└────────────────────────────────────────────────────────────  ┘
```

The distinction between the System High and Compartmented modes is captured by the fact that in the Compartmented mode all of the software proxies capable of altering need-to-know controls are trusted not to misuse this ability. Note that in practice this is usually achieved by arranging that the 'untrusted' software cannot alter the controls.

```
┌─ Compartmented ──────────────────────────────────────────┐
│  SYSTEM                                                    │
│ ┌────────────────────────────────────────────────────────
│ │                                                         │
│ │ (DirectClearances ∪ ExternalClearances) ×              │
│ │     (dom OutputClasses) ⊆ _ ≀ _                        │
│ │ ∃ ntk :dom OutputNTKs ·                                │
│ │    ¬( DirectNames ∪ ExternalNames ⊆ ntk )              │
│ │ NTKProxyConfidence ≠ {}                                │
│ │ rng NTKProxyConfidence × {NTKfaithful} ⊆ _ ≀ _         │
│ └────────────────────────────────────────────────────────
└────────────────────────────────────────────────────────────┘
```

The feature which distinguishes the Multi-Level mode from the others is that not all of the users have formal security clearance for all of the information and technical security functionality is present which is capable of maintaining accurate security labels. Thus for every inherent security class on the system the information can be output labelled at that class. Such functionality is capable of preventing the users from accessing information for which they are not cleared.

Note that this proposed definition of the Multi-Level Mode of operation also requires that if there are users with no need-to-know for information there must be some technical security controls to prevent them from gaining access.

```
┌─ Multi-Level ────────────────────────────────────────────┐
│  SYSTEM                                                    │
│ ┌────────────────────────────────────────────────────────
│ │                                                         │
│ │ ¬((DirectClearances ∪ ExternalClearances) ×            │
│ │     (dom OutputClasses) ⊆ ⊒ )                          │
│ │ ∀ c : dom OutputClasses · c ∈ OutputClasses( c )       │
│ │ ∃ ntk :dom OutputNTKs ·                                │
│ │    ¬( DirectNames ∪ ExternalNames ⊆ ntk )              │
│ │ ⇒  NTKProxyConfidence ≠ {}                             │
│ └────────────────────────────────────────────────────────
└────────────────────────────────────────────────────────────┘
```

A system can be insecure for two reasons. Firstly, it is insecure for there to be no functionality to maintain accurate security labels and yet have users with insufficient formal security clearance. Secondly, it is insecure to have users with no need-to-know for information, and yet have no technical security controls to prevent them from gaining access.

```
┌─ InsecureClass ─────────────────────────────────────────────┐
│ SYSTEM                                                       │
│                                                              │
├──────────────────────────────────────────────────────────────┤
│ ¬((DirectClearances ∪ ExternalClearances) ×                  │
│     (dom OutputClasses) ⊆ ⪰)                                 │
│ rng OutputClasses = { { LUB ( dom OutputClasses ) } }        │
└──────────────────────────────────────────────────────────────┘


┌─ InsecureNTK ───────────────────────────────────────────────┐
│ SYSTEM                                                       │
│                                                              │
├──────────────────────────────────────────────────────────────┤
│ ∃ ntk :dom OutputNTKs •                                      │
│     ¬( DirectNames ∪ ExternalNames ⊆ ntk )                   │
│ NTKProxyConfidence = {}                                      │
└──────────────────────────────────────────────────────────────┘
```

```
Insecure ≙ InsecureClass ∨ InsecureNTK
```

As discussed earlier, this model of a system recognises the existence of the UK Occasional Access rule. This permits people limited access to information for which they have a genuine need-to-know, but are not formally cleared. A system which requires this rule to be invoked in a controlled manner will need to contain security functionality which is capable of maintaining accurate security labels on information. Thus, the definitions above place such a system as operating in the Multi-Level mode. However, in a computer with software acting on behalf of the human users, the precise difference between a system which requires the Occasional Access rule to be invoked and an insecure system is unclear.

These five types of system partition the model of a system given in this paper. Thus, all systems which conform to the model described in Section 4 will meet exactly one of the above definitions. An informal justification for this theorem is given as Annex B. This contains a table listing the combinations of criteria and identifies the corresponding mode.

```
⊢ < Dedicated, SystemHigh, Compartmented, Multi-Level,
    Insecure > partition SYSTEM
```

6 Discussion and Further Definition

Systems which meet the definition of a particular mode of operation can have different technical security requirements. In particular, the definitions of both System High and Compartmented allow systems within the mode to have either accurate labelling of output or to label at the level of the highest security class on the system. This could be a potential source of confusion and ambiguity whenever the mode of operation is used as a shorthand to describe a system.

Furthermore, systems may meet different modes of operation definitions depending upon where the system boundary is drawn with respect to the direct and external users. For example a system could be Compartmented if only the direct users were counted, and yet be Multi-Level if the clearances of all the people who could access the system via an interconnection, i.e. external users, were considered.

However, even when all the users have been taken into consideration, and all have formal security clearances, a system may still require accurate labelling of output. In other words, accurate labelling of output may be required in systems other than those which operate in the Multi-Level mode (as defined in this paper). Such a situation arises quite naturally where there is a requirement for a system to pass its outputs into an environment where there will be people who are not fully cleared.

This section proposes three further terms which can be used to more fully characterise a system. These are derived from the model given in this paper, and describe the 'boundary mode', the 'output class mode' and the 'output need-to-know' mode' of a system.

6.1 Boundary Mode

As discussed above, a system may meet different modes of operation depending upon where the boundary has been drawn with respect to the direct and external users. The problem partly results from the fact that the official terminology does not precisely define the users of a system. In terms of the model of a system used in this paper, choosing just the direct users who are under the direct control of the system management may give one mode, whilst including the external users gives another. Such a situation could occur if an interconnection requirement for a system arises at a late stage in its procurement.

This paper proposes that systems which have not included external users in their mode of operation be referred to as *Introspective*, since the system boundary has been drawn between its direct and external users. It is proposed that a system which does consider both kinds of user be called *Inclusive*.

```
┌─ Introspective ─────────────────────┐
│ SYSTEM                               │
├──────────────────────────────────────┤
│ ExternalNames \ DirectNames ≠ {}     │
└──────────────────────────────────────┘

┌─ Inclusive ─────────────────────────┐
│ SYSTEM                               │
├──────────────────────────────────────┤
│ ExternalNames \ DirectNames = {}     │
└──────────────────────────────────────┘
```

⊢ < Introspective, Inclusive > partition SYSTEM

6.2 Output Class Mode

An output class mode for a system is proposed. This characterises the potential recipients of the outputs from the system with respect to the security clearances which they hold. Four modes are defined, *Isolated*, *Connected* and *StrongBounded*, and a mode corresponding to a system with an insecure boundary.

In determining the output class mode for a system, the clearances of the potential recipients are considered with respect to the highest security class contained within the system. It is important to note that they are not just compared with the security classes of the outputs they should receive.

An Isolated system is one where all of the possible recipients of output have sufficient clearance for all of the security classes contained on the system. Thus, no technical security functionality within the system is necessary, since labels are not required to control access to outputs. Without technical security functionality to maintain separation between security classes, all the outputs will be labelled at the level of the highest. Such a system can be considered to be isolated with respect to security classes, since it does interact with people who are not cleared for all of its information.

```
┌─ Isolated ──────────────────────────────────────────────┐
│ SYSTEM                                                   │
├──────────────────────────────────────────────────────────┤
│                                                          │
│ RecipientClearances x (dom OutputClasses) ⊆ _ ≥ _        │
│ rng OutputClasses = { { LUB dom OutputClasses } }        │
└──────────────────────────────────────────────────────────┘
```

A Connected system is one where the outputs may enter an environment where there are potential recipients who are not formally cleared for all of the information on the system. Thus, the system needs to provide accurate labels on its outputs in order to ensure that the environment to which it passes responsibility for information is able to make appropriate access control decisions.

```
┌─ Connected ─────────────────────────────────────────────┐
│ SYSTEM                                                   │
├──────────────────────────────────────────────────────────┤
│                                                          │
│ ¬( RecipientClearances x (dom OutputClasses)  ⊆ _ ≥ _ )  │
│ ∀ c : dom OutputClasses  ·  c ∈ OutputClasses( c )       │
└──────────────────────────────────────────────────────────┘
```

A system would have an insecure boundary if there were potential recipients of output who were not cleared for all of the classes of information on the system, and yet the system did not contain any security functionality to ensure that security labels were accurate.

```
┌─ InsecureBoundary ──────────────────────────────────────────────┐
│ SYSTEM                                                           │
│                                                                  │
├──────────────────────────────────────────────────────────────────┤
│ ¬( RecipientClearances × (dom OutputClasses)  ⊆ _ ≩ _ )          │
│ rng OutputClasses = { { LUB ( dom OutputClasses ) } }            │
│ # dom OutputClasses ≠ 1                                          │
│                                                                  │
└──────────────────────────────────────────────────────────────────┘
```

There is one final case to consider. This is where all the potential recipients of outputs have sufficient clearance for all of the information on the system, and yet the system maintains accurate security labels on the various classes of information in the system. Such a situation could be needed if there were authorised users (as opposed to the recipients of output) with insufficient clearance.

```
┌─ StrongBounded ─────────────────────────────────────────────────┐
│ SYSTEM                                                           │
│                                                                  │
├──────────────────────────────────────────────────────────────────┤
│ RecipientClearances × { dom OutputClasses }  ⊆ _ ≩ _            │
│ ∀ c : dom OutputClasses  ·  c ∈ OutputClasses( c )              │
│ # dom OutputClasses ≠ 1                                          │
│                                                                  │
└──────────────────────────────────────────────────────────────────┘
```

⊢ < Isolated, Connected, StrongBounded, InsecureBoundary >
        partition SYSTEM

6.3   Output Need-to-Know Mode

Finally, an output need-to-know mode is proposed. This is similar to the output class mode, except that the potential recipients of the outputs are considered with respect to their need-to-know for information. Five modes are defined, *Continuous*, *Linked*, *Discrete* and *StrongNTKBounded*, together with a mode corresponding to a system with an insecure need-to-know boundary.

A Continuous system is defined to be one where all the potential recipients of outputs have a need-to-know for all of the information within the system. Thus, no technical security functionality is required to ensure that the external environment, either electronic or human, can make appropriate access control decisions. Such a system could be considered as continuous, because the boundary between the electronic systems, or between the electronic and human world, is not significant.

```
┌─ Continuous ──────────────────────────────────────────────────┐
│ SYSTEM                                                         │
├───────────────────────────────────────────────────────────────┤
│ ∀ ntk : dom OutputNTKs · RecipientNames ⊆ ntk                  │
│ NTKProxyConfidence = {}                                        │
└───────────────────────────────────────────────────────────────┘
```

A Linked system is defined to be one where there are potential recipients of output who do not have a need-to-know for all of the information, and where the threat is such that 'weak' need-to-know controls are sufficient. The system contains security controls to provide need-to-know labelling which may be misused by software acting on behalf of the users, i.e. without their authority. Thus, the need-to-know markings applied to output could be inappropriate. Such a type of system can be referred to as linked with its external environments. Thus, there is a weak boundary between the system and the environment of its outputs.

```
┌─ Linked ──────────────────────────────────────────────────────┐
│ SYSTEM                                                         │
├───────────────────────────────────────────────────────────────┤
│ ∃ ntk : dom OutputNTKs · ∃ u : RecipientNames · u ∉ ntk        │
│ ∃ c : rng NTKProxyConfidence · ¬( c ≥ NTKfaithful )            │
└───────────────────────────────────────────────────────────────┘
```

Thirdly, a system can be considered to be a discrete entity with external interfaces requiring 'strong' need-to-know controls. Such controls ensure that the environments which take over responsibility for the protection of information can make appropriate decisions. In this case there are potential recipients of outputs who do not have a need-to-know for all of the information on the system. The system contains security controls for need-to-know which cannot be altered inappropriately by the software acting on behalf of its users.

```
┌─ Discrete ────────────────────────────────────────────────────┐
│ SYSTEM                                                         │
├───────────────────────────────────────────────────────────────┤
│ ∃ ntk : dom OutputNTKs · ∃ u : RecipientNames · u ∉ ntk        │
│ NTKProxyConfidence ≠ {}                                        │
│ rng NTKProxyConfidence × { NTKfaithful } ⊆ _ ≥ _               │
└───────────────────────────────────────────────────────────────┘
```

A system is insecure across its boundary to external environments if there are potential recipients who do not have a need-to-know for all of the information on the system, and yet the system has no technical security functionality to provide need-to-know controls.

```
┌─ InsecureNTKBoundary ──────────────────────────────────┐
│ SYSTEM                                                  │
├─────────────────────────────────────────────────────────┤
│ ∃ ntk : dom OutputNTKs  ·  ∃ u : RecipientNames  ·  u ∉ ntk │
│ NTKProxyConfidence = {}                                 │
└─────────────────────────────────────────────────────────┘
```

The final case to consider is where all the potential recipients of output have a need-to-know for all of the information on the system, and yet the system contains some need-to-know controls. This situation could be needed if the authorised users (as opposed to the recipients of output) do not all have a need-to-know for the information on the system.

```
┌─ StrongNTKBounded ──────────────────────────────────────┐
│ SYSTEM                                                  │
├─────────────────────────────────────────────────────────┤
│ ∀ ntk : dom OutputNTKs  ·  RecipientNames ⊆ ntk         │
│ NTKProxyConfidence ≠ {}                                 │
└─────────────────────────────────────────────────────────┘
```

⊢ < Continuous, Linked, Discrete, StrongNTKBounded,
    InsecureNTKBoundary> **partition** SYSTEM

7 Conclusions

This paper has considered the standard UK glossary definitions of the modes of operation for secure systems. A mathematical model of a system has been proposed and precise definitions for Dedicated, System High, Compartmented and Multi-Level have been given in terms of this model. New, orthogonal, definitions have been proposed which can be used to describe the differences between various kinds of system which have the same mode of operation.

Therefore, this paper concludes that it is possible to devise finer-grained descriptions of a system than the standard modes of operation currently provide. What remains for future work is to determine whether the finer-grained descriptions proposed in this paper can be usefully applied to the problems of determining the appropriate security functionality and assurance requirements which are encountered in real system procurements.

A second conclusion from the work presented in this paper concerns the value of the use of formal methods. The development of the mathematical model of a system required the issues of the boundary of a system and its users to be explored in depth. Furthermore, the mathematical specification has underpinned the development of the ideas contained in this paper. Whether or not the proposed definitions of the existing and new modes are appropriate, the mathematical specification provides a solid foundation for further discussions in this area. It is concluded that the use of mathematical modelling can be an effective tool in the development of the conceptual foundations and terminology for the science of Computer Security.

8 References

1. CESG Computer Security Memorandum 1, Glossary of Computer Security Terms, Issue 2.2, November 1993

2. Guidance for Applying the Department of Defense Trusted Computer System, Evaluation Criteria in Specific Environments, CSC-STD-003-85, June 1985

3. H O Lubbes: COMPUSEC, A Personal View, Proceedings of the 9th Annual Computer Security Applications Conference, Orlando, Florida, December 6 - 10, 1993

4. D E Bell, L J LaPadula: Secure Computer Systems: Mathematical Foundations, MTR-2547, Volume 1, November 1973; Secure Computer Systems: A Mathematical Model, MTR-2547 Volume II, November 1973; Secure Computer Systems: A Refinement of the Mathematical Model, MTR-2547 Volume III, April 1974; and Secure Computer System: Unified Exposition and Multics Interpretation, MTR-2997, January 1976

5. J M Spivey: The Z Notation: a Reference Manual, 2nd Edition, Prentice Hall International, 1992

6. S R Wiseman, C L Robinson and M M Adams: A Mathematical Definition of Access Control, DRA report DRA/CIS/CSE2/94007, April 1994

7. J A Goguen, J Meseguer: Security Policies and Security Models, Proceedings of the 1982 Symposium on Security and Privacy, Oakland, California, April 1982

Annex A: An Overview of the Z Notation

Z is a mathematical notation that has been developed by the Programming Research Group at Oxford University. The underlying basis of Z is standard set theory, and it makes use of the associated notation. Properties about sets are described using predicate calculus. A Z specification is structured into self contained parts using schemas.

$[A]$	introduction of a new set, called A
$\{\}$	set, with no members
$a \in A$	a is a member of the set A
$a \notin A$	a is not a member of the set A
$A \subseteq B$	A is a subset of the set B (possibly equal)
$A \cup B$	union of members of the sets A and B

$A \setminus B$	members of set A which are not in set B
$A \times B$	set consisting of all the possible pairings of members of A and B
$x : T$	declaration, x is an element drawn from the set T
$\mathbb{P}\ A$	powerset, i.e. the set of all possible subsets of A (including empty set)
$\mathbb{P}_1\ A$	powerset, excluding empty set
AS <u>partition</u> A	the set of sets AS are disjoint sets and cover A

A relation may be viewed as a set of ordered pairs. Functions are a special type of relation where there is a single element in the range for each element of the domain. Thus, the operators defined for sets are applicable to both functions and relations.

dom r	domain of relation, r, i.e. set of all the first elements of the ordered pairs
rng r	range of a relation, r, i.e. set of all the second elements of the ordered pairs
$f : A \rightarrow B$	f is a total function, i.e. domain is all possible members of the set A
$f : A \nrightarrow B$	f is a partial function, i.e. domain is not necessarily all of the set A
r : partial_order A	r is an ordered relation where all pairs of elements are not necessarily comparable
$P \vee Q$	either predicate P holds or Q does
$\neg P$	predicate P does not hold
$P \Rightarrow Q$	if P holds then Q does
$\forall\ x:T \cdot P$	for all x of type T predicate P holds
$\exists\ x:T \cdot P$	there exists an x of type T for which predicate P holds
$\vdash P$	P is a theorem

declaration ——— predicates	An axiomatic definition. The declarations are global and the predicates define properties about them. The predicates are optional.
name ——— signature ——— predicates	A schema. The signature declares some variables and their types. The predicates define some properties about them. The declarations from one schema are made available to another by including the name of the schema in the signature. They are in scope until the end of the schema. The predicates are conjoined with those of the new schema.
$S \triangleq T$	schemas S and T are equivalent

Annex B: Modes of Operation

The table below lists the possible combinations of the mode of operation partitioning criteria and gives the mode of operation for each. Certain combinations represent insecure systems, and where this is the case a note gives the reason. The table also indicates where the combination of clearance and need-to-know suggests that the UK Occasional Access rule is being applied.

Users Cleared: all   all users (direct and external) cleared for all security classes on the system

                   some   at least one not cleared

Users NTK: all   all users (direct and external) have a need-to-know for all information on the system

                   some   at least one does not have a need-to-know for something

NTK Labels: none   no technical security functionality to control access based on need-to-know

                  weak   need-to-know mechanisms vulnerable to inappropriate use by untrusted software

                 strong need-to-know mechanisms not vulnerable

Class Labels: high   all output must be labelled at highest security class on system

                  accurate security functionality present to maintain accurate security class labels

Users Cleared	Users NTK	NTK Labels	Class Labels	Mode
all	all	none	high	DEDICATED
all	all	none	accurate	DEDICATED
all	all	weak	high	DEDICATED
all	all	weak	accurate	DEDICATED
all	all	strong	high	DEDICATED
all	all	strong	accurate	DEDICATED
all	some	none	high	insecure[NTK]
all	some	none	accurate	insecure[NTK]
all	some	weak	high	SYSTEM HIGH
all	some	weak	accurate	SYSTEM HIGH
all	some	strong	high	COMPARTMENTED
all	some	strong	accurate	COMPARTMENTED

some	all	none	high	insecure[CLASS]
some	all	none	accurate	MULTI-LEVEL[OAR]
some	all	weak	high	insecure[CLASS]
some	all	weak	accurate	MULTI-LEVEL[OAR]
some	all	strong	high	insecure[CLASS]
some	all	strong	accurate	MULTI-LEVEL[OAR]
some	some	none	high	insecure[NTK and CLASS]
some	some	none	accurate	insecure[NTK]
some	some	weak	high	insecure[CLASS]
some	some	weak	accurate	MULTI-LEVEL
some	some	strong	high	insecure[CLASS]
some	some	strong	accurate	MULTI-LEVEL

[NTK]This combination is insecure because although not all users need-to-know all the information, no technical security controls are applied to prevent them getting access.

[CLASS]This combination is insecure because although not all users are cleared, no controls are applied.

[OAR]This combination suggests that the Occasional Access rule applies since although not all users are cleared for all the information, all have a need-to-know.

Database I

Mark-and-Sweep Garbage Collection in Multilevel Secure Object-Oriented Database Systems*

Alessandro Ciampichetti[1], Elisa Bertino[2] and Luigi Mancini[1]

[1] Dipartimento di Informatica e Scienze dell'Informazione,
Università di Genova, Viale Benedetto XV 3, 16132 Genova, Italy
email: {ciampi,mancini}@disi.unige.it
[2] Dipartimento di Scienze dell'Informazione,
Università di Milano, Via Comelico 39, 20135 Milano, Italy
email: bertino@hermes.mc.dsi.unimi.it

Abstract. In this paper, the introduction of garbage collection techniques in a multilevel secure object-oriented database system is discussed; in particular, the attention is focused on mark-and-sweep collectors. A secure garbage collection scheme guarantees referential integrity and avoids potential covert channels arising from object deletion.
Keywords: object-oriented database systems, mandatory access control, garbage collection, object deletion, mark-and-sweep.

1 Introduction

Issues related to security and to privacy have not been widely investigated in the area of Object-Oriented Database Systems (OODBSs). Models have been proposed for mandatory access control [11] and for discretionary access control OODBSs [17]. In particular, discretionary access control provided by several commercial OODBSs is not able to protect data against certain types of attacks, known as *Trojan Horses*. Mandatory access control is safer then discretionary access control in that the former is able to protect data from Trojan Horses operating at different security levels. However, even mandatory access control is not able to always protect data from illegal accesses that exploit *covert channels* [3]. Therefore, recent research in database security has been directed towards defining architectures, techniques and algorithms to protect data against covert channels. An example along this direction is represented by concurrency control mechanisms specifically designed for multilevel secure relational DBSs [14]. The problem of developing DBSs able to guard against sophisticated type of illegal accesses, has been dealt so far only in the area of relational DBSs. Some of the solutions developed for relational DBSs can be directly applied to OODBSs; however, new security problems may arise that are

---

* The work reported in this paper is partially supported by CNR under Grant n. 94.00450.CT12, by NATO under Collaborative Research Grant n. 930888, and by the Italian M.U.R.S.T.

specific to OODBSs. In particular, object deletion and garbage collection are operations that could be exploited as covert channels.

Because of the relevance of garbage collection in object stores, several algorithms both centralized and distributed have been proposed (see [10, 15], for example). This paper continues the work in secure garbage collection reported in [2]. The main differences are summarized as follows. First, some issues related to storage covert channels and delete operations are analyzed in more detail here. Second, the problem of timing channels is solved by taking into account integrity, availability and confidentiality requirements. Finally, in [2] the copying approach to garbage collection was used, whereas the scheme discussed here is based on the mark- and-sweep technique. The use of different techniques shows that the approach based on untrusted collectors [2] is valid in general regardless of the particular garbage collection technique employed. Other solutions making various assumptions on the structure of the object store are discussed in [4].

The remainder of this paper is organized as follows. Section 2 summarizes the message filter approach. Section 3 introduces object deletion in multilevel environments. Section 4 describes our secure garbage collection scheme, whereas Section 5 draws some conclusions from the research reported in this paper and provides directions for future research efforts.

2 The Message Filter Approach

This section recalls the basic concepts of multilevel security and describes the message filter approach [11], since our aim is to introduce a garbage collector in a secure OODBS employing the message filter approach. In the Bell-LaPadula model [1], the system consists of a set O of *objects* (passive entities), a set S of *subjects* (active entities), and a partially ordered set *Lev* of *security levels* with a partial ordering relation $\leq$. A (security) level l_i is said to be *dominated* by another level l_j if $l_i \leq l_j$. Moreover, a level l_i is strictly dominated by a level l_j, denoted as $l_i < l_j$, if $l_i \leq l_j$ and $i \neq j$. Two mappings F and F_S are defined from O and S, respectively, to *Lev* that associate each object as well as every subject with a security level. That is, $\forall o \in O, F(o) \in Lev$, and $\forall s \in S, F_S(s) \in Lev$. A secure system enforces the Bell-LaPadula principles that can be stated as follows:

1. a subject s is allowed to read an object o only if $F(o) \leq F_S(s)$ (no read-up);
2. a subject s is allowed to write an object o only if $F_S(s) \leq F(o)$ (no write-down).

The second principle is also known as the **-property* and prevents leakage of information due to Trojan Horses. Additional details can be found in [5].

The Bell-LaPadula model has been applied to the object model by means of the message filter approach. In the following, this approach is described. An OODBS is defined as a set of objects exchanging information via messages. An object consists of an object identifier (OID) and of a set of attributes, whose values represent the *state* of the object. Moreover, an object has a set of methods that are used to manipulate the state of the object. Hence, an object is both a subject and an object with respect to the Bell-LaPadula terminology [3]. An object can be primitive (like an integer, or a character) or non-primitive. A non-primitive object is an object in which the value of an attribute can be a primitive object or an OID. Whenever an object o has as value of one of its attributes the OID of an object o', we say that o *references* o' and that o' is *referenced* by o. Given an object o, a security level is assigned to the entire object o.

A message consists of three components: *name, parameters* and *reply*. Each message is associated with a method that is activated upon the reception of the message. A special type of object, called *user object*, represents a user session within the system, and can invoke methods spontaneously. An object, as part of the execution of a method, can send messages to other objects. Each message has a *sender* and a *receiver* object. Access to internal attributes, object creation and invocation of internal methods are all performed by having an object sending a message to itself. In particular, there exist three *primitive* messages, named *read, write* and *create*, which an object sends to itself in order to access internal attributes or to perform object creation respectively. An object sends a message m by invoking a system primitive $send(m, id)$, where id is the OID of the receiver object.

The state of an object can only be accessed by sending messages. This consideration is the basis of the message filter approach. Indeed, a message filter intercepts every message sent by any object in the system and decides how to handle the message. Mandatory access control is enforced by the message filter on the basis of the following two rules:

1. if the sender of a message is at a strictly higher level than the level of the receiver, the method is executed by the receiver in *restricted mode* (no update can be performed);
2. if the sender of a message is at a strictly lower level then the level of the receiver, the method is executed in *unrestricted (normal) mode*, but the returned value is always *nil*. To prevent timing channels, the *nil* value is returned to the sender before actually executing the method.

Principle 1 ensures that a subject does not write down, whereas principle 2 ensures that a subject does not read up. The message filter approach introduces two additional constraints: (1) the security level of an instance must dominate the class security level, and (2) the security level of a subclass must dominate the superclass security level.

Since its purpose is to enforce the security, the message filter has to be trusted, that is, it is embedded in the *Trusted Computing Base (TCB)* [3]. It is worth noting that the implementation of the message filter must also meet the following requirements, discussed in more detail in Section 4.3: (i) the creation of high-level objects could be exploited to establish timing channels; and (ii) OIDs must be generated in a secure fashion [16].

---

[3] In the following, the term "subject" will still be used to emphasize the actual method executions rather than the data hold by an object.

3 Implicit and Explicit Deletion

Existing OODBSs use different approaches for the implementation of the delete operation. There are two categories of OODBSs: those that allow subjects to perform explicit delete operations (e.g., Orion [8]) and those that employ a garbage collection mechanism to remove objects that are not any more reachable from other objects (e.g., O_2 [7] and Gemstone [13]). Note that a garbage collector is a piece of software that deletes objects no more reachable.

Whenever storage can be deallocated, the problem of dangling references may arise. A *dangling reference* occurs when there is a reference to storage that has been deallocated. It is a logical error to use dangling references, and it makes the system rise run-time errors.

The following example shows how dangling references can be exploited to establish a covert channel. If object o' in Figure 1(a) is deleted by a subject at level L_2, a dangling reference appears in object o at level L_1, Figure 1(b). A subject at level L_1 could infer the deletion of object o' by trying to send a write message to the object. On the basis of the result of such an operation (run-time error or successful update), the subject receives one bit of information from a higher security level. A subject at level L_2 could delete a subset of the objects referenced by the objects at level L_1, and a subject at level L_1 could try to access all higher-level objects resulting in a set of unsuccessful-successful updates. Hence, an arbitrary string of bits of reserved information could be transmitted from a higher security level. In a garbage collection environment, an untrusted collector, which acts on the entire database, could intentionally remove the object o' at level L_2 to establish a covert channel. Hence, upwards dangling references must be avoided. Note that this simple example only states *what* needs to be done by a secure system to prevent such covert channels.

In the following, by "high-level (low-level) object" it is meant "object with higher (lower) classification than those of the objects considered".

4 Secure Mark-and-Sweep Garbage Collection

In the following, the attention is focused on the interaction between garbage collection and the message filter. The garbage collection is concerned with automatically reclaiming storage that was once used but is no longer needed. The collector is invoked periodically or when a memory overflow arises. Our goal is to achieve referential integrity in multilevel OODBSs by means of mark-and-sweep garbage collection without compromising security. A mark-and-sweep collector follows the pointers in the heap marking any object that is reached (*marking phase*), then it collects all unmarked objects (*sweeping phase*) scanning the heap sequentially. The marking phase starts from the *root objects*, that is, the objects containing information always needed. The root objects are the "entry points" for a security level. A serious drawback with conventional garbage collection mechanisms is that the collector would have to access objects at various security levels; this would require the collector to be trusted. However, theoretically secure solutions could produce complex implementations impractical to be verified

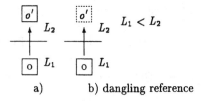

a)   b) dangling reference

Fig. 1. Dangling references and covert channels

secure. We propose a different approach which does not require the collector to be trusted.

A mark-and-sweep collection algorithm can be augmented with *generations* to improve performance [12, 22]. Hence, a marking collector can also be used to manage large stable heaps; this is an important requirement for a collection algorithm to be widely employed. Moreover, various algorithms have been developed for efficiently scanning the heap [18, 20, 21].

4.1 Overview of the Approach

The overall garbage collection scheme is similar to that described in [2]. A multilevel trusted collector can be implemented employing a TCB which controls the behaviour of single-level untrusted collectors, that is, root objects and an untrusted garbage collector GC_l for each security level l are required. The untrusted collectors are objects whose behaviour is under the control of the message filter. They cooperate among themselves and behave as a multilevel trusted collector. As a consequence of this fact, each collector can only read user or system information at its security level or at lower levels. Moreover, since the collector GC_l executes a write operation in order to mark an object, it is only able to mark an object at levels higher or equal to l.

In Figure 2, the interactions among the collectors and the message filter are shown with the help of a simple security lattice. In the following, an object at level l is said to be *(non) locally reachable* if it can(not) be reached starting from the root objects of level l. The garbage collection is managed in a stop-the-world fashion: activities are suspended, garbage is collected and then activities are restarted. Each collector GC_l executes the marking phase for the security level l, while the unmarked objects are collected (i.e. deleted) subsequently in all security levels by the TCB during the sweeping phase. In particular, the collector GC_l does not mark an object o at level l or higher if and only if all references to o from other objects at level l have been removed.

In [2] the interactions among the message filter and the collectors were not addressed, and a *Trusted Collection Monitor* controlled the activations and the behaviour of the collectors. Here, the message filter is logically subdivided into two modules: the Garbage Collection Module (GCM) that activates the collectors and deletes the garbage, and the Message Filtering Module (MFM) that

$$Unclassified < Confidential < Secret < TopSecret$$

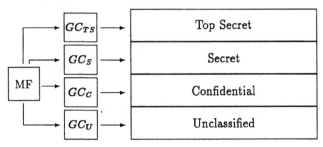

Fig. 2. Message Filter and Garbage Collectors

acts as the basic message filter. The GCM activates the collectors GC_l by sending them a message, say DETECT. A method *detect* which performs the marking phase is associated with this message.

The collector GC_l cannot consider the OIDs from objects at security levels higher than l because of the no read-up constraint. Therefore, dangling references could appear at security levels higher than l after the garbage collection is completed. Indeed, an object at level l which is not locally reachable and which is not referenced by any low-level object, is not marked by the collectors at levels lower or equal to l; hence, such an object will be deleted during the sweeping phase at level l. The key of our approach to maintain referential integrity is that whenever an object o at level l, which is to be deleted from its security level, is referenced by an object at level l', $l < l'$, the collector $GC_{l'}$ creates a copy of o at level l', that is, a new object is created at level l' and data are copied into the new object. The following subsection will show in more detail how the proposed garbage collection scheme works.

4.2 Untrusted Marking Collectors

Since the aim of our approach is to avoid explicit deletion, it does not make sense to define a deletion message for each object (i.e. a primitive message). Indeed, in a garbage collection environment the system (here, the GCM) must collect garbage and delete objects, while subjects can only read and update objects. Moreover, an important requirement for a system to be secure is the *object reuse* [3], that is, the basic storage elements (e.g., disk sectors, memory pages, etc.) must be cleared prior to their assignment to a subject so that no intentional or unintentional data scavenging [4] takes place. The storage elements can be cleared when deallocated. Hence, the delete operation is required to be a

---

[4] Accesses to system resources such as memory pages and disk sectors no more allocated.

trusted operation implemented as part of the TCB and it is invoked by the GCM and not by the collectors as in [2]. However, in order to avoid all the storage covert channels, some issues have to be analyzed that in [2] were not addressed. Storage covert channels are illegal channels established via the exploitation of the dynamic allocation of memory or via data scavenging. For example, a high-level subject could establish such a covert channel by saturating the memory to prevent the normal computation of a low-level subject, which, in turn, could infer high-level information. To overcome this drawback, the following solution is proposed. The system memory (volatile and non volatile) is divided into a number of fixed partitions, one for each security level. Moreover, subjects at level l can allocate memory only from the partition assigned to level l and the creation of a high-level object is performed at the level requested for the new object. Hence, there is no way for a subject at level l to interfere with the memory allocation performed at a lower or incomparable security level.

Achieving Referential Integrity In Section 4.1, we have outlined the problem of potential dangling references in high-level objects arising from the garbage collection. The solution we propose is the following. The collector GC_l is activated if and only if all the collectors $GC_{l'}$, $l' < l$, have terminated the local marking phase. If an object is unmarked after the marking phase is ended at its security level, it is copied [5] at higher security levels once it is reached during the marking phase at such levels, that is, when a downwards OID referencing it is found at higher levels. Note that the copying operations can be performed by the collectors, since they obey the Bell-LaPadula principles. The copy c created at level l is marked by the collector GC_l since it is a useful information at that level. The marking phase at level l continues by traversing the OIDs eventually stored in c.

To avoid redundant copies, it is sufficient to create a copy of an unmarked low-level object o at the lowest levels where o is needed. For example, if object o is referenced from levels L_1 and L_2, such that $L_1 < L_2$, a copy of o could be created only at level L_1. Then, the OID referencing o and stored at level L_2 should only be updated with the OID of the copy stored at level L_1. When dealing with incomparable levels, a copy is generated for each level, as the example in Figure 3 shows. Note that the sweeping phases must be postponed till the marking phase ends in all security levels, otherwise the copying of a low-level object o could not be executed, since o could have been previously deleted.

If an object o if referenced only from incomparable levels, a copy of o is created at each of such levels. If the consistency among the copies of o is not needed, then the copies can be treated as independent objects. Otherwise, the copies of o must be kept consistent, and any further update must be denied. For the former case, the garbage collection scheme proposed so far works well. In the latter case, a problem arises. Indeed, the fact that a copy of a low-level is read-only can be exploited to signal a bit of information between two subjects

---

[5] In the following, as previously stated, by "copy" we mean the creation of a new object and the copying of data into it.

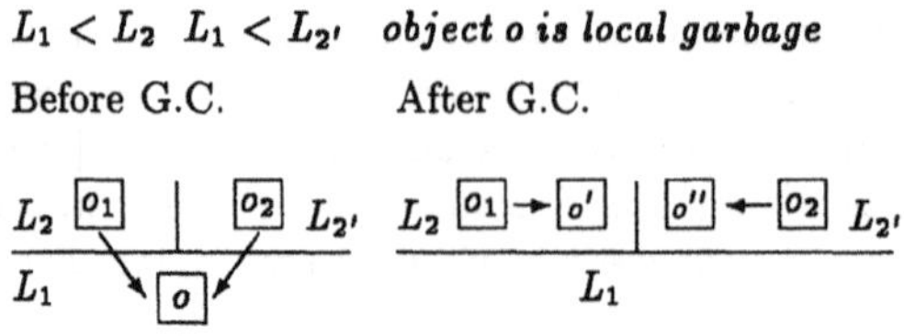

$L_1 < L_2$ $L_1 < L_{2'}$ *object o is local garbage*

Before G.C. After G.C.

Fig. 3. Copying objects at incomparable security levels

at incomparable security levels. A simple and radical solution is the following. When a collector GC_l creates a copy of a low-level object o, GC_l sets the copy of o as read-only, regardless of the existence of other objects referencing o from levels incomparable with l. This information is used by the MFM to avoid further write accesses. If a malicious collector GC_l does not set a copy of a low-level object as read-only, no covert channel can be established. Indeed, the collector GC_l has no information about the objects stored at levels higher (or incomparable) than l. Note that if each subject in the system is allowed to create read-only objects, data can be kept consistent without compromising confidentiality.

The copying operations can be performed with the help of a hash table associated with each security level. Such tables, called *Copy Tables*, are read and updated by the collectors. In particular, the collector GC_l builds at level l a Copy Table [6] to store pairs of related OIDs of the form (*old-oid, new-oid*), where *old-oid* is the OID of a low-level unmarked object, and *new-oid* is the OID of its copy created at level l by the collector GC_l. The Copy Table ct at level l is read by the collectors at levels higher than l to avoid redundant copies and does not survive a collection cycle, that is, during the marking phase the collector GC_l does not mark ct. Moreover, we assume that when ct is created its OID is available at higher levels. Hence, the collectors at higher levels can read ct and do not copy it as any other unmarked low-level object is.

Visiting the Security Lattice The collectors are activated visiting the security levels hierarchy on the basis of a sequence $(l_1, \ldots, l_n)$ called *visit-sequence*, such that l_1 is the lowest security level, l_n the highest, and for each l_i ($1 < i \leq n$) and for each l_j ($1 \leq j < i$), $l_j < l_i$ or $l_j <> l_i$ (incomparable). A visit-sequence is a static list associated with a given database. When level l is visited, the collector GC_l is activated and after its termination the next security level in the visit-sequence is visited. As the marking phase is ended for all the security levels, the GCM deletes all unmarked objects, that is, performs the sweeping phase for each security level. In Figure 4, an example of this approach is shown. Object o_1 at level L_3 is not marked by the collector GC_{L3}. Hence, a copy o'_1 of object o_1

---

[6] Except for the lowest level in the security lattice. Indeed, this level has no downwards OIDs.

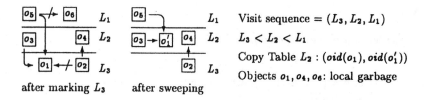

after marking L_3 after sweeping

Fig. 4. Achieving referential integrity with garbage collection

is created at level L_2 by the collector GC_{L2} that adds the pair $(oid(o_1), oid(o_1'))$ in the Copy Table at level L_2. The OID stored in object o_5 at level L_1 and referencing object o_1 is updated with the OID of the copy o_1' stored at level L_2. This update is performed by the collector GC_{L1} that reads the OID of object o_1' from the Copy Table at level L_2. Note that object o_4 is not locally reachable at level L_2, but it is referenced by object o_2. Hence, the collector GC_{L3} marks object o_4 during the marking phase at level L_3 (write-up is allowed); thus, object o_4 is not deleted during the sweeping phase at level L_2.

The Garbage Collection Module In Figure 5, the GCM is described. The procedure *Mark* carries on the marking phase for each security level on the basis of the *visit-sequence*. The collectors are invoked by sending them the message DETECT (variable *msg*); for this purpose the OID of each collector is needed (variable *id*). The message filter can directly access any object and its methods, hence the message DETECT can be sent in a simpler way to the relevant garbage collector. In particular, the GCM does not use the system primitive *send* used by subjects; rather, it uses a system primitive *mf-send* that performs asynchronous method invocations.

Since the marking phase is executed autonomously by all collectors that are untrusted components, a collector GC_l could delay the completion of the marking phase to signal some information to low-level collectors which, in turn, can evaluate the time elapsed between two consecutive garbage collection cycles. In order to meet the NCSC covert channel capacity guidelines [6] for B3/A1 classes, we propose the following solution. The overall garbage collection time must be long enough to prevent timing channels with high-capacity bandwidth. To accomplish this requirement, the execution time of each marking phase is forced to be longer than a pre-defined lower bound, called *min-run*, which can be the same for each security level. Since the upper bound for the bandwidth of timing channels is 100 bit per second (bps) [6], *min-run* can be assigned a value that does not cause performance penalty.

The performance of the marking phase can be improved by allowing the parallel execution of collectors at incomparable security levels. The GCM should be modified for this purpose; in particular, the visit-sequence should be used in a different manner. Indeed, it is only needed that the collector GC_l starts the local

```
Mark( )
{
    let lev = first(visit-sequence);
    while lev ≠ null do
    {
        let msg = (DETECT, ( ), detect-reply);
        let id = oid(GC_l);
        mf-send(msg, id);
        if min-run not expired then wait(min-run);
        let lev = next(visit-sequence);
    };
};
Sweep(l: level) {
    for each unmarked object o in l do {
        let id = oid(o);
        clear-mem(id); % clears memory
        delete-object(id); % deallocates memory
    };
    if min-sweep not expired then wait(min-sweep);
};
```

Garbage Collection Module

$\qquad$ *Marking Phase* : **Mark()**

$\qquad$ *Sweeping Phase* : forall security level l do **Sweep(l)**

Fig. 5. Garbage Collection Module

marking phase if and only if all the collectors at level l', $l' < l$, have terminated.

The sweeping phase starts after the termination of the *Mark* procedure, and is performed in parallel at all security levels by the trusted procedure *Sweep*. Note that there is no synchronization requirement among the sweeping phases. Since the procedure *Sweep* is executed under the control of the GCM, a collector cannot signal information during the sweeping phase by means of timing channels. For example, a solution similar to the above based on the use of a lower bound on execution time (*min-sweep*) can be adopted. In order to reduce the bandwidth of timing channels to 0 bps, the GCM can fix a time limit for the execution of each collector. After such a time-out is expired, the GCM aborts the collector at level l which has not yet completed the marking phase. If a collector ends the marking phase within the time limit, the GCM waits for the time-out to be expired. In such a way, any illegal behaviour of a collector is hidden to all the lower (or incomparable) security levels. However, this solution has several drawbacks. First, it is needed that the sweeping phase is executed for a security level l only if the collector GC_l ends its marking phase within the time-out fixed by the GCM. Indeed, since the procedure *Sweep* is executed under the control of the GCM, a collector cannot signal information during the sweeping phase by means of timing channels. For example, a solution similar to the above one based on the use of time-outs can be adopted by evaluating the maximum time needed for the sweeping phase of a single security level. Second, if a time-out occurs at level l, there is no certainty that the corresponding collector has already marked every high-level object according to existing low references. Hence, the sweeping phase cannot be executed for all levels that dominate l. Finally, the time limit for level l is not simple to be chosen, since it is rather difficult to evaluate the time a collector needs to create the copies of low-elevel unmarked objects. Moreover, increasing the time limits may lead to serious performance penalty.

4.3 Remarks on the Message Filter Approach

The MFM is similar to the original message filter. However, in this section we outline some implementation issues.

- The fact that OIDs must be unique may lead to a covert channel. When an object is created, the new OID must be different from the OIDs that are already in use, including those belonging to higher or incomparable level objects. How much information the object requesting the creation gets depends on the mechanism used to assign OIDs to a new object. This problem and some solutions are well known [16]. Here, we assume that an OID is concatenated with the security level (or some encoding of it) at which the referenced object is stored; hence, the message filter knows the security level associated with an OID without accessing the referenced object. Therefore, run-time errors caused by accesses to maliciously deleted objects are avoided. Such run-time errors could generate a covert channel like that described in Section 3.
- Create messages must be properly controlled. Indeed, a timing channel could be established on the basis of the timing of the reply (i.e. the OID of the new object). The solution we propose is that a subject s at level l requesting a creation at level l', $l < l'$, *immediately* receives the new OID, while the creation itself is executed asynchronously. Potential dangling references can be managed by the message filter as explained before, and errors possibly occurred during the creation do not prevent subject s from immediately receiving the new OID.

The solutions stated above have a drawback. Indeed, no acknowledge is returned to a subject sending a message through an upwards OID or creating an object at higher levels. Hence, communication from a low- to a high-level subject may be unreliable in that it is based on assurance of high probability that the information will arrive error free and will be processed correctly. One way to circumvent this drawback is to provide a controlled stream of acknowledgements to the low- level as described in [9]. However, upwards dangling references, possibly generated by Trojan Horses planted inside the collectors, must be managed providing either an acknowledgement and not filtering a run-time error, or avoiding object deletion. In the latter case, the TCB can record the references pointing an object at level

l from objects at level l', $l' < l$, via a trusted reference counting stored at level l. In this way, the GCM is able to avoid the deletion of an object o when o is referenced by low-level objects.

In some proposals, write-ups are not allowed. In this case, the message filter can be simplified, since no upwards OID is allowed. Hence, all messages sent to high-level objects are treated as messages sent among incomparable levels, that is, a *nil* reply is immediately returned to the sender of the message [11]. Moreover, a collector does not need to mark high-level objects. Consider Figure 4; object o_2 could not reference object o_4 and this object would be deleted during the sweeping phase at level L_2. However, the OIDs and create messages must be properly managed. In particular, a subject s at level l can still create an object at level l', $l < l'$, but the OID of the new object will not be returned to s.

4.4   Correctness

The problem of defining a secure garbage collection scheme has been analyzed so far disregarding implementation details. However, most covert channels arise from the exploitation of system resources for a given implementation. Hence, the implementation must be accurate and must satisfy the requirements of the security policy [3]. Nevertheless, single-level collectors can be easily layered onto a TCB; the advantages of a layered implementation are analyzed in [19]. In particular, no additional security proofs for the collectors is required because they are controlled by the message filter as any other object in the database. We make this more clear with the following considerations.

Each collector can only read information (user or system information) at its security level or at lower levels. Moreover,

1. the collector GC_l cannot execute explicit delete operations, nor it can cause the deletion of an object at level l', $l' < l$, (the *-property should be violated for this purpose);
2. all messages sent by means of *illegal references* [7] are ineffective because they are blocked by the MFM that returns immediately the value *nil* as reply, even if the receiver object has been deleted.

The above considerations assume that the collectors are correct with respect to memory consistency. Suppose now that a collector incorrectly executes the marking phase:

– the collector GC_l could intentionally avoid marking an object reachable only at level l. Then, the GCM would delete it. Therefore, the collector GC_l could generate dangling references in memory. However, such dangling references would only concern objects at the same security level or higher. Hence, no covert channel could be established. By contrast, the collector GC_l cannot mark an unreachable object because it cannot access the object at all.

---

[7] OIDs between incomparable levels.

- The collector GC_l could avoid the marking of an object o at level l', $l < l'$ reachable only from level l. In this case, an upwards dangling reference could appear at level l since o would be deleted during the sweeping phase of level l' if no restriction is applied on objects referenced by low-level objects (cf. Section 4.3). Nevertheless, such a dangling reference could not be exploited to establish a covert channel because of two reasons: (i) the collector GC_l itself creates the dangling reference and (ii) the MFM avoids run-time errors (cf. Section 4.3).
- The collector GC_l could avoid the copying of an unmarked low-level object, but this would only generate dangling references at level l.
- Information stored in a Copy Table at level l concern level l or lower levels; hence, a Copy Table cannot be used for the illegal transfer of information.
- The overall garbage collection time has a lower bound. Hence, the collector GC_l has no way to establish a timing channel with high-capacity bandwidth.
- The behaviour of the collector GC_l with respect to memory allocation is not different from that of any other subject at level l.

In conclusion, the confidentiality is achieved even if the collectors are intentionally designed and implemented incorrectly. Note that dangling references, possibly occurring when activities restart, are similar to programming errors in the source code of a collector. That is, if a dangling reference occurs, then there exist a collector that does not work properly. Hence, since collectors must be tested before being employed, it seems difficult that such a problem occurs. Moreover, the programmers developing the collectors know the restrictions enforced on the collectors activity, hence there is no reason to implement a collector that generates dangling references, since it is known by the programmers that there is no way to establish a covert channel.

5 Conclusions

In this paper, the introduction of garbage collection techniques in multilevel secure OODBSs has been discussed. Such an approach guarantees referential integrity and avoids covert channels due to object deletion via a careful control of the garbage collection execution. The use of untrusted garbage collectors simplifies design, implementation and testing (formal and operative) of the TCB. Moreover, untrusted collectors give the system more flexibility. Indeed, the collectors can be thought as "black boxes" that manage memory and that are controlled by the TCB, disregarding implementation and garbage collection techniques.

The basic ideas under the scheme proposed can be used with different garbage collection techniques [2]. In particular, the garbage collection scheme proposed in [2] can be reused. There is still interesting work to be do in this area, such as the design and efficient implementation of the message filter and the garbage collectors, and the study of different activation strategies for the collectors. We are currently investigating a garbage collection scheme in which the collectors acts concurrently.

References

1. Bell D., LaPadula L., *"Secure Computer Systems: Unified Exposition and Multics Interpretation"*, Technical Report ESD-TR-75-306, MTR-2997, MITRE, Bedford, Massachusetts, 1975.
2. Bertino E., Mancini L. V., Jajodia S., *"Collecting Garbage in Multilevel Secure Object Stores"*, Proc. IEEE Symp. on Research in Security and Privacy, Oakland, CA, May 1994.
3. Chokhani S., *"Trusted Products Evaluation"*, Comm. of the ACM, vol. 35, no. 7, July, 1992, pp. 66-76.
4. Ciampichetti A., *"Object Deletion and Garbage Collection in Secure Object-Oriented DBMSs"*, (in Italian), Master Thesis, Department of Computer Science, University of Genova, Italy, October 1993.
5. Denning D. E., *"Cryptography and Data Security"*, Addison Wesley Editions, Reading, Massachusetts, 1982.
6. Department of Defense, *"Trusted Computer System Evaluation Criteria"*, DOD 5200.28-STD, Washington DC, Usa, December 1985.
7. Deux O., et al., *"The Story of O_2"*, IEEE Transactions on Knowledge and Data Engineering, vol. 2, no. 1, 1990, pp. 91-108.
8. Kim W., et al., *"Architecture of the ORION Next-Generation Database System"*, IEEE Transactions on Knowledge and Data Engineering, vol. 2, no. 1, 1990, pp. 109-124.
9. Kang H. M., Moskowitz I. S., *"A Pump for Rapid, Reliable, Secure Communication"*, 1st ACM Conf. - Computer and Comm. Security, pp. 119-129, Va, Usa, November 1993.
10. Kolodner E., Liskov B., Weihl W., *"Atomic Garbage Collection: Managing a Stable Heap"*, Proc. ACM-SIGMOD International Conference on Management of Data, Boston, Oregon, May-June 1989.
11. Jajodia S., Kogan B., *"Integrating an Object-Oriented Data Model with Multilevel Security"*, Proc. 1990 IEEE Computer Society Symp. on Research in Security and Privacy, May 1990.
12. Lieberman H., Hewitt C., *"A real-time Garbage Collector based on the Lifetime of Objects"*, Comm. of the ACM, Vol. 26, No. 6, June 1983.
13. Maier D., et al., *"Development of an Object-Oriented DBS"*, Proc. OOPSLA 1st Conference, Portland, Oregon, October 1986.
14. Maimone W. T., Greenberg I. B., *"Single-Level Multiversion Schedulers for Multilevel Secure Database Systems"*, Proc. IEEE Computer Society Symp. on Research in Security and Privacy, Oakland, California, May 1990.
15. Mancini L. V., Shrivastava S. K. , *"Fault-Tolerant Reference Counting for Garbage Collection in Distributed Systems"*, The Computer Journal, vol. 34, no. 6, 1991.
16. Millen J. K., Lunt T. F., *"Security for Object-Oriented Database Systems"*, Proc. IEEE Computer Society Symp. on Research in Security and Privacy, Oakland, California, May 1992.
17. Rabitti F., Bertino E., Kim W., Woelk D., *"A Model of Authorization for Object-Oriented and Semantic Database Systems"*, ACM Transactions on Database Systems, vol. 16, no. 1, March 1991.
18. Schorr H., Waite W. M., *"An Efficient Machine-Independent Procedure for Garbage Collection in Various List Structures"*, Comm. of the ACM, vol. 10, n. 8, pp. 501-506, 1967.

19. Shockly W. R., Schell R. R., *"TCB Subsets for Incremental Evaluation"*, Proc. 2nd AIAA Conference on Computer Security, December 1987.
20. Thorelli L. E., *"Marking Algorithms"*, Bit, vol. 12, n. 4, pp. 555-568, 1972.
21. Thorelli L. E., *"A Fast Compactifying Garbage Collector"*, Bit, vol. 16, n. 4, pp. 426-441, 1976.
22. Zorn B., *"Comparing Mark-and-Sweep and Stop-and-Copy Garbage Collection"*, Comm. of the ACM, 1990, pp. 87-98.

Decomposition of Multilevel Objects in an Object-Oriented Database

N. Boulahia-Cuppens, F. Cuppens, A. Gabillon, K. Yazdanian

ONERA / CERT
2 avenue Edouard Belin
31055 Toulouse cedex
France

nora@tls-cs.cert.fr, cuppens@tls-cs.cert.fr, gabillon@tls-cs.cert.fr, yazdanian@tls-cs.cert.fr

Abstract

For many reasons, multilevel relations are decomposed. Several decomposition algorithms have been proposed but we show that many difficulties would appear when implementing them - especially performance loss and problems to propagate low classified updates to higher classified re lations. In this paper, we propose a security model which provides means to protect all characteristics of an object including object existence, attribute tuple values and attribute set values and we show how to decompose a multilevel object oriented database which supports these complex multilevel objects into a collection of single level databases. This idea is similar to the idea already proposed for multilevel relational databases. However, our approach takes fully advantage of the object oriented model. Hence, we claim that the kernelized architecture we suggest for object oriented databases does not suffer from the drawbacks noticed for relational systems based on this architecture. In particular, it does not cause important performance losses and the semantics of update operations is straightforward in comparison with the one previously developed for multi-level relations.

1. Introduction

For many years, much database security research work has been trying to extend the classical relational model to obtain multi-level relations. In this context, the 1982 Air Force Summer Study [Air83] suggested three different architectures for building secure multilevel database management systems. These architectures differ from how the multilevel data is physically stored. The first architecture is called the *kernelized* DBMS. Most of the current research in secure databases are based on this architecture [Hin75,Gro76,Den87,Gar90,Hai90]. In this architecture, the multilevel database is partitioned into singlelevel databases which are stored separately. The second architecture is called the *distributed* DBMS in [Air83] or the *replicated* DBMS in [Jaj90b]. In this architecture, there is a database at each security class which contains all data whose classifications are less or equal to the database security class; each database is associated with a separate DBMS. As its name suggests, in the *replicated* architecture, we need means to replicate lower data in all databases containing higher level data. There are only a few research projects which are based on this architecture [Fro89, McC92]. The third architecture is based on integrity lock technology. As noticed in [Jaj90b], this last architecture is vulnerable to Trojan Horse attacks and we will no longer consider this approach in the rest of this paper.

Another problem which has also been deeply investigated in the past is how access classes should be assigned to data stored in relations. The proposals have ranged from assigning access class to relations, assigning access class to individual tuples in a relation or assigning access class to individual attributes of each tuple. If the architecture of the database is the kernelized or replicated DBMS, then in both case we need to decompose the multilevel relations. In the kernelized architecture, the goal is to obtain a collection of single-level base relations which are then physically stored in the database. In the replicated architecture, the goal is to extract relations which contain all data at or below each security level. The difficulties of the decomposition depend on how classifications are assigned to data. If classifications are assigned to relations or tuples, then the decomposition is straightforward. On the other hand, if classifications are assigned to attributes, this decomposition it turns out is not trivial. In this context, several decomposition algorithms have been proposed in particular by Denning et *al.* [Den87], Jajodia and Sandhu [Jaj90a,Jaj91].

More recently, the object oriented model was defined and it is already starting to root as the new generation of database systems. Object oriented databases present important advantages over classical database systems, in particular, through the notions of encapsulation and inheritance, they are fundamentally designed to reduce the difficulty of managing complex data. They also include the notion of methods which are general programs that are associated with an object class to perform specific computation.

Several proposals have appeared in the literature dealing with security models for object-oriented databases and it seems that we are involved in debate similar to that about relational databases, namely how to assign access classes to data stored in objects. Some proposals consider that every object must be assigned a unique classification that applies to all its content (attributes and methods) [Mil92] or only to the passive content (attributes) [Jaj90c]. The advantage of this approach is the simplicity with which security policies can be stated and enforced. However, as objects are used to model real world entities, it may seem somewhat restrictive that all objects have only a single security level. Hence, other proposals introduce also a finer grain of classification in assigning a classification to each pair (attribute, value) [Kee89,Var91]. This approach allows us to easily represent multilevel entities in the object oriented database, but some researchers consider that multilevel objects are likely to introduce overwhelming difficulties (cf. [Lun90] for instance) or try to demonstrate that restricting objects to be single level does not have to imply that it would not be still possible to represent multilevel entities [Jaj90c].

In this paper, we propose an approach for a secure multilevel object oriented database management system which supports multilevel entities. The central idea is to decompose a multilevel object oriented database into a collection of single level databases and is similar to the idea already proposed for multilevel relational databases. However, our approach takes full advantage of the object oriented model. Hence, we guess that the kernelized architecture we suggest for object oriented databases does not suffer from the drawbacks noticed for relational systems based on this architecture. In particular, it only causes a marginal performance loss.

The remainder of this paper is organized as follows. In section 2, we propose a brief survey of several algorithms proposed to decompose multi-level relations, focussing on the difficulties generated by the implementation of these algorithms. In section 3, we informally describe the main principles of the object oriented model we may use to simplify the decomposition of multilevel objects. In section 4, we develop a security model for object oriented databases based on these principles. This model provides means to protect all characteristics of an object including object existence, attribute tuple values and attribute set values. We also give formal operational semantics for update operations which turn out to be straightforward in comparison to the one previously developed for multi-level relations [Jaj90d]. Finally, section 6 concludes the paper on further work that remains to be done.

2. Decomposition of Multilevel relations

In this section, we will discuss only the case where security classifications are assigned to individual data elements of the tuples of a relation. According to this approach, let $r(A_k, A_1,...,A_n)$ be a classical relation (without classification) where A_K is a primary key. This relation is extended by the following relation:

$$R(A_K, C_{AK}, A_1, C_1,..., A_n, C_n, TC)$$

where each C_i is a classification attribute for A_i and TC is the tuple-class attribute.

In order to provide consistency for data at different access classes, including polyinstantiated data[1], it is necessary to extend the classical integrity constraints of the relational model. In particular, to properly deal with the polyinstantiation problem, previous research work suggested adding several integrity constraints. The first one is the so-called *polyinstantiation integrity constraint* which prohibits polyinstantiation of an attribute within a single access class [Den87]:

[PI-FD] R satisfies FD polyinstantiation integrity if and only if we have for all A_i in R:

$$A_K, C_{AK}, C_i \rightarrow A_i$$

This property stipulates that the user-specified key A_K, in conjunction with the classification attributes C_{AK} and C_i, functionally determines the value of the A_i attribute.

Another integrity constraint in case of polyinstantiation is the *one tuple per tuple-class* constraint [San90]:

[PI-tuple-class] R satisfies tuple-class polyinstantiation integrity if and only if we have for all $A_i \notin A_K$:

$$A_K, C_{AK}, TC \rightarrow A_i$$

The idea of this property is that although we have several polyinstantiated tuples for the same key A_K there should be only one such tuple per tuple-class.

In [Cup92], we showed that the combination of PI-FD and PI-tuple-class provides good control of polyinstantiated relations: it admits only relation instances which represent consistent versions of reality for each access class and rules out all other instances.

For many reasons, multilevel relations are decomposed. For instance, in the SeaView project which is based on a kernelized DBMS, the goal is to obtain a collection of single-level base relations which are then physically stored in the

---

1. Polyinstantiation refers to the simultaneous existence of multiple tuples with the same primary key A_K, where the multiple instantiations are distinguished by their classification.

database. Another reason is that, even though the relation $r(A_K, A_1,...,A_n)$ is in the third normal form (3NF), the multilevel relation $R(A_K, C_{AK}, A_1, C_1,..., A_n, C_n, TC)$ is not in 3NF (and not even in 2NF). This fact is due to the PI-FD integrity constraint and was first observed by Denning in [Den88]. The foreseeable consequences of this problem are well-known: redundancy of information and anomalies according to update operations. To avoid these problems, we have to decompose the relation.

Several decomposition algorithms have been proposed in the literature. The first one was used in the SeaView project [Den87]. As noted by Jajodia and Sandhu in [Jaj91], there are many problems with this decomposition algorithm and its related recovery algorithm used to reconstruct the original relation from decomposed fragments. In particular, due to the limitations set by the decomposition algorithm, several realistic and useful interpretations of the database cannot be represented in SeaView. Moreover, the recovery algorithm is based on complex and expensive outer joins and introduces spurious tuples. Jajodia and Sandhu have also proposed two different decompositions respectively in [Jaj90a] and [Jaj91]. We now propose a brief overview of these alogorithms.

2.1 First decomposition algorithm of Jajodia and Sandhu

In [Jaj90a], Jajodia and Sandhu have given a modified version of the SeaView decomposition and recovery algorithms. If we apply their algorithm to the following instance of the relation *Personage* where *Name* is the primary key:

Fig. 1 Personage

Name	C_1	Date_of_birth	C_2	Father	C_3	TC
Louis XIV	U	1638	U	Louis XIII	U	U
Iron-Mask	U	1639	U	Louis XIII	S	S
Duc du Maine	U	1670	U	Marquis de Montespan	U	U
Duc du Maine	U	1670	U	Louis XIV	C	C

we obtain nine single-level relations:

$$D_{1, U}$$

Name	C_1	C_2	C_3
Louis XIV	U	U	U
Iron-Mask	U	U	U
Duc du Maine	U	U	U

$$D_{1, C}$$

Name	C_1	C_2	C_3
Duc du Maine	U	U	C

$$D_{1, S}$$

Name	C_1	C_2	C_3
Iron-Mask	U	U	S

Fig. 2 Primary key group relations

$$D_{2,U}$$

Name	C_1	Date_of_birth	C_2
Louis XIV	U	1638	U
Iron-Mask	U	1639	U
Duc du Maine	U	1670	U

$$D_{2,C}$$

Name	C_1	Date_of_birth	C_2

$$D_{2,S}$$

Name	C_1	Date_of_birth	C_2

$$D_{3,U}$$

Name	C_1	Father	C_2
Louis XIV	U	Louis XIII	U
Iron-Mask	U	NULL	U
Duc du Maine	U	Marquis de Montespan	U

$$D_{3,C}$$

Name	C_1	Father	C_2
Duc du Maine	U	Louis XIV	C

$$D_{3,S}$$

Name	C_1	Father	C_2
Iron-Mask	U	Louis XIII	S

Fig. 3 Attribute group relations

If we compare this decomposition algorithm with the one proposed in the SeaView project, then it is possible to reconstruct the original relation without using outer join and introducing spurious tuples. We also showed in [Cup92] that this decomposition algorithm is consistent with the decomposition in 3NF of the multilevel relation with respect to PI-FD and PI-tuple-class. This means that this decomposition would not introduce redundancy of information and anomalies according to update operations. However, a major drawback is that it is necessary to break the initial "conceptual schema" of the relational database. Hence, we may think that every multilevel DBMS based on this decomposition algorithm would suffer from poor performance, because satisfying queries would involve repeated joins of relations and natural join is an expensive operation. Finally, notice that this decomposition algorithm has associated, in relation $D_{3,U}$, Iron-Mask's father with a Null value whose semantics is not perfectly clear (see section 2.3 for a discussion).

2.2 Second decomposition algorithm of Jajodia and Sandhu

In [Jaj91], Jajodia and Sandhu proposed a second decomposition algorithm for breaking a multilevel relation into single-level ones. If we apply this algorithm to the above instance of the relation *Personage*, then we would obtain only three single-level relations:

$$D_U$$

Name	C_1	Date_of_birth	C_2	Father	C_3
Louis XIV	U	1638	U	Louis XIII	U
Iron-Mask	U	1639	U	NULL	U
Duc du Maine	U	1670	U	Marquis de Montespan	U

$$D_C$$

Name	C_1	Date_of_birth	C_2	Father	C_3
Duc du Maine	U	1670	U	Louis XIV	C

$$D_S$$

Name	C_1	Date_of_birth	C_2	Father	C_3
Iron-Mask	U	1639	U	Louis XIII	S

Fig. 4

The major advantage of this algorithm compared to the one in section 2.1 is that the associated recovery algorithm does not use joins to reconstruct the initial multilevel relation but only unions. However, this decomposition is not a decomposition in 3NF with respect to the PI-FD integrity constraint. This means that these single-level relations are not in 3NF and that it is necessary to replicate some updates at several classification levels. For instance, if an unclassified user updates Duc du Maine's date of Birth from 1670 to 1671, then this update must be propagated in both D_U and D_C relations. Moreover, in some situations, it is not clear how to propagate an update performed at a lower level to higher levels. For instance, let us assume that a confidential user wants to update Iron-Mask's date of birth from 1639 to 1638. We need first to update the D_C relation as follows:

Fig. 5 D_C

Name	C_1	Date_of_birth	C_2	Father	C_3
Duc du Maine	U	1670	U	Louis XIV	C
Iron-Mask	U	1638	C	NULL	U

Now, the exact change to D_S depends on the propagation rules. In [Jaj90d], Jajodia and Sandhu suggest two possibilities. In the first case called the minimal propagation rule, D_S is not updated:

Fig. 6 D_S

Name	C_1	Date_of_birth	C_2	Father	C_3
Iron-Mask	U	1639	U	Louis XIII	S

In the second case, called the interpreted propagation rule, D_S is updated as follows:

Fig. 7 D_S

Name	C_1	Date_of_birth	C_2	Father	C_3
Iron-Mask	U	1639	U	Louis XIII	S
Iron-Mask	U	1638	C	Louis XIII	S

Notice that this last case is not acceptable in our approach because it violates PI-tuple-class: there are two tuples with the same primary key associated with a secret tuple class. A third possibility, not mentioned in [Jaj90d], would be to update D_S as follows:

Fig. 8 D_S

Name	C_1	Date_of_birth	C_2	Father	C_3
Iron-Mask	U	1638	C	Louis XIII	S

We argue that it is probably the best propagation. We provide the following interpretation: 1638 is the actual Iron-Mask's date of birth and 1639 becomes a cover story. The objective is to hide at the unclassified level that Louis XIV and the Iron-Mask have the same date of birth which might partially disclose that Louis XIV and the Iron-Mask are twins. In observing figure 8, a secret user would learn the actual date of birth and father of the Iron-Mask.

However, we agree that the propagation of updates in multilevel relations is not completely clear. In particular if we use the algorithm of section 2.1, we have also to propagate the confidential update of Iron-Mask's date of birth in secret relation $D_{1,S}$ and $D_{2,S}$ to obtain the instance proposed in figure 8. This means that the decomposition in 3NF with respect to PI-FD and PI-tuple-class is not sufficient to avoid the propagation according to this update. We will show below that we can propose a clearer semantics within the object oriented model.

2.3 Synthesis

As has been pointed out before (for instance in [Air83,Gra90]), relational databases based on the kernelized architecture would suffer from poor performance. The algorithm of section 2.1 is the best illustration of this problem since even queries involving data at a single level necessitate repeated joins as soon as multiple attributes must be accessed. The second algorithm of section 2.2 provides better performance in this case and works well when queries involve data only at a single level. However, both algorithms need to decompose any query involving multilevel data into single-level queries and to combine answers from each single-level database by using repeated joins of relations. As natural join is an expensive operation, satisfying multilevel relational queries lead to a performance loss.

Another problem is that it is difficult to propose a clear semantics for updates in multilevel databases. The next section shows how to take advantage of the object oriented model to cope with these difficulties.

Finally, notice that both decomposition algorithms of sections 2.1 and 2.2 introduce null values. It may seem that there is an analogy between this null value and some kind of incomplete information, i.e. information about an attribute which can be unknown at a given time. However, the semantics in the present case is not exactly the same but rather: "data exists but is not available at this level". Jajodia and Sandhu in [San91] suggest using a particular value denoted "restricted" to represent this kind of incomplete information. In the following, we prefer to use more informative values called "level-value" (see [BCGY93]). For instance, in using these "level-values" in the algorithm of section 2.2, we would decompose the tuple *<Iron-Mask, U, 1639, U, Louis XIII, S>* as follows:

D_U

Name	C_1	Date_of_birth	C_2	Father	C_3
Iron-Mask	U	1639	U	"Secret"	U

$$D_S$$

Name	C_1	Date_of_birth	C_2	Father	C_3
Iron-Mask	U	1639	U	Louis XIII	S

Fig. 9

"Secret" is a "level-value" whose semantics is: "data exists but is secret".

3. Decomposition of Multi-level objects

3.1 Lessons learned from the relational model

Let us consider a classical relation (without classification) $r(A_k, A_1,...,A_n)$, its multilevel extension $R(A_K, C_{AK}, A_1, C_1,..., A_n, C_n, TC)$ and analyze the meaning of each level of classification associated with this multilevel relation. In the classical relation r, the key A_K is used to uniquely identify a given real world entity. In the multilevel relation R the key may be polyinstantiated. This means that the following instance of the relation *Personage* is allowed:

Fig. 10

Name	C_1	Date_of_birth	C_2	Father	C_3	TC
Iron-Mask	U	1639	U	Louis XIII	S	S
Iron-Mask	S	1670	S	Louis XIV	S	S

A possible interpretation would be to consider that the two tuples are pertaining to two distinct personages, the first one identified by *(Iron-Mask, U)*, the second one by *(Iron-Mask, S)*. This type of polyinstantiation is called entity polyinstantiation in [Lun91]. It means that, in the multilevel relation R, it is now the pair (A_K, C_{AK}) which is used to uniquely identify a real world entity. There are several techniques to avoid entity polyinstantiation, in particular we can partition the domain of the primary key among the classification levels. For instance, the personages whose names begin with "S-" are secret. Hence, we can rename the secret Iron-Mask as follows:

Fig. 11

Name	C_1	Date_of_birth	C_2	Father	C_3	TC
Iron-Mask	U	1639	U	Louis XIII	S	S
S-Iron-Mask	S	1670	S	Louis XIV	S	S

In this case, an unclassified user who tries to insert a personage whose name begins with "S-" is always rejected (without creating a covert channel). Using this technique, it is again possible to use the key A_K to uniquely identify an entity in the multilevel relation R.

Now let us analyze the PI-tuple-class integrity constraint. The idea is that a multilevel database is designed to represent the actual universe and, in our case, we consider that the universe is multilevel. Our objective is to partition this universe into single-level databases corresponding to each security level. These single-level databases are the views of the universe by users at the corresponding levels. The PI-tuple-class integrity constraint says that although we have several polyinstantiated tuples for the same entity there should be only one such tuple (i.e. one view of this entity) in each single-level database. The tuple class is used to uniquely identify the view of the entity at a given security level. For instance, let us consider the following instance of our relation *Personage*:

Fig. 12

Name	C_1	Date_of_birth	C_2	Father	C_3	TC
Melle de Blois	U	1677	U	Marquis de Montespan	U	U
Melle de Blois	U	1677	U	Louis XIV	S	S

The first tuple whose tuple class is U represents the view of the personage Mademoiselle de Blois at the unclassified level and the second tuple whose tuple class is S represents the view of the same personage at the secret level. Notice that in this instance, there is no explicit view of Mademoiselle de Blois at the confidential level.

Finally, let us analyze the PI-FD integrity constraint. The idea is that, although we have several polyinstantiated tuples for the same entity, if the classification of a given attribute is the same in two such tuples, then the attribute value should be the same in the two tuples. Actually, we may consider, in this case, that these two tuples share the same attribute value. However, we cannot dynamically represent this attribute sharing in the relational model and we have showed that the static representation of the multilevel relations leads to anomalies according to update operations. We now show that the object oriented model provides ways to avoid this problem.

3.2 Application to the object oriented model

The main advantage of the object oriented model compared to the relational model is that it is possible to create several objects which share the same sub-object. For instance, let us consider the following object class (without multilevel classification) and three instances of this class:

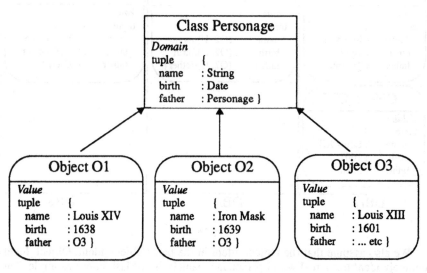

Fig. 13

The objects O1 and O2 share the same father, namely the object O3. This means that, if the object O3 is updated, then the attribute father of both objects O1 and O2 would also be automatically updated. We use this possibility to efficiently represent multilevel objects. For instance, let us consider the following multilevel instance of the relation *Personage*:

Fig. 14

Name	C_1	Date_of_birth	C_2	Father	C_3	TC
Lousi XIV	U	1638	U	Louis XIII	U	U
Iron-Mask	U	1639	U	Louis XIII	S	S
Louis XIII	U	1601	U	... etc	U	U

In our object oriented approach, this multilevel relation will be represented as in figure 15. We propose the following interpretation of this figure. There are three distinct objects (O2, U), (O2, C) and (O2, S) whose names are Iron-Mask. These three objects are respectively the view of the personage called Iron-Mask at the unclassified, confidential and secret levels. The pair (Object_ident, Object_level) is used to uniquely identify the view of the personage at a given security level. There is an analogy between the Object_level is this pair and the tuple class in the relational model.

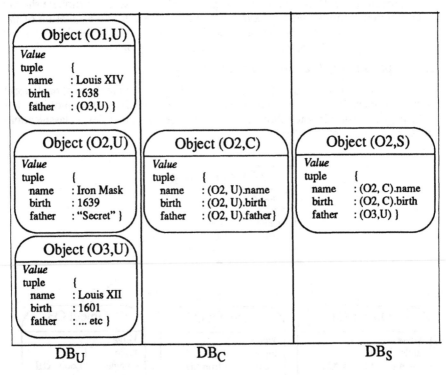

Fig. 15

We also assume that the Object_ident in the pair (Object_ident, Object_level) uniquely identifies a real world personage, namely Iron-Mask in our example. This means that we reject entity polyinstantiation in our model. For this purpose, we assume that the set of object identifiers is partitioned into several pairwise disjoint subsets associated with each security level. This technique is similar to the one suggested for the relational model. For instance, the personages whose object identifiers begin with "S-" are secret.

Each object (O2, U), (O2, C) and (O2, S) is actually a single-level object which may be physically stored in a single-level database, viz. respectively unclassified, confidential and secret. However, notice that dynamic links are created between these objects. For instance, in the confidential view (O2, C), there is a pointer to the unclassified name stored in (O2, U). This means that if an unclassified user updates the name of (O2, U), this update will be automatically propagated to the instance (O2, C) and (O2, S) through the respective pointers.

Notice also that a confidential view of object O2 is explicitly created even though the pointers make it actually identical to the unclassified view (O2, U). However, let us now assume that a confidential user wants to update Iron-Mask's date of Birth from 1639 to 1638. The confidential view of object O2 is updated as follows:

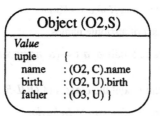

```
Object (O2,C)

Value
tuple      {
  name     : (O2, U).name
  birth    : 1638
  father   : (O2, U).father}
```

Fig. 16

The secret view is not explicitly updated. However, as there is a pointer from the date of birth of (O2, S) to the date of birth of (O2, C), the secret view is implicitly updated with the new confidential date of birth. Hence, the secret view becomes similar to the relation instance proposed in figure 8 - without using propagation. Notice that it would also be possible to construct another secret view before updating for instance:

```
Object (O2,S)

Value
tuple      {
  name     : (O2, C).name
  birth    : (O2, U).birth
  father   : (O3, U) }
```

Fig. 17

In this case, the secret view would remain unchanged because there is an explicit pointer from the date_of_birth of (O2, S) to the unclassified date of birth of (O2, U). And in this case, the secret view would become similar to the relation instance proposed in figure 6 - again without using propagation. The choice between the view of (O2, S) in figure 15 or figure 17 depends on particular situations. The main advantage of our object oriented approach over the relational model, it that it is possible for a user to explicitly choose which representation he prefers. However, we stress that, in many situations, figure 15 is probably the best representation. In the remainder of this paper, we develop a security model for object oriented databases called the MultiView model based on the principles of section 3.2.

4. The MultiView model

4.1 Object Oriented Model

In this section we suggest some preliminary definitions that sum up the main characteristics of the object oriented model. These definitions are not sufficient to fully describe the object oriented model. Indeed, we only provide the definitions we need to define our security model. A fully stated definition of the object oriented model may be found for example in [Ban92].

4.1.1 Definitions

Let *OODB* be an Object Oriented DataBase.

Definition NS 1. We can model the *objects* of *OODB* as a partial function,

$$Object \in Ident \rightarrowtail Value$$

Ident is a set of object identifiers and *Value* is a set of *values*.

A *value* may be:

- A primitive value belonging to a predefined set (Integer, String ...).
- A tuple-value i.e a set of object attributes i.e a subset of the ObjectAttribute relation.
- An object identifier.
- A set of values which are of the same domain.

An *object* of *OODB* is a pair *o = (id, value)* of the *Object* function.

Definition NS 2. We can model the *object attributes* of *OODB* as a relation,

$$ObjectAttribute \in AttributeName \leftrightarrow Value$$

AttributeName is a set of attribute names.

An *object attribute* is a pair *o_att = (a_name,value)* of the *ObjectAttribute* relation.

Definition NS 3. We can model the *classes* of *OODB* as a partial function,

$$Class \in ClassName \rightarrowtail Domain \times Behavior$$

ClassName is a set of class names, *Domain* is a set of *domains* and *Behavior* is *P(Method)*, with *Method* being the set of the *methods* of *OODB*.

A *domain* may be:

- A predefined set (Integer, String ...).
- A class name.
- A tuple i.e a set of class attributes i.e a subset of the ClassAttribute relation.
- P(d) if d denotes a domain.

A *class* of *OODB* is a pair *c =(c_name, (domain, behavior))* of the *Class* function

Definition NS 4. We can model the *class attributes* of *OODB* as a relation,

$$ClassAttribute \in AttributeName \leftrightarrow Domain$$

A *class attribute* is a pair $c\_att = (a\_name, domain)$ of the *ClassAttribute* relation.

Definition NS 5.   We can model the *methods* of *OODB* as a relation,

$Method \in Signature \leftrightarrow Body$

Signature is the set of the *signatures* of *OODB*. *Body* is the set of the program *bodies* of *OODB*.

We can model the *signatures* of *OODB* as a relation,

$Signature \in MethodName \times P(Domain) \leftrightarrow Domain$

MethodName is a set of method names.

A *signature* is a pair $s = ((m\_name, \{d_1, ..., d_i, ..., d_n\}), d)$ of the *Signature* relation. It is usually noted like the following:

$m\_name \times d_1 \times ... \times d_n \rightarrow d$

$d_1, ..., d_i, ..., d_n$ denote the domains of the method parameters and d denotes the domain of the value returned by the method.

A *body* is a program written in some programming langage.

A *method* is a pair $m = (signature, body)$ of the *Method* relation. A method describes a behavior of a set of objects encapsulated in a class.

Definition NS 6.   The database *schema* is defined by the *Class* relation and the *inherit* function.

$Schema = (Class, inherit)$

For a given class, the inherit function return its *superclass*[1]:

$inherit \in Class \rightarrow Class$

Definition NS 7.   The database *OODB* is defined as a triple.

$OODB = (Object, Schema, Instance)$

Instance is a function. For a given object, it returns the class where the object was created.

$Instance \in Object \rightarrow Class$

A class looks like a pattern object. The value of an object of a given class must be compatible with the domain of the class.

4.2 Assumptions of our approach.

Before we present the MultiView model, we have to make some assumptions. These assumptions are to define what pieces of information of an object oriented database we assign with a security level:

4.2.1 Schema protection

Rule 1.   We assume that the schema of the database is not protected.

---

1. To simplify this definition, we ignore the multiple inheritance

Every user can see the overall database schema. Only objects are concerned with classifications. Notice it does not mean that some part of the database schema would not need to be protected, but the MultiView model we present in this article does not provide this possibility. In future work we will extend the MultiView model to be able to protect some part of the database schema.

4.2.2 Objects protection

Rule 2. Object identifiers are assigned with a security level.

The object-identifier classification is used to hide the *existence* of an object to the subjects who are not sufficiently cleared. For example, existence of the two objects *id1* and *id2* represented in figure 18 are not protected since the security level assigned to their object identifier is unclassified.

The protection of Object values is a problem subject to debate. Some proposals consider [Jaj90c] that every object must be assigned with a unique classification that applies to all its attributes. In this case, we deal with *singlelevel* objects. Other approaches [Kee89] consider that every object attributes must be assigned with a security level. In this case we deal with *multilevel* objects. In our case, we think that an object may represent a complex real world entity so it may possibly not be uniquely classified as a whole. That is why we think that a secured multilevel object oriented database must provide a mechanism to manage multilevel entities. However, as stated in definition NS1, an object value may be other than a set of attributes i.e a tuple value. Indeed, it may be also a primitive value, an identifier value or a set value. Moreover, the value of a given attribute may be itself a complex value i.e a tuple value or a set value. We need then to detail precisely through some examples which grain of classification we consider :

Rule 3. If the object value is an *atomic* value i.e an object identifier or a primitive value then this object value is a grain of classification and is assigned with a single security level.

This object value classification represents the sensitivity of the association of the object identifier with the value.

As an example, let us look at figure 18. The value of the object *id1* is unclassified. It means that the information "the value of the object id1 is king of France" is unclassified.

The next rule deals with both the case where an *object value* is a *tuple value* and the case where an *attribute value* is itself a *tuple value*. In this case we have two possibilities: the grain of classification may be the tuple value as a whole or each attribute value of the tuple value may be itself a grain of classification.

Rule 4. If the value of an object or an attribute is a *tuple value* then this value may be either a *singlelevel* tuple value i.e it may be uniquely classified as a whole, or a *multilevel* tuple value i.e each of its object attribute values may be assigned with its own security level.

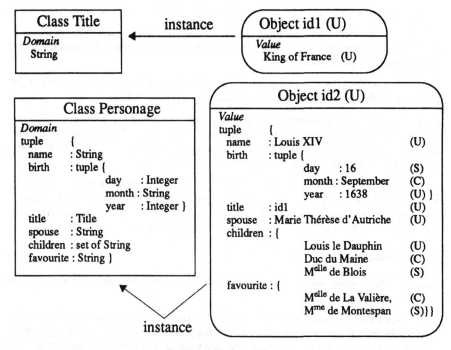

Fig. 18 Multilevel Object

The object attribute value classification represents the sensitivity of the association of the object attribute name with the value. As an example let us look at figure 18. In this figure, we have a multilevel object id2 i.e the object value of id2 is a multilevel tuple value. Some of the attribute values of this multilevel tuple values are atomic values; each of these atomic values is assigned with a single security level. Thus, the name, the spouse and the title of id2 are atomic values and are unclassified. The birth value is itself a tuple value. Morerover this birth tuple value is multilevel, so it is not protected as a whole; each of the attribute values of this multilevel value is assigned with its own security level. The year of birth is unclassified, the month of birth is confidential and the day of birth is secret. The other attribute values of the object value of id2 are studied below.

The next rule deals with both the case where an *object value* is a *set value* and the case where an *attribute value* is itself a *set value*. As in the previous case we have one alternative : the grain of classification may be the set value as a whole or each value included in the set value may be itself a grain of classification.

Rule 5.   If the value of an object or an attribute is a *set value* then this value may be either a *single-level* set value, i.e it may be uniquely classified as a whole, or a *multilevel* set value, i.e each of its values may be assigned with its own security level.

For instance in figure 18, the children of Louis XIV is a multilevel set value. Louis le Dauphin is an unclassified child. He is the son of the queen Marie Thérèse d'Autriche, spouse of Louis XIV, therefore, he is the rightful heir to the throne. On the other hand Duc du Maine and Mademoiselle de Blois are the children of the favourite Madame de Montespan, therefore they are classified children.

Finally notice that the two following integrity constraints must be enforced:

Rule 6. The object-identifier must always be assigned with a classification which is dominated by the greatest lower bound of the classifications appearing in the corresponding object value.

With this integrity constraint, a subject must be first authorized to observe the existence of the object before being authorized to access its value.

Rule 7. If an object identifier is assigned with a security level equal to C_{id}, any reference to it must be assigned with a security level equal or dominating the security level C_{id}, or may be included in a single-level value (tuple or set) assigned with a security level equal or dominating the security level C_{id}.

Without this integrity constraint, a user could learn the existence of an object even if he is not allowed to know of its existence. For example, in figure 18, if the security level assigned to the identifier id1 had been confidential or secret, then the title attribute in the object id2 could not have been unclassified.

4.2.3 Cover stories

Rule 8. Each value *which is a grain of classification* may be associated with a *cover story.*

It means that for example a single-level tuple value may be associated with a cover story whereas a multilevel tuple value may not because it is not a grain of classification. On the other hand, each attribute value of this multilevel tuple value may be associated with a cover story, provided the attribute value is itself a grain of classification.

In the SODA model [Kee89] cover stories are managed by using the so called *polyinstantiation* technique. It means that every value which is a grain of classification may depend on the level of classification. For instance, in figure 18, the favourite of Louis XIV is Mademoiselle de La Valière for confidential users, whereas the favourite of the king is Madame de Montespan for secret users. The value "Mademoiselle de La Valière" is used to hide from confidential users that the new favourite of the king is Madame de Montespan. Notice that the value of the favourite attribute is a polyinstantiated value but is not a set value as is the child attribute. Indeed, the domain of the favourite attribute is String, whereas the domain of the child attribute is set of String.

We have shown that the previous rules 2 to 8 allow us to have a great expressive power concerning information protection. Indeed, we can represent complex and structured multilevel objects. Notice we could have built a TCB to manage these multilevel objects as such. Some proposals [Kee89] suggest building such a TCB. In our concern, we explain in [BCGY93] why we think that such a TCB is not realistic because it would lead to deeply modifying the object management layer which would downgrade performances, and it would lead to managing multilevel transactions which would make the database vulnerable to covert channels. In the MultiView model, we split up these multilevel objects into single-level objects that are stored in different single-level databases. Our objective is to define a realistic security policy which can be implemented without downgrading too much the performances of an existing OODBMS and without modifying a lot this existing OODBMS. We will see in the next section that this decomposition preserves this great expressive power concerning information protection. Moreover, we will see that the MultiView model can manage cover stories without making the interpretation of the data difficult, as is the case in the SODA model [Kee89].

4.3 Definitions

The MultiView model is based on the decomposition of a n-level Object Oriented Database into n single level databases. Each database corresponds to a given level of classification. This decomposition allows us to provide the user with a view of the database compatible with his clearance or the level of classification he chooses to perform his transaction. Then, for each object of the n-level Object Oriented Database it corresponds to *n* views, this is the reason why we called this model "MultiView".

The changes we perform on the non-secure model to obtain the MultiView model are natural and straightforward. We deal with objects having several levels of classification, so it is natural to have several single-level databases. Each object can appear in several databases with the same identifier but with possibly different values. So its identifier is not sufficient to uniquely identify it. It is then straightforward to associate with the object identifier a level of classification to uniquely identify this object according to its sensitivity. Thus, definitions NS1 and NS7 of the non-secure model are changed into definitions MV1 and MV7 in the MultiView Model.

Let *OODB* be an Object Oriented Database.

Definition MV 1. We can model the *objects* of *OODB* as a partial function,

$Object \in Ident \times Level \rightarrow Value$

Ident is a set of object identifiers. *Value* is a set of *values* and *Level* is a set of partially ordered security levels. $Level = \{l_1, ..., l_i, ..., l_n\}$

A *value* may be:

- *A primitive value belonging to a predefined set (Integer, String ...).*
- *A tuple-value i.e a set of object attributes i.e a subset of the ObjectAttribute relation.*
- *An object identifier i.e a pair (identifier, level)*
- *A pointer value i.e an expression being an access path to a value stored in an object of OODB. Object identifiers are a kind of pointer value.*
- *A set of values which are of the same domain.*
- *A level value taken in the following set: $\{"l_1", ..., "l_i", ..., "l_n"\}$. Each "$l_i$" corresponds to the l_i security level.*
- *An algebraic expression.*

An *object* of *OODB* is a pair $o = ((id, l), value)$ of the *Object* function.

Definition MV 7. The database *OODB* is defined as a triple.

$OODB = (<OODB_{l1}, ..., OODB_{li}, ... OODB_{ln}>, Schema, Instance)$

$l_i, i \in [1,n]$ is a classification level. Each classified database is a set of objects whose classification level is l_i, that is $OODB_{li} \in P(Object)$.

Instance is a function. For a given object, it returns the class where the object was created.

$Instance \in Object \rightarrow Class$

A class looks like a pattern object. The value of an object of a given class must be compatible with the domain of the class.

Finally notice:

- A pointer value is compatible with its corresponding class domain provided its evaluation is a value compatible with this domain.
- A "level value" is compatible with any domain.
- The evaluation result of an algebraic expression standing for a value must be a value compatible with the corresponding class domain.

4.4 Object Creation

Object creation must respect the following rules:

Rule 9. Let O be a real world entity that must be created and let c_{id} be the existence classification of this entity, then an object view of O must be *first* created in the corresponding $OODB_{cid}$.

Rule 10. A user who wants to create an object (O, l_i) in $OODB_{li}$ must set his working security level to l_i. Of course the user's clearance must dominate the l_i level.

Rule 11. Let O be a real world entity. Let (O, l_i) be an object view of this entity being created in $OODB_{li}$. Let v be a value being a grain of classification of O. Let l_v be the security level assigned to v: Let v_i be the corresponding value of v in the object view (O, l_i) [1]. Because v_i may be equal to a pointer or an algebraic expression, we denote *Evaluation(v_i)* the evaluation result of v_i:

1. **If v is not a value of a multilevel set value then :**
   - If $l_i \geq l_v$ then *Evaluation(v_i)* $= v$.
   - If $l_i < l_v$ then *Evaluation(v_i)* is equal to a cover story or a special "l_j" level value such that $l_i < l_j$. Notice that *the* level value "l_j" is not necessarily equal to "l_v". The decision to use a cover story or a level value is taken by the object creator.

2. **If v is a value of a multilevel set value *mvset* :**
   - If $l_i \geq l_v$ then $v \in$ *Evaluation($mvset_i$)*.
   - If $l_i < l_v$ then $v \notin$ *Evaluation($mvset_i$)*.

Let us see through an example how creation is performed in the MultiView model. Let us consider the two real world entities id1 and id2 in figure 18. Existence of these entities is not protected, so an unclassified view of each entity must be first created in the unclassifed database $OODB_U$ according to rule 9. A user who wants to create these two objects must set his working security level to unclassified according to rule 10. Creations of these two unclassified objects are then performed according to rule 11.

(Id1, U) creation:

As the whole value of the entity id1 is unclassified, the value of (id1, U) is equal to the actual value of the entity id1 (figure 19). The creation of id1 thanks to the MultiView model is then complete.

(id2, U) creation (figure 19):

---

1. More generaly, if *val* is any value included in the object value of O, then val_k represents the corresponding value of *val* in the object view (O, l_k).

Unclassified grains of classification:

Unclassified grains of classification of the entity id2 are introduced in the object view (id2, U):

- The name, the year of birth, the title and the spouse are introduced in (id2, U).
- The child Louis le Dauphin is introduced in the child attribute set value.

Protected grains of classification:

- Since the month of birth is confidential, it is replaced by the "confidential" level value in (id2, U). This is to tell unclassified users that the month of birth of Louis XIV is confidential. In the same way, since the day of birth is secret, it is replaced by the "secret" level value in (id2, U).
- As the favourite of the king is classified it is replaced by a level value in (id2, U). However this level value is "confidential" whereas the favourite is secret. This means that this "confidential" level value is in fact a kind of cover story. It tells unclassified users that the favourite of Louis XIV is confidential whereas it is secret. The choice of this "confidential" level value will be explained in section 4.5.
- Duc du Maine and Melle de Blois are protected, so both of these values are discarded in the child attribute set value of (id2, U).

(id2, C) creation (figure 19):

Once the unclassified view of the entity id2 is created, the user must create other views of this entity, according to the following rule:

Rule 12. To fully create a multilevel entity, a user must create an object view of this entity at every security level which appears in the multilevel entity.

Notice that the user may create these other views in any order, but it may be easier to create successively these views from the lowest classification to the highest classification.

According to rule 12, the user must create the confidential view of the entity id2. According to rule 10 the user must set his working level to confidential. Creation is then performed according to rule 11.

Unclassified grains of classification

Unclassified grains of classification are accessed by pointer values toward (id2, U):

Since the name, the year of birth, the title and the spouse are unclassified, each of them is replaced in (id2, C) by a pointer value toward the corresponding value in (id2, U).

Notice that these pointer values are not mandatory. For instance, rule 11 would not prevent the user from directly introducing the name, the year of birth, the title and the spouse in the confidential object view. However, it is better to replace each of these values by a pointer value. Indeed, such pointer values are used to avoid replicating the data and, as we will see in the update section, they provide us with a means to automatically propagate to high levels the updates performed at a low level.

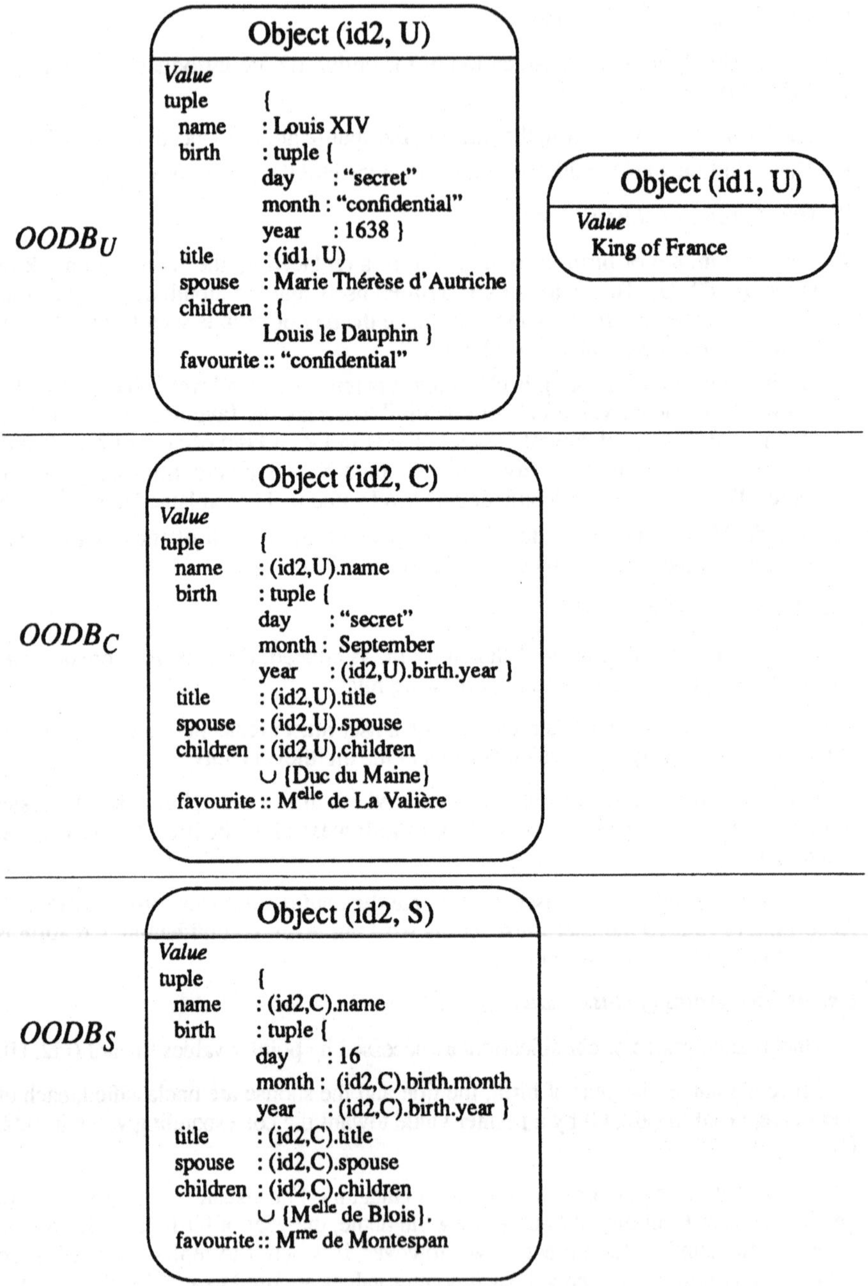

Object (id2, U)

Value
tuple   {
  name   : Louis XIV
  birth   : tuple {
    day   : "secret"
    month : "confidential"
    year   : 1638 }
  title   : (id1, U)
  spouse : Marie Thérèse d'Autriche
  children : {
    Louis le Dauphin }
  favourite :: "confidential"

$OODB_U$

Object (id1, U)

Value
King of France

Object (id2, C)

Value
tuple   {
  name   : (id2,U).name
  birth   : tuple {
    day   : "secret"
    month : September
    year   : (id2,U).birth.year }
  title   : (id2,U).title
  spouse   : (id2,U).spouse
  children : (id2,U).children
    ∪ {Duc du Maine}
  favourite :: Melle de La Valière

$OODB_C$

Object (id2, S)

Value
tuple   {
  name   : (id2,C).name
  birth   : tuple {
    day   : 16
    month : (id2,C).birth.month
    year   : (id2,C).birth.year }
  title   : (id2,C).title
  spouse   : (id2,C).spouse
  children : (id2,C).children
    ∪ {M^{elle} de Blois}.
  favourite :: Mme de Montespan

$OODB_S$

Fig. 19 Multilevel Database.

- The child attribute set value of (id2, C) is replaced by an algebraic expression including a pointer value toward the whole child attribute set value of (id2, U). This pointer value stands for the unclassified view of Louis XIV's children. To obtain the confidential view of Louis XIV's children, "Duc du Maine" is added to this unclassified set. The evaluation result of the expression is of course {Louis le Dauphin, Duc du Maine}.

Confidential grains of classification

Confidential grains of classification of the entity id2 are introduced in the object view (id2, C):

- Since it is confidential the month of birth is introduced in (id2, C).
- Since it is confidential, the child Duc du Maine appears in the evaluation result of the expression assigned to the child attribute set value of (id2, C).

Secret grains of classifications

- Since the day of birth is secret, it is replaced by the "secret" level value in (id2, C).
- In (id2, C), the favourite attribute value is a cover story to make the confidential users believe that the favourite of the king is still Mademoiselle de La Valière whereas she has been superseded by Madame de Montespan.
- Melle de Blois is secret, then this value is discarded in the child attribute set value of (id2, C).

(id2, S) creation (figure 19):

Finally, the user must create the secret view of the entity id2. According to rule 10 the user must set his working level to secret. Creation is then performed according to rule 11.

Lower protected grains of classification

Lower protected grains of classification are accessed by pointer values toward (id2, C):

- Since the name, the year of birth, the title and the spouse are unclassified, each of them is replaced in (id2, S) by a pointer value toward the corresponding value in (id2, C).

Notice that the user could have introduced pointer values towards the unclassified object view (id2, U). We will see in the update section why we think that such a representation is not convenient.

- Since the day of birth is confidential, it is replaced in (id2, S) by a pointer value toward the corresponding value in (id2, C).

This explains why it is better to create the confidential view of id2 before creating the secret view of id2, otherwise such a pointer value would temporarily refer to an inexisting object view.

- The child attribute set value of (id2, S) is replaced by an expression including a pointer value toward the whole child attribute set value of (id2, C). This pointer value stands for the confidential view of Louis XIV's children. To obtain the secret view of Louis XIV's children, Melle de Blois is added to this confidential set. The evaluation result of the expression is, of course, {Louis le Dauphin, Duc du Maine, Melle de Blois}.

Secret grains of classification

Secret grains of classification of the entity id2 are introduced in the object view (id2, S):

- Since the day of birth is secret, it is introduced in (id2, S).
- Since the child Melle de Blois is secret, it appears in the evaluation result of the expression assigned to the child attribute set value of (id2, S).
- Since the favourite of the king is secret, it is introduced in (id2, S)

The creation of id2 thanks to the MultiView model is then complete.

Notice that in this mechanism of object creation, the user must create himself each object view of the multilevel object. In [BCGY93], we present another mechanism of creation which is slightly different: Once the lowest classified view of a multilevel object is created by the user, other higher classified views of the same multilevel object are automatically created. Each of these higher classified views is pointing per default to the directly lower classified object view. Any of these default pointers can later be overwritten by any user if he has the required clearance.

Let us see now how consultation is carried out with the MultiView model.

4.5 Consultation

To access some data of OODB, a user must first choose a current security level to initiate a transaction. Of course, this level must be compatible with his clearance. Then the user's read access rights are defined by the following rule:

Rule 13. If a user starts a transaction at security level l_i, then this user may read any $OODB_{lj}$ such as $l_j \le l_i$.

As an example, let us consider a user who wants to consult the multilevel object *id2*. Suppose this user initiates an unclassified transaction. This user may then read $OODB_U$. So the user can learn the following (figure 19):

- The user learns the name, the year of birth and the spouse of id2.
- Thanks to the title identifier value, the user learns that Louis XIV is the king of France.
- The user learns that Louis XIV is the father of Louis le Dauphin, but the user cannot know the other children.
- Thanks to level values, the user learns that the month of birth is confidential and that the day of birth is secret. Thanks to a "confidential" level value, he learns that the identification of the king's favourite is "confidential". In fact, as we will see below, the king's favourite is secret.

Now let us suppose a user initiates a confidential transaction to see the confidential view of id2. This user may then read $OODB_C$. So the user can learn the following (figure 19):

- The user learns the month of birth of Louis XIV.
- A pointer is evaluated every times a user or a program access it. Thus, thanks to the pointers to the unclassified view, the user can learn the name, the year of birth, the spouse and the title of id2.
- The user learns that Louis XIV is the father of two children. One of them is Louis le Dauphin, the other one is Duc du Maine.
- Thanks to a "secret" level value, the user learns that the day of birth is secret.

- The user believes that Melle de La Valière is the king's favourite. He cannot know that Melle de La Valière has been superseded by Madame de Montespan.

As is stated in rule 14, this confidential user may also read OODB$_U$. Therefore this user may see the unclassified view of id2 and compare this view with the confidential view of id2. Thus, the user can see precisely which data is unclassified and which data is confidential. The user sees that the confidential and the unclassified values of the king's favourite are respectively Melle de La Valière and the "confidential" level value. Now the actual king's favourite is Mme de Montespan which is secret. This explains why it is better to set the unclassified favourite attribute value to "confidential" instead of "secret". Indeed a "secret" level value might disclose to confidential users that perhaps Melle de La Valière is not the favourite of the king.

Now let us suppose a user initiates a secret transaction to see the secret view of id2. This user may then read OODB$_S$. So the user can learn the following (figure 19):

- The user learns the day of birth of Louis XIV.
- Thanks to the pointer to the confidential view od id2, the user learns the month of birth of id2.
- Thanks to the pointers to the confidential view od id2 and thanks to the pointers from the confidential view of id2 to the unclassified view of id2, the user can learn the name, the year of birth, the spouse and the title of id2.
- The user learns that Louis XIV is the father of three children: Louis le Dauphin, Duc du Maine and Melle de Blois.
- The user learns that Mme de Montespan is the king's favourite.

Notice that, as it is stated in rule 14, this secret user may also read OODB$_C$ and OODB$_U$.

Notice also that in order to access an attribute value of a high-level object view, several levels of indirection (pointers) may have to be processed, thus our approach may cause a performance loss. However, compared with joins in the relational case, it is a marginal loss of performance.

4.6 Updating

Let us now see through an example how updating is performed with the MultiView model. To update some data of OODB, a user must first choose a current security level to initiate a transaction. Of course, this level must be compatible with his clearance. Then the user's write access rights are defined by the following rule:

Rule 14. If a user starts a transaction at security level l_i, then this user may only update data of $OODB_{li}$.

As an example, let us consider a user who wants to update the object view (id2, U). This user wants to set the spouse attribute to NULL value because the queen Marie Thérèse d'Autriche is dead (she died in 1683). According to the previous rule, the user must initiate an unclassified transaction and then may update the spouse attribute of (id2, U) (figure 20).

The user need not propagate this update to the higher levels. Indeed, this update is automatically propagated to the higher levels thanks to the pointer from the confidential spouse attribute to the unclassified spouse attribute and thanks to the pointer from the secret spouse attribute to the confidential spouse attribute.

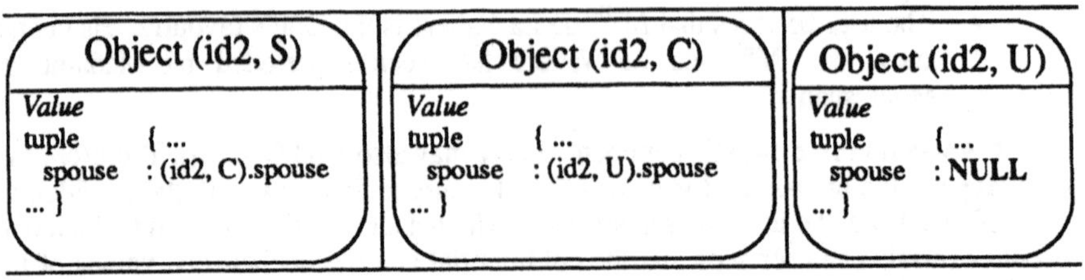

Fig. 20

Now in 1683, Louis XIV secretly married again with Mme de Maintenon. Suppose a secret user wants to insert this secret information in the database. According to rule 14, the user must initiate a secret transaction. He may then update the spouse attribute of (id2, S) (figure 21).

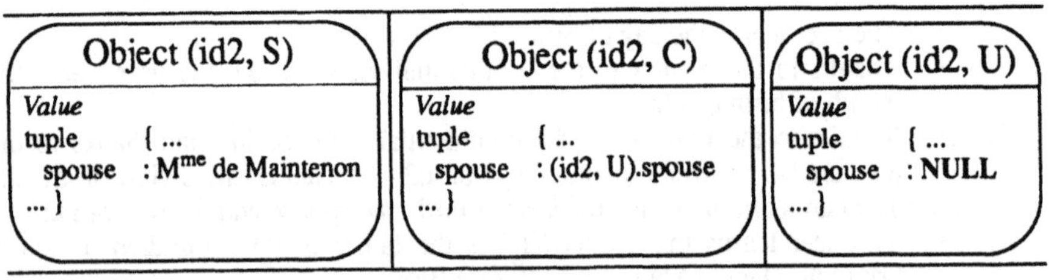

Fig. 21

The pointer to the confidential database is broken. Mme de Maintenon is now Louis XIV's spouse. This is secret information. The NULL value stands now for a cover story. It tells unclassified and confidential users that Louis XIV has no wife.

4.7 Deletion

We assume that every object view may be deleted without any restriction. Only the following rule must be enforced:

Rule 15. Let O be a real world entity. Let (O, l_i) an object view of this entity to be deleted. To delete this view, a user must set his working level to security level l_i.

As an example, let us consider a user who wants to delete the confidential view (id2, C). According to the previous rule, the user must initiate a confidential transaction and may then delete (id2, C) .

We can see in figure 22 that (id2, C) is deleted. This deletion means that pointer values from (id2, S) to (id2, C) become dangling references. Thus the OODB is no longer consistent since some pointer values reference data which do not exist any longer. To avoid such inconsistency, it would be necessary to update these pointer values in a way which makes the whole database consistent. [Ber94] suggests an approach to preserve referential integrity while ensuring that confidentiality is not violated.

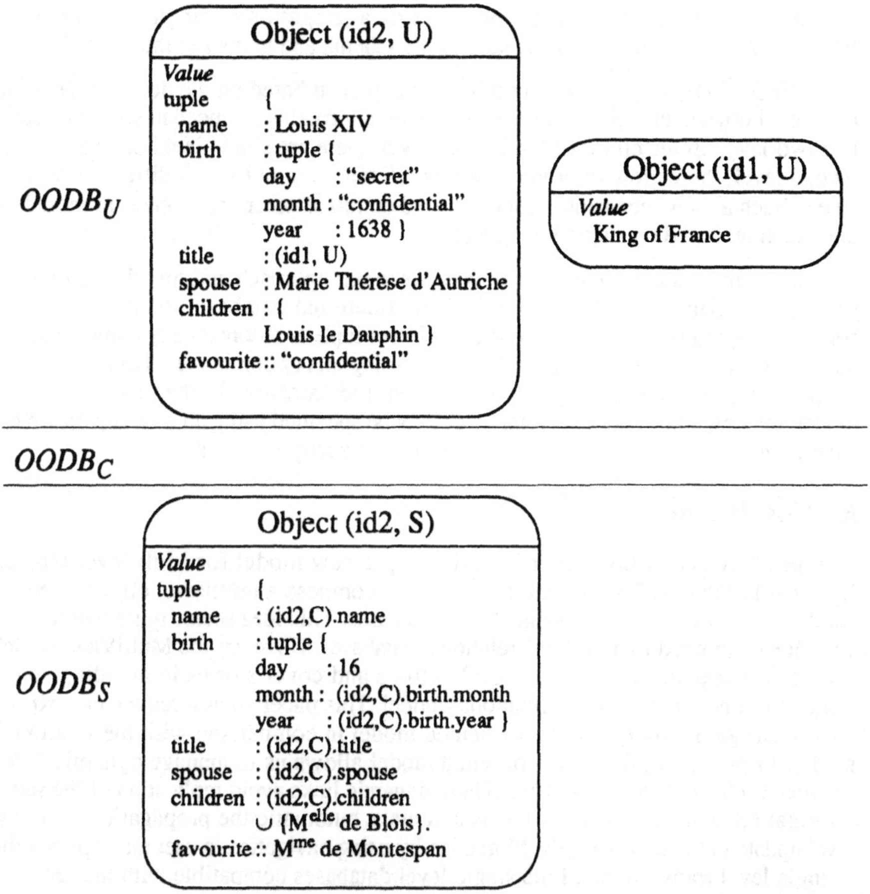

```
┌─────────────────────────────────────┐
│            Object (id2, U)           │
├─────────────────────────────────────┤
│ Value                                │
│ tuple      {                         │
│   name     : Louis XIV               │
│   birth    : tuple {                 │         ┌──────────────────────┐
│              day    : "secret"       │         │    Object (id1, U)    │
│              month : "confidential"  │         ├──────────────────────┤
│              year   : 1638 }         │         │ Value                │
│   title    : (id1, U)                │         │ King of France       │
│   spouse   : Marie Thérèse d'Autriche│         └──────────────────────┘
│   children : {                       │
│              Louis le Dauphin }      │
│   favourite :: "confidential"        │
└─────────────────────────────────────┘
```

$OODB_U$

───

$OODB_C$

───

```
┌─────────────────────────────────────┐
│            Object (id2, S)           │
├─────────────────────────────────────┤
│ Value                                │
│ tuple      {                         │
│   name     : (id2,C).name            │
│   birth    : tuple {                 │
│              day   : 16              │
│              month : (id2,C).birth.month │
│              year  : (id2,C).birth.year } │
│   title    : (id2,C).title           │
│   spouse   : (id2,C).spouse          │
│   children : (id2,C).children        │
│              ∪ {Melle de Blois}.     │
│   favourite :: Mme de Montespan      │
└─────────────────────────────────────┘
```

$OODB_S$

Fig. 22   Deletion of (id2, C)

5. Comparison with related works.

In [Jaj90c], Jajodia and Kogan try also to demonstrate that it is possible to represent multilevel entities by using single level entities. This motivation is similar to ours. However, our approach drastically differs from the one proposed in [Jaj90c]. In this paper, we assume that the database schema is not protected, so everybody is aware of the existence of every attribute. This assumption is removed in the approach used in [Jaj90c]. We argue that a complete model for multilevel object oriented databases must provide the possibility to hide some part of the database schema. Hence, it would be interesting to combine our model with the approach suggested in [Jaj90c]. However, as it is pointed out by [Mil92], in the case where the schema is protected, some difficulties may appear when creating a multilevel object because a process needs to access the higher classified schema to create the view of the unclassified instance at higher classified levels.

Two other approaches to support multilevel objects by decomposing them into single-level objects were proposed by [Mil92] and [Ber93]. In particular [Ber93] suggests to represent multilevel objects using aggregation of single-level objects. However this approach requires to modify the schema and to rewrite the methods.

In [BCGY94], we suggest to combine an approach based on the decomposition of multilevel objects into single level objects with a virtual view mechanism. This leads to a two-level architecture. At the bottom level, there are single-level objects. At the second level, there are virtual views which references to objects of different security levels. Such a view mechanism could be used on top of other approaches, proposed in the literature, based on single-level objects.

Finally, there are some connections between our approach and the 'derive option' proposed in [Hai91] to design a multilevel relational database. the derive option permits a user to require that the value at a lower tuple is automatically copied up into the attribute of a higher level tuple. However, using this option in the relationnal model deeply complicates the retrieval of data from the database. In the object-oriented model, the down-pointing data references may be specified using an access path which enables the lower classified attribute values to be directly retrieved.

6. Conclusion

Our objective in this paper is to develop a new model for Multilevel Object Oriented Databases. The central idea was to decompose a multilevel object oriented database into a collection of single level databases. This idea seems quite natural and was already applied to multilevel relational databases. However the MultiView model provides means to support multilevel entities and cover stories in avoiding some difficulties encountered in the relational model. This paper shows that we can expect significant gains from the object oriented model in comparison with the relational model. In particular, the object oriented model allows us to manage dynamic links between each single level database. These dynamic links avoid replication of the same information at several security levels and make automatic the propagation of a low level update to the higher levels. Moreover, by using navigation, a user may see, within a single level transaction, all the single level databases compatible with the security level of the transaction.

We also show in this paper how the MultiView model allows us to manage very complex multilevel entities. Structured attribute tuple values as well as attribute set values are taken into account in the MultiView model. However this work could be extended in one major direction. Indeed, we could include the possibility of classifying some parts of the object oriented database schema, for instance the existence of a secret attribute or the existence of a secret method. This extension would provide us with a complete multilevel security model for object oriented databases which copes with any security requirement.

Acknowledgement

We would like to thank the STEI for its support, Jill Manning for her help, and the anonymous referees for their comments on a previous draft of this paper.

References :

[Air83]   Air Force Studies Board. Multilevel Data Management Security. Committee on Multilevel Data Management Security. National Research Council. 1983.

[Ban92]   F. Bancilhon, C. Delobel and P. Kanellakis. Building an Object-

Oriented Database System. Morgan Kaufmann 1992.

[Ber93]   E. Bertino and S. Jajodia. Modeling Multilevel Entities Using Single-level Objects. Proc. of the Third Conference on Deductive and Object-Oriented Databases. Springer-Verlag Lecture Notes in Computer Science, Vol. 760. December 1993.

[Ber94]   E. Bertino, L. Mancini and S. Jajodia. Collecting Garbage in Multilevel Secure Object Stores. Proc. of the 1994 IEEE Symposium on Research in Security and Privacy. Oakland. 1994.

[BCGY93]   N. Boulahia-Cuppens, F. Cuppens, A. Gabillon, K. Yazdanian. Multiview Model for MultiLevel Object-Oriented Database. Proc. of the Ninth Annual Computer Security Applications Conference. Orlando, Florida. December 1993.

[BCGY94]   N. Boulahia-Cuppens, F. Cuppens, A. Gabillon, K. Yazdanian. Virtual View Model to Design a Secure Object-Oriented Database. Proc. of the 17th National Computer Security Conference. Baltimore, Maryland. October 1994.

[Cup92]   F. Cuppens, K. Yazdanian. A "Natural" Decomposition of Multi-level Relations. Proc. of the 1992 IEEE Symposium on Research in Security and Privacy. Oakland. 1992.

[Den87]   D. Denning, T. Lunt, R. Shell, M. Heckman and W. Shockley. A Multilevel Relational Data Model. IEEE Symposium on Research in Security and Privacy. Oakland. 1987.

[Den88]   D. Denning. Lessons learned from modeling a Secure Multilevel Relational Database System. Database Security I : Status and Prospects. C. Landwehr. (North-Holland). 1988.

[Fro89]   J. Frosher and C. Meadows. Achieving a Trusted Database Management System Using Parallelism. Database Security II : Status and Prospects. Elsevier Science Publisher B.V. (North-Holland). IFIP 1989.

[Gar90]   C. Garvey, T. Hinke, N. Jensen, J. Solomon and A. Wu. A Layered TCB Implementation versus the Hinke-Schaefer Approach. Database Security III : Status and Prospects. Elsevier Science Publisher B.V. (North-Holland). IFIP 1990.

[Gra90]   R. Graubart. A Comparison of Three Secure DBMS Architectures. In Database Security III, Status and Prospects. North-Holland 1990.

[Gro76]   M. Grohn. A model of protected data management system. ESD-TR-76-289. Bedford Mass. I. P. Sharp Associates ltd. 1976.

[Hai90]   J.T. Haigh, R.C. O'Brien, P.D. Stachour and D.L. Toups. The LDV Approach to Database Security. Database Security III : Status and Prospects. Elsevier Science Publisher B.V. (North-Holland). IFIP 1990.

[Hai91]   J.T. Haigh, R.C. O'Brien, D. J. Thomsen. The LDV Secure Relational DBMS Model. Database Security IV : Status and Prospects. Elsevier Science Publisher B.V. (North-Holland). IFIP 1991.

[Hin75]   T. Hinke and M. Schaeffer. Secure data management system. RADC-TR-75-266. System Development Corporation. 1975.

[Jaj90a]   S. Jajodia and R. Sandhu. Polyinstantiation Integrity in Multilevel Relations. IEEE Symposium on Research in Security and Privacy. Oakland. 1990.

[Jaj90b]   S. Jajodia , B. Kogan. Transaction Processing in Multilevel Secure Database Using the Replicated Architecture. Proc. of the 1990 IEEE Symposium on Research in Security and Privacy. 1990.

[Jaj90c]   S. Jajodia and B. Kogan. Integrating an object-oriented data model with multi-level security. Proc. of the 1990 IEEE Symposium on Security and Privacy. 1990.

[Jaj90d]   S. Jajodia and R. Sandhu and E. Sibley. Update Semantics for Multilevel Relations. Proc. of the Sixth Annual Computer Security Applications Conference. Tucson Arizona. 1990.

[Jaj91]   S. Jajodia and R. Sandhu. A novel Decomposition of Multilevel Relations Into Single-level Relations. IEEE Symposium on Research in Security and Privacy. Oakland. 1991.

[Kee89]   T.F. Keefe, W.T. Tsai and M.B. Thuraisingham. SODA : A Secure Object-Oriented Database System. Computer & Security, Vol 8, N°6, 1989.

[Lun90]   T.F. Lunt. Multilevel Security for Object-Oriented Database Systems. Database Security III : Status and Prospects. Elsevier Science Publisher B.V. (North-Holland). IFIP 1990.

[Lun91]   T.F. Lunt. Polyinstantiation: an Inevitable Part of a Multilevel World. Proc. of the IEEE Workshop on Computer Security Foundations. Franconia, New Hampshire. June 1991.

[Mil92]   J.K. Millen and T.F. Lunt. Security for Object-Oriented Database Systems. Proc. of the 1992 IEEE Symposium on Research in Security and Privacy. 1992.

[McC92]   C. McCollum and L. Notargiacomo. Distributed concurrency control with optional data replication. Database Security V : Status and Prospects. Elsevier Science Publisher B.V. (North-Holland). IFIP 1992.

[San90]   R. Sandhu and S. Jajodia and T. Lunt. A New Polyinstantiation Integrity Constraint for Multilevel Relations. Proc of the Computer Security Foundations Workshop III. Franconia 1990.

[San91]   R. Sandhu and S. Jajodia. Honest Databases That Can Keep Secrets. Proc. of the 14th National Computer Security Conference. 1991

[Var91]   V. Varadharajan and S. Black. Multilevel Security in a Distributed Object-Oriented System. Computer & Security, 10 (1991).

Supporting Object-based High-assurance Write-up in Multilevel Databases for the Replicated Architecture

Roshan K. Thomas[1] and Ravi S. Sandhu[2]
[1]Odyssey Research Associates
301 A Dates Drive
Ithaca, NY 14850-1313, USA
[2]George Mason University
ISSE Department, MS 4A4
Fairfax, VA 22030-4444, USA*

Abstract. We discuss the support of high-assurance write-up actions in multilevel secure object-oriented databases under the replicated architecture. In this architecture, there exists a separate untrusted single-level database for each security level. Data is replicated across these databases (or containers), as each database stores a copy of all the data whose class is dominated by that of the database. Our work utilizes an underlying message filter based object-oriented security model. Supporting message-based write-up actions with synchronous semantics directly impacts confidentiality, integrity, and performance issues. Also, an important concern in the replicated architecture is the maintenance of the mutual consistency of the replicated data. In this paper we offer solutions to support write-up actions while preserving the conflicting goals of confidentiality, integrity, and efficiency and at the same time demonstrate how the effects of updates arising from write-up actions are replicated correctly to guarantee such mutual consistency. Finally, we wish to emphasize that our elaboration of the message filter model demands minimum functionality from the TCB that is hosted within the trusted front end (TFE), and further requires no trusted subjects (i.e. subjects who are exempted, perhaps partially, from the usual mandatory controls). Collectively, these make verification of our solutions easier, since we have the assurance that covert channels cannot be introduced through the TFE.

Keywords: Replicated architecture, object-oriented databases, write-up, serial correctness, message-filtering, signaling channels.

1 Introduction

The replicated architecture for multilevel secure database management systems (mls DBMSs) has lately experienced a resurgence in the research community.

* The work of both authors was partially supported by the National Security Agency through contract MDA904-92–C-5140. We are indebted to Pete Sell, Howard Stainer and Mike Ware for their support and encouragement in making this work possible.

It represents one of the three architectures identified by the Woods Hole study organized by the U.S. Air Force [19]. These architectures were motivated by the need to build multilevel secure DBMSs from existing untrusted DBMSs. The distinguishing feature of the replicated architecture is that lower level data is replicated at higher levels. To be more precise, for any given security level, a physically separate DBMS is used to manage data at or below the level. In our further discussions, we use the term "container" to be synonymous with "database". These backend databases are untrusted, and rely on a trusted front end (TFE) that hosts the trusted computing base (TCB), for access mediation. The replicated architecture, as elaborated for a simple lattice, is shown in figure 1. Thus an object classified at U and stored in the first container is replicated across the other containers 2, 3, and 4. Such replicas when stored at containers 2, 3, and 4, are no longer considered to be at level U, rather are classified at the level of their respective containers. However, as far as applications are concerned, these replicas make up one logical object and is thus identified by a single object identifier.

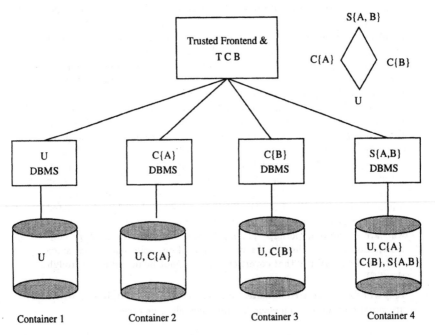

Fig. 1. The replicated architecture illustrating containers for a simple lattice

The advantages and security of the replicated architecture stem from the fact that users (or subjects acting on their behalf) at different levels are physically isolated from one another, and that a user is able to accomplish all tasks (multilevel queries and updates at his/her level) from the data stored at a single

DBMS. This is because a properly cleared user who logs in to the system at security level l, will be assigned to the DBMS at l. All data that is classified below levels l and stored at the lower level databases is replicated, and thus available, at the DBMS at l. Thus, for example, security threats from covert channels due to read-down operations in multilevel queries do not arise in this architecture.

The benefits of the replicated architecture come at the cost (and complexity) of the replica control schemes needed to keep the replicas of the data mutually consistent. To make this architecture commercially viable, these schemes would not only have to be efficient, but in addition must be secure (in that they do not introduce covert channels). It is important to note that covert channels can be introduced in this architecture only through the TFE.

Replica and concurrency control algorithms for relational databases under the replicated architecture have appeared in recent literature [1, 4, 5, 7, 11]. These algorithms have contributed to a better understanding of the complexity that arises due to the interaction between concurrency control, replication, and multilevel security. Perhaps the most significant advancement in this area was reported in [1]. Here it was observed that many algorithms for the replicated architecture could produce schedules that are not serializable, due to the distributed nature of decision making and synchronization. The authors in [1] pursue two approaches to address this. The first calls for global synchronization while the second restricts the security structure to avoid such synchronization.

In this paper, we turn our attention to object-oriented databases. With the ever increasing interest in object-oriented databases, we believe our effort here is timely, and one that we hope will provide impetus for further work in the area. The object-oriented security model that we utilize in this paper is based on a message filter component in the TCB that mediates messages sent between objects at various security levels [6]. The elaboration of this message filter object-oriented security model for trusted subject and kernelized architectures has been reported elsewhere in the literature [14, 15, 16]. In this paper, we elaborate the message-filtering functions under the replicated architecture, and in particular, focus on write-up actions. The solutions presented here are not prone to the problems reported in [1] since we use a forkstamping scheme for centralized decision making.

The rest of this paper is organized as follows. Section 2 presents some background material covering object-oriented databases and the message filter model. Section 3 explores the implications of the message filtering approach to security, for the replicated architecture. Section 4 discusses how the activity of a single user session is replicated across containers, while section 5 discusses how such sessions are synchronized across containers. Finally, section 6 concludes the paper.

2 Background

In this section we give some background to the message filter object-oriented security model and the concurrency and synchronization problems that arise when write-up actions are supported.

2.1 The Message Filter Model

The message filter model is one of several proposals addressing mandatory security in multilevel object-oriented databases that have appeared in the recent literature [6, 8, 9, 12, 13, 18]. The model [6, 14, 15, 16] is based on the view that the task of enforcing mandatory confidentiality essentially reduces to that of controlling and filtering the exchange of messages between objects. Objects and messages thus constitute the main entities in the model. Every object is assigned a single classification. The security policy is captured in a filtering algorithm, and enforced by a message filter component.

The message filter algorithm is given in figure 2. (In this and other algorithms, the % symbol is used to delimit comments.) Cases (1) through (4) deal with abstract messages, which are processed by application and user-defined methods. Cases (5) through (7) deal with primitive messages, which are directly processed by system defined methods. In case (1), the sender and receiver are at the same security level, and the message g_1 and its reply are allowed to pass. In case (2) the levels are incomparable and thus the filter blocks the message from getting to the receiver object, and further injects a NIL reply. Case (3) involves a receiver at a higher level than the sender. The message is allowed to pass but the filter discards the actual reply, and substitutes a NIL instead. In case (4), the receiver object is at a lower level than the sender and the filter allows both the message and the reply to pass unaltered.

In cases (1), (3), and (4) the method in the receiver object is invoked at a security level given by the variable *rlevel*. The intuitive significance of *rlevel* is that it keeps track of the least upper bound (lub) of all objects encountered in a chain of method invocations, going back to the root of the chain. The value of *rlevel* needs to be computed for each receiver method invocation. In cases (1) and (4) the *rlevel* of the receiver method is the same as the *rlevel* of the sender method. In case (3), *rlevel* is the least upper bound of the *rlevel* of the sender method, and the classification of the receiver object. The purpose of *rlevel* is to implement the notion of restricted method invocations so as to prevent write-down violations. It is easy to see that if t_i is a method invocation in object o_i then $rlevel(t_i) \geq L(o_i)$. We say that a method invocation t_i has a *restricted status* if $rlevel(t_i) > L(o_i)$. When t_i is restricted, it can no longer update the state of the object o_i, it belongs to.

The message filtering algorithm presented above can be thought of as an abstract, non-executable, specification of the filtering functions. A close examination of the execution and implementation requirements for such a specification bring several issues to the forefront. In particular, dealing with the timing of replies to write-up messages (case 3 of the filtering algorithm) requires careful attention to potential downward signaling channels [14, 15, 16, 17]. Such channels are opened up if a low level sender method is resumed on the termination of the higher receiver method and receipt of the NIL reply. The solutions pursued in [15, 16, 17] have been to return instantaenous NIL replies and to execute

% let $g_1 = (h_1, (p_1, \ldots, p_k), r)$ be the message sent from object o_1 to object o_2 where

% h_1 is the message name, $p_1, \ldots, p_k$ are message parameters, r is the return value

if $o_1 \neq o_2 \lor h_1 \notin \{read, write, create\}$ then case
% i.e., g_1 is a non-primitive message

(1) $L(o_1) = L(o_2)$:   % let g_1 pass, let reply pass
                             invoke t_2 with $rlevel(t_2) \leftarrow rlevel(t_1)$;
                             $r \leftarrow$ reply from t_2; return r to t_1;

(2) $L(o_1) <> L(o_2)$:   % block g_1, inject NIL reply
                             $r \leftarrow$ NIL; return r to t_1;

(3) $L(o_1) < L(o_2)$:   % let g_1 pass, inject NIL reply, ignore actual reply
                             $r \leftarrow$ NIL; return r to t_1;
                             invoke t_2 with $rlevel(t_2) \leftarrow \text{lub}[L(o_2), rlevel(t_1)]$;
                             % where lub denotes least upper bound
                             discard reply from t_2;

(4) $L(o_1) > L(o_2)$:   % let g_1 pass, let reply pass
                             invoke t_2 with $rlevel(t_2) \leftarrow rlevel(t_1)$;
                             $r \leftarrow$ reply from t_2; return r to t_1;

end case;

if $o_1 = o_2 \land h_1 \in \{read, write, create\}$ then case
% i.e., g_1 is a primitive message
% let v_i be the value that is to be bound to attribute a_i

(5) $g_1 = (read, (a_j), r)$: % allow unconditionally
                             $r \leftarrow$ value of a_j; return r to t_1;

(6) $g_1 = (write, (a_j, v_j), r)$: % allow if status of t_1 is unrestricted
                             if $rlevel(t_1) = L(o_1)$
                                 then $[a_j \leftarrow v_j; r \leftarrow \text{SUCCESS}]$
                                 else $r \leftarrow$ FAILURE;
                             return r to t_1;

(7) $g_1 = (create, (v_1, \ldots, v_k, S_j), r)$: % allow if status of t_1 is unrestricted relative to S_j
                             if $rlevel(t_1) \leq S_j$
                                 then [CREATE i with values $v_1, \ldots, v_k$ and $L(i) \leftarrow S_j$; $r \leftarrow i$]
                                 else $r \leftarrow$ FAILURE;
                             return r to t_1;

end case;

Fig. 2. Message filtering algorithm

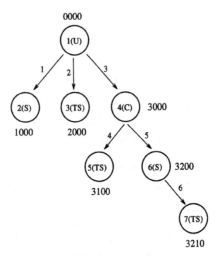

Fig. 3. A tree of concurrent computations with forkstamps

the methods (computations) in the sender and receiver objects concurrently on issuing write-up messages. Now if the application being modeled calls for synchronous message passing semantics, the challenge then is to synchronize the concurrent computations to achieve equivalence to a sequential (synchronous) execution. When such equivalence can be guaranteed, we say that the concurrent computations preserve *serial correctness*. If serial correctness cannot be guaranteed, the integrity of the database may be compromised. Lastly, it should be noted that the signaling channel threat does not exist in kernelized architectures. But it turns out that synchronous semantics are not implementable in such architectures as there exists no trusted subjects.[2] Hence concurrent computations are still the most efficient way to process write-up messages requiring synchronous semantics.

2.2 Concurrency, Scheduling and Serial Correctness

We now elaborate on concurrency and serial correctness in more general terms. We can visualize the set of concurrent computations issued by a user as belonging to a *user session* and forming a tree such as the one shown in figure 3. The label on the arrows indicate the order in which the messages and the associated computations (methods) would be processed in a serial (synchronous) execution. Note that this order can be derived by a depth-first traversal of the

---

[2] The term "trusted" is used often in the literature to convey one of two different notions of trust. In the first case, it conveys the fact that something is trusted to be correct. In the second case, we mean that some subject is exempted from mandatory confidentiality controls; in particular the simple-security and ∗-properties in the Bell-Lapadula framework. It is the latter sense of trust that we refer to in this paper.

tree. Serial correctness requires that a computation such as 3(TS) in the tree, see all the latest updates of lower level computations to its left, and no updates of lower level computations to its right. Thus 3(TS) should see the latest updates of 2(S) but not of 4(C) and 6(S). This is achieved with the help of a multi-version synchronization scheme that ensures that the versions of objects at levels C (confidential) and S (secret) that are available to 3(TS) are the ones that existed before 4(C) and 6(S) were created (forked). Further, serial correctness also mandates that a computation such as 3(TS) not get ahead of earlier forked ones to its left. Thus 3(TS) should not be started until 2(S) and its children (if any) have terminated.

If no system component has a global snapshot (such as that embedded in a tree) of the entire set of computations, then we need to explicitly capture the global serial order of messages and computations. This can be done by a scheme that assigns a unique forkstamp to each computation, as shown in figure 3. Starting with an initial forkstamp of 0000 for the root, every subsequent child of the root is given a forkstamp by progressively incrementing the most significant digit of this initial stamp by one. To generalize this for the entire tree, we require that with increasing levels, a less significant digit be incremented.

We can now succinctly state the requirements for serial correctness in terms of the following constraints that need to hold whenever a computation c is started at a level l:

- **Correctness-constraint 1:** There cannot exist any earlier forked computation (i.e. with a smaller forkstamp) at level l, that is pending execution;
- **Correctness-constraint 2:** All current non-ancestral as well as future executions of computations that have forkstamps smaller than that of c, would have to be at levels higher or incomparable to l;
- **Correctness-constraint 3:** At each level below l, the object versions read by c would have to be the latest ones created by computations such as k, that have the largest forkstamp that is still less than the forkstamp of c. If k is an ancestor of c, then the latest version given to c is the one that was created by k just before c was forked.

From the above discussion it should be clear that we need to enforce some discipline on concurrent computations as arbitrary concurrency makes synchronization difficult and could lead to the violation of serial correctness (thereby affecting the integrity of objects). A scheduling strategy which guarantees serial correctness and at the same time enforces some discipline on concurrency, must take into account the following considerations.

- The scheduling strategy itself must be secure in that it should not introduce any signaling channels.
- The amount of unnecessary delay a computation experiences before it is started should be reduced.

The first condition above requires that a low-level computation never be delayed waiting for the termination of another one at a higher or incomparable level. If this were allowed, a potential for a signaling channel is again opened up. The second consideration admits a family of scheduling strategies offering varying degrees of performance. Informally, we say a computation is unnecessarily delayed if it is denied immediate execution on being forked, for reasons other than the violation of serial correctness.

We now consider two scheduling strategies that appear to approach the ends of a spectrum of secure (and correct) scheduling strategies, and a third one that lies somewhere in the middle of such a spectrum. These schemes that lie at the ends of this spectrum are referred to as *conservative* and *aggressive* schemes, and they are governed by the following invariants, respectively.

Inv-conservative: *A computation is executing at a level l only if all computations at lower levels, and all computations with smaller fork stamps at level l, have terminated.*

Inv-aggressive: *A computation is executing at a level l only if all non-ancestor computations (in the corresponding computation tree) with smaller fork stamps at levels l or lower, have terminated.*

Given a lattice of security levels, the conservative scheme essentially reduces to executing computations on a level-by-level basis in forkstamp order, starting at the lowest level in the lattice. At any point, only computations at incomparable levels can be concurrently executing. However, with the aggressive scheme, we are not following a level-by-level approach. Rather, a forked computation is denied immediate execution only if (at the time of fork) there exists at least one non-ancestral lower level computation with an earlier (smaller) forkstamp, that has not terminated. If denied execution, such a computation is queued and later released for execution when this condition is no longer true (as a result of one or more terminations). Figures 4 and 5 illustrate the progressive execution of the tree of concurrent computations in figure 3 under the conservative and aggressive strategies, respectively. In each of these figures, the termination of one or more computations (indicated by shaded circles) advances the tree to the next stage. As can be seen in these figures, the tree progresses to termination fastest under the aggressive scheme, since it induces no unnecessary delays. We conjecture that there exists several other variations of the above three scheduling schemes. Finally, it is important to note that the security of these schemes stem from the fact a low level computation is never suspended (delayed) because of a higher one.

3   Message-filtering in the Replicated Architecture

When we consider the implementation of message filtering in the replicated architecture, the very nature of the architecture poses a different and unique set of problems. We have to deal with security and integrity aspects of processing data within a single container as well as multiple containers.

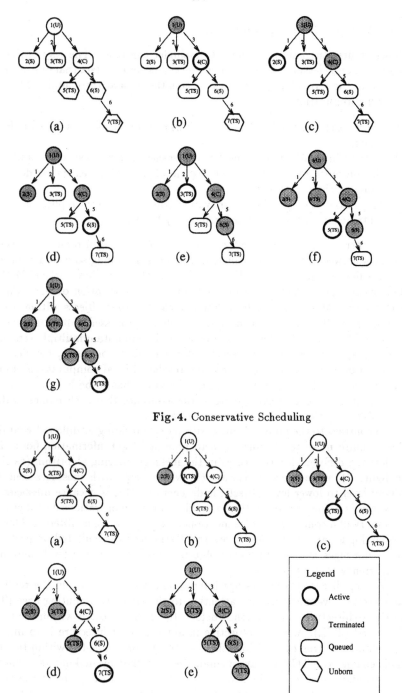

Fig. 4. Conservative Scheduling

Fig. 5. Aggressive Scheduling

3.1 Message-filtering Revisited

Consider first the issues pertinent to a singler container. The way objects are replicated and classified at the various containers, and the fact that only a subject cleared to the level of a container can access the data at the container, have the following implications:

1. There exists no need for message filtering between objects at a single container.
2. Method invocations resulting from messages sent between objects at a single container can be processed sequentially, as there exists no downward signaling channel threat.
3. There exists the need for integrity mechanisms to prevent replicas at a single container from being updated arbitrarily by subjects.

In other words, we do not enforce any message filtering or mandatory security controls between objects at a single container, since doing so would require access mediation mechanisms to be imported into the individual backend DBMS's. This clearly goes against the original spirit and motivation of the replicated architecture. Messages sent from low replicas to other objects within a single container result in method invocations which are processed sequentially according to RPC semantics. Hence there is no need to maintain multiple versions of objects. Also, covert channel threats do not exist, as only subjects cleared to the level of a container can observe the results of local computations. Finally, the lack of mandatory controls within a container has to be balanced with adequate integrity mechanisms giving us the assurance that such replicas will not be updated by the local subjects at a container.

In contrast to the above, dealing with objects residing at different containers does require message filtering so as to prevent illegal information flows. If we review the different filtering cases in the message filtering algorithm (as shown in figure 2), we now see that case (4) which deals with messages sent from higher level to lower level objects, is degenerate. This is because messages sent downwards in the security lattice to enable read-down operations do not cross the boundary of a container, and as mentioned before, involve no filtering. Messages sent to higher and incomparable levels will still need to be filtered. In particular, when messages are sent to higher objects (residing at higher level containers), concurrency may again arise.

Having discussed the message filtering and security issues in the replicated architecture, we now turn our attention to the trusted computing base (TCB) in the architecture. As mentioned before, the TCB is hosted within the trusted front end (TFE). A design objective in any secure architecture is to minimize the number of trusted functions that need to be implemented within the TCB. This enables the TCB to have a small size, and thereby making its verification and validation easier. In light of this, is it possible to implement the various coordination and replica control algorithms while keeping the size of the TCB small? In later sections, we present replica control and coordination schemes that require minimal functionality from the TCB. To be more precise, the role of the

TCB reduces basically to that of a router of messages from lower level to higher containers. In particular, the TCB requires no trusted (multilevel) subjects or data structures. All scheduling and coordination is achieved through single-level subjects at the backend databases. In other words, this portion of the front-end TCB could be implemented using a kernelized architecture.

3.2 Serial Correctness and Replica Control

Recall from our previous discussion that sending messages between objects at a single container involves no message filtering, while sending messages to objects across containers does call for filtering. When filtering is involved concurrency is once again inevitable and we have to ensure that the concurrent computations executing across the various containers preserve serial correctness. We now investigate the interplay between serial correctness, the various scheduling algorithms, and replica control.

We had earlier presented three constraints as sufficient conditions to guarantee serial correctness of concurrent computations. Correctness constraints 1 and 2 are required to govern the scheduling of concurrent computations while the third constraint governs how versions should be assigned to process read-down requests. Constraints 1 and 2 would now have to be interpreted for computations executing across containers. For example, when a computation c is started at a level l (container C_l), constraint 2 would now read: *All current non-ancestral as well as future executions of computations that have forktamps smaller than that of c, would have to be at containers for level l or higher.* Also, the fact that there are no trusted subjects in our implementation means that there will no central coordination of the computations executing across the various containers. Hence the implementation of the various scheduling algorithms would have to be inherently distributed. Finally, correctness-constraint 3 also has to reinterpreted for the replicated architecture as we no longer maintain versions of objects. The original requirement that a computation c reading down obtain the versions of lower level objects consistent with a sequential execution, now maps to the requirement that the various updates (also called update projections in the literature) producing these different versions be shipped and applied to $c's$ container before it starts executing. This last constraint thus has a direct implication on the replica control schemes that would be utilized for the architecture.

In order to reason about update projections and their effect on serial correctness, we introduce the notion of *r-transactions*. This is done only for ease of exposition. Our solutions do not impose or mandate any particular model of transactions. Transactions allow us to conveniently group sequences of updates, and in particular those that need to be incrementally propagated to higher containers. We use the prefix "r" which stands for "replicated", to distinguish this notion of transactions from others in the literature. We drop the prefix when it is clear from the context that we are referring to r-transactions.

In the object model of computing, every message in is received at an object and results in the invocation of a method defined in that object. We refer to such an object as the home object of the method. The subsequent activity (reads and updates) within the boundary of a home object can be modeled as belonging to a r-transaction. Every message in a message chain can be mapped to a corresponding transaction. This leads to a hierarchical (tree) model of transactions for a user session. We consider the root message as starting a root transaction. The root transaction in turn issues other transactions which we see as its descendants in the tree. Figure 6 illustrates the transaction tree for a computation tree.

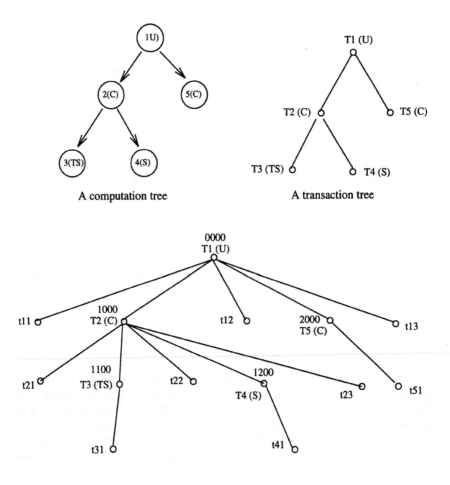

A computation tree

A transaction tree

The corresponding subtransaction tree

Fig. 6. A transaction tree and its subtransaction mapping

A depth-first (left-to-right) traversal of a transaction tree starting with the root transaction, will give the sequence in which the transactions are issued and started within a user session. To illustrate how serial correctness is to be maintained within a session and in the context of the replicated architecture, we need to zoom in and take a magnified look at the transaction tree. This is because a transaction may make its partial results visible to other transactions at different containers. Consider any subtree in figure 6 such as the one rooted at transaction T_2. A child of T_2, such as T_3, is allowed to see (read down) only part of the updates made by T_2. To be more precise, it is only those updates made by T_2 up to the point T_3 was issued. The second child T_4 will be allowed to see all the updates seen by T_6, and in addition those made by T_2 between the interval that T_3 and T_4 were issued.

To model and visualize partial visibilities within transaction boundaries, we introduce *r-subtransactions* as finer units of transactions. The second and larger tree in figure 6 illustrates a subtransaction tree derived from the original transaction tree. A transaction such as T_2 is now chopped up into three subtransactions $t_{2,1}$, $t_{2,2}$, $t_{2,3}$. The subtransaction $t_{2,1}$ represents all the updates by T_2 until transaction T_3 was issued. Subtransaction $t_{2,2}$ similarly represents the updates between the interval that transactions T_3 and T_4 were issued. Finally, the subtransaction $t_{2,3}$ accounts for all the remaining activity in T_2 before it committed. A subtransaction is seen as having a relatively short lifetime, and is required to commit before any sibling subtransactions to the right, or child transactions (and implicitly subtransactions) are started. The operations issued by a subtransaction are said to be *atomic operations*. Such operations never cross the boundary of their relevant home object and cannot lead to the sending of further messages (or the issuing of transactions) to other objects. Serial correctness requires that an individual transaction, such as T_4 see all the updates of all subtransactions below its level that will be encountered in a depth-first search of the subtransaction tree starting with the root and ending in T_4. Thus for T_4 this will include subtransactions $t_{1,1}$, $t_{2,1}$, and $t_{2,2}$. The updates of all these subtransactions except $t_{2,2}$ would have to be seen by the left sibling of T_4, which is transaction T_3, and thus would have already been applied logically at the relevant containers before T_4 was issued.

We formally define these and other notions below:

Definition 1. We consider a *subtransaction* to be a totally ordered set of atomic operations. We define a *transaction* T_i to be a partial order $(s_i, <_{T_i})$ such that:

1. s_i is a set of operations, and each operation may be a subtransaction or another transaction $T_j = (s_j, <_{T_j})$.
2. The relation $<_{T_i}$ orders at least all conflicting atomic operations in s_i.

Definition 2. We define the *replica-set* of a transaction T_j at level j to be the set of updates of subtransactions at or below level j that will be seen by T_j in a sequential execution (or depth-first search) of the tree.

Definition 3. We define the *propagation-list* of a transaction T_j to be those updates in the replica-set of T_j that have not been seen by T_i, where T_i was the last transaction that was issued before T_j in a sequential execution. These updates are those made by subtransactions at levels lower than j, and to the right of T_i and to the left of T_j (in the subtransaction tree).

In figure 6, the replica-set of transaction T_4 will consist of the updates issued by subtransactions $t_{1,1}$, $t_{2,1}$, and $t_{2,2}$. The propagation-list of T_4 will consist of the updates issued by subtransaction $t_{2,2}$.

Now in the replicated architecture, the transactions in a subtransaction tree execute across containers. Whenever an object in a low container issues a write-up request, a message will be sent upwards in the lattice, and routed by the TFE to the appropriate high level container. Such a message will be received by an object in the higher level container and eventually result in the invocation of a method. Before this method can be invoked (i.e., before the corresponding transaction can be started), we need to do the following:

1. Determine if it is safe to begin execution of the transaction;
2. Make sure that the propagation-list of the transaction has been applied at the local container.

The first consideration above arises from the fact that the transactions (methods) generated by a session execute across the various containers in a distributed fashion, and this may lead to transactions at higher containers starting prematurely (when compared to centralized sequential execution). We thus require the start-up of transactions to be governed by some invariant. Once a transaction is allowed to start (i.e., doing so would not violate the invariant), the replica control scheme should ensure that the relevant propagation-list (set of update projections) is applied at the local container of the transaction.

Before concluding our discussion on serial correctness and replica control, we note that in the replicated architecture serial correctness alone is insufficient to guarantee the mutual consistency of replicated data. This is because serial correctness can be guaranteed by shipping update projections only to the containers which have forked transactions for a session. In other words, if a transaction was not forked for a level, the replicas at the container for the level could be out-of-date, and we would still not violate serial correctness. The scheduling algorithms that we present in the next section not only guarantee serial correctness, but in addition ensure that when a session terminates, all containers will be mutually consistent. When such consistency is guaranteed, we say that the algorithms preserve the *final-state equivalence* of all the containers.

4 Intra-session Scheduling

In this section we discuss how we can combine replica control to ensure final-state equivalence with scheduling strategies. As in the kernelized architecture, the conservative scheme involves less complexity and is thus easier to implement. Due to the lack of space we discuss only the aggressive scheduling scheme. We begin by clarifying some aspects related to the execution and failure semantics of transactions, as well as some of the necessary data structures to be maintained by individual containers.

A r-transaction, as described here, is characterized by the property of failure atomicity. Hence if any of the subtransactions of a transactions fails or aborts, we have to abort the entire corresponding transaction. This would also require that we undo the effects of any committed earlier subtransactions. To avoid this, and still guarantee failure atomicity, we allow a transaction to commit only if all its subtransactions commit. The updates of committed subtransactions are made permanent in the database only when the parent transaction commits. Also, we take the commit of the root transaction to imply that the entire session has committed.

To implement our scheduling strategies and replica control schemes, every container C_j at level j maintains the following data structures for an active user session:

Activation-queue$_j$:   this is a priority queue of transactions that is maintained according to the forkstamp;

Projection-queue$_j$:   a queue which stores update projections (propagation-lists) by their forkstamps;

Transaction-history$_i$: this is a list maintained for each level $i < j$, and maintains for every transaction forked from level i, its id, forkstamp, status and other information.

When transactions start issuing other transactions at higher levels, the relevant propagation-lists (update projections) are incrementally shipped to higher containers and stored in their projection queues. When a scheduling scheme calls for a transaction to be started, it is dequeued from the local activation queue and the relevant update projections are applied to the container just before transaction starts.

4.1 Implementing Aggressive Scheduling

We now briefly discuss the implementation of the aggressive scheduling scheme. A transaction history (listed above) is required to be maintained at every container and keeps track of the forked transactions at dominated levels. It is important to note that this history itself is a replicated data structure and snapshot. The need for the maintenance of this history arises from the fact that a container cannot read-down information at lower level containers. Recall that the front-end in the replicated architecture sends messages only in an upwards direction in the lattice. Hence the relevant information has to be gathered with the help of snapshots maintained by constantly sending messages upwards in the lattice. It is the sending of such messages and the maintenance of snapshots such as transaction histories that add to the complexity of implementing the aggressive scheduling scheme.

The aggressive scheduling algorithm is governed by the following invariant: **Inv-aggressive-replicated:** *A transaction is executing at a container at level l only if all non-ancestor transactions (in the corresponding transaction tree) with smaller fork stamps at containers for levels l or lower, have terminated.*

The description of the scheduling algorithms is similar to that of the kernelized architecture [17], with the difference that we now have to post update projections at the right time to the appropriate containers. A container always looks at its transaction histories for dominated levels to see if the start-up of the next transaction would violate the above invariant. The detailed algorithms are presented in figures 7,8,11, and 12. In these algorithms % is a delimiter for comments.

When a write-up message is issued and a transaction is forked at a level, the transaction-history at this level is updated (see the fork procedure in figure 7). We then check to see if the update projections from the parent issuing the write-up can be applied to the local container and also if the forked transaction can be allowed to start. If doing so would violate serial correctness, the update projections are queued in the local projection-queue and the forked transaction is queued in the local activation-queue. A queued transaction is later started or "woken up" by the termination of a running transaction. When a transaction terminates (see figure 9), its updates are posted to the local as well as higher containers. If serial correctness is not violated, relevant update projections from the projection-queue may also be applied to the local container. We then check to see if transactions at the local and higher containers can be started as a result of this most recent termination. To release or start queued transactions at higher levels, a WAKE-UP message is sent to the higher level containers through the trusted front end (TFE). It is important to note that a WAKE-UP message is sent to higher containers only if there exists queued transactions and their release would not violate serial correctness and the invariant. As such when a container receives a WAKE-UP message from a lower level, it knows that its activation queue is not empty and proceeds unconditionally to start the next transaction at the head of the activation queue (see procedure for WAKE-UP processing in figure 8). Before a transaction is actually started, the projection queue is examined and all entries with a forkstamp less than that of the transaction are emptied and applied to the local container (as shown in figure 10).

Proofs

For brevity, we omit the proofs to demonstrate that that our algorithms preserve serial correctness. The arguments are similar to those made for the aggressive scheme under the kernelized architecture [17]. However, the requirement for these algorithms to preserve final-state equivalence is unique to this architecture. We state and prove this as a theorem.

Theorem 4. *The aggressive scheme preserves final-state-equivalence.*

Proof:
By induction on the number of possible terminations, n, in a session.
Basis: Consider the basis with $n = 1$. In this case we have only one termination, that of the root transaction. The procedure **term-rep-agg** in figure 9 processes terminate requests, and calls for the update projection of the root transaction

```
Procedure fork-rep-agg(level-parent, level-create, forkstamp, update-projection)
{
%Let level-create be the level of the local transaction and container
Create a new transaction tt at level-create with identifier id;

%Initialize variables for tt
       tt.id ← id;
       tt.level-parent ← level-parent;
       tt.level-create ← level-create;
       tt.forkstamp ← forkstamp;
       tt.status ← 'non-terminated';

%Update local transaction history
append(transaction-history_{level−parent} , tt);

%See if the update projection from the parent can be applied at the local container and
%if tt can be started immediately
If ∀ l ≤ level-create, ¬∃ any transaction c ∈ transaction-history_l :
       (c.level-create ≤ level-create ∧ c.forkstamp < tt.forkstamp
       ∧ c.status = 'non-terminated')
       then
          apply update-projection to local container;
          start-rep(tt);
       else
          %This is a priority queue maintained in forkstamp order
          enqueue(projection-queue, update-projection, forkstamp);
          %This is also a priority queue of transactions waiting to be activated
          enqueue(activation-queue, tt);
end-if
}
end procedure fork-rep-agg;
```

Fig. 7. Processing **fork** requests under aggressive scheduling

```
Procedure wake-up-rep-agg
{
%Let tt be the transaction at the head of the local activation-queue
dequeue(activation-queue, tt);
start-rep(tt);
}
end procedure wake-up-rep-agg;
```

Fig. 8. Processing **wake-up** requests under aggressive scheduling

---

Procedure term-rep-agg(level-term, last-update, term-forkstamp, last-forkstamp)
{
%*Record the termination of transaction tt at level-term*
For each level l < level-term **do**
  If (*pp* ∈ transaction-history$_l$ ∧ pp.forkstamp = tt.forkstamp)
    then *tt*.status ← 'terminated'; **End-If End-For**

%*Update local container with the last set of updates issued by tt*
apply the updates in last-update to local container;
%*Post these updates to higher levels*
term-flag ← 'true';
For each level > level-term **do**
  post-update-rep-agg(level, last-update, increment(last-forkstamp), term-flag, tt);
End-For

%*See if the update projections for last-updates from lower levels can be applied*
quit-flag ← 'false';
For all levels l ≤ level-term **do**
  If ∃ any transaction q ∈ transaction-history$_l$:(q.status = 'not-terminated' ∧
  q.level-create ≤ level-term) **then** quit-flag ← 'true';**exit for**;**end-If**; **end-For**;

If quit-flag = 'false' **then**
  Repeat
    dequeue (projection-queue, update-projection);
    apply update-projection to local container;
  Until projection-queue = empty; **exit procedure**; **End-If**

%*Check if a queued transaction at level level-term can be started*
%*Let mm be the transaction at the head of the activation queue*
If the activation-queue is not empty
then If ∀ l, l ≤ level-term, ¬∃ any transaction c ∈ transaction-history$_l$:
    (c.forkstamp < *mm*.forkstamp ∧ c.status = 'not-terminated')
    then dequeue(activation-queue, *mm*); start-rep(*mm*); **End-If End-If**

%*Check if a transaction at levels ≥ level-term can be started*
For all levels l ≤ level-term **do**
  If ∃ a transaction c ∈ transaction-history$_l$ with c.level-create > level-term ∧
  c.forkstamp > tt.forkstamp: ¬∃ any non-ancestor transaction k
  with (level(k) ≤ level(c) ∧ k.forkstamp < c.forkstamp ∧
  transaction-history$_{level(k)}$.k.status = 'not-terminated')
  % *We checked to see if c was not preceded by a lower-level active or queued*
  % *non-ancestor transaction in any of the transaction-histories searched*
  then Send a WAKE-UP message to the container at level(c); **End-If End-For**
} **end procedure** term-rep-agg;

Fig. 9. Processing **terminate** requests under aggressive scheduling

```
Procedure start-rep(tt)
{
%Let tt be the transaction to be started
counter ← 1;
Repeat
%Treat the projection-queue at the level of tt as a list and examine it
element-wise
    Read (projection-queue[counter], pp);
    If pp.forkstamp ≤ tt.forkstamp
      then
        apply pp to local container;
        delete (projection-queue, pp);
    End-If
    counter ← counter + 1;
Until counter = length-of(projection-queue);

%Begin executing tt
execute(tt);
}
end procedure start-rep;
```

Fig. 10. Updating the local container before starting a transaction

```
Procedure post-update-rep-agg(local-level, update-projection, forkstamp,
term-flag, tt)
{
%See if the posted update can be applied
If ∀ l ≤ local-level, ¬∃ any transaction c ∈ transaction-history_l:
    (c.level-create ≤ local-level ∧ c.forkstamp ≤ tt.forkstamp
    ∧ c.status = 'non-terminated')
    then
        apply update-projection to local container;
    else
        %This is a priority queue maintained in forkstamp order
        enqueue(projection-queue, update-projection, forkstamp);
end-if

If term-flag = 'true'
then %Record the termination of transaction tt
transaction-history_{tt.level-parent}.tt.status ← 'terminated';
end-if
}
end procedure post-update-rep-agg;
```

Fig. 11. Processing posted updates

Procedure record-new-transaction(*transaction, level-parent*)

{

% Update local transaction history for level level-parent

append(transaction-history$_{level-parent}$, transaction);

}

end procedure record-transaction;

Fig. 12. Recording the fork of computations at lower levels

to be posted to the local container as well as all higher containers. Each higher container, on receiving the projection, will find that there are no lower level transactions with smaller forkstamps than the terminated root, and apply the update projection from its queue. Each higher container will thus be brought up-to-date with the updates of the root transaction and thus preserving final-state equivalence.

Induction Step: For the induction hypothesis, assume that when n is equal to m, final-state equivalence is guaranteed. For the induction step, let $n = m + 1$. In other words, there are $m + 1$ possible terminations, and given that the first m terminations preserve final-state equivalence, we have to show that the $m + 1^{th}$ termination preserves final-state equivalence. Consider the transaction t_{m+1} at container C_{m+1} that causes the $m+1^{th}$ termination. By the induction hypothesis, we are guaranteed that C_{m+1} will receive all update projections from dominated containers. Some of these projections would be applied to the contents of C_{m+1} as soon as they are received, while others will be queued in the projection queue (as shown in procedure **post-update-rep-agg** of figure 11). When t_{m+1} starts, all the queued update projections originating from lower level transactions with smaller forkstamps than t_{m+1} would also be applied to C_{m+1}. Finally when t_{m+1} terminates all remaining update projections will be emptied and applied to C_{m+1} along with its last-updates. This guarantees the mutual consistency of container C_{m+1} will all lower level containers. It now remains to show that mutual consistency is preserved with containers higher than C_{m+1}. This follows from the fact when t_{m+1} terminates, all its update projection would be sent to all higher containers where they would be subsequently applied. Thus final-state equivalence is preserved across all $m + 1$ terminations, and this concludes the proof. □

5   Inter-session Synchronization

Having discussed various intra-scheduling schemes, we now turn our attention to inter-session concurrency control in the the replicated architecture. We do not address the issue of concurrency control between sessions at a single container, rather focus on multiple containers. Every container is assumed to provide some local concurrency control.

We assume the following:

- Every container C_j at level j, uses some local concurrency control scheme L_j.
- All containers share a system-low real-time clock. This is a reasonable assumption since the replicated architecture is not for a distributed system, but rather to be implemented on a single (central) machine. The value read from this clock is used to maintain a global serial order for sessions and transactions.

We discuss three approaches to inter-session synchronization and concurrency control that provide increasing degrees of concurrency across user sessions. To elaborate, consider the four sessions S_a, S_b, S_c, and S_d as shown in figure 13(a). Sessions S_a and S_b originate at container C_U at level U, while S_c and S_d originate at containers C_C and C_S at levels C and S respectively. The different transactions generated by these sessions are shown in the figure. For example, session S_a generates transactions T_{a1} at level U, T_{a2} at level C, and T_{a3} at level S. Figures 13 (a), 13 (b), and 13 (c) depict the histories that could be generated by the three inter-session schemes, at the various containers.

In the first scheme, sessions are serialized in a global order that is equivalent to the serialization events of the sessions. If L_j is based on two phase locking, we can use the lock point, which is the last lock step of the root transaction of the session, as its serialization event. If the local concurrency control scheme, L_j is based on timestamping, the timestamp assigned to S_j or the root transaction can be used for the serialization event. In the second approach, this serial order can be successively redefined to interleave incoming newer sessions without affecting the mutual consistency or correctness of the replicas and updates. In the third approach we relax the serial order for the sessions, and instead serialize transactions on a level-by-level basis.

Protocol 1: Globally serial sessions

When a session S_j starts at a container j (i.e., the root transaction executes C_j), the following protocol is observed:

1. S_j makes its resource requests to the local concurrency controller, and its transactions compete with other local sessions that start at C_j.
2. When S_j reaches its serialization event as governed by L_j, the real-time clock is read and its value used to form a *serial-stamp* for S_j.
3. The serial-stamp of S_j is broadcast to all higher level containers.
4. When S_j commits, a *commit-session* message is broadcast to all higher containers. This message may be piggy-backed with the *commit-transaction* message from the root transaction of S_j.

On receiving the serial-stamp from a container at a lower level, a container, C_k at level k, observes the following rules:

5. All local sessions originating at C_k, and having a smaller serial-stamp than that of S_j, are allowed to commit according to their serial-stamps, and subsequently propagate their updates to containers at levels higher than k.

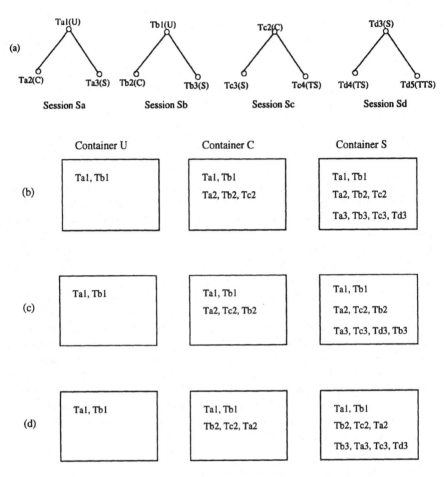

Fig. 13. Illustrating histories with various inter-session synchronization schemes

6. The updates and transactions of S_j are allowed to proceed.
7. All local sessions at C_k having a greater serial-stamp than S_j are allowed to commit only after the *commit-session* notification of S_j is received, and its updates applied as in step 2 above, to C_k.

Several optimizations and variations on the above protocol are possible. It is obvious that the protocol provides minimum concurrency between sessions. In particular, the scheme offers very poor performance if transactions are of long durations. To elaborate, consider what happens if session S_b has sent its serial-stamp to container C but does not commit for a long time. If timestamping is used for the serialization events of sessions at container C, a local session S_c starting at container C_C after the serial-stamp of S_a has been received, will be assigned a greater serial-stamp. Hence, S_c will not be allowed to commit until

S_b sends its *commit-transaction* message. The decrease in such concurrency is directly proportional to the size of the window between the serialization and commit events of session S_b.

We can easily improve the performance of the above scheme if S_c were allowed to go ahead and commit even if the *commit-session* message has not been received from S_b. This is possible if S_b has not updated the container C_C at level C so far. We can then re-assign to S_c an earlier serial-stamp than that of S_b. Figure 13(b) shows a possible history at the various containers with protocol 1, and figure 13(c) shows how the updates of session S_c can be placed ahead of S_b at container C by giving S_c an earlier serial-stamp than S_b. It is important to note that the relative order between the sessions S_a and S_b is still maintained, but only that S_c is now allowed to come between them. This idea is summarized in protocol 2 below.

Protocol 2: Globally serial sessions with successively redefinable serial-orders

Steps 1 through 6 of Protocol 1 still apply to Protocol 2, but step 7 is modified as below.

When a container C_k receives the serial-stamp from a session S_j at a lower container C_j, the following rules are followed:

7'. If there exists a session S_k that has the smallest serial-stamp among the sessions at C_k that have reached their serialization events but not yet committed, and such that S_k has a serial-stamp greater than S_j, then do:

    (a) If session S_j has not yet updated C_k, then reassign a serial-stamp to S_k that is smaller than the stamp of S_j.

    (b) Broadcast this new serial-stamp to all higher containers.

    (c) Allow S_k to update C_k and propagate its updates to higher containers.

The ability of protocols 1 and 2 above, to ensure the mutual consistency of the replicas at the various containers, can be attributed to the way updates are processed. To be more specific, the updates represented in the propagation-lists sent by various sessions, are processed at every container in strict serial-stamp order. A single serial-stamp is associated with the entire set of transactions (updates) that belong to a session.[3] In other words, a session is the basic unit of concurrency for interleaving updates from multiple sessions. To put it another way, the histories of the updates generated by protocols 1 and 2, guarantee that the individual transactions of two sessions, where each session starts at a different container, cannot be interleaved with each other in any of these histories.

---

[3] We assume that such associations are kept in some data structure. We also assume that a transaction such as T_{c2} in figure 13(c), running at the container C_C, cannot update the local replicas of data stored at the lower container C_U. Protocols 1 and 2 can guarantee mutual consistency only to the extent that integrity safeguards are available to prevent such events.

A further improvement to protocol 2 and protocol 1 which we might call protocol 3, can be achieved if the global serial order that is maintained for sessions, is relaxed. Transactions are now serialized in some order on a level-by-level basis. This allows us to exploit more fine-grained concurrency within the structure of a session. The unit of concurrency now is no longer a session, but rather of finer granularity, and thus a transaction. Of course, the key here is exploit such fine-grained concurrency without compromising the mutual consistency of the replicas. The intuition behind this approach is illustrated in figure 13(d). Thus we see that the transactions at level U, namely $T_{a,1}$ and $T_{b,1}$ are serialized in the same order at all the containers. However, transactions at level C, namely $T_{a,2}$, $T_{c,2}$, $T_{b,2}$ are serialized in a different order. In particular, the updates from session S_b now come before sessions S_a and S_c. Protocol 2 can easily be modified so that the updates at each level are serialized independently, and made known to the higher containers. Unlike protocols 1 and 2, level-initiator transactions now have to compete with other transactions at the various containers to access data. When an individual transaction reaches it serialization event, the real-time clock is read to form a transaction-serial-stamp, which is subsequently broadcast to higher containers. Mutual consistency of the replicas is achieved by ensuring that updates in the propagation-lists are applied in strict transaction-serial-stamp order.

We now briefly discuss the correctness of the above protocols. Space constraints prevent us from giving a full-blown formal proof here. A well known correctness criterion for replicated data is *one-copy serializability* [2]. Protocols 1 and 2 guarantee what one might call *one-copy* **session** *serializability*. This gives the illusion that the sessions originating at the different containers execute serially on a one-copy, non-replicated, database. The interactions between transactions as governed by one-copy session serializability is much more restrictive in terms of concurrency and interleaving than one-copy serializability, but implicitly guarantees the latter. The final variation, ie., protocol 3, is less restrictive than the other two protocols and does not guarantee one-copy session serializability, but instead maintains one-copy serializability.

6 Summary and Conclusions

In this paper, we have addressed the issue of replica control for object-oriented databases. The elaboration of the message filter model for the replicated architecture required that we handle replica control for updates and computations generated within a session, as well as synchronization for multiple user sessions. Collectively, object-orientation and the support of write-up actions have impacted the solutions presented in this paper. These solutions thus differ from others presented for the replicated architecture within the context of traditional (relational) database systems.

The solutions presented here increase the commercial viability of the replicated architecture as well as object-oriented databases, for applications and environments that require multilevel security. The approach taken here requires minimum functionality from the TCB (that is hosted within the TFE) and more significantly, requires no multilevel (trusted) subjects. The potential for covert channels to be exploited within the TFE is thus eliminated.

There exists several avenues for future work. Inter-session synchronization and concurrency control warrant further investigation. In particular, it would be interesting to look at type-specific and semantic concurrency control across user sessions in the multilevel context. We would also like to investigate if it is possible to maintain atomicity of an entire session without violating confidentiality? That is, all of the component transactions in a session commit or abort without any impact on security (confidentiality). As observed by Mathur and Keefe in [10], atomicity and security seem to be conflicting requirements. If a session has component transactions at many levels, we cannot guarantee atomicity without introducing covert channels. At best we can only hope to reduce the bandwidth of such channels. Perhaps the approach would be to build a model that support write-up actions and at the same time minimizes such channels.

References

1. P. Ammann and S. Jajodia. Planar lattice security structures for multi-level replicated databases. *Proc. of the Seventh IFIP 11.3 Workshop on Database Security*, Vancouver, Huntsville, Alabama, September 1993.
2. P.A. Bernstein, V. Hadzilacos, and N. Goodman. *Concurrency Control and Recovery in Database Systems*, Addison-Wesley Publ. Co., Inc., Reading, MA, 1987.
3. B. Blaustein, S. Jajodia, C.D. McCollum, and L. Notargiacomo. A model of atomicity for multilevel transactions. *Proc. of the 1993 IEEE Symposium on Security and Privacy*, pp. 120–134, May 1993.
4. O. Costich. Transaction processing using an untrusted scheduler in a multilevel database with replicated architecture, *Database Security V, Status and Prospects*, C.E Landwehr and S. Jajodia (Editors), Elsevier Science Publishers B.V. (North-Holland), Amsterdam, 1992.
5. O. Costich and J. McDermott. A multilevel transaction problem for multilevel secure database systems and its solution for the replicated architecture. *Proc. of the 1992 IEEE Symposium on Security and Privacy*, pp. 192–203, May 1992.
6. S. Jajodia and B. Kogan. Integrating an object-oriented data model with multilevel security. *Proc. of the 1990 IEEE Symposium on Security and Privacy*, pp. 76–85, May 1990.
7. Sushil Jajodia and Boris Kogan, "Transaction processing in multilevel-secure databases using replicated architecture." *Proc. IEEE Symposium on Security and Privacy*, Oakland, California, May 1990, pages 360–368.
8. T.F. Keefe and W.T. Tsai. Prototyping the SODA security model. *Proc. 3rd IFIP WG 11.3 Workshop on Database Security*, September 1989.
9. T.F. Keefe, W.T. Tsai, and M.B. Thuraisingham. A multilevel security model for object-oriented systems. *Proc. 11th National Computer Security Conference*, pp. 1–9, October 1988.
10. A.G. Mathur and T.F. Keefe. The concurrency control and recovery problem for multilevel update transactions in MLS systems. *To appear in the Proc. of the Computer Security Foundations Workshop*, Franconia, New Hampshire, 1993.

11. J. McDermott, S. Jajodia, and R. Sandhu. A single-level scheduler for the replicated architecture for multilevel-secure databases. *Proc. of the Seventh Annual Computer Security Applications Conference*, San Antonio, TX, 1991.

12. J.K. Millen and T.F. Lunt. Security for object-oriented database systems. In *Proc. of the 1992 IEEE Symposium on Security and Privacy*, pp 260-272, May 1992.

13. M. Morgenstern A security model for multilevel objects with bidirectional relationships. *Database Security IV, Status and Prospects*, S. Jajodia and C.E Landwehr (Editors), Elsevier Science Publishers B.V. (North-Holland)

14. R.S. Sandhu, R. Thomas, and S. Jajodia. A Secure Kernelized Architecture for Multilevel Object-Oriented Databases. *Proc. of the IEEE Computer Security Foundations Workshop IV*, pp. 139-152, June 1991.

15. R.S. Sandhu, R. Thomas, and S. Jajodia. Supporting timing-channel free computations in multilevel secure object-oriented databases. *Proc. of the IFIP 11.3 Workshop on Database Security*, Sheperdstown, West Virginia, November 1991.

16. R.K. Thomas and R.S. Sandhu. Implementing the message filter object-oriented security model without trusted subjects. *Proc. of the IFIP 11.3 Workshop on Database Security*, Vancouver, Canada, August 1992.

17. R.K. Thomas and R.S. Sandhu. A Kernelized Architecture for Multilevel Secure Object-oriented Databases Supporting Write-up. *Journal of Computer Security*, Volume 2, No. 3, IOS Press, Netherlands, 1994.

18. M.B. Thuraisingham. A multilevel secure object-oriented data model. *Proc. 12th National Computer Security Conference*, pp. 579–590, October 1989.

19. Multilevel data management security. Committee on Multilevel Data Management Security, Air Force Studies Board, National Research Council, Washington, D.C., 1983.

Database II

Database II

Aggregation in Relational Databases: Controlled Disclosure of Sensitive Information

Amihai Motro, Donald G. Marks, and Sushil Jajodia

Department of Information and Software Systems Engineering
George Mason University
Fairfax, VA 22030-4444

Abstract. It has been observed that often the release of a limited part of an information resource poses no security risks, but the relase of a sufficiently large part of that resource might pose such risks. This problem of controlled disclosure of sensitive information is an example of what is known as the *aggregation* problem. In this paper we argue that it should be possible to articulate specific secrets within a database that should be protected against overdisclosure, and we provide a general framework in which such controlled disclosure can be achieved. Our methods foil any attempt to attack these predefined secrets by disguising queries as queries whose definitions do not resemble secrets, but whose answers nevertheless "nibble" at secrets. Our methods also foil attempts to attack secrets by breaking queries into sequences of smaller requests that extract information less conspicuously. The accounting methods we employ to thwart such attempts are shown to be both accurate and economical.

1 Introduction

The most common approach to secrets is to specify the information that must be protected, and to devise mechanisms that forbid disclosure of *any* of this information to unauthorized users. In the environment of relational databases, secret information is often defined via *views*. Models for *multi-level security* are used to classify both users and information according to a variety of secrecy levels, and *authorization* algorithms ensure that classified information is made available only to users with the appropriate classification [1].

However, it has been observed that often the release of a *limited* part of an information resource poses no security risks, but the relase of a sufficiently large part of that resource might pose such risks. In the environment of relational databases, this implies that the release of a limited number of tuples would be permitted, but once this number exceeds a predetermined threshold, security might be breached. This problem of controlled disclosure of sensitive information is an example of what is known as the *aggregation* problem [5, 3, 6, 7, 2, 4].

The work of Motro was supported in part by NSF Grant No. IRI-9007106 and by ARPA grant, administered by the Office of Naval Research under Grant No. N0014-92-J-4038. The work of Jajodia was supported in part by NSF Grant No. IRI-9303416.

A typical example is that of the Secret Government Agency (SGA) Phonebook. In this example, the entire phonebook is a classified document that is not available without the appropriate clearance; yet, individual phonebook entries are available to inquiring callers. In theory this may appear to be contradictory, because with a sufficient number of queries it should be possible to extract all the information in the phonebook. In practice, however, these queries are handled by operators who can recognize repetitive querying; also, the low bandwidth of these extractions serve to protect the phonebook from substantial disclosures. A small example of such a phonebook is shown in Fig. 1.

Name	Tel	Div	Mail	Bldg	Room
A. Long	x1234	A	m404	1	307
P. Smith	x1111	B	m303	2	610
E. Brown	x2345	B	m101	3	455
C. Jones	x1234	A	m202	1	307
M. Johnson	x1234	B	m101	3	103
B. Stevenson	x2222	A	m202	1	305
S. Quinn	x2222	C	m606	3	101
R. Helmick	x1234	A	m404	1	307
A. Facey	x1122	C	m505	2	400
S. Sheets	x2345	B	m101	3	103

Fig. 1. The Phonebook Example

An approach for preventing overdisclosure of such a database is to *monitor* the number of database tuples that are being given away [2]; in this example, where the total number of tuples is 10, it could be determined that only 3 tuples should be disclosed to the same user.

Yet, it is conceivable that we would be willing to disclose an *unlimited* number of telephone numbers, but only a limited number of division affiliations (say, because these affiliations disclose the amount of effort devoted to particular projects). Similarly, we might be willing to disclose any number of telephone numbers, but limit the disclosure of telephone numbers of employees in division A (because we would like to prevent users from estimating the size of this division). In other words, rather than protect the entire database from overdisclosure, we argue that it should be possible to articulate those specific aggregates that are sensitive, and protect only these aggregates from overdisclosure.

In this paper we describe a scheme for aggregation control that provides this flexibility. Our scheme uses general *views* to define the secrets that can be disclosed to a limited degree, and associates a threshold value with each such view. We shall refer to these views as *sensitive concepts* (or simply *concepts*). Clearly, if a view is defined to be a concept, then any view that incorporates this concept (a "larger" concept) should be protected as well.

This approach allows to define a variety of sensitive concepts. For example, with the database of Fig. 1:

1. To limit the disclosure of the total number of employees to five, the concept π_{Name} is assigned the threshold 5.
2. To prevent disclosure of information regarding the division to which employees belong, the concept $\pi_{Name,Div}$ is assigned the threshold 0. Note that any view that includes the attributes *Name, Div* would be protected as well!
3. To limit the disclosure of occupants in Building 1 to at most three employees, the concept $\pi_{Name}\sigma_{Bldg=1}$ is assigned the threshold 3.

Attacks on sensitive concepts (i.e., secrets that may be disclosed partially) may be disguised by either of two strategies (or a combination of both):

1. Queries are broken down into sequences of *smaller* requests that extract information less conspicuously.
2. Queries are disguised as other queries whose definitions do not resemble secrets, but whose answers nevertheless extract information covered by secrets.

Any system that permits controlled disclosure of secrets must be able to recognize both of these strategies.

Consider the above concept limiting to 3 the disclosure of occupants of building 1. A query to list the names and buildings of all employees at mailstop m202 retrieves 2 employees in Building 1 (Jones and Stevenson). A second query to list the names, telephone numbers and buildings of employees at room 307 retrieves 3 employees (Long, Jones and Hemlick). Any mechanism for protecting concepts must recognize that these apparently dissimilar queries in effect might be "nibbling" at the same sensitive concept.

The first strategy can be foiled by keeping track of the total number of tuples from a concept that have already been disclosed to every user. Thus, it is mostly a question of continuous accounting. Yet, this accounting is often subject to gross inaccuracies. When queries Q_1 and Q_2 retrieve n_1 and n_2 tuples, respectively, the number of tuples disclosed would be taken as $n_1 + n_2$. In effect, if the queries overlap, the number is smaller; for example, if $Q_1 = Q_2$ (the same query is repeated), the number of tuples disclosed is only n_1. In the previous example, the number of building 1 occupants disclosed by both queries is not 5, but 4, because Jones was included in both queries. This inaccuracy may be corrected by keeping record of the *actual* tuples that have been disclosed; for example, by maintaining a set of tuple identifiers. The disadvantage is that with very large databases such record keeping becomes very costly.

The method we describe foils the first strategy by continuous accounting, which is precise yet economical: it keeps accurate account of the number of tuples disclosed without maintaining the entire set of these tuples.[1]

The second attack strategy poses a more serious challenge. As an example, assume that the set of employees working in division A is a sensitive concept

---

[1] Incidentally, since we wish to protect arbitrary views, it would not have been even possible to use tuple identifiers to keep track of the tuples that have been disclosed.

and consider a query on the employees in building 1. Apparently, this query is unrelated to the concept, and therefore should be allowed. Yet, the set of employees in building 1 is identical to the set of employees in division A. By answering this query, the system will be giving away the *contents* of a sensitive concept, although the *definition* of this set of values (as formulated by the user) is quite different from its definition as a sensitive concept.

Consider a database view V and its materialization v in a specific database instance. V and v are often called, respectively, the *intensional definition* (or simply intension) and the *extensional definition* (or simply extension) of a view.[2] Given V (and assuming the proper permissions), v is easily and uniquely determined. It is much more difficult, however, to determine V from v. Indeed, there may be numerous intensional definitions of a view that evaluate to the same view extension. The problem of finding for a given view intension V another view intension V' that shares the same extension v is known as *intensional answering* [9]. In that context, the finding of alternative intensional definitions to a query is considered *cooperative* behavior: provide users with additional characterizations of their answers. In this context, finding alternative intensional definitions to a query is intended to be *uncooperative*: given a query, the system would search for alternative intensional definitions that "cover" the same information as the query, but correspond to sensitive concepts; if found, the user may be attempting to attack a concept using the second strategy.

Given a query, our method will detect whether it trespasses a sensitive concept, regardless of the statement of the query. Thus, our method thwarts the second strategy as well.

In summary, we provide a general framework in which sensitive information can be defined flexibly. To protect sensitive concepts from excessive disclosure, for each concept and for each user our method keeps track of the number of tuples that has already been disclosed. Each incoming query is compared with each predefined concept to determine whether it might trespass that concept. If so, the number of *new* tuples thus disclosed is computed and added to the number of tuples already disclosed, and, depending on the relationship of this counter to the threshold, the query is either permitted or rejected. Our accounting is both accurate and economical.

Our discussion is limited to databases that are single relations and to queries and concepts that are projection-selection views, where all selections are conjunctions of simple clauses of the form *attribute* = *value*. We conjecture that our method can be extended to overcome these limitations.

Section 2 establishes the formal framework with definitions of queries, concepts and concept disclosure by queries. Section 3 describes a basic algorithm for disclosure control, and Section 4 describes two improvements. Section 5 concludes this paper with a brief summary and discussion of future research directions.

---

[2] The terms are derived from the notions of *intensive* and *extensive* descriptions of information [10].

2 The Model

We adopt the usual definition of relational databases, but restrict our attention to databases that are *single* relations, and to *projection-selection* views, where all selections are conjunctions of simple clauses of the form *attribute = value*. We denote the database scheme $R = (A_1, \ldots, A_n)$.

2.1 Queries, Concepts and Patterns

A *query* is a view. Its extension in the present database instance is the *answer* to the query. Queries are defined by users and describe the information they are seeking. A *concept* is also a view. Concepts are defined in the system and describe the information that needs to be protected.

Views (queries or concepts) may be syntactically different, but yet describe the same information. Consider the example database scheme $Emp = (Name,$ $Tel,$ $Div,$ $Mail,$ $Bldg,$ $Room)$ and these two views:

1. $\pi_{Name,Room}\,\sigma_{(Room=103)\wedge(Div=B)}$
2. $\pi_{Name}\,\sigma_{(Room=103)\wedge(Div=B)}$

Both view definitions are identical, except that the latter view does not project a selection attribute which is projected by the former (*Room*). Nevertheless, because the values of selection attributes are known (in this case, the constant value 103), there is no difference in the information these views describe. Consequently, we shall always assume that views are defined in their *expanded* form, where the projection attributes include all the selection attributes. Thus, in the above example, both views would be interpreted as

$$\pi_{Name,Div,Room}\,\sigma_{(Room=103)\wedge(Div=B)}$$

A *pattern* is a formal notation for views. A pattern is an n-tuple $p_1, \ldots, p_n$, where n is the number of attributes in the database scheme, and each p_i is defined as follows

$$p_i = \begin{cases} a & \text{if the selection formula includes } A_i = a \\ * & \text{if } A_i \text{ is a projection attribute which is not a selection attribute} \\ - & \text{otherwise} \end{cases}$$

Because the projection attributes are assumed to include the selection attributes, patterns record only the projection attributes that are *not* selection attributes.

For example, all three view definitions above are represented by this pattern

$$(*, -, B, -, -, 103,)$$

Note that $*$ indicates an attribute of the database which is *unaffected* by the view: it is neither restricted nor removed. This notation resembles the notation for meta-tuples used in [8].

2.2 Concept Disclosure

Let U and V be views of database scheme D.

The selection condition of U is *at least as restrictive* as the selection restriction of V, if every clause $A_i = a$ in V's selection condition also appears in U's selection condition. The selection conditions of U and V are *contradictory*, if U's selection condition includes the clause $A_i = a$ and V's selection condition includes the clause $A_i = b$, for some attribute A_i and two different constants a and b.

U *overlaps* V, if their selection conditions are not contradictory, and U's projection attributes contain V's projection attributes. When U overlaps V, then the extension of U could be processed by another view that will remove the extra attributes. Some of the resulting tuples may be in the extension of V.

U *overlays* V, if U's selection condition is at least as restrictive as the selection condition of V, and U's projection attributes contain V's projection attributes. Obviously, when U overlays V, it also overlaps V. However, when the extension of U is processed by another view that removes the extra attributes, *all* the resulting tuples will be in the extension of V.

The overlap and overlay relationships are illustrated schematically in Fig. 2, in which U_1 overlaps V and U_2 overlays V.

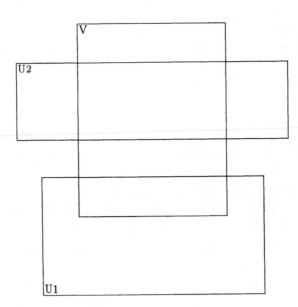

Fig. 2. Overlapping and Overlaying

Assume that U overlaps V. The *restriction* of V to U, denoted $V \mid U$, is the view obtained from V by appending to its selection condition the selection condition of U. The *exclusion* of U from V, denoted $V \mid \neg U$, is the view obtained from V by appending to its selection condition the *negation* of the selection condition of U.[3] Obviously, $V = (V \mid U) \cup (V \mid \neg U)$.

Let C be a concept view and let Q be a query view. Q *discloses* C, if Q overlaps C. Intuitively, a query discloses a concept, if its result could be processed by another query, to possibly derive tuples from the protected concept.

As an example, with the previous database scheme, consider this concept

$$C = \pi_{Name,Div,Room}\,\sigma_{(Room=103)\wedge(Div=B)}$$
(names of those in division B and in room 103)

and these three queries

1. $Q_1 = \pi_{Name,Tel,Div,Room}\,\sigma_{(Room=103)\wedge(Div=B)\wedge(Tel=x2345)}$
   (names of those in room 103, in division B, and with telephone x2345)
2. $Q_2 = \pi_{Name,Div,Room}\,\sigma_{Div=B}$
   (names and rooms of those in division B)
3. $Q_3 = \pi_{Name,Div,Room}\,\sigma_{Room=102}$
   (names and divisions of those in room 102)

Q_1 discloses C, because applying the query $\pi_{Name,Div,Room}$ to the result of Q_1 may yield some tuples in C. Q_2 discloses C in its entirety, because applying the query $\sigma_{Room=103}$ to the result of Q_2 yields all the tuples of C. Q_3 does not disclose any tuples of C because their selection conditions contradict.

The disclosure relationship between a query and a concept is illustrated schematically in Fig. 3. Notice that a concept protects its tuples, but not its subtuples; i.e., a query on a *subset* of the concept's projection attributes does not disclose the concept. On the other hand, a query on a *superset* of the attributes would disclose the concept (unless their selection conditions are contradictory).

As mentioned earlier, disclosure control requires that the number of tuples disclosed from a given concept does not exceed a certain predetermined number. For each concept C we define three integer values called *concept total, concept threshold* and *concept counter*, and denoted respectively, N, T and D. N denotes the total number of tuples in the extension of this concept, T denotes the maximal number of tuples that may be disclosed from this concept, and D denotes the number of tuples from this concept that have already been disclosed. If $T \geq N$, then the concept is *unrestricted*; we shall assume that none of the concepts are unrestricted. As queries are processed, the database system must keep track of D to ensure that $D \leq T$. The number of tuples in the extension of a view V will be denoted $\|V\|$; e.g., $\|C\| = N$.

---

[3] Note that the resulting selection condition is no longer a simple conjunction.

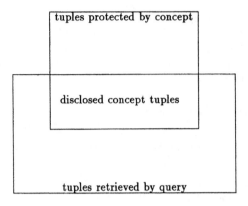

Fig. 3. Disclosure relationships between a query and a concept

3   Aggregation Control

Given a concept C with its three counters and given a query Q, our goal is to determine whether the request should be satisfied or not, and update the counters as appropriate. The main problem is to determine *how many tuples of C does Q disclose?* Once this question is answered, the rest is mostly bookkeeping.

To answer this question, we consider the patterns that represent Q and C. Let

$$C = (c_1, \ldots, c_n)$$
$$Q = (q_1, \ldots, q_n)$$

We establish a relationship between each element of the query pattern q_i and the corresponding element of the concept pattern c_i. Recall that a pattern element could be a constant or $*$ or $-$. A constant a indicates that A_i is a selection attribute and the selection condition is $A_i = a$, $*$ indicates that A_i is a projection attribute which is not a selection attribute, and $-$ indicates that A_i is neither a selection attribute nor a projection attribute.

We now define overlapping and restriction at the level of pattern elements. An element q_i of the query pattern *overlaps* the corresponding element c_i of the concept pattern, if either

1. q_i is a constant and c_i is either the same constant or $*$ or $-$.
2. q_i is $*$.
3. q_i and c_i are both $-$.

Thus, the query element q_i overlaps the concept element c_i in all but two situations: (1) when the query and the concept have contradictory selection conditions, or (2) when the attribute A_i is protected by the concept, but not requested by the query. Intuitively, if q_i overlaps c_i, and all the other pattern elements in both the query and the concept are ∗ (reflecting unaffected attributes), then the query Q overlaps the concept C.

Assume that q_i overlaps c_i. The *restriction* of c_i to q_i is defined as follows:

$$r_i = \begin{cases} q_i \text{ if } q_i \text{ is a constant} \\ c_i \text{ otherwise} \end{cases}$$

Intuitively, if the query element q_i overlaps the concept element c_i, and all the other pattern elements in both the query and the concept are ∗ (reflecting unaffected attributes), then the pattern with r_i in position i and ∗ everywhere else describes the restriction of concept C to the query Q.

In general, a query Q overlaps a concept C, if all their corresponding pattern elements overlap. Similarly, the restriction of a concept C to a query Q is obtained from the restrictions of the corresponding pattern elements. Thus, by considering "in parallel" all the pattern elements, we can determine whether Q discloses C, and define the precise subview of C that is disclosed by Q. This discussion is summarized in the following theorem.

Theorem (disclosure). *Let C be a concept with pattern $(c_1, \dots, c_n)$ and Q a query with pattern $(q_1, \dots, q_n)$. Then*

1. *Q possibly discloses tuples of C, if q_i overlaps c_i, for all $1 \leq i \leq n$.*
2. *The set of C tuples disclosed by Q is given by the pattern $(r_1, \dots, r_n)$, where r_i is the restriction of c_i to q_i.*

This theorem suggests a basic algorithm for disclosure control, shown in Fig. 4. The input to this algorithm is a set $C_1, \dots, C_m$ of protected concepts, each with its associated counters N_i, T_i and D_i, and a query Q. The algorithm also uses a temporary counter M_i for each concept. When it terminates, the value of *permit* indicates whether the answer to Q should be presented to the user or not.

Essentially, the overhead incurred in authorizing Q is the determination whether Q overlaps C_i and, if it does, the derivation of $C_i \mid Q$ from Q. As the theorem suggests, overlapping is discovered by a simple comparison of the patterns. The derivation of the disclosed tuples $C_i \mid Q$ from the answer set Q is also quite simple. Altogether, the complexity of this algorithm (excluding the cost of materializing Q) is $O(m \cdot n \cdot k)$, where m is the number of concepts, n is the number of attributes, and k is the size of the answer.

Referring to the example in Fig. 1, there are 4 employees in division A. Assume that only 3 employees in this division may be disclosed, and that one such employee has already been disclosed. The concept pattern and counters are

$$C_1 = (*, *, A, *, *, *)$$
$$N_1 = 4$$
$$T_1 = 3$$
$$D_1 = 1$$

Algorithm (disclosure)
$permit := true$
materialize Q
$i := 0$
while $permit$ **and** $i < m$
do
    $i := i + 1$
    $M_i := 0$
    if Q overlaps C_i
    then
        $M_i := \|C_i \mid Q\|$
        if $D_i + M_i > T_i$
        then
            $permit := false$
            break
        endif
    endif
done
if $permit$
then
    for $i = 1, \ldots m$
    do
        $D_i := D_i + M_i$
    done
endif

Fig. 4. Basic algorithm for disclosure control

Consider now the query that requests complete information on the employees whose telephone number is x1234 and whose mail stop is m404. The query and query pattern are

$$\sigma_{(Tel=x1234)\wedge(Mail=m404)}$$
$$Q \doteq (*, x1234, *, m404, *, *)$$

The restriction of C_1 to Q is described by the pattern

$$R = (*, x1234, A, m404, *, *)$$

R's extension has two tuples, so the query is accepted and D_1 is updated to 3.

    As another example, the telephone number x1234 is assigned to 4 employees. Assume that only 3 employees with this number may be disclosed, and that two have already been disclosed. The concept pattern and counters are

$$C_2 = (*, x1234, -, -, -, -)$$
$$N_2 = 4$$
$$T_2 = 3$$
$$D_2 = 2$$

Consider now the query that requests the location of the telephone whose number is x1234. The query and query pattern are

$$\pi_{Tel,Bldg,Room}\, \sigma_{Tel=x1234}$$
$$Q = (-, x1234, -, -, *, *)$$

Q does not overlap C_2, so it is permitted.

4 Improvements

Assume a concept C. First, consider a query Q_1 that overlaps C by m_1 tuples. Algorithm **disclosure** increments the counter D of disclosed tuples by m_1. Consider now a second query Q_2 that overlaps C by m_2 tuples. The algorithm will increment D by m_2. This continues until D reaches the threshold value T, when further queries that overlap C would be denied.

Yet, it is entirely possible that some of (or all) the tuples disclosed by Q_2 have already been disclosed by Q_1. In other words, possibly the user is being "charged" twice for the same tuples, and is thus approaching the threshold faster than warranted.

To rectify this, we offer the following improvement. With each concept C we associate a *predicate* P that describes the concept tuples that have already been disclosed. P is initialized to *true*. Assume that $Q_1, \ldots, Q_p$ have already been processed when Q_{p+1} is received, and let $\alpha_1, \ldots, \alpha_p$ denote their respective selection conditions. The present value of P would be $\alpha_1 \vee \cdots \vee \alpha_p$. After computing the restriction of C to Q_{p+1}, we exclude from it the view σ_P. The tuples in this new query are those that have *not* been delivered already. This improvement is incorporated into a new algorithm, shown in Fig. 5.

The input to this algorithm is a set $C_1, \ldots, C_m$ of protected concepts, each with its associated predicate P_i and counters N_i, T_i and D_i, and the query Q whose selection predicate is α. When the algorithm terminates, the value of *permit* indicates whether the answer to Q should be presented to the user or not.

Again, the overhead incurred in authorizing Q is the determination whether Q overlaps C_i and, if it does, the derivation of $(C_i \mid Q) \mid \neg\sigma_{P_i}$ from Q. Again, these are simple procedures, and the complexity of the algorithm is $O(m \cdot n \cdot k \cdot p)$, where n, m and k are as before, and p is the number of queries already processed.

We have assumed that the collection of protected concepts $C_1, \ldots, C_m$ is essentially *unstructured* and have ignored any possible relationships among these concepts. At times, the concepts to be protected form specific structures; recognizing these structures could help improve the performance of the disclosure control algorithms.

Assume an organization with three divisions called A, B and C, and the following limitations on disclosure: 20 employees in division A, 15 in division B, 10 in division C, but not more than 30 employees in total. These limitations are described in four concepts:

Algorithm (improve1)
$permit := true$
materialize Q
$i := 0$
while $permit$ **and** $i < m$
do
    $i := i + 1$
    $M_i := 0$
    if Q overlaps C_i
    then
        $M_i := \|(C_i \mid Q) \mid \neg\sigma_{P_i}\|$
        if $D_i + M_i > T_i$
        then
            $permit := false$
            break
        endif
    endif
done
if $permit$
then
    for $i = 1, \ldots m$
    do
        $P_i := P_i \wedge \alpha$
        $D_i := D_i + M_i$
    done
endif

Fig. 5. Disclosure control algorithm with accurate bookkeeping

1. $C_1 = \pi_{Name,Div}\sigma_{Div=A}$
   $T_1 = 20$
2. $C_2 = \pi_{Name,Div}\sigma_{Div=B}$
   $T_2 = 15$
3. $C_3 = \pi_{Name,Div}\sigma_{Div=C}$
   $T_3 = 10$
4. $C_4 = \pi_{Name}$
   $T_4 = 30$

With respect to the mutual relationships of these four views, we note that

1. Each of the concepts C_1, C_2, and C_3 *overlays* the concept C_4.
2. The restrictions $C_4 \mid C_1$, $C_4 \mid C_2$, $C_4 \mid C_3$ *partition* C_4.

Thus, every disclosure from one of first three concepts corresponds to a disclosure from C_4 (and disclosure from C_4 corresponds to a disclosure from exactly one of the first three concepts). Consequently, the disclosure control algorithm only needs to compare a query Q against the first three concepts. Increments of D_1,

Algorithm (improve2)
materialize Q
$permit := true$
for every leaf concept C_i
do
$\qquad M_i := 0$
$\qquad$**if** Q overlaps C_i
$\qquad$**then**
$\qquad\qquad M_i := \|(C_i \mid Q) \mid \neg\sigma_{P_i}\|$
$\qquad\qquad$**if** $D_i + M_i > T_i$
$\qquad\qquad$**then**
$\qquad\qquad\qquad permit := false$
$\qquad\qquad\qquad$**break**
$\qquad\qquad$**else**
$\qquad\qquad\qquad$**for** every ancestor C_j of C_i
$\qquad\qquad\qquad$**do**
$\qquad\qquad\qquad\qquad M_j := M_i$
$\qquad\qquad\qquad\qquad$**if** $D_j + M_j > T_j$
$\qquad\qquad\qquad\qquad$**then**
$\qquad\qquad\qquad\qquad\qquad permit := false$
$\qquad\qquad\qquad\qquad\qquad$**break**
$\qquad\qquad\qquad\qquad$**endif**
$\qquad\qquad\qquad$**done**
$\qquad\qquad$**endif**
$\qquad$**endif**
$\qquad$**if** $\neg permit$
$\qquad$**then**
$\qquad\qquad$**break**
$\qquad$**endif**
done
if $permit$
then
$\qquad$**for** $i = 1, \ldots m$
$\qquad$**do**
$\qquad\qquad D_i := D_i + M_i$
$\qquad\qquad$**if** C_i is leaf concept
$\qquad\qquad$**then**
$\qquad\qquad\qquad P_i := P_i \wedge \alpha$
$\qquad\qquad$**endif**
$\qquad$**done**
endif

Fig. 6. Disclosure control algorithm with concept hierarchy

D_2 or D_3 should also trigger identical increments to D_4 (and a comparison of D_4 with T_4).

This improvement is incorporated into a new algorithm, shown in Fig. 6. The input to this algorithm is a *hierarchy* $C_1, \ldots, C_m$ of protected concepts, each with its associated predicate P_i and counters N_i, T_i and D_i, and the query Q whose selection predicate is α. When the algorithm terminates, the value of *permit* indicates whether the answer to Q should be presented to the user or not. The complexity of the algorithm is $O(m \cdot n \cdot k \cdot p + m^2)$.

Note that it is not necessary to maintain the predicates P_i for non-leaf concepts: tuples newly disclosed from leaf concepts are guaranteed to be newly disclosed from ancestor concepts.

5 Conclusion

We addressed the problem of controlled disclosure of sensitive information. We defined a model in which any view of the database can be defined as a sensitive concept, and we offered simple and efficient algorithms that accurately monitor the disclosure of these predefined concepts. With these algorithms, any query by a user of the database is noted for its effect on the set of predefined concepts; any "nibble" into a concept is recorded, and once these "nibbles" add up to a substantial part of a concept (as defined by a threshold), future queries are rejected. Even queries that are apparently unrelated to sensitive concepts are monitored for their effect on these concepts, thus foiling any strategy of disguising queries through alternative formulations.

Much work remains to be done, and we mention here several directions. First, we are interested in extending this work to remove the simplifying assumptions that have been made on the relations and on the definitions of concepts and queries. Also, the selection of concepts and thresholds needs to be considered more carefully. For example, thresholds must be assigned *consistently*; e.g., the threshold for a "broader" concept must be larger than the threshold for any of its "subconcepts".

Our discussion has been limited to "static" databases; i.e., when considering a sequence of queries by the same user, we assumed that the extensions of concepts do not change via insertions or deletions of tuples. Further research is required to extend this work to "dynamic" databases.

Finally, we assumed that all sensitive information has been *predefined* as concepts, and challenged every attack against these concepts. Hence, we can only detect attacks on information that has already been recognized as sensitive. A more challenging direction is to conclude from users queries whether they are attempting to "converge" on a concept which so far has been unclassified, thus alerting the system to the possibility of security "holes".

Acknowledgement. The authors are grateful to the anonymous referees for their important corrections and suggestions.

References

1. D. E. Denning. *Cryptography and Data Security*. Addison Wesley, Reading, Massachusetts, 1982.
2. J.T. Haigh, R.C. O'Brian, P.D. Stachour, and D.L. Toups. The LDV approach to security. In D.L. Spooner and C. Landwehr, editors, *Database Security III: Status and Prospects*, pages 323–339. North Holland, Amsterdam, 1990.
3. T.N. Hinke. Inference aggregation deduction in database management systems. In *Proceedings of IEEE Symposium on Security and Privacy*, pages 96–106, April 1988.
4. S. Jajodia. Inference problems in secure database management systems. Technical Report MTR 92W0000052, The MITRE Corporation, McLean, Virginia, June 1992.
5. T.Y. Lin. Database, aggregation and security algebra. In *Proceedings of the 4th IFIP Working Conference on Database Security*, September 1990.
6. T.F. Lunt. Aggregation and inference: Facts and fallacies. In *Proceedings of IEEE Symposium on Security and Privacy*, pages 102–109, May 1989.
7. T.F. Lunt and R.A. Whitehurst. The Sea View formal top level specifications. Technical report, Computer Science Laboratory, SRI International, February 1988.
8. A. Motro. Integrity = validity + completeness. *ACM Transactions on Database Systems*, 14(4):480–502, December 1989.
9. A. Motro. Intensional answers to database queries. *IEEE Transactions on Knowledge and Data Engineering*, 6(3):444–454, June 1994.
10. D. C. Tsichritzis and F. H. Lochovsky. *Data Models*. Prentice Hall, Englewood Cllifs, New Jersey, 1982.

Information Flow Controls vs
Inference Controls:
An Integrated Approach

F. Cuppens[1] and G. Trouessin[2]

[1] ONERA-CERT, 2 Av. E. Belin, 31055 Toulouse Cedex, France,
email: cuppens@tls-cs.cert.fr
[2] CESSI CNAM-TS, 14 Place Saint Etienne, 31000 Toulouse, France

Abstract. This paper proposes a formal method for modeling database
security based on a logical interpretation of two problems: the (internal)
information flow controls and the (external) information inference controls. Examples are developed that illustrate the inability of "classical"
security models such as non-interference and non-deducibility to completely take into account the inference problem, because both are too
constraining: the former model leads to the existence problem, whereas
the latter one leads to the elimination problem. The causality model,
which has been developed to solve the information flow control problem
by considering that "what is known, must be permitted to be known",
does not also explicitly take into account the inference problem. But we
show that it is possible to extend causality so that inference can in fact
be solved by formalizing the security policy consistency in the following
way "any information must not be both permitted and forbidden, to be
known". However, some difficulties remain if we do not consider that a
subject can perform not only valid derivations but also plausible derivations. In particular, we show that classical solutions to the inference
problem such as use of polyinstantiated databases are not plainly satisfactory, unless the security policy is able to estimate how it is plausible
that an abductive reasoning can occur.
Keywords: Security model, Information flow control, Database security,
Inference control, Modal logic.

Introduction

An application that has been of particular interest since the beginning of work on
secure computer systems is the implementation of a secure database management
system (DBMS). To design and construct a secure DBMS, we need a formal
model in order to define the security requirements, to have a precise description
of the behavior desired of the security relevant portions of the DBMS and to
have a means to prove that these portions of the DBMS are secure with respect
to the security requirements.

The initial works of Hinke and Schaefer [26] and Grohn [22] provide an interpretation of the Bell and LaPadula model [2] for a relational DBMS. These first
applications of a security model to a DBMS are still restrictive because the Bell

and LaPadula model was not designed to deal with several important problems, among them we state:

1. Information can be passed by subtle and indirect means which the Bell and LaPadula model cannot detect.
2. Users can derive secret information from that to which they have legal access.

Afterwards, non-interference [21] and non-deducibility [34] models have been developed. They present formal frameworks which try to solve these problems. Concurrently, several realizations of secure databases were initiated. These projects generally enclose a formal verification of the database operations against the security properties of the policy model. This is, in particular, the case of the Seaview [14, 15] and LDV [24] projects.

The Seaview verification effort is described in [37]. The Seaview specifications contain a formal policy model of the security requirements for multilevel secure databases as well as an abstract description of the database operations. Seaview does not use a classical model of information flow control such as non-interference or non-deducibility but rather an ad-hoc model. In this model, to infer that the global system is secure, it must be proved that the initial state is secure and that each command is secure. To prove that a command is secure, it must be proved that it satisfies the *secure-states* and *secure-transitions* predicates. To prove the former predicate, fourteen properties must be satisfied and to prove the latter, sixteen properties must be satisfied. The problem with the formal security policy model used by Seaview is the absence of a general definition of the security constraints such as that proposed in non-interference and non-deducibility models.

On the other hand, the LDV project is controlled by the basic LOCK policy which satisfies the requirements of the non-interference formal model. This approach provides good assurance that the design is secure. However, we consider that classical models of information flow (such as non-interfence and non-deducibility) are too constraining to realistically take into account the security problems in a DBMS. Section 1 states through examples this point of view. In section 2, we show that in order to have a correct model of the security requirements in a DBMS, it is more convenient to split up the problem of confidentiality into two sub-problems:

1. Internal information flow controls.
2. Inference control.

This decomposition was already suggested by Denning in [13]. In fact, our previous analysis in [9] shows that non-interfence and non-deducibility models try to jointly solve these two sub-problems, but we consider that they do not provide a satisfactory solution to any of them.

In sections 3 and 4, we give a logical interpretation of these two problems. To analyze the confidentiality of a system in a logical context, we need a formal definition of three concepts:

- The knowledge of each subject, we denote it K_A.

- The permission to know of each subject, we denote it PK_A.
- The prohibition to know of each subject, we denote it FK_A.

In the context of the logic of security, confidentiality is defined by a logical formula $K_A\varphi \rightarrow PK_A\varphi$ that could be read:

If A knows φ then A should be permitted to know that φ

In [4], we provide a semantics for this logical formula which leads to a new security condition called causality. In section 3, we show that the security enforced via causality provides a satisfactory solution to the problem of **internal** information flow control but it does not deal with the inference control problem. Therefore, the aim of section 4 is to show how to extend causality in order to take into account this problem. We show that in the context of the logic of security, inference control is defined by the formula $\neg(PK_A\varphi \wedge FK_A\varphi)$ that could be read:

A cannot both have the permission to know φ and the prohibition to know φ

The enforcement of this condition guarantees that no inference channel exists which uses valid derivation. Thus, by combining the causality and consistency requirements, we obtain a general and complete formal method for modeling database security. However, some difficulties remain because a subject can also perform plausible derivations. In particular, we analyze some potential solutions such as the incompleteness and/or the polyinstantiation of the database. We can show that with the help of abductive reasoning some information can be illegally deduced, as stated in [18], unless some supplementary measures have been taken, such as imprecise assessment of potential abductive information. Finally, section 5 concludes on further work that remains to be done.

1 Drawbacks of "classical" information flow models

It is generally considered (see [23] for instance) that computer security is concerned with the transmission of information through a computer system. Goguen and Meseguer with non-interference [21] and, following them, Sutherland with non-deducibility [34] presented frameworks for identifying general flows of information through a computer system, and suggested policies that would disallow some of them.

Actually, the main difference between non-interference and non-deducibility is that these definitions do not agree on information flows that must be disallowed. However, we can bring out several common points between these two definitions:

1. At the initial time, each subject A perfectly knows all the possible behaviors (traces) of the system. Then, A observes the system by performing inputs and receiving outputs. Thus, for each trace t of the system, A has a partial view of this trace that we called the restriction of t to A and we write it $t\lceil A$. Finally, we can define what A can infer from its observation in trace t by defining its **knowledge** in t:

A subject A knows a piece of information φ in a given trace t if and only if φ is true in all traces t' such that $t\lceil A = t'\lceil A$ (that is to say t and t' are indistinguishable according to A's observation).

2. For each subject A, both non-interference and non-deducibility aim to protect a given set of secret information (see Figure 1). According to these two definitions, this set is the sequence of inputs performed by another user B. In [3], we showed that, for these two definitions, the protection of this set of secret information means the enforcement of an **ignorance** condition for A, that is to say:

   - **non-interference:** B does not interfere with A if and only if A **does not know** that B has performed any input in the system.
   - **non-deducibility:** A does not deduce anything on B if and only if for every possible behavior[3] b_i of B, A **does not know** whether B had a behavior different from b_i.

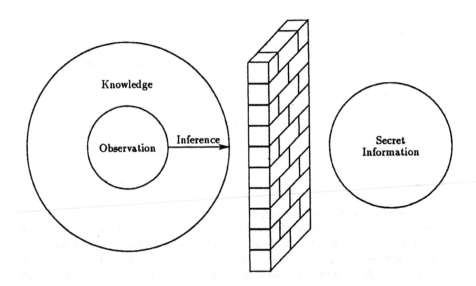

Fig. 1. Classical representation of confidentiality

In [4], we showed that there exist several problems with non-interference and non-deducibility when we use these definitions to control information flow through a computer system. In particular, we showed that these definitions disallow any kind of dependency between unclassified information and secret infor-

---

[3] b_i is a possible behavior of B if and only if there exists a trace t such that the sequence of inputs performed by B in trace t is equal to b_i, i.e. $t\lceil B_i = b_i$

mation. Moreover, these definitions require implicit assumptions on the subjects' behavior:

- For non-interference, it is always possible that B does not perform any input.
- For non-deducibility, inputs performed by A and B are always compatible.

In this paper, we want to show that, due to these problems, these two definitions are not adapted to model database security.

1.1 Example 1: The existence problem with non-interference

Let us consider, in this first example issued from [28], an ordinary database relation, *Mission*, with three attributes, *Starship*, *Objective* and *Destination*, with *Starship* being the key: this means that for each starship there is at most one tuple in the *Mission* relation giving us the *Starship*'s unique *Objective* and unique *Destination*. For example, the tuple ⟨*Intergalactic, Exploration, Talos*⟩ denotes that the starship *Intergalactic* has set out for an *Exploration* of *Talos*. This entire tuple gives us the mission of *Intergalactic*, as shown in Table 1.

Starship	Objective	Destination
Enterprise	Spying	Rigel
Intergalactic	Exploration	Talos

Table 1. The ordinary *Mission* relation

Let us now consider a multilevel relation which attempts to represent the same information as in the ordinary *Mission* relation, but in a context in which all the facts recorded in the database, denoted DB, are classified according to their confidentiality level. Suppose that there are only two classification levels: the high level or *Secret* level (denoted S) and the low level or *Unclassified* level (denoted U). Following the example issued from [28], each attribute value of each tuple can be associated with a given confidentiality level so that the previous *Mission* relation becomes a new multilevel *SOD* relation (as shown in Table 2). Each tuple of the *SOD* relation can also be associated with a classification, the *Tuple Classification* (or *TC*), which is the highest classification level of the classification levels of all the attribute values of the tuple (as indicated in Table 2).

Then, it is possible to decompose a multilevel relation in a set of single-level relations [28, 11]. In the case of the example shown in Table 2, it can thus be considered that two distinct databases (DB_S and DB_U) are managed by the secure DBMS to represent the original database DB:

- DB_S contains the *Secret* data of DB to which only any *Secret* user, $user_S$, has access;

Starship		Objective		Destination		TC
Enterprise	U	Spying	S	Rigel	S	S
Intergalactic	U	Exploration	U	Talos	U	U

Table 2. The multilevel *SOD* relation

- DB_U contains the *Unclassified* data of *DB* to which both any *user_S* and any *Unclassified* user, *user_U*, have access;

Each of these two databases is able to give its own answer to the following request:

Request1:   SELECT ⟨*Starship, Objective, Destination*⟩ FROM *SOD*
Answer1.S: ⟨*Enterprise, Spying, Rigel*⟩   (if *user_S* has sent *Request1* to DB_S)
                 ⟨*Intergalactic, Exploration, Talos*⟩
Answer1.U: ⟨*Intergalactic, Exploration, Talos*⟩
                                                      (if *user_U* has sent *Request1* to DB_U)

and each database can also give its own answer to the following request:

Request2:   SELECT ⟨*Starship*⟩ FROM *SOD*
Answer2.S: ⟨*Enterprise*⟩   (if *user_S* has sent *Request2* to DB_S)
                 ⟨*Intergalactic*⟩
Answer2.U: ⟨*Enterprise*⟩   (if *user_U* has sent *Request2* to DB_U)
                 ⟨*Intergalactic*⟩

Let us assume that *DB* is complete with respect to *SOD* (as it is the case in Table 2). This means that if a given *Starship* is stored in *DB* then its *Objective* and *Destination* are also stored in *DB*. Since $DB = DB_S \cup DB_U$, "*DB is globally complete with respect to SOD*" means that *SOD* is represented in, either DB_S, or DB_U, or both. In other words:

$$[\forall star, (Starship(star) \in DB) \Rightarrow (\exists obj, \exists dest, SOD(star, obj, dest) \in DB)]$$

or equivalently:

$$[\forall star, (Starship(star) \in DB) \Rightarrow (\exists obj, \exists dest, SOD(star, obj, dest) \in DB_S$$
$$\vee \ SOD(star, obj, dest) \in DB_U)]$$

Suppose now that *user_U* sends the following request to DB_U:

Request3:   SELECT ⟨*Destination*⟩ FROM *SOD*
                 WHERE *Starship = Enterprise*
Answer3a.U: Unknown   (if *user_U* has sent *Request3* to DB_U)

Although such an answer does not seem to provide any information, *user_U* can use the hypothesis that *DB* is complete to build the following reasoning.

From:

$$K_{user_U}[\forall star, (Starship(star) \in DB)$$
$$\Rightarrow (\exists obj, \exists dest, SOD(star, obj, dest) \in DB)]$$

and by considering the information given by *Answer2.U*:

$$K_{user_U}[Starship(Enterprise) \in DB]$$

user_U can derive that:

$$K_{user_U}[\exists obj, \exists dest, SOD(Enterprise, obj, dest) \in DB]$$

and from *Answer3a.U*:

$$K_{user_U}[\forall dest, Destination(Enterprise, dest) \notin DB_U]$$

Finally, by using the fact that $DB = DB_U \cup DB_S$, *user_U* can derive that:

$$K_{user_U}[\exists dest, Destination(Enterprise, dest) \in DB_S]$$

If the hypothesis is made that *Secret* tuples are only introduced in *DB* by the way of *Secret* inputs[4], this kind of reasoning subsumes that another user, *user_S* (whose clearance is *Secret*), has performed some secret input in *DB* (in *DB_S* to be more precise). In [9], we obtain a similar result in developing a different argumentation based on the *restricted* value first introduced by Sandhu and Jajodia in [31]. Now, let us consider that the non-interference model is used, this means that:

- *user_U* must not know that *Enterprise*'s destination is *Rigel*, because the classification level of the destination of *Enterprise* is secret;
- *user_U* must not even know that the classification level of *Enterprise*'s destination is secret, because this would imply that a secret input has been performed. In our example, from the non-interference point of view, the security constraint is not satisfied because an input/output sequence (i.e., *Request2-Answer2.U-Request3-Answer3a.U*) can interfere with a higher input/output sequence (namely the insert in *DB_S* of the secret tuple $\langle Enterprise, Spying, Rigel \rangle$).

Generally, to avoid this kind of problem which occurs when we apply the non-interference model, the polyinstantiation technique is systematically employed. In particular, this is the case of the LDV project, which is based on the non-interference model. However, it is important to be able to consider that the existence of secret information is not always secret. As it is stated in [33], it would be better to consider that *"unless otherwise specified in a secrecy constraint, the system need not hide the existence of classified data in the database (PS#6: Security Policy Statement #6)"*. This means that polyinstantiation must not be automatically employed but only when explicitly specified in the security policy.

---

[4] This hypothesis is an integrity constraint used by most multilevel databases

1.2 Example 2: The elimination problem with non-deducibility

Let us now consider for this second example an extension of the previous example[5]. This extension concerns an additional relation, denoted STR, that indicates for each *Starship* its *Category*, that is to say its unique *Type* and its unique *Range* (as shown in Table 3).

Starship		Type		Range		TC
Enterprise	U	Quick-and-light	U	20000	U	U
Intergalactic	U	Slow-and-heavy	U	50000	U	U

Table 3. Two instances of the STR relation

Each attribute of this relation must not be obligatorily classified because it is only considered that the mission (i.e., *Objective* and *Destination*) of a starship can be confidential, but not its category (i.e., *Type* and *Range*).

Even if $user_U$ does not know the secret destination of *Enterprise*, from the knowledge of *Enterprise*'s range, he can nevertheless eliminate some of the originally possible destinations of *Enterprise* (see Figure 2). For instance, if Talos is a destination more than 20000 distant, then $user_U$ knows that $\neg Dest(Enterprise, Talos)$. From the non-deducibility point of view, the security constraint is not satisfied because $user_U$ can deduce that some destinations are impossible (i.e, he can eliminate some possible behavior of secret users).

Faced with this problem, a possible solution would be to change classifications, for instance to consider that $SR(Enterprise, 20000)$ is secret information. Nevertheless, to consider that $SR(Enterprise, 20000)$ is unclassified information may be necessary because this piece of information is related to the technical characteristics of Enterprise and is perhaps widely distributed and well-known information.

Actually, from the non-deducibility point of view, a confidential piece of information cannot be partially determined by unclassified information. However, it can be interesting to state that only a portion of this piece of information must be confidential (see for instance [7]). For example, only the confidentiality must be preserved for the two high-order bits, or for all the odd-order bits. The pertinence of such confidentiality constraints becomes obvious if they are applied to information such as the *employee's salary*. This approach can also be applied at a higher granularity level: at a byte level, or even at the level of the elementary pieces of information within a global and more complex data structure.

---

[5] A similar example was developed in [9]

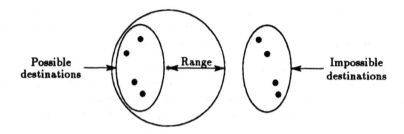

Fig. 2. The possible/impossible destinations of *Enterprise*

1.3 Synthesis

The examples of sections 1.1 and 1.2 illustrate that it is possible to differentiate several types of inference:

1. **Exact inference.** This inference occurs when a secret piece of information is exactly determined by a user whose clearance is unclassified.
2. **Partial inference.** It occurs when a user whose clearance is unclassified can reduce the set of possible values that can be assigned to a classified datum. This problem was first studied in [7]. Example of section 1.2 is an example of partial inference.
3. **Existential inference.** It occurs when a user whose clearance is unclassified derives the existence of a secret piece of information. Example of section 1.1 is an example of existential inference.

Most current research works focus on exact inference (for instance [35, 19, 17, 25]) and do not take into account the two other types of inference. We guess that these types of inference are equally important but are difficult to represent for at least two reasons :

1. To take into account these two types of inference, we need representing existential, disjunctive or negative information. Languages used in standard DBMS or in classical provers such as PROLOG do not provide these facilities. However, several researchers are currently developing this kind of extension (see for instance [12, 27, 30]).
2. It is clear that the exact inference of a secret piece of information is always a threat to confidentiality. Hence the security policy must prevent all exact inferences. On the other hand, every partial or existential inference does not necessarily represent a threat to confidentiality. For instance, let us assume that Paul's salary is equal to 10000 and this piece of information is classified at secret. Let us assume that an unclassified user can derive that this salary is between 9990 and 10010. It is a partial inference of Paul's salary and we can think that the security administrator will consider that this partial inference is not allowed. However, let us now assume that, in another situation, this

unclassified user can only infer that Paul's salary is greater that the SMIC[6].
It is another kind of partial inference of Paul's salary but it is clear that the
security administrator cannot prevent from this partial inference.

Hence, to properly take into account partial and existential inferences, we
must develop means which would allow the security administrator to precisely
define which information is unclassified and which information is secret. It is
only after doing so that we can distinguish acceptable states from unacceptable
ones.

Notice that non interference and non deducibility properties respectively reject all existential inferences and partial inferences. This is the reason why we
claim that these two security properties are too constraining to model database
security.

2　A formal method to solve the different problems

When we want to correctly analyze problems we have to solve, it is important
to come back to the concept of security policy for confidentiality. In this paper,
we only consider the case of mandatory access control. An organization defines
a mandatory access control policy which is applied to a set of sentences[7] $\mathcal{L}$ that
represents the knowledge domain of the organization and a set of subjects $\mathcal{A}$
members of this organization. For each subject $A \in \mathcal{A}$, the policy divides the set
of sentences $\mathcal{L}$ into two subsets:

1. The set of sentences $R(A)$ for which A is explicitly permitted to have an
   access.
2. The set of sentences $F(A)$ for which A is explicitly forbidden to have an
   access.

We do not assume that the policy is necessarily complete. This means that some
sentences of $\mathcal{L}$ may not belong to either $R(A)$ or $F(A)$. For instance, let us take
the example of the multilevel security policy. Some sentences $s \in \mathcal{L}$ receives a
classification $l(s)$ and each subject $A \in \mathcal{A}$ receives a clearance $L(A)$. The sets
$R(A)$ and $F(A)$ are then defined by:

$$R(A) = \{s \in \mathcal{L} \mid l(s) \leq L(A)\}$$

$$F(A) = \{s \in \mathcal{L} \mid \neg(l(s) \leq L(A))\}$$

In the following, we will assume that $R(A)$ is a consistent set of sentences. On
the other hand, $F(A)$ is not necessarily consistent. We can then, as proposed by
Dennings in [13], state two problems:

---

[6] The SMIC is the minimum salary allowed in France

[7] By a set of sentences, we mean a full first order language with a set of predicates,
logical connectors (conjunction, disjunction, negation, implication) and existential
and universal quantifiers.

1. Internal information flow controls.
2. Inference controls.

It is well known (see [29] for instance) that a computer system can be used to transmit information[8] not only by a direct access to a given piece of information but also by subtle and indirect means. Internal information flow controls are concerned with these leakages of information. To prohibit these leakages, we will show in section 3 that the system must control the permission to know any piece of information. This is a problem of knowledge conformity of an agent A with respect to its rights: A must only know pieces of information for which A has received a clearance.

When information derived from confidential data must be declassified for wider distribution, another leakage of information can occur: a user can use lower sensitive information stored in the database to which he can legally have an access to derive higher sensitive information. This leakage of information is called the inference problem. In this case, internal information controls as described above are not sufficient. Indeed, the flow of information is outside the computer system. Actually, we will show in section 4 that the inference problem does not occur if the security policy is correctly defined. This means we must verify, beside dividing $\mathcal{L}$, that the sets $R(A)$ and $F(A)$ are defined in a consistent manner (see Figure 3).

It is important to notice that the pioneering work of Bell and LaPadula deals essentially with internal flow controls and it does not take into account anymore the inference control. On the other hand, the majority of models designed to ensure information flow control (in particular non-interference and non-deducibility) jointly deal with the two problems.

The comparative study performed in [4] showed that these models do not provide a satisfactory control of internal flows of information. We also think that these models do not propose a satisfactory solution to inference control. Examples of sections 1.1 and 1.2 illustrate this point of view.

3 Internal information flow control

When reasoning about security, it is important to have a precise notion of what a subject **knows** and what a subject is **permitted to know**. Generally, what a subject A knows is represented by a modal operator denoted K_A. This modal operator was extensively studied and now has a well established semantics. We briefly recalled this semantics in section 1.

In our model, what a subject A is permitted to know is represented by another modal operator PK_A. This approach was first suggested by Glasgow and McEwen in [20]. In [4], we proposed a formal semantics for this modal operator. Intuitively, A is permitted to know φ if and only if A learns φ by playing the role of a user cleared to know the unclassified set of sentences $R(A)$. Hence, by identifying the authorized role of A with the unclassified set of sentences $R(A)$, we have:

$$PK_A\varphi \equiv K_{R(A)}\varphi$$

---

[8] By information, we mean a consistent subset of the language $\mathcal{L}$, i.e. a theory.

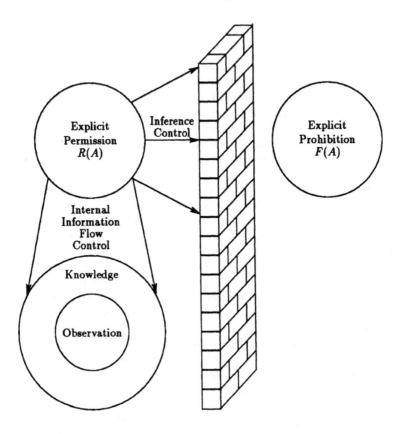

Fig. 3. The two problems to solve

A system is secure with respect to A if and only if the formula $K_A\varphi \rightarrow PK_A\varphi$ is valid (true in every traces of the system). This definition of security can be equivalently stated by the following requirement on the traces of the system:

Causality: For all traces t and t'
$$\text{If } t\lceil R(A) = t'\lceil R(A) \text{ then } t\lceil A = t'\lceil A$$

that is to say: the information A can observe should only depend on the information A is permitted to know. This means that causality rules out every non-authorized flow of information inside the computer system. In particular, causality controls every non-authorized indirect flows such as covert channels. In [4], we formally compare this definition of security with the classical definition of absence of information flow as non-interference and non-deducibility. It appears that causality has several advantages:

1. The explicit representation of time in the model proposed in [4] enables every covert channels to be controlled including timing channels.

2. Causality forces the system to be deterministic. This could appear as a draw-back of the approach, however, it also enables every probabilistic covert channels to be controlled [9].

3. Causality does not include the tranquillity principle and provides efficient conditions to control the dynamic assignment of security levels and to per-form secure downgradings [5].

4. It is possible to state the Brewer-Nash and Foley policies using the model of causality [8].

5. Causality has the hook-up property and we even propose an extension of this result in case of asynchronous composition [6]. This enables the security of a system to be analyzed in a modular way.

6. Causality does not require implicit assumptions on the subject's behavior. This enables the security of every non-input total systems to be analyzed [4].

7. Causality allows some kind of dependencies between unclassified information and secret information.

Thanks to these advantages (especially the two last points), causality does not rule out interesting system's behaviors, in particular those presented in sections 1.1 and 1.2. However, this can also lead to paradoxical examples in which a secure system copies high sensitivity inputs to low sensitivity outputs. These paradoxical situations exist when the information flow actually occurs externally, in the environment. Indeed, causality only provides a solution to the problem of internal information flow.

Similarly, let us analyze the security of the two examples proposed in sections 1.1 and 1.2. In both cases, the unclassified user, $user_U$, receives an answer computed by BD_U, and BD_U only contains information that $user_U$ is legally permitted to know. So, the output provided to $user_U$ only depends on unclassified information and, in that case, the internal flows of information are secure. Consequently, according to causality, these two examples are always secure.

As we have already suggested in section 1.3, the security administrator may specify that these two examples are actually insecure and he would consider in this case that the causality point of view is too optimistic. However, this only means that causality does not deal with the inference problem. In the following section, we show how to extend causality in order to take into account this problem.

4 Inference control

The inference problem in multilevel databases can be defined by the following: a user A can derive higher sensitive information, from lower sensitive information to which A has legally access. This problem seems a priori easy to solve because we can believe that it is sufficient to arbitrarily divide the set of relevant sentences $\mathcal{L}$ (those on which the multilevel security policy applies) into a set $R(A)$ of A's explicit permission and a set $F(A)$ of A's explicit prohibition. Actually, the problem is much more tedious because each subject A can use its own permission to know some information but also general rules and common knowledge of the real world to derive new information (which are eventually forbidden). So, it must be verified, beside dividing $\mathcal{L}$, that the sets $R(A)$ and $F(A)$ were defined in a consistent manner. In order to correctly analyze this problem, we need a formal definition of the following concepts:

- The permission to know of each subject. We have already proposed a formal semantics for this concept for controlling internal flows of information. It is considered, with this semantics, that a subject A is permitted to know every given piece of information φ_0 for which A is explicitly permitted to have an access, i.e.:

$$\text{If } \varphi_0 \in R(A) \text{ then } PK_A\varphi_0$$

Moreover, A is implicitly authorized to perform valid derivation, i.e.:

$$\text{If } PK_A\varphi \text{ and } PK_A(\varphi \to \psi) \text{ then } PK_A\psi$$

that could be read: if A is permitted to know φ and if A is permitted to know $(\varphi \to \psi)$, then A is authorized to perform the derivation. Hence, A is permitted to know ψ.

- The prohibition to know of each subject, we denote it FK_A. We must formally define this concept. As in the case of the permission to know, the semantics of FK_A must enforce that a subject A is forbidden to know any given piece of information φ_0 for which A is explicitly forbidden to have an access, i.e.:

$$\text{If } \varphi_0 \in F(A) \text{ then } FK_A\varphi_0$$

Moreover, there exist implicit prohibitions[9], for instance:

$$\text{If } FK_A\varphi \text{ or } FK_A\psi \text{ then } FK_A(\varphi \wedge \psi)$$

that could be read: if A is forbidden to know φ or if A is forbidden to know ψ then A is implicitly forbidden to know the conjunction of φ and ψ. Notice, that the converse:

$$\text{If } FK_A(\varphi \wedge \psi) \text{ then } FK_A\varphi \text{ or } FK_A\psi$$

is generally not valid. For instance, think of the aggregation problem in which two pieces of information are more sensitive together than separate. The following sentence states another implicit prohibition:

$$\text{If } FK_A(\varphi \vee \psi) \text{ then } FK_A\varphi \text{ and } FK_A\psi$$

---

[9] We refer to [10] for a detailed presentation of a complete set of such implicit prohibitions.

that could be read: if A is forbidden to know the disjunctive data $\varphi \vee \psi$, then A is also implicitly forbidden to know more informative data such as φ or ψ. This last axiom allows us to control a partial disclosure of information. For instance, let us assume that Paul's salary is equal to 10000 and that the security administrator actually specifies that the unclassified user A is forbidden to know that Paul's salary is between 8000 and 15000, that is to say:

$$FK_A(Salary(Paul, 8000) \vee ... \vee Salary(Paul, 15000))$$

Hence, in using the above axiom, A is also implicitly forbidden to reduce the set of values belonging to the interval $[8000, 15000]$. On the other hand, the converse of this axiom:

$$\text{If } FK_A\varphi \text{ and } FK_A\psi \text{ then } FK_A(\varphi \vee \psi)$$

is generally not valid. For instance, if the security administrator states that:

$$\forall sal, SMIC \leq sal \rightarrow FK_A Salary(Paul, sal)$$

then we cannot infer that:

$$FK_A(Salary(Paul, SMIC)$$
$$\vee \ Salary(Paul, SMIC + 1) \vee Salary(Paul, SMIC + 2) \vee ...)$$

that could be read: A is forbidden to know that Paul's salary is greater than the SMIC, which is common knowledge to any user in France.
Similarly, we do not consider that the following instance is an implicit prohibition:

$$\text{If } FK_A\varphi(c) \text{ then } FK_A(\exists x, FK_A\varphi(x)) \text{ (where } c \text{ is a given constant)}$$

This sentence could be read: if A is forbidden to know a secret piece of information $\varphi(c)$ (for instance $Destination(Enterprise, c)$), then A should not be always implicitly forbidden to know the existence of this secret piece of information. Notice that this assumption is made in the non-interference model. In our approach, it is the role of the security policy to explicitly specify the case for which the existence of a secret piece of information is also secret.

Notice also, that we do not consider that we have:

$$FK_A\varphi \equiv \neg PK_A\varphi$$

that could be read: A is forbidden to know φ if and only if A is not permitted to know φ. Indeed, we want to consider that there exists explicit permission to have an access (from which we derive what a subject is permitted to know) and explicit prohibition to have an access (from which we derive what a subject is forbidden to know). Generally, in reasoning about normative propositions, it is not assumed that $FK_A\varphi \equiv \neg PK_A\varphi$, especially when one wants to analyze the consistency of a given set of normative propositions (see [1] for instance). This is exactly the case of the inference problem. This problem occurs when the security policy is not defined in a consistent way. This means that, if we want to avoid this problem, we must enforce the validity of the following sentence:

$$\neg(PK_A\varphi \wedge FK_A\varphi)$$

This sentence could be read: A cannot both have the permission to know φ and the prohibition to know φ. The enforcement of this condition guarantees that A cannot deduce forbidden information from permitted information by performing valid derivations. However, some difficulties remain because A can also perform plausible derivation. Through the following examples, we illustrate some of these problems and define possible solutions to solve them.

4.1 Example 3: Pseudo-consistency due to DB's incompleteness

When requests are sent to the secure DBMS that manages the SOD relation described in *Example 1*, answers that are formulated by this secure DBMS can depend on several parameters:

1. The clearance level of the user who sends the request to the DBMS (i.e., *Unclassified* or *Secret*).
2. The "characteristic" of the database (i.e., complete or incomplete).
3. The "characteristic" of the security policy that is applied to insure the internal information flow controls and, possibly, the inference controls.
4. The method that is used to avoid such inferences (i.e., with or without polyinstantiation).

It can thus be interesting to look at the inference problem in these different contexts, in order to be able to define some possible solutions to solve that inference problem. Let us consider that the security policy is defined so that $user_U$ is forbidden to know any secret piece of information and is also forbidden to know the existence of such secret information.

A first solution to enforce the security policy consistency is to consider that DB could be incomplete, this means that:

$\exists star, [Starship(star) \in DB] \wedge$
$(\ [(\exists obj, Objective(star, obj) \in DB) \wedge (\forall dest, Destination(star, dest) \notin DB)]$
$\vee [(\forall obj, Objective(star, obj) \notin DB) \wedge (\exists dest, Destination(star, dest) \in DB)]$
$\vee [(\forall obj, Objective(star, obj) \notin DB) \wedge (\forall dest, Destination(star, dest) \notin DB)]\ )$

When it is stated that $(\exists x, \forall y, Attribute(x, y) \notin DB)$, where *Attribute* means in the present example *Objective* or *Destination*, it is sometimes considered [27] that y is an undetermined value, denoted *Null* (see Table 4).

When DB is incomplete, the answer sent by the DBMS to $user_U$ for *Request3* is:

Request3:   SELECT ⟨*Destination*⟩ FROM *SOD*
                     WHERE *Destination* = *Enterprise*
Answer3b.U: *Null*

Starship		Objective		Destination		TC
Enterprise	U	Spying	S	Rigel	S	S
Enterprise	U	Null	U	Null	U	U
Intergalactic	U	Exploration	U	Talos	U	U

Table 4. The multilevel *SOD* relation when *DB* is incomplete

This means that DB_U does not know the answer either, because there (perhaps) exists a response, in the real world, that DB does not know or, because there (actually) exists a response, in the real world and in DB, that $user_U$ cannot know because it is unknown by DB_U, and only known by DB_S.

From the assumption that DB could be incomplete, and by combining the *Answer2.U* and *Answer3b.U*, $user_U$ can deduce that:

$$K_{user_U}[(\exists dest, (Destination(Enterprise, dest) \in DB_S) \land (dest \neq Null))$$
$$\lor(\forall dest, Destination(Enterprise, dest) \notin DB)]$$

The incompleteness of DB could be considered as a satisfying approach from the security policy point of view because there is no inconsistency, since $user_U$ is not sure that there is a *Secret* destination for *Enterprise*; and, from the non-interference point of view this approach is really satisfying because there is no interference of DB_S on DB_U.

But if it is now considered that the probability, the possibility or the plausibility (let us more generally say the "certainty factor") of the fact $[\forall dest, Destination(Enterprise, dest) \notin DB]$ is very small, then there remains the eventuality that the security policy can be inconsistent, exactly as in the case previously studied with the DB's completeness. Such a small certainty factor for the fact $[\forall dest, Destination(Enterprise, dest) \notin DB]$ could be obtained by $user_U$ with external information to DB, as it is stated in [18]. In fact, $user_U$ can suppose that the DBMS either does not know the real answer to *Request3*, or does not want to give him the response. He can go further in his reasoning by considering the second hypothesis, if he has access to external information, and thus build some abductive reasoning. Such external facts could be for examples:

- the fact that *Enterprise* will live soon, in a few days, and that the mission of any starship (and of course it's destination) must be known for some administrative reasons and thus recorded in the database (in DB_S in the present case) at least a few days before the date of the departure of the starship (let us say half a week);
- or the fact that $user_U$ has, or someone has for him, physically observed a great deal of activity all around *Enterprise*, signifying that this starship will live soon for a well-known mission;
- or also the fact that, usually, any starship does never stay idle more than a few days (let us say one week), and that *Enterprise* arrived five or six days ago.

To avoid such an abductive reasoning, another method could be used, *Polyinstantiation* (as it is often the case), but some management tools could nevertheless be very useful for the security manager to assess these certainty factors, for each fact such as: *"Enterprise will live soon"*, as it will be shown at the end of the next example.

4.2 Example 4: Pseudo-consistency due to DB's polyinstantiation

Consider now that the database is complete again but polyinstantiated (as shown in Table 5):

$$\forall star \quad [\exists obj, \exists dest, SOD(star, obj, dest) \in DB_S]$$
$$\Rightarrow [\exists obj', \exists dest', SOD(star, obj', dest') \in DB_U \wedge$$
$$(obj' \neq obj) \wedge (dest' \neq dest)]$$

Starship		Objective		Destination		TC
Enterprise	U	Spying	S	Rigel	S	S
Enterprise	U	Exploration	U	Talos	U	U
Intergalactic	U	Exploration	U	Talos	U	U

Table 5. The multilevel polyinstantiated *SOD* relation

This means that each fact that exists in DB_S must also exist in DB_U, with a distinct value for each attribute. The security policy is the same as in *Example 3*, i.e.:

$$FK_{user_U}[Destination(Enterprise, Rigel)] \wedge$$
$$FK_{user_U}[\exists dest, FK_{user_U}Destination(Enterprise, dest)]$$

Therefore, the answer sent by DB_U to $user_U$ for *Request3* is:

Request3:   SELECT $\langle Destination \rangle$ FROM *SOD*
                WHERE *Starship* $=$ *Enterprise*
Answer3c. U: $\langle Talos \rangle$

From the fact that DB is complete and polyinstantiated, $user_U$ can only be sure that:
$$\exists dest, Destination(Enterprise, dest) \in DB_U$$

However, if $user_U$ has access to contradictory external facts, he could suppose that another destination for *Enterprise* might exist, only known from DB_S. Hence, in the case of DB's polyinstantiation, the abductive reasoning is still possible. Indeed, even if $user_U$, by some kind of external observation, can suppose that *Enterprise* will live soon (exactly as in the case where DB is incomplete), he can nevertheless believe that the DBMS wants him to be mislead (see [18] for a more complete example).

It can thus be seen that some assistance tools may be very useful to the security manager for the assessment of the certainty factors of the different external facts that could be used for building some abductive reasoning. According to the external facts and their certainty factors, it is thus much easier to decide if any knowledge permitted to, or inferred by, $user_U$ is consistent with his explicit prohibitions.

4.3 The use of uncertainty to control abductive reasoning

As we have shown, respectively, in *Example 3* and *Example 4*, DB's incompleteness and DB's polyinstantiation are sometimes insufficient to avoid any effective information inference, in particular when abductive reasoning is possible. In both cases, we consider that uncertainty/certainty factors could be used to better appreciate such effective inference. Different types of uncertainty/certainty factors can be used (i.e., based, for example, on the possibility theory [38], or on the theory of evidence [32]); but, at the present step of our work, the following features of such uncertainty reasoning can be stated for any type of uncertainty/certainty factors:

- Uncertain and/or imprecise information can easily be represented in a linguistic form (which is very near to the natural language).
- The ordinal versus cardinal, and qualitative versus quantitative, aspects of uncertain and/or imprecise information are privileged.
- The mathematical frameworks that can be used, such as the possibility theory, are less normative than those classically used for representing certainty, such as probabilities.
- Uncertain and/or imprecise information can easily be combined, and thus updated, when represented in such a possibilistic framework.

This new type of approach used for representing, and evaluating the uncertainty/certainty of information stored in the system was already stated before (see for instance [36]) as a prospective research work for the assessment of the confidentiality preservation, referring in that case to the possibility theory [38, 16]. Independently, the same approach was also stated as an interesting solution to the abductive reasoning problem, in particular in relational DBMS [19, 18], referring in that case to the Dempster-Shafer theory [32].

So, when it is possible, only qualitative assessment is privileged faced to quantitative one. One advantage of such a representation is that it is much easier to combine distinct pieces of information and then compute the resulting certainty factor of the updated or resulting piece of information because the possibilistic or plausibilistic framework is less normative than the traditional probabilistic framework. This is mainly due to the following two reasons:

- The notion of independence of elementary events is not necessary to be able to compute the uncertainty/certainty factors of the piece of information issued from the combination of such elementary events.

– The fact that the sum of the certainty factors of two complementary events is not obligatorily equal to the unity (i.e., it is not always completely sure that either a given event, e, or its contrary, $\bar{e}$, will occur).

5 Conclusion

In this paper, we propose a general and complete method for modeling database security by splitting up the enforcement of a security policy into two sub-problems:

– The internal information flow controls enforced via causality.
– The inference controls enforced via policy consistency.

We think that this decomposition provides a better understanding of the confidentiality problem. Notice that this method is not limited to the design of a secure database management system. Actually, it could apply to any information management system as soon as it is possible to give a formal correspondence between the objects stored in the system (such as tuples in the case of a relational DBMS) and formula in first order logic. However, much work remains to be done. First of all, we have formally defined the concept of prohibition to know some information using modal logic and possible world semantics. This formalism was presented in [10]. The aim is to build a tool the security manager could use to verify the consistency of the security policy he has defined. A possible scenario that could provide effective assistance for security managers could be the following:

1. The tool can prove that, a low user cannot, by using valid reasoning, derive higher sensitive information from lower sensitive information. We can conclude that no inference channel inside the security policy exists.
2. If no inference channel exists, then, for a given higher sensitive piece of information, the tool can use abductive reasoning to find what information α the low subject needs to assume in order to derive this higher sensitive piece of information.
3. The tool asks the security manager whether it is plausible that a low subject might assume α. In a more ambitious scenario, the tool can use plausible reasoning in order to put itself in the position of the database security manager who tries to answer this question.

Finally, notice that, in this paper, we focus on mandatory access control and we do not consider discretionary access controls. It could be interesting to see whether the method we proposed can be applied to both kinds of access (mandatory and discretionary).

Acknowledgement

We would like to thank the DRET for its support, Jill Manning for her help, and the anonymous referees for their comments on a previous draft of this paper.

References

1. C. E. Alchourron. Philosophical Foundations of Deontic Logic and its Practical Applications in Computational Contexts. In *Proc. of the First International Workshop on Deontic Logic in Computer Science*, Amsterdam, The Netherlands, 1991. Invited Lecture.

2. D. Bell and L. LaPadula. Secure Computer Systems: Unified Exposition and Multics Interpretation. Technical Report ESD-TR-75-306, MTR-2997, MITRE, Bedford, Mass, 1975.

3. P. Bieber and F. Cuppens. Computer Security Policies and Deontic Logic. In *Proc. of the First International Workshop on Deontic Logic in Computer Science*, Amsterdam, The Netherlands, 1991.

4. P. Bieber and F. Cuppens. A Logical View of Secure Dependencies. *Journal of Computer Security*, 1(1):99–129, 1992.

5. P. Bieber and F. Cuppens. Secure Dependencies with Dynamic Level Assignments. In *Proc. of the computer security foundations workshop*, Franconia, 1992.

6. N. Boulahia-Cuppens and F. Cuppens. Asynchronous composition and required security condition. In *IEEE Symposium on Security and Privacy*, Oakland, 1994.

7. E. Cohen. Information Transmission in Sequential Programs. In *Foundations of Secure Computation*. Academic Press, 1978.

8. F. Cuppens. A modal logic framework to solve aggregation problems. In S. Jajodia and C. Landwehr, editors, *Database Security, 5: Status and Prospects*. North-Holland, 1992. Results of the IFIP WG 11.3 Workshop on Database Security.

9. F. Cuppens. A Logical Analysis of Authorized and Prohibited Information Flows. In *IEEE Symposium on Security and Privacy*, Oakland, 1993.

10. F. Cuppens and R. Demolombe. Normative Conflicts in a Confidentiality Policy. In *ECAI-94 Workshop on Artificial Normative Reasoning*, Amsterdam, The Netherlands, 1994.

11. F. Cuppens and K. Yazdanian. A "Natural" Decomposition of Multi-level Relations. In *IEEE Symposium on Security and Privacy*, Oakland, 1992.

12. R. Demolombe and L. Fariñas del Cerro. Efficient representation of incomplete information. In J. Schmidt and C Thanos, editors, *Foundations of Knowledge Base Management*. Springer Verlag, 1990.

13. D. Denning. *Cryptography and Data Security*. Addison-Wesley, 1982.

14. D. Denning, T. Lunt, R. Shell, M. Heckman, and W. Shockley. A Multilevel Relational Data Model. In *IEEE Symposium on Security and Privacy*, Oakland, 1987.

15. D. Denning, T. Lunt, R. Shell, W. Shockley, and M. Heckman. The SeaView Security Model. In *IEEE Symposium on Security and Privacy*, Oakland, 1988.

16. D. Dubois and H. Prade. *Possibility Theory: an approach to computerized processing of uncertainty*. Plenum Press, 1988.

17. T. Garvey, T. Lunt, X. Qian, and M. Stickel. Toward a Tool to Detect and Eliminate Inference Problems in the Design of Multilevel Databases. In *Proc. of the Sixth IFIP WG 11.3 Working Conference on Database Security*, Vancouver, 1992.

18. T. D. Garvey and T. F. Lunt. Cover Stories for Database Security. In S. Jajodia and C. Landwehr, editors, *Database Security, 5: Status and Prospects*. North-Holland, 1992. Results of the IFIP WG 11.3 Workshop on Database Security.

19. T. D. Garvey, T. F. Lunt, and M. E. Stickel. Abductive and Approximate Reasoning Models for Characterizing Inference Channels. In *Proc. of the computer security foundations workshop*, Franconia, 1991.

20. J. Glasgow and G. McEwen. Reasoning about knowledge and permission in secure distributed systems. In *Proc. of the computer security foundations workshop*, Franconia, 1988.

21. J. Goguen and J. Meseguer. Unwinding and Inference Control. In *IEEE Symposium on Security and Privacy*, Oakland, 1984.

22. M. J. Grohn. A model of a protected data management system. Technical Report ESD-TR-76-289, I. P. Sharp Associates Ltd., Bedford, Mass, 1976.

23. J. Guttman and M. Nadel. What needs securing. In *Proc. of the computer security foundations workshop*, Franconia, 1988.

24. J. T. Haigh, R. C. O'Brien, P. D. Stachour, and D. L. Toups. The LDV Approach to Database Security. In D. L. Spooner and C. Landwehr, editors, *Database Security, III: Status and Prospects*. North-Holland, 1990. Results of the IFIP WG 11.3 Workshop on Database Security.

25. T. H. Hinke. Inference Aggregation Detection in Database Management Systems. In *IEEE Symposium on Security and Privacy*, Oakland, 1988.

26. T. H. Hinke and M. Schaeffer. Secure data management system. Technical Report RADC-TR-75-266, System Development Corporation, 1975.

27. T. Imielinski and W. Lipski. Incomplete information in relational databases. *JACM*, 31(4), October 1984.

28. S. Jajodia and R. Sandhu. Polyinstatiation Integrity in Multilevel Relations. In *IEEE Symposium on Security and Privacy*, Oakland, 1990.

29. B. W. Lampson. A note on the confinement problem. *Communication of the Association for Computing Machinery*, 16(10):613–615, 1973.

30. K.-C. Liu and R. Sunderraman. General indefinite and maybe information in relational databases. In R. Ritter, editor, *Information processing 89*, pages 809–814, New-York, 1989. Elsevier.

31. R. Sandhu and S. Jajodia. Honest Databases That Can Keep Secrets. In *Proceedings of the 14th National Computer Security Conference*, Washington, D.C., 1991.

32. G. Shafer. *A Mathematical Theory of Evidence*. Princeton University Press, 1976.

33. G. W. Smith. Multilevel Secure Database Design: A Practical Application. In *Fifth Annual Computer Security Applications Conference*, Tucson, Arizona, 1989.

34. D. Sutherland. A Model of Information. In *Proceedings of the 9th National Computer Security Conference*, 1986.

35. B. Thuraisingham, W. Ford, M. Collins, and J. O'Keefe. Design and implementation of a database inference controller. *Data & Knowledge Engineering*, 11(3), December 1993.

36. G. Trouessin. Quantitative Evaluation of Confidentiality by Entropy Calculation. In *Proc. of the computer security foundations workshop*, Franconia, 1991.

37. R. A. Whitehurst and T. F. Lunt. The Seaview Verification. In *Proc. of the computer security foundations workshop*, Franconia, 1989.

38. L. A. Zadeh. Fuzzy Sets as a Basis for a Theory of Possibility. *Fuzzy Sets and Systems*, 1, 1978.

List of Authors

Lecture Notes in Computer Science

For information about Vols. 1–798
please contact your bookseller or Springer-Verlag

Vol. 835: W. M. Tepfenhart, J. P. Dick, J. F. Sowa (Eds.), Conceptual Structures: Current Practices. Proceedings, 1994. VIII, 331 pages. 1994. (Subseries LNAI).

Vol. 836: B. Jonsson, J. Parrow (Eds.), CONCUR '94: Concurrency Theory. Proceedings, 1994. IX, 529 pages. 1994.

Vol. 837: S. Wess, K.-D. Althoff, M. M. Richter (Eds.), Topics in Case-Based Reasoning. Proceedings, 1993. IX, 471 pages. 1994. (Subseries LNAI).

Vol. 838: C. MacNish, D. Pearce, L. Moniz Pereira (Eds.), Logics in Artificial Intelligence. Proceedings, 1994. IX, 413 pages. 1994. (Subseries LNAI).

Vol. 839: Y. G. Desmedt (Ed.), Advances in Cryptology - CRYPTO '94. Proceedings, 1994. XII, 439 pages. 1994.

Vol. 840: G. Reinelt, The Traveling Salesman. VIII, 223 pages. 1994.

Vol. 841: I. Prívara, B. Rovan, P. Ružička (Eds.), Mathematical Foundations of Computer Science 1994. Proceedings, 1994. X, 628 pages. 1994.

Vol. 842: T. Kloks, Treewidth. IX, 209 pages. 1994.

Vol. 843: A. Szepietowski, Turing Machines with Sublogarithmic Space. VIII, 115 pages. 1994.

Vol. 844: M. Hermenegildo, J. Penjam (Eds.), Programming Language Implementation and Logic Programming. Proceedings, 1994. XII, 469 pages. 1994.

Vol. 845: J.-P. Jouannaud (Ed.), Constraints in Computational Logics. Proceedings, 1994. VIII, 367 pages. 1994.

Vol. 846: D. Shepherd, G. Blair, G. Coulson, N. Davies, F. Garcia (Eds.), Network and Operating System Support for Digital Audio and Video. Proceedings, 1993. VIII, 269 pages. 1994.

Vol. 847: A. L. Ralescu (Ed.) Fuzzy Logic in Artificial Intelligence. Proceedings, 1993. VII, 128 pages. 1994. (Subseries LNAI).

Vol. 848: A. R. Krommer, C. W. Ueberhuber, Numerical Integration on Advanced Computer Systems. XIII, 341 pages. 1994.

Vol. 849: R. W. Hartenstein, M. Z. Servít (Eds.), Field-Programmable Logic. Proceedings, 1994. XI, 434 pages. 1994.

Vol. 850: G. Levi, M. Rodríguez-Artalejo (Eds.), Algebraic and Logic Programming. Proceedings, 1994. VIII, 304 pages. 1994.

Vol. 851: H.-J. Kugler, A. Mullery, N. Niebert (Eds.), Towards a Pan-European Telecommunication Service Infrastructure. Proceedings, 1994. XIII, 582 pages. 1994.

Vol. 852: K. Echtle, D. Hammer, D. Powell (Eds.), Dependable Computing – EDCC-1. Proceedings, 1994. XVII, 618 pages. 1994.

Vol. 853: K. Bolding, L. Snyder (Eds.), Parallel Computer Routing and Communication. Proceedings, 1994. IX, 317 pages. 1994.

Vol. 854: B. Buchberger, J. Volkert (Eds.), Parallel Processing: CONPAR 94 – VAPP VI. Proceedings, 1994. XVI, 893 pages. 1994.

Vol. 855: J. van Leeuwen (Ed.), Algorithms – ESA '94. Proceedings, 1994. X, 510 pages. 1994.

Vol. 856: D. Karagiannis (Ed.), Database and Expert Systems Applications. Proceedings, 1994. XVII, 807 pages. 1994.

Vol. 857: G. Tel, P. Vitányi (Eds.), Distributed Algorithms. Proceedings, 1994. X, 370 pages. 1994.

Vol. 858: E. Bertino, S. Urban (Eds.), Object-Oriented Methodologies and Systems. Proceedings, 1994. X, 386 pages. 1994.

Vol. 859: T. F. Melham, J. Camilleri (Eds.), Higher Order Logic Theorem Proving and Its Applications. Proceedings, 1994. IX, 470 pages. 1994.

Vol. 860: W. L. Zagler, G. Busby, R. R. Wagner (Eds.), Computers for Handicapped Persons. Proceedings, 1994. XX, 625 pages. 1994.

Vol: 861: B. Nebel, L. Dreschler-Fischer (Eds.), KI-94: Advances in Artificial Intelligence. Proceedings, 1994. IX, 401 pages. 1994. (Subseries LNAI).

Vol. 862: R. C. Carrasco, J. Oncina (Eds.), Grammatical Inference and Applications. Proceedings, 1994. VIII, 290 pages. 1994. (Subseries LNAI).

Vol. 863: H. Langmaack, W.-P. de Roever, J. Vytopil (Eds.), Formal Techniques in Real-Time and Fault-Tolerant Systems. Proceedings, 1994. XIV, 787 pages. 1994.

Vol. 864: B. Le Charlier (Ed.), Static Analysis. Proceedings, 1994. XII, 465 pages. 1994.

Vol. 865: T. C. Fogarty (Ed.), Evolutionary Computing. Proceedings, 1994. XII, 332 pages. 1994.

Vol. 866: Y. Davidor, H.-P. Schwefel, R. Männer (Eds.), Parallel Problem Solving from Nature - PPSN III. Proceedings, 1994. XV, 642 pages. 1994.

Vol 867: L. Steels, G. Schreiber, W. Van de Velde (Eds.), A Future for Knowledge Acquisition. Proceedings, 1994. XII, 414 pages. 1994. (Subseries LNAI).

Vol. 868: R. Steinmetz (Ed.), Multimedia: Advanced Teleservices and High-Speed Communication Architectures. Proceedings, 1994. IX, 451 pages. 1994.

Vol. 869: Z. W. Raś, Zemankova (Eds.), Methodologies for Intelligent Systems. Proceedings, 1994. X, 613 pages. 1994. (Subseries LNAI).

Vol. 870: J. S. Greenfield, Distributed Programming Paradigms with Cryptography Applications. XI, 182 pages. 1994.

Vol. 871: J. P. Lee, G. G. Grinstein (Eds.), Database Issues for Data Visualization. Proceedings, 1993. XIV, 229 pages. 1994.

Vol. 873: M. Naftalin, T. Denvir, M. Bertran (Eds.), FME '94: Industrial Benefit of Formal Methods. Proceedings, 1994. XI, 723 pages. 1994.

Vol. 874: A. Borning (Ed.), Principles and Practice of Constraint Programming. Proceedings, 1994. IX, 361 pages. 1994.

Vol. 875: D. Gollmann (Ed.), Computer Security – ESORICS 94. Proceedings, 1994. XI, 469 pages. 1994.

Vol. 876: B. Blumenthal, J. Gornostaev, C. Unger (Eds.), Human-Computer Interaction. Proceedings, 1994. IX, 239 pages. 1994.